The Norton Introduction to

POETRY

SIXTH EDITION

The Norton Introduction to
POETRY

SIXTH EDITION

J. Paul Hunter
The University of Chicago

W • W • NORTON & COMPANY • NEW YORK • LONDON

Composition by Vail-Ballou Composition.
Manufacturing by Courier Corp.
Cover illustration: Wayne Thiebaud, *California Hillside*. Courtesy Allan Stone Gallery,
New York City.

Library of Congress Cataloging-in-Publication Data

The Norton introduction to poetry / [edited by] J. Paul Hunter. —6th ed.
p.   cm.
Includes index.
1. Poetry—Collections.   I. Hunter, J. Paul, date.
PN6101.N6   1995
808.1—dc20
95-4817
ISBN 0-393-96822-7 (pbk.)

W. W. Norton & Company, Inc., 500 Fifth Avenue, New York, N.Y. 10110
W. W. Norton & Company Ltd., 10 Coptic Street, London WC1A 1PU

1 2 3 4 5 6 7 8 9 0

CONTENTS

v

Evaluating Poetry   457

Reading More Poetry   473

WRITING ABOUT POETRY

FOREWORD TO THE
SIXTH EDITION

Reading is action. Even though it is often done quietly and alone, reading is a profoundly social activity, and a vigorous and demanding one. There is nothing passive about reading; it requires attention, energy, an act of will. Texts have the potential for meaning, implication, response, and result; but the reader must activate them, give them life, and turn them from quiet print into a lively interplay of ideas and feelings. Reading makes things happen, usually in the mind and imagination, but sometimes in the larger world as well, for the process of reading involves not just the consciousness of the self but an awareness of the other—what is beyond the self. Reading doesn't just happen to you; you have to do it, and doing it involves decision, reaching out, discovery, awareness. Reading is an act of power, and learning how to get the most out of its possibilities can be an invigorating activity. For all its association with quietness, solitude, and the sedentary life, reading involves—at its deepest level—action and interaction.

Through all of its editions, *The Norton Introduction to Poetry* has been committed to helping students learn to read and enjoy poetry. This edition, like those before it, offers many different ways of building and reinforcing the skills of reading; in addition to studying poetry in terms of its elements, this book emphasizes reading works in different contexts—authorial, historical, and cultural. I have strengthened the offering of texts in contextual groups in this edition with the addition of a new chapter, "The Author's Work in Context: Adrienne Rich." Also, I have strengthened the connection between reading and writing at several points throughout the book. The introductory chapter first treats the reading experience generally, then works to involve students in examining their own responses as a first step toward writing about poetry. Three student papers offer a variety of responses to selected writing suggestions. And as in previous editions, I have provided many new selections.

But the Sixth Edition remains more than a grab-bag of good things to read. The book offers in a single volume a complete course in reading and writing about poetry. It is both an anthology and a textbook—a teaching anthology—for the indispensable course in which college student and college teacher begin to read poetry, and to write about it, seriously together.

The works are arranged in order to introduce a reader to the study of poetry. *Poetry: Reading, Responding, Writing* treats the purpose and nature of poetry, the reading experience, and the first steps one takes to begin writing about it. This is followed by the eight-chapter section called *Understanding the Text*, in which poems are analyzed by questions of craft, the so-called elements of poetry; this section ends with a chapter entitled "The Whole Text," which makes use of all or most of the analytical aids offered in the previous chapters, putting them together to see the work as a whole. The third section, *Exploring Contexts*, suggests some ways of seeing a work of literature interacting with its temporal and cultural contexts and reaching out beyond the page.

The sections on reading, analyzing, and placing the work in context are followed by guidance in taking that final and extremely difficult step—evaluation. *Evaluating Poetry* discusses how one would go about assessing the merits of two poems, not to offer definitive judgments, a litmus test, or even a checklist or formula, but to show how one goes about bringing to consciousness, defining, modifying, articulating, and negotiating one's judgments about a work of poetry.

Reading More Poetry is a reservoir of additional examples, for independent study or a different approach. The book's arrangement seeks to facilitate the reader's movement from narrower to broader questions, mirroring the way people read—wanting to learn more as they experience more.

The Norton Introduction to Poetry offers a full section on *Writing about Poetry*. In it I deal both with the writing process as applied to literary works—choosing a topic, gathering evidence, developing an argument, and so forth—and with the varieties of a reader's written responses, from copying and paraphrasing to analysis and interpretation: I explore not merely the hows, but the whats and whys as well.

In this section I also offer a discussion of critical approaches, designed to provide the student with a basic overview of contemporary critical theory, as well as an introduction to its terminology.

The Sixth Edition includes 433 poems, 142 of which are new. It has been infused with selections familiar and fresh, with newly included works by Ai, Elizabeth Alexander, Agha Shahid Ali, John Ashbery, Anna Laetitia Barbauld, April Bernard, Earle Birney, Elizabeth Bishop, Louise Bogan, Roo Borson, Emily Brontë, Gwendolyn Brooks, Mary, Lady Chudleigh, Judith Ortiz Cofer, Wendy Cope, Hart Crane, H. D., T. S. Eliot, Louise Erdrich, Carolyn Forché, John Gay, Louise Glück, Thomas Gray, Robert Hass, Barbara Howes, Erica Jong, Donald Justice, Archibald Lampman, Irving Layton, James Merrill, Edna St. Vincent Millay, Marianne Moore, Erin Mouré, Susan Musgrave, Ricardo Pau-Llosa, Katherine Philips, Alberto Alvaro Ríos, Sir Charles G. D. Roberts, Muriel Rukeyser, Duncan Campbell Scott, Leslie Marmon Silko, Richard Snyder, Derek Walcott, Edmund Waller, and Walt Whitman, among others.

Certain editorial procedures that proved their usefulness in earlier editions have been retained. First of all, the works are annotated, as is customary in Norton anthologies; the notes are informational and not interpretative, for the aim is to help readers understand and appreciate the work, not to dictate a meaning or a response. In order to avoid giving the impression that all poetry was written at the same time, I have noted at the right margin after each selection the date of first book publication (or, when preceded by a *p*, first periodical publication or, when the date appears at the left margin, the year of composition).

In all my work on this edition I have been guided by teachers in other English departments and in my own, by students who wrote me as the author of the textbook they were using, and by those who were able to approach me after class as their teacher: I hope that with such help I have been able to offer you a solid and stimulating introduction to the experience of poetry.

Acknowledgments   I would like to thank my teachers, for their example in the love of literature and in the art of sharing that love; my students, for their patience as I am learning from them to be a better teacher of poetry; my wife and children, for their understanding when the work of preparing this text made me seem less than a perfectly loving husband and father.

I would also like to thank my colleagues, many of whom have taught my book and evaluated my efforts, for their constant encouragement and enlightenment. Of my colleagues at the University of Chicago, I would like especially to thank Robert von Hallberg, Michelle Hawley, Jonathan Martin, Anne Elizabeth Murdy, Janel Mueller, Vicky Olwell, Richard Strier, and John Wright. For their help in selecting papers by student writers, I would like to thank Geneva Ballard, Theresa Budniakiewicz, Rebecca S. Ries, and Avantika Rohatgi, of Indiana University—Purdue University at Indianapolis, and Thomas Miller, Tilly Warnock, Lisa-Anne Culp, Loren Goodman, Brendan McBryde, and Ruthe Thompson, at the University of Arizona. I also thank the students whose papers I include: Meaghan E. Parker and Kimberly Smith. For their work on the *Instructor's Guide*, I thank Gayla McGlamery and Bryan Crockett, Loyola College in Baltimore.

And I thank also Elizabeth Alkagond, Columbia College; M. Allen, Bakersfield College; Marjorie Allen, LaSalle University; Preston Allen, Miami-Dade Community College; Sally Allen, North Georgia College; Bruce Anawalt, Washington State University; Anne Andrews, Mississippi State University; Charles Angel, Bridgewater State College; Booker Anthony, Fayetteville State University; Robert Arledge, Southern University at New Orleans; Michael Atkinson, University of Cincinnati; Janet Auten, American University; Sylvia Baer, Gloucester County College; Raymond Bailey, Bishop State Community College; Lee Baker, High Point College; Harold Bakst, Minneapolis Community College; Nancy Barendse, Christopher Newport College; Chris Barkley, Palomar College; Linda Barlow, Fayetteville State University; William Barnette, Prestonsburg Community College; Dr. Barney, Citrus College; E. Barnton, California State University, Bakersfield; Harry E. Batty, University of Maine; Shawn Beaty, Hokkaido University; Nancy Beers, Temple University; Linda Bensel-Meyers, University of Tennessee, Knoxville; Lawrence Berkoben, California State University; Tracey Besmark, Ashland Community College; Barbara Bird, St. Petersburg Community College; Lillian Bisson, Marymount College; Clark Blaise, University of Iowa; T. E. Blom, University of British Columbia; Roy L. Bond, University of Texas at Dallas; Steven Bouler, Tuskegee University; Veleda Boyd, Tarleton State University; Helen Bridge, Chabot College; Sandra Brim, North Georgia College; Loretta Brister, Tarleton State University; Patrick Broderick, Santa Rosa Junior College; Robert Brophy, California State University, Long Beach; Theresa Brown, Tufts University; William Brown, Philadelphia College of Textiles and Science; Virginia Brumbach, Eastfield College; C. Bryant, Colby College; Edward Burns, William Paterson College of New Jersey; Daniel Cahill, University of Northern Iowa; Martha Campbell, St. Petersburg Community College at Tarpon Springs; William Campbell, Monroe Community College; D. Cano, Santa Monica Community College; Nathan Carb, Rowan College of New Jersey; Roger Carlstrom, Yakima Valley Community College; Martha Carpentier, Seton Hall University; Anne Carr, Southeast Community College; Conrad Carroll, Northern Kentucky University; Gisela Casines, Florida International University; Ahwadhesh Chaudhary, Texas College; Dr. Clark, Citrus College; John Clower, Indiana University–Purdue University at Indianapolis; Steven Cole, Temple University; Cindy Collins, Fullerton College; Kathleen Collins, Creighton University; Marianne Conroy, McGill University; Pat Conner, Memphis State University; Martha Cook, Longwood College; Holly Cordova, Contra Costa College; Susan Cornett, St. Petersburg Community College at Tarpon Springs; Brian Corrigan, North Georgia College; Betty Corum, Owensboro Community College; Beverly Cotton, Cerritos College; Delmar Crisp, Wesleyan College; Virginia Critchlow, Monroe Community College; Carol Cunningham-Ruiz, Bakersfield College; Lennett Daigle, North Georgia College; Christopher Dark, Tarleton State University; Vivian Davis, Eastfield College; Hugh Dawson, University of San Francisco; Martha Day, Richard Bland College; George Diamond, Moravian College; Helen DiBona, North Carolina Central University; Sister Mary Colleen Dillon, Thomas More College; Marvin Diogenes, University of Arizona; Frank Dobson, Indiana University–Purdue University at Indianapolis; Minna Doskow, Rowan College of New Jersey; Donald Dowdey, Virginia Wesleyan College; Bonnie Duncan, Upper Iowa University; Timothy Dykstal, Auburn University; Wayne Eason, University of North Carolina at Charlotte; Larry Eby, Emory University; Paula Eckard, University of North Carolina at Charlotte; Mary Eiser, Kauai Community College; Marianne Eismann, Wake Forest University; Joyce Ellis, North Carolina Central University; Reed Ellis, St. John's Community College; Peggy Endel, Florida International University; James Erickson, Wichita State University; Dessagene Ewing, Delaware County Community College; Jim Ewing, North Georgia College; Sasha Feinstein, Indiana University; Charles Feldstein, Florida Community College at Jacksonville; Norman Feltes, York University; Jean Fields, Lindenwood College; Mildred Flynn, South Dakota University; Eileen Foley, University of Maine; Dolores Formicella, Delaware County Community College; Elsa Ann Gaines, North Georgia College; Dennis Gaitner, Frostburg State University; Reloy Garcia, Creighton University; Joseph Glaser, Western Kentucky University; Andrea Glebe, University of Nevada; Karen Gleeman, Normandale Community College; C. Golliher, Victor Valley College; Douglas Gordon, Christopher Newport College; Donna Gormly, Eastfield College; Kathryn Graham, Virginia Polytechnic Institute and State University; Pat Gregory, Community College of Philadelphia; Ann Grigsby, University of New Mexico; Alan Grob, Rice University; Lynda Haas, Hillsborough Community College; Florence Halle, Memphis State University; Jerry Harris, Western Oregon State College; Sydney Harrison, Manatee Community College; Joan Hartman, William Patterson College; Charles Hatten, Bellarmine College;

Bruce Henderson, Fullerton College; Nancy Henry, SUNY at Binghamton; David Hernandez, Eastfield College; Robert Herzog, Monroe Community College; Laura Higgs, Clemson University; David Hill, SUNY College at Oswego; Robert Hipkiss, California State University; David Hoegberg, Indiana University–Purdue University at Indianapolis; Eartha Holley, Delaware State University; R. C. Hoover, Wenatchee Valley College; Roger Horn, Charles County Community College; L. C. Howard, Skyline College; Erlene Hubly, University of Northern Iowa; William Hudson, Radford University; David Hufford, Iowa Western Community College; Deirdre Hughes, Fullerton College; Dr. Humphrey, Citrus College; Kathryn Montgomery Hunter, Northwestern University School of Medicine; Lisa Hunter, University of Wisconsin Medical School; P. Hunter, Los Angeles Valley College; Edelina Huntley, Appalachian State University; Robert Huntley, Washington and Lee University; Sharon Irvin, Florida Institute of Technology; Sylvia Iskander, University of Southwestern Louisiana; Eleanor James, Montgomery County Community College; Anne Johnson, Jacksonville State University; Christopher Johnson, Missouri Valley College; Craig Johnson, Hillsborough Community College; Darryl Johnson, St. Cloud State University; Dolores Johnson, Seattle University; Karen Johnson, Indiana University–Purdue University at Indianapolis; Dr. Jones, Citrus College; Grace Jones, Owensboro Community College; Walter Kalaidjian, St. Cloud State University; Frank Kastor, Wichita State University; E. Kenney, Colby College; Don King, Central Washington University; Andrew Kirk, University of California, Davis; John Klijinski, Idaho State University; William Klink, Charles County Community College; Michael Krasny, San Francisco State University; Anne Krause, Yakima Valley Community College; Harold Kuglemass, Onondaga Community College; Stuart Kurland, Muhlenberg College; Donald Lawler, East Carolina University; Lynn Lewis, Memphis State University; Vincent J. Liesenfeld, University of Oklahoma; Jun Liu, California State University, Los Angeles; Travis Livingston, Tarleton State University; Lillian Liwag-Sutcliffe, Old Dominion University; Mary Lowe-Evans, University of West Florida; Michael Lund, Longwood College; Kathleen Lyons, Bellarmine College; Thomas Mack, University of South Carolina; Patricia MacVaugh, Lehigh County Community College; Emory Maiden, Appalachian State University; Christina Malcolmson, Bates College; Dexter Marks, Jersey City State College; William Martin, Tarleton State University; Frank Mason, University of South Florida; Pam Mathis, North Arkansas Community College; Laura May, St. Petersburg Community College; Katherine Maynard, Rider College; R. McAllister, Victor Valley College; Kathleen McCloy, Shoreline Community College; Betty J. McCommas, Ouachita Baptist University; Clare McDonnell, Neumann College; Frank McLaughlin, Ramapo College; Thomas McLaughlin, Appalachian State University; William McMahon, Western Kentucky University; Terrence McNally, Northern Kentucky University; Alan McNarie, University of Hawaii; Nyan McNeill, Foothill College; Jay Meek, University of North Dakota; Ivan Melada, University of New Mexico; Donna Melancon, Xavier University; Linda Merions, LaSalle University; Darlene Mettler, Wesleyan College; R. Metzger, Los Angeles Valley College; Brian Michaels, Diane Middlebrook (Stanford University) St. John's

Community College; Daniel Miller, Northern Kentucky University; George Miller, University of Delaware; Ron Miller, University of West Florida; Leslie Mittelman, California State University, Long Beach; Rosa Mizerski, West Valley College; Rosemary Moffett, Elizabethtown Community College; Warren Moore, Loyola College; Mike Moran, University of Georgia; Dean Morgan, Olympic College; William Morgan, Illinois State University; William Morris, University of South Florida; Sharon Morrow, University of Southern Indiana; Renate Muendel, West Chester University; Gordon Mundell, University of Nebraska; David Murdoch, Rochester Institute of Technology; Carol Murphy, Roanoke College; Thomas Murray, Trenton State College; Joseph Nacca, Community College of Finger Lakes; Joseph Nasser, Rochester Institute of Technology; Mary Neil, Eastfield College; Kay Nelson, St. Cloud University; Dorothy Newman, Southern University; Lee Nicholson, Modesto Junior College; Mimi Nicholson, University of Southern Indiana; Elizabeth Nollen, West Chester University; Dale Norris, Des Moines Community College; Robert Ochsner, University of Maryland at Baltimore; Sarah Oglesby, Madisonville Community College; Francis Olley, Saint Joseph's University; Ann Olson, Central Washington University; Regina Oost, Wesleyan College; Mildred Orenstein, Drexel University; Kathleen O'Shea, Monroe Community College; Thornton Penfield, Southern University; Christopher Penna, University of Delaware; Rita Perkins, Camden County College; Donald Peterson, City College of San Francisco; Steven Phelan, Rollins College; Randall Popken, Tarleton State University; Robert Post, University of Washington; Pamela Postma, University of North Carolina at Greensboro; Linda Ray Pratt, University of Nebraska; Ross Primm, Columbia College; Richard Quaintance, Rutgers University; James Randall, Coe College; Rosemary Raynal, Davidson College; Mary Rea, Indiana University–Purdue University at Indianapolis; Thomas Redshaw, University of St. Thomas; Ron Reed, Hazard Community College; Donna Reiss, Tidewater Community College; Alan Richardson, Boston College; Ann Richey, Virginia Polytechnic Institute and State University; Joan Richmond, Tarleton State University; Harold Ridley, LeMoyne College; Leonard Roberts, Northampton Area Community College; Douglas Robinson, University of Mississippi; J. Robinson, Victor Valley College; Beate Rodewald, Palm Beach Atlantic College; Ruben Rodriguez, Tarleton State University; Owen Rogal, St. Ambrose University; Eva Rosenn, Wesleyan College; William Rossiter, Flathead Valley College; Connie Rothwell, University of North Carolina; Don Rud, Texas Tech University; Don Russ, Kennesaw State College; Charles J. Rzepka, Boston University; Christina Savage, Long Beach City College; Vicki Scannell, Pierce College; Paul Schacht, SUNY College at Geneseo; Steven Scherwatzky, Merrimack College; Marie Schiebold, Skyline College; Ronald Schleifer, University of Oklahoma; Linda Schmidt, Iowa Western Community College; Roger Schmidt, Idaho State College; Michael Schoenecke, Texas Tech University; Jane Schultz, Indiana University–Purdue University at Indianapolis; Lucille Schultz, University of Cincinnati; Carolyn Segal, Lehigh University; JoAnn Seiple, University of North Carolina; Bill Senior, Broward Community College; Pat Shalter, Reading Area Community College; Lewis Sheffler, Missouri Valley College; Richard

Siciliano, Charles County Community College; Odette Sims, Modesto Junior College; Judy Jo Small, North Carolina State University; Louise Smith, University of Massachusetts; Peter Smith, Wesleyan College; Stephen Smith, LaSalle University; Thomas Sonith, Widener University; B. Spears, Victor Valley College; Dr. Spencer, California State University, Bakersfield; Rich Sprouse, North Georgia College; Ann Spurlock, Mississippi State University; David Stacey, Missouri Valley College; Nancy Stahl, Indiana University–Purdue University at Indianapolis; Jamie Steckelberg, University of North Dakota; James Stick, Des Moines Community College; Bruce Stillians, University of Hawaii; McKay Sundwall, East Carolina University; Kathryn Swanson, Augsburg College; John Taylor, College of Marin; Judith Taylor, Northern Kentucky University; David Thibodaux, University of Southwestern Louisiana; Victor Thompson, Thomas Nelson Community College; Charles Thornbury, College of St. Benedict; Mike Thro, Tidewater Community College; Kathleen Tickner, Brevard Community College; Edna Troiano, Charles County Community College; Gail Tubbs, Washington College; Richard Turner, Indiana University–Purdue University at Indianapolis; Teresa Tweet, Augustana College; D. Unrue, University of Nevada; Margaret Vail, Xavier University; Diana Valdina, Cayuga County Community College; Kenneth Vandover, Lincoln University; Eleanor Vassal, St. Petersburg Community College; Tim Viator, North Georgia College; Richard Victor, Saddleback College; Jeanne Walker, University of Delaware; Cynthia Wall, University of Virginia; Leslie Wallace, DeAnza College; W. Wallis, Los Angeles Valley College; R. Warkentin, California State University, Dominguez Hills; David Weekes, Eastern Washington University; Edwin Weihe, Seattle University; Ronald Wendling, Saint Joseph's University; Agnes Whitsel, Mercer University; Keith Wicker, Henderson Community College; Inga Wiehl, Yakima Valley College; Waller Wigginton, Idaho State University; Arthur Williams, Louisiana School for Mathematics, Science and the Arts; Jack Williams, California State University; James Wilson, University of Southwestern Louisiana; Sharon Wilson, Fort Hays State University; Sandra Witt, University of Northern Iowa; Susan Wolstenholme, Cayuga County Community College; Strohn Woodward, University of Maine; James Wyatt, Lindsey Wilson College; Linda Yakle, St. Petersburg Community College; and Dr. Zounes, Los Angeles Valley College.

I would like to thank my friends at W. W. Norton & Company, especially the late John Benedict and the late Barry Wade, to whom I dedicate this revision, and also Allen Clawson, Carol Hollar-Zwick, Marian Johnson, Kate Lovelady, John Mardirosian, Fred McFarland, Diane O'Connor, Nancy Palmquist, David Sutter, Ann Tappert, Candace Watt, and Kurt Wildermuth.

J.P.H.

The Norton Introduction to

POETRY

SIXTH EDITION

▼ ▼ ▼

Poetry: Reading, Responding, Writing

f you're already a reader of poetry, you know: poetry reading is not just an intellectual and bookish activity; it is about feeling. Reading poetry well means responding to it: if you respond on a feeling level, you are likely to read more accurately, with deeper understanding, and with greater pleasure. And, conversely, if you read poetry accurately, and with attention to detail, you will almost certainly respond—or learn how to respond—to it on an emotional level. Reading poetry involves conscious articulation through language, and reading and responding come to be, for experienced readers of poetry, very nearly one. But those who teach poetry—and there are a lot of us, almost all enthusiasts about both poetry as a subject and reading as a craft—have discovered something else: writing about poetry helps both the reading and the responding processes. Responding involves remembering and reflecting as well. As you recall your own past and make associations between things in the text and things you already know and feel, you will not only respond more fully to a particular poem, but improve your reading skills more generally. Your knowledge and life experience informs your reading of what is before you, and allows you to connect things within the text—events, images, words, sounds—so that meanings and feelings develop and accumulate. Prior learning creates expectations: of pattern, repetition, association, or causality. Reflecting on the text—and on expectations produced by themes and ideas in the text— re-creates old feelings but directs them in new, often unusual ways. Poems, even when they are about things we have no experience of, connect to things we do know and order our memories, thoughts, and feelings in new and newly challenging ways.

A course in reading poetry can help you to be a better, more fully sensitive and responsive person: that's the larger goal. But the more immediate goal—and the route to the larger one—is to make you a better reader of texts and a more precise and careful writer yourself. Close attention to one text makes you appreciate, and understand, textuality and its possibilities more generally.

READING   Poems, perhaps even more than other texts, can sharpen your reading skills because they tend to be so compact, so fully dependent on concise expressions of feeling. In poems, ideas and feelings are packed tightly into just a few lines. The experiences of life are very concentrated here, and meanings emerge quickly, word by word. Poems often show us the very process of putting feelings into a language that can be shared with others—to *say* feelings in a communicable way. Poetry can be intellectual too, explaining and exploring ideas, but its focus is more often on how people feel than how they think. Poems work out a sharable language for feeling, and one of poetry's most insistent virtues involves its attempt to express the inexpressible. How can anyone, for example, put into words what it means to be in love? or how it feels to lose someone one cares about? Poetry tries, and it often captures exactly the shade of emotion that feels just right to a reader. No single poem can be said to express all the things that love or death feels like, or means, but one of the joys of experiencing poetry occurs when we read a poem and want to say, "Yes, that is just what it is like; I know exactly what that line means but I've never been able to express it so well." Poetry can be the voice of our feelings even when our minds are speechless with grief or joy. Reading is no substitute for living, but it can make living more abundant and more available.

Here are two poems that talk about the sincerity and depth of love between two people. Each is written as if it were spoken by one person to his or her lover, and each is definite and powerful about the intensity and quality of love; but the poems work in quite different ways—the first one asserting the strength and depth of love, the second implying intense feeling by reminiscing about events in the relationship between the two people.

ELIZABETH BARRETT BROWNING

How Do I Love Thee?

How do I love thee? Let me count the ways.
I love thee to the depth and breadth and height
My soul can reach, when feeling out of sight

For the ends of Being and ideal Grace.
I love thee to the level of every day's   5
Most quiet need, by sun and candlelight.
I love thee freely, as men strive for Right;
I love thee purely, as they turn from Praise;
I love thee with the passion put to use
In my old griefs, and with my childhood's faith.   10
I love thee with a love I seemed to lose
With my lost saints—I love thee with the breath,
Smiles, tears of all my life!—and, if God choose,
I shall but love thee better after death.   1850

JAROLD RAMSEY

The Tally Stick

Here from the start, from our first of days, look:
I have carved our lives in secret on this stick
of mountain mahogany the length of your arms
outstretched, the wood clear red, so hard and rare.
It is time to touch and handle what we know we share.   5

Near the butt, this intricate notch where the grains
converge and join: it is our wedding.
I can read it through with a thumb and tell you now
who danced, who made up the songs, who meant us joy.
These little arrowheads along the grain,   10
they are the births of our children. See,
they make a kind of design with these heavy crosses,
the deaths of our parents, the loss of friends.

Over it all as it goes, of course, I
have chiseled Events, History—random   15
hashmarks cut against the swirling grain.
See, here is the Year the World Went Wrong,
we thought, and here the days the Great Men fell.
The lengthening runes of our lives run through it all.

See, our tally stick is whittled nearly end to end;   20
delicate as scrimshaw, it would not bear you up.
Regrets have polished it, hand over hand.
Yet let us take it up, and as our fingers
like children leading on a trail cry back
our unforgotten wonders, sign after sign,   25
we will talk softly as of ordinary matters,
and in one another's blameless eyes go blind.   p. 1977

The first poem is direct, but fairly abstract. It lists several ways in which the poet feels love and connects them to some noble ideas of higher obligations—to justice (line 7), for example, and to spiritual aspiration (lines 2–4). It suggests a wide range of things that love can mean and notices a variety of emotions. It is an ardent statement of feeling and asserts a permanence that will extend even beyond death. It contains admirable thoughts and memorable phrases that many lovers would like to hear said to themselves. What it does not do is say very much about what the relationship between the two lovers is like on an everyday basis, what experiences they have had together, what distinguishes their relationship from that of other devoted or ideal lovers. Its appeal is to our general sense of what love is like and how intense feelings can be; it does not offer everyday details. Love may differ from person to person and even from moment to moment, and so can poems about love.

"The Tally Stick" is much more concrete. The whole poem concentrates on a single object that, like "How Do I Love Thee?," "counts" or "tallies" the ways in which this couple love one another. This stick stands for their love and becomes a kind of physical reminder of it: its natural features—the notches and arrowheads and cross marks (lines 6, 10, and 12) along with the marks carved on it (lines 15–16, 20–21)—indicate events in the story of the relationship. (We could say that the stick *symbolizes* their love; later on, we will look at a number of terms like this that can be used to make it easier to talk about some aspects of poems, but for now it is enough to notice that the stick serves the lovers as a reminder of some specific details of their love.) It is a special kind of reminder to them because its language is "secret" (line 2), something they can share privately (except that we as readers of the poem are sort of looking over their shoulders, not intruding but sharing their secret). The poet interprets the particular features of the stick as standing for particular events—their wedding and the births of their children, for example—and carves marks into it as reminders of other events (lines 15ff.). The stick itself becomes a very personal object, and in the last stanza of the poem it is as if we watch the lovers touching the stick together and reminiscing over it, gradually dissolving into their emotions and each other as they recall the "unforgotten wonders" (line 25) of their lives together.

Both poems are powerful statements of feelings, each in its own way. Various readers will respond differently to each poem; the effect these poems have on their readers will lead some to prefer one and some the other. Personal preference does not mean that objective standards for poetry cannot be found (some poems are better than others, and later we will look in detail at features that help us to evaluate poems), but we need have no preconceived standard that all poetry must be one thing or another or work in one particular way. Some good poems are quite abstract, others quite specific. Any poem that helps us to articulate and clarify human feelings and ideas has a legitimate claim on us as readers.

Both "How Do I Love Thee?" and "The Tally Stick" are written as if they were addressed to the partner in the love relationship, and both talk directly about the intensity of the love. The poem below talks only indirectly about the quality and intensity of love. It is written as if it were a letter from a woman to her husband who has gone on a long journey on business. It directly expresses how much she misses him and indirectly suggests how much she cares about him.

EZRA POUND

The River-Merchant's Wife: A Letter

(after Rihaku[1])

While my hair was still cut straight across my forehead
I played about the front gate, pulling flowers.
You came by on bamboo stilts, playing horse,
You walked about my seat, playing with blue plums.
And we went on living in the village of Chokan: 5
Two small people, without dislike or suspicion.

At fourteen I married My Lord you.
I never laughed, being bashful.
Lowering my head, I looked at the wall.
Called to, a thousand times, I never looked back.   10

At fifteen I stopped scowling,
I desired my dust to be mingled with yours
For ever and for ever and for ever.
Why should I climb the look out?

At sixteen you departed,   15
You went into far Ku-to-yen, by the river of swirling eddies,
And you have been gone five months.
The monkeys make sorrowful noise overhead.

You dragged your feet when you went out.
By the gate now, the moss is grown, the different mosses,   20
Too deep to clear them away!

1. The Japanese name for Li Po, an eighth-century Chinese poet. Pound's poem is a loose paraphrase of Li Po's.

The leaves fall early this autumn, in wind.
The paired butterflies are already yellow with August
Over the grass in the West garden;
They hurt me. I grow older.
If you are coming down through the narrows of the river Kiang,
Please let me know beforehand,
And I will come out to meet you
    As far as Cho-fu-Sa.

25

1915

The "letter" tells us only a few facts about the nameless merchant's wife: that she is about sixteen and a half years old, that she married at fourteen and fell in love with her husband a year later, that she is now very lonely. About their relationship we know only that they were childhood playmates in a small Chinese village, that their marriage originally was not a matter of personal choice, and that the husband unwillingly went away on a long journey five months ago. But the words tell us a great deal about how the young wife feels, and the simplicity of her language suggests her sincere and deep longing. The daily noises she hears seem "sorrowful" (line 18), and she worries about the dangers of the far-away place where her husband is, thinking of it in terms of its perilous "river of swirling eddies" (line 16). She thinks of how moss has grown up over the unused gate, and more time seems to her to have passed than actually has (lines 22–25). Nostalgically she remembers their innocent childhood, when they played together without deeper love or commitment (lines 1–6), and contrasts that with her later satisfaction in their love (lines 11–14) and with her present anxiety, loneliness, and desire. We do not need to know the details of the geography of the river Kiang or how far Cho-fu-Sa is to sense that her wish to see him is very strong, that her desire is powerful enough to make her venture beyond the ordinary geographical bounds of her existence so that their reunion will come sooner. The closest she comes to a direct statement about her love is her statement that she desired that her dust be mingled with his "For ever and for ever and for ever" (lines 12–13). But her single-minded vision of the world, her perception of even the beauty of nature as only a record of her husband's absence and the passage of time, and her plain, apparently uncalculated language about her rejection of other suitors and her shutting out of the rest of the world all show her to be committed, desirous, nearly desperate for his presence. In a different sense, she has also counted the ways that she loves her man.

Here is another poem about marriage, equally about dependency but with a very different set of attitudes and feelings.

MARY, LADY CHUDLEIGH

To the Ladies

Wife and servant are the same,
But only differ in the name:
For when that fatal knot is tied,
Which nothing, nothing can divide,
When she the word *Obey* has said,   5
And man by law supreme has made,
Then all that's kind is laid aside,
And nothing left but state and pride.
Fierce as an eastern prince he grows,
And all his innate rigor shows: 10
Then but to look, to laugh, or speak,
Will the nuptial contract break.
Like mutes, she signs alone must make,
And never any freedom take,
But still be governed by a nod,   15
And fear her husband as her god:
Him still must serve, him still obey,
And nothing act, and nothing say,
But what her haughty lord thinks fit,
Who, with the power, has all the wit.   20
Then shun, oh! shun that wretched state,
And all the fawning flatterers hate.
Value yourselves, and men despise:
You must be proud, if you'll be wise.   1703

This poem is addressed directly to a specific audience, and presence becomes as abhorrent here as absence does in the previous poem. Marriage here is an oppressor and the husband the personification of oppression; the poem blurs distinctions between discourses, insisting that "Wife" and "servant" mean the same thing because they testify to parallel relationships of mastery and obedience. Unlike the river-merchant's wife in the previous poem, this speaker is angry and feels betrayed by events; rather than speak of her own specific experiences and feelings, she tries to arouse feelings in an audience she counts on to recognize a repeated pattern and habit of marital experience.

Poems can be about the meaning of a relationship or about disappointment just as easily as about emotional fulfillment, and poets are often very good at suggesting the contradictions and uncertainties in relationships. Like other people, poets often find love quaint or downright funny, too, mainly because it involves human beings who, however serious their intentions and concerns, are often inept, uncertain, and self-contradictory—in short, human. Showing us ourselves as others see us is one of the more useful tasks that poems perform, but the poems that result can be just as entertaining and pleasurable as they are educational. Here is a poem that imagines a very strange scene, a kind of fantasy of what happens when we *think* too much about sex or love, and it is likely to leave us laughing, whether or not we take it seriously as a statement of human anxiety and of the tendency to intellectualize too much.

TOM WAYMAN

Wayman in Love

At last Wayman gets the girl into bed.
He is locked in one of those embraces
so passionate his left arm is asleep
when suddenly he is bumped in the back.
"Excuse me," a voice mutters, thick with German.
Wayman and the girl sit up astounded
as a furry gentleman in boots and a frock coat
climbs in under the covers.

"My name is Doktor Marx," the intruder announces
settling his neck comfortably on the pillow.
"I'm here to consider for you the cost of a kiss."
He pulls out a notepad. "Let's see now,
we have the price of the mattress, this room must be rented,
your time off work, groceries for two,
medical fees in case of accidents . . ."

"Look," Wayman says,
"couldn't we do this later?"
The philosopher sighs, and continues: "You are affected too, Miss.
If you are not working, you are going to resent
your dependent position. This will influence
I assure you, your most intimate moments . . ."

"Doctor, please," Wayman says. "All we want
is to be left alone."
But another beard, more nattily dressed,
is also getting into the bed.
There is a shifting and heaving of bodies
as everyone wriggles out room for themselves.
"I want you to meet a friend from Vienna,"
Marx says. "This is Doktor Freud."

The newcomer straightens his glasses,   30
peers at Wayman and the girl.
"I can see," he begins,
"that you two have problems . . ."   1973

RESPONDING   The poems we have looked at so far all describe,
though in quite different ways, feelings associated with loving or being
attached to someone and the expression—either physical or verbal—of those
feelings. Watching how poems work out a language for feeling can help us to
work out a language for our own feelings, but the process is also reciprocal:
being conscious of feelings we already have can lead us into poems more
surely and with more satisfaction. Readers with a strong romantic bent—and
with strong yearnings or positive memories of desire—will be likely to find
"The Tally Stick" and "The River-Merchant's Wife: A Letter" easy to respond
to and like, while those more skeptical of human institutions and male habits
will find not only the anger but the formulation of argument in "To the
Ladies" attractive.

   Poems can be about all kinds of experiences, and not all the things we find
in them will replicate (or even relate to) experiences we may have individually
had. But sharing through language will often enable us to get in touch with
feelings—of love or anger, fear or confidence—we did not know we had. The
next few poems involve another, far less pleasant set of feelings than those usu-
ally generated by love, but even here, where our experience may be limited,
we are able to respond, to feel the tug of emotions within us that we may not
be fully aware of. In the following poem, a father struggles to understand and
control his grief over the death of a seven-year-old son. We don't have to be a
father or to have lost a loved one to be aware of—and even share—the speak-
er's pain because our own experiences will have given us some idea of what
such a loss would feel like. And the words and strategies of the poem may alert
us to expectations that our previous experiences with death may activate.

BEN JONSON

On My First Son

Farewell, thou child of my right hand,[2] and joy;
My sin was too much hope of thee, loved boy:
Seven years thou wert lent to me, and I thee pay,

---

2. A literal translation of the son's name, Benjamin.

Exacted by thy fate, on the just[3] day.
O could I lose all father now! for why
5 Will man lament the state he should envý,
To have so soon 'scaped world's and flesh's rage,
And, if no other misery, yet age?
Rest in soft peace, and asked, say, "Here doth lie
10 Ben Jonson his[4] best piece of poetry."
For whose sake henceforth all his vows be such
As what he loves may never like too much.   1616

This poem's attempts to rationalize the boy's death are quite conventional. Although the father tries to be comforted by pious thoughts, his feelings keep showing through. The poem's beginning—with its formal "farewell" and the rather distant-sounding address to the dead boy ("child of my right hand")— cannot be sustained for long: both of the first two lines end with bursts of emotion. It is as if the father is trying to explain the death to himself and to keep his emotions under control, but cannot quite manage it. Even the punctuation suggests the way his feelings compete with conventional attempts to put the death into some sort of perspective that will soften the grief, and the comma near the end of each of the first two lines marks a pause that cannot quite hold back the overflowing emotion. But finally the only "idea" that the poem supports is that the father wishes he did not feel so intensely; in the fifth line he fairly blurts that he wishes he could lose his fatherly emotions, and in the final lines he resolves never again to "like" so much that he can be this deeply hurt. Philosophy and religion offer their useful counsels in this poem, but they prove far less powerful than feeling. Rather than drawing some kind of moral about what death means, the poem presents the actuality of feeling as inevitable and nearly all-consuming.

The poem that follows similarly tries to suppress the rawness of feelings about the death of a loved one, but here the survivor is haunted by memories of his wife when he sees a physical object—a vacuum cleaner—that he associates with her.

HOWARD NEMEROV

The Vacuum

The house is so quiet now
The vacuum cleaner sulks in the corner closet,

---

3. Exact; the son died on his seventh birthday, in 1603.   4. Ben Jonson's (a common Renaissance form of the possessive).

Its bag limp as a stopped lung, its mouth
Grinning into the floor, maybe at my
Slovenly life, my dog-dead youth.   5

I've lived this way long enough,
But when my old woman died her soul
Went into that vacuum cleaner, and I can't bear
To see the bag swell like a belly, eating the dust
And the woolen mice, and begin to howl   10

Because there is old filth everywhere
She used to crawl, in the corner and under the stair.
I know now how life is cheap as dirt,
And still the hungry, angry heart
Hangs on and howls, biting at air.   1955   15

The poem is about a vacuum in the husband's life, but the title refers most
obviously to the vacuum cleaner that, like the tally stick we looked at earlier,
seems to stand for many of the things that were once important in the life he
had together with his wife. The cleaner is a reminder of the dead wife ("my
old woman," line 7) because of her devotion to cleanliness. But to the surviv-
ing husband buried in the filth of his life it seems as if the machine has
become almost human, a kind of ghost of her: it "sulks" (line 2), it has lungs
and a mouth (line 3), and it seems to grin, making fun of what has become of
him. He "can't bear" (line 8) to see it in action because it then seems too
much alive, too much a reminder of her life. The poem records his paralysis,
his inability to do more than discover that life is "cheap as dirt" without her
ordering and cleansing presence for him. At the end it is *his* angry heart that
acts like the haunting machine, howling and biting at air as if he has merged
with her spirit and the physical object that memorializes her. This poem puts a
strong emphasis on the stillness of death and the way it makes things seem to
stop; it captures in words the hurt, the anger, the inability to understand, the
vacuum that remains when a loved one dies and leaves a vacant space. But
here we do not see the body or hear a direct good-bye to the dead person;
rather we encounter the feeling that lingers and won't go away, recalled
through memory by an especially significant object, a mere thing but one that
has been personalized to the point of becoming nearly human in itself. (The
event described here is, by the way, fictional; the poet's wife did not in fact die.
Like a dramatist or writer of fiction, the poet may simply *imagine* an event in
order to analyze and articulate how such an event might feel in certain circum-
stances.)

Here is another poem about the death of a loved one:

SHARON OLDS

The Glass

I think of it with wonder now,
the glass of mucus that stood on the table
next to my father all weekend. The cancer
is growing fast in his throat now,
5 and as it grows it sends out pus like the
sun sending out flares, those pouring
tongues. So my father has to gargle, hack,
spit a mouth full of thick stuff
into the glass every ten minutes or so,
10 scraping the rim up his lower lip to
get the last bit off his skin, then he
sets the glass down on the table and it
sits there, like a glass of beer foam,
shiny and faintly golden, he gurgles and
15 coughs and reaches for it again and
gets the heavy sputum out,
full of bubbles and moving around like yeast—
he is like some god producing food from his own mouth.
He himself can eat nothing anymore,
20 just a swallow of milk sometimes,
cut with water, and even then it
can't always get past the tumor,
and the next time the saliva comes up it's
chalkish and ropey, he has to roll it in his
25 throat to form it and get it up and dis-
gorge the elliptical globule into the cup—
and the wonder to me is that it did not disgust me,
that glass of phlegm that stood there all day and
filled slowly with compound globes and I'd
30 empty it and it would fill again and
shimmer there on the table until the
room seemed to turn around it
in an orderly way, a model of the solar system
turning around the gold sun,
35 my father the dark earth that used to
lie at the center of the universe
now turning with the rest of us
around the bright glass of spit
on the table, these last mouthfuls.

1990

Like "The Vacuum," "The Glass" reflects on a loved one through unconventional images, material objects that suggest pain and unpleasantness rather than joy and love. The "glass" of the title is not a mirror that reflects a beautiful face, not a crafted objet d'art, but rather a simple tumbler, and it is full of mucus—not a very appealing object. The loved one, the father of the person who is speaking the poem, is dying of cancer, and the indicators of his condition are painfully detailed. The sights and sounds are disgusting rather than pleasant; the body fluids are pus and spit, and the human sounds are gargling, gurgling, and hacking. It is almost as if the poem tries to create a picture as ugly as possible, for the father's physical struggle just to swallow and spit is chronicled moment by painful moment. "[T]he wonder to me," says the daughter who views the daily struggle and records it for us in the poem, "is that it did not disgust me" (line 27), and the poem transforms the central object of disgust ("that glass of phlegm," line 28) into something that stands for the daughter's love and the father's ability to accept it even in his deteriorating condition. The daughter's act of staying and emptying the glass represents not only fortitude and loyalty but the steadying influence of stability and predictability. She begins to see the glass itself—its regular filling and emptying of life and coming death—as a kind of center around which human activity revolves "in an orderly way" (line 33). The father, once the center of the family's universe, now seems to move with the others "around" (line 38) the fact of death as represented by the glass. It is an awful picture—awful in its details, awful in its implications of loss—but it is also beautiful in its own way. The poem shows that life and love can be portrayed, explained, and imprinted on our memories by even the most unattractive events, objects, and words.

Sometimes poems are a way of confronting feelings. Sometimes they explore feelings in detail and try to intellectualize or rationalize them. At other times, poems generate responses by recalling an experience many years in the past. In the following two poems, for example, memories of childhood provide perspective on two very different kinds of events. In the first, written as if the person speaking the poem were in the fifth grade, a child's sense of death is portrayed through her exploration of a photograph that makes her grandfather's earlier presence vivid to her memory—a memory that lingers primarily through smell and touch. In the second poem, another childhood memory—this time of overshoes—takes an adult almost physically back into childhood. As you read the two poems, keep track of (or perhaps even jot down) your responses. How much of your feeling is due to your own past experiences? In which specific places? What family photographs do you remember most vividly? What feelings did they invoke that make them so memorable? How are your memories different from those expressed in "Fifth Grade Autobiography"? in "The Fury of Overshoes"? Which feelings expressed in each poem are similar to your own? Where do your feelings differ most strongly? How would you articulate your responses to memories differently? In what ways does an awareness of your similar—and different—experiences and feelings make you a better reader of the poem?

RITA DOVE

Fifth Grade Autobiography

I was four in this photograph fishing
with my grandparents at a lake in Michigan.
My brother squats in poison ivy.
His Davy Crockett cap
5   sits squared on his head so the raccoon tail
flounces down the back of his sailor suit.

My grandfather sits to the far right
in a folding chair,
and I know his left hand is on
10   the tobacco in his pants pocket
because I used to wrap it for him
every Christmas. Grandmother's hips
bulge from the brush, she's leaning
into the ice chest, sun through the trees
15   printing her dress with soft
luminous paws.

I am staring jealously at my brother;
the day before he rode his first horse, alone.
I was strapped in a basket
20   behind my grandfather.
He smelled of lemons. He's died—

but I remember his hands.   1989

ANNE SEXTON

The Fury of Overshoes

They sit in a row
outside the kindergarten,
black, red, brown, all
with those brass buckles.
5   Remember when you couldn't
buckle your own

overshoe
or tie your own
shoe
or cut your own meat   10
and the tears
running down like mud
because you fell off your
tricycle?
Remember, big fish,   15
when you couldn't swim
and simply slipped under
like a stone frog?
The world wasn't
yours.   20
It belonged to
the big people.
Under your bed
sat the wolf
and he made a shadow   25
when cars passed by
at night.
They made you give up
your nightlight
and your teddy   30
and your thumb.
Oh overshoes,
don't you
remember me,
pushing you up and down   35
in the winter snow?
Oh thumb,
I want a drink,
it is dark,
where are the big people,   40
when will I get there,
taking giant steps
all day,
each day,
and thinking   45
nothing of it?   1974

There is much more going on in the poems that we have glanced at than
we have taken time to consider, but even the quickest look at these poems sug-
gests something of the range of feelings that poems can offer—the depth of
feeling, the clarity, the experience that may be articulately and precisely
shared. Not all poems are as accessible as those we've looked at so far, and

even the ones that are accessible usually yield themselves to us more readily and more completely if we approach them systematically by developing specific reading habits and skills—just as someone learning to play tennis systematically learns the rules, the techniques, the things to watch out for that are distinctive to the pleasures and hazards of that skill or craft. It helps if you develop a sense of what to expect, and the chapters that follow will help you to an understanding of the things that poets can do—and thus of what poems can do for you.

But knowing what to expect isn't everything, and I have one bit of advice to offer every prospective reader of poetry before going any further: Be open. Be open to new experience, be open to new feelings, be open to new ideas. Every poem in the world is a potential new experience, and no matter how sophisticated you become, you can still be surprised (and delighted) by new poems— and by rereading old ones. Good poems bear many, many rereadings, and often one discovers something new with every new reading. Be willing to let poems surprise you when you come to them; let them come on their own terms, let them be themselves. If you are open to poetry, you are open to much that the world can offer you.

No one can give you a method that will offer you total experience of all poems. But because many characteristics of an individual poem are characteristics that one poem shares with other poems, there are guidelines that can prompt you to ask the right questions. The chapters that follow will help you in detail with a variety of problems, but meanwhile here is a checklist of some things to remember:

1. *Read the syntax literally.* What the words say literally in normal sentences is only a starting point, but it is the place to start. Not all poems use normal prose syntax, but most of them do, and you can save yourself embarrassment by paraphrasing accurately (that is, rephrasing what the poem literally says, in plain prose) and not simply free-associating from an isolated word or phrase.

2. *Articulate for yourself what the title, subject, and situation make you expect.* Poets often use false leads and try to surprise you by doing shocking things, but defining expectation lets you be conscious of where you are when you begin.

3. *Identify the poem's situation.* What is said is often conditioned by where it is said and by whom. Identifying the speaker and his or her place in the situation puts what he or she says in perspective.

4. *Find out what is implied by the traditions behind the poem.* Verse forms,

poetic kinds, and metrical patterns all have a frame of reference, traditions of the way they are usually used and for what. For example, the anapest (two unstressed syllables followed by a stressed one, as in the word "Tennessee") is usually used for comic poems, and when poets use it "straight" they are aware of their "departure" and are probably making a point by doing it.

5. *Bother the reference librarian.* Look up anything you don't understand: an unfamiliar word (or an ordinary word used in an unfamiliar way), a place, a person, a myth, an idea—anything the poem uses. When you can't find what you need or don't know where to look, ask for help.

6. *Remember that poems exist in time, and times change.* Not only the meanings of words, but whole ways of looking at the universe vary in different ages. Consciousness of time works two ways: your knowledge of history provides a context for reading the poem, and the poem's use of a word or idea may modify your notion of a particular age.

7. *Take a poem on its own terms.* Adjust to the poem; don't make the poem adjust to you. Be prepared to hear things you do not want to hear. Not all poems are about your ideas, nor will they always present emotions you want to feel. But be tolerant and listen to the poem's ideas, not only to your desire to revise them for yourself.

8. *Be willing to be surprised.* Things often happen in poems that turn them around. A poem may seem to suggest one thing at first, then persuade you of its opposite, or at least of a significant qualification or variation.

9. *Assume there is a reason for everything.* Poets do make mistakes, but in poems that show some degree of verbal control it is usually safest to assume that the poet chose each word carefully; if the choice seems peculiar to us, it is often *we* who are missing something. Try to account for everything in a poem and see what kind of sense you can make of it. Poets make choices; try to figure out a coherent pattern that explains the text as it stands.

10. *Argue.* Discussion usually results in clarification and keeps you from being too dependent on personal biases and preoccupations that sometimes mislead even the best readers. Talking a poem over with someone else (especially someone very different) can expand your perspective.

WRITING ABOUT POEMS   If you have been keeping notes on your personal responses to the poems you've read, you have already taken an important step toward writing about them. There are many different ways to write about poems, just as there are many different things to say. (The chapter

in the back of the book on *Writing About Literature* suggests many different
kinds of topics.) But all writing begins from a clear sense of the poem itself and
your responses to it, so the first steps (long before formally sitting down to
write) are to read the poem over several times and keep notes on the things
that strike you and the questions that remain.

Formulating a clear series of questions will usually help lead you to an
appropriate approach to the poem and to a good topic. Learning to ask the
right questions can save you a lot of time. Some questions—the kinds of ques-
tions implied in the ten guidelines for reading listed above (pp. 16–17)—are
basic and more or less apply to all poems. But each poem makes demands of
its own, too, because of its distinctive way of going about its business, so you
will usually want to make a list of what seem to you the crucial questions for
that poem. Here are—just to give you an example—some questions that could
be useful in leading you to a paper topic on the first of the poems printed at
the end of this chapter.

1. How does the title affect your reading of and response to the poem?
2. What is the poem about?
3. What makes the poem interesting to read?
4. Who is the speaker? What role does the speaker have in the poem?
5. What effect does the poem have on you as a reader? Do you think the
poet intended to have such an effect?
6. What is distinctive about the poet's use of language? Which words espe-
cially contribute to the poem's effect?

What *is* poetry? Let your definition be cumulative as you read more and
more poems. No dictionary definition will cover all that you find, and it is
better to discover for yourself poetry's many ingredients, its many effects, its
many ways of acting. What can it do for you? Wait and see. Begin to add up its
effects after you have read carefully—after you have studied and reread—a hun-
dred or so poems; that will be a beginning, and you will be able to add to that
total as long as you continue to read new poems or reread old ones.

▾   ▾   ▾

WILLIAM SHAKESPEARE

[Let me not to the marriage of true minds]

Let me not to the marriage of true minds
Admit impediments.[5] Love is not love
Which alters when it alteration finds,
Or bends with the remover to remove:
Oh, no! it is an ever-fixéd mark,   5
That looks on tempests and is never shaken;
It is the star to every wandering bark,
Whose worth's unknown, although his height be taken.[6]
Love's not Time's fool, though rosy lips and cheeks
Within his bending sickle's compass come;   10
Love alters not with his brief hours and weeks,
But bears it out even to the edge of doom.
If this be error and upon me proved,
I never writ, nor no man ever loved.   1609

ANNE BRADSTREET

To My Dear and Loving Husband

If ever two were one, then surely we.
If ever man were loved by wife, then thee;
If ever wife was happy in a man,
Compare with me ye women if you can.
I prize thy love more than whole mines of gold,   5
Or all the riches that the East doth hold.
My love is such that rivers cannot quench,
Nor aught but love from thee give recompense.
Thy love is such I can no way repay;
The heavens reward thee manifold, I pray.   10
Then while we live, in love let's so persever,
That when we live no more we may live ever.   1678

---

5. The Marriage Service contains this address to the witnesses: "If any of you know cause or just impediments why these persons should not be joined together. . . ."   **6.** I.e., measuring the altitude of stars (for purposes of navigation) is not a measurement of value.

W. B. YEATS

A Last Confession

What lively lad most pleasured me
Of all that with me lay?
I answer that I gave my soul
And loved in misery,
5 But had great pleasure with a lad
That I loved bodily.

Flinging from his arms I laughed
To think his passion such
He fancied that I gave a soul
10 Did but our bodies touch,
And laughed upon his breast to think
Beast gave beast as much.

I gave what other women gave
That stepped out of their clothes,
15 But when this soul, its body off,
Naked to naked goes,
He it has found shall find therein
What none other knows,

And give his own and take his own
20 And rule in his own right;
And though it loved in misery
Close and cling so tight,
There's not a bird of day that dare
Extinguish that delight.   1933

EDNA ST. VINCENT MILLAY

[I, being born a woman and distressed]

I, being born a woman and distressed
By all the needs and notions of my kind,
Am urged by your propinquity to find
Your person fair, and feel a certain zest
5 To bear your body's weight upon my breast:
So subtly is the fume of life designed,
To clarify the pulse and cloud the mind,
And leave me once again undone, possessed.
Think not for this, however, the poor treason
10 Of my stout blood against my staggering brain,
I shall remember you with love, or season

My scorn with pity,—let me make it plain:
I find this frenzy insufficient reason
For conversation when we meet again.   1923

GALWAY KINNELL

After Making Love We Hear Footsteps

For I can snore like a bullhorn
or play loud music
or sit up talking with any reasonably sober Irishman
and Fergus will only sink deeper
into his dreamless sleep, which goes by all in one flash,   5
but let there be that heavy breathing
or a stifled come-cry anywhere in the house
and he will wrench himself awake
and make for it on the run—as now, we lie together,
after making love, quiet, touching along the length of our bodies,   10
familiar touch of the long-married,
and he appears—in his baseball pajamas, it happens,
the neck opening so small
he has to screw them on, which one day may make him wonder
about the mental capacity of baseball players—   15
and says, "Are you loving and snuggling? May I join?"
He flops down between us and hugs us and snuggles himself to sleep,
his face gleaming with satisfaction at being this very child.

In the half darkness we look at each other
and smile   20
and touch arms across his little, startlingly muscled body—
this one whom habit of memory propels to the ground of his making,
sleeper only the mortal sounds can sing awake,
this blessing love gives again into our arms.   1980

CAROL JANE BANGS

Touching Each Other's Surfaces

Skin meeting skin, we want to think
we know each other scientifically;
we want to believe
it is objective knowledge
gives this conviction of intimacy,   5
makes us say it feels so right.
That mole below your shoulder blade,

the soft hair over my thighs—
we examine our bodies with the precision
known only to lovers or surgeons,
all those whose profession is explication,
who have to believe their own words.
And yet, having memorized each turning,
each place where bone strains or bends,
each hollow, each hair, each failure of form,
we still encounter that stubborn wall,
that barrier which hides an infinite vastness
the most sincere gesture can't find.

Nor does emotion take us further
than the shared heat of bodies
aware of themselves,
the flattery of multiple desires.
We rest in each other's arms unexplained
by these currents of feeling rushing past
like ripples over a pool of water
whose substance never changes,
reflecting each wave, each ribboned crossing,
without being really moved.
We search each other's eyes so long
beyond our own reflections,
finding only the black centers,
the immeasurable interior we'll
never reach with candle,
never plumb with love.
Perhaps it is just this ignorance,
this absence of certainty, lack of clear view,
more than anything, brings us together,
draws us into and through each other
to the unknown inside us all,
that gray space from which
what we know of ourselves
emerges briefly, casts a transient
shadow across the earth
and learns to believe in itself just enough
to believe in some one else.   1983

LI-YOUNG LEE

Persimmons

In sixth grade Mrs. Walker
slapped the back of my head
and made me stand in the corner

for not knowing the difference
between *persimmon* and *precision*.   5
How to choose

persimmons. This is precision.
Ripe ones are soft and brown-spotted.
Sniff the bottoms. The sweet one
will be fragrant. How to eat: 10
put the knife away, lay down newspaper.
Peel the skin tenderly, not to tear the meat.
Chew the skin, suck it,
and swallow. Now, eat
the meat of the fruit,   15
so sweet,
all of it, to the heart.

Donna undresses, her stomach is white.
In the yard, dewy and shivering
with crickets, we lie naked,   20
face-up, face-down.
I teach her Chinese.
Crickets: *chiu chiu.* Dew: I've forgotten.
Naked: I've forgotten.
Ni, wo: you and me.   25
I part her legs,
remember to tell her
she is beautiful as the moon.

Other words
that got me into trouble were   30
fight and *fright, wren* and *yarn.*
Fight was what I did when I was frightened,
fright was what I felt when I was fighting.
Wrens are small, plain birds,
yarn is what one knits with.   35
Wrens are soft as yarn.
My mother made birds out of yarn.
I loved to watch her tie the stuff;
a bird, a rabbit, a wee man.

Mrs. Walker brought a persimmon to class   40
and cut it up
so everyone could taste
a *Chinese apple.* Knowing
it wasn't ripe or sweet, I didn't eat
but watched the other faces.   45

My mother said every persimmon has a sun
inside, something golden, glowing,
warm as my face.

Once, in the cellar, I found two wrapped in newspaper,
50   forgotten and not yet ripe.
I took them and set both on my bedroom windowsill,
where each morning a cardinal
sang, *The sun, the sun.*

Finally understanding
55   he was going blind,
my father sat up all one night
waiting for a song, a ghost.
I gave him the persimmons,
swelled, heavy as sadness,
60   and sweet as love.

This year, in the muddy lighting
of my parents' cellar, I rummage, looking
for something I lost.
My father sits on the tired, wooden stairs,
65   black cane between his knees,
hand over hand, gripping the handle.

He's so happy that I've come home.
I ask how his eyes are, a stupid question.
All gone, he answers.

70   Under some blankets, I find a box.
Inside the box I find three scrolls.
I sit beside him and untie
three paintings by my father:
Hibiscus leaf and a white flower.
75   Two cats preening.
Two persimmons, so full they want to drop from the cloth.

He raises both hands to touch the cloth,
asks, *Which is this?*

This is persimmons, Father.

80   *Oh, the feel of the wolftail on the silk,*
the strength, the tense
precision in the wrist.
I painted them hundreds of times
eyes closed. These I painted blind.
85   *Some things never leave a person:*
scent of the hair of one you love,
the texture of persimmons,
in your palm, the ripe weight.

                                                  1986

AUDRE LORDE

Recreation

Coming together
it is easier to work
after our bodies
meet
paper and pen   5
neither care nor profit
whether we write or not
but as your body moves
under my hands
charged and waiting   10
we cut the leash
you create me against your thighs
hilly with images
moving through our word countries
my body   15
writes into your flesh
the poem
you make of me

Touching you I catch midnight
as moon fires set in my throat   20
I love you flesh into blossom
I made you
and take you made
into me.   1978

ERIN MOURÉ

Thirteen Years

I am in a daydream of my uncle,
his shirt out at his daughter's wedding,
white scoop of the shirt-tail bobbing
on the dance floor & him in it, no,
his drunk friend pawing me, it was *his* shirt dangling,   5
I forgot this
my youngest cousin in his dress pants downing straight whisky,
& me too, tying tin cans to his sister's car.
The sour taste of it. Drink this, he said.

I am wondering how we live at all   10
or if we do.

The puppy we grew up with came from the same uncle's farm.
His shirt-tail beneath his suit jacket, dancing.
The friend of the family touching my new chest.
15 They told me not to say so.
I'll drive you to the motel, he said, his breath close.
No. Be nice to him, they said, & waved me off from the table.
I was so scared.
Everyone had been drinking. Including me. Thirteen years old.
20 Who the hell did my cousin marry.
I tell you.   1988

▼   ▼   ▼

QUESTIONS

1. Did you notice that "To the Ladies" was written in 1703? Were you at all surprised by your response to it when you read it? If not, does the date of publication modify your response? Why?

2. How did you respond to "Thirteen Years"? What message is the speaker trying to get across to us? How does she feel about herself and her relatives as she recounts this adolescent experience?

WRITING SUGGESTIONS

1. Jot down your responses to all of the marriage poems at the beginning of this chapter. Which one most accurately expresses your ideal of a good marriage? Why do you think so? What does your choice say about you?

2. Choose one of the poems on death, and write a letter to the grieving relative (the speaker) in which you offer condolences and comfort.

▽ ▽ ▽

Understanding the Text

1 TONE

Poetry is full of surprises. Poems express anger or outrage just as effectively as love or sadness, and good poems can be written about going to a rock concert or having lunch or cutting the lawn, as well as about making love or gazing at a cloudless sky or smelling flowers. Even poems on "predictable" subjects can surprise us with unpredicted attitudes, unusual events, or a sudden twist. Knowing that a poem is about some particular subject—love, for example, or death—may give us a general idea of what to expect, but it never tells us altogether what we will find in a particular poem. Responding to a poem fully means being open to the poem and its surprises, being willing to let the poem guide us to its own stances, feelings, and ideas. Letting a poem speak to us means being willing to listen to *how* the poem says what it says—hearing the tone of voice implied in the way the words are spoken.

The following two poems—one about death and one about love—express rather different ideas and feelings from the poems we have read so far.

MARGE PIERCY

Barbie Doll

This girlchild was born as usual
and presented dolls that did pee-pee
and miniature GE stoves and irons

27

and wee lipsticks the color of cherry candy.
Then in the magic of puberty, a classmate said:
You have a great big nose and fat legs.

She was healthy, tested intelligent,
possessed strong arms and back,
abundant sexual drive and manual dexterity.
She went to and fro apologizing.
Everyone saw a fat nose on thick legs.

She was advised to play coy,
exhorted to come on hearty,
exercise, diet, smile and wheedle.
Her good nature wore out
like a fan belt.
So she cut off her nose and her legs
and offered them up.

In the casket displayed on satin she lay
with the undertaker's cosmetics painted on,
a turned-up putty nose,
dressed in a pink and white nightie.
Doesn't she look pretty? everyone said.
Consummation at last.
To every woman a happy ending.   1973

W. D. SNODGRASS

Leaving the Motel

Outside, the last kids holler
Near the pool: they'll stay the night.
Pick up the towels; fold your collar
Out of sight.

Check: is the second bed
Unrumpled, as agreed?
Landlords have to think ahead
In case of need,

Too. Keep things straight: don't take
The matches, the wrong keyrings—
We've nowhere we could keep a keepsake—
Ashtrays, combs, things

That sooner or later others
Would accidentally find.
Check: take nothing of one another's
And leave behind

Your license number only,
Which they won't care to trace;
We've paid. Still, should such things get lonely,
Leave in their vase   20

An aspirin to preserve
Our lilacs, the wayside flowers
We've gathered and must leave to serve
A few more hours;

That's all. We can't tell when   25
We'll come back, can't press claims,
We would no doubt have other rooms then,
Or other names.   1968

The first poem has the strong note of sadness that characterizes many death
poems, but its emphasis is not on the girl's death but on the disappointments
in her life. The only "scene" in the poem (lines 19–23) portrays the unnamed
girl at rest in her casket, but the still body in the casket contrasts not with vital-
ity but with frustration and anxiety: her life since puberty (lines 5–6) had been
full of apologies and attempts to change her physical appearance and emo-
tional makeup. The rest she achieves in death is not, however, a triumph,
despite what people say (line 23). Although the poem's last two words are
"happy ending," this girl without a name has died in embarrassment and with-
out fulfillment, and the final lines are ironic, meaning the opposite of what
they say. The cheerful comments at the end lack force and truth because of
what we already know; we understand them as ironic because they underline
how unhappy the girl was and how false her cosmeticized corpse is to the sad
truth of her life.

The poem's concern is to suggest the falsity and destructiveness of those
standards of female beauty that have led to the tragedy of the girl's life. In an
important sense, the poem is not really *about* death at all in spite of the fact
that the girl's death and her repaired corpse are central to it. As the title sug-
gests, the poem dramatizes how standardized, commercialized notions of femi-
ninity and prettiness can be painful and destructive to those whose bodies do
not precisely fit the conformist models, and the poem attacks vigorously those
conventional standards and the widespread, unthinking acceptance of them.

"Leaving the Motel" similarly goes in quite a different direction from many
poems on the subject of love. Instead of expressing assurance about how love
lasts and endures, or about the sincerity and depth of affection, this poem
describes a parting of lovers after a brief sexual encounter. But it does not
emphasize sexuality or eroticism in the meeting of the nameless lovers (we see

them only as they prepare to leave), nor does it suggest why or how they have found each other, or what either of them is like as a person. Its focus is on how careful they must be not to get caught, how exact and calculating they must be in their planning, how finite and limited their encounter must be, how sealed off this encounter is from the rest of their lives. The poem relates the tiny details the lovers must think of, the agreements they must observe, and the ritual checklist of their duties ("Check . . . Keep things straight . . . Check . . . ," lines 5, 9, 15). Affection and sentiment have their small place in the poem (notice the care for the flowers, lines 19–24, and the thought of "pressing claims," line 26), but the emphasis is on temporariness, uncertainty, and limits. The poem is about an illicit, perhaps adulterous, sexual encounter, but there is no sex in the poem, only a kind of archeological record of lust.

Labeling a poem as a "love poem" or a "death poem" is primarily a matter of convenience; such categories indicate the **subject** of a poem or the event or **topic** it chooses to engage. But as the poems we have been looking at suggest, poems that may be loosely called love poems or death poems may differ widely from one another, express totally different attitudes or ideas, and concentrate on very different aspects of the subject. The main advantages of grouping poems in this way for study is that a reader can become conscious of individual differences: a reading of two poems side by side may suggest how each is distinctive in what it has to say and how it says it.

What a poem has to say is often called its **theme,** the kind of statement it makes about its subject. We could say, for example, that the theme of "Leaving the Motel" is that illicit love is secretive, careful, transitory, and short on emotion and sentiment, or that secret sexual encounters tend to be brief, calculated, and characterized by restrained and insecure feelings. The theme of a poem may be expressed in several different ways, and poems often have more than one theme. "Barbie Doll" suggests that commercialized standards destroy human values; that rigid and idealized notions of normality cripple those who are different; that people are easily and tragically led to accept evaluations thrust upon them by others; that American consumers tend to be conformists, easily influenced in their outlook by advertising and by commercial products; that children who do not conform to middle-class standards and notions don't have a chance. The poem implies each of these statements, and all are quite central to it. But none of these statements individually nor all of them together would fully express or explain the poem itself. To state the themes in such a brief and abstract way—though it may be helpful in clarifying what the poem does and does not say—never does justice to the experience of the poem, the way it works on us as readers, the way we respond. Poems affect us in all sorts of ways—emotional and psychological as well as rational—and often a poem's dramatization of a story, an event, or a moment bypasses our rational responses and affects us far more deeply than a clear and logical argument would.

Sometimes poems express feelings directly and quite simply:

LINDA PASTAN

love poem

I want to write you
a love poem as headlong
as our creek
after thaw
when we stand   5
on its dangerous
banks and watch it carry
with it every twig
every dry leaf and branch
in its path   10
every scruple
when we see it
so swollen
with runoff
that even as we watch   15
we must grab
each other
and step back
we must grab each
other or   20
get our shoes
soaked we must
grab each other   1988

The directness and simplicity of this poem suggest how the art and craft of poems work. The poem expresses the desire to write a love poem even as the love poem itself begins to proceed; the desire and the resultant poem exist side by side, and in reading the poem we seem to watch the poet's creative process at work in developing appropriate metaphors and means of expression. The poem must be "headlong" (line 2), to match the power of a love that needs to be compared to the irresistible forces of nature. The poem should, like the love it expresses and the swollen creek it describes, sweep everything along, and it should represent (and reproduce) the sense of watching that the lovers have when they observe natural processes at work. The poem, like the action it represents, has to suggest to readers the kind of desire that grabbing each other means to the lovers.

The lovers in this poem seem, at least to themselves, to own the world they observe, when in fact they are controlled by it. The creek on whose banks they stand is "our creek" (line 3), but what they observe as they watch its rising currents requires them ("must," lines 16, 19, 22) to "grab each other" over and over again. It is as if their love is part of nature itself, which subjects them to forces larger than themselves. Everything—twigs, leaves, branches, scruples—is carried along by the powerful currents after the "thaw" (line 4), and the poem replicates the repeated action of the lovers as if to power along observant readers just as the lovers are powered along by what they see. But the poem (and their love) admits dangers too; it is the fact of danger that propels the lovers to each other. The poem suggests that love provides a kind of haven, but the haven hardly involves passivity or peace; instead, it requires the kind of grabbing that means activity and boldness and deep passion. Love here is no quiet or simple matter even if the expression of it in poems can be direct and based on a simple observation of experience. The "love poem" itself—linked as it is with the headlong currents of the creek from which the lovers are protecting themselves—even represents that which is beyond love and that therefore both threatens it and at the same time makes it happen. The power of poetry is thus affirmed at the center of the poem, but what poetry is about (love and life) is suggested to be more important. Poetry makes things happen but is not itself a substitute for life, just a means to make it more energetic and meaningful.

Poems, then, differ widely from one another even when they share a common subject. And the subjects of poetry also vary widely. It isn't true that there are certain "poetic" subjects and that there are others that aren't appropriate to poetry. Any human activity, thought, or feeling can be the subject of poetry. Poetry often deals with beauty and the softer, more attractive human emotions, but it can deal with ugliness and less attractive human conduct as well, for poetry seeks to represent human beings and human events, showing us ourselves not only as we would like to be but as we are. Good poetry gets written about all kinds of topics, in all kinds of forms, with all kinds of attitudes. Here, for example, is a poem about a prison inmate—and about the conflict between individual and societal values.

ETHERIDGE KNIGHT

Hard Rock Returns to Prison from the Hospital for the Criminal Insane

Hard Rock was "known not to take no shit
From nobody," and he had the scars to prove it:
Split purple lips, lumped ears, welts above
His yellow eyes, and one long scar that cut
Across his temple and plowed through a thick   5
Canopy of kinky hair.

The WORD was that Hard Rock wasn't a mean nigger
Anymore, that the doctors had bored a hole in his head,
Cut out part of his brain, and shot electricity
Through the rest. When they brought Hard Rock back,   10
Handcuffed and chained, he was turned loose,
Like a freshly gelded stallion, to try his new status.
And we all waited and watched, like indians at a corral,
To see if the WORD was true.

As we waited we wrapped ourselves in the cloak   15
Of his exploits: "Man, the last time, it took eight
Screws to put him in the Hole."[1] "Yeah, remember when he
Smacked the captain with his dinner tray?" "He set
The record for time in the Hole—67 straight days!"
"Ol Hard Rock! man, that's one crazy nigger."   20
And then the jewel of a myth that Hard Rock had once bit
A screw on the thumb and poisoned him with syphilitic spit.

The testing came, to see if Hard Rock was really tame.
A hillbilly called him a black son of a bitch
And didn't lose his teeth, a screw who knew Hard Rock   25
From before shook him down and barked in his face.
And Hard Rock did *nothing*. Just grinned and looked silly,
His eyes empty like knot holes in a fence.

And even after we discovered that it took Hard Rock
Exactly 3 minutes to tell you his first name,   30
We told ourselves that he had just wised up,
Was being cool; but we could not fool ourselves for long,
And we turned away, our eyes on the ground. Crushed.
He had been our Destroyer, the doer of things
We dreamed of doing but could not bring ourselves to do,   35
The fears of years, like a biting whip,
Had cut grooves too deeply across our backs.   1968

1. Solitary confinement. *Screws*: guards.

The picture of Hard Rock as a kind of hero to other prison inmates is established early in the poem through a retelling of the legends circulated about him; the straightforward chronology of the poem sets up the mystery of how he will react after his "treatment" in the hospital. The poem identifies with those who wait; they are hopeful that Hard Rock's spirit has not been broken by surgery or shock treatments, and the lines crawl almost to a stop with disappointment in stanza 4. The *"nothing"* (line 27) of Hard Rock's response to teasing and taunting and the emptiness of his eyes ("like knot holes in a fence," line 28) reduce the heroic hopes and illusions to despair. The final stanza recounts the observers' attempts to reinterpret, to hang onto hope that their symbol of heroism could stand up against the best efforts to tame him, but the spirit has gone out of the hero-worshipers too, and the poem records them as beaten, conformed, deprived of their spirit as Hard Rock has been of his. The poem records the despair of the hopeless, and it protests against the cruel exercise of power that can curb even as rebellious a figure as Hard Rock.

The following poem is equally full of anger and disappointment, but it expresses its attitudes in a very different way.

WILLIAM BLAKE

London

I wander through each chartered street,
Near where the chartered Thames does flow,
And mark in every face I meet
Marks of weakness, marks of woe.

5   In every cry of every man,
In every Infant's cry of fear,
In every voice, in every ban,
The mind-forged manacles I hear.

How the Chimney-sweeper's cry
10 Every black'ning Church appalls;
And the hapless Soldier's sigh
Runs in blood down Palace walls.

But most through midnight streets I hear
How the youthful Harlot's curse
15 Blasts the new-born Infant's tear,
And blights with plagues the Marriage hearse.   1794

The poem gives a strong sense of how London feels to this particular observer; it is cluttered, constricting, oppressive. The wordplay here articulates and connects the strong emotions he associates with London experiences. The repeated words—"every," for example, or "cry"—intensify the sense of total despair in the city and weld connections between things not necessarily related—the cries of street vendors, for example, with the cries for help. The twice-used word "chartered" implies strong feelings too. The streets, instead of seeming alive with people or bustling with movement, are rigidly, coldly determined, controlled, cramped. Likewise the river seems as if it were planned, programmed, laid out by an oppressor. In actual fact, the course of the Thames had been altered (slightly) by the government before Blake's time, but most important is the word's emotional force, the sense it projects of constriction and artificiality: the person speaking experiences London as if human artifice had totally altered nature. Moreover, according to the poem, people are victimized, "marked" by their confrontations with urbanness and the power of institutions: the "Soldier's sigh" that "runs in blood down Palace walls" vividly suggests, through a metaphor that visually depicts the speaker's feelings, both the powerlessness of the individual and the callousness of power. The "description" of the city has clearly become, by now, a subjective, highly emotional, and vivid expression of how the speaker feels about London and what it represents to him.

Another thing about "London": at first it looks like an account of a personal experience, as if the speaker is describing and interpreting as he goes along: "I wander through each chartered street." But soon it is clear that he is describing many wanderings, putting together impressions from many walks, re-creating a typical walk—which shows him "every" person in the streets, allows him to generalize about the churches being "appalled" (literally, made white) by the cry of the representative Chimney-sweeper, and leads to his conclusions about soldiers, prostitutes, and infants. What we are given is not a personal record of an event, but a representation of it, as it seems in retrospect—not a story, not a narrative or chronological account of events, but a dramatization of self that compresses many experiences into one.

"London" is somber in spite of the poet's playfulness with words. Wordplay may be witty and funny if it calls attention to its own cleverness, but here it involves the discovery of unsuspected (but meaningful) connections between things. The term **tone** is used to describe the attitude a poem takes toward its subject and theme. If the theme of a poem is *what* the poem says, the tone involves *how* one says it. The tone of "London" is sad, despairing, and angry; reading "London" aloud, one would try to show in one's voice the strong feelings that the poem expresses, just as one would try to reproduce tenderness and caring and passion in reading aloud "The Tally Stick" or "How Do I Love Thee?"

The following two poems involve animals, although both of them place their final emphasis on what human beings are like: the animal in each case is only the means to the end of exploring human nature. The poems share a common assumption that animal behavior may appear to reflect human habits and conduct and may reveal much about ourselves, and in each case the character central to the poem is revealed to be surprisingly unlike the way she thinks of herself. But the poems are very different from one another. Read each poem aloud, and try to imagine what each main character is like. What tones of voice do you use to help express the character of the killer in the first poem? What demands on your voice does the second poem make?

MAXINE KUMIN

Woodchucks

Gassing the woodchucks didn't turn out right.
The knockout bomb from the Feed and Grain Exchange
was featured as merciful, quick at the bone
and the case we had against them was airtight,
both exits shoehorned shut with puddingstone,[2]
but they had a sub-sub-basement out of range.

Next morning they turned up again, no worse
for the cyanide than we for our cigarettes
and state-store Scotch, all of us up to scratch.
They brought down the marigolds as a matter of course
and then took over the vegetable patch
nipping the broccoli shoots, beheading the carrots.

The food from our mouths, I said, righteously thrilling
to the feel of the .22, the bullets' neat noses.
I, a lapsed pacifist fallen from grace
puffed with Darwinian pieties for killing,
now drew a bead on the littlest woodchuck's face.
He died down in the everbearing roses.

Ten minutes later I dropped the mother. She
flipflopped in the air and fell, her needle teeth
still hooked in a leaf of early Swiss chard.
Another baby next. O one-two-three
the murderer inside me rose up hard,
the hawkeye killer came on stage forthwith.

There's one chuck left. Old wily fellow, he keeps
me cocked and ready day after day after day.

2. A mixture of cement, pebbles, and gravel.

All night I hunt his humped-up form. I dream
I sight along the barrel in my sleep.
If only they'd all consented to die unseen
gassed underground the quiet Nazi way.   30

1972

ADRIENNE RICH

Aunt Jennifer's Tigers

Aunt Jennifer's tigers prance across a screen,
Bright topaz denizens of a world of green.
They do not fear the men beneath the tree;
They pace in sleek chivalric certainty.

Aunt Jennifer's fingers fluttering through her wool   5
Find even the ivory needle hard to pull.
The massive weight of Uncle's wedding band
Sits heavily upon Aunt Jennifer's hand.

When Aunt is dead, her terrified hands will lie
Still ringed with ordeals she was mastered by.   10
The tigers in the panel that she made
Will go on prancing, proud and unafraid.   1951

If you read "Woodchucks" aloud, how would your tone of voice change from beginning to end? What tone would you use to read the ending? How does the hunter feel about her increasing attraction to violence? Why does the poem begin by calling the gassing of the woodchucks "merciful" and end by describing it as "the quiet Nazi way"? What names does the hunter call herself? How does the name-calling affect your feelings about her? Exactly when does the hunter begin to *enjoy* the feel of the gun and the idea of killing? How does the poet make that clear?

Why are tigers a particularly appropriate contrast to the quiet and subdued manner of Aunt Jennifer? What words used to describe the tigers seem particularly significant? In what ways is the tiger an opposite of Aunt Jennifer? In what ways does it externalize her secrets? Why are Aunt Jennifer's hands described as "terrified"? What clues does the poem give about why Aunt Jennifer is so afraid? How does the poem make you feel about Aunt Jennifer? about her tigers? about her life? How would you describe the tone of the poem? How does the poet feel about Aunt Jennifer?

Twenty years after writing "Aunt Jennifer's Tigers," Adrienne Rich said this about the poem:

In writing this poem, composed and apparently cool as it is, I thought I was creating a portrait of an imaginary woman. But this woman suffers from the opposition of her imagination, worked out in tapestry, and her life style, "ringed with ordeals she was mastered by." It was important to me that Aunt Jennifer was a person as distinct from myself as possible—distanced by the formalism of the poem, by its objective, observant tone—even by putting the woman in a different generation. In those years formalism was part of the strategy—like asbestos gloves, it allowed me to handle materials I couldn't pick up bare-handed.[3]

Not often do we have such an explicit comment on a poem by its author, and we don't actually have to have it to understand and experience the force of the poem (although such a statement may clarify why the author chose particular modes of presentation and how the poem fits into the author's own patterns of thinking and growing). Most poems contain within them what we need to know in order to tap the human and artistic resources they offer us.

Subject, theme, and tone: each of these categories gives us a way to begin considering poems and showing how one poem differs from another. Comparing poems on the same subject, or with a similar theme or tone, can lead to a clearer understanding of each individual poem and can refine our responses to the subtleties of individual differences. The title of a poem ("Leaving the Motel," for example) or the way the poem first introduces its subject often can give us a sense of what to expect, but we need to be open to surprise too. No two poems are going to be exactly alike in their effect on us; the variety of possible poems multiplies when you think of all the possible themes and tones that can be explored within any single subject. Varieties of feeling often coincide with varieties of thinking, and readers open to the pleasures of the unexpected may find themselves learning, growing, becoming more sensitive to ideas and human issues as well as more articulate about feelings and thoughts they already have.

▾ ▾ ▾

ALAN DUGAN

Elegy

I know but will not tell
you, Aunt Irene, why there

---

3. From "When We Dead Awaken: Writing as Re-Vision," a talk given in December 1971 at the Women's Forum of the Modern Language Association.

are soapsuds in the whiskey:
Uncle Robert had to have
a drink while shaving. May   5
there be no bloodshed in your house
this morning of my father's death
and no unkept appearance
in the living, since he has
to wear the rouge and lipstick   10
of your ceremony, mother,
for the first and last time:
father, hello and goodbye.   1963

DOROTHY PARKER

Comment

Oh, life is a glorious cycle of song,
A medley of extemporanea;
And love is a thing that can never go wrong;
And I am Marie of Rumania.   1926

SIR WALTER RALEGH

The Author's Epitaph, Made By Himself

Even such is time, which takes in trust
Our youth, our joys, and all we have,
And pays us but with age and dust,
Who in the dark and silent grave
When we have wandered all our ways   5
Shuts up the story of our days,
And from which earth, and grave, and dust
The Lord shall raise me up, I trust.   1628

CAROLYN FORCHÉ

Reunion

Just as he changes himself, in the end eternity changes him.
—MALLARMÉ

On the phonograph, the voice
of a woman already dead for three

decades, singing of a man
who could make her do anything.
On the table, two fragile
glasses of black wine,
a bottle wrapped in its towel.
It is that room, the one
we took in every city, it is
as I remember: the bed, a block
of moonlight and pillows.
My fingernails, pecks of light
on your thighs.
The stink of the fire escape.
The wet butts of cigarettes
you crushed one after another.
How I watched the morning come
as you slept, more my son
than a man ten years older.
How my breasts feel, years
later, the tongues swishing
in my dress, some yours, some
left by other men.
Since then, I have always
wakened first, I have learned
to leave a bed without being
seen and have stood
at the washbasins, wiping oil
and salt from my skin,
staring at the cupped water
in my two hands.
I have kept everything
you whispered to me then.
I can remember it now as I see you
again, how much tenderness we could
wedge between a stairwell
and a police lock, or as it was,
as it still is, in the voice
of a woman singing of a man
who could make her do anything.

1981

APHRA BEHN

On Her Loving Two Equally

I

How strong does my passion flow,
Divided equally twixt[4] two?
Damon had ne'er subdued my heart
Had not Alexis took his part;
Nor could Alexis powerful prove,   5
Without my Damon's aid, to gain my love.

II

When my Alexis present is,
Then I for Damon sigh and mourn;
But when Alexis I do miss,
Damon gains nothing but my scorn.   10
But if it chance they both are by,
For both alike I languish, sigh, and die.

III

Cure then, thou mighty wingéd god,[5]
This restless fever in my blood;
One golden-pointed dart take back: 15
But which, O Cupid, wilt thou take?
If Damon's, all my hopes are crossed;
Or that of my Alexis, I am lost.   1684

ROBERT HAYDEN

Those Winter Sundays

Sundays too my father got up early
and put his clothes on in the blueblack cold,
then with cracked hands that ached
from labor in the weekday weather made
banked fires blaze. No one ever thanked him.   5

I'd wake and hear the cold splintering, breaking.
When the rooms were warm, he'd call,
and slowly I would rise and dress,
fearing the chronic angers of that house,

---

4. Between.   5. Cupid, who, according to myth, shot darts of lead and of gold at the hearts of lovers, corresponding to false love and true love, respectively.

10   Speaking indifferently to him,
     who had driven out the cold
     and polished my good shoes as well.
     What did I know, what did I know
     of love's austere and lonely offices?   1966

SYLVIA PLATH

Daddy

You do not do, you do not do
Any more, black shoe
In which I have lived like a foot
For thirty years, poor and white,
5   Barely daring to breathe or Achoo.

Daddy, I have had to kill you.
You died before I had time—
Marble-heavy, a bag full of God,
Ghastly statue with one gray toe
10   Big as a Frisco seal

And a head in the freakish Atlantic
Where it pours bean green over blue
In the waters off beautiful Nauset.[6]
I used to pray to recover you.
15   Ach, du.[7]

In the German tongue, in the Polish town
Scraped flat by the roller
Of wars, wars, wars.
But the name of the town is common.
20   My Polack friend

Says there are a dozen or two.
So I never could tell where you
Put your foot, your root,
I never could talk to you.
25   The tongue stuck in my jaw.

It stuck in a barb wire snare.
Ich, ich, ich, ich,
I could hardly speak.
I thought every German was you.
30   And the language obscene

---

6. An inlet on Cape Cod.   7. "Oh, you" in German. Plath often portrays herself as Jewish and her oppressors as German. *Ich* (below): German for "I."

An engine, an engine
Chuffing me off like a Jew.
A Jew to Dachau, Auschwitz, Belsen.[8]
I began to talk like a Jew.
I think I may well be a Jew.   35

The snows of the Tyrol,[9] the clear beer of Vienna
Are not very pure or true.
With my gypsy-ancestress and my weird luck
And my Taroc[1] pack and my Taroc pack
I may be a bit of a Jew.   40

I have always been scared of *you*,
With your Luftwaffe,[2] your gobbledygoo.
And your neat moustache
And your Aryan eye, bright blue.
Panzer-man, panzer-man, O You—   45

Not God but a swastika
So black no sky could squeak through.
Every woman adores a Fascist,
The boot in the face, the brute
Brute heart of a brute like you.   50

You stand at the blackboard, daddy,
In the picture I have of you,
A cleft in your chin instead of your foot
But no less a devil for that, no not
Any less the black man who   55

Bit my pretty red heart in two.
I was ten when they buried you.
At twenty I tried to die
And get back, back, back to you.
I thought even the bones would do   60

But they pulled me out of the sack,
And they stuck me together with glue.
And then I knew what to do.
I made a model of you,
A man in black with a Meinkampf[3] look   65

And a love of the rack and the screw.
And I said I do, I do.
So daddy, I'm finally through.
The black telephone's off at the root,
The voices just can't worm through.   70

---

8. Sites of World War II German death camps.   9. Alpine region in Austria and northern Italy.
The snow there is, legendarily, as pure as the beer is clear in Vienna.   1. Tarot, playing cards
used mainly for fortune-telling.   2. German air force.   3. The title of Adolf Hitler's autobiog-
raphy and manifesto (1925–27); German for "my struggle."

If I've killed one man, I've killed two—
The vampire who said he was you
And drank my blood for a year,
Seven years, if you want to know.
Daddy, you can lie back now.

There's a stake in your fat black heart
And the villagers never liked you.
They are dancing and stamping on you.
They always *knew* it was you.
Daddy, daddy, you bastard, I'm through.

1966

SUSAN MUSGRAVE

You Didn't Fit

for my father

You wouldn't fit in your coffin
but to me it was no surprise.
All your life you had never fit in
anywhere; you saw no reason to
begin fitting now.

When I was little I remember
a sheriff coming. You were
taken to court because your
false teeth didn't fit and you
wouldn't pay the dentist. It was
your third set, you said none of them
fit properly. I was afraid then
that something would take you from me
as it has done now: death
with a bright face and teeth that
fit perfectly.

A human smile that shuts me out.
The Court, I remember, returned
your teeth, now marked an exhibit.
You were dismissed with costs—
I never understood. The teeth were
terrible. We liked you better
without them.

We didn't fit, either, into your
life or your loneliness, though you

tried, and we did too. Once
I wanted to marry you, and then left;
I'm still the child who won't fit
into the arms of anyone, but is
always reaching.   30

I was awkward for years, my bones
didn't fit in my body but stuck out
like my heart—people used to comment
on it. They said I was very good
at office parties where you took me   35
and let others do the talking—the
crude jokes, the corny men—I saw
how they hurt you and I loved you
harder than ever.

Because neither of us fit. Later you   40
blamed me, said "You must fit in,"
but I didn't and I still think
it made you secretly happy.

Like I am now: you won't fit in your
coffin. My mother, after a life   45
of it, says, "This is the last straw."
And it is. We're all clutching.   1985

SUSAN GLICKMAN

Beauty

Maybe there are no easy deaths but Grandpa's
was terrible. The scuttling crab-wise crawl
of the disease eating him
for months, a slow insult.
The scotch-and-nicotine smell of him   5
gone off, festering,
so that even he flinched from his skin,
that strange dank leather
clammy as a wet groundsheet
stretched over his bones.   10
Bones he'd kept modestly hidden
in his patriarch's bulk, his executive jowls,
all naked and poor
in plain view—my fierce private grandfather
exposed.   15

My mother was afraid of him:
his *Sit up straight!* his *Girls*

don't go to college.
My sister, only little when he died, remembers
a scowling giant whose moustache spoiled
his kisses.
And he *was* fierce, his longshoreman's fists,
but with me he was always courtly. We discussed things.
And Grandpa, you were right,
which I knew even then, about beauty.
It comes from inside, you said (But I was only
twelve, desperate for power, afraid I might never
have any) *It has nothing to do
with fashion.*

We were sitting in your wood-panelled den, the TV on
to *Bonanza* or *Perry Mason,* your favourites,
and talking. And I knew you were right.
But even now I can feel that hard little knot, that "no,"
stuck in my throat like a candy
stolen from your secret cupboard and swallowed guiltily
and whole, that knot of stubbornness which, like the candy,
like everything I took from you, silver dollars, a complete set
of Dickens, your gold pen, was mine
from inside, my true inheritance.   1990

JONATHAN SWIFT

A Description of a City Shower

    Careful observers may foretell the hour
(By sure prognostics) when to dread a shower:
While rain depends,[4] the pensive cat gives o'er
Her frolics, and pursues her tail no more
Returning home at night, you'll find the sink[5]
Strike your offended sense with double stink.
If you be wise, then go not far to dine;
You'll spend in coach hire more than save in wine.
A coming shower your shooting corns presage,
Old achés throb, your hollow tooth will rage.
Sauntering in coffeehouse is Dulman[6] seen;
He damns the climate and complains of spleen.
    Meanwhile the South, rising with dabbled wings,
A sable cloud athwart the welkin flings,
That swilled more liquor than it could contain,
And, like a drunkard, gives it up again.

---

4. Impends, is imminent.   5. Sewer.   6. A type name (from "dull man").

Brisk Susan whips her linen from the rope,
While the first drizzling shower is borne aslope:
Such is that sprinkling which some careless quean[7]
Flirts on you from her mop, but not so clean: 20
You fly, invoke the gods; then turning, stop
To rail; she singing, still whirls on her mop.
Not yet the dust had shunned the unequal strife,
But, aided by the wind, fought still for life,
And wafted with its foe by violent gust,   25
'Twas doubtful which was rain and which was dust.
Ah! where must needy poet seek for aid,
When dust and rain at once his coat invade?
Sole coat, where dust cemented by the rain
Erects the nap, and leaves a mingled stain.   30
    Now in contiguous drops the flood comes down,
Threatening with deluge this devoted town.
To shops in crowds the daggled females fly,
Pretend to cheapen[8] goods, but nothing buy.
The Templar spruce, while every spout's abroach,[9]   35
Stays till 'tis fair, yet seems to call a coach.
The tucked-up sempstress walks with hasty strides,
While streams run down her oiled umbrella's sides.
Here various kinds, by various fortunes led,
Commence acquaintance underneath a shed.   40
Triumphant Tories and desponding Whigs
Forget their feuds, and join to save their wigs.
Boxed in a chair the beau impatient sits,
While spouts run clattering o'er the roof by fits,
And ever and anon with frightful din   45
The leather sounds; he trembles from within.
So when Troy chairmen bore the wooden steed,
Pregnant with Greeks impatient to be freed
(Those bully Greeks, who, as the moderns do,
Instead of paying chairmen, run them through),[1]   50
Laocoön struck the outside with his spear,
And each imprisoned hero quaked for fear[2]
    Now from all parts the swelling kennels[3] flow,
And bear their trophies with them as they go:
Filth of all hues and odors seem to tell   55
What street they sailed from, by their sight and smell.
They, as each torrent drives with rapid force,
From Smithfield or St. Pulchre's shape their course,
And in huge confluence joined at Snow Hill ridge,

---

7. Wench, slut.   8. Bargain for. *Daggled:* spattered with mud.   9. Pouring out water. *The Templar:* a young man studying law.   1. Run them through with swords.   2. *The Aeneid,* II, 40–53.   3. Open gutters in the middle of the street.

60 Fall from the conduit prone to Holborn Bridge.[4]
Sweepings from butchers' stalls, dung, guts, and blood,
Drowned puppies, stinking sprats[5] all drenched in mud,
Dead cats, and turnip tops, come tumbling down the flood. 110

THOMAS GRAY

Elegy Written in a Country Churchyard

The curfew tolls the knell of parting day,
    The lowing herd wind slowly o'er the lea,
The plowman homeward plods his weary way,
    And leaves the world to darkness and to me.

5 Now fades the glimmering landscape on the sight,
    And all the air a solemn stillness holds,
Save where the beetle wheels his droning flight,
    And drowsy tinklings lull the distant folds;

Save that from yonder ivy-mantled tower
10   The moping owl does to the moon complain
Of such, as wandering near her secret bower,
    Molest her ancient solitary reign.

Beneath those rugged elms, that yew tree's shade,
    Where heaves the turf in many a moldering heap,
15 Each in his narrow cell forever laid,
    The rude[6] forefathers of the hamlet sleep.

The breezy call of incense-breathing Morn,
    The swallow twittering from the straw-built shed,
The cock's shrill clarion, or the echoing horn.[7]
20   No more shall rouse them from their lowly bed.

For them no more the blazing hearth shall burn,
    Or busy housewife ply her evening care;
No children run to lisp their sire's return,
    Or climb his knees the envied kiss to share.

25 Oft did the harvest to their sickle yield,
    Their furrow oft the stubborn glebe[8] has broke;
How jocund did they drive their team afield!
    How bowed the woods beneath their sturdy stroke!

Let not Ambition mock their useful toil,
30   Their homely joys, and destiny obscure;

4. *Smithfield*: site of cattle and sheep markets at the foot of Snow Hill. *St. Pulchre's*: church of St. Sepulchre. Holborn Conduit drained into a foul-smelling sewer at Holborn Bridge.   5. Small herrings.   6. Unlearned.   7. The hunter's horn.   8. Soil.

Nor Grandeur hear with a disdainful smile
    The short and simple annals of the poor.

The boast of heraldry,[9] the pomp of power,
    And all that beauty, all that wealth e'er gave,
Awaits alike the inevitable hour.   35
    The paths of glory lead but to the grave.

Nor you, ye proud, impute to these the fault,
    If Memory o'er their tomb no trophies[1] raise,
Where through the long-drawn aisle and fretted[2] vault
    The pealing anthem swells the note of praise   40

Can storied urn or animated[3] bust
    Back to its mansion call the fleeting breath?
Can Honor's voice provoke the silent dust,
    Or Flattery soothe the dull cold ear of Death?

Perhaps in this neglected spot is laid   45
    Some heart once pregnant with celestial fire;
Hands that the rod of empire might have swayed,
    Or waked to ecstasy the living lyre.

But Knowledge to their eyes her ample page
    Rich with the spoils of time did ne'er unroll;   50
Chill Penury repressed their noble rage,
    And froze the genial current of the soul.

Full many a gem of purest ray serene,
    The dark unfathomed caves of ocean bear:
Full many a flower is born to blush unseen,   55
    And waste its sweetness on the desert air.

Some village Hampden,[4] that with dauntless breast
    The little tyrant of his fields withstood;
Some mute inglorious Milton here may rest,
    Some Cromwell guiltless of his country's blood.   60

The applause of listening senates to command,
    The threats of pain and ruin to despise,
To scatter plenty o'er a smiling land,
    And read their history in a nation's eyes,

Their lot forbade: nor circumscribed alone   65
    Their growing virtues, but their crimes confined;
Forbade to wade through slaughter to a throne,
    And shut the gates of mercy on mankind,

---

9. Noble birth.   1. An ornamental or symbolic group of figures depicting the achievements of the deceased.   2. Decorated with intersecting lines in relief.   3. Lifelike. *Storied urn*: a funeral urn with an epitaph or pictured story inscribed on it.   4. John Hampden (1594–1643), who, both as a private citizen and as a member of Parliament, zealously defended the rights of the people against the autocratic policies of Charles I.

The struggling pangs of conscious truth to hide,
    To quench the blushes of ingenuous shame,
70   Or heap the shrine of Luxury and Pride
    With incense kindled at the Muse's flame.

Far from the madding crowd's ignoble strife,
    Their sober wishes never learned to stray;
75   Along the cool sequestered vale of life
    They kept the noiseless tenor of their way.

Yet even these bones from insult to protect
    Some frail memorial still erected nigh,
With uncouth rhymes and shapeless sculpture decked,[5]
80   Implores the passing tribute of a sigh.

Their name, their years, spelt by the unlettered Muse,
    The place of fame and elegy supply:
And many a holy text around she strews,
    That teach the rustic moralist to die.

85 For who to dumb Forgetfulness a prey,
    This pleasing anxious being e'er resigned,
Left the warm precincts of the cheerful day,
    Nor cast one longing lingering look behind?

On some fond breast the parting soul relies,
90   Some pious drops the closing eye requires;
Even from the tomb the voice of Nature cries,
    Even in our ashes live their wonted fires.

For thee, who mindful of the unhonored dead
    Dost in these lines their artless tale relate;
95   If chance, by lonely contemplation led,
    Some kindred spirit shall inquire thy fate,

Haply some hoary-headed swain may say,
    "Oft have we seen him at the peep of dawn
Brushing with hasty steps the dews away
100   To meet the sun upon the upland lawn.

"There at the foot of yonder nodding beech
    That wreathes its old fantastic roots so high,
His listless length at noontide would he stretch,
    And pore upon the brook that babbles by.

105 "Hard by yon wood, now smiling as in scorn,
    Muttering his wayward fancies he would rove,
Now drooping, woeful wan, like one forlorn,
    Or crazed with care, or crossed in hopeless love.

"One morn I missed him on the customed hill,
110   Along the heath and near his favorite tree;

---

5. Cf. "the storied urn or animated bust" dedicated inside the church to "the proud" (line 41).

Another came; nor yet beside the rill,
   Nor up the lawn, nor at the wood was he;

"The next with dirges due in sad array
   Slow through the churchway path we saw him borne.
Approach and read (for thou canst read) the lay,   115
   Graved on the stone beneath yon aged thorn."

The Epitaph

Here rests his head upon the lap of Earth
   A youth to Fortune and to Fame unknown.
Fair Science[6] frowned not on his humble birth,
   And Melancholy marked him for her own.   120

Large was his bounty, and his soul sincere,
   Heaven did a recompense as largely send:
He gave to Misery all he had, a tear,
   He gained from Heaven ('twas all he wished) a friend.

No farther seek his merits to disclose,   125
   Or draw his frailties from their dread abode
(There they alike in trembling hope repose),
   The bosom of his Father and his God.

ca. 1742–50   1751

RICHARD EBERHART

The Groundhog

In June, amid the golden fields,
I saw a groundhog lying dead.
Dead lay he; my senses shook,
And mind outshot our naked frailty.
There lowly in the vigorous summer   5
His form began its senseless change,
And made my senses waver dim
Seeing nature ferocious in him.
Inspecting close his maggots' might
And seething cauldron of his being,   10
Half with loathing, half with a strange love,
I poked him with an angry stick.
The fever rose, became a flame
And Vigour circumscribed the skies,
Immense energy in the sun,   15
And through my frame a sunless trembling.

6. Learning.

My stick had done nor good nor harm.
Then stood I silent in the day
Watching the object, as before;
20 And kept my reverence for knowledge
Trying for control, to be still,
To quell the passion of the blood;
Until I had bent down on my knees
Praying for joy in the sight of decay.
25 And so I left; and I returned
In Autumn strict of eye, to see
The sap gone out of the groundhog,
But the bony sodden hulk remained.
But the year had lost its meaning,
30 And in intellectual chains
I lost both love and loathing,
Mured up[7] in the wall of wisdom.
Another summer took the fields again
Massive and burning, full of life,
35 But when I chanced upon the spot
There was only a little hair left,
And bones bleaching in the sunlight
Beautiful as architecture;
I watched them like a geometer,[8]
40 And cut a walking stick from a birch.
It has been three years, now.
There is no sign of the groundhog.
I stood there in the whirling summer,
My hand capped a withered heart,
45 And thought of China and of Greece,
Of Alexander in his tent;
Of Montaigne in his tower,
Of Saint Theresa[9] in her wild lament.   1936

WILLIAM BLAKE

The Tyger

Tyger! Tyger! burning bright
In the forests of the night,
What immortal hand or eye
Could frame thy fearful symmetry?

7. Confined.   8. Geometrician, one skilled in measuring properties and arrangement.
9. Alexander the Great, ancient king of Macedonia and conqueror of the East; Michel de Montaigne, the Renaissance French essayist who used a tower near his house for a study; and St. Theresa of Spain, famous for intense trances and visions.

In what distant deeps or skies   5
Burnt the fire of thine eyes?
On what wings dare he aspire?
What the hand dare seize the fire?

And what shoulder, & what art,
Could twist the sinews of thy heart?   10
And when thy heart began to beat,
What dread hand? & what dread feet?

What the hammer? what the chain?
In what furnace was thy brain?
What the anvil? what dread grasp   15
Dare its deadly terrors clasp?

When the stars threw down their spears[1]
And water'd heaven with their tears,
Did he smile his work to see?
Did he who made the Lamb make thee?   20

Tyger! Tyger! burning bright
In the forests of the night,
What immortal hand or eye
Dare frame thy fearful symmetry?

1790–92   1794

▼ ▼ ▼

TONE A Glossary

subject: the general or specific area of concern of a poem; also called topic
theme: the statement a poem makes about its subject
tone: the attitude a poem takes toward its subject and theme
topic: see subject

QUESTIONS

1. Consider carefully how the tone of "Those Winter Sundays" is created. What activities of the father inspire the son's admiration? Which words of the

---

1. "Threw down" is ambiguous and may signify that the stars either "surrendered" or "hurled down" their spears.

son are especially effective in suggesting his attitude toward his father? Why is the phrase "what did I know" repeated in line 13? What are the connotations of the word "austere" in line 14? How old does the son seem to be at the time the poem is written? How can you tell?

2. What information presented in Sylvia Plath's "Daddy" explains the poem's attitude toward Daddy? What other charges are made or implied against Daddy? What tonal purpose is served by the portrayal of Daddy as a Nazi? What adjectives would you use to describe the basic tone of voice in which the poem is spoken?

3. What attitude does "Elegy" take toward Aunt Irene? toward Uncle Robert? toward the mother? toward the father? How can you tell about the attitudes toward each? What individual words or factual details help to suggest the attitudes? Is "Elegy" an appropriate title for the poem? Why?

4. In Blake's poem "The Tyger," why is the "Tyger" described as "burning bright"? What is implied by such a strong visual image? What different attitudes does the poem imply toward the tiger? Are the attitudes contradictory? How do you feel about the tiger by the end of the poem?

WRITING SUGGESTIONS

1. Paraphrase—that is, put into different words line by line and stanza by stanza—Behn's "On Her Loving Two Equally." Summarize the poem's basic statement in one sentence. How accurately do your paraphrase and summary represent the tone of the poem?

2. Compare the tone of voice used in reading "Leaving the Motel" aloud to that in "Reunion." Pick out three or four key words from each poem that seem to help control the tone. Then, concentrating on the words you have isolated, write a short essay, of no more than 600 words, in which you compare the tones of the two poems.

2 SPEAKER

P oems are personal. The thoughts and feelings they express belong to a
specific person, and however general or universal their sentiments
seem to be, poems come to us as the expression of an individual
human voice. That voice is often the voice of the poet. But not always. Poets
sometimes create a "character" just as writers of fiction or drama do—people
who speak for them only indirectly. A character may, in fact, be very different
from the poet, just as a character in a play or story is different from the author,
and that person, the **speaker** of the poem, may express ideas or feelings very dif-
ferent from the poet's own. In the following poem, *two* individual voices in fact
speak, and it is clear that, rather than himself speaking directly to us, the poet,
Thomas Hardy, has chosen to create two speakers, both female, each of whom
has a distinctive voice, personality, and character.

THOMAS HARDY

The Ruined Maid

"O 'Melia,[1] my dear, this does everything crown!
Who could have supposed I should meet you in Town?
And whence such fair garments, such prosperi-ty?"—
"O didn't you know I'd been ruined?" said she.

—"You left us in tatters, without shoes or socks,   5
Tired of digging potatoes, and spudding up docks;[2]
And now you've gay bracelets and bright feathers three!"—
"Yes: that's how we dress when we're ruined," said she.

—"At home in the barton[3] you said 'thee' and 'thou,'
And 'thik oon,' and 'theäs oon,' and 't'other'; but now   10
Your talking quite fits 'ee for high compa-ny!"—
"Some polish is gained with one's ruin," said she.

—"Your hands were like paws then, your face blue and bleak
But now I'm bewitched by your delicate cheek,
And your little gloves fit as on any la-dy!"—   15
"We never do work when we're ruined," said she.

1. Short for Amelia.   2. Spading up weeds.   3. Farmyard.

—"You used to call home-life a hag-ridden dream,
And you'd sigh, and you'd sock;[4] but at present you seem
To know not of megrims[5] or melancho-ly!"—
"True. One's pretty lively when ruined," said she.

20

—"I wish I had feathers, a fine sweeping gown,
And a delicate face, and could strut about Town!"—
"My dear—a raw country girl, such as you be,
Cannot quite expect that. You ain't ruined," said she.

1866

The first voice, that of a young woman who has remained back on the farm, is designated typographically (that is, by the way the poem is printed): there are dashes at the beginning and end of each of her speeches. She speaks the first part of each stanza, usually the first three lines. The second young woman, a companion and co-worker on the farm in years gone by, regularly gets the last line in each stanza (and in the last stanza, two lines), so it is easy to tell who is talking at every point. Also, the two speakers are just as clearly distinguished by what they say, how they say it, and what sort of person each proves to be. The nameless stay-at-home shows little knowledge of the world, and everything surprises her: seeing her former companion at all, but especially seeing her well clothed, cheerful, and polished; and as the poem develops she shows increasing envy of her more worldly friend. She is the "raw country girl" (line 23) that the other speaker says she is, and she still speaks the country dialect ("fits 'ee," line 11, for example) that she notices her friend has lost (lines 9–11). The "ruined" young woman ('Melia), on the other hand, says little except to keep repeating the refrain about having been ruined, but even the slight variations she plays on that theme suggest her sophistication and amusement at her farm friend, although she still uses a rural "ain't" at the end. We are not told the full story of their lives (was the ruined young woman thrown out? did she run away from home or work?), but we know enough (that they've been separated for some time, that the stay-at-home did not know where the other had gone) to allow the dialogue to articulate the contrast between them. The style of speech of each speaker then does the rest.

It is equally obvious that there is a speaker (or, in this case, actually a singer) in stanzas 2 through 9 of this poem:

---

4. Deliver angry blows.   5. Migraine headaches.

X. J. KENNEDY

In a Prominent Bar in Secaucus One Day

To the tune of "The Old Orange Flute" or the tune of
"Sweet Betsy from Pike"

In a prominent bar in Secaucus[6] one day
Rose a lady in skunk with a topheavy sway,
Raised a knobby red finger—all turned from their beer—
While with eyes bright as snowcrust she sang high and clear:

"Now who of you'd think from an eyeload of me   5
That I once was a lady as proud as could be?
Oh I'd never sit down by a tumbledown drunk
If it wasn't, my dears, for the high cost of junk.

"All the gents used to swear that the white of my calf
Beat the down of a swan by a length and a half.   10
In the kerchief of linen I caught to my nose
Ah, there never fell snot, but a little gold rose.

"I had seven gold teeth and a toothpick of gold.
My Virginia cheroot was a leaf of it rolled
And I'd light it each time with a thousand in cash—   15
Why the bums used to fight if I flicked them an ash.

"Once the toast of the Biltmore,[7] the belle of the Taft,
I would drink bottle beer at the Drake, never draft,
And dine at the Astor on Salisbury steak
With a clean tablecloth for each bite I did take.   20

"In a car like the Roxy[8] I'd roll to the track,
A steel-guitar trio, a bar in the back,
And the wheels made no noise, they turned over so fast,
Still it took you ten minutes to see me go past.

"When the horses bowed down to me that I might choose,   25
I bet on them all, for I hated to lose.
Now I'm saddled each night for my butter and eggs
And the broken threads race down the backs of my legs.

"Let you hold in mind, girls, that your beauty must pass
Like a lovely white clover that rusts with its grass.   30
Keep your bottoms off barstools and marry you young
Or be left—an old barrel with many a bung.

6. A small town on the Hackensack River in New Jersey, a few miles west of Manhattan.   7. Like
the Taft, Drake, and Astor, a once-fashionable New York hotel.   8. A luxurious old New York
theater and movie house, the site of many "world premieres" in the heyday of Hollywood.

"For when time takes you out for a spin in his car
You'll be hard-pressed to stop him from going too far

35   And be left by the roadside, for all your good deeds,
Two toadstools for tits and a face full of weeds."

All the house raised a cheer, but the man at the bar
Made a phonecall and up pulled a red patrol car
And she blew us a kiss as they copped her away

40   From that prominent bar in Secaucus, N.J.   1961

Again, we learn about the character primarily through her own words, although we don't have to believe everything she tells us about her past. From her introduction in the first stanza we get some general notion of her appearance and condition, but it is she who tells us that she is a junkie (line 8), a prostitute (line 27), and that her face and figure are pretty well shot (lines 32, 36). That information could make her a sad case, and the poem might lament her state or allow her to lament it, but instead the poem presents her in a light and friendly way. She is anxious to give advice and sound moral (line 31, for example), but she's also enormously cheerful about herself, and her spirit repeatedly bursts through her song. Her performance gives her a lot of pleasure as she exaggerates outrageously about her former luxury and prominence, and even her departure in a patrol car she chooses to treat as a grand exit, throwing a kiss to her audience. The comedy is bittersweet, perhaps, but she is allowed to present herself, through her own words and attitudes, as a likable character—someone who has survived life's disappointments and retained her dignity and her sense of theatricality. The glorious fiction of her life, narrated with energy and polish in the manner of a practiced and accomplished liar, betrays some rather naive notions of good taste and luxurious living (lines 18–26). But this "lady in skunk" has a picturesque and engaging style, a refreshing sense of humor about herself, and a flair for drama. Like the cheap fur she wears, her experiences in what she considers high life satisfy her sense of style and celebration. The self-portrait accumulates, almost completely through how she talks about herself, and the poet develops our attitude toward her by allowing her to recount her story herself, in her own words—or rather in words chosen for her by the author.

The following poem uses the idea of speaker in a very different way and for quite different tonal purposes.

ADRIENNE RICH

Letters in the Family

I: Catalonia, 1936

Dear Parents:
                    I'm the daughter
you didn't bless when she left,
an unmarried woman wearing a khaki knapsack
with a poor mark in Spanish.
                              I'm writing now
from a plaster-dusted desk in a town   5
pocked street by street with hand grenades,
some of them, dear ones, thrown by me.
This is a school: the children are at war.
You don't need honors in schoolroom Spanish here
to be of use and my right arm   10
's as strong as anyone's. I sometimes think
all languages are spoken here,
even mine, which you got zero in.
Don't worry. Don't try to write. I'm happy,
if you could know it.
                      Rochelle.   15

II: Yugoslavia, 1944[9]

Dear Chana,
              where are you now?
Am sending this pocket-to-pocket
(though we both know pockets we'd hate to lie in).
They showed me that poem you gave Reuven,
about the match: 20
Chana, you know, I never was
for martyrdom. I thought we'd try our best,
ragtag mission that we were,
then clear out if the signals looked too bad.
Something in you drives things ahead for me   25
but if I can I mean to stay alive.
We're none of us giants, you know,
just small, frail, inexperienced romantic people.

---

9. "See *Hannah Senesh: Her Life and Diary* (New York: Schocken, 1973). Born in Budapest, 1921, Hannah Senesh became a Zionist and emigrated to Palestine at the age of eighteen; her mother and brother remained in Europe. In 1943, she joined an expedition of Jews who trained under the British to parachute behind Nazi lines in Europe and connect with the partisan underground, to rescue Jews in Hungary, Romania, and Czechoslovakia. She was arrested by the Nazis, imprisoned, tortured, and executed in November 1944. Like the other letter-writers, 'Esther' is an imagined person.

   See also Ruth Whitman's long poem, *The Testing of Hannah Senesh* (Detroit: Wayne State University Press, 1986)." (Rich's note)

But there are things we learn.
You know the sudden suck of empty space
between the jump and the ripcord pull?
I hate it. I hate it so,
I've hated you for your dropping
ecstatically in free-fall, in the training,
your look, dragged on the ground, of knowing
precisely why you were there.
                              My mother's
still in Palestine. And yours
still there in Hungary. Well, there we are.
When this is over—
                    I'm
your earthbound friend to the end, still yours—
                                        Esther.

III: Southern Africa, 1986

Dear children:
                    We've been walking nights
a long time over rough terrain,
sometimes through marshes. Days we hide
under what bushes we can find.
Our stars steer us. I write
on my knee by a river with a weary hand,
and the weariness will come through
this letter that should tell you
nothing but love. I can't say where we are,
what weeds are in bloom, what birds cry at dawn.
The less you know the safer.
But not to know how you are going on—
Matile's earache, Emma's lessons, those tell-tale
eyes and tongues, so quick—are you remembering
to be brave and wise and strong?
At the end of this hard road
we'll sit all together at one meal
and I'll tell you everything: the names
of our comrades, how the letters
were routed to you, why I left.
And I'll stop and say, "Now you,
grown so big, how was it for you, those times?
Look, I know you in detail, every inch of each
sweet body, haven't I washed and dried you
a thousand times?"
                    And we'll eat and tell our stories
together. That is my reason.
                    Ma.   1989

As in "The Ruined Maid," this poem uses different voices, and here they are clearly distinguished as different "historical" characters—Rochelle, Esther, and "Ma," women from three separate places and times who in letter form tell their own stories. In each case, the individual story is part of some larger historical moment, and although all three characters are (as the author's footnote points out) fictional, the three stories together present a kind of history of female heroism in difficult cultural moments.

Read the poem aloud and notice how different in tone the three voices sound; each woman has distinctive expressions and syntax of her own. All are in part defined by their relationships to families left behind, but all are defined even more fully by their own idealistic determination to resist the larger social and political forces in the cultures where they are at the time they write their letters. Telling stories, the pleasure identified by the third speaker as the ultimate purpose of her actions (lines 56–62), is important to all three speakers as a way of defining themselves in relation to their families; to the poem, the telling of separate stories by the different speakers becomes the collective means to exemplify the power of women in history in action.

Some speakers in poems are not, however, nearly so heroic or attractive, and some poems create a speaker who makes us dislike him or her, also because of what the poet makes him or her say, as the following poem does. Here the speaker, as the title implies, is a monk, but he shows himself to be most unmonklike: mean, self-righteous, and despicable.

ROBERT BROWNING

Soliloquy of the Spanish Cloister[1]

> Gr-r-r—there go, my heart's abhorrence!
>   Water your damned flower-pots, do!
> If hate killed men, Brother Lawrence,
>   God's blood, would not mine kill you!
> What? your myrtle-bush wants trimming?   5
>   Oh, that rose has prior claims—
> Needs its leaden vase filled brimming?
>   Hell dry you up with its flames!
>
> At the meal we sit together:
>   *Salve tibi!*[2] I must hear   10
> Wish talk of the kind of weather,
>   Sort of season, time of year:

1. Monastery.   2. "Hail to thee" (Latin). Italics usually indicate the words of Brother Lawrence.

> *Not a plenteous cork-crop: scarcely*
> *Dare we hope oak-galls,*[3] *I doubt:*
> *What's the Latin name for "parsley"?*
> What's the Greek name for Swine's Snout?

Whew! We'll have our platter burnished,
    Laid with care on our own shelf!
With a fire-new spoon we're furnished,
    And a goblet for ourself,
Rinsed like something sacrificial
    Ere 'tis fit to touch our chaps[4]—
Marked with L. for our initial!
    (He-he! There his lily snaps!)

Saint, forsooth! While brown Dolores
    —Squats outside the Convent bank
With Sanchicha, telling stories,
    Steeping tresses in the tank,
Blue-black, lustrous, thick like horsehairs,
    —Can't I see his dead eye glow,
Bright as 'twere a Barbary corsair's?[5]
    (That is, if he'd let it show!)

When he finishes refection,[6]
    Knife and fork he never lays
Cross-wise, to my recollection,
    As do I, in Jesu's praise.
I the Trinity illustrate,
    Drinking watered orange-pulp—
In three sips the Arian[7] frustrate;
    —While he drains his at one gulp.

Oh, those melons? If he's able
    We're to have a feast! so nice!
One goes to the Abbot's table,
    All of us get each a slice.
How go on your flowers? None double?
    Not one fruit-sort can you spy?
Strange!—And I, too, at such trouble,
    —Keep them close-nipped on the sly!

There's a great text in Galatians,
    Once you trip on it, entails
Twenty-nine distinct damnations,[8]
    One sure, if another fails:
If I trip him just a-dying,
    Sure of heaven as sure can be,

15
20
25
30
35
40
45
50

---

3. Abnormal growth on oak trees, used for tanning.   **4.** Jaws.   **5.** African pirate's.   **6.** A meal.   **7.** A heretical sect that denied the Trinity.   **8.** Galatians 5:15–23 provides a long list of possible offenses, but they do not add up to 29.

Spin him round and send him flying   55
    Off to hell, a Manichee?[9]

Or, my scrofulous French novel
    On gray paper with blunt type!
Simply glance at it, you grovel
    Hand and foot in Belial's gripe:[1]   60
If I double down its pages
    At the woeful sixteenth print,
When he gathers his greengages,
    Ope a sieve and slip it in't?

Or, there's Satan!—one might venture   65
    ledge one's soul to him, yet leave
Such a flaw in the indenture
    –As he'd miss till, past retrieve,
Blasted lay that rose-acacia
    We're so proud of! *Hy, Zy, Hine . . .*[2]   70
'St, there's Vespers! *Plena gratiâ*
    Ave, Virgo.[3] Gr-r-r—you swine!   1842

Not many poems begin with a growl, and this harsh sound turns out to be
fair warning that we are about to get to know a real beast, even though he is in
the clothing of a religious man. In line 1, he has already shown himself to hold
a most uncharitable attitude toward his fellow monk, Brother Lawrence, and
by line 4 he has uttered two profanities and admitted his intense feelings of
hatred and vengefulness. His ranting and roaring is full of exclamation points
(four in the first stanza!), and he reveals his own personality and character
when he imagines curses and unflattering nicknames for Brother Lawrence or
plots malicious jokes on him. By the end, we have accumulated no knowledge
of Brother Lawrence that makes him seem a fit target for such rage (except that
he is pious, dutiful, and pleasant—perhaps enough to make this sort of speaker
despise him), but we have discovered the speaker to be lecherous (stanza 4),
full of false piety (stanza 5), malicious in trivial matters (stanza 6), ready to use
his theological learning to sponsor damnation rather than salvation (stanza 7),
a closet reader and viewer of pornography within the monastery (stanza 8)—
even willing to risk his own soul in order to torment Brother Lawrence (last
stanza).

The speaker is made to characterize himself; the details accrue and accu-
mulate into a fairly full portrait, and here we do not have even an opening and

9. A heretic. According to the Manichean heresy, the world was divided into the forces of good and
evil, equally powerful.   1. In the clutches of Satan.   2. Possibly the beginning of an incanta-
tion or curse.   3. The opening words of the *Ave Maria*, here reversed: "Full of grace, Hail,
Virgin" (Latin).

closing "objective" description (as in "In a Prominent Bar") or another speaker (as in "The Ruined Maid") to give us perspective. Except for the moments when the speaker mimics or parodies Brother Lawrence (usually in italic type), we have only the speaker's own words and thoughts. But that is enough; the poet has controlled them so carefully that we clearly know what he thinks of the speaker he has created—that he is a mean-spirited, vengeful hypocrite, a thoroughly disreputable and unlikable character. The whole poem has been about him and his attitudes; the point of the poem has been to characterize the speaker and develop in us a dislike of him and what he stands for—total hypocrisy.

In reading a poem like this aloud, we would want our voice to suggest all the unlikable features of a hypocrite. We would also need to suggest, through the tone of voice we used, the author's contemptuous mocking of the rage and hypocrisy, and we would want, like an actor, to create strong disapproval in the hearer. The poem's words (the ones the author has given to the speaker) clearly imply those attitudes, and we would want our voice to express them. Usually there is much more to a poem than the identification and characterization of the speaker, but in many cases it is necessary to identify the speaker and determine his or her character before we can appreciate what else goes on in the poem. And sometimes, as here, in looking for the speaker of the poem, we come near to the center of the poem itself.

Sometimes the effect of a poem depends on our recognizing the temporal position of the speaker as well as her or his identity. The following poem, for example, quickly makes plain that a childhood experience is at the center of the action and that the speaker is female:

TESS GALLAGHER

Sudden Journey

Maybe I'm seven in the open field—
the straw-grass so high
only the top of my head makes a curve
of brown in the yellow. Rain then.
First a little. A few drops on my
wrist, the right wrist. More rain.
My shoulders, my chin. Until I'm looking up
to let my eyes take the bliss.
I open my face. Let the teeth show. I
pull my shirt down past the collar-bones.
I'm still a boy under my breast spots.

I can drink anywhere. The rain. My
skin shattering. Up suddenly, needing
to gulp, turning with my tongue, my arms out
running, running in the hard, cold plenitude   15
of all those who reach earth by falling.   1984

The sense of adventure and wonder here has a lot to do with the childlike
syntax and words at the beginning of the poem. Sentences are short, observa-
tions direct and simple. The rain becomes exciting and blissful and totally
absorbing as the child's actions and reactions take over the poem in lines 2–13.
But not all of the poem takes place in a child's mind in spite of the precise and
impressive re-creation of childish responses and feelings. The opening line
makes clear that we are sliding into a supposition of the past; "maybe I'm
seven" makes clear that we, as conspiring adults, are pretending ourselves into
earlier time. And at the end the word "plenitude"—crucial to interpreting the
poem's full effect and meaning—makes clear that we are finding an adult per-
spective on the incident. Elsewhere, too, the adult world gives the incident
meaning. In line 12, for example, the joke about being able to drink anywhere
depends on an adult sense of what being a boy might mean. The "journey" of
the poem's title is not only the little girl's running in the rain but also the adult
movement into a past re-created and newly understood.

The speaker in the following poem positions herself very differently, but we
do not get a very full sense of her until the poem is well along. As you read, try
to imitate the tone of voice you think this kind of person would use. Exactly
when do you begin to feel that you know what she is like?

DOROTHY PARKER

A Certain Lady

Oh, I can smile for you, and tilt my head,
   And drink your rushing words with eager lips,
And paint my mouth for you a fragrant red,
   And trace your brows with tutored finger-tips.
When you rehearse your list of loves to me,   5
   Oh, I can laugh and marvel, rapturous-eyed.
And you laugh back, nor can you ever see
   The thousand little deaths my heart has died.
And you believe, so well I know my part,
   That I am gay as morning, light as snow,   10
And all the straining things within my heart
   You'll never know.

Oh, I can laugh and listen, when we meet,
    And you bring tales of fresh adventurings—
15   Of ladies delicately indiscreet,
      Of lingering hands, and gently whispered things.
And you are pleased with me, and strive anew
    To sing me sagas of your late delights.
Thus do you want me—marveling, gay, and true—
20   Nor do you see my staring eyes of nights.
And when, in search of novelty, you stray,
    Oh, I can kiss you blithely as you go . . .
And what goes on, my love, while you're away,
    You'll never know.   1937

To whom does the speaker seem to be talking? What sort of person is he? How do you feel about him? Which habits and attitudes of his do you like least? How soon can you tell that the speaker is not altogether happy about his conversation and conduct? In what tone of voice would you read the first 22 lines aloud? What attitude would you try to express toward the person spoken to? What tone would you use for the last two lines? How would you describe the speaker's personality? What aspects of her behavior are most crucial to the poem's effect?

It is easy to assume that the speaker in a poem is an extension of the poet. Is the speaker in this poem Dorothy Parker? Maybe. A lot of Parker's poems present a similar world-weary posture and a kind of cynicism about romantic love (look, for example, at "Comment" on p. 39). But the poem is hardly an example of self-revelation, a giving away of personal secrets. If it were, it would be silly, not to say risky, to address her lover in a way that gives damaging facts about a pose she has been so careful to set up.

In poems such as "The Ruined Maid," "In a Prominent Bar," and "Solilo-quy of the Spanish Cloister," we are in no danger of mistaking the speaker for the poet, once we have recognized that poets may create speakers who partici-pate in specific situations much as in fiction or drama. When there is a pointed discrepancy between the speaker and what we know of the poet— when the speaker is a woman, for example, and the poet is a man—we know we have a created speaker to contend with and that the point (or at least *one* point) in the poem is to observe the characterization carefully. In "A Certain Lady" we may be less sure, and in other poems the discrepancy between speaker and poet may be even more uncertain. What are we to make, for exam-ple, of the speaker in "Woodchucks" in the previous chapter? Is that speaker the real Maxine Kumin? At best (without knowing something quite specific about the author) we can only say "maybe" to that question. What we can be sure of is the sort of person the speaker is portrayed to be—someone (man? or woman?) surprised to discover feelings and attitudes that contradict values apparently held confidently. And that is exactly what we need to know for the poem to have its effect.

A similar kind of self-mocking of the speaker is present in the following poem, but here the mockery is put to less revelatory, more comic ends.

A. R. AMMONS

Needs

I want something suited to my special needs
I want chrome hubcaps, pin-on attachments
and year round use year after year
I want a workhorse with smooth uniform cut,
dozer blade and snow blade & deluxe steering   5
wheel
I want something to mow, throw snow, tow
and sow with
I want precision reel blades
I want a console styled dashboard   10
I want an easy spintype recoil starter
I want combination bevel and spur gears, 14
gauge stamped steel housing and
washable foam element air cleaner
I want a pivoting front axle and extrawide   15
turf tires
I want an inch of foam rubber inside a vinyl
covering
and especially if it's not too much, if I
can deserve it, even if I can't pay for it   20
I want to mow while riding.   1970

The poet here may be teasing himself about his desire for comfort and ease—and showing how readily advertisements and catalog descriptions manipulate us. But the speaker doesn't have to be the author for the teasing to work. In fact, the effect is to tease those attitudes no matter who holds them by teasing a speaker who illustrates the attitudes. It doesn't matter to the poem whether the speaker is the poet himself or some totally invented character. If the speaker is a version of the poet himself—perhaps a *side* of his personality that he is exploring—the portrait is still fictional in an important sense. The poem presents not a whole human being (*no* poem could do that) but only a version of him—a mood perhaps, an aspect, an attitude, a part of that person. The poet presents someone with an obsession, in this case a small and not very damaging one, and allows him to spout phrases as if he were reciting from an ad or a sales catalog. The "portrait" is made more comic by a clear sense the poem projects that what we have is only a part of the person, an interest grown too intense, gone askew, gotten out of proportion, something that happens to most of us from time to time. All we know about the speaker is that he has a one-track mind, that he is obsessed by his own luxurious comfort. He may not even be a "he": there is nothing in the poem that makes us certain that the speaker is male. It is customary to think of the speaker in a poem written by a man as "he" and in a poem written by a woman as "she" (as in Maxine Kumin's "Woodchucks") unless the poem presents contrary evidence, but it is merely a convenience, a habit, nothing more.

Even when poets present themselves as if they were speaking directly to us in their own voices, their poems present only a partial portrait, something considerably less than the full personality and character of the poet. Even when there is not an obviously created character—someone with distinct characteristics that are different from those of the poet—strategies of characterization are used to present the person speaking in one way and not another. Even in a poem like the following one, which contains identifiable autobiographical details, it is still a good idea to talk of the speaker instead of the poet, although here it is probable that the poet is writing about a personal, actual experience.

WILLIAM WORDSWORTH

She Dwelt among the Untrodden Ways

> She dwelt among the untrodden ways
>   Beside the springs of Dove,[4]
> A Maid whom there were none to praise
>   And very few to love:
>
> A violet by a mossy stone
>   Half hidden from the eye!
> —Fair as a star, when only one
>   Is shining in the sky.
>
> She lived unknown, and few could know
>   When Lucy ceased to be;
> But she is in her grave, and, oh,
>   The difference to me!

5

10

1800

It is hard to say whether this poem is more about Lucy or about how the speaker feels about her death. Her simple life, far removed from fame and

4. A small stream in the Lake District in northern England, near where Wordsworth lived in Dove Cottage at Grasmere.

known only to a few, is said nevertheless to have been beautiful. We know lit-
tle about her beyond her name and where she lived, in a beautiful but then-
isolated section of northern England. We don't know if she was young or old,
only that the speaker thinks of her as "fair" and compares her to a "violet by a
mossy stone." What we do know is that the speaker is deeply pained by her
death, so deeply that he is almost inarticulate with grief, lapsing into simple
exclamation ("oh," line 11) and unable to articulate the "difference" that her
death makes.

Did Lucy actually live? Was she a friend of the poet? We don't know; the
poem doesn't tell us, and even biographers of Wordsworth are unsure. What
we do know is that Wordsworth was able to represent grief over the death very
powerfully. Whether the speaker is the historical Wordsworth or not, that
speaker is a major focus of the poem, and it is his feelings that the poem iso-
lates and expresses. We need to recognize some characteristics of the speaker
and be sensitive to his feelings for the poem to work.

The following poem similarly seems to draw upon an actual occurrence
and present a speaker who is the poet herself.

SHARON OLDS

The Lifting

Suddenly my father lifted up his nightie, I
turned my head away but he cried out
Shar!, my nickname, so I turned and looked.
He was sitting in the high cranked-up hospital bed with the
gown up, around his neck,   5
to show me the weight he had lost. I looked
where his solid ruddy stomach had been
and I saw the skin fallen into loose
soft hairy rippled folds
lying in a pool of folds   10
down at the base of his abdomen,
the gaunt torso of a big man
who will die soon. Right away
I saw how much his hips are like mine,
the long, white angles, and then   15
how much his pelvis is shaped like my daughter's,
a chambered whelk-shell hollowed out,
I saw the folds of skin like something
poured, a thick batter, I saw
his rueful smile, the cast-up eyes as he   20
shows me his old body, he knows

I will be interested, he knows I will find him
appealing. If anyone had told me I would sit
by him and he would pull up his nightie and I would look
at him, his naked body, the thick   2
bud of his glans, his penis in all that
dark hair, look at him
in affection and uneasy wonder
I would not have believed it. But now I can still
see the tiny snowflakes, white and   3
night-blue, on the cotton of the gown as it
rises the way we were promised at death it would rise,
the veils would fall from our eyes, we would know everything.

                                                            1990

Other poems by Olds written at about the same time also recount moments
in the approaching death of a father—compare, for example, "The Glass" on
p. 12—and the similar situations may suggest that the poet was herself strug-
gling with such an event. But even if we were to read enough about the poet's
life to be sure that the poem was based on an actual event, we would still have
to be careful about assuming that the speaker was, plainly and simply, the poet
herself. It may well be that the "I" in this poem is very close to the historical
Sharon Olds in 1990, but we are still well advised as readers to think of the
speaker in the poem as the woman characterized specifically in the text and
not necessarily as altogether identical to the poet.

The poems we have looked at in this chapter—and the group that follows
at the end of the chapter—all suggest the value of beginning the reading of
any poem with a simple question: Who is speaking and what do we know
about him or her? Putting together the evidence that the poem presents in
answer to this question can often take us a long way into the poem. For some
poems, this question won't help a great deal because the speaking voice is too
indistinct or the character behind the poem too scantily presented, but in
many cases asking this question will lead you toward the central experience the
poem offers.

▼   ▼   ▼

HENRY REED

Lessons of the War

JUDGING DISTANCES

Not only how far away, but the way that you say it
Is very important. Perhaps you may never get
The knack of judging a distance, but at least you know
How to report on a landscape: the central sector,
The right of arc and that, which we had last Tuesday,   5
    And at least you know

That maps are of time, not place, so far as the army
Happens to be concerned—the reason being,
Is one which need not delay us. Again, you know
There are three kinds of tree, three only, the fir and the poplar,   10
And those which have bushy tops to; and lastly
    That things only seem to be things.

A barn is not called a barn, to put it more plainly,
Or a field in the distance, where sheep may be safely grazing.
You must never be over-sure. You must say, when reporting: 15
At five o'clock in the central sector is a dozen
Of what appear to be animals; whatever you do,
    Don't call the bleeders *sheep.*

I am sure that's quite clear; and suppose, for the sake of example,
The one at the end, asleep, endeavors to tell us   20
What he sees over there to the west, and how far away,
After first having come to attention. There to the west,
On the fields of summer the sun and the shadows bestow
    Vestments of purple and gold.

The still white dwellings are like a mirage in the heat,   25
And under the swaying elms a man and a woman
Lie gently together. Which is, perhaps, only to say
That there is a row of houses to the left of arc,
And that under some poplars a pair of what appear to be humans
    Appear to be loving.   30

Well that, for an answer, is what we might rightly call
Moderately satisfactory only, the reason being,
Is that two things have been omitted, and those are important.
The human beings, now: in what direction are they,
And how far away, would you say? And do not forget   35
    There may be dead ground in between.

There may be dead ground in between; and I may not have got
The knack of judging a distance; I will only venture

A guess that perhaps between me and the apparent lovers,
(Who, incidentally, appear by now to have finished,)
At seven o'clock from the houses, is roughly a distance
   Of about one year and a half.

4⁰

1946

AUDRE LORDE

Hanging Fire

I am fourteen
and my skin has betrayed me
the boy I cannot live without
still sucks his thumb
in secret
how come my knees are
always so ashy
what if I die
before morning
and momma's in the bedroom
with the door closed.

I have to learn how to dance
in time for the next party
my room is too small for me
suppose I die before graduation
they will sing sad melodies
but finally
tell the truth about me
There is nothing I want to do
and too much
that has to be done
and momma's in the bedroom
with the door closed.

Nobody even stops to think
about my side of it
I should have been on Math Team
my marks were better than his
why do I have to be
the one
wearing braces
I have nothing to wear tomorrow
will I live long enough
to grow up
and momma's in the bedroom
with the door closed.

1978

JUDITH ORTIZ COFER

The Changeling

As a young girl
vying for my father's attention,
I invented a game that made him look up
from his reading and shake his head
as if both baffled and amused.   5

In my brother's closet, I'd change
into his dungarees—the rough material
molding me into boy shape; hide
my long hair under an army helmet
he'd been given by Father, and emerge   10
transformed into the legendary Ché[5]
of grown-up talk.

Strutting around the room,
I'd tell of life in the mountains,
of carnage and rivers of blood,   15
and of manly feasts with rum and music
to celebrate victories *para la libertad*.[6]
He would listen with a smile
to my tales of battles and brotherhood
until Mother called us to dinner.   20

She was not amused
by my transformations, sternly forbidding me
from sitting down with them as a man.
She'd order me back to the dark cubicle
that smelled of adventure, to shed   25
my costume, to braid my hair furiously
with blind hands, and to return invisible,
as myself,
to the real world of her kitchen.   1993

JOHN BETJEMAN

In Westminster Abbey[7]

Let me take this other glove off
As the *vox humana*[8] swells,

5. Ché Guevara (1928–1967), martyred companion of Fidel Castro.   6. "For freedom" (Spanish).   7. Gothic church in London in which English monarchs are crowned and famous Englishmen are buried (see lines 5, 39–40).   8. Organ tones that resemble the human voice.

And the beauteous fields of Eden
    Bask beneath the Abbey bells.
Here, where England's statesmen lie,
Listen to a lady's cry.

Gracious Lord, oh bomb the Germans.
    Spare their women for Thy Sake,
And if that is not too easy
    We will pardon Thy Mistake.
But, gracious Lord, whate'er shall be,
Don't let anyone bomb me.

Keep our Empire undismembered
    Guide our Forces by Thy Hand,
Gallant blacks from far Jamaica,
    Honduras and Togoland;
Protect them Lord in all their fights,
And, even more, protect the whites.

Think of what our Nation stands for,
    Books from Boots[9] and country lanes,
Free speech, free passes, class distinction,
    Democracy and proper drains.
Lord, put beneath Thy special care
One-eighty-nine Cadogan Square.[1]

Although dear Lord I am a sinner,
    I have done no major crime;
Now I'll come to Evening Service
    Whensoever I have the time.
So, Lord, reserve for me a crown,
And do not let my shares go down.

I will labor for Thy Kingdom,
    Help our lads to win the war,
Send white feathers to the cowards[2]
    Join the Women's Army Corps,[3]
Then wash the Steps around Thy Throne
In the Eternal Safety Zone.

Now I feel a little better,
    What a treat to hear Thy Word
Where the bones of leading statesmen,
    Have so often been interred.
And now, dear Lord, I cannot wait
Because I have a luncheon date.

    1940

9. A chain of London pharmacies.   1. Presumably where the speaker lives, in a fairly fashionable area.   2. White feathers were sometimes given, or sent, to men not in uniform, to suggest that they were cowards and should join the armed forces.   3. The speaker uses the old World War I name (Women's Army Auxiliary Corps) of the Auxiliary Territorial Service, an organization that performed domestic (and some foreign) defense duties.

AI

Twenty-year Marriage

You keep me waiting in a truck
with its one good wheel stuck in the ditch,
while you piss against the south side of a tree.
Hurry. I've got nothing on under my skirt tonight.
That still excites you, but this pickup has no windows   5
and the seat, one fake leather thigh,
pressed close to mine is cold.
I'm the same size, shape, make as twenty years ago,
but get inside me, start the engine;
you'll have the strength, the will to move.   10
I'll pull, you push, we'll tear each other in half.
come on, baby, lay me down on my back.
Pretend you don't owe me a thing
and maybe we'll roll out of here,
leaving the past stacked up behind us;   15
old newspapers nobody's ever got to read again.   1973

WILLIAM SHAKESPEARE

[When my love swears that she is made of truth]

When my love swears that she is made of truth,
I do believe her, though I know she lies,
That she might think me some untutored youth,
Unlearnèd in the world's false subtleties.
Thus vainly thinking that she thinks me young,   5
Although she knows my days are past the best,[4]
Simply[5] I credit her false-speaking tongue:
On both sides thus is simple truth suppressed.
But wherefore says she not she is unjust?[6]
And wherefore say not I that I am old?   10
Oh, love's best habit[7] is in seeming trust,
And age in love loves not to have years told.
    Therefore I lie with her and she with me,
    And in our faults by lies we flattered be.   1599

---

4. Shakespeare was thirty-five or younger when he wrote this sonnet.   5. Like a simpleton.
6. Unfaithful.   7. Appearance, deportment.

SYLVIA PLATH

Mirror

I am silver and exact. I have no preconceptions.
Whatever I see I swallow immediately
Just as it is, unmisted by love or dislike.
I am not cruel, only truthful—
The eye of a little god, four-cornered.
Most of the time I meditate on the opposite wall.
It is pink, with speckles. I have looked at it so long
I think it is a part of my heart. But it flickers.
Faces and darkness separate us over and over.

Now I am a lake. A woman bends over me,
Searching my reaches for what she really is.
Then she turns to those liars, the candles or the moon.
I see her back, and reflect it faithfully.
She rewards me with tears and an agitation of hands.
I am important to her. She comes and goes.
Each morning it is her face that replaces the darkness.
In me she has drowned a young girl, and in me an old woman
Rises toward her day after day, like a terrible fish.

1961

GWENDOLYN BROOKS

We Real Cool

THE POOL PLAYERS,
SEVEN AT THE GOLDEN SHOVEL.

We real cool. We
Left school. We

Lurk late. We
Strike straight. We

Sing sin. We
Thin gin. We

Jazz June. We
Die soon.

1950

SIR THOMAS WYATT

They Flee from Me

They flee from me, that sometime did me seek,
With naked foot stalking in my chamber.
I have seen them, gentle, tame, and meek,
That now are wild, and do not remember
That sometime they put themselves in danger   5
To take bread at my hand; and now they range,
Busily seeking with a continual change.

Thankéd be Fortune it hath been otherwise,
Twenty times better; but once in special,
In thin array, after a pleasant guise,   10
When her loose gown from her shoulders did fall,
And she me caught in her arms long and small.[8]
And therewith all sweetly did me kiss
And softly said, "Dear heart, how like you this?"

It was no dream, I lay broad waking.   15
But all is turned, thorough[9] my gentleness,
Into a strange fashion of forsaking;
And I have leave to go, of her goodness,
And she also to use newfangleness.[1]
But since that I so kindely[2] am servéd,   20
I fain[3] would know what she hath deservéd.   1557

ADRIENNE RICH

[My mouth hovers across your breasts][4]

3.

My mouth hovers across your breasts
in the short grey winter afternoon
in this bed   we are delicate
and tough   so hot with joy we amaze ourselves
tough   and delicate   we play rings   5
around each other   our daytime candle burns
with its peculiar light   and if the snow
begins to fall outside   filling the branches
and if the night falls   without announcement

8. Slender.   9. Through.   1. Fondness for novelty.   2. In a way natural to women.
3. Eagerly.   4. This poem is taken from Rich's series "Tracking Poems."

10 these are the pleasures of winter
sudden, wild and delicate   your fingers
exact   my tongue exact at the same moment
stopping to laugh at a joke
my love   hot on your scent   on the cusp of winter

1983–85   1986

STEPHEN DUNN

Dancing with God

At first the surprise
of being singled out,
the dance floor crowded
and me not looking my best,
5 a too-often-worn dress
and the man with me
a budding casualty
of one repetition too much.
God just touched his shoulder
10 and he left.
Then the confirmation of
an old guess:
God was a wild god,
into the most mindless rock,
15 but graceful,
looking—this excited me—
like no one I could love,
cruel mouth, eyes evocative
of promises unkept.
20 I never danced better, freer,
as if dancing were my way
of saying how easily
I could be with him, or apart.
When the music turned slow
25 God held me close
and I felt for a moment
I'd mistaken him,
that he was Death
and this the famous embrace
30 before the lights go out.
But God kept holding me
and I him
until the band stopped
and I stood looking at a figure
35 I wanted to slap

or forgive for something,
I couldn't decide which.
He left then, no thanks,
no sign
that he'd felt anything   40
more than an earthly moment
with someone who could've been
anyone on earth.
To this day I don't know why
I thought he was God,   45
though it was clear
there was no going back
to the man who brought me,
nice man
with whom I'd slept   50
and grown tired,
who danced wrong,
who never again
could do anything right.   1989

STEVIE SMITH

I Remember

It was my bridal night I remember,
An old man of seventy-three
I lay with my young bride in my arms,
A girl with t.b.
It was wartime, and overhead   5
The Germans were making a particularly heavy raid on Hampstead.
What rendered the confusion worse, perversely
Our bombers had chosen that moment to set out for Germany.
Harry, do they ever collide?
I do not think it has ever happened,   10
Oh my bride, my bride.   1957

SEAMUS HEANEY

The Outlaw

Kelly's kept an unlicensed bull, well away
From the road: you risked fine but had to pay

The normal fee if cows were serviced there.
Once I dragged a nervous Friesian on a tether

Down a lane of alder, shaggy with catkin,
Down to the shed the bull was kept in.

I gave Old Kelly the clammy silver, though why
I could not guess. He grunted a curt 'Go by

Get up on that gate.' And from my lofty station
I watched the business-like conception.

The door, unbolted, whacked back against the wall.
The illegal sire fumbled from his stall

Unhurried as an old steam engine shunting,
He circled, snored and nosed. No hectic panting,

Just the unfussy ease of a good tradesman;
Then an awkward, unexpected jump, and

His knobbed forelegs straddling her flank,
He slammed life home, impassive as a tank,

Dropping off like a tipped-up load of sand.
'She'll do,' said Kelly and tapped his ash-plant

Across her hindquarters. 'If not, bring her back.'
I walked ahead of her, the rope now slack

While Kelly whooped and prodded his outlaw
Who, in his own time, resumed the dark, the straw.   1969

MARGARET ATWOOD

Death of a Young Son by Drowning

He, who navigated with success
the dangerous river of his own birth
once more set forth

on a voyage of discovery
into the land I floated on
but could not touch to claim.

His feet slid on the bank,
the currents took him;
he swirled with ice and trees in the swollen water

and plunged into distant regions,
his head a bathysphere;
through his eyes' thin glass bubbles

he looked out, reckless adventurer
on a landscape stranger than Uranus
we have all been to and some remember.

There was an accident; the air locked,
he was hung in the river like a heart.
They retrieved the swamped body,

cairn of my plans and future charts,
with poles and hooks   20
from among the nudging logs.

It was spring, the sun kept shining, the new grass
leapt to solidity;
my hands glistened with details.

After the long trip I was tired of waves.   25
My foot hit rock. The dreamed sails
collapsed, ragged.

    I planted him in his country
    like a flag.   1970

SAMUEL TAYLOR COLERIDGE

This Lime-Tree Bower My Prison[5]

Well, they are gone, and here must I remain,
This lime-tree bower my prison! I have lost
Beauties and feelings, such as would have been
Most sweet to my remembrance even when age
Had dimmed mine eyes to blindness! They, meanwhile,   5
Friends, whom I never more may meet again,
On springy[6] heath, along the hilltop edge,
Wander in gladness, and wind down, perchance,
To that still roaring dell, of which I told;
The roaring dell, o'erwooded, narrow, deep,   10
And only speckled by the midday sun;
Where its slim trunk the ash from rock to rock
Flings arching like a bridge;—that branchless ash,
Unsunned and damp, whose few poor yellow leaves
Ne'er tremble in the gale, yet tremble still,   15
Fanned by the waterfall! and there my friends
Behold the dark green file of long lank weeds,[7]
That all at once (a most fantastic sight!)
Still nod and drip beneath the dripping edge
Of the blue clay-stone.

---

5. Coleridge wrote the poem during a visit to his cottage by some friends; an accident on the way of their arrival prevented him from accompanying them on walks, during one of which the poem is set. 6. "Elastic, I mean." (Coleridge's note) 7. Plants usually called adder's tongue or hart's tongue.

20   Now, my friends emerge
         Beneath the wide wide Heaven—and view again
         The many-steepled tract magnificent
         Of hilly fields and meadows, and the sea,
         With some fair bark, perhaps, whose sails light up
25   The slip of smooth clear blue betwixt two Isles
         Of purple shadow! Yes! they wander on
         In gladness all; but thou, methinks, most glad,
         My gentle-hearted Charles![8] for thou hast pined
         And hungered after Nature, many a year,
30   In the great City pent,[9] winning thy way
         With sad yet patient soul, through evil and pain
         And strange calamity! Ah! slowly sink
         Behind the western ridge, thou glorious Sun!
         Shine in the slant beams of the sinking orb,
35   Ye purple heath-flowers! richlier burn, ye clouds!
         Live in the yellow light, ye distant groves!
         And kindle, thou blue Ocean! So my friend
         Struck with deep joy may stand, as I have stood,
         Silent with swimming sense; yea, gazing round
40   On the wide landscape, gaze till all doth seem
         Less gross than bodily; and of such hues
         As veil the Almighty Spirit, when yet he makes
         Spirits perceive his presence.

                                 A delight
         Comes sudden on my heart, and I am glad
45   As I myself were there! Nor in this bower,
         This little lime-tree bower, have I not marked
         Much that has soothed me. Pale beneath the blaze
         Hung the transparent foliage; and I watched
         Some broad and sunny leaf, and loved to see
50   The shadow of the leaf and stem above
         Dappling its sunshine! And that walnut-tree
         Was richly tinged, and a deep radiance lay
         Full on the ancient ivy, which usurps
         Those fronting elms, and now, with blackest mass
55   Makes their dark branches gleam a lighter hue
         Through the late twilight: and though now the bat
         Wheels silent by, and not a swallow twitters,
         Yet still the solitary humble-bee
         Sings in the bean-flower! Henceforth I shall know
60   That Nature ne'er deserts the wise and pure;
         No plot so narrow, be but Nature there,
         No waste so vacant, but may well employ

---

8. The poem is addressed to Charles Lamb, one of the visiting friends.   9. Lamb was a clerk at the India House, London.

Each faculty of sense, and keep the heart
Awake to Love and Beauty! and sometimes
'Tis well to be bereft of promised good,   65
That we may lift the soul, and contemplate
With lively joy the joys we cannot share.
My gentle-hearted Charles! when the last rook[1]
Beat its straight path along the dusky air
Homewards, I blessed it! deeming its black wing   70
(Now a dim speck, now vanishing in light)
Had crossed the mighty orb's dilated glory,
While thou stood'st gazing; or, when all was still,
Flew creeking o'er thy head, and had a charm
For thee, my gentle-hearted Charles, to whom   75
No sound is dissonant which tells of Life.   1797

WALT WHITMAN

[I celebrate myself, and sing myself]

I celebrate myself, and sing myself,
And what I assume you shall assume,
For every atom belonging to me as good belongs to you.

I loafe and invite my soul,
I lean and loafe at my ease observing a spear of summer grass.   5

My tongue, every atom of my blood, form'd from this soil, this air,
Born here of parents born here from parents the same, and their parents the
    same,
I, now thirty-seven years old in perfect health begin,
Hoping to cease not till death.

Creeds and schools in abeyance,   10
Retiring back a while sufficed at what they are, but never forgotten,
I harbor for good or bad, I permit to speak at every hazard,
Nature without check with original energy.   1855, 1881

▼   ▼   ▼

SPEAKER **A Glossary**

speaker: the person, not necessarily the author, who is the voice of the
poem

---

1. Crow.

QUESTIONS

1. In "Lessons of the War: Judging Distances," what indicators are there that different voices speak within the poem? Where, exactly, do the changes of speaker take place? How would you characterize each speaker? What words or phrases are especially effective in establishing the different speakers' characters and values?

2. What, precisely, do we know about the speaker in "Hanging Fire"? How much self-confidence does she have? How can you tell? How does she feel about herself?

3. List all the facts we know about the speaker of "In Westminster Abbey." Which facts are especially important in our view of her? Explain the significance of the poem's setting.

4. Characterize the speaker in "The Outlaw." What in particular fascinates him about the breeding operation? What, exactly, does he see? How do the two participants respond to the central event? How do the observers respond? Why does the poem describe the path to Kelly's so fully? Why does the "nervous Friesian" have to be dragged? Why is the money paid to Kelly described as "clammy silver" (line 7)? Why does the speaker decide to employ an "unlicensed bull"? What or whom does the title of the poem refer to?

5. What kind of journey does the mother make in "Death of a Young Son by Drowning"? How are the son's and mother's journeys related? Explain the final image in lines 28–29.

WRITING SUGGESTIONS

1. In your college library, do some basic research on Westminster Abbey—its location and appearance, its history, its symbolic status in England. Look up some brief summary (an encyclopedia entry will do) of the effects of World War II on London. Then write a two-page essay on the importance of setting to the tone of "In Westminster Abbey."

2. The speakers in "Needs" and "The Outlaw" both reveal themselves to have desires and needs that they are not themselves fully conscious of. Analyze carefully just what elements in the poem make clear to us the "secret" aspects of their characters. Compare the character of the speaker (and the strategies used to characterize her) in Maxine Kumin's "Woodchucks" (p. 36). Choose either "Needs" or "The Outlaw" to compare in detail with "Woodchucks," and

write a short (600–700 word) essay in which you characterize the speakers in the two poems, making clear what kind of attitude each poem develops toward its speaker.

3. Analyze carefully the way "Mirror" is narrated. Evaluate the strategy of using a nonhuman speaker through which to present the words of the poem. Write a brief, two-paragraph account of the poem in which you explain the advantages and disadvantages of its choice of speaker.

4. Make a list of all the "facts" we learn about the speaker in "Twenty-year Marriage." What, exactly, is the setting of the poem? How much do we know about the husband? How much do we learn about the marriage? What is the speaker's attitude toward tonight? toward the marriage? toward the past? Once you are clear about exactly what is going on in the poem, write an answer, as if written by the husband.

3 SITUATION AND SETTING

Questions about the speaker ("Who?" questions) in a poem almost always lead to questions of "Where?" "When?" and "Why?" Identifying the speaker usually is, in fact, part of a larger process of defining the entire imagined **situation** in a poem: What is happening? Where is it happening? Who is the speaker speaking to? Who else is present? Why is this event occurring? In order to understand the dialogue in "The Ruined Maid," for example, we need to recognize that the friends are meeting after an extended period of separation, and that they meet in a town setting rather than the rural area in which they grew up together. We infer (from the opening lines) that the meeting is accidental, and that no other friends are present for the conversation. The poem's whole "story" depends on their situation: after leading separate lives for some time they have some catching up to do. We don't know what specific town is involved, or what year, season, or time of day because those details are not important to the poem's effect. But crucial to the poem are the where and when questions that define the situation and relationship of the two speakers, and the answer to the why question—that the meeting is by chance—is important too. In another poem we looked at in the previous chapter, "A Certain Lady," the specific moment and place are not important, but we do need to notice that the "lady" is talking to (or having an imaginary conversation with) her lover and that they are talking about a relationship of some duration.

Sometimes a *specific* time and place (**setting**) may be important. The "lady in skunk" sings her life story "in a prominent bar in Secaucus," a smelly and unfashionable town in New Jersey, but on no particular occasion ("one day"). In "Soliloquy of the Spanish Cloister," the setting (a monastery) adds to the irony because of the gross inappropriateness of such sentiments and attitudes in a supposedly holy place, and the setting of "In Westminster Abbey" similarly helps us to judge the speaker's ideas, attitudes, and self-conception.

The title of the following poem suggests that place may be important, and it is, although you may be surprised to discover exactly what exists at this address and what uses the speaker makes of it.

JAMES DICKEY

Cherrylog Road

Off Highway 106
At Cherrylog Road I entered
The '34 Ford without wheels,
Smothered in kudzu,[1]
With a seat pulled out to run   5
Corn whiskey down from the hills,

And then from the other side
Crept into an Essex
With a rumble seat of red leather
And then out again, aboard   10
A blue Chevrolet, releasing
The rust from its other color,

Reared up on three building blocks.
None had the same body heat;
I changed with them inward, toward   15
The weedy heart of the junkyard,
For I knew that Doris Holbrook
Would escape from her father at noon

And would come from the farm
To seek parts owned by the sun   20
Among the abandoned chassis,
Sitting in each in turn
As I did, leaning forward
As in a wild stock-car race

In the parking lot of the dead.   25
Time after time, I climbed in
And out the other side, like
An envoy or movie star
Met at the station by crickets.
A radiator cap raised its head,   30

Become a real toad or a kingsnake
As I neared the hub of the yard,
Passing through many states,
Many lives, to reach
Some grandmother's long Pierce-Arrow   35
Sending platters of blindness forth

1. A rapidly growing vine, introduced from Japan to combat erosion but now covering whole fields and groves of trees, especially in the deep South.

From its nickel hubcaps
And spilling its tender upholstery
On sleepy roaches,
40   The glass panel in between
Lady and colored driver
Not all the way broken out,

The back-seat phone
Still on its hook.
45   I got in as though to exclaim,
"Let us go to the orphan asylum,
John; I have some old toys
For children who say their prayers."

I popped with sweat as I thought
50   I heard Doris Holbrook scrape
Like a mouse in the southern-state sun
That was eating the paint in blisters
From a hundred car tops and hoods.
She was tapping like code,

55   Loosening the screws,
Carrying off headlights,
Sparkplugs, bumpers,
Cracked mirrors and gear-knobs,
Getting ready, already,
60   To go back with something to show

Other than her lips' new trembling
I would hold to me soon, soon,
Where I sat in the ripped back seat
Talking over the interphone,
65   Praying for Doris Holbrook
To come from her father's farm

And to get back there
With no trace of me on her face
To be seen by her red-haired father
70   Who would change, in the squalling barn,
Her back's pale skin with a strop,
Then lay for me

In a bootlegger's roasting car
With a string-triggered 12-gauge shotgun
75   To blast the breath from the air.
Not cut by the jagged windshields,
Through the acres of wrecks she came
With a wrench in her hand,

Through dust where the blacksnake dies
80   Of boredom, and the beetle knows

The compost has no more life.
Someone outside would have seen
The oldest car's door inexplicably
Close from within:

I held her and held her and held her,   85
Convoyed at terrific speed
By the stalled, dreaming traffic around us,
So the blacksnake, stiff
With inaction, curved back
Into life, and hunted the mouse   90

With deadly overexcitement,
The beetles reclaimed their field
As we clung, glued together,
With the hooks of the seat springs
Working through to catch us red-handed   95
Amidst the gray breathless batting

That burst from the seat at our backs.
We left by separate doors
Into the changed, other bodies
Of cars, she down Cherrylog Road   100
And I to my motorcycle
Parked like the soul of the junkyard

Restored, a bicycle fleshed
With power, and tore off
Up Highway 106, continually   105
Drunk on the wind in my mouth,
Wringing the handlebar for speed,
Wild to be wreckage forever.   1964

The *exact* location of the junkyard is not important (there is no Highway 106 near the real Cherrylog Road in North Georgia), but we do need to know that the setting is rural, that the time is summer and that the summer is hot, and that moonshine whiskey is native to the area. Following the story is no problem once we have sorted out these few facts, and we are prepared to meet the cast of characters: Doris Holbrook, her red-haired father, and the speaker. About each we learn just enough to appreciate the sense of vitality, adventure, and power that constitute the major effects of the poem.

The situation of lovemaking in another setting than the junkyard would not produce the same effects, and the exotic sense of a forbidden meeting in this unlikely place helps to re-create the speaker's sense of the episode. For him, it is memorable (notice all the tiny details he remembers), powerful (notice his reaction when he gets back on his motorcycle), dreamlike (notice the sense of time standing still, especially in lines 85–89), and important (notice how the speaker perceives his environment as changed by their lovemaking, lines 88–91 and 98–100). The wealth of details about setting also helps us to raise other, related questions. Why does the speaker fantasize about being shot by the father (lines 72–75)? Why, in a poem so full of details, do we find out so little about what Doris Holbrook looks like? What gives us the sense that this incident is a composite of episodes, an event that was repeated many times? What gives us the impression that the events occurred long ago? What makes the speaker feel so powerful at the end? What does he mean when he talks of himself as being "wild to be wreckage forever"? All of the poem's attention to the speaker's reactions, reflections, and memories is intricately tied up with the particulars of setting. Making love in a junkyard is crucial to the speaker's sense of both power and wreckage, and to him Doris is merely a matter of excitement, adventure, and pale skin, appreciated because she makes the world seem different and because she is willing to take risks and to suffer for meeting him like this. The more we probe the poem with questions about situation, the more likely we are to catch the poem's full effect.

The plot of "Cherrylog Road" is fairly easy to sort out, but its effect is more complex than the simple story suggests. The next poem we will look at is, at first glance, much more difficult to follow. Part of the difficulty is that the poem is from an earlier age and its language and syntax may seem a bit unfamiliar, and part is because the action in the poem is so closely connected to what is being said. But its opening lines—addressed to someone who is resisting the speaker's suggestions—disclose the situation, and gradually we can figure out the scene: a man is trying to convince a woman that they should make love. When a flea happens by, the speaker uses it for an unlikely example; it becomes part of his argument. And once we recognize the situation, we can readily follow (and be amused by) the speaker's witty and intricate argument.

JOHN DONNE

The Flea

Mark but this flea, and mark in this[2]
How little that which thou deny'st me is;
It sucked me first, and now sucks thee,
And in this flea our two bloods mingled be;

---

2. Medieval preachers and rhetoricians asked their hearers to "mark" (look at) an object that illustrated a moral or philosophical lesson they wished to emphasize.

Thou know'st that this cannot be said   5
A sin, nor shame, nor loss of maidenhead.
    Yet this enjoys before it woo,
    And pampered[3] swells with one blood made of two,
    And this, alas, is more than we would do.[4]

Oh stay, three lives in one flea spare,   10
Where we almost, yea more than, married are.
This flea is you and I, and this
Our marriage bed, and marriage temple is;
Though parents grudge, and you, we're met
And cloistered in these living walls of jet.   15
    Though use[5] make you apt to kill me,
    Let not to that, self-murder added be,
    And sacrilege, three sins in killing three.

Cruel and sudden, hast thou since
Purpled thy nail in blood of innocence?   20
Wherein could this flea guilty be,
Except in that drop which it sucked from thee?
Yet thou triumph'st, and say'st that thou
Find'st not thyself, nor me, the weaker now;
    'Tis true; then learn how false, fears be;   25
    Just so much honor, when thou yield'st to me,
    Will waste, as this flea's death took life from thee.   1633

The scene in "The Flea" develops almost as it would in the theater. Action occurs even as the poem is being written. Between stanzas 1 and 2, the woman makes a move to kill the flea (as stanza 2 opens, the speaker is trying to stop her), and between stanzas 2 and 3 she has squashed the flea with her fingernail. Once we make sense of what the speaker says, the action is just as clear from the words as if we had stage directions in the margin. All of the speaker's verbal cleverness and all of his specious arguments follow from the situation, and in this poem (as in "Soliloquy of the Spanish Cloister" or "In Westminster Abbey") we watch as if we were observing a scene in a play. The speaker is, in effect, giving a dramatic monologue for our benefit.

    Neither time nor place is important to "The Flea," except that the speaker and his friend must be assumed to be in the same place and to have the leisure for some playfulness. The situation could occur anywhere a man, a woman, and a flea could be together: indoors, outdoors, morning, evening, city, country, in cottage or palace, on a boat or in a bedroom. We do know, from the

---

3. Fed luxuriously.   4. According to contemporary medical theory, conception involved the literal mingling of the lovers' blood.   5. Habit.

date of publication of the poem (1633), that the poet was writing about people of almost four centuries ago, but the conduct he describes might equally happen in later ages. Only the habits of language (and perhaps the speaker's religious attitudes) date the poem; the situation could just as easily be set in any age or place.

The two poems that follow have simpler plots, but in each case the heart of the poem is in the basic situation:

RITA DOVE

Daystar

She wanted a little room for thinking:
but she saw diapers steaming on the line,
a doll slumped behind the door.

So she lugged a chair behind the garage
to sit out the children's naps.

Sometimes there were things to watch—
the pinched armor of a vanished cricket,
a floating maple leaf. Other days
she stared until she was assured
when she closed her eyes
she'd see only her own vivid blood.

She had an hour, at best, before Liza appeared
pouting from the top of the stairs.
And just *what* was mother doing
out back with the field mice? Why,

building a palace. Later
that night when Thomas rolled over and
lurched into her, she would open her eyes
and think of the place that was hers
for an hour—where
she was nothing,
pure nothing, in the middle of the day.

1986

LINDA PASTAN

To a Daughter Leaving Home

When I taught you
at eight to ride
a bicycle, loping along
beside you
as you wobbled away   5
on two round wheels,
my own mouth rounding
in surprise when you pulled
ahead down the curved
path of the park,   10
I kept waiting
for the thud
of your crash as I
sprinted to catch up,
while you grew   15
smaller, more breakable
with distance,
pumping, pumping
for your life, screaming
with laughter,   20
the hair flapping
behind you like a
handkerchief waving
goodbye.   1988

Both these poems involve motherhood, but they take entirely different
stances about it and have very different tones. The mother in "Daystar" is over-
whelmed by the demands of young children and needs a room of her own. All
she can manage, however, is a brief hour in a chair behind the garage. The sit-
uation is virtually the whole story here. Nothing really happens except that
daily events (washing diapers, picking up toys, looking at crickets and leaves,
explaining the world to children, having sex) crowd her brief private hour and
make it precious. Being "nothing" (lines 21 and 22) takes on great value in
these circumstances, and the poem makes much of the setting: an isolated
chair behind the garage. Setting in poems often means something much more
specific about a particular culture or social history, but here time and place are
given value by the circumstances of the situation for one frazzled mother.

The particulars of time and place in "To a Daughter Leaving Home" are
even less specific, but the incident the poem describes happened a long time

ago, and it is important to notice that its vividness in the poem is a function of memory. The mother is the speaker here, and we are told very little about her, at least directly. But she is thinking back nostalgically to a moment long ago when her daughter made an earlier (but briefer) departure from home, and the poem implies the occasion for her doing so. The daughter now is old enough to "leave" home in a full sense; the poem does not tell us why or what the present circumstances are, but the title tells us the situation. We may infer quite a bit about the speaker here—her affection for the daughter, the kind of mother she has been, her anxiety at the new departure that seems to reflect the earlier wobbly ride into the distance—but as in "Daystar" the poem is all situation. There are almost no details of present action, and we have no specific information about place or time for either the remembered event or the present one.

Some poems, however, depend heavily on historical specifics and a knowledge of actual places and events. The following poem, for example, depends not only on knowing some facts about a particular event but on the parallels between that event and circumstances surrounding the poet and his immediate readers.

JOHN MILTON

On the Late Massacre in Piedmont

Avenge, O Lord, thy slaughtered saints, whose bones
　　Lie scattered on the Alpine mountains cold;
　　Even them who kept thy truth so pure of old
　　When all our fathers worshiped stocks and stones,
5　Forget not: in thy book record their groans
　　Who were thy sheep and in their ancient fold
　　Slain by the bloody Piemontese that rolled
　　Mother with infant down the rocks. Their moans
The vales redoubled to the hills, and they
10　　To heaven. Their martyred blood and ashes sow
　　O'er all th' Italian fields, where still doth sway
The triple tyrant:[6] that from these may grow
　　A hundredfold, who having learnt thy way
　　Early may fly the Babylonian woe.[7]

1673

6. The Pope's tiara featured three crowns.　　7. In Milton's day, Protestants often likened the Roman Church to Babylonian decadence, called the church "the whore of Babylon," and read Revelation 17 and 18 as an allegory of its coming destruction.

The "slaughtered saints" were members of the Waldensians—a heretical sect that had long been settled in southern France and northern Italy (the Piedmont). Though a minority, the Waldensians were allowed freedom of worship until 1655, when their protection under the law was taken away and locals attacked them, killing large numbers. This poem, then, is not a private meditation, but rather a public statement about a well-known "news" event. The reader, to fully understand the poem and respond to it meaningfully, must therefore be acquainted with its historical context, including the massacre itself and the significance it had for Milton and his English audience.

Milton wrote the poem shortly after the Piedmont massacre of 1655 became known in England, and implicit in its "meaning" is a parallel Milton's readers would have felt between the events in the Piedmont and current English politics. Milton signals the analogy early on by calling the dead Piedmontese "saints," the term then regularly used by English Protestants of the Puritan stamp to describe themselves, and to thereby assert their belief that every individual Christian—not just those few "special" religious heroes singled out in the Catholic tradition—lived a heroic life. By identifying the Waldensians with the English Puritans—their beliefs were in some ways quite similar, and both were minorities in a larger political and cultural context—Milton was warning his fellow Puritans that, if the Stuart monarchy were reestablished, what had just happened to the Waldensians could happen to them as well. Following the Restoration in 1660, tight restrictions were in fact placed on the Puritan "sects" under the new monarchy. In lines 12 and 14, the poem alludes to dangers of religious rule by dominant groups by invoking standard images of Catholic power and persecution; the heir to the English throne (who succeeded to the throne as Charles II in 1660) was spending his exile in Catholic Europe and was, because of his sympathetic treatment of Catholic associates and friends, thought perhaps to be himself a Catholic. Chauvinistic Englishmen, who promoted rivalries with Catholic powers like France, considered him a traitor.

Many poems, like this one, make use of historical occurrences and situations to create a widely evocative set of angers, sympathies, and conclusions. Sometimes a poet's intention in recording a particular moment or event is to commemorate it or comment upon it. A poem written about a specific occasion is usually called an **occasional poem,** and such a poem is **referential;** that is, it *refers* to a certain historical time or event. Often it is hard to place ourselves fully enough in another time or place to imagine sympathetically what a particular historical moment would have been like, and even the best poetic efforts do not necessarily transport us there. For such poems we need, at the

least, specific historical information—plus a willingness on our part as readers
to be transported, by a name, a date, or a dramatic situation.

Time or place may, of course, be used much less specifically and still be
important to a poem; frequently a poem's setting draws upon common notions
of a particular time or place. Setting a poem in a garden, for example, or writ-
ing about apples almost inevitably reminds us of the Garden of Eden because
it is part of the Western heritage of belief or knowledge. Even people who
don't read at all or who lack Judeo-Christian religious commitments are likely
to know about Eden, and a poet writing in our culture can count on that. An
allusion is a reference to something outside the poem that carries a history of
meaning and strong emotional associations. (There's a longer account of allu-
sion in Chapter 11.) For example, gardens may carry suggestions of innocence
and order, or temptation and the Fall, or both, depending on how the poem
handles the allusion. Well-known places from history or myth may be popu-
larly associated with particular ideas or values or ways of life.

The place involved in a poem is its **spatial setting,** and the time is its **tem-
poral setting.** The temporal setting may involve a specific date or an era, a sea-
son of the year or a time of day. We tend, for example, to think of spring as a
time of discovery and growth, and poems set in spring are likely to make use of
that association; morning usually suggests discovery as well—beginnings, vital-
ity, the world fresh and new—even to those of us who in reality take our wak-
ing slow. Temporal or spatial setting is often used to influence our expectation
of theme and tone, although the poet may then go on to surprise us by making
something very different of our expectation. Setting is often an important factor
in creating the mood in poems just as in stories, plays, or films. Often the
details of setting have a lot to do with the way we ultimately respond to the
poem's subject or theme, as in this poem:

SYLVIA PLATH

Point Shirley

From Water-Tower Hill to the brick prison
The shingle booms, bickering under
The sea's collapse.
Snowcakes break and welter. This year
5   The gritted wave leaps
The seawall and drops onto a bier

Of quahog chips,[8]
Leaving a salty mash of ice to whiten

In my grandmother's sand yard. She is dead,
Whose laundry snapped and froze here, who   10
Kept house against
What the sluttish, rutted sea could do.
Squall waves once danced
Ship timbers in through the cellar window;
A thresh-tailed, lanced   15
Shark littered in the geranium bed—

Such collusion of mulish elements
She wore her broom straws to the nub.
Twenty years out
Of her hand; the house still hugs in each drab   20
Stucco socket
The purple egg-stones: from Great Head's knob
To the filled-in Gut
The sea in its cold gizzard ground those rounds.

Nobody wintering now behind   25
The planked-up windows where she set
Her wheat loaves
And apple cakes to cool. What is it
Survives, grieves
So, over this battered, obstinate spit   30
Of gravel? The waves'
Spewed relics clicker masses in the wind,

Gray waves the stub-necked eiders ride.
A labor of love, and that labor lost.
Steadily the sea   35
Eats at Point Shirley. She died blessed,
And I come by
Bones, bones only, pawed and tossed,
A dog-faced sea.
The sun sinks under Boston, bloody red.   40

I would get from these dry-papped stones
The milk your love instilled in them.
The black ducks dive.
And though your graciousness might stream,
And I contrive,   45
Grandmother, stones are nothing of home
To that spumiest dove.
Against both bar and tower the black sea runs.   1960

8. Chips from quahog clam shells, common on the New England coast.

One does not have to know the New England coast by personal experience to find it vividly re-created in Plath's poem. A reader who knows that coast or another like it may have an advantage in being able to respond more quickly to the poem's precision of description, but the poem does not depend on the reader's having such knowledge. The precise location of Point Shirley, near Boston, is not especially important, but visualization of the setting is. Crucial to the poem's tone and mood is the sense of the sea as aggressor, a force powerful enough to change the contours of the coast and invade the privacy of yards and homes. The energy, relentlessness, and impersonality of the sea met their match, though only temporarily, in the speaker's grandmother, who "[k]ept house against / What the sluttish, rutted sea could do" (lines 11–12). The grandmother *belonged* in this setting, and it seemed hers, but twenty years of her absence (since her death) now begin to show. Still, the marks of her obstinacy and love are there, although ultimately doomed by the sea's more enduring power.

Details—and how they are amassed—are important here rather than historic particulars of time and place. The grays and whites and drab colors of the sea and its leavings provide both a visual sense of the scene and the mood for the poem. The stubbornness that the speaker admired in the grandmother comes to seem a part of that tenacious grayness. Nothing happens rapidly here; things wear down. Even the "bloody red" (line 40) of the sun's setting—an ominous sign that adds a vivid fright to the dullness rather than brightening it— makes promises that seem slow and long-term. The toughness of the boarded-up house is a monument to the grandmother's loving care and becomes a way for the speaker to touch her human spirit, but the poem's final emphasis is on the relentless black sea, which continues to run against the landmarks and fortresses that had been identified with the setting in the very first line.

Questions about situation and setting begin as simple questions of identification but often become more complex when we sort out all the implications. Often it takes only a moment to determine a poem's situation, but it may take much longer to discover all of the things that time and place imply, for their meanings may depend upon visual details, or upon actual historical occurrences, or upon habitual ways of thinking about certain times and places—or all three at once. As you read the following poem, notice how the setting— another shore—prepares us for the speaker's moods and ideas, and then watch how the movement of his mind is affected by what he sees.

MATTHEW ARNOLD

Dover Beach[9]

The sea is calm tonight.
The tide is full, the moon lies fair
Upon the straits; on the French coast the light
Gleams and is gone; the cliffs of England stand,
Glimmering and vast, out in the tranquil bay.   5
Come to the window, sweet is the night-air!
Only, from the long line of spray
Where the sea meets the moon-blanched land,
Listen! you hear the grating roar
Of pebbles which the waves draw back, and fling,   10
At their return, up the high strand,
Begin, and cease, and then again begin,
With tremulous cadence slow, and bring
The eternal note of sadness in.

Sophocles long ago   15
Heard it on the Aegean, and it brought
Into his mind the turbid ebb and flow
Of human misery;[1] we
Find also in the sound a thought,
Hearing it by this distant northern sea.   20

The Sea of Faith
Was once, too, at the full, and round earth's shore
Lay like the folds of a bright girdle furled.
But now I only hear
Its melancholy, long, withdrawing roar,   25
Retreating, to the breath
Of the night-wind, down the vast edges drear
And naked shingles[2] of the world.

Ah, love, let us be true
To one another! for the world, which seems   30
To lie before us like a land of dreams,
So various, so beautiful, so new,
Hath really neither joy, nor love, nor light,
Nor certitude, nor peace, nor help for pain;
And we are here as on a darkling plain   35
Swept with confused alarms of struggle and flight,
Where ignorant armies clash by night.

ca. 1851

---

9. At the narrowest point on the English Channel. The lights on the French coast (lines 3–4) would be about 20 miles away.   1. In *Antigone*, lines 583–91, the chorus compares the fate of the house of Oedipus to the waves of the sea.   2. Pebble-strewn beaches.

Exactly what is the dramatic situation in "Dover Beach"? How soon are you aware that someone is being spoken to? How much are we told about the person spoken to? How would you describe the speaker's mood? What does the speaker's mood have to do with time and place? Do any details of present place and time help to account for his tendency to talk repeatedly of the past and the future? How important is it to the poem's total effect that the beach here involves an international border? What particulars of the Dover Beach seem especially important to the poem's themes? to its emotional effects?

Sometimes time and place may carry even greater resonance in a poem because pieces of history are recovered or rehearsed. In the following poem, for example, the whole history of Manifest Destiny ultimately is invoked in a situation that at first only seems to involve a quiet walk in a California small town. Here the "clear night in Live Oak" (line 1) quickly allows us to see large episodes in American and Mexican history.

ADRIENNE RICH

Walking down the Road

On a clear night in Live Oak you can see
the stars glittering low as from the deck
of a frigate.
In Live Oak without pavements you can walk
5 the fronts of old homesteads, past tattered palms,
original rosebushes, thick walnut trees
ghosts of the liveoak groves
the whitemen cleared. On a night like this
the old California thickens and bends
10 the Baja streams out like lava-melt
we are no longer the United States
we're a lost piece of Mexico
maybe dreaming the destruction
of the Indians, reading the headlines,
15 how the gringos marched into Mexico City
forcing California into the hand
of Manifest Destiny, law following greed.
And the pale lies trapped in the flickering boxes
here in Live Oak tonight, they too follow.
20 One thing follows on another, that is time:
Carmel in its death-infested prettiness,
thousands of skeletons stacked in the *campo santo:*[3]

3. Sacred field, cemetery (Spanish).

the spring fouled by the pickaxe:
the flag dragged on to the moon:
the crystal goblet smashed: grains of the universe   25
flashing their angry tears, here in Live Oak.   1989

Not all poems have an identifiable situation or setting, just as not all poems have a speaker who is entirely distinct from the author. Poems that simply present a series of thoughts and feelings directly, in a contemplative, meditative, or reflective way, may not set up any kind of action, plot, or situation at all, preferring to speak directly without the intermediary of a dramatic device. But most poems depend crucially upon a sense of place, a sense of time, and an understanding of human interaction in scenes that resemble the strategies of drama or film. And questions about these matters will often lead you to define not only the "facts" but also the feelings central to a poem's design upon us.

▼   ▼   ▼

ROBERT BROWNING

My Last Duchess

FERRARA[4]

That's my last Duchess painted on the wall,
Looking as if she were alive. I call
That piece a wonder, now: Frà Pandolf's hands[5]
Worked busily a day, and there she stands.
Will't please you sit and look at her? I said   5
"Frà Pandolf" by design, for never read
Strangers like you that pictured countenance,
The depth and passion of its earnest glance,
But to myself they turned (since none puts by
The curtain I have drawn for you, but I)   10
And seemed as they would ask me, if they durst,
How such a glance came there; so, not the first
Are you to turn and ask thus. Sir, 'twas not
Her husband's presence only, called that spot
Of joy into the Duchess' cheek: perhaps   15

---

4. Alfonso II, Duke of Ferrara in Italy in the mid-16th century, is the presumed speaker of the poem, which is loosely based on historical events. The duke's first wife—whom he had married when she was 14—died under suspicious circumstances at 17, and he then negotiated through an agent (to whom the poem is spoken) for the hand of the niece of the Count of Tyrol in Austria.   5. Frà Pandolf is, like Claus (line 56), fictitious.

Frà Pandolf chanced to say "Her mantle laps
Over my lady's wrist too much," or "Paint
Must never hope to reproduce the faint
Half-flush that dies along her throat": such stuff
Was courtesy, she thought, and cause enough
For calling up that spot of joy. She had
A heart—how shall I say?—too soon made glad,
Too easily impressed; she liked whate'er
She looked on, and her looks went everywhere.
Sir, 'twas all one! My favor at her breast,
The dropping of the daylight in the West,
The bough of cherries some officious fool
Broke in the orchard for her, the white mule
She rode with round the terrace—all and each
Would draw from her alike the approving speech,
Or blush, at least. She thanked men,—good! but thanked
Somehow—I know not how—as if she ranked
My gift of a nine-hundred-years-old name
With anybody's gift. Who'd stoop to blame
This sort of trifling? Even had you skill
In speech—which I have not—to make your will
Quite clear to such an one, and say, "Just this
Or that in you disgusts me; here you miss,
Or there exceed the mark"—and if she let
Herself be lessoned so, nor plainly set
Her wits to yours, forsooth, and made excuse,
—E'en then would be some stooping; and I choose
Never to stoop. Oh sir, she smiled, no doubt,
Whene'er I passed her; but who passed without
Much the same smile? This grew; I gave commands;
Then all smiles stopped together. There she stands
As if alive. Will't please you rise? We'll meet
The company below, then. I repeat,
The Count your master's known munificence
Is ample warrant that no just pretense
Of mine for dowry will be disallowed;
Though his fair daughter's self, as I avowed
At starting, is my object. Nay, we'll go
Together down, sir. Notice Neptune, though,
Taming a sea-horse, thought a rarity,
Which Claus of Innsbruck cast in bronze for me!

1842

JAROLD RAMSEY

Hunting Arrowheads

Under the throbbing power lines, whose steel towers
stalk the ridge like servile dinosaurs in traces,
I find a perfect arrowhead—obsidian,
a deadly leaf, whose shaping branch was a human hand.
They say in many tribes the blind were specialists   5
at knapping tools, and as I lick the stone and taste
the mineral centuries beyond its single flight
I picture a man, led out to a boulder by a child,
a man with the milky eyes of trachoma, who turns with the sun
all day as his hands, busy with deerhorn flaker and rawhide,   10
empower the brittle stone to fly true and kill.
He sings, endlessly, *ya-ta-ta*
                    ya-ta-ta
                         ya-ta-ta
and the ring of subtracted flakes around him grows, as he dreams
of the hunt to which his flawless weapons go.

I sometimes think my true calling is finding arrowheads—   15
like Thoreau, I seem to have a knack, the mind aimless
and alert, the cricket heart easy in the harmlessness
of the search—like poetry, perhaps. *We are injurious*
to no one, doing our things, I hear New America
singing its anthem—but neither do we help, do we?   20
Do I? What's incumbent on me way up here?
Without a memory, cicadas sing all day.
Brother, were you there when they crucified
our neighbor? Was I there when they took him from the street?
Because we die we must be sorry for each other;   25
we must help each other; by throngs our human hearts are tried.

Shattered glass gleams on the sidewalks, on the streets.
Is the pattern of our lives to be read there, then,
where we live, a great desultory flaking
from some ultimate crystal? In the city, the senses   30
jangle, they turn away, grudge us the physical world.
It is a terrible price to pay. Once, after a summer
in these hills, I found my children in a parking lot,
under a web of power lines, searching for arrowheads in the gravel.

1989

LOUISE GLÜCK

Labor Day

Requiring something lovely on his arm
Took me to Stamford, Connecticut, a quasi-farm,
His family's; later picking up the mammoth
Girlfriend of Charlie, meanwhile trying to pawn me off
On some third guy also up for the weekend.
But Saturday we still were paired; spent
it sprawled across that sprawling acreage
Until the grass grew limp
With damp. Like me. Johnston-baby, I can still see
The pelted clover, burrs' prickle fur and gorged
Pastures spewing infinite tiny bells. You pimp.

1969

RICHARD SNYDER

A Mongoloid Child Handling Shells on the Beach

She turns them over in her slow hands,
as did the sea sending them to her;
broken bits from the mazarine maze,
they are the calmest things on this sand.
The unbroken children splash and shout,
rough as surf, gay as their nesting towels.
But she plays soberly with the sea's
small change and hums back to it its slow vowels.

1971

ELIZABETH ALEXANDER

Boston Year

My first week in Cambridge a car full of white boys
tried to run me off the road, and spit through the window,
open to ask directions. I was always asking directions
and always driving: to an Armenian market
in Watertown to buy figs and string cheese, apricots,
dark spices and olives from barrels, tubes of paste
with unreadable Arabic labels. I ate
stuffed grape leaves and watched my lips swell in the mirror.
The floors of my apartment would never come clean.

Whenever I saw other colored people 10
in bookshops, or museums, or cafeterias, I'd gasp,
smile shyly, but they'd disappear before I spoke.
What would I have said to them? Come with me? Take
me home? Are you my mother? No. I sat alone
in countless Chinese restaurants eating almond 15
cookies, sipping tea with spoons and spoons of sugar.
Popcorn and coffee was dinner. When I fainted
from migraine in the grocery store, a Portuguese
man above me mouthed: "No breakfast." He gave me
orange juice and chocolate bars. The color red 20
sprang into relief singing Wagner's *Walküre*.[6]
Entire tribes gyrated and drummed in my head.
I learned the samba from a Brazilian man
so tiny, so festooned with glitter I was certain
that he slept inside a filigreed, Fabergé egg. 25
No one at the door: no salesmen, Mormons, meter
readers, exterminators, no Harriet Tubman,
no one. Red notes sounding in a grey trolley town. 1990

DOROTHY LIVESAY

Green Rain

I remember long veils of green rain
Feathered like the shawl of my grandmother—
Green from the half-green of the spring trees
Waving in the valley.

I remember the road 5
Like the one which leads to my grandmother's house,
A warm house, with green carpets,
Geraniums, a trilling canary
And shining horse-hair chairs;
And the silence, full of the rain's falling 10
Was like my grandmother's parlor
Alive with herself and her voice, rising and falling—
Rain and wind intermingled.

I remember on that day
I was thinking only of my love 15
And of my love's house.
But now I remember the day
As I remember my grandmother.
I remember the rain as the feathery fringe of her shawl. p. 1929

---

6. One of four operas in *Der Ring des Nibelungen (The Ring of the Nibelung)* by German composer Richard Wagner (1813–1883).

EMILY BRONTË

The Night-Wind

In summer's mellow midnight,
A cloudless moon shone through
Our open parlor window
And rosetrees wet with dew.

I sat in silent musing,
The soft wind waved my hair:
It told me Heaven was glorious,
And sleeping Earth was fair.

I needed not its breathing
To bring such thoughts to me,
But still it whispered lowly,
"How dark the woods will be!

"The thick leaves in my murmur
Are rustling like a dream,
And all their myriad voices
Instinct[7] with spirit seem."

I said, "Go, gentle singer,
Thy wooing voice is kind,
But do not think its music
Has power to reach my mind.

"Play with the scented flower,
The young tree's supple bough,
And leave my human feelings
In their own course to flow."

The wanderer would not leave me;
Its kiss grew warmer still —
"O come," it sighed so sweetly,
"I'll win thee 'gainst thy will.

"Have we not been from childhood friends?
Have I not loved thee long?
As long as thou hast loved the night
Whose silence wakes my song.

"And when thy heart is laid at rest
Beneath the church-yard stone
I shall have time enough to mourn
And thou to be alone."

September 11, 1840   1850

7. Infused.

JOHN ASHBERY

City Afternoon

A veil of haze protects this
Long-ago afternoon forgotten by everybody
In this photograph, most of them now
Sucked screaming through old age and death.

If one could seize America   5
Or at least a fine forgetfulness
That seeps into our outline
Defining our volumes with a stain
That is fleeting too

But commemorates   10
Because it does define, after all:
Gray garlands, that threesome
Waiting for the light to change,
Air lifting the hair of one
Upside down in the reflecting pool.   1975   15

APRIL BERNARD

Praise Psalm of the City-Dweller

for C. B.

Lift your heads, all you peoples, to the wet heat rising in the airshaft,
to the pigeon feathers scattered on the sills, to the grey
triangle of sky that drifts like a soft, wet shawl

For this is the day of the heat, when yellow sedans herd like goats,
when the smell of the body contains its own joyful death   5

See how the young men of the city weep and fall upon one another's
shoulders, see how they turn their shining faces away from us who stand
encumbered by the changing sky

There was a place made, a clearing in the wilderness of bricks,
where they gathered to sing—the microphone warbled,   10
the hot smell of tar and hope fanned in wings of smoke

Shout singing in your praises, all you peoples, for there will be more
days like this, when the mouths of all the dogs fall open, pink
and quivering, and the cats lie down like lambs and close their eyes

While the hot grey heat rises like tissue from the skin, accumulating   15
in clouds of tears, there will be more days

Break the stick across your knee, O my brother, begin again
in the heat of further days   1993

ARCHIBALD LAMPMAN

In November

The hills and leafless forests slowly yield
  To the thick-driving snow. A little while
  And night shall darken down. In shouting file
The woodmen's carts go by me homeward-wheeled,
Past the thin fading stubbles, half concealed,
  Now golden-gray, sowed softly through with snow,
  Where the last ploughman follows still his row,
Turning black furrows through the whitening field.
Far off the village lamps begin to gleam,
  Fast drives the snow, and no man comes this way;
    The hills grow wintry white, and bleak winds moan
    About the naked uplands. I alone
  Am neither sad, nor shelterless, nor gray,
Wrapped round with thought, content to watch and dream.   1888

5

10

SUSAN MUSGRAVE

I Am Not a Conspiracy
Everything Is Not Paranoid
The Drug Enforcement Administration Is
Not Everywhere

Paul comes from Toronto on Sunday
to photograph me here in my
new image. We drive to a cornfield
where I stand looking uncomfortable.
The corn-god has an Irish accent—
I can hear him whispering, "Whiskey!"

And the cows. They, too, are in the
corn, entranced like figures in effigy.
Last summer in Mexico I saw purses at the
market made from unborn calfskin—
I've been wondering where they came from
ever since, the soft skins I ran my hands
down over, that made me feel like shuddering.

I was wrong. The corn-god is whispering
"Cocaine!" He is not Irish, after all,
but D.E.A. wanting to do business. He

5

10

15

demands to know the names of all my friends,
wants me to tell him who's dealing.

I confess I'm growing restless as the
camera goes on clicking, standing naked in the   20
high-heel shoes I bought last summer in Mexico.
"We want names," say the cows, who suddenly
look malevolent. They are tearing the ears
off the innocent corn. They call it an
investigation.   25

Paul calls to them, "Come here, cows!"
though I don't even want them in the picture.
What Paul sees is something different from
me; my skin feels like shuddering when those
cows run their eyes down over me.   30

"But didn't you smuggle this poem into Canada?"
asks the cow with the mirrored sunglasses.
"As far as we can tell, this is not a
Canadian poem. Didn't you write it
in Mexico?"   1985   35

WILLIAM SHAKESPEARE

[Full many a glorious morning have I seen]

Full many a glorious morning have I seen
Flatter the mountain-tops with sovereign eye,
Kissing with golden face the meadows green,
Gilding pale streams with heavenly alchymy;
Anon permit the basest clouds to ride   5
With ugly rack[8] on his celestial face,
And from the forlorn world his visage hide,
Stealing unseen to west with this disgrace:
Even so my sun one early morn did shine,
With all-triumphant splendor on my brow;   10
But, out! alack! he was but one hour mine,
The region cloud hath mask'd him from me now.
    Yet him for this my love no whit disdaineth;
    Suns of the world may stain when heaven's sun staineth.   1609

8. Moss.

JOHN DONNE

The Good-Morrow

I wonder, by my troth, what thou and I
    Did, till we loved? were we not weaned till then?
But sucked on country pleasures, childishly?
    Or snorted we in the Seven Sleepers' den?[9]
5   'Twas so; but[1] this, all pleasures fancies be.
If ever any beauty I did see,
Which I desired, and got,[2] twas but a dream of thee.

And now good-morrow to our waking souls,
    Which watch not one another out of fear;
10 For love, all love of other sights controls,
    And makes one little room an everywhere.
Let sea-discoverers to new worlds have gone,
Let maps to other,[3] worlds on worlds have shown,
Let us possess one world, each hath one, and is one.

15 My face in thine eye, thine in mine appears,[4]
    And true plain hearts do in the faces rest;
Where can we find two better hemispheres,
    Without sharp north, without declining west?
Whatever dies was not mixed equally,[5]
20 If our two loves be one, or, thou and I
Love so alike that none do slacken, none can die.   1633

MARILYN CHIN

Aubade

The candle that would not burn
will never share its glory.

Waking is this easy:
Sunday; Haunauma Bay,[6] your birthday,
and we—too comfortable to notice
the sea forging inward,

5 that before the picture window
our special pine, dwarfed and hunched

9. According to tradition, seven Christian youths escaped Roman persecution by sleeping in a cave for 187 years. *Snorted:* snored.   1. Except for.   2. Sexually possessed. *Beauty:* beautiful woman.   3. Other people.   4. I.e., each is reflected in the other's eyes.   5. Perfectly mixed elements, according to scholastic philosophy, were stable and immortal.   6. On Oahu, east of Honolulu.

through decades of seastorm and salty air,
has uprooted to die in the rain.

And in our sleep, the years have proceeded toward the horizon
like a school of uninteresting driftwood   10
or tortoises plodding disconsolately
to find what lurks at the edge.

What lurks there might be disaster:
the charred aftermath of Rome and Cathay, or
more deceptive, a sea of new aquatic flora   15
bathed in eternal dawn light.

But today as clouds give way to sunshine,
we wake as tourists of yet another decade.
Our tongues stale with last night's lovemaking,
our eyes bleared with tomorrow's dreams.   20

For now, let each candle gutter, as they do
and celebrate earth's mundane surprises:
family, lovers, friends,
clams in the mudflat for the taking.   1987

JONATHAN SWIFT

A Description of the Morning

Now hardly here and there a hackney-coach[7]
Appearing, showed the ruddy morn's approach.
Now Betty[8] from her master's bed had flown,
And softly stole to discompose her own.
The slip shod 'prentice from his master's door   5
Had pared the dirt, and sprinkled round the floor.
Now Moll had whirled her mop with dext'rous airs,
Prepared to scrub the entry and the stairs.
The youth with broomy stumps began to trace
The kennel-edge[9] where wheels had worn the place.   10
The small-coal man[1] was heard with cadence deep,
Till drowned in shriller notes of chimney-sweep:
Duns[2] at his lordship's gate began to meet;
And brick-dust Moll had screamed through half the street.[3]
The turnkey now his flock returning sees,   15

7. Hired coach. *Hardly:* Scarcely; i.e., they are just beginning to appear.   8. A stock name for a servant girl. Moll (lines 7, 14) is a frequent lower-class nickname.   9. Edge of the gutter that ran down the middle of the street. *Trace:* "To find old Nails." (Swift's note)   1. A seller of coal and charcoal.   2. Bill collectors.   3. Selling ·powdered brick that was used to clean knives.

Duly let out a-nights to steal for fees.[4]
The watchful bailiffs take their silent stands,[5]
And schoolboys lag with satchels in their hands.   p. 1709

SYLVIA PLATH

Morning Song

Love set you going like a fat gold watch.
The midwife slapped your footsoles, and your bald cry
Took its place among the elements.

Our voices echo, magnifying your arrival. New statue.
5   In a drafty museum, your nakedness
Shadows our safety. We stand round blankly as walls.

I'm no more your mother
Than the cloud that distils a mirror to reflect its own slow
Effacement at the wind's hand.

10   All night your moth-breath
Flickers among the flat pink roses. I wake to listen:
A far sea moves in my ear.

One cry, and I stumble from bed, cow-heavy and floral
In my Victorian nightgown.
15   Your mouth opens clean as a cat's. The window square

Whitens and swallows its dull stars. And now you try
Your handful of notes;
The clear vowels rise like balloons.   1961

▾   ▾   ▾

SITUATION AND SETTING A Glossary

allusion: a reference to a text or myth, outside the poem itself, that carries
  its own history of meaning
occasional poem: a poem written about or for a specific occasion, public
  or private
referential: making use of a specific historical moment or event
setting: the time and place of the poem's action
situation: the context of the poem's action, what is happening when the
  poem begins

---

4. Jailers collected fees from prisoners for their keep and often let them out at night so they could
steal to pay expenses.   5. Looking for those on their "wanted" lists.

> **spatial setting:** the place of a poem
> **temporal setting:** the time of a poem

QUESTIONS

1. What facts do we actually have about the speaker of "My Last Duchess"? On what basis do we form our evaluation of him? How does the setting contribute to the characterization? At what point in reading the poem do you become aware of the precise situation?

2. How much do we know about the child in "A Mongoloid Child Handling Shells on the Beach"? What do each of the following words contribute to the portrait of her: "slow" (lines 1, 8), "unbroken" (line 5), "soberly" (line 7), "hums" (line 8)? How does the boisterousness of the other children help to characterize the main character? What does the seaside setting contribute to the poem? What is the poem's tone?

3. What is the plot of "Labor Day"? How long ago did the central events occur? How can you tell? In what ways has the speaker's attitudes toward the events changed?

4. What do we come to know about the speaker in "Boston Year"? about the other residents of Boston? What kinds of attitudes toward her tastes does the speaker encounter? toward her color? What kind of year was it, all things considered? How is Boston itself characterized? What details in the poem justify the final images of red and gray?

WRITING SUGGESTIONS

1. Choose one of the poems you've read in this chapter and try to connect it to an experience in your own life that has helped you to appreciate the poem. Write a page or two explaining how the poem speaks to your particular situation.

2. What, exactly, happens in "The Good-Morrow"? How does the speaker feel about his lover? about the night of love? about himself? What is the evidence for his feelings about each of these things? What does the dawn have to do with the speaker's state of mind? with the tone of the poem? Write a brief two-page paper about the significance of the time setting.

3. Consult at least three handbooks of literary terms, and compare their definitions of *aubade* and *aube*. Consider the poems at the end of this chapter by Shakespeare, Donne, Chin, Swift, and Plath. Choose *one* of these poems and analyze how closely it relates to the tradition of morning poems described in the handbooks. Write a short essay (no more than two pages long) in which you explain how the poem achieves its effects by employing and modifying or rejecting the standard expectations of how mornings are to be described in poetry.

4. Consult a handbook of classical literature, and find out how Roman poets represented sunrises mythologically. (Hint: look up Phoebus, then—guided by the handbook or a reference librarian—look at several poems in which Phoebus or his fiery car is described in detail.) Consider carefully the opening lines of Swift's "A Description of the Morning." Write a short account (no more than three paragraphs) of how Swift's first two lines work: in what ways do they use and modify the standard mythological expectations? What do you make of the comparison of modern ordinary life to mythic patterns? What kind of evaluation of modern life (or of mythology) seems to be implied?

STUDENT WRITING

Below is an excerpt from one student's first response to Linda Pastan's "To a Daughter Leaving Home." The student's assignment was similar to Writing Suggestion number 1. Note how she asks Pastan questions about meaning as a way of articulating her own response to and questions about the poem.

A Letter to an Author

Kimberly Smith

Dear Linda,

    I read your poem "To a Daughter Leaving Home" and it really grabbed my attention. I felt as if I were in your head knowing exactly how you felt when you wrote it. It was a feeling that a father, mother or even a child could understand.

I also understand that you were born in New York, as I was. After reading the poem and finding out that we were born in the same place, I felt a connection to you. I came to Tucson from New Jersey and it was a very big culture shock. Knowing you are from the east gave me an easy feeling, a feeling of home.

I can remember back when I learned how to ride a bike. My father gave me the incentive that if I could ride to him without falling, then he would take me out for a lobster dinner. So, I did. I was ten and I got on that bike and peddled away until I could catch my balance and my Dad could let me go. I know now that learning to ride my bike meant more than my father watching me ride down the road. It was a symbol of freedom and growing up. It was time for my parents to let go a little more. I saw that same feeling in your poem also. Is that what you meant? Did you intend the bike image to portray a feeling of growing up and moving along in life?

It seemed to me that you wrote the poem to represent stages of a child's life. The first stage is from the beginning to the line "on two round wheels" (line 6). This stage, I believe, is when a baby is learning to walk and he or she wobbles around until getting the hang of it. The second stage is until the line "sprinted to catch up" (line 14). These are the elementary years and maybe junior high, when the child is trying to be on her own and do things for herself. I can remember this stage very well. I thought that I was at an age where I did not need my parents' help anymore. I used to say, "Mom, I am eleven years old and I am old enough to stay alone. I don't need a baby-sitter." The next stage, which I believe is one of the biggest changes in a child's life, ends at the line "with laughter" (line 20). This stage, to me, is very clearly marked high school. The idea about growing more distant I related to very well. That is because I definitely grew up a lot and learned a lot during high school. I got a car and finally felt like an individual, with her own mind. I was able to make my own decisions which was very important to me.

The language you have chosen is very simple, just like the stages of a child's life. Your sentences are short and to the point. I believe that you arranged the poem in the way you did to show a balance. The arrangement of the poem on paper is straight, just like a bike ride and just as parents want their child's life to be. I believe that you chose your words very carefully. For example, "thud" (line 12) has a deep and powerful meaning. It coincides with the last word of the poem, "goodbye" (line 24). Thud is a very final word as if you fell and you heard a big thud. "Goodbye" (line 24) has that same meaning here. You get a feeling of the end instead of just a new beginning. That is what I felt when I read those words. Did you intend to show that same connection between the words "thud" (line 12) and "goodbye" (line 24) that I saw?

There is one impression that I am getting from you in your poem that I do not agree with. I am not sure if you are intending this, but I got the feeling that you have the idea that as children go farther away that they become more fragile. That may be true in some cases, but if children are brought up in an environment that they are held in a glass box all of their life, then, in that case, it is definitely about time that they moved out on their own. Everyone is going to make mistakes but they only mean something if you can fix them yourself. I always tell my father that I appreciate his advice but sometimes I need to figure things out on my own and that making mistakes is all about growing up.

I learned a lot from your poem. I hope you enjoy my comments and feelings.

Yours truly,
Kimberly Smith

4 LANGUAGE

Fiction and drama depend upon language just as poetry does, but in a poem almost everything comes down to the particular meanings and implications of individual words. In stories and plays, we are likely to keep our attention primarily on character and plot—what is happening in front of us or in the action as we imagine it in our minds—and although words are crucial to how we imagine the characters and how we respond to what happens to them, we are not as likely to pause over any one word as we may need to in a poem. Because poems often are short and use only a few words, a lot depends on every single one. Poetry sometimes feels like prose that is distilled: only the most essential words are there. Just barely enough is said to communicate in the most basic way, using the most elemental signs of meaning and feeling—and each chosen for exactly the right shade of meaning. But elemental does not necessarily mean simple, and these signs may be very rich in their meanings and complex in their effects.

Precision and Ambiguity

Let's look first at two poems that create some of their major effects by emphasizing a single key word.

RICHARD ARMOUR

Hiding Place

A speaker at a meeting of the New York State Frozen Food Locker Association declared that the best hiding place in event of an atomic explosion is a frozen-food locker, where "radiation will not penetrate."[1]

—NEWS ITEM

Move over, ham
And quartered cow,

1. Before home freezers became popular, many Americans rented lockers in specially equipped commercial buildings.

My Geiger says
    The time is now.

Yes, now I lay me   5
    Down to sleep,
And if I die,
    At least I'll keep.   1954

YVOR WINTERS

At the San Francisco Airport

to my daughter, 1954

This is the terminal: the light
Gives perfect vision, false and hard;
The metal glitters, deep and bright.
Great planes are waiting in the yard—
They are already in the night.   5

And you are here beside me, small,
Contained and fragile, and intent
On things that I but half recall—
Yet going whither you are bent.
I am the past, and that is all.   10

But you and I in part are one:
The frightened brain, the nervous will,
The knowledge of what must be done,
The passion to acquire the skill
To face that which you dare not shun.   15

The rain of matter upon sense
Destroys me momently. The score:
There comes what will come. The expense
Is what one thought, and something more—
One's being and intelligence.   20

This is the terminal, the break.
Beyond this point, on lines of air,
You take the way that you must take;
And I remain in light and stare—
1954   In light, and nothing else, awake.   25

In "Hiding Place," almost all the poem's comedy depends on the final word, "keep." In the child's prayer that the poem echoes, to "pray the Lord my soul to keep" does not exactly involve cold storage (though it implies, theologically, a distinct lack of afterlife heat), and so the poem depends upon an outrageous double meaning. The key word is chosen because it can mean more than one thing; in this case, the importance of the word involves its **ambiguity** (an ability to mean more than one thing) rather than its **precision** (exactness).

In the second poem, the several possible meanings of a single word are probed more soberly and thoughtfully. What does it *mean* to be in a place called a "terminal"? the poem asks. As the parting of father and daughter is explored, carefully, the place of parting and the means of transportation begin to take on meanings larger than their simple referential ones. The poem is full of contrasts—young and old, light and dark, past and present, security and adventure. The father ("I am the past," line 10) remains in the light, among known objects and experience familiar to his many years; the daughter is about to depart into the night, the unknown, the uncertain future. But they both share a sense of the necessity of the parting, of the need for the daughter to mature, gain knowledge, acquire experience. Is she going off to school? to college? to her first job? We don't know, but her plane ride clearly means a new departure and a clean break with childhood, dependency, the past.

So much depends upon the word "terminal." It refers to the airport building, of course, but it also implies a boundary, an extremity, an end, something that is limited, a place where a connection is broken. Important as well is the unambiguous meaning of certain words, i.e., what these other words **denote**. The final stanza is articulated flatly, as if the speaker has recovered completely from the momentary confusion of stanza 4, when "being and intelligence" are lost in the emotion of the parting itself. The words "break," "point," "way," and "remain" are almost completely unemotional and colorless; they do not make value judgments or offer personal views, but rather define and describe. The sharp articulation of the last stanza stresses the **denotations** of the words employed. It is as if the speaker is trying to disengage himself from the emotion of the situation and just give the facts.

Words, however, are more than hard blocks of meaning on whose sense everyone agrees. They also have a more personal side, and they carry emotional force and shades of suggestion. The words we use indicate not only what we mean but how we feel about it, and we choose words that we hope will engage others emotionally and persuasively, in conversation and daily usage as well as in poems. A person who holds office is, quite literally (and unemotionally), an "officeholder," a word that clearly denotes what he or she does. But if we want to convince someone that an officeholder is wise, trustworthy, and deserving of political support we may call that person a "political leader" or perhaps a "statesman"; whereas if we want to promote distrust or contempt of officeholders we might call them "politicians" or "bureaucrats" or "political hacks." These latter words have clear **connotations**—suggestions of emotional coloration that imply our attitude and invite a similar one on the part of our hearers. What words **connote** can be just as important to a poem as what they denote, although some poems depend primarily on denotation and some more on connotation.

"At the San Francisco Airport" seems to depend primarily on denotation; the speaker tries to *specify* the meanings and implications of the parting with his daughter, and his tendency to split categories neatly for the two of them at first contributes to the sense of clarity and certainty which the speaker wants to project. He is the past (line 10) and what remains (line 24); he has age and experience, his life is the known quantity, he stands in the light. She, on the other hand, is committed to the adventure of going into the night; she seems small, fragile, and her identity exists in the uncertain future. Yet the connotations of some words carry strong emotional force as well as clear definition: that the daughter seems "small" and "fragile" to the speaker suggests his fear for her, something quite different from her sense of adventure. The neat, clean categories keep breaking down, and the speaker's feelings keep showing through. In stanza 1, the speaker tells us that the light in the terminal gives "perfect vision" but he also notices, indirectly, its artificial quality: it is "false" and "hard," suggesting the limits of the rationalism he tries to maintain. That artificial light shines over most of the poem and honors the speaker's effort, but the whole poem represents his struggle, and in stanza 4 the signals of disturbance are very strong as, despite an insistence on a vocabulary of calculation, his rational facade collapses completely. If we have observed his verbal strategies carefully, we should not be surprised to find him at the end just *staring* in the artificial light, merely awake, although the poem has shown him to be unconsciously awake to much more than he will candidly admit.

"At the San Francisco Airport" is an unusually intricate and complicated poem, and it offers us, if we are willing to examine very precisely its carefully crafted fabric, an unusually rich insight into how complex it is to be human and to have human feelings and foibles when we think we must be rational machines. But connotations can work more simply. The following epitaph, for example, even though it describes the mixed feelings one person has about another, depends heavily on the common connotations of fairly common words.

WALTER DE LA MARE

Slim Cunning Hands

Slim cunning hands at rest, and cozening eyes—
Under this stone one loved too wildly lies;
How false she was, no granite could declare;
　　　Nor all earth's flowers, how fair.　　　　　　　1950

What the speaker in "Slim Cunning Hands" remembers about the dead woman—her hands, her eyes—tells part of the story; her physical presence was clearly important to him, and the poem's other nouns—stone, granite, flowers—all remind us of her death and its finality. All these words denote objects having to do with rituals that memorialize a departed life. Granite and stone connote finality as well, and flowers connote fragility and suggest the shortness of life (which is why they have become the symbolic language of funerals). The way the speaker talks about the woman expresses, in just a few words, the complexity of his love for her. She was loved, he says, too "wildly"—by him perhaps, and apparently by others. The excitement she offered is suggested by the word, and also the lack of control. The words "cunning" and "cozening" help us interpret both her wildness and falsity; they suggest her calculation, cleverness, and untrustworthiness as well as her skill, persuasiveness, and ability to please. And the word "fair," a simple yet very inclusive word, suggests how totally attractive the speaker finds her: her beauty is just as incapable of being expressed by flowers as her fickleness is of being expressed in something as permanent as stone. Simple words here tell us perhaps all we need to know of a long story—or at least the speaker's version of it.

Words like "fair" and "cozening" are clearly loaded; they imply more emotionally than they literally mean. They have strong, clear connotations and tell us what to think, what evaluation to make, and they suggest the basis for the evaluation. Both words in the title of the following poem turn out to be key ones in its meaning and effect:

PAT MORA

Gentle Communion

Even the long-dead are willing to move.
Without a word, she came with me from the desert.

Mornings she wanders through my rooms
making beds, folding socks.

Since she can't hear me anymore,   5
Mamande[2] ignores the questions I never knew
to ask, about her younger days, her red
hair, the time she fell and broke her nose
in the snow. I will never know.

When I try to make her laugh,   10
to disprove her sad album face, she leaves
the room, resists me as she resisted
grinning for cameras, make-up, English.

While I write, she sits and prays,
feet apart, legs never crossed,   15
the blue housecoat buttoned high
as her hair dries white, girlish
around her head and shoulders.

She closes her eyes, bows her head,
and like a child presses her hands together,   20
her patient flesh steeple, the skin
worn, like the pages of her prayer book.

Sometimes I sit in her wide-armed
chair as I once sat in her lap.
Alone, we played a quiet I Spy.   25
She peeled grapes I still taste.

She removes the thin skin, places
the luminous coolness on my tongue.
I know not to bite or chew. I wait
for the thick melt,   30
our private green honey.   1991

Neither of the words in the title appears in the text itself, but both resonate
throughout the poem. "Communion" is the more powerful of the words; here,
it comes to imply the close ritualized relationship between the speaker and
"Mamande." Mamande has long been dead but now returns, recalling to the
speaker a host of memories and providing a sense of history and family iden-
tity. To the speaker, the reunion has a powerful value, reminding her of rituals,
habits, and beliefs that "place" her and affirm her heritage. The past is strong
in the speaker's mind and in the poem. Many details are recalled from album
photographs—the blue housecoat (line 16), the sad face (line 11), the white
hair that was once red (lines 7–8 and 17), the posture at prayer (lines 19–22),

2. A child's conflation of *mama grande* (Spanish for "grandmother").

the big chair (lines 23–24), the plain old-fashioned style (line 13)—and the speaker's childhood memories fade into them as she recalls a specific intimate moment.

The full effect of the word "communion"—which describes an intimate moment of union and a ritual—comes only in the final lines when the speaker remembers the secret of the grapes and recalls their sensuous feel and taste. The moment brings together the experience of different generations and cultures and represents a sacred sharing: the Spanish grandmother had resisted English, modernity, and show (line 13), and the speaker is a poet, writing (and publishing) in English, but the two have a common "private" (line 31) moment ritually shared and forever memorable. At the end, too, the full sense of "gentle" becomes evident—a word that sums up the softness, quietness, and understatedness of the experience, the personal qualities of "Mamande," and the unpretentious but dignified social level of the family heritage. Throughout the text, other words—ordinary, simple, and precise—are chosen with equal care to suggest the sense of personal dignity, revealed identity, and verbal power that the speaker comes to accept as her own. Look especially at the words "move" (line 1), "steeple" (line 21), and "luminous" (line 28).

In the two poems that follow we can readily see why the specific words are chosen because, although both poems express a male preference for the same sort of feminine appearance, the grounds of appeal are vastly different.

BEN JONSON

Still to Be Neat[3]

Still[4] to be neat, still to be dressed,
As you were going to a feast;
Still to be powdered, still perfumed;
Lady, it is to be presumed,
5 Though art's hid causes are not found,
All is not sweet, all is not sound.

Give me a look, give me a face
That makes simplicity a grace;
Robes loosely flowing, hair as free;
10 Such sweet neglect more taketh me
Than all th' adulteries of art.
They strike mine eyes, but not my heart.   1609

3. A song from Jonson's play *The Silent Woman* (1609–10).   4. Continually.

ROBERT HERRICK

Delight in Disorder

A sweet disorder in the dress
Kindles in clothes a wantonness.
A lawn[5] about the shoulders thrown
Into a fine distractiön;
An erring lace, which here and there   5
Enthralls the crimson stomacher,[6]
A cuff neglectful, and thereby
Ribbands[7] to flow confusedly;
A winning wave, deserving note,
In the tempestuous petticoat;   10
A careless shoestring, in whose tie
I see a wild civility;
Do more bewitch me than when art
Is too precise[8] in every part.   1648

The poem "Still to Be Neat" begins by describing a woman who looks too neat and orderly; she seems too perfect to be believed, the speaker says, and he has to assume that there is a reason for such overly fastidious grooming, that she is covering up something. He worries that something is wrong under-neath—that not all is "sweet" and "sound." "Sweet" could mean several things; its meaning becomes clearer when it is repeated in the next stanza in a more specific context. "Sound" begins to suggest the speaker's moral earnestness: it is a strong word, implying a suspicion that something is deeply wrong.

When "sweet" is repeated in line 10, it has taken on specific attributes from what the speaker has said about things he likes in a less calculated physical appearance. Now it appears to mean easy, attractive, unpremeditated. And when the speaker springs "adulteries" on us in the next line as a description of the woman's cosmeticizing, it is clear what he fears—that the appearance of the too neat, too made-up woman covers serious flaws, that she is trying to appear as someone she is not. "Adulteries" suggests the addition of something foreign, something unlike her own nature, and it is a strong, disapproving word. The "soundness" he had worried about involves her integrity; his objec-tion is certainly moral, probably sexual. He wants a woman to be simple and chaste; he wants women to be just what they seem to be.

The speaker in "Delight in Disorder" wants his women easy and simple

5. Scarf of fine linen.   6. Ornamental covering for the breasts.   7. Ribbons.   8. In the 16th and 17th centuries Puritans were often called Precisians because of their fastidiousness.

too, but for different reasons. He finds disorder "sweet" (line 1), and seems almost to be answering the first speaker, providing a different rationale for artless appearance. His grounds of preference are clear early: his support of "wantonness" (line 2) is close to the opposite in its moral suppositions of the first speaker's disapproval of "adulteries." This speaker wants a careless look because he thinks it's sexy, and many of the words he chooses suggest sensuality and availability: "distraction" (line 4), "erring" (line 5), "tempestuous" (line 10), "wild" (line 12). The speakers in the two poems read informality of dress very differently and have very different expectations of the person who dresses in a particular way. We find out quite a lot about each speaker. Their common subject allows us to see clearly how different they are, and how what one sees is in the eye of the beholder, how values and assumptions are built into the words one chooses even for description. Jonson has created a speaker who wants an informally clad woman who has a natural grace and ease of manner because she is confident of herself, dependable, and chaste. Herrick has created a speaker who finds informality of dress fetching and sexy and indicative of sensuality and availability.

Words are the starting point for all poetry, and almost every word is likely to be significant, either denotatively, connotatively, or both. Poets who know their craft pick each word with care to express exactly what needs to be expressed and to suggest every emotional shade that the poem is calculated to evoke in us. Often individual words qualify and amplify one another—suggestions clarify other suggestions, and meanings grow upon meanings—and thus the way the words are put together can be important too. Notice, for example, that in "Slim Cunning Hands" the final emphasis is on how *fair* in appearance the woman was; the speaker's last word describes the quality he can't forget in spite of her lack of a different kind of fairness and his distrust of her, the quality that, even though it doesn't justify everything else, mitigates all the disappointment and hurt.

That word does not stand all by itself, however, any more than any other word in a poem can be considered all alone. Every word exists within larger units of meaning—sentences, patterns of comparisons and contrasts, the whole poem—and where the word is and how it is used are often important. The final word or words may be especially emphatic (as in "Slim Cunning Hands"), and words that are repeated take on a special intensity, as "terminal" does in "At the San Francisco Airport" or as "chartered" and "cry" do in "London" (p. 34). Certain words often stand out, because they are used in an unusual way (like "chartered" in "London" or "adulteries" in "Still to Be Neat") or because they are given an artificial prominence—through unusual sentence structure, for example, or because the title calls special attention to them.

Sometimes word choice in poems is less dramatic and less obviously "significant" but equally important. Simple appropriateness is often, in fact, what makes the words in a poem work, and when words do not call special attention to themselves they are sometimes the most effective. Precision of denotation may be just as impressive and productive of specific effects as the resonance or ambiguous suggestiveness of connotation. Often poems achieve their power by a combination of verbal effects, setting off elaborate figures of speech (which we will discuss shortly) or other complicated strategies with simple words chosen to mark exact actions, moments, or states of mind. Notice, for example, how carefully the following poem produces its complex description of emotional patterns by delineating precise stages (which are then elaborated) of feeling.

EMILY DICKINSON

[After great pain, a formal feeling comes—]

After great pain, a formal feeling comes —
The Nerves sit ceremonious, like Tombs —
The stiff Heart questions was it He, that bore,
And Yesterday, or Centuries before?

The Feet, mechanical, go round —   5
Of Ground, or Air, or Ought —
A Wooden way
Regardless grown,
A Quartz contentment, like a stone —

This is the Hour of Lead —   10
Remembered, if outlived,
As Freezing Persons recollect the Snow —
ca. 1862   First — Chill — then Stupor — then the letting go —

In the following poem, notice how the title calls upon us to wonder, from the beginning, how playful and how patterned the boy's bedtime romp with his father is. As you read it, try to be conscious of the emotional effects created by the choice of words that seem to be key ones. Which words establish the bond between the two males?

THEODORE ROETHKE

My Papa's Waltz

The whiskey on your breath
Could make a small boy dizzy;
But I hung on like death:
Such waltzing was not easy.

5 We romped until the pans
Slid from the kitchen shelf;
My mother's countenance
Could not unfrown itself.

The hand that held my wrist
10 Was battered on one knuckle;
At every step you missed
My right ear scraped a buckle.

You beat time on my head
With a palm caked hard by dirt,
15 Then waltzed me off to bed
Still clinging to your shirt.   1948

Exactly what is the situation in "My Papa's Waltz"? What are the economic circumstances in the family? How can you tell? What indications are there of the family's social class? of the father's line of work? How would you characterize the speaker? How does the poem indicate his pleasure in the bedtime ritual? Which words suggest the boy's excitement? Which suggest his anxiety? How can you tell how the speaker feels about his father? What clues are there about what the mother is like? How can you tell that the experience is remembered at some years' distance? What clues are there in the word choice that an adult is remembering a childhood experience? In what sense is the poem a tribute to memories of the father? How would you describe the poem's tone?

The subtlety and force of word choice is sometimes very much affected by **word order,** the way the sentences are put together. Sometimes poems are driven to unusual word order because of the demands of rhyme and meter, but ordinarily poets use word order very much as prose writers do, to create a particular emphasis. When an unusual word order is used, you can be pretty sure that something there merits special attention. Notice the odd constructions in the second and third stanzas of "My Papa's Waltz"—the way the speaker talks about the abrasion of buckle on ear in line 12, for example. He does not say that the buckle scraped his ear, but rather puts it the other way round—a big difference in the kind of effect created, for it avoids placing blame and refuses to specify any unpleasant effect. Had he said that the buckle scraped his ear—the normal way of putting it—we would have to worry about the fragile ear. The **syntax** (sentence structure) of the poem channels our feeling and helps to control what we think of the "waltz."

The most curious part of the poem is the second stanza, for it is there that the silent mother appears, and the syntax there is peculiar in two places. In lines 5–6, the connection between the romping and the pans falling is stated oddly: "We romped *until* the pans / Slid from the kitchen shelf." The speaker does not say that they knocked down the pans or imply that there was awkwardness, but he does suggest energetic activity and duration. He implies intensity, almost design—as though the romping would not be complete until the pans fell. And the sentence about the mother—odd but effective—makes her position clear. She is a silent bystander in this male ritual, and her frown seems molded on her face. It is not as if she is frightened or angry but as if she too is performing a ritual, holding a frown on her face as if it is part of her role in the ritual, as well as perhaps a facet of her stern character. The syntax implies that she *has to* maintain the frown, and the falling of the pans almost seems to be for her benefit. She disapproves, but she is still their audience.

Word order is not always as complicated or crucial as it is in "My Papa's Waltz," but poets often manipulate the ordinary prose order of a sentence to make a specific point or create a specific emphasis or effect. In the passage below from *Paradise Lost*, for example, notice how the syntax first sets a formal tone for the passage, then calls attention to the complexities of theology that it expresses, and (in lines 44ff.) imitates, by holding back key elements of the grammar, the Fall that is being described.

Sometimes poems create, as well, a powerful sense of the way minds and emotions work by varying normal syntactical order in special ways. Listen, for example, in the following poem to the speaker's sudden loss of vocal control in the midst of what seems to be a calm analysis of her feelings about sexual behavior.

SHARON OLDS

Sex Without Love

How do they do it, the ones who make love
without love? Beautiful as dancers,
gliding over each other like ice-skaters

over the ice, fingers hooked
inside each other's bodies, faces
red as steak, wine, wet as the
children at birth whose mothers are going to
give them away. How do they come to the
come to the   come to the   God   come to the
still waters, and not love
the one who came there with them, light
rising slowly as steam off their joined
skin? These are the true religious,
the purists, the pros, the ones who will not
accept a false Messiah, love the
priest instead of the God. They do not
mistake the lover for their own pleasure,
they are like great runners: they know they are alone
with the road surface, the cold, the wind,
the fit of their shoes, their over-all cardio-
vascular health—just factors, like the partner
in the bed, and not the truth, which is the
single body alone in the universe
against its own best time.   1984

The poem starts calmly enough, with a simple rhetorical question implying
that the speaker just cannot understand sex without love. The second through
fourth lines compare such sexual activity with some distant aesthetic, with two
carefully delineated examples, and the speaker—although plainly disapprov-
ing—seems coolly, almost chillingly, in control of the analysis and evaluation.
But by the end of the fourth line, something begins to seem odd: "hooked"
seems too ugly and extreme a way to characterize the lovers' fingers, however
much the speaker may disapprove, and by line 6, the syntax seems to break
down. How does "wine" fit the syntax of the line? Is it parallel with "steak,"
another example of redness? or is it somehow related to the last part of the sen-
tence, parallel with "faces"? But neither of these possibilities quite works. At
best, the punctuation is faulty; at worst the speaker's mind is working too fast
for the language it can generate, scrambling its images. We can't yet be quite
sure what is going on, but by the ninth line the lack of control is manifest with
the compulsive repeating (three times) of "come to the" and the interjected
"God."

Such verbal behavior—here concretized by the way the poem orders its
words—invites us to reevaluate the speaker's moralism relative to her emo-
tional involvement with the issues and with her representation of sexuality
itself. The speaker's values, as well as those who have sex without love, become
a subject for evaluation.

Words are the basic building materials of poetry. They are of many kinds and are used in many different ways and in different—sometimes surprising—combinations. Words are seldom simple, even when we know their meanings and recognize their syntax as conventional and transparent. The careful examination of them individually and collectively is a crucial part of the process of reading poems, and learning exactly what kinds of questions to ask about the words that poems use and how poems use them is one of the most basic—and rewarding—skills a reader of poetry can develop.

Here is a group of poems illustrating varieties of word usages and word orders. The discussion of language continues later in this chapter with an explanation of figures of speech.

▼　▼　▼

GERARD MANLEY HOPKINS

Pied Beauty[9]

Glory be to God for dappled things—
　　For skies of couple-color as a brinded[1] cow;
　　　　For rose-moles all in stipple[2] upon trout that swim;
Fresh-firecoal chestnut-falls;[3] finches' wings;
　　Landscape plotted and pieced—fold, fallow, and plow;　　　　5
　　　　And all trades, their gear and tackle and trim.
All things counter, original, spare, strange;
　　Whatever is fickle, freckled (who knows how?)
　　　　With swift, slow; sweet, sour; adazzle, dim;
He fathers-forth whose beauty is past change:　　　　10
　　　　　　　　Praise him.　　　　　　　　　1877

ROBERT GRAVES

The Naked and the Nude

　　For me, the naked and the nude
　　(By lexicographers construed
　　As synonyms that should express
　　The same deficiency of dress
　　Or shelter) stand as wide apart　　　　5
　　As love from lies, or truth from art.

9. Particolored beauty: having patches or sections of more than one color.　1. Streaked or spotted.　2. Rose-colored dots or flecks.　3. Fallen chestnuts as red as burning coals.

Lovers without reproach will gaze
On bodies naked and ablaze;
The Hippocratic[4] eye will see
In nakedness, anatomy;
And naked shines the Goddess when
She mounts her lion among men.[5]

The nude are bold, the nude are sly
To hold each treasonable eye.
While draping by a showman's trick
Their dishabille in rhetoric,
They grin a mock-religious grin
Of scorn at those of naked skin.

The naked, therefore, who compete
Against the nude may know defeat;
Yet when they both together tread
The briary pastures of the dead,
By Gorgons[6] with long whips pursued,
How naked go the sometime nude!

1958

WILLIAM CARLOS WILLIAMS

The Red Wheelbarrow

so much depends
upon

a red wheel
barrow

glazed with rain
water

beside the white
chickens.

1923

CAROLYN KIZER

Bitch

Now, when he and I meet, after all these years,
I say to the bitch inside me, don't start growling.

---

4. Hippocrates (c. 460–375 B.C.) is traditionally considered the father of medicine.   5. In *The White Goddess*, Graves glosses the title figure as "Muse, the Mother of all living." Riding a lion symbolizes, according to Graves, the sexual dominance of the goddess.   6. In Greek mythology, female monsters who had snakes on their heads instead of hair and whose glance could turn mortals to stone.

He isn't a trespasser anymore,
Just an old acquaintance tipping his hat.
My voice says, "Nice to see you," 5
As the bitch starts to bark hysterically.
He isn't an enemy now,
Where are your manners, I say, as I say,
"How are the children? They must be growing up."
At a kind word from him, a look like the old days, 10
The bitch changes her tone: she begins to whimper.
She wants to snuggle up to him, to cringe.
Down, girl! Keep your distance
Or I'll give you a taste of the choke-chain.
"Fine, I'm just fine," I tell him. 15
She slobbers and grovels.
After all, I am her mistress. She is basically loyal.
It's just that she remembers how she came running
Each evening, when she heard his step;
How she lay at his feet and looked up adoringly 20
Though he was absorbed in his paper;
Or, bored with her devotion, ordered her to the kitchen
Until he was ready to play.
But the small careless kindnesses
When he'd had a good day, or a couple of drinks, 25
Come back to her now, seem more important
Than the casual cruelties, the ultimate dismissal.
"It's nice to know you are doing so well," I say.
He couldn't have taken you with him;
You were too demonstrative, too clumsy, 30
Not like the well-groomed pets of his new friends.
"Give my regards to your wife," I say. You gag
As I drag you off by the scruff,
Saying, "Goodbye! Goodbye! Nice to have seen you again."   1984

E. E. CUMMINGS

[in Just-][7]

in Just-
spring   when the world is mud-
luscious the little
lame balloonman

whistles   far   and wee 5

---

7. *Chansons innocentes* I.

and eddieandbill come
running from marbles and
piracies and it's
spring

10   when the world is puddle-wonderful

the queer
old balloonman whistles
far   and   wee
and bettyandisbel come dancing

15   from hop-scotch and jump-rope and
it's
spring
and
      the

20   goat-footed

balloonMan   whistles
far
and
wee[8]   1923

RICARDO PAU-LLOSA

Foreign Language

Every object is a room
you walk words into.
Take an apple, its windows peeling.
In your hands the apple's
5   door opens a crack
and the words barge through
like salesmen confident of a kill.
The gerund opens the mail,
the verb's hands rumble through
10   the refrigerator, an adverb
caresses the daughter's knee,
the noun, its feet on the sofa,
says everything is as it should be.
Teeth tear through the walls of the apple
15   like a plane crashing in the suburbs.
The mouth is full of a wet white word

8. Pan, whose Greek name means "everything," is traditionally represented with a syrinx (or the pipes of Pan). The upper half of his body is human, the lower half goat, and as the father of Silenus he is associated with the spring rites of Dionysus.

you can't pronounce, a pronoun
reading the newspaper in the living room.
When you bit, you never knew what hit you.   1992

SUSAN MUSGRAVE

Hidden Meaning

Imagine hailing a taxi
and the driver is a poet.
You could say, "Tell me a poem
and take me to Costa Rica."
As you drive away.   5

Imagine getting into a taxi
where the driver is a *real* poet.
You could quote Robert Penn Warren
without feeling ridiculous: "Driver,
do you truly, truly know what flesh is?"   10

Imagine getting into a taxi
and it's snowy Saskatchewan
and the poet has not made a dollar.
The snow goes on falling
and now you're both stuck in it; poetry   15
gets you nowhere faster than anything.

Imagine breaking into a taxi
and finding two poets frozen together.
You'd look at one another as if the world
had meaning for the first time, hidden   20
meaning, and wouldn't it be a kind
of terrible occasion.   1991

HEATHER McHUGH

Two St. Petersburgs

I. RUSSIA

The statue turned
upon a chain; beneath its broken knees
were thirty feet of air. Under its sway
of handwide eye stood, ludicrous,

a pedestal with only
feet on top. And under that

ranged real but little people, tiny
uprightnesses, all
abruptly free. Freely they milled,
collectively buzzed. They
feuded over food, they fell
in love anew, had words anew, had different
differences than heretofore. The differences were free

to spread; an air of half-lights made
for deep misgivings in the minds
of brand-new sunshade salesmen . . .

II. FLORIDA

The desk clerk's disposition is
professionally sunny. In the waterbed room I can ask
to be tied up, but nicely; you know
nooses that release.

Detachment has apartments and
attachment has departments. We can order
long and cool, or quick and hot. Or quick
and cool or long and hot. But can we

pull ourselves together? Keep the living daylights ever-
loving? Kill the cough?
For broken is a place
where something gave; a joint's

a place where something moved.
And eloquent is just
a mess of hinge and sign: a MO where the TEL
is not yet fallen off . . .   1993

EMILY DICKINSON

[I dwell in Possibility—]

I dwell in Possibility—
A fairer House than Prose—
More numerous of Windows—
Superior—for Doors—

Of Chambers as the Cedars—
Impregnable of Eye—
And for an Everlasting Roof
The Gambrels[9] of the Sky—

9. Roofs with double slopes.

Of Visitors—the fairest—
For Occupation—This—   10
The spreading wide my narrow Hands
ca. 1862   To gather Paradise—

JOHN MILTON

from Paradise Lost[1]

I

Of man's first disobedience, and the fruit[2]
Of that forbidden tree whose mortal taste
Brought death into the world, and all our woe,
With loss of Eden, till one greater Man
Restore us, and regain the blissful seat,   5
Sing, Heav'nly Muse,[3] that, on the secret top
Of Oreb, or of Sinai, didst inspire
That shepherd who first taught the chosen seed
In the beginning how the Heav'ns and Earth
Rose out of Chaos: or, if Sion hill   10
Delight thee more, and Siloa's brook that flowed
Fast[4] by the oracle of God, I thence
Invoke thy aid to my adventurous song,
That with no middle flight intends to soar
Above th' Aonian mount,[5] while it pursues   15
Things unattempted yet in prose or rhyme.
And chiefly thou, O Spirit,[6] that dost prefer
Before all temples th' upright heart and pure,
Instruct me, for thou know'st; thou from the first
Wast present, and, with mighty wings outspread,   20

1. The opening lines of Books I and II and a short passage from Book III. The first passage states the poem's subject, and the second describes Satan's beginning address to the council of fallen angels meeting to discuss strategy; in the third, God is looking down from Heaven at his new human creation and watching Satan approach the Earth.   2. The apple, but also the consequences. 3. Addressing one of the muses and asking for aid is a convention for the opening lines of an epic; Milton complicates the standard procedure here by describing sources and circumstances of Judeo-Christian revelation rather than specifically invoking one of the nine classical muses. Sinai is the spur of Mount Oreb, where Moses ("That shepherd," line 8, who was traditionally regarded as author of the first five books of the Bible) received the Law; Sion hill and Siloa (lines 10–11), near Jerusalem, correspond to the traditional mountain (Helicon) and springs of classical tradition. Later, in Book VII, Milton calls upon Urania, the muse of astronomy, but he does not mention by name the muse of epic poetry, Calliope.   4. Close.   5. Mt. Helicon, home of the classical muses. 6. The divine voice that inspired the Hebrew prophets. Genesis 1:2 says that "the Spirit of God moved upon the face of the waters" as part of the process of Creation; Milton follows tradition in making the inspirational and communicative function of God present in Creation itself. The passage echoes and merges many biblical references to Creation and divine revelation.

Dovelike sat'st brooding on the vast abyss,
And mad'st it pregnant: what in me is dark
Illumine; what is low, raise and support;
That, to the height of this great argument,[7]
25   I may assert Eternal Providence,
And justify the ways of God to men.
    Say first (for Heav'n hides nothing from thy view,
Nor the deep tract of Hell), say first what cause
Moved our grand parents, in that happy state,
30   Favored of Heav'n so highly, to fall off
From their Creator, and transgress his will
For one restraint, lords of the world besides?[8]
Who first seduced them to that foul revolt?
Th' infernal serpent; he it was, whose guile,
35   Stirred up with envy and revenge, deceived
The mother of mankind, what time[9] his pride
Had cast him out from Heav'n, with all his host
Of rebel angels, by whose aid, aspiring
To set himself in glory above his peers,
40   He trusted to have equaled the Most High,
If he opposed; and with ambitious aim
Against the throne and monarchy of God,
Raised impious war in Heav'n and battle proud,
With vain attempt. Him the Almighty Power
45   Hurled headlong flaming from th' ethereal sky,
With hideous ruin and combustion down
To bottomless perdition, there to dwell
In adamantine chains and penal fire,
Who durst defy th' Omnipotent to arms.[1]

     ✻   ✻   ✻

II

High on a throne of royal state, which far
Outshone the wealth of Ormus and of Ind,[2]
Or where the gorgeous East with richest hand
Show'rs on her kings barbaric pearl and gold,
5   Satan exalted sat, by merit raised
To that bad eminence; and, from despair
Thus high uplifted beyond hope, aspires
Beyond thus high, insatiate to pursue
Vain war with Heav'n, and by success[3] untaught,
10   His proud imaginations thus displayed:
    "Powers and Dominions, Deities of Heav'n,

---

7. Subject.   8. In all other respects. *For:* because of.   9. When.   1. After invoking the muse and giving a brief summary of the poem's subject, an epic regularly begins *in medias res* (in the midst of things).   2. India. *Ormus:* Hormuz, an island in the Persian Gulf, famous for pearls.   3. Outcome, either good or bad.

For since no deep within her gulf can hold
Immortal vigor, though oppressed and fall'n,
I give not Heav'n for lost. From this descent
Celestial virtues rising will appear   15
More glorious and more dread than from no fall,
And trust themselves to fear no second fate.
Me though just right and the fixed laws of Heav'n
Did first create your leader, next, free choice,
With what besides, in council or in fight,   20
Hath been achieved of merit, yet this loss,
Thus far at least recovered, hath much more
Established in a safe unenvied throne
Yielded with full consent. The happier state
In Heav'n, which follows dignity, might draw   25
Envy from each inferior; but who here
Will envy whom the highest place exposes
Foremost to stand against the Thunderer's aim
Your bulwark, and condemns to greatest share
Of endless pain? Where there is then no good   30
For which to strive, no strife can grow up there
From faction; for none sure will claim in hell
Precédence, none, whose portion is so small
Of present pain, that with ambitious mind
Will covet more. With this advantage then   35
To union, and firm faith, and firm accord,
More than can be in Heav'n, we now return
To claim our just inheritance of old,
Surer to prosper than prosperity
Could have assured us; and by what best way,   40
Whether of open war or covert guile,
We now debate; who can advise, may speak."

*   *   *

III

*   *   *

Now had th' Almighty Father from above,   56
From the pure empyrean where he sits
High throned above all height, bent down his eye,
His own works and their works at once to view:
About him all the sanctities of Heav'n[4]   60
Stood thick as stars, and from his sight received
Beatitude past utterance; on his right
The radiant image of his glory sat,
His only Son. On earth he first beheld
Our two first parents, yet the only two   65
Of mankind, in the happy garden placed,

4. The hierarchies of angels.

Reaping immortal fruits of joy and love,
Uninterrupted joy, unrivaled love,
In blissful solitude. He then surveyed
70   Hell and the gulf between, and Satan there
Coasting the wall of Heav'n on this side Night
In the dun air sublime,[5] and ready now
To stoop[6] with wearied wings and willing feet
On the bare outside of this world, that seemed
75   Firm land embosomed without firmament,
Uncertain which, in ocean or in air.   1667

Metaphor and Simile

The language of poetry is almost always visual and pictorial. Rather than
depending primarily on abstract ideas and elaborate reasoning, poems depend
mainly upon concrete and specific words that create images in our minds.
Poems thus help us to see things fresh and new, or to feel them suggestively
through our other physical senses, such as hearing or touch. But, most often,
poetry uses the sense of sight in that it helps us form, in our minds, visual
impressions, images that communicate more directly than concepts. We "see"
yellow leaves on a branch, a father and son waltzing precariously, or two lovers
sitting together on the bank of a stream, so that our response begins from a
vivid impression of exactly what is happening. Some people think that those
media and arts that challenge the imagination of a hearer or reader—radio
drama, for example, or poetry—allow us to respond more fully than those
(such as television or theater) that actually show things more fully to our physi-
cal senses. Certainly they leave more to our imagination, to our mind's eye.

But being visual does not just mean describing, telling us facts, indicating
shapes, colors, and specific details and giving us precise discriminations
through exacting verbs, nouns, adverbs, and adjectives. Often the vividness of
the picture in our minds depends upon comparisons. What we are trying to
imagine is pictured in terms of something else familiar to us, and we are asked
to think of one thing as if it were something else. Many such comparisons, or
figures of speech, in which something is pictured or figured forth in terms of
something already familiar to us, are taken for granted in daily life. Things we
can't see or that aren't familiar to us are imaged as things we already know; for
example, God is said to be like a father, Italy is said to be shaped like a boot,

5. Aloft in the twilight atmosphere.   6. Swoop down, like a bird of prey.

life is compared to a forest, a journey, or a sea. Poems use **figurative language** much of the time. A poem may insist that death is like a sunset or sex like an earthquake or that the way to imagine how it feels to be spiritually secure is to think of the way a shepherd takes care of his sheep. The pictorialness of our imagination may *clarify* things for us—scenes, states of mind, ideas—but at the same time it stimulates us to think of how those pictures make us *feel*. Pictures, even when they are mental pictures or imagined visions, may be both denotative and connotative, just as individual words are: they may clarify and make precise, and they may channel our feelings.

In the poem that follows, the poet helps us to visualize the old age and approaching death of the speaker by making comparisons with familiar things—the coming of winter, the approach of sunset, and the dying embers of a fire.

WILLIAM SHAKESPEARE

[That time of year thou mayst in me behold]

That time of year thou mayst in me behold
When yellow leaves, or none, or few, do hang
Upon those boughs which shake against the cold,
Bare ruined choirs, where late the sweet birds sang.
In me thou see'st the twilight of such day   5
As after sunset fadeth in the west;
Which by and by[1] black night doth take away,
Death's second self,[2] that seals up all in rest.
In me thou see'st the glowing of such fire,
That on the ashes of his youth doth lie,   10
As the deathbed whereon it must expire,
Consumed with that which it was nourished by.
This thou perceiv'st, which makes thy love more strong,
To love that well which thou must leave ere long.   1609

The first four lines of "That time of year" evoke images of the late autumn; but notice that the poet does not have the speaker say directly that his physical condition and age make him resemble autumn. He draws the comparison without stating that it is a comparison: you can see, he says, my own state in the coming of winter, when the leaves are almost all off the trees. The speaker por-

1. Shortly.   2. Sleep.

trays himself *indirectly* by talking about the passing of the year. The poem uses **metaphor**; that is, one thing is pictured *as if* it were something else. "That time of year" goes on to another metaphor in lines 5–8 and still another in lines 9–12, and each of the metaphors contributes to our understanding of the speaker's sense of his old age and approaching death. More important, how-ever, is the way the metaphors give us feelings, an emotional sense of the speak-er's age and of his own attitude toward aging. Through the metaphors we come to understand, appreciate, and to some extent share the increasing sense of anxiety and urgency that the poem expresses. Our emotional sense of the poem is largely influenced by the way each metaphor is developed and by the way each metaphor leads, with its own kind of internal logic, to another.

The images of late autumn in the first four lines all suggest loneliness, loss, and nostalgia for earlier times. As in the rest of the poem, our eyes are imag-ined to be the main vehicle for noticing the speaker's age and condition; the phrase "thou mayst in me behold" (line 1) introduces what we are asked to see, and in both lines 5 and 9 we are similarly told "In me thou see'st. . . ." The pic-ture of the trees shedding their leaves suggests that autumn is nearly over, and we can imagine trees either with yellow leaves, or without leaves, or with just a trace of foliage remaining—the latter perhaps most feelingly suggesting the bleakness and loneliness that characterize the change of seasons, the ending of the life cycle. But other senses are invoked too. The boughs shaking against the cold represent an appeal to our tactile sense, and the next line appeals to our sense of hearing, although only as a reminder that the birds no longer sing. (Notice how exact the visual representation is of the bare, or nearly bare, limbs, even as the cold and the lack of birds are noted; birds lined up like a choir on risers would have made a striking visual image on the barren limbs one above the other, but now there is only the *reminder* of what used to be. The present is quiet, bleak, trembly, and lonely.)

The next four lines are slightly different in tone, and the color changes. From a black-and-white landscape with a few yellow leaves, we come upon a rich and almost warm reminder of a faded sunset. But a somber note does enter the poem in these lines through another figure of speech, **personifica-tion**, which involves treating an abstraction, such as death or justice or beauty, as if it were a person. The poem is talking about the coming of night and of sleep, and Sleep is personified and identified as the "second self" of Death (that is, as a kind of "double" for death). The main emphasis is on how night and sleep close in on our sense of twilight, and only secondarily does a reminder of death enter the poem. But it does enter.

The third metaphor—that of the dying embers of a fire—begins in line 9 and continues to color and warm the bleak cold that the poem began with, but it also sharpens the reminder of death. The three main metaphors in the poem work in a way to make our sense of old age and approaching death more familiar, but also more immediate: moving from barren trees, to fading twilight, to dying embers suggests a sensuous increase of color and warmth, but also an increasing urgency. The first metaphor involves a whole season, or at least a segment of one, a matter of days or possibly weeks; the second involves the passing of a single day, reducing the time scale to a matter of minutes, and the third draws our attention to that split second when a glowing ember fades into a gray ash. The final part of the fire metaphor introduces the most explicit sense of death so far, as the metaphor of embers shifts into a direct reminder of death. Embers which had been a metaphor of the speaker's aging body now themselves become, metaphorically, a deathbed; the vitality that nourishes youth is used up just as a log in a fire is. The urgency of the reminder of coming death has now peaked. It is friendlier but now seems immediate and inevitable, a natural part of the life process, and the final two lines then make an explicit plea to make good and intense use of the remaining moments of human relationship.

"That time of year" represents an unusually intricate use of images to organize a poem and focus its emotional impact. Not all poems are so skillfully made, and not all depend on such a full and varied use of metaphor. But most poems use metaphors for at least part of their effect, and often a poem is based on a single metaphor that is fully developed as the major way of making the poem's statement and impact, as in the following poem about the role of a mother and wife.

LINDA PASTAN

Marks

My husband gives me an A
for last night's supper,
an incomplete for my ironing,
a B plus in bed.
My son says I am average,   5
an average mother, but if
I put my mind to it
I could improve.
My daughter believes
in Pass / Fail and tells me   10
I pass. Wait 'til they learn
I'm dropping out.

1978

The speaker in "Marks" is obviously not thrilled with the idea of continually being judged, and the metaphor of marks (or grades) as a way of talking about her performance of roles in the family suggests her irritation. The list of the roles implies the many things expected of her, and the three different systems of marking (letter grades, categories to be checked off on a chart, and pass / fail) detail the difficulties of multiple standards. The poem retains the language of schooldays all the way to the end ("learn," line 11; "dropping out," line 12), and the major effect of the poem depends on the irony of the speaker's surrendering to the metaphor the family has thrust upon her; if she is to be judged as if she were a student, she retains the right to leave the system. Ironically, she joins the system (adopts the metaphor for herself) in order to defeat it.

The following poem depends from the beginning—even from its title—on a single metaphor and the values associated with it.

DAVID WAGONER

My Father's Garden

On his way to the open hearth where white-hot steel
Boiled against furnace walls in wait for his lance
To pierce the fireclay and set loose demons
And dragons in molten tons, blazing
Down to the huge satanic caldrons,
Each day he would pass the scrapyard, his kind of garden.

In rusty rockeries of stoves and brake drums,
In grottoes of sewing machines and refrigerators,
He would pick flowers for us: small gears and cogwheels
With teeth like petals, with holes for anthers,
Long stalks of lead to be poured into toy soldiers,
Ball bearings as big as grapes to knock them down.

He was called a melter. He tried to keep his brain
From melting in those tyger-mouthed mills
Where the same steel reappeared over and over
To be reborn in the fire as something better
Or worse: cannons or cars, needles or girders,
Flagpoles, swords, or plowshares.

But it melted. His classical learning ran
Down and away from him, not burning bright.
His fingers culled a few cold scraps of Latin
And Greek, *magna sine laude*,[3] for crosswords

---

3. Without great distinction; a reversal of the usual *magna cum laude*.

And brought home lumps of tin and sewer grills
As if they were his ripe prize vegetables.   1987

    The poem is a tribute to the speaker's father and the things he understands
and values in his ordinary, workingman's life. The father is a "melter" (line 13)
in the steel mills (lines 14–15), and what he values are the things made from
what he helps to produce. His avocation has developed from his vocation: he
collects metal objects from the scrapyard and brings them home just as some
other men would pick flowers for their families. The scrapyard is, says the
speaker, "his kind of garden" (line 6). The life led by the father has been a
hard one, but he shows love for his children in the only way he knows how—
by bringing home things that mean something to him and that can be made
into toys his children will come to value. Describing these scraps as the prod-
ucts of his garden—"As if they were his ripe prize vegetables" (line 24)—has
the effect of making them seem home-grown, carefully tended, nurtured by
the father into a useful beauty. Instead of crude and ugly pieces of scrap, they
become—through the metaphor of the poem—examples of value and beauty
corresponding to the warm feelings the speaker has for a father who did what
he could with what he knew and what he had.

    Poets often are self-conscious and explicit about the ways they use language
metaphorically, and sometimes (as in the following poem) they celebrate the
richness of language that makes their art possible:

ROBERT FRANCIS

Hogwash

The tongue that mothered such a metaphor
Only the purest purist could despair of.

Nobody ever called swill sweet but isn't
Hogwash a daisy in a field of daisies?

What beside sports and flowers could you find   5
To praise better than the American language?

Bruised by American foreign policy
What shall I soothe me, what defend me with

But a handful of clean unmistakable words—
Daisies, daisies, in a field of daisies?   1965   10

The poet here claims little for his own invention and not much for the art of poetry, insisting that the American language itself is responsible for miraculous conceptions. The poet plays cheerfully here with what words offer—the pun on "purest" and "purist" (line 2), for example, and the taunting (but misleading) similarity of the beginnings of "swill" and "sweet" (line 3)—but insists that poems and poets only articulate things already realized in common speech, where metaphors are "mothered" (line 1). "Hogwash," although never explicitly glossed or discussed in the poem, is the primary example: What *does* "hogwash" mean? How do hogs wash themselves and in what? to what purpose and effect? How did the term get invented as a metaphor, and what are its visual implications? And what is it doing as an example of beauty in a poem about "clean unmistakable words" (line 9)? But then the poem plays even more fully with "daisy" (lines 4 and 10) as metaphor and idiomatic expression. A "daisy" is a great success, a breakthrough, a beaut, a perfect example, and the word "hogwash" is such a daisy, an instance of such a success: a "daisy in a field of daisies," a success of successes, a wonder in a language full of wonders.

Not everything American, according to this poem, is as praiseworthy as its language, and the word "hogwash" ultimately has its context established in the poem's fourth stanza when the speaker finally tells us why the word is so soothing and so pertinent. Poets, the poem says, need words and metaphors that are not always images of beauty because the world is full of things that are not altogether beautiful, and metaphors of ugliness can be "daisies" too.

Not all poets feel as positive as Robert Francis claims to be here about the raw materials they have to work with in language. Ultimately, of course, the modesty of the poet's claims about his own inventiveness becomes as comic as the metaphor of "hogwash" itself and the poem's characterization of foreign policy, for it is the poem that makes this particular use of the metaphor, no matter where or when it was invented: the wit belongs to the poem, not the language. Poets make use of whatever idioms, expressions, inherited metaphors, and traditions of language come their way, and they turn them to their own uses, sometimes quite surprisingly.

The difficulty of conveying what some experiences are like and how we feel about them sometimes leads poets to startling comparisons and figures of speech that may at first seem far-fetched but that, in one way or another, do in fact suggest the quality of the experience or the feelings associated with it. Sometimes they use a series of metaphors, as if no single act of visualization will serve but several together may suggest the full complexity of the experience or cumulatively define the feeling precisely. Metaphors open up virtually endless possibilities of comparison, giving words a chance to be more than

words, offering our mind's eye a challenge to keep up with the fertile and artic-
ulate imagination of writers who make it their business to see things that ordi-
nary people miss, noticing the most surprising likenesses and conveying
feelings more powerfully than politicians usually do.

Sometimes, in poetry as in prose, comparisons are made explicitly, as in the
following poem.

ROBERT BURNS

A Red, Red Rose

O, my luve's like a red, red rose
That's newly sprung in June.
O, my luve is like the melodie
That's sweetly played in tune.

As fair art thou, my bonnie lass,   5
So deep in luve am I;
And I will luve thee still, my dear,
Till a' the seas gang[4] dry.

Till a' the seas gang dry, my dear,
And the rocks melt wi' the sun;   10
And I will luve thee still, my dear,
While the sands o' life shall run.

And fare thee weel, my only luve,
And fare thee weel a while!
And I will come again, my luve,   15
Though it were ten thousand mile.   1796

The first four lines make two explicit comparisons: the speaker says that his
love is "like a rose" and "like a melodie." Such *explicit* comparison is called a
simile, and usually (as here) the comparison involves the words "like" or "as."
Similes work much as do metaphors, except that they usually are used more
passingly, more incidentally; they make a quick comparison and usually do not
elaborate, whereas metaphors often extend over a long section of a poem (in
which case they are called **extended metaphors**) or even over the whole poem,
as in "Marks" (in which case they are called **controlling metaphors**).

The two similes in "A Red, Red Rose" assume that we already have a favor-
able opinion of roses and of melodies. Here the poet does not develop the com-

4. Go.

parison or even remind us of attractive details about roses or tunes. He pays the quick compliment and moves on. Similes sometimes develop more elaborate comparisons than this and occasionally even control long sections of a poem (in which case they are called **analogies**), but usually a simile is briefer and relies more fully on something we already know. The speaker in "My Papa's Waltz" says that he hung on "like death"; he doesn't have to explain or elaborate the comparison: we know the anxiety he refers to.

Like metaphors, similes may imply both meaning and feeling; they may both explain something and invoke feelings about it. All figurative language involves an attempt to clarify something *and* to help readers feel a certain way about it. Saying that one's love is like a rose implies a delicate and fragile beauty and invites our senses into play so that we can share sensuously a response to fragrant appeal and soft touch, just as the shivering boughs and dying embers in "That time of year" explain separation and loss at the same time that they allow us to share the cold sense of loneliness and the warmth of old friendship.

Once you are alerted to look for them you will find figures of speech in poem after poem; they are among the most common devices through which poets share their vision with us.

The following poem uses a variety of metaphors to describe sexual experiences.

ADRIENNE RICH

Two Songs

1

Sex, as they harshly call it,
I fell into this morning
at ten o'clock, a drizzling hour
of traffic and wet newspapers.
I thought of him who yesterday
clearly didn't
turn me to a hot field
ready for plowing,
and longing for that young man
pierced me to the roots
bathing every vein, etc.[5]
All day he appears to me

5. See the opening lines of the Prologue to Chaucer's *Canterbury Tales.*

touchingly desirable,
a prize one could wreck one's peace for.
I'd call it love if love   15
didn't take so many years
but lust too is a jewel
a sweet flower and what
pure happiness to know
all our high-toned questions   20
breed in a lively animal.

2

That "old last act"!
And yet sometimes
all seems post coitum triste[6]
and I a mere bystander.   25
Somebody else is going off,
getting shot to the moon.
Or, a moon-race!
Split seconds after
my opposite number lands   30
I make it—
we lie fainting together
at a crater-edge
heavy as mercury in our moonsuits
till he speaks   35
in a different language
yet one I've picked up
through cultural exchanges . . .
we murmur the first moonwords:
Spasibo.[7] *Thanks. O.K.*   1964   40

The first "song" begins straightforwardly as narration ("Sex . . . I fell into this morning / at ten o'clock"), but the vividness of sex and desire is communicated mostly by figure. The narrator describes her body as "a hot field / ready for plowing" (lines 7–8)—quite unlike her resistant body yesterday—and her longing is also described by metaphor, in this case an elaborate one borrowed from another poem. After so sensual and urgent a beginning, the song turns more thoughtful and philosophical, but even the intellectual sorting between love and lust comes to depend on figures: lust is a "jewel" (line 17) and a "flower" (line 18). After the opening pace and excitement those later metaphors seem calm and tame, moving the poem from the lust of its beginning to

---

6. Sadness after sexual union.   7. Russian for "thanks."

a contemplative reflection on the value and beauty of momentary physical pleasures.

The second song depends on two closely related metaphors, and here the metaphors for sex are highly self-conscious and a little comic. The song begins on a plaintive note, considering the classic melancholic feeling after sex; the speaker pictures herself as isolated, left out, "a bystander" (line 25), while someone else is having sexual pleasure. This pleasure of others is described through two colloquial expressions (both metaphors) for sexual climax: "going off" (line 26) and "getting shot to the moon" (line 27). Suddenly the narrator pretends to take sex as space travel seriously and creates a metaphor of her own: sexual partners running a "moon-race" (line 28). The rest of the poem enacts the metaphor in the context of the space race between the United States and Russia in the early 1960s. The race, not exactly even but close enough, is described in detail, and the speaker tells her story in a self-conscious comic way. These are international relations, foreign affairs, and the lovers appropriately say their thank-yous separately in Russian and English, then communicate an international "O.K."

▼ ▼ ▼

RANDALL JARRELL

The Death of the Ball Turret Gunner[8]

From my mother's sleep I fell into the State,
And I hunched in its belly till my wet fur froze.
Six miles from earth, loosed from its dream of life,
I woke to black flak and the nightmare fighters.
When I died they washed me out of the turret with a hose.   1945

5

LINDA PASTAN

Erosion

We are slowly
undermined. Grain

8. "A ball turret was a plexiglass sphere set into the belly of a B-17 or B-24 and inhabited by two .50 caliber machine-guns and one man, a short, small man. When this gunner tracked with his machine-guns a fighter attacking his bomber from below, he revolved with the turret; hunched upside-down in his little sphere, he looked like the foetus in the womb. The fighters which attacked him were armed with cannon firing explosive shells. The hose was a steam hose." (Jarrell's note)

by grain . . .
inch by inch . . .
slippage.   5
It happens as we watch.
The waves move their long row
of scythes over the beach.

It happens as we sleep,
the way the clock's hands   10
move continuously
just out of sight,
but more like an hourglass
than a clock,
for here sand   15
is running out.

We wake to water.
Implacably lovely
is this view
though it will swallow   20
us whole, soon
there will be
nothing left
but view.

We have tried a seawall.   25
We have tried prayer.
We have planted grasses
on the bank, small tentacles
hooks of green that catch
on nothing. For the wind   30
does its work, the water
does its sure work.

One day the sea will simply
take us. The children
press their faces to the glass   35
as if the windows were portholes,
and the house fills
with animals: two dogs,
a bird, cats—we are becoming
an ark already.   40

The gulls will follow
our wake.
We are made of water anyway,
I can feel it in the yielding
of your flesh, though sometimes   45
I think that you are sand,
moving slowly, slowly
from under me.   1988

HART CRANE

Forgetfulness

Forgetfulness is like a song
That, freed from beat and measure, wanders.
Forgetfulness is like a bird whose wings are reconciled,
Outspread and motionless, —
5 A bird that coasts the wind unwearyingly.

Forgetfulness is rain at night,
Or an old house in a forest, — or a child.
Forgetfulness is white, — white as a blasted tree,
And it may stun the sybil into prophecy,
10 Or bury the Gods.

I can remember much forgetfulness.   p. 1918

CAROLYN FORCHÉ

Taking Off My Clothes

I take off my shirt, I show you.
I shaved the hair out under my arms.
I roll up my pants, I scraped off the hair
on my legs with a knife, getting white.

5 My hair is the color of chopped maples
My eyes dark as beans cooked in the south.
(Coal fields in the moon on torn-up hills)

Skin polished as a Ming bowl
showing its blood cracks, its age, I have hundreds
10 of names for the snow, for this, all of them quiet.

In the night I come to you and it seems a shame.
to waste my deepest shudders on a wall of a man.

You recognize strangers,
think you lived through destruction.
15 You can't explain this night, my face, your memory.

You want to know what I know?
Your own hands are lying.   1976

THEODORE ROETHKE

Elegy for Jane

(MY STUDENT, THROWN BY A HORSE)

I remember the neckcurls, limp and damp as tendrils;
And her quick look, a sidelong pickerel smile;
And how, once startled into talk, the light syllables leaped for her,
And she balanced in the delight of her thought,
A wren, happy, tail into the wind,   5
Her song trembling the twigs and small branches.
The shade sang with her;
The leaves, their whispers turned to kissing;
And the mould sang in the bleached valleys under the rose.

Oh, when she was sad, she cast herself down into such a pure depth,   10
Even a father could not find her:
Scraping her cheek against straw;
Stirring the clearest water.

My sparrow, you are not here,
Waiting like a fern, making a spiney shadow.   15
The sides of wet stones cannot console me,
Nor the moss, wound with the last light.

If only I could nudge you from this sleep,
My maimed darling, my skittery pigeon.
Over this damp grave I speak the words of my love: 20
I, with no rights in this matter,
Neither father nor lover.   1953

AGHA SHAHID ALI

The Dacca Gauzes

> . . . for a whole year he sought
> to accumulate the most exquisite
> Dacca gauzes.
> —OSCAR WILDE / *The Picture*
> *of Dorian Gray*

Those transparent Dacca gauzes
known as woven air, running
water, evening dew:

a dead art now, dead over
a hundred years. "No one   5
now knows," my grandmother says,

"what it was to wear
or touch that cloth." She wore
it once, an heirloom sari from

10 her mother's dowry, proved
genuine when it was pulled, all
six yards, through a ring.

Years later when it tore,
many handkerchiefs embroidered
15 with gold-thread paisleys

were distributed among
the nieces and daughters-in-law.
Those too now lost.

In history we learned: the hands
20 of weavers were amputated,
the looms of Bengal silenced,

and the cotton shipped raw
by the British to England.
History of little use to her,

25 my grandmother just says
how the muslins of today
seem so coarse and that only

in autumn, should one wake up
at dawn to pray, can one
30 feel that same texture again.

One morning, she says, the air
was dew-starched: she pulled
it absently through her ring.   1987

JOHN DONNE

[Batter my heart, three-personed God . . .][9]

Batter my heart, three-personed God; for You
As yet but knock, breathe, shine, and seek to mend;
That I may rise and stand, o'erthrow me, and bend
Your force, to break, blow, burn, and make me new.
5 I, like an usurped town, to another due,
Labor to admit You, but Oh, to no end!

9. *Holy Sonnets,* 14.

Reason, Your viceroy[1] in me, me should defend,
But is captived, and proves weak or untrue.
Yet dearly I love You, and would be loved fain,[2]
But am betrothed unto Your enemy: 10
Divorce me, untie or break that knot again,
Take me to You, imprison me, for I,
Except You enthrall me, never shall be free,
Nor ever chaste, except You ravish me.   1633

ANONYMOUS[3]

The Twenty-third Psalm

The Lord is my shepherd; I shall not want.
He maketh me to lie down in green pastures: he leadeth me beside
    the still waters.
He restoreth my soul: he leadeth me in the paths of righteousness
    for his name's sake.
Yea, though I walk through the valley of the shadow of death,
    I will fear no evil: for thou art with me;
    thy rod and thy staff they comfort me.
Thou preparest a table before me in the presence of mine enemies:
    thou anointest my head with oil; my cup runneth over.   5
Surely goodness and mercy shall follow me all the days of my life:
    and I will dwell in the house of the Lord for ever.

Symbol

The word "symbol" is often used sloppily and sometimes pretentiously, but properly used the term suggests one of the most basic things about poems— their ability to get beyond what words signify and make larger claims about meanings in the verbal world. All words go beyond themselves. They are not simply a collection of sounds: they signify something beyond their sounds, often things or actions or ideas. Words describe not only a verbal universe but a world in which actions occur, acts have implications, and events mean. Sometimes words not only signify something beyond themselves—a rock or a tree or a cloud—but symbolize something as well—solidity or life or dreams.

---

1. One who rules as the representative of a higher power.   2. Gladly.   3. Traditionally attributed to King David. The English translation printed here is from the King James Version.

Words can—when their implications are agreed on by tradition, convention, or habit—stand for things beyond their most immediate meanings or significations and become symbols, and even simple words that have accumulated no special power from previous use may be given special significance in special circumstances—either in poetry or in life itself.

A **symbol** is, put simply, something that stands for something else. The everyday world is full of common examples; a flag, a logo, a trademark, or a skull and crossbones all suggest things beyond themselves, and everyone is likely to understand what their display is meant to indicate, whether or not the viewer shares a commitment to what the object represents. In common usage a prison is a symbol of confinement, constriction, and loss of freedom, and in specialized traditional usage a cross may symbolize oppression, cruelty, suffering, death, resurrection, triumph, or the intersection of two separate things, traditions, or ideas (as in crossroads and crosscurrents, for example). The specific symbolic significance is controlled by the context; a reader may often decide what it is by looking at contiguous details in the poem and by examining the poem's attitude toward a particular tradition or body of beliefs. A star means one kind of thing to a Jewish poet and something else to a Christian poet, still something else to a sailor or actor. In a very literal sense, words themselves are all symbols (they stand for an object, action, or quality, not just for letters or sounds), but symbols in poetry are said to be those words and groups of words that have a range of reference beyond their literal signification or denotation.

Poems sometimes create a symbol out of a thing, action, or event that has no previously agreed upon symbolic significance. In the following poem, for example, a random gesture is given symbolic significance.

SHARON OLDS

Leningrad Cemetery, Winter of 1941[1]

That winter, the dead could not be buried.
The ground was frozen, the gravediggers weak from hunger,
the coffin wood used for fuel. So they were covered with something
and taken on a child's sled to the cemetery
in the sub-zero air. They lay on the soil,
some of them wrapped in dark cloth
bound with rope like the tree's ball of roots
when it waits to be planted; others wound in sheets,
their pale, gauze, tapered shapes

1. The 900-day siege of Leningrad during World War II began in September 1941.

stiff as cocoons that will split down the center 10
when the new life inside is prepared;
but most lay like corpses, their coverings
coming undone, naked calves
hard as corded wood spilling
from under a cloak, a hand reaching out 15
with no sign of peace, wanting to come back
even to the bread made of glue and sawdust,
even to the icy winter, and the siege. p. 1979

All of the corpses—frozen, neglected, beginning to be in disarray—vividly stamp upon our minds a sense of the horrors of war, and the detailed picture of the random, uncounted clutter of bodies is likely to stick in our minds long after we have finished reading the poem. Several of the details are striking, and the poem's language heightens our sense of them. The corpses wound in sheets, for example, are described in "their pale, gauze, tapered shapes," and they are compared to cocoons that one day will split and emit new life; and the limbs that dangle loose when the coverings come undone are said to be "hard as corded wood spilling." But clearly the most memorable sight is the hand dangling from one corpse that is coming unwrapped, for the poet invests that hand with special significance, giving its gesture *meaning.* The hand is described as "reaching out . . . wanting to come back": it is as if the dead can still gesture even if they cannot speak, and the gesture seems to signify the desire of the dead to come back at any price. They would be glad to be alive, even under the grim conditions that attend the living in Leningrad during this grim war. Suddenly the grimness that we—living—have been witnessing pales by comparison with what the dead have lost simply by being dead. The hand has been made to *symbolize* the desire of the dead to return, to be alive, to be still among us, anywhere. The hand reaches out in the poem as a gesture that means; the poet has made it a symbol of desire.

The whole array of dead bodies in the poem might be said to be symbolic as well. As a group, they stand for the human waste that the war has produced, and their dramatic visual presence on the scene provides the poem with a dramatic visualization of how war and its requirements have no time for decency, not even the decency of burial. The bodies are a symbol in the sense that they stand for what the poem as a whole asserts.

The poem that follows also arises out of a historical moment, but this time the event is a personal one that the poet gives a significance by the interpretation he puts upon it.

JAMES DICKEY

The Leap

The only thing I have of Jane MacNaughton
Is one instant of a dancing-class dance.
She was the fastest runner in the seventh grade,
My scrapbook says, even when boys were beginning
To be as big as the girls,
But I do not have her running in my mind,
Though Frances Lane is there, Agnes Fraser,
Fat Betty Lou Black in the boys-against-girls
Relays we ran at recess: she must have run

Like the other girls, with her skirts tucked up
So they would be like bloomers,
But I cannot tell; that part of her is gone.
What I do have is when she came,
With the hem of her skirt where it should be
For a young lady, into the annual dance
Of the dancing class we all hated, and with a light
Grave leap, jumped up and touched the end
Of one of the paper-ring decorations

To see if she could reach it. She could,
And reached me now as well, hanging in my mind
From a brown chain of brittle paper, thin
And muscular, wide-mouthed, eager to prove
Whatever it proves when you leap
In a new dress, a new womanhood, among the boys
Whom you easily left in the dust
Of the passionless playground. If I said I saw
In the paper where Jane MacNaughton Hill,

Mother of four, leapt to her death from a window
Of a downtown hotel, and that her body crushed-in
The top of a parked taxi, and that I held
Without trembling a picture of her lying cradled
In that papery steel as though lying in the grass,
One shoe idly off, arms folded across her breast,
I would not believe myself. I would say
The convenient thing, that it was a bad dream
Of maturity, to see that eternal process

Most obsessively wrong with the world
Come out of her light, earth-spurning feet
Grown heavy: would say that in the dusty heels
Of the playground some boy who did not depend
On speed of foot, caught and betrayed her.

Jane, stay where you are in my first mind:
It was odd in that school, at that dance.
I and the other slow-footed yokels sat in corners
Cutting rings out of drawing paper   45

Before you leapt in your new dress
And touched the end of something I began,
Above the couples struggling on the floor,
New men and women clutching at each other
And prancing foolishly as bears: hold on   50
To that ring I made for you, Jane—
My feet are nailed to the ground
By dust I swallowed thirty years ago—
While I examine my hands.   1967

Memory is crucial to "The Leap." The fact that Jane MacNaughton's grace-
ful leap in dancing class has stuck in the speaker's mind for all these years
means that this leap was important to him, meant something to him, stood for
something in his mind. For the speaker, the leap is an "instant" and the "only
thing" he has of Jane. Its grace and ease are what he remembers, and he strug-
gles at several points to articulate its meaning (lines 15–26, 44–50), but even
without articulation or explanation it is there in his head as a visual memory, a
symbol for him of something beyond himself, something he cannot do, some-
thing he wanted to be. What that leap had stood for, or symbolized, was bold-
ness, confidence, accomplishment, maturity, the ability to go beyond her
fellow students in dancing class—the transcending of childhood by someone
beginning to be a woman. Her feet now seem "earth-spurning" (line 38) in that
original leap, and they separate her from everyone else. Jane MacNaughton
was beyond the speaker's abilities and any attempt he could make to articulate
his hopes, but not beyond his dreams. And even before articulation, she sym-
bolized that dream.

The leap to her death seems cruelly ironic in the context of her earlier
leap. In memory she is suspended in air, as if there were no gravity, no coming
back to earth, as if life could exist as dream. And so the photograph, re-created
in precise detail, is a cruel dashing of the speaker's dream—a detailed record
of the ending of a leap, a denial of the suspension in which his memory had
held her. His dream is grounded; her mortality is insistent. But what the
speaker wants to hang on to (line 42) is still that symbolic moment which,
although now confronted in more mature implications, will never be alto-
gether replaced or surrendered.

The leap is ultimately symbolic in the *poem*, too, not just in the speaker's mind. In the poem (and for us as readers) the symbolism of the leap is double: the first leap is aspiration, and the second is frustration of high hopes; the two are complementary, one unable to be imagined without the other. The poem is horrifying in some ways, a dramatic reminder that human beings don't ultimately transcend their mortality, their limits, no matter how heroic or unencumbered by gravity they may seem to an observer. But it is not altogether sad and despairing either, partly because it notices and affirms the validity of the original leap and partly because another symbol is created and elaborated in the poem. That symbol is the paper chain.

The chain connects Jane to the speaker both literally and figuratively. It is, in part, *his* paper chain which she had leaped to touch in dancing class (lines 18–19), and he thinks of her first leap as "touch[ing] the end of something I began" (line 47). He and the other "slow-footed," earthbound "yokels" (line 44) were the makers of the chain, and thus they are connected to her original leap, just as a photograph glimpsed in the paper connects the speaker to her second leap. The paper in the chain is "brittle" (line 21), and its creators seem dull artisans compared to the artistic performer that Jane was. They are heavy and left in the dust (lines 25, 52–53), and she is "light" (line 16) and able to transcend them but even in transcendence touching their lives and what they are able to do. And so the paper chain becomes the poem's symbol of linkage, connecting lower accomplishment to higher possibility, the artisan to the artist, material substance to the act of imagination. And the speaker at the end examines the hands that made the chain because those hands certify his connection to her and the imaginative leap she had made for him. The chain thus symbolizes not only the lower capabilities of those who cannot leap like the budding Jane could, but (later) the connection with her leap as both transcendence and mortality. Like the leap itself, the chain has been elevated to special meaning, given symbolic significance, by the poet's treatment of it. A leap and a chain have no necessary significance in themselves to most of us—at least no significance that we have all agreed upon together—but they may be given significance in specific circumstances or a specific text.

But some objects and acts do have a significance built in because of past usage. Over the years some things have acquired an agreed-upon significance, an accepted value in our minds. They already stand for something before the poet cites them; they are **traditional symbols.** Their uses in poetry have to do with the fact that poets can count on a recognition of their traditional suggestions and meanings outside the poem, and the poem does not have to propose or argue a particular symbolic value. Birds, for example, traditionally symbolize flight, freedom from confinement, detachment from earthbound limits, the ability to soar beyond rationality and transcend mortal limits. Traditionally, birds have also been linked with imagination, especially poetic imagination, and poets often identify with them as pure and ideal singers of songs, as in Keats's "Ode to a Nightingale." One of the most traditional symbols is the rose. It may be a simple and fairly plentiful flower in its season, but it has been allowed to stand for particular qualities for so long that to name it raises predictable expectations. Its beauty, delicacy, fragility, shortness of life, and depth of color have made it a symbol of the transitoriness of beauty, and countless poets have counted on its accepted symbolism—sometimes to compliment a friend (as Burns does in "A Red, Red Rose") or sometimes to make a point about the nature of symbolism. The following poem draws on, in a quite traditional way, the traditional meanings.

JOHN CLARE

Love's Emblem

Go, rose, my Chloe's[2] bosom grace:
    How happy should I prove,
Could I supply that envied place
    With never-fading love.

Accept, dear maid, now summer glows,   5
    This pure, unsullied gem,
Love's emblem in a full-blown rose,
    Just broken from the stem.

Accept it as a favorite flower
    For thy soft breast to wear;   10
'Twill blossom there its transient hour,
    A favorite of the fair.

Upon thy cheek its blossom glows,
    As from a mirror clear,
Making thyself a living rose,   15
    In blossom all the year.

It is a sweet and favorite flower
    To grace a maiden's brow,
Emblem of love without its power—
    A sweeter rose art thou.   20

---

2. A standard "poetic" name for a woman in traditional love poetry.

The rose, like hues of insect wing,
   May perish in an hour;
'Tis but at best a fading thing,
   But thou'rt a living flower.

The roses steeped in morning dews
   Would every eye enthrall,
But woman, she alone subdues;
   Her beauty conquers all.   1873

     The speaker in "Love's Emblem" sends the rose to Chloe to decorate her bosom (lines 1, 10) and reflect the blush of her cheek and brow (lines 13, 18), and he goes on to mention some of the standard meanings: the rose is pure (line 6), transitory (line 11), fragrant, beautiful, and always appreciated (line 17). The poet need not elaborate or argue these things; he counts on the tradition, habits of mind built on familiarity and repetition. To say that the rose is an emblem of love is to say that it traditionally symbolizes love, and the speaker expects Chloe to accept his gift readily; she will understand it as a compliment, a pledge, and a bond. She will understand, too, that her admirer is being conventional and complimentary in going on to call her (and women in general) a rose (line 20), except that her qualities are said to be more lasting than those of a momentary flower.
     Poems often use traditional symbols to invoke predictable responses—in effect using shortcuts to meaning and power by repeating acts of signification and symbolization sanctioned by time and habit. But often poets examine the tradition even as they employ it, and sometimes they revise or reverse meanings built into the tradition. Some of the poems at the end of this chapter question the usual meanings of roses in poetry and evaluate as they go. Symbols do not necessarily stay the same over time, and poets often turn even the most traditional of symbols to their own original uses. Knowing the traditions of poetry—reading a lot of poems and observing how they tend to use certain words, metaphors, and symbols—can be very useful in reading new poems, but traditions modify and individual poems do highly individual things. Knowing the past never means being able to predict new texts with confidence. Symbolism makes things happen, but individual poets and texts determine what will happen and how.
     Sometimes symbols—traditional or not—become so insistent in the world of a poem that the larger referential world is left almost totally behind. In such cases the symbol is everything, and the poem does not just *use* symbols but

becomes a **symbolic poem,** usually a highly individualized one dependent on an internal system introduced by the individual poet.

Here is an example of such a poem:

WILLIAM BLAKE

The Sick Rose[3]

O rose, thou art sick.
The invisible worm
That flies in the night
In the howling storm

Has found out thy bed   5
Of crimson joy,
And his dark secret love
Does thy life destroy.   1794

The poem does not seem to be about a rose, but about what the rose represents—not in this case something altogether understandable through the traditional meanings of rose.

We know that the rose is usually associated with beauty and love, often with sex; and here several key terms have sexual connotations: "bed," "worm," and "crimson joy." The violation of the rose by the worm is the poem's main concern; the violation seems to have involved secrecy, deceit, and "dark" motives, and the result is sickness rather than the joy of love. The poem is sad; it involves a sense of hurt and tragedy, nearly of despair. The poem cries out against the misuse of the rose, against its desecration, implying that instead of a healthy joy in sensuality and sexuality, in this case, there has been destruction and hurt because of misunderstanding and repression and lack of sensitivity.

But to say so much about this poem I have had to extrapolate from other poems by this poet, and have introduced information from outside the poem. Fully symbolic poems often require that, and thus they ask us to go beyond the formal procedures of reading that we have discussed so far. As presented in this poem, the rose is not part of the normal world that we ordinarily see, and it is symbolic in a special sense. The poet does not simply take an object from that everyday world and give it special significance, making it a symbol in the same

---

3. In Renaissance emblem books, the scarab beetle, worm, and rose are closely associated: the beetle feeds on dung, and the smell of the rose is fatal to it.

sense that the leap is a symbol, or the corpse's hand. Here the rose seems to belong to its own world, a world made entirely inside the poem or the poet's head. The rose is not referential or not primarily so. The whole poem is symbolic; it is not paraphrasable; it lives in its own world. But what is the rose here a symbol of? In general terms, we can say from what the poem tells us; but we may not be as confident as we can be in the more nearly everyday world of "The Leap" or "Leningrad Cemetery, Winter of 1941," poems that contain actions we recognize from the world of probabilities in which we live. In "The Sick Rose," it seems inappropriate to ask the standard questions: What rose? Where? Which worm? What are the particulars here? In the world of this poem worms can fly and may be invisible. We are altogether in a world of meanings that have been formulated according to a particular system of knowledge and code of belief. We will only feel comfortable and confident in that world if we read many poems written by the poet (in this case William Blake) within the same symbolic system.

Negotiation of meanings in symbolic poems can be very difficult indeed. The skill of reading symbolic poems is an advanced skill that depends on special knowledge of authors and of the special traditions they work from, but the symbols you will usually find in poems are referential, and these meanings are readily discoverable from the careful study of the poems themselves, as in poems like "The Leap" and "Love's Emblem."

▼   ▼   ▼

EDMUND WALLER

Song

Go, lovely rose!
Tell her that wastes her time and me
   That now she knows,
When I resemble[4] her to thee,
How sweet and fair she seems to be.

Tell her that's young,
And shuns to have her graces spied,
   That hadst thou sprung
In deserts, where no men abide,
Thou must have uncommended died.

4. Compare.

Small is the worth
Of beauty from the light retired;
   Bid her come forth,
Suffer herself to be desired,
And not blush so to be admired.   15

   Then die! that she
The common fate of all things rare
   May read in thee;
How small a part of time they share
That are so wondrous sweet and fair!   1645   20

JOHN GAY

[Virgins are like the fair Flower in its Lustre] (*from* The Beggar's Opera)

Virgins are like the fair Flower in its Lustre,
Which in the Garden enamels the Ground;
Near it the Bees in Play flutter and cluster,
And gaudy Butterflies frolick around.
But, when once pluck'd, 'tis no longer alluring,   5
To Covent-Garden[5] 'tis sent, (as yet sweet,)
There fades, and shrinks, and grows past all enduring,
Rots, stinks, and dies, and is trod under feet.   1728

EMILY DICKINSON

[Go not too near a House of Rose—]

Go not too near a House of Rose—
The depredation of a Breeze
Or inundation of a Dew
Alarms its walls away—

Nor try to tie the Butterfly,   5
Nor climb the Bars of Ecstasy,
In insecurity to lie
ca. 1878   Is Joy's insuring quality.

---

5. A fruit and vegetable market in London (but also a haven for prostitutes).

WILLIAM CARLOS WILLIAMS

Poem

The rose fades
and is renewed again
by its seed, naturally
but where

5   save in the poem
shall it go
to suffer no diminution
of its splendor   1962

ALFRED, LORD TENNYSON

Now Sleeps the Crimson Petal[6]

Now sleeps the crimson petal, now the white;
Nor waves the cypress in the palace walk;
Nor winks the gold fin in the porphyry font;[7]
The firefly wakens; waken thou with me.

5   Now droops the milk-white peacock like a ghost,
And like a ghost she glimmers on to me.

Now lies the Earth all Danaë[8] to the stars,
And all thy heart lies open unto me.

Now slides the silent meteor on, and leaves
10   A shining furrow, as thy thoughts in me.

Now folds the lily all her sweetness up,
And slips into the bosom of the lake;
So fold thyself, my dearest, thou, and slip
Into my bosom and be lost in me.   1847

DOROTHY PARKER

One Perfect Rose

A single flow'r he sent me, since we met.
All tenderly his messenger he chose;

6. A song from *The Princess*.   7. Stone fishbowl. *Porphyry*: a red stone containing fine white crystals.   8. A princess, confined in a tower, seduced by Zeus after he became a shower of gold in order to gain access to her.

Deep-hearted, pure, with scented dew still wet—
    One perfect rose.

I knew the language of the floweret;   5
    "My fragile leaves," it said, "his heart enclose."
Love long has taken for his amulet
    One perfect rose.

Why is it no one ever sent me yet
    One perfect limousine, do you suppose?   10
Ah no, it's always just my luck to get
    One perfect rose.

                                                                    1937

KATHA POLLITT

Two Fish

Those speckled trout we glimpsed in a pool last year
you'd take for an image of love: it too should be
graceful, elusive, tacit, moving surely
among half-lights of mingled dim and clear,
forced to no course, of no fixed residence,   5
its only end its own swift elegance.
What would you say
if you saw what I saw the other day:
that pool heat-choked and fevered where sick blue
bubbled green scum and blistered water lily?   10
A white like a rolled-back eye or fish's belly
I thought I saw far out—but doubtless you
prefer to think our trout had left together
to seek a place with less inclement weather.

                                                                    1981

JORIE GRAHAM

The Geese

Today as I hang out the wash I see them again, a code
as urgent as elegant,
tapering with goals.
For days they have been crossing. We live beneath these geese

as if beneath the passage of time, or a most perfect heading.   5
Sometimes I fear their relevance.
Closest at hand,
between the lines,

the spiders imitate the paths the geese won't stray from,
imitate them endlessly to no avail:
things will not remain connected,
will not heal,

and the world thickens with texture instead of history,
texture instead of place.
Yet the small fear of the spiders
binds and binds

the pins to the lines, the lines to the eaves, to the pincushion bush,
as if, at any time, things could fall further apart
and nothing could help them
recover their meaning. And if these spiders had their way,

chainlink over the visible world,
would we be in or out? I turn to go back in.
There is a feeling the body gives the mind
of having missed something, a bedrock poverty, like falling

without the sense that you are passing through one world,
that you could reach another
anytime. Instead the real
is crossing you,

your body an arrival
you know is false but can't outrun. And somewhere in between
these geese forever entering and
these spiders turning back,

this astonishing delay, the everyday, takes place.   1980

ROO BORSON

After a Death

Seeing that there's no other way,
I turn his absence into a chair.
I can sit in it,
gaze out through the window.
I can do what I do best
and then go out into the world.
And I can return then with my useless love,
to rest,
because the chair is there.   1989

GEORGE PEELE

A Farewell to Arms[9]

His golden locks time hath to silver turned;
    Oh, time too swift, oh, swiftness never ceasing!
His youth 'gainst time and age hath ever spurned,[1]
    But spurned in vain; youth waneth by increasing.
Beauty, strength, youth, are flowers but fading seen;   5
Duty, faith, love, are roots, and ever green.

His helmet now shall make a hive for bees,
    And lover's sonnets turned to holy psalms,
A man-at-arms must now serve on his knees,
    And feed on prayers, which are age his[2] alms;   10
But though from court to cottage he depart,
His saint is sure of his unspotted heart.

And when he saddest sits in homely cell,
    He'll teach his swains this carol for a song:
Blest be the hearts that wish my sovereign well,   15
    Cursed be the souls that think her any wrong!
Goddess, allow this aged man his right,
To be your beadsman[3] now, that was your knight.   1590

HOWARD NEMEROV

The Town Dump

"The art of our necessities is strange,
That can make vile things precious."[4]

A mile out in the marshes, under a sky
Which seems to be always going away
In a hurry, on that Venetian land threaded
With hidden canals, you will find the city
Which seconds ours (so cemeteries, too,   5
Reflect a town from hillsides out of town),
Where Being most Becomingly[5] ends up
Becoming some more. From cardboard tenements,
Windowed with cellophane, or simply tenting
In paper bags, the angry mackerel eyes

---

9. From *Polyhymnia*, a verse description of a 1590 jousting tournament on Queen Elizabeth's birthday. Sir Henry Lee, who had for years been the queen's champion in such contests, retired that year (at age 60) in favor of a younger man.   1. Kicked.   2. Age's (a common Elizabethan possessive form).   3. One who prays for the soul of another (OED).   4. *King Lear*, Act III, scene 2, 70–71.   5. "Being" and "Becoming" have been, since Heraclitus, the standard antinomies in Western philosophy, standing for (respectively) the eternal and that which changes.

Glare at you out of stove-in, sunken heads
Far from the sea; the lobster, also, lifts
An empty claw in his most minatory
Of gestures; oyster, crab, and mussel shells
Lie here in heaps, savage as money hurled
Away at the gate of hell. If you want results,
These are results.
        Objects of value or virtue,
However, are also to be picked up here,
Though rarely, lying with bones and rotten meat,
Eggshells and mouldy bread, banana peels
No one will skid on, apple cores that caused
Neither the fall of man nor a theory
Of gravitation.[6] People do throw out
The family pearls by accident, sometimes,
Not often; I've known dealers in antiques
To prowl this place by night, with flashlights, on
The off-chance of somebody's having left
Derelict chairs which will turn out to be
By Hepplewhite,[7] a perfect set of six
Going to show, I guess, that in any sty
Someone's heaven may open and shower down
Riches responsive to the right dream; though
It is a small chance, certainly, that sends
The ghostly dealer, heavy with fly-netting
Over his head, across these hills in darkness,
Stumbling in cut-glass goblets, lacquered cups,
And other products of his dreamy midden[8]
Penciled with light and guarded by the flies.

For there are flies, of course. A dynamo
Composed, by thousands, of our ancient black
Retainers, hums here day and night, steady
As someone telling[9] beads, the hum becoming
A high whine at any disturbance; then,
Settled again, they shine under the sun
Like oil-drops, or are invisible as night,
By night,
        All this continually smoulders,
Crackles, and smokes with mostly invisible fires
Which, working deep, rarely flash out and flare,
And never finish. Nothing finishes;
The flies, feeling the heat, keep on the move.

---

6. According to legend, Sir Isaac Newton's discovery of the principle of gravitation followed his being hit on the head by a falling apple.   7. A late 18th-century cabinet maker and furniture designer, famed for his simplification of neoclassic lines. No pieces known to have been actually made by Hepplewhite survive.   8. Refuse heap. (The term is usually used to describe those primitive refuse heaps that have been untouched for centuries and in which archeologists dig for shards and artifacts of older cultures.)   9. Counting.

Among the flies, the purefying fires,
The hunters by night, acquainted with the art
Of our necessities, and the new deposits
That each day wastes with treasure, you may say
There should be ratios. You may sum up   55
The results if you want results. But I will add
That wild birds, drawn to the carrion and flies,
Assemble in some numbers here, their wings
Shining with light, their flight enviably free,
Their music marvelous, though sad, and strange.   1958   60

▼   ▼   ▼

Language A Glossary

ambiguity: the ability to mean more than one thing

analogy: a comparison based on certain resemblances between things that are otherwise unlike

connotation: what is suggested by a word, apart from what it explicitly describes

connote: to suggest something in addition to explicit meaning

controlling metaphors: metaphors that dominate or organize an entire poem

denotation: a direct and specific meaning (as distinct from implication)

denote: to mean or stand for

extended metaphors: detailed and complex metaphors that extend over a long section of a poem

figurative language: language that uses figures of speech

figures of speech: comparisons in which something is pictured or figured forth in other, more familiar terms

metaphor: one thing pictured as if it were something else, suggesting a likeness or analogy between them

personification (or **prosopopeia**): treating an abstraction as if it were a person, endowing it with human-like qualities

precision: exactness, accuracy of language or description

simile: a direct, explicit comparison of one thing to another, and usually using the words "like" or "as" to draw the connection

symbol: something that stands for something else

symbolic poem: a poem in which the use of symbols is so pervasive and internally consistent that the larger referential world is distanced, if not forgotten

syntax: the formal arrangement of words in a sentence

traditional symbols: symbols that, through years of usage, have acquired an agreed-on significance, an accepted meaning

word order: the positioning of words in relation to one another

QUESTIONS

1. List all of the neologisms and other unusual words in "Pied Beauty." Find the most precise synonym you can for each. How can you tell exactly what these words contribute to the poem? Explain the effects of the repeated consonant sounds (alliteration) and repeated vowel sounds (assonance) in the poem. What are the advantages of making up original words to describe highly individualized effects? What are the disadvantages?

2. Compare "I dwell in Possibility—" with two other Dickinson poems, "A narrow Fellow in the Grass" (p. 200) and "After great pain, a formal feeling comes—." What patterns of word use do you see in the three poems? What kinds of vocabulary do they have in common? what patterns of syntax? what strategies of organization?

3. Read aloud the passage from *Paradise Lost*. Then ask a friend to read the passage aloud as well. As the friend reads, note which words—and which choices of word order—provide especially useful guides for reading aloud. Make a list of all the lines in which the "normal" word order would be different if the poem were not written in a metrical form designed for reading aloud. In each case in which the poem uses unusual word order, try to figure out exactly what effect is produced by the variation.

4. Characterize as fully as you can the speaker in "Batter my heart, three-personed God." Explain how the metaphor of invasion and resistance works in the poem. What effect does this central metaphor have on our conception of the speaker? Explain the terms "imprison" (line 12) and "enthrall" (line 13). Explain "chaste" and "ravish" (line 14). How do these two sets of terms relate to the poem's central metaphor?

5. List every term in "The Twenty-third Psalm" that relates to the central metaphor of sheepherding. Explain the metaphors of anointing and the over-full cup in line 5. (If you have trouble with this metaphor and do not understand the historical/cultural reference, ask a reference librarian to guide you to biblical commentaries that explain the practices referred to here.) What is the "house of the Lord" (line 6), and how does it relate to the basic metaphor of the psalm? (Again, if you are not sure of the historical/cultural reference, consult biblical commentaries or other historical sources on social and economic structures of the ancient Middle East.)

6. List all of the material objects and human activities in "A Farewell to Arms" that symbolize the active world of the knight. List all the objects and activities that symbolize the contemplative life of the beadsman. What,

according to the poem, are the relative values of the "golden" and "silver" (line 1) worlds?

7. Compare the symbolism of the fish and seafood in "The Town Dump" with that of the two trout in "Two Fish."

WRITING SUGGESTIONS

1. Read back through the poems you have read so far in the course, and pick out one in which a single word seems to you crucial to that poem's total effect. Write a short essay in which you work out carefully how the poem's meaning and tone depend upon that one word.

2. With the help of a reference librarian, find several pictures of B-17 bombers, and study carefully the design and appearance of the ball turret. Try to find a picture of the gunner at work in the turret, and note carefully his body position. Explain, in a paragraph, how the poem uses the visual details of the ball turret to create the fetal and birth metaphors in the poem.

3. Consider carefully the symbolism of the trout in "Two Fish." Exactly how do the fish become symbolic to the lovers? How do they become invested with meaning? What do this year's trout look like? Is the difference between last year's trout and this year's in the fish themselves or in their settings? What power does the weather have over the fish? What is the implied moral for the lovers? What does each lover believe about what the trout represent? What are the temperamental differences between the two lovers? What does the poem conclude about the "meaning" of the fish? Write an essay of about three pages in which you show how the poem opens and develops the question of what "symbols" mean.

4. With the help of a reference librarian, find at least half a dozen more poems that are about roses. Read them all carefully, and make a list of all the things that the rose seems to stand for in the poems. Write a paragraph about each poem showing how a specific symbolism for rose is established.

5 THE SOUNDS OF POETRY

A lot of what happens in a poem happens in your mind's eye, but some of it happens in your voice. Poems are full of sounds and silences as well as words and sentences that are meaningful. Besides choosing words for their meanings, poets sometimes choose words because they involve certain sounds, and poems use sound effects to create a mood or establish a tone, just as films do. Sometimes the sounds of words are crucial to what is happening in the text of the poem.

The following poem explores the sounds of a particular word, tries them on, and analyzes them in relation to the word itself.

HELEN CHASIN

The Word *Plum*

The word *plum* is delicious

pout and push, luxury of
self-love, and savoring murmur

full in the mouth and falling
5   like fruit

taut skin
pierced, bitten, provoked into
juice, and tart flesh

question
10   and reply, lip and tongue
of pleasure.   1968

The poem savors the sounds of the word as well as the taste and feel of the fruit itself. It is almost as if the poem is tasting the sounds and rolling them carefully on the tongue. The second and third lines even replicate the *p, l, uh,* and *m* sounds of the word while at the same time imitating the squishy sounds of eating the fruit. Words like "delicious" and "luxury" sound juicy, and other words imitate sounds of satisfaction and pleasure—"murmur," for example. Even the process of eating is in part re-created aurally. The tight, clipped sounds of "taut skin / pierced" suggest the way teeth sharply break the skin and

174

slice quickly into the solid flesh of a plum, and as the tartness is described, the words ("provoked," "question") force the lips to pucker and the tongue and palate to meet and hold, as if the mouth were savoring a tart fruit. The poet is having fun here re-creating the various sense appeals of a plum, teasing the sounds and meanings out of available words. The words must mean something appropriate and describe something accurately first of all, of course, but when they can also imitate the sounds and feel of the process, they can do double duty. Not all poems manipulate sound as consciously or as fully as "The Word *Plum*," but many poems at least contain passages in which the sounds of life are reproduced by the human voice reading the poem. To get the full effect of this poem—and of many others—reading aloud is essential; that way, you can pay attention to the vocal rhythms and articulate the sounds as the poem calls for them to be reproduced by the human voice.

Almost always a poem's effect will be helped by reading it aloud, using your voice to pronounce the words so that the poem becomes a spoken communication. Historically, poetry began as an oral phenomenon, and often poems that seem very difficult when looked at silently come alive when they are turned into sound. Early bards chanted their verses, and the music of poetry—its cadences and rhythms—developed from this kind of performance. Often performances of primitive poetry (and sometimes in later ages) were accompanied by some kind of musical instrument. The rhythms of any poem become clearer when you say or hear them.

Poetry is, almost always, a vocal art, dependent on the human voice to become its full self (for some exceptions look at the shaped verse in Chapter 7). In a sense, it begins to exist as a real phenomenon when a reader reads and actualizes it. Poems don't really achieve their full meaning when they merely exist on a page; a poem on a page is more a score or set of stage directions for a poem than a poem itself. Sometimes, in fact, it is hard to experience the poem at all unless you hear it. A good poetry reading might easily convince you of the importance of a good voice sensitive to the poem's requirements, but you can also persuade yourself by reading poems aloud in the privacy of your own room. An audience is even better, however, because then there is someone to share the pleasure in the sounds themselves and consider what they imply. At its oral best, much poetry is communal.

MONA VAN DUYN

What the Motorcycle Said

Br-r-r-am-m-m, rackety-am-m, OM, *Am:*
All—r-r-room, r-r-ram, ala-bas-ter—
Am, the world's my oyster.

I hate plastic, wear it black and slick,
hate hardhats, wear one on my head,
that's what the motorcycle said.

Passed phonies in Fords, knocked down billboards, landed
on the other side of The Gap, and Whee,
bypassed history.

When I was born (The Past), baby knew best.
They shook when I bawled, took Freud's path,
threw away their wrath.

R-r-rackety-am-m. *Am.* War, rhyme,
soap, meat, marriage, the Phantom Jet
are shit, and like that.

Hate pompousness, punishment, patience, am into Love,
hate middle-class moneymakers, live on Dad,
that's what the motorcycle said.

Br-r-r-am-m-m. It's Nowsville, man. Passed Oldies, Uglies,
Straighties, Honkies. I'll never be
mean, tired or unsexy.

Passed cigarette suckers, souses, mother-fuckers,
losers, went back to Nature and found
how to get VD, stoned.

Passed a cow, too fast to hear her moo, "I rolled
our leaves of grass into one ball.
I am the grassy All."

Br-r-r-am-m-m, rackety-am-m, OM, *Am:*
All—gr-r-rin, oooohgah, gl-l-utton—
Am, the world's my smilebutton.

1973

Saying this poem as if you were a motorcycle with the power of speech
(sort of) is part of the poem's fun, and the rich, loud sounds of a motorcycle
revving up concentrate and intensify the effect and enrich the pleasure. It's a
shame not to hear a poem like this aloud; a lot of it is missed if you don't try to
imitate the sounds or to pick up the motor's rhythms in the poem. A perfor-

mance here is clearly worth it: a human being as motorcycle, motorcycle as human being.

And it's a good poem, too. It does something interesting, important, and maybe a bit subversive. The speaking motorcycle seems to take on the values of some of its riders, the noisy and obtrusive ones that readers are most likely to associate with motorcycles. The riders made fun of here are themselves sort of mindless and mechanical; they are the sort who have cult feelings about their group, who travel in packs, and who live no life beyond their machines. The speaking motorcycle, like such riders, grooves on power and speed, lives for the moment, and has little respect for people, the past, institutions, or for anything beyond its own small world. It is self-centered, modish, ignorant, and inarticulate; but it is proud as well, mighty proud, and feels important in its own sounds. That's what the motorcycle says.

The following poem uses sound effects efficiently, too.

KENNETH FEARING

Dirge

1-2-3 was the number he played but today the number came 3-2-1;
Bought his Carbide at 30, and it went to 29; had the favorite at Bowie[1] but the track was slow—

O executive type, would you like to drive a floating-power, knee-action, silk-upholstered six? Wed a Hollywood star? Shoot the course in 58? Draw to the ace, king, jack?
O fellow with a will who won't take no, watch out for three cigarettes on the same, single match; O democratic voter born in August under Mars, beware of liquidated rails—

Denouement to denouement, he took a personal pride in the certain, certain way he lived his own, private life,   5
But nevertheless, they shut off his gas; nevertheless, the bank foreclosed; nevertheless, the landlord called; nevertheless, the radio broke,

And twelve o'clock arrived just once too often,
Just the same he wore one gray tweed suit, bought one straw hat, drank one straight Scotch, walked one short step, took one long look, drew one deep breath,
Just one too many,

1. A racetrack in Maryland. *Carbide*: the Union Carbide Corporation.

10   And wow he died as wow he lived,
Going whop to the office and blooie home to sleep and biff got married and
    bam had children and oof got fired,
Zowie did he live and zowie did he die,

With who the hell are you at the corner of his casket, and where the hell're we
    going on the right-hand silver knob, and who the hell cares walking second
    from the end with an American Beauty[2] wreath from why the hell not,

Very much missed by the circulation staff of the New York Evening Post; deeply,
    deeply mourned by the B.M.T.[3]
15   Wham, Mr. Roosevelt; pow, Sears Roebuck; awk, big dipper; bop, summer rain;
    Bong, Mr., bong, Mr., bong, Mr., bong.

                                                                    1935

As the title implies, "Dirge" is a kind of musical lament, in this case for a
certain sort of businessman who took a lot of chances and saw his investments
and life go down the drain in the depression of the early 1930s. Reading this
poem aloud is a big help partly because it contains expressive cartoon words
that echo the action, words like "oof" and "blooie" (which primarily carry their
meaning in their sounds, for they have practically no literal or referential mean-
ing). Reading aloud also helps us notice that the poem employs rhythms much
as a song would and that it frequently shifts its pace and mood. Notice how
carefully the first two lines are balanced, and then how quickly the rhythm
shifts as the "executive type" begins to be addressed directly in line 3. (Line 2 is
long and dribbles over in the narrow pages of a book like this; a lot of the lines
here are especially long, and the irregularity of the line lengths is one aspect of
the special sound effects the poem creates.) In the direct address, the poem
first picks up a series of advertising features, which it recites in rapid-fire order
rather like the advertising phrases in "Needs" (p. 67). In stanza 3 here, the
rhythm shifts again, but the poem gives us helpful clues about how to read.
Line 5 sounds like prose and is long, drawn out, and rather dull (rather like its
subject), but line 6 sets up a regular (and monotonous) rhythm with its
repeated "nevertheless," which punctuates the rhythm like a drumbeat: "But
nevertheless, *tuh-tuh-tuh-tuh-tuh*; nevertheless, *tuh-tuh-tuh-tuh*; nevertheless,
tuh-tuh-tuh-tuh; nevertheless *tuh-tuh-tuh-tuh-tuh*." In the next stanza, the repet-
itive phrasing comes again, this time guided by the word "one" in cooperation
with other words of one syllable: "wore *one* gray tweed suit, bought *one* straw
hat, *tuh* one *tuh-tuh*, *tuh* one *tuh-tuh*, *tuh* one *tuh-tuh*, *tuh* one *tuh-tuh*." And
then a new rhythm and a new technique in stanza 5 as the language of comic

2. A variety of rose.   3. A New York City subway line.

books is imitated to describe in violent, exaggerated terms the routine of his life. You have to say words like "whop" and "zowie" aloud and in the rhythm of the whole sentence to get the full effect of how boring his life is, no matter how he tries to jazz it up with exciting words. And so it goes—repeated words, shifting rhythms, emphasis on routine and averageness—until the final bell ("Bong . . . bong . . . bong . . . bong") tolls rhythmically for the dead man in the final clanging line.

Sometimes sounds in poems just provide special effects, rather like a musical score behind a film, setting mood and getting us into an appropriate frame of mind. But often sound and meaning go hand in hand, and the poet finds words that in their sounds echo the action. A word that captures or approximates the sound of what it describes, such as "splash" or "squish" or "murmur" is called an **onomatopoeic** word, and the device itself is called **onomatopoeia**. And similar things can be done poetically with pacing and rhythm, sounds and pauses. The punctuation, the length of vowels, and the combination of consonant sounds help to control the way we read so that we imitate what is being described. The poems at the end of this discussion (pp. 185–201) suggest several ways that such imitations of pace and pause may occur: by echoing the lapping of waves on a shore, for example ("Like as the waves"), or reproducing the rhythms of a musical style ("Queen of the Blues" or "Dear John, Dear Coltrane").

Here is a classic passage in which a skillful poet talks about the virtues of making the sound echo the sense—and shows at the same time how to do it:

ALEXANDER POPE

Sound and Sense[4]

> But most by numbers[5] judge a poet's song,   337
> And smooth or rough, with them, is right or wrong;
> In the bright muse though thousand charms conspire,[6]
> Her voice is all these tuneful fools admire,   340
> Who haunt Parnassus[7] but to please their ear,
> Not mend their minds; as some to church repair,
> Not for the doctrine, but the music there.
> These, equal syllables[8] alone require,

4. From *An Essay on Criticism*, Pope's poem on the art of poetry and the problems of literary criticism. The passage excerpted here follows a discussion of several common weaknesses of critics; failure to regard an author's intention, for example, or overemphasis on clever metaphors and ornate style.   5. Meter, rhythm, sound.   6. Unite.   7. A mountain in Greece, traditionally associated with the muses and considered the seat of poetry and music.   8. Regular accents.

345   Though oft the ear the open vowels tire,
      While expletives[9] their feeble aid do join,
      And ten low words oft creep in one dull line,
      While they ring round the same unvaried chimes,
      With sure returns of still expected rhymes.
350   Where'er you find "the cooling western breeze,"
      In the next line, it "whispers through the trees";
      If crystal streams "with pleasing murmurs creep,"
      The reader's threatened (not in vain) with "sleep."
      Then, at the last and only couplet fraught
355   With some unmeaning thing they call a thought,
      A needless Alexandrine[1] ends the song,
      That, like a wounded snake, drags its slow length along.
      Leave such to tune their own dull rhymes, and know
      What's roundly smooth, or languishingly slow;
360   And praise the easy vigor of a line,
      Where Denham's strength and Waller's[2] sweetness join.
      True ease in writing comes from art, not chance,
      As those move easiest who have learned to dance.
      'Tis not enough no harshness gives offense,
365   The sound must seem an echo to the sense:
      Soft is the strain when Zephyr[3] gently blows,
      And the smooth stream in smoother numbers flows;
      But when loud surges lash the sounding shore,
      The hoarse, rough verse should like the torrent roar.
370   When Ajax[4] strives, some rock's vast weight to throw,
      The line too labors, and the words move slow;
      Not so, when swift Camilla[5] scours the plain,
      Flies o'er th' unbending corn, and skims along the main.
      Hear how Timotheus'[6] varied lays surprise,
375   And bid alternate passions fall and rise!
      While, at each change, the son of Libyan Jove[7]
      Now burns with glory, and then melts with love;
      Now his fierce eyes with sparkling fury glow,
      Now sighs steal out, and tears begin to flow:
380   Persians and Greeks like turns of nature[8] found,
      And the world's victor stood subdued by sound!
      The pow'r of music all our hearts allow,
      And what Timotheus was, is DRYDEN now.   1711

9. Filler words, such as "do."   1. A six-foot line, sometimes used in pen-tameter poems to vary
the pace mechanically. Line 357 is an alexandrine.   2. Sir John Denham and Edmund Waller,
17th-century poets credited with perfecting the heroic couplet.   3. The west wind.   4. A
Greek hero of the Trojan War, noted for his strength.   5. A woman warrior in *The Aeneid*.
6. The court-musician of Alexander the Great, celebrated in a famous poem by Dryden (see line
383) for the power of his music over Alexander's emotions.   7. In Greek tradition, the chief god
of any people was often given the name Zeus (Jove), and the chief god of Libya (the Greek name
for all of Africa) was called Zeus Ammon. Alexander visited his oracle and was proclaimed son of
the god.   8. Similar alternations of emotion.

A lot of things are going on here simultaneously. The poem uses a number of echoic or onomatopoeic words, and pleasant and unpleasant consonant sounds are used in some lines to underline a particular point or add some mood music. When the poet talks about a particular weakness in poetry, he illustrates it at the same time—by using open vowels (line 345), expletives (line 346), monosyllabic words (line 347), predictable rhymes (lines 350–53), or long, slow lines (line 357). And the good qualities of poetry he talks about and illustrates as well (line 360, for example). But the main effects of the passage come from an interaction of several strategies at once. The effects are fairly simple and easy to spot, but their causes involve a lot of poetic ingenuity. In line 340, for example, a careful cacophonous effect is achieved by the repetition of the $\overline{oo}$ vowel sound and the repetition of the *l* consonant sound together with the interruption (twice) of the rough *f* sound in the middle; no one wants to be caught admiring that music when the poet gets through with us, but the careful harmony of the preceding sounds has set us up beautifully. And the pace of lines 347, 357, and 359 is carefully controlled by clashing consonant sounds as well as by the use of long vowels. Line 347 moves incredibly slowly and seems much longer than it is because almost all the one-syllable words end in a consonant that refuses to blend with the beginning of the next word, making the words hard to say without distinct, awkward pauses between them. In lines 357 and 359, long vowels such as those in "wounded," "snake," "slow," "along," "roundly," and "smooth" help to slow down the pace, and the trick of juxtaposing awkward, unpronounceable consonants is again employed. The commas also provide nearly a full stop in the midst of these lines to slow us down still more. Similarly, the harsh lashing of the shore in lines 368–69 is partly accomplished by onomatopoeia, partly by a shift in the pattern of stress, which creates irregular waves in line 368, and partly by the dominance of rough consonants in line 369. (In Pope's time, the English *r* was still trilled gruffly so that it could be made to sound extremely rrrough and harrrsh.) Almost every line in this passage demonstrates how to make sound echo sense.

As "Sound and Sense" and "Dirge" suggest, sound is most effectively manipulated in poetry when the rhythm of the voice is carefully controlled so that not only are the proper sounds heard, but they are heard at precisely the right moment. Pace and rhythm are nearly as important to a good poem as they are to a good piece of music. The human voice naturally develops certain rhythms in speech; some syllables and some words receive more stress than others, and a careful poet controls the flow of stresses so that, in many poems, a certain basic rhythm develops almost like a quiet percussion instrument in the background. Not all poems are metered, and not all metered poems follow a single dominant rhythm, but many poems are written in one pervasive pattern, and it is useful to look for patterns of stress.

Here is a poem that names and illustrates many of the meters. If you hear someone reading it aloud and chart the unstressed (˘) and stressed (‾) syllables you should have a chart similar to that done by the poet himself in the text.

SAMUEL TAYLOR COLERIDGE

Metrical Feet

LESSON FOR A BOY

Trōchĕe trīps frŏm lōng tŏ shōrt;[9]
From long to long in solemn sort
Slōw Spōndēe stālks; strōng fōot! yet ill able
Ēvĕr tŏ cōme ŭp wĭth Dāctўl trĭsyllăblĕ.
Ĭāmbĭcs mārch frŏm shōrt tŏ lōng —
With ă lēap ănd ă bōund thĕ swĭft Ānăpĕsts thrōng;
One syllable long, with one short at each side,
Ămphĭbrăchўs hāstes wĭth ă stātelў stride —
Fīrst ănd lāst bēĭng lōng, mĭddlĕ shōrt, Ămphĭmācer
Strīkes hĭs thūndērĭng hōofs līke ă prōud hĭgh-brĕd Rācer.
If Derwent[1] be innocent, steady, and wise,
And delight in the things of earth, water, and skies;
Tender warmth at his heart, with these meters to show it,
With sound sense in his brains, may make Derwent a poet —
May crown him with fame, and must win him the love
Of his father on earth and his Father above.
          My dear, dear child!
Could you stand upon Skiddaw,[2] you would not from its whole ridge
See a man who so loves you as your fond S. T. COLERIDGE.

1806

The following poem exemplifies **dactylic** rhythm (‾ ˘ ˘, or a stressed sylla-
ble followed by two unstressed ones).

---

9. The long and short marks over syllables are Coleridge's.   1. Written originally for Coleridge's son Hartley, the poem was later adapted for his younger son, Derwent.   2. A mountain in the lake country of northern England (where Coleridge lived in his early years), near the town of Derwent.

WENDY COPE

Emily Dickinson

Higgledy-piggledy
Emily Dickinson
Liked to use dashes
Instead of full stops.

Nowadays, faced with such   5
Idiosyncrasy,
Critics and editors
Send for the cops.   1986

Limericks rely on **anapestic** meter (⌣⌣‾, or two unstressed syllables fol-
lowed by a stressed one), although usually the first two syllables are in iambic
meter (see below).

ANONYMOUS

[A staid schizophrenic named Struther]

A staid schizophrenic named Struther,
When told of the death of his brother,
   Said: "Yes, I am sad;
   It makes me feel bad,
But then, I still have each other."   5

The following poem is composed in the more common **trochaic** meter (‾⌣,
a stressed syllable followed by an unstressed one).

SIR JOHN SUCKLING

Song

Why so pale and wan, fond Lover?
   Prithee why so pale?

Will, when looking well can't move her,
  Looking ill prevail?
  Prithee why so pale?

Why so dull and mute, young Sinner?
  Prithee why so mute?
Will, when speaking well can't win her,
  Saying nothing do 't?
  Prithee why so mute?

Quit, quit, for shame, this will not move,
  This cannot take her;
If of her self she will not love,
  Nothing can make her,
  The Devil take her.   1646

The basic meter in the following poem, as in "Sound and Sense," is the most common one in English, **iambic** (⌣−, an unstressed syllable followed by a stressed one).

JOHN DRYDEN

To the Memory of Mr. Oldham[3]

Farewell, too little, and too lately known,
Whom I began to think and call my own;
For sure our souls were near allied, and thine
Cast in the same poetic mold with mine.
One common note on either lyre did strike,
And knaves and fools we both abhorred alike.
To the same goal did both our studies drive;
The last set out the soonest did arrive.
Thus Nisus fell upon the slippery place,
While his young friend performed and won the race.[4]
O early ripe! to thy abundant store
What could advancing age have added more?
It might (what nature never gives the young)
Have taught the numbers[5] of thy native tongue.
But satire needs not those, and wit will shine
Through the harsh cadence of a rugged line.[6]
A noble error, and but seldom made,

3. John Oldham (1653–1683), who like Dryden (see lines 3–6) wrote satiric poetry.   4. In Vergil's *Aeneid* (Book V), Nisus (who is leading the race) falls and then trips the second runner so that his friend Euryalus can win.   5. Rhythms.   6. In Dryden's time, *r*'s were pronounced with a harsh, trilling sound.

When poets are by too much force betrayed.
Thy generous fruits, though gathered ere their prime,
Still showed a quickness; and maturing time   20
But mellows what we write to the dull sweets of rhyme.
Once more, hail and farewell; farewell, thou young,
But ah too short, Marcellus[7] of our tongue;
Thy brows with ivy, and with laurels bound;
But fate and gloomy night encompass thee around.   1684   25

Once you have figured out the basic rhythm of a poem, you can often find some interesting things by looking carefully at the departures from the pattern. Departures from the basic iambic meter of "To the Memory of Mr. Oldham," for example, suggest some of the imaginative things that poets can do within the apparently very restrictive requirements of traditional meter. Try marking the stressed and unstressed syllables in "To the Memory of Mr. Oldham" and then look carefully at each place that varies from the basic iambic pattern. Which of these variations call special attention to a particular sound or action being talked about in the poem? Which ones specifically mimic or echo the sense? Which variations seem to exist primarily for emphasis? Which ones seem primarily intended to mark structural breaks in the poem?

▾ ▾ ▾

GWENDOLYN BROOKS

Queen of the Blues

Mame was singing
At the Midnight Club.
And the place was red
With blues.
She could shake her body   5
Across the floor.
For what did she have
To lose?

She put her mama
Under the ground   10
Two years ago.

7. The nephew of the Roman emperor Augustus; he died at 20, and Vergil celebrated him in *The Aeneid*, Book VI.

(Was it three?)
She covered that grave
With roses and tears.
(A handsome thing
15   To see.)

She didn't have any
Legal pa
To glare at her,
To shame
20   Her off the floor
Of the Midnight Club.
Poor Mame.

She didn't have any
Big brother
25   To shout
"No sister of mine ! . . ."
She didn't have any
Small brother
To think she was everything
30   Fine.

She didn't have any
Baby girl
With velvet
Pop-open eyes.
35   She didn't have any
Sonny boy
To tell sweet
Sonny boy lies.

"Show me a man
40   What will love me
Till I die.
Now show me a man
What will love me
45   Till I die.
Can't find no such a man
No matter how hard
You try.
Go 'long, baby.
50   Ain't a true man left
In Chi.

"I loved my daddy.
But what did my daddy
Do?
55   I loved my daddy.

But what did my daddy
Do?
Found him a brown-skin chicken
What's gonna be
Black and blue. 60

"I was good to my daddy.
Gave him all my dough.
I say, I was good to my daddy.
I gave him all of my dough.
Scrubbed hard in them white folks' 65
Kitchens
Till my knees was rusty
And so'."

The M.C. hollered,
"Queen of the blues 70
Folks, this is strictly
The queen of the blues!"
She snapped her fingers.
She rolled her hips.
What did she have 75
To lose?

But a thought ran through her
Like a fire.
"Men don't tip their
Hats to me. 80
They pinch my arms
And they slap my thighs.
But when has a man
Tipped his hat to me?"

Queen of the blues! 85
Queen of the blues!
Strictly, strictly,
The queen of the blues!

Men are low down
Dirty and mean. 90
Why don't they tip
Their hats to a queen? 1945

MICHAEL HARPER

Dear John, Dear Coltrane

a love supreme, a love supreme[8]
a love supreme, a love supreme

Sex fingers toes
in the marketplace
near your father's church
in Hamlet, North Carolina—[9]
witness to this love
in this calm fallow
of these minds,
there is no substitute for pain:
genitals gone or going,
seed burned out,
you tuck the roots in the earth,
turn back, and move
by river through the swamps,
singing: *a love supreme, a love supreme;*
what does it all mean?
Loss, so great each black
woman expects your failure
in mute change, the seed gone.
You plod up into the electric city—
your song now crystal and
the blues. You pick up the horn
with some will and blow
into the freezing night:
a love supreme, a love supreme—

Dawn comes and you cook
up the thick sin 'tween
impotence and death, fuel
the tenor sax cannibal
heart, genitals and sweat
that makes you clean—
a love supreme, a love supreme—

Why you so black?
cause I am
why you so funky?
cause I am

8. Coltrane wrote "A Love Supreme" in response to a spiritual experience in 1957, which led to his quitting heroin and alcohol. The record was released in 1965.   9. Coltrane's birthplace. His family shared a house with Coltrane's grandfather, who was the minister of St. Stephen's AME Zion Church there.

why you so black
cause I am
why you so sweet?
cause I am
why you so black? 40
cause I am
a love supreme, a love supreme:

So sick
you couldn't play *Naima*,[1]
so flat we ached 45
for song you'd concealed
with your own blood,
your diseased liver gave
out its purity,
the inflated heart 50
pumps out, the tenor kiss,
tenor love:
a love supreme, a love supreme—
a love supreme, a love supreme— 1970

WILLIAM SHAKESPEARE

[Like as the waves make towards the pebbled shore]

Like as the waves make towards the pebbled shore,
So do our minutes hasten to their end,
Each changing place with that which goes before,
In sequent toil all forwards do contend.[2]
Nativity, once in the main[3] of light, 5
Crawls to maturity, wherewith being crowned,
Crooked[4] eclipses 'gainst his glory fight,
And Time that gave doth now his gift confound.[5]
Time doth transfix[6] the flourish set on youth
And delves the parallels[7] in beauty's brow, 10
Feeds on the rarities of nature's truth,
And nothing stands but for his scythe to mow.
And yet to times in hope[8] my verse shall stand,
Praising thy worth, despite his cruel hand. 1609

---

1. A song Coltrane wrote for and named after his wife, recorded in 1959.   2. Struggle. *Sequent:*
successive.   3. High seas. *Nativity:* newborn life.   4. Perverse.   5. Bring to nothing.
6. Pierce.   7. Lines, wrinkles.   8. In the future.

JAMES MERRILL

Watching the Dance

1. BALANCHINE'S[9]

Poor savage, doubting that a river flows
But for the myriad eddies made
By unseen powers twirling on their toes,

Here in this darkness it would seem
You had already died, and were afraid.
Be still. Observe the powers. Infer the stream.

2. DISCOTHEQUE.

Having survived entirely your own youth,
Last of your generation, purple gloom
Investing you, sit, Jonah,[1] beyond speech,

And let towards the brute volume VOOM whale
mouth
VAM pounding viscera VAM VOOM
A teenage plankton luminously twitch.

1967

ALFRED, LORD TENNYSON

Break, Break, Break

Break, break, break,
    On thy cold gray stones, O Sea!
And I would that my tongue could utter
    The thoughts that arise in me.

O, well for the fisherman's boy,
    That he shouts with his sister at play!
O, well for the sailor lad,
    That he sings in his boat on the bay!

And the stately ships go on
    To their haven under the hill;
But O for the touch of a vanished hand,
    And the sound of a voice that is still!

9. George Balanchine (1904–1983), Russian-born ballet choreographer and teacher.   1. According to Jonah 4, Jonah sat in gloom near Nineveh after its residents repented and God decided to spare the city from destruction.

Break, break, break,
　　At the foot of thy crags, O Sea!
But the tender grace of a day that is dead   15
　　Will never come back to me.

ca. 1834

BEN JONSON

Slow, Slow, Fresh Fount[2]

Slow, slow, fresh fount, keep time with my salt tears;
Yet slower, yet, O faintly, gentle springs!
List to the heavy part the music bears.
Woe weeps out her division,[3] when she sings.
　　Droop herbs and flowers;   5
　　Fall grief in showers;
　　Our beauties are not ours.
　　　　O, I could still,
Like melting snow upon some craggy hill,
　　Drop, drop, drop, drop,   10
Since nature's pride is now a withered daffodil.   1600

THOMAS NASHE

A Litany in Time of Plague

　　Adieu, farewell, earth's bliss;
　　This world uncertain is;
　　Fond[4] are life's lustful joys;
　　Death proves them all but toys;[5]
　　None from his darts can fly;   5
　　I am sick, I must die.
　　　　Lord, have mercy on us!

　　Rich men, trust not in wealth,
　　Gold cannot buy you health;
　　Physic himself must fade.   10
　　All things to end are made,
　　The plague full swift goes by;

---

2. This lyric, from Jonson's play *Cynthia's Revels,* is a lament sung by Echo for Narcissus, who was entranced by his own reflection and ultimately transformed into a flower.　　3. Grief at parting, but also a rapid melodic passage of music.　　4. Foolish.　　5. Trifles.

I am sick, I must die.
    Lord, have mercy on us!

15 Beauty is but a flower
Which wrinkles will devour;
Brightness falls from the air;
Queens have died young and fair;
Dust hath closed Helen's eye.
20 I am sick, I must die.
    Lord, have mercy on us!

Strength stoops unto the grave,
Worms feed on Hector brave;
Swords may not fight with fate,
25 Earth still holds ope her gate.
"Come, come!" the bells do cry.
I am sick, I must die.
    Lord, have mercy on us.

Wit with his wantonness
30 Tasteth death's bitterness;
Hell's executioner
Hath no ears for to hear
What vain art can reply.
I am sick, I must die.
35   Lord, have mercy on us.

Haste, therefore, each degree,
To welcome destiny;
Heaven is our heritage,
Earth but a player's stage;
40 Mount we unto the sky.
I am sick, I must die.
    Lord, have mercy on us.   1600

STEVIE SMITH

Our Bog is Dood

Our Bog is dood, our Bog is dood,
They lisped in accents mild,
But when I asked them to explain
They grew a little wild.
5 How do you know your Bog is dood
My darling little child?

We know because we wish it so
That is enough, they cried,
And straight within each infant eye

Stood up the flame of pride,   10
And if you do not think it so
You shall be crucified.

Then tell me, darling little ones,
What's dood, suppose Bog is?
Just what we think, the answer came,   15
Just what we think it is.
They bowed their heads. Our Bog is ours
And we are wholly his.

But when they raised them up again
They had forgotten me   20
Each one upon each other glared
In pride and misery
For what was dood, and what their Bog
They never could agree.

Oh sweet it was to leave them then,   25
And sweeter not to see,
And sweetest of all to walk alone
Beside the encroaching sea,
The sea that soon should drown them all,
That never yet drowned me.   1950   30

LEWIS CARROLL

Jabberwocky[6]

'Twas brillig, and the slithy toves
    Did gyre and gimble in the wabe;
All mimsy were the borogoves,
        And the mome raths outgrabe.

"Beware the Jabberwock, my son!   5
    The jaws that bite, the claws that catch!
Beware the Jubjub bird, and shun
        The frumious Bandersnatch!"

He took his vorpal sword in hand:
    Long time the manxome foe he sought—   10
So rested he by the Tumtum tree,
        And stood awhile in thought.

---

6. Of the "hard words" in this poem, Carroll wrote: "Humpty-Dumpty's theory, of two meanings packed into one word like a portmanteau, seems to me the right explanation for all. For instance, take the two words 'fuming' and 'furious.' Make up your mind that you will say both words, but leave it unsettled which you will say first. . . . If you have that rarest of gifts, a perfectly balanced mind, you will say "frumious.'"

And as in uffish thought he stood,
  The Jabberwock, with eyes of flame,
Came whiffling through the tulgey wood,
    And burbled as it came!

One, two! One, two! And through and through
  The vorpal blade went snicker-snack!
He left it dead, and with its head
    He went galumphing back.

"And hast thou slain the Jabberwock?
  Come to my arms, my beamish boy!
O frabjous day! Callooh! Callay!"
    He chortled in his joy.

'Twas brillig, and the slithy toves
  Did gyre and gimble in the wabe;
All mimsy were the borogoves,
    And the mome raths outgrabe.   1871

DONALD JUSTICE

Counting the Mad

This one was put in a jacket,
This one was sent home,
This one was given bread and meat
But would eat none,
And this one cried No No No No
All day long.

This one looked at the window
As though it were a wall,
This one saw things that were not there,
This one things that were,
And this one cried No No No No
All day long.

This one thought himself a bird,
This one a dog,
And this one thought himself a man,
An ordinary man,
And cried and cried No No No No
All day long.   1960

EDGAR ALLAN POE

The Raven

Once upon a midnight dreary, while I pondered, weak and weary,
Over many a quaint and curious volume of forgotten lore,
While I nodded, nearly napping, suddenly there came a tapping,
As of some one gently rapping, rapping at my chamber door.
" 'Tis some visitor," I muttered, "tapping at my chamber door—   5
         Only this, and nothing more."

Ah, distinctly I remember it was in the bleak December,
And each separate dying ember wrought its ghost upon the floor.
Eagerly I wished the morrow;—vainly I had sought to borrow
From my books surcease of sorrow—sorrow for the lost Lenore—   10
For the rare and radiant maiden whom the angels name Lenore—
         Nameless here for evermore.

And the silken sad uncertain rustling of each purple curtain
Thrilled me—filled me with fantastic terrors never felt before;
So that now, to still the beating of my heart, I stood repeating   15
" 'Tis some visitor entreating entrance at my chamber door;—
Some late visitor entreating entrance at my chamber door;
         This it is, and nothing more."

Presently my soul grew stronger; hesitating then no longer,
"Sir," said I, "or Madam, truly your forgiveness I implore;   20
But the fact is I was napping, and so gently you came rapping,
And so faintly you came tapping, tapping at my chamber door,
That I scarce was sure I heard you"—here I opened wide the door;—
         Darkness there, and nothing more.

Deep into that darkness peering, long I stood there wondering, fearing,   25
Doubting, dreaming dreams no mortal ever dared to dream before;
But the silence was unbroken, and the darkness gave no token,
And the only word there spoken was the whispered word, "Lenore!"
This I whispered, and an echo murmured back the word, "Lenore!"—
         Merely this, and nothing more.   30

Back into the chamber turning, all my soul within me burning,
Soon I heard again a tapping somewhat louder than before.
"Surely," said I, "surely that is something at my window lattice;
Let me see, then, what thereat is, and this mystery explore—
Let my heart be still a moment and this mystery explore;—   35
         'Tis the wind and nothing more!"

Open here I flung the shutter, when, with many a flirt and flutter,
In there stepped a stately raven of the saintly days of yore;
Not the least obeisance made he; not an instant stopped or stayed he;
But, with mien of lord or lady, perched above my chamber door—   40

Perched upon a bust of Pallas[7] just above my chamber door—
Perched, and sat, and nothing more.

Then this ebony bird beguiling my sad fancy into smiling,
By the grave and stern decorum of the countenance it wore,
45   "Though thy crest be shorn and shaven, thou," I said, "art sure no craven,
Ghastly grim and ancient raven wandering from the Nightly shore—
Tell me what thy lordly name is on the Night's Plutonian shore!"
Quoth the raven, "Nevermore."

Much I marvelled this ungainly fowl to hear discourse so plainly,
50   Though its answer little meaning—little relevancy bore,
For we cannot help agreeing that no living human being
Ever yet was blessed with seeing bird above his chamber door—
Bird or beast upon the sculptured bust above his chamber door,
With such name as "Nevermore."

But the raven, sitting lonely on the placid bust, spoke only
55   That one word, as if his soul in that one word he did outpour.
Nothing farther then he uttered—not a feather then he fluttered—
Till I scarcely more than muttered "Other friends have flown before—
On the morrow *he* will leave me, as my hopes have flown before."
60   Then the bird said "Nevermore."

Startled at the stillness broken by reply so aptly spoken,
"Doubtless," said I, "what it utters is its only stock and store
Caught from some unhappy master whom unmerciful Disaster
Followed fast and followed faster till his songs one burden bore—
65   Till the dirges of his Hope that melancholy burden bore
Of 'Never—nevermore.'"

But the raven still beguiling all my sad soul into smiling,
Straight I wheeled a cushioned seat in front of bird and bust and door;
Then, upon the velvet sinking, I betook myself to linking
70   Fancy unto fancy, thinking what this ominous bird of yore—
What this grim, ungainly, ghastly, gaunt, and ominous bird of yore
Meant in croaking "Nevermore."

This I sat engaged in guessing, but no syllable expressing
To the fowl whose fiery eyes now burned into my bosom's core;
75   This and more I sat divining, with my head at ease reclining
On the cushion's velvet lining that the lamplight gloated o'er,
But whose velvet violet lining with the lamplight gloating o'er,
She shall press, ah, nevermore!

Then, methought, the air grew denser, perfumed from an unseen censer
80   Swung by angels whose faint foot-falls tinkled on the tufted floor.
"Wretch," I cried, "thy God hath lent thee—by these angels he hath sent thee

---

7. Athena, the Greek goddess of wisdom.

Respite—respite and nepenthe[8] from thy memories of Lenore!
Quaff, oh quaff this kind nepenthe and forget this lost Lenore!"
           Quoth the raven, "Nevermore."

"Prophet!" said I, "thing of evil!—prophet still, if bird or devil!—   85
Whether Tempter sent, or whether tempest tossed thee here ashore,
Desolate, yet all undaunted, on this desert land enchanted—
On this home by Horror haunted—tell me truly, I implore—
Is there—*is* there balm in Gilead?[9]—tell me—tell me, I implore!"
           Quoth the raven, "Nevermore."   90

"Prophet!" said I, "thing of evil—prophet still, if bird or devil!
by that Heaven that bends above us—by that God we both adore—
Tell this soul with sorrow laden if, within the distant Aidenn,
It shall clasp a sainted maiden whom the angels name Lenore—
Clasp a rare and radiant maiden whom the angels name Lenore."   95
           Quoth the raven, "Nevermore."

"Be that word our sign of parting, bird or fiend!" I shrieked upstarting—
"Get thee back into the tempest and the Night's Plutonian shore!
Leave no black plume as a token of that lie thy soul hath spoken!
Leave my loneliness unbroken!—quit the bust above my door!   100
Take thy beak from out my heart, and take thy form from off my door!"
           Quoth the raven, "Nevermore."

And the raven, never flitting, still is sitting, still is sitting
On the pallid bust of Pallas just above my chamber door;
And his eyes have all the seeming of a demon's that is dreaming,   105
And the lamp-light o'er him streaming throws his shadow on the floor;
And my soul from out that shadow that lies floating on the floor
           Shall be lifted—nevermore!   1844

GERARD MANLEY HOPKINS

Spring and Fall:

to a young child

Márgarét áre you gríeving
Over Goldengrove unleaving?
Leáves, like the things of man, you
With your fresh thoughts care for, can you?
Áh! ás the heart grows older   5
It will come to such sights colder
By and by, nor spare a sigh

8. A drug reputed by the Greeks to cause forgetfulness or sorrow.   9. Cf. Jeremiah 8:22.

Though worlds of wanwood leafmeal[1] lie;
And yet you will weep and know why.
Now no matter, child, the name:
Sórrow's spríngs áre the same.
Nor mouth had, no nor mind, expressed
What heart heard of, ghost[2] guessed:
It ís the blight man was born for,
It is Margaret you mourn for.

10

15   1880

JUDITH WRIGHT

"Dove-Love"

The dove purrs—over and over the dove
purrs its declaration. The wind's tone
changes from tree to tree, the creek on stone
alters its sob and fall, but still the dove
goes insistently on, telling its love
        "I could eat you."

And in captivity, they say, doves do.
Gentle, methodical, starting with the feet
(the ham-pink succulent toes
on their thin stems of rose),
baring feather by feather the wincing meat:
        "I could eat you."

That neat suburban head, that suit of grey,
watchful conventional eye and manicured claw—
these also rhyme with us. The doves play
on one repetitive note that plucks the raw
helpless nerve, their soft "I do. I do.
        I could eat you."

1962

MARGE PIERCY

To Have Without Holding

Learning to love differently is hard,
love with the hands wide open, love
with the doors banging on their hinges,
the cupboard unlocked, the wind
roaring and whimpering in the rooms
rustling the sheets and snapping the blinds

5

1. Broken up, leaf by leaf (analogous to "piecemeal"). *Wanwood*: pale, gloomy woods.   2. Soul.

that thwack like rubber bands
in an open palm.

It hurts to love wide open
stretching the muscles that feel   10
as if they are made of wet plaster,
then of blunt knives, then
of sharp knives.

It hurts to thwart the reflexes
of grab, of clutch; to love and let   15
go again and again. It pesters to remember
the lover who is not in the bed,
to hold back what is owed to the work
that gutters like a candle in a cave
without air, to love consciously,   20
conscientiously, concretely, constructively.

I can't do it, you say it's killing
me, but you thrive, you glow
on the street like a neon raspberry,
You float and sail, a helium balloon   25
bright bachelor's button blue and bobbing
on the cold and hot winds of our breath,
as we make and unmake in passionate
diastole and systole the rhythm
of our unbound bonding, to have   30
and not to hold, to love
with minimized malice, hunger
and anger moment by moment balanced.   1980

IRVING LAYTON

The Way the World Ends

Before me on the dancestand
A god's vomit or damned by his decrees
The excited twitching couples shook and
Wriggled like giant parentheses.

A pallid Canadienne   5
Raised a finger and wetted her lip,
and echoing the nickelodeon
'Chip,' she breathed drowsily, 'Chip, chip.'

Aroused, her slavish partner
Smiled, showed his dentures through sodapop gas,   10
And 'chip' he said right back to her
And 'chip, chip' she said and shook her ass.

Denture to denture, 'Pas mal'[3]
They whispered and were glad, jerked to and fro:
Their distorted bodies like bits of steel
Controlled by that throbbing dynamo.

They stomped, flung out their arms, groaned;
And in a flash I saw the cosmos end
And last of all the black night cover this:
'Chip, chip' and a shake of the ass.

1956

EMILY DICKINSON

[A narrow Fellow in the Grass]

A narrow Fellow in the Grass
Occasionally rides—
You may have met Him—did you not
His notice sudden is—

The Grass divides as with a Comb—
A spotted shaft is seen—
And then it closes at your feet
And opens further on—

He likes a Boggy Acre
A Floor too cool for Corn—
Yet when a Boy, and Barefoot—
I more than once at Noon

Have passed, I thought, a Whip lash
Unbraiding in the Sun
When stooping to secure it
It wrinkled, and was gone—

Several of Nature's People
I know, and they know me—
I feel for them a transport
Of cordiality—

But never met this Fellow
Attended, or alone
Without a tighter breathing
And Zero at the Bone—

1866

3. Not bad (French).

ROBERT HERRICK

To the Virgins, to Make Much of Time

Gather ye rosebuds while ye may,
　Old time is still a-flying;
And this same flower that smiles today
　Tomorrow will be dying.

The glorious lamp of heaven, the sun,　　　　　　5
　The higher he's a-getting,
The sooner will his race be run,
　And nearer he's to setting.

That age is best which is the first,
　When youth and blood are warmer;　　　　　　10
But being spent, the worse, and worst
　Times still succeed the former.

Then be not coy, but use your time,
　And, while ye may, go marry;
For, having lost but once your prime,　　　　　　15
　You may forever tarry.　　　　　　　　　1648

JEAN TOOMER

Reapers

Black reapers with the sound of steel on stones
Are sharpening scythes. I see them place the hones[4]
In their hip-pockets as a thing that's done,
And start their silent swinging, one by one.
Black horses drive a mower through the weeds　　　5
And there, a field rat, startled, squealing bleeds.
His belly close to ground. I see the blade,
Blood-stained, continue cutting weeds and shade.　　1923

▼　▼　▼

4. Instruments for sharpening blades.

THE SOUNDS OF POETRY A Glossary

anapestic: two unstressed syllables followed by a stressed one
dactylic: a stressed syllable followed by two unstressed ones
iambic: an unstressed syllable followed by a stressed one
onamatopoeia: a word capturing or approximating the sound of what it describes
trochaic: a stressed syllable followed by an unstressed one

QUESTIONS

1. Read "Persimmons" (p. 22) and Galway Kinnell's "Blackberry Eating" (p. 469), and compare their sound effects with those in "The Word *Plum.*" How visual an image does each poem create? To what purposes does Li-Young Lee put the visual qualities of the persimmon? Which other of the five senses are evoked in each poem? to what specific purpose?

2. Read the following poems aloud: "Break, Break, Break," "A Litany in Time of Plague," and "The Raven." As you read each, try to be especially conscious of the way punctuation and spacing guide your pauses and of the pace you develop as you become accustomed to the prevailing rhythms of the poem.

3. Scan—that is, mark all of the stressed syllables and chart their pattern— "Like as the waves make towards the pebbled shore." What variations do you find on the basic iambic pentameter pattern? What functions do the variations perform in each case?

4. Read "To the Virgins, to Make Much of Time" aloud. Then have some-one else read it aloud to you. Compare the *pace* of the readings. Compare the stress on particular words and syllables. To what extent does the basic metrical pattern in the poem come to control the voice? Do you notice more similari-ties in the two readings as you and the other reader progress through the poem? why?

WRITING SUGGESTIONS

1. Read "Sound and Sense" over carefully twice—once silently and once aloud—and then mark the stressed and unstressed syllables. Draw up a chart indicating, line by line, exactly what the patterns of stress are, and then single out all the lines that have major variations from the basic iambic pentameter pattern. Pick out half a dozen lines with variations that seem to you worthy of comment, and write a paragraph on each in which you show how the metrical pattern contributes to the specific effects achieved in that line. (You will probably notice that in most of the lines other strategies also contribute to the sound effects, but confine your discussion to the achievement through metrical pattern.)

2. Try your hand at writing limericks in imitation of "A staid schizophrenic named Struther" (study the rhythmic patterns and line lengths carefully, and imitate them exactly in your poem). Begin your limerick with "There once was a ———— named ————" (use a name for which you think you can find a comic rhyme).

3. Scan line by line Suckling's "Song." In an essay of no more than 500 words, show in detail how the varied metrical pattern in the final stanza abruptly changes the tone of the poem and reverses the poem's direction.

4. Read "Anglosaxon Street" (p. 262) aloud. Then go through the poem line by line and pick out half a dozen words and patterns of sound that seem to you especially effective in creating vocal effects. Analyze carefully the effects created by each of these words or word groups, and try to account for exactly how the passage works. Then, using these examples as the primary (though not necessarily the exclusive) basis, write a three-page paper on the uses of sound in the poem.

6 INTERNAL STRUCTURE

P roper words in proper places": that is the way one great writer of English prose (Jonathan Swift) described good writing. Finding appropriate words is not the easiest of tasks for a poet, and already we have looked at some of the implications for readers of the verbal choices a poet makes. But a poet's decision about where to put those words—how to arrange them for maximum effect—is also difficult, for individual words, metaphors, and symbols not only exist as part of a phrase or sentence or rhythmic pattern but also as part of the larger whole of the poem itself. How are the words to be ordered and the poem organized? What will come first and what last? What will be its "plot"? How will it be conceived as a whole? How is some sort of structure to be created? What principle or idea of organization will inform the poem? How are words, sentences, images, ideas, and feelings to be put together into something that holds together, seems complete, and will have a certain effect upon us as readers?

Looking at these questions from the point of view of the poet (What shall I plan? Where shall I begin?) can help the reader notice the effect of structural decisions. Every poem is different from every other one, and independent, individual decisions must therefore be made about how to organize. But there are also patterns of organization that poems fall into, sometimes because of the subject matter, sometimes because of the effect intended, sometimes for other reasons. Often poets consciously decide on a particular organizational strategy; sometimes they may reach instinctively for one or happen into a structure that suits the needs of the moment, one onto which a creator can hang the words and sentences one by one and group by group.

When there is a story to be told, the organization of a poem may be fairly simple. Here, for example, is a poem that tells a fairly simple story, largely in chronological fashion (first . . . and then . . .):

EDWIN ARLINGTON ROBINSON

Mr. Flood's Party

Old Eben Flood, climbing alone one night
Over the hill between the town below
And the forsaken upland hermitage

That held as much as he should ever know
On earth again of home, paused warily.   5
The road was his and not a native near;
And Eben, having leisure, said aloud,
For no man else in Tilbury Town to hear:

"Well, Mr. Flood, we have the harvest moon
Again, and we may not have many more;   10
The bird is on the wing, the poet says,[1]
And you and I have said it here before.
Drink to the bird." He raised up to the light
The jug that he had gone so far to fill,
And answered huskily: "Well, Mr. Flood,   15
Since you propose it, I believe I will."

Alone, as if enduring to the end
A valiant armor of scarred hopes outworn
He stood there in the middle of the road
Like Roland's ghost winding a silent horn.[2]   20
Below him, in the town among the trees,
Where friends of other days had honored him,
A phantom salutation of the dead
Rang thinly till old Eben's eyes were dim

Then, as a mother lays her sleeping child   25
Down tenderly, fearing it may awake
He set the jug down slowly at his feet
With trembling care, knowing that most things break;
And only when assured that on firm earth
It stood, as the uncertain lives of men   30
Assuredly did not, he paced away,
And with his hand extended paused again:

"Well, Mr. Flood, we have not met like this
In a long time; and many a change has come
To both of us, I fear, since last it was   35
We had a drop together. Welcome home!"
Convivially returning with himself,
Again he raised the jug up to the light;
And with an acquiescent quaver said:
"Well, Mr. Flood, if you insist, I might.   40

"Only a very little, Mr. Flood—
For auld lang syne. No more, sir; that will do."
So, for the time, apparently it did,
And Eben evidently thought so too;
For soon amid the silver loneliness   45

1. Edward Fitzgerald, in "The Rubáiyat of Omar Khayyám" (more or less a translation of an Arab original), so describes the "Bird of Time."   2. In French legend Roland's powerful ivory horn was used to warn his allies of impending attack.

Of night he lifted up his voice and sang,
Secure, with only two moons listening,
Until the whole harmonious landscape rang—

50 "For auld lang syne." The weary throat gave out,
The last word wavered, and the song was done.
He raised again the jug regretfully
And shook his head, and was again alone.
There was not much that was ahead of him,
And there was nothing in the town below—
55 Where strangers would have shut the many doors
That many friends had opened long ago.   1921

The fairly simple **narrative structure** here is based on the gradual unfolding of the story. Old Eben is introduced and "placed" in relation to the town and his home, and then the "plot" unfolds: he sits down in the road, reviews his life, reflects on the present, and has a drink. Several drinks, in fact, as he thinks about passing time and growing old; and he sings and considers going "home." Not much happens really: what we get is a vignette of Mr. Flood between two places and two times, but there *is* action, and the poem's movement—its organization and structure—depends on it: Mr. Flood in motion, in stasis, and then, again, contemplating motion. Here is story, and chronological movement, such as it is. You could say that a narrative of sort takes place (rather like that in "Cherrylog Road" [p. 87]), though sparely. The poem's organization—its structural principle—involves the passing of time, action moving forward, a larger story being revealed by the few moments depicted here.

"Mr. Flood's Party" presents about as much story as a short poem ever does, but as with most poems the emphasis is not really on the developing action— which all seems fairly predictable once we "get" who Eben is, how old he is, and what "position" he occupies in the communal memory of Tilbury Town and vice versa. Rather, the movement forward in time dictates the shape of the poem, determines the way it presents its images, ideas, themes. There's an easy-to-follow chronology here, and nearly everything takes place within it: you could say that a story is told—with a beginning, middle, and end—and that time structures how the revelation of facts takes place.

But even here, in one of the most simple of narrative structures, there are complications to be noted. One complication is in the use of time itself, for "old" time and "present" time seem posed against each other as a structural principle too, one in tension with the chronological movement: Eben's past, as contrasted with his present and limited future, focuses the poem's attention, and in some ways the contrast between what was and what is seems even more important than the brief movement through present time that gets the most obvious attention in the poem. Then, too, "character"—Eben's character and that of the townspeople of later generations—gets a lot of the poem's attention, even as the chronology moves forward. More than one structural principle is at work here. We may identify the main movement of the poem as chronological and its principal structure as narrative, but to be fair and full in our discussion we have to note several other competing organizational forces at work, principles of comparison and contrast, for example, and of descriptive elaboration.

Most poems work with this kind of complexity, and identifying a single structure behind any poem involves a sense of what kind of organizational principle makes it work—while at the same time recognizing that other principles repeatedly, perhaps continually, compete for our attention. A poem's *structure* involves its conceptual framework—what principle best explains its organization and movement—and it is often useful to identify one particular structure that gives the poem its shape. But it is well to recognize from the start that most poems follow paradigmatic models loosely. As with other "elements" of a poem, finding an appropriate label to describe the structure of a particular poem can help in analyzing the poem's other aspects, but there is nothing magic in the label itself.

Purely narrative poems are often very long, much longer than can be included in a book like this, and often there are many features that are not, strictly speaking, closely connected to the narrative or linked to a strict chronology. Very often a poem moves on from a narrative of an event to some sort of commentary or reflection upon it, as in "Auto Wreck" (p. 220). Reflection can be included along the way or may be implicit in the way the story is narrated, as in "Woodchucks" (p. 36), where our major attention is more on the narrator and her responses than on the events in the story as such.

Just as poems sometimes take on a structure rather like that of a story, they sometimes borrow the structures of plays. The following poem has a **dramatic structure**; it consists of a series of scenes, each of which is presented vividly and in detail:

HOWARD NEMEROV

The Goose Fish

On the long shore, lit by the moon
To show them properly alone,

Two lovers suddenly embraced
So that their shadows were as one.
The ordinary night was graced
For them by the swift tide of blood
That silently they took at flood.
And for a little time they prized
    Themselves emparadised.

Then, as if shaken by stage-fright
Beneath the hard moon's bony light,
They stood together on the sand
Embarrassed in each other's sight
But still conspiring hand in hand,
Until they saw, there underfoot,
As though the world had found them out,
The goose fish turning up, though dead,
    His hugely grinning head.

There in the china light he lay,
Most ancient and corrupt and gray.
They hesitated at his smile,
Wondering what it seemed to say
To lovers who a little while
Before had thought to understand,
By violence upon the sand,
The only way that could be known
    To make a world their own.

It was a wide and moony grin
Together peaceful and obscene;
They knew not what he would express,
So finished a comedian
He might mean failure or success,
But took it for an emblem of
Their sudden, new and guilty love
To be observed by, when they kissed,
    That rigid optimist.

So he became their patriarch,
Dreadfully mild in the half-dark.
His throat that the sand seemed to choke,
His picket teeth, these left their mark
But never did explain the joke
That so amused him, lying there
While the moon went down to disappear
Along the still and tilted track
    That bears the zodiac.

1955

The first stanza sets the scene—a sandy shore in moonlight—and presents, in fact, the major action of the poem. The rest of the poem dramatizes the lovers' reactions: their initial embarrassment and feelings of guilt (stanza 2), their attempt to interpret the goose fish's smile (stanza 3), their decision to make him, whatever his meaning, the "emblem" of their love (stanza 4), and their acceptance of the fish's ambiguity and of their own relationship (stanza 5). The five stanzas do not exactly present five different scenes, but they do present separate dramatic moments, even if only a few minutes apart. Almost like a play of five very short acts, the poem traces the drama of the lovers' discovery of themselves, of their coming to terms with the meaning of their action. As in many plays, the central event (their love-making) is not the central focus of the drama, although the drama is based upon that event and could not take place without it. Here, that event is depicted only briefly but very vividly through figurative language: "they took at flood" the "swift tide of blood," and the immediate effect is to make them briefly feel "emparadised." But the poem concentrates on their later reactions, not on the act of love itself.

Their sudden discovery of the fish is a rude shock and injects a grotesque, almost macabre note into the poem. From a vision of paradise, the poem seems for a moment to turn toward a gothic horror story when the lovers discover that they have, after all, been seen—and by such a ghoulish spectator. The last three stanzas gradually re-create the intruder in their minds, as they are forced to admit that their act of love does not exist in isolation as they had at first hoped, and they begin to see it as part of a continuum, as part of their relationship to the larger world, even (at the end) putting it into the context of the rotating world and its seasons as the moon disappears into its zodiac. In retrospect, we can see that even at the moment of passion they were in touch with larger processes controlled by the presiding mood (the "swift tide of blood"), but neither the lovers nor we had understood their act as such then, and the poem is about their gradual recognition of their "place" in time and space.

Stages of feeling and knowing rather than specific visual scenes are responsible for the poem's progress, and its dramatic structure depends upon internal perceptions and internal states of mind rather than dialogue and events. Visualization and images help to organize the poem too. Notice in particular how the two most striking visual features of the poem—the fish and the moon—are presented stanza by stanza. In stanza 1, the fish is not yet noticed, and the moon exists plain; it is only mentioned, not described, and its light serves as a stage spotlight to assure not center-stage attention, but rather total privacy: it is a kind of lookout for the lovers. The stage imagery, barely suggested by the light in stanza 1, is articulated in stanza 2, and there the moon is said to be "hard" and its light "bony'"; its features have characteristics that seem more appropriate to the fish, which has now become visible. In stanza 3, the moon's light has come to seem fragile ("china") as it is said to expose the fish directly; the role of the moon as lookout and protector seems abandoned, or at least endangered. No moon appears in stanza 4, but the fish's grin is described as "wide and moony," almost as if the two onlookers, one earthly and dead, the other heavenly and eternal, had become merged in the poem, as they nearly had been by the imagery in stanza 2. And by stanza 5, the fish has become a friend—by now he is a comedian, optimist, emblem, and a patriarch of their love—and his new position in collaboration with the lovers is presided over by the moon going about its eternal business. The moon has provided the stage light for the poem and the means by which not only the fish but the meaning of the lovers' act has been discovered. The moon has also helped to organize the poem, partly as a dramatic accessory, partly as imagery.

The following poem is also dramatic, but it seems to represent a composite of several similar experiences (compare Blake's "London" [p. 34] and Dickey's "Cherrylog Road" [p. 87]) rather than a single event—a fairly common pattern in dramatic poems:

PHILIP LARKIN

Church Going

Once I am sure there's nothing going on
I step inside, letting the door thud shut.
Another church: matting, seats, and stone,
And little books; sprawlings of flowers, cut
For Sunday, brownish now; some brass and stuff
Up at the holy end; the small neat organ;
And a tense, musty, unignorable silence,
Brewed God knows how long. Hatless, I take off
My cycle-clips in awkward reverence,

Move forward, run my hand around the font.
From where I stand, the roof looks almost new—
Cleaned, or restored? Someone would know: I don't.
Mounting the lectern, I peruse a few
Hectoring large-scale verses, and pronounce
"Here endeth" much more loudly than I'd meant.
The echoes snigger briefly. Back at the door
I sign the book, donate an Irish sixpence,
Reflect the place was not worth stopping for.

Yet stop I did: in fact I often do,
And always end much at a loss like this,   20
Wondering what to look for; wondering, too,
When churches fall completely out of use
What we shall turn them into, if we shall keep
A few cathedrals chronically on show,
Their parchment, plate and pyx in locked cases,   25
And let the rest rent-free to rain and sheep.
Shall we avoid them as unlucky places?

Or, after dark, will dubious women come
To make their children touch a particular stone;
Pick simples³ for a cancer; or on some   30
Advised night see walking a dead one?
Power of some sort or other will go on
In games, in riddles, seemingly at random;
But superstition, like belief, must die,
And what remains when disbelief has gone?   35
Grass, weedy pavement, brambles, buttress, sky,

A shape less recognizable each week,
A purpose more obscure. I wonder who
Will be the last, the very last, to seek
This place for what it was; one of the crew   40
That tap and jot and know what rood-lofts⁴ were?
Some ruin-bibber,⁵ randy for antique,
Or Christmas-addict, counting on a whiff
Of gown-and-bands and organ-pipes and myrrh?
Or will he be my representative,   45

Bored, uninformed, knowing the ghostly silt
Dispersed, yet tending to this cross of ground
Through suburb scrub because it held unspilt
So long and equably what since is found
Only in separation—marriage, and birth,   50
And death, and thoughts of these—for whom was built
This special shell? For, though I've no idea
What this accoutered frowsty barn is worth,
It pleases me to stand in silence here;

A serious house on serious earth it is,   55
In whose blent air all our compulsions meet,
Are recognized, and robed as destinies.
And that much never can be obsolete,
Since someone will forever be surprising
A hunger in himself to be more serious,   60

3. Medicinal herbs.   4. Galleries atop the screens (on which crosses are mounted) that divide
the naves or main bodies of churches from the choirs or chancels.   5. Literally, ruin-drinker:
someone extremely attracted to antiquarian objects.

And gravitating with it to this ground,
Which, he once heard, was proper to grow wise in,
If only that so many dead lie round.   1955

Ultimately, the poem's emphasis is upon what it means to visit churches, what sort of phenomenon church buildings represent, and what is to be made of the fact that "church going" (in the usual sense of the word) has declined so much. The poem uses a *different* sort of church going (visitation by tourists) to consider larger philosophical questions about the relationship of religion to culture and history. The poem is, finally, a rather philosophical one about the directions of English culture, and through an enumeration of religious objects and rituals it reviews the history of how we got to our present historical circumstance. It tells a kind of story first, through one lengthy dramatized scene, in order to comment later on what the place and the experience may mean, and the larger conclusion derives from the particulars of what the speaker does and touches. The action is really over by the end of stanza 2, and that action, we are told, stands for many such visits to similar churches; after that, all is reflection and discussion, five stanzas' worth.

"Church Going" is a curious poem in many ways. It goes to a lot of trouble to characterize its speaker, who seems a rather odd choice as a commentator on the state of religion. His informal attire (he takes off his cycle-clips at the end of stanza 1) and his not exactly worshipful behavior do not at first make us expect him to be a serious philosopher about what all this means. He is not disrespectful or sacrilegious, and before the end of stanza 1 he has tried to describe the "awkward reverence" he feels, but his overly somber imitation of part of the service stamps him as playful, a little satirical, and as a tourist here, not someone who regularly drops in for prayer or meditation in the usual sense. And yet those early details do give him credentials, in a way; he clearly knows the names of religious objects and has some of the history of churches in his grasp. Clearly he does this sort of church going often ("Yet stop I did; in fact I often do," line 19) because he wonders seriously what it all means— now—in comparison to what it meant to religious worshipers in times past. Ultimately, he takes the church itself seriously and its cultural meaning and function just as seriously (lines 55ff.), and understands the importance of the church in the history of his culture. In this poem, the drama is, relatively speaking, brief, but it gives a context for the more digressive and rambling freefloating reflections that grow out of the dramatic experience.

Sometimes poems are organized by contrasts, setting one thing up conveniently against another that is quite different. Look, for example, at the two worlds in the following poem, and notice how carefully the contrasts between the two worlds are developed.

PAT MORA

Sonrisas

I live in a doorway
between two rooms, I hear
quiet clicks, cups of black
coffee, *click, click* like facts
    budgets, tenure, curriculum,   5
from careful women in crisp beige
suits, quick beige smiles
that seldom sneak into their eyes.

I peek
in the other room señoras   10
in faded dresses stir sweet
milk coffee, laughter whirls
with steam from fresh *tamales*
    sh, sh, mucho ruido,[6]
they scold one another,   15
press their lips, trap smiles
in their dark, Mexican eyes.   1986

Here different words, habits, and values characterize the different worlds of the two sets of characters, and the poem is largely organized on the basis of the contrasts between them. The meaning of the poem (the difference between the two worlds) is very nearly the same as the structure itself.

Poems often have **discursive structures** too; that is, they are sometimes organized like a treatise, an argument, or an essay. "First," they say, "and second . . . and third. . . ." This sort of 1-2-3 structure takes a variety of forms depending on what one is enumerating or arguing. Here, for example, is a poem that is about three people who have died. The poem honors all three, but makes clear and sharp distinctions between them. As you read the poem, try to articulate just what sort of person each of the three is represented to be.

6. A lot of noise.

JAMES WRIGHT

Arrangements with Earth for
Three Dead Friends

Sweet earth, he ran and changed his shoes to go
Outside with other children through the fields.
He panted up the hills and swung from trees
Wild as a beast but for the human laughter
5   That tumbled like a cider down his cheeks.
Sweet earth, the summer has been gone for weeks,
And weary fish already sleeping under water
Below the banks where early acorns freeze.
Receive his flesh and keep it cured of colds.
10 Button his coat and scarf his throat from snow.

And now, bright earth, this other is out of place
In what, awake, we speak about as tombs.
He sang in houses when the birds were still
And friends of his were huddled round till dawn
15 After the many nights to hear him sing.
Bright earth, his friends remember how he sang
Voices of night away when wind was one.
Lonely the neighborhood beneath your hill
Where he is waved away through silent rooms.
20 Listen for music, earth, and human ways.

Dark earth, there is another gone away,
But she was not inclined to beg of you
Relief from water falling or the storm.
She was aware of scavengers in holes
25 Of stone, she knew the loosened stones that fell
Indifferently as pebbles plunging down a well
And broke for the sake of nothing human souls.
Earth, hide your face from her where dark is warm.
She does not beg for anything, who knew
30 The change of tone, the human hope gone gray.   1957

Why, in stanza 1, is the earth represented as a parent? What does
addressing the earth here as "sweet" seem to mean? How does the address to
earth as "bright" fit the dead person described in stanza 2? In what different
senses is the person described in stanza 3 "dark"? Why is the earth asked to
give attention secretly to this person? Exactly what kind of person was she?
How does the poem make you feel about her? Is there any cumulative point in
describing three such different people in the same poem? What is accom-

plished by having the poem's three stanzas addressed to various aspects of earth? Similar discursive structures help to organize poems such as Shelley's "Ode to the West Wind" (p. 224), where the wind is shown driving a leaf in Part I, a cloud in Part II, a wave in Part III, and then, after a summary and statement of the speaker's ambitious hope in Part IV, is asked to make the speaker a lyre in Part V.

Poems may borrow their organizational strategies from many places, imitating chronological, visual, or discursive shapes in reality or in other works of art. Sometimes poems strive to be almost purely descriptive of someone or something (using **descriptive structures**), in which case organizational decisions have to be made much as a painter or photographer would make them, deciding first how the whole scene should look, then putting the parts into proper place for the whole. But there are differences demanded by the poetic medium: a poem has to present the details sequentially, not all at once as an actual picture more or less can, so the poet must decide where the description starts (at the left? center? top?) and what sort of movement to use (linear across the scene? clockwise?). But if having words instead of paint or film has some disadvantages, it also has particular assets: figurative language can be a part of description, or an adjunct to it. A poet can insert a comparison at any point without necessarily disturbing the unity of what he or she describes.

Some poems use **imitative structures,** mirroring as exactly as possible the structure of something that already exists as an object and can be seen — another poem perhaps, as in Koch's "Variations on a Theme by William Carlos Williams" (p. 376). Or a poem may use **reflective** (or **meditative) structures,** pondering a subject, theme, or event, and letting the mind play with it, skipping (sometimes illogically but still usefully) from one sound to another, or to related thoughts or objects as the mind receives them.

Here is a poem that involves several different organizational principles but ultimately takes its structure from an important emotional shift in the speaker's attitude as her mind reviews, ponders, and rethinks events of long ago.

SHARON OLDS

The Victims

When Mother divorced you, we were glad. She took it and
took it, in silence, all those years and then
kicked you out, suddenly, and her
kids loved it. Then you were fired, and we

5   grinned inside, the way people grinned when
Nixon's helicopter lifted off the South
Lawn for the last time.[7] We were tickled
to think of your office taken away,
your secretaries taken away,
10   your lunches with three double bourbons,
your pencils, your reams of paper. Would they take your
suits back, too, those dark
carcasses hung in your closet, and the black
noses of your shoes with their large pores?
15   She had taught us to take it, to hate you and take it
until we pricked with her for your
annihilation, Father. Now I
pass the bums in doorways, the white
slugs of their bodies gleaming through slits in their
20   suits of compressed silt, the stained
flippers of their hands, the underwater
fire of their eyes, ships gone down with the
lanterns lit, and I wonder who took it and
took it from them in silence until they had
25   given it all away and had nothing
left but this.   1984

"The Victims" divides basically into two parts. In the first two-thirds of the poem (from line 1 to the middle of line 17), the speaker evokes her father (the "you" of lines 1, 3, etc.), who had been guilty of terrible habits and behavior when the speaker was young and was kicked out suddenly and divorced by the speaker's mother (lines 1–3). He was then fired from his job (line 4) and lost his whole way of life (lines 8–12), and the speaker (taught by the mother, lines 15–17) recalls celebrating every defeat and every loss ("we pricked with her for your annihilation," lines 16–17). The mother is regarded as a victim ("she took it and took it, in silence, all those years" [lines 1–2]), and the speaker forms an indivisible unit with her and the other children ("her kids," lines 3–4). They are the "we" of the first part of the poem. They were "glad" (line 1) at the divorce; they "loved it" (line 4) when the mother kicked out the father; they "grinned" (line 5) when the father was fired; they were "tickled" (line 7) when he lost his job, his secretaries, and his daily life. Only at the end of the first section does the speaker (now older but remembering what it was like to be a child) recognize that the mother was responsible for the easy, childish vision of the father's guilt ("she had taught us to take it, to hate you and take it" [line

7. When Richard Nixon resigned the U.S. presidency on August 8, 1974, his exit from the White House (by helicopter from the lawn) was televised live.

15]); nevertheless, all sympathy in this part of the poem is with the mother and her children, while all of the imagery is entirely unfavorable to the father. The family reacted to the father's misfortunes the way observers responded to the retreat in disgrace of Richard Nixon from the U.S. presidency. The father seems to have led a luxurious and insensitive life, with lots of support in his office (lines 8–11), fancy clothes (lines 12–14), and decadent lunches (line 10); his artificial identity seemed haunting and daunting (lines 11–14) to the speaker as child.

But in line 17, the poem shifts focus and shifts gears. The "you" in the poem is now, suddenly, "Father." A bit of sympathy begins to surface for "bums in doorways" (line 18), who begin to seem like victims too; their bodies are "slugs" (line 19), their suits are made of residual waste pressed into regimented usefulness (lines 19–20), and their hands are constricted into mechanical "flippers" (line 21). Their eyes contain fire (line 22), but it is as if they retain only a spark of life in their submerged and dying state. The speaker has not forgotten the cruelty and insensitivity remembered in the first part of the poem, but the blame seems to have shifted somewhat and the father is not the only villain, nor are the mother and children the only victims. Look carefully at how the existence of street people recalls earlier details about the father, how sympathy for his plight is elicited from us, and how the definition of victim shifts.

Imagery, words, attitudes, and narrative are different in the two parts of the poem, and the second half carefully qualifies the first, as if to illustrate the more mature and considered attitudes of the speaker in her older years—a qualification of the easy imitation of the earlier years when the mother's views were thoroughly dominant and seemed sensible and adequate. Change has governed the poem's structure here; differences in age, attitude, and tone are supported by entirely different sets of terms, attitudes, and versions of causality.

The paradigms (or models) for organizing poems are, finally, not all that different from those of prose. It may be easier to organize something short rather than something long, but the question of intensity becomes comparatively more important in shorter works. Basically, the problem of how to organize one's material is, for the writer, first of all a matter of deciding what kind of thing one wants to create, of having its purposes and effects clearly in mind. That means that every poem will differ somewhat from every other, but it also means that patterns of purpose—narrative, dramatic, discursive, descriptive, imitative, or reflective—may help writers organize and formulate their ideas. A consciousness of purpose and effect can help the reader see *how* a poem proceeds toward its goal. Seeing how a poem is organized is, in turn, often a good way of seeing where it is going and what its real concerns and purposes may be. Often a poem's organization helps to make clear the particular effects that the poet wishes to generate. In a good poem, means and end are closely related, and a reader who is a good observer of one will be able to discover the other.

▾   ▾   ▾

ANONYMOUS

Sir Patrick Spens

The king sits in Dumferling toune,[8]
    Drinking the blude-reid[9] wine:
"O whar will I get guid sailor,
    To sail this ship of mine?"

5   Up and spake an eldern knicht,
    Sat at the king's richt knee:
"Sir Patrick Spens is the best sailor
    That sails upon the sea."

The king has written a braid[1] letter
10   And signed it wi' his hand,
And sent it to Sir Patrick Spens,
    Was walking on the sand.

The first line that Sir Patrick read,
    A loud lauch[2] lauched he;
15   The next line that Sir Patrick read,
    The tear blinded his ee.[3]

"O wha is this has done this deed,
    This il deed done to me,
To send me out this time o' the year,
20   To sail upon the sea?

"Make haste, make haste, my merry men all,
    Our guid ship sails the morn."
"O say na sae,[4] my master dear,
    For I fear a deadly storm.

25   "Late, late yestre'en I saw the new moon
    Wi' the auld moon in her arm,
And I fear, I fear, my dear mastér,
    That we will come to harm."

---

8. Town.   9. Blood-red.   1. Broad: explicit.   2. Laugh.   3. Eye.   4. Not so.

O our Scots nobles were richt laith[5]
   To weet their cork-heeled shoon,[6]
But lang owre a'[7] the play were played   30
   Their hats they swam aboon.[8]

O lang, lang, may their ladies sit,
   Wi' their fans into their hand,
Or ere they see Sir Patrick Spens   35
   Come sailing to the land.

O lang, lang, may the ladies stand
   Wi' their gold kems[9] in their hair,
Waiting for their ain[1] dear lords,
   For they'll see them na mair.   40

Half o'er, half o'er to Aberdour
   It's fifty fadom deep,
And there lies guid Sir Patrick Spens
   Wi' the Scots lords at his feet.   Probably 13th cent.

T. S. ELIOT

Journey of the Magi[2]

"A cold coming we had of it,
Just the worst time of the year
For a journey, and such a long journey:
The ways deep and the weather sharp,
The very dead of winter."[3]   5
And the camels galled, sore-footed, refractory,
Lying down in the melting snow.
There were times we regretted
The summer palaces on slopes, the terraces,
And the silken girls bringing sherbet.   10
Then the camel men cursing and grumbling
And running away, and wanting their liquor and women,
And the night-fires going out, and the lack of shelters,
And the cities hostile and the towns unfriendly
And the villages dirty and charging high prices: 15
A hard time we had of it.
At the end we preferred to travel all night,
Sleeping in snatches,
With the voices singing in our ears, saying
That this was all folly.   20

---

5. Right loath: very reluctant.   6. To wet their cork-heeled shoes. Cork was expensive, and therefore such shoes were a mark of wealth and status.   7. Before all.   8. Their hats swam above them.   9. Combs.   1. Own.   2. The wise men who followed the star of Bethlehem. See Matthew 2:1–12.   3. An adaptation of a passage from a 1622 sermon by Lancelot Andrewes.

Then at dawn we came down to a temperate valley,
Wet, below the snow line, smelling of vegetation;
With a running stream and a water-mill beating the darkness,
And three trees on the low sky,[4]
25 And an old white horse galloped away in the meadow.
Then we came to a tavern with vine-leaves over the lintel,
Six hands at an open door dicing for pieces of silver,
And feet kicking the empty wine-skins.
But there was no information, and so we continued
30 And arrived at evening, not a moment too soon
Finding the place; it was (you may say) satisfactory.

All this was a long time ago, I remember,
And I would do it again, but set down
This set down
35 This: were we led all that way for
Birth or Death? There was a Birth, certainly,
We had evidence and no doubt. I had seen birth and death,
But had thought they were different; this Birth was
Hard and bitter agony for us, like Death, our death.
40 We returned to our places, these Kingdoms,[5]
But no longer at ease here, in the old dispensation,
With an alien people clutching their gods.
I should be glad of another death.   1927

KARL SHAPIRO

Auto Wreck

Its quick soft silver bell beating, beating,
And down the dark one ruby flare
Pulsing out red light like an artery,
The ambulance at top speed floating down
5 Past beacons and illuminated clocks
Wings in a heavy curve, dips down,
And brakes speed, entering the crowd.
The doors leap open, emptying light;
Stretchers are laid out, the mangled lifted
10 And stowed into the little hospital.
Then the bell, breaking the hush, tolls once,

---

4. Suggestive of the three crosses of the Crucifixion (Luke 23:32–33). The Magi see several objects that suggest later events in Christ's life: pieces of silver (see Matthew 26:14–16), the dicing (see Matthew 27:35), the white horse (see Revelation 6:2 and 19:11–16), and the empty wine-skins (see Matthew 9:14–17, possibly relevant also to lines 41–42).   5. The Bible only identifies the wise men as "from the East," and subsequent tradition has made them kings. In Persia, magi were members of an ancient priestly caste.

And the ambulance with its terrible cargo
Rocking, slightly rocking, moves away,
As the doors, an afterthought, are closed.

We are deranged, walking among the cops   15
Who sweep glass and are large and composed.
One is still making notes under the light.
One with a bucket douches ponds of blood
Into the street and gutter.
One hangs lanterns on the wrecks that cling,   20
Empty husks of locusts, to iron poles.

Our throats were tight as tourniquets,
Our feet were bound with splints, but now,
Like convalescents intimate and gauche,
We speak through sickly smiles and warn   25
With the stubborn saw of common sense,
The grim joke and the banal resolution.
The traffic moves around with care,
But we remain, touching a wound
That opens to our richest horror.   30
Already old, the question Who shall die?
Becomes unspoken Who is innocent?

For death in war is done by hands;
Suicide has cause and stillbirth, logic;
And cancer, simple as a flower, blooms.   35
But this invites the occult mind,
Cancels our physics with a sneer,
And spatters all we knew of denouement
Across the expedient and wicked stones.   1942

W. S. MERWIN

Burning the Cat

In the spring, by the big shuck-pile
Between the bramble-choked brook where the copperheads
Curled in the first sun, and the mud road,
All at once it could no longer be ignored.
The season steamed with an odor for which   5
There has never been a name, but it shouted above all.
When I went near, the wood-lice were in its eyes
And a nest of beetles in the white fur of its armpit.
I built a fire there by the shuck-pile
But it did no more than pop the beetles   10
And singe the damp fur, raising a stench
Of burning hair that bit through the sweet day-smell.

Then thinking how time leches after indecency,
Since both grief is indecent and the lack of it,
15   I went away and fetched newspaper,
And wrapped it in kerosene and put it in
With the garbage on a heaped nest of sticks:
20   It was harder to burn than the peels of oranges,
Bubbling and spitting, and the reek was like
Rank cooking that drifted with the smoke out
Through the budding woods and clouded the shining dogwood.
But I became stubborn: I would consume it
Though the pyre should take me a day to build
25   And the flames rise over the house. And hours I fed
That burning, till I was black and streaked with sweat;
And poked it out then, with charred meat still clustering
Thick around the bones. And buried it so
As I should have done in the first place, for
30   The earth is slow, but deep, and good for hiding;
I would have used it if I had understood
How nine lives can vanish in one flash of a dog's jaws,
A car or a copperhead, and yet how one small
Death, however reckoned, is hard to dispose of.   1955

DENISE LEVERTOV

What Were They Like?

1) Did the people of Viet Nam
   use lanterns of stone?
2) Did they hold ceremonies
   to reverence the opening of buds?
5   3) Were they inclined to rippling laughter?
4) Did they use bone and ivory,
   jade and silver, for ornament?
5) Had they an epic poem?
6) Did they distinguish between speech and singing?

10   1) Sir, their light hearts turned to stone.
   It is not remembered whether in gardens
   stone lanterns illumined pleasant ways.
2) Perhaps they gathered once to delight in blossom,
   but after the children were killed
15   there were no more buds.
3) Sir, laughter is bitter to the burned mouth.
4) A dream ago, perhaps. Ornament is for joy.
   All the bones were charred.

5) It is not remembered. Remember,
   most were peasants; their life   20
   was in rice and bamboo.
   When peaceful clouds were reflected in the paddies
   and the water buffalo stepped surely along terraces,
   maybe fathers told their sons old tales.
   When bombs smashed the mirrors   25
   there was time only to scream.
6) There is an echo yet, it is said,
   of their speech which was like a song.
   It is reported their singing resembled
   the flight of moths in moonlight.   30
   Who can say? It is silent now.   1966

ROO BORSON

Save Us From

Save us from night,
from bleak open highways
without end, and the fluorescent
oases of gas stations,
from the gunning of immortal   5
engines past midnight,
when time has no meaning,
from all-night cafés,
their ghoulish slices of pie,
and the orange ruffle on the   10
apron of the waitress,
the matching plastic chairs,
from orange and brown and
all unearthly colors,
banish them back to the test tube,   15
save us from them,
from those bathrooms with a
moonscape of skin in the mirror,
from fatigue, its merciless brightness,
when each cell of the body stands on end,   20
and the sensation of teeth,
and the mind's eternal sentry,
and the unmapped city
with its cold bed.
Save us from insomnia,   25
its treadmill,
its school bells and factory bells,

from living-rooms like the tomb,
their plaid chesterfields
30   and galaxies of dust,
from chairs without arms,
from any matched set of furniture,
from floor-length drapes which
close out the world,
35   from padded bras and rented suits,
from any object in which horror is concealed.
Save us from waking after nightmares,
save us from nightmares,
from other worlds,
40   from the mute, immobile contours
of dressers and shoes,
from another measureless day, save us.   1989

WILLIAM CARLOS WILLIAMS

The Dance

In Brueghel's great picture, The Kermess,[6]
the dancers go round, they go round and
around, the squeal and the blare and the
tweedle of bagpipes, a bugle and fiddles
5   tipping their bellies (round as the thick-
sided glasses whose wash they impound)
their hips and their bellies off balance
to turn them. Kicking and rolling about
the Fair Grounds, swinging their butts, those
10   shanks must be sound to bear up under such
rollicking measures, prance as they dance
in Brueghel's great picture, The Kermess.   1944

PERCY BYSSHE SHELLEY

Ode to the West Wind

I

O wild West Wind, thou breath of Autumn's being,
Thou, from whose unseen presence the leaves dead
Are driven, like ghosts from an enchanter fleeing,

6. A drawing by Pieter Brueghel the elder (1525?–1569).

Yellow, and black, and pale, and hectic red,
Pestilence-stricken multitudes: O thou, 5
Who chariotest to their dark wintry bed

The wingéd seeds, where they lie cold and low,
Each like a corpse within its grave, until
Thine azure sister of the Spring shall blow

Her clarion[7] o'er the dreaming earth, and fill 10
(Driving sweet buds like flocks to feed in air)
With living hues and odors plain and hill:

Wild Spirit, which art moving everywhere;
Destroyer and preserver; hear, oh, hear!

II

Thou on whose stream, mid the steep sky's commotion, 15
Loose clouds like earth's decaying leaves are shed,
Shook from the tangled boughs of Heaven and Ocean,

Angels[8] of rain and lightning: there are spread
On the blue surface of thine aëry surge,
Like the bright hair uplifted from the head 20

Of some fierce Maenad,[9] even from the dim verge
Of the horizon to the zenith's height,
The locks of the approaching storm. Thou dirge

Of the dying year, to which this closing night
Will be the dome of a vast sepulcher, 25
Vaulted with all thy congregated might

Of vapors, from whose solid atmosphere
Black rain, and fire, and hail will burst: oh, hear!

III

Thou who didst waken from his summer dreams
The blue Mediterranean, where he lay, 30
Lulled by the coil of his crystálline streams,

Beside a pumice isle in Baiae's bay,[1]
And saw in sleep old palaces and towers
Quivering within the wave's intenser day,

All overgrown with azure moss and flowers 35
So sweet, the sense faints picturing them! Thou
For whose path the Atlantic's level powers

7. Trumpet-call.   8. Messengers.   9. A frenzied female votary of Dionysus, the Greek god of vegetation and fertility who was supposed to die in the fall and rise again each spring.   1. Where Roman emperors had erected villas, west of Naples.

Cleave themselves into chasms, while far below
The sea-blooms and the oozy woods which wear
40 The sapless foliage of the ocean, know

Thy voice, and suddenly grow gray with fear,
And tremble and despoil themselves:[2] oh, hear!

IV

If I were a dead leaf thou mightest bear;
If I were a swift cloud to fly with thee;
45 A wave to pant beneath thy power, and share

The impulse of thy strength, only less free
Than thou, O uncontrollable! If even
I were as in my boyhood, and could be

The comrade of thy wanderings over Heaven,
50 As then, when to outstrip thy skyey speed
Scarce seemed a vision; I would ne'er have striven

As thus with thee in prayer in my sore need.
Oh, lift me as a wave, a leaf, a cloud!
I fall upon the thorns of life! I bleed!

55 A heavy weight of hours has chained and bowed
One too like thee: tameless, and swift, and proud.

V

Make me thy lyre, even as the forest is:
What if my leaves are falling like its own!
The tumult of thy mighty harmonies

60 Will take from both a deep, autumnal tone,
Sweet though in sadness. Be thou, Spirit fierce,
My spirit! Be thou me, impetuous one!

Drive my dead thoughts over the universe
Like withered leaves to quicken a new birth!
65 And, by the incantation of this verse,

Scatter, as from an unextinguished hearth
Ashes and sparks, my words among mankind!
Be through my lips to unawakened earth

The trumpet of a prophecy! O Wind,
70 If Winter comes, can Spring be far behind?   1820

---

2. "The vegatation at the bottom of the sea . . . sympathizers with that of the land in the change of
seasons." (Shelley's note)

MARGARET ATWOOD

Siren Song

This is the one song everyone
would like to learn: the song
that is irresistible:

the song that forces men
to leap overboard in squadrons   5
even though they see the beached skulls

the song nobody knows
because anyone who has heard it
is dead, and the others can't remember.

Shall I tell you the secret   10
and if I do, will you get me
out of this bird suit?

I don't enjoy it here
squatting on this island
looking picturesque and mythical   15

with these two feathery maniacs,
I don't enjoy singing
this trio, fatal and valuable.

I will tell the secret to you,
to you, only to you.   20
Come closer. This song

is a cry for help: Help me!
Only you, only you can,
you are unique

at last. Alas   25
it is a boring song
but it works every time.   1974

LOUISE BOGAN

Cartography

As you lay in sleep
I saw the chart
Of artery and vein
Running from your heart,

Plain as the strength
Marked upon the leaf
Along the length,
Mortal and brief,

Of your gaunt hand.
I saw it clear:
The wiry brand
Of the life we bear

Mapped like the great
Rivers that rise
Beyond our fate
And distant from our eyes.   1941

▼   ▼   ▼

INTERNAL STRUCTURE   A Glossary

descriptive structure: determined by the requirements of describing someone or something

discursive structure: organized in the form of a treatise, argument, or essay

dramatic structure: consisting of a series of scenes, each of which is presented vividly and in detail

imitative structure: mirroring as exactly as possible the structure of something that already exists as an object and can be seen

narrative structure: based on a straightforward chronological framework

reflective/meditative structure: pondering a subject, theme, or event, and letting the mind play with it, skipping from one sound to another, or to related thoughts or objects as the mind receives them

---

QUESTIONS

1. How many different "scenes" can you identify in "Sir Patrick Spens"? Where does each scene begin and end? How are the transitions made from scene to scene? How is the "fading" effect between scenes accomplished?

2. Why does the last line of "The Dance" repeat the first line? How do the line breaks early in the poem help to control the poem's rhythm and pace? What differences do you notice in the choice of words early in the poem and then later? How is the poem organized?

3. What words and patterns are repeated in the different stanzas of "Ode to

the West Wind"? What differences are there from stanza to stanza? What "prog-ress" does the poem make? In what sense is the poem "revolutionary" or "cycli-cal"? What contribution to the structure of the poem do the sound patterns make? How do the rhymes and repeated stanza patterns contribute to the tone of the poem? to its meaning?

4. Look back over the poems you have read earlier in the course, and pick out one of them that seems to you particularly effective in the way it is put together. Read it over several times and consider carefully how it is organized, i.e., what principles of structure it uses. What does the choice of speaker, situa-tion, and setting have to do with its structure? What other artistic decisions seem to you crucial in creating the poem's structure?

WRITING SUGGESTIONS

1. After doing the reading and analysis suggested in question 4 above, write a detailed essay in which you consider fully the structural principles at work in the poem. The length of your essay will depend on the length of the poem you choose—but also on the complexity of its structure.

2. Look back at "Cherrylog Road" (p. 87) and reread it carefully. Then look for another poem in which memory of a much earlier event plays an important structural function. Compare the poems in detail, noting how (in each case) memory influences the way the event is reconstructed. What details of the event are in each case omitted in the retelling? What parts are lengthened or dwelt upon? What, in each case, is the point of having the event recalled later rather than from an immediate recollection?

Write a three- or four-page essay comparing the structuring function of memory in the two poems, noting in each case exactly how the structural prin-ciples at work in the poem help to create the poem's final tone.

STUDENT WRITING

Below is one student's response to the first Writing Suggestion. The student focuses primarily on the phrases in "The Victims" that involve "taking" as he describes the structure of the poem.

Structure and Language in "The Victims"
by Sharon Olds

In Sharon Olds' poem "The Victims" we hear a
son or daughter, already grown, speaking to a
father whom he/she lost as a result of divorce.
It reads like part accusation and part
confession. As the poem progresses attitudes such
as bitterness and spite toward the father soften,
and at the end the reader is left with the same
ambivalent feelings as the speaker herself[1]
feels.

The poem is divided into two parts, from line
1 to line 17 and from there to the end. The first
portion is in many ways a narration, the story
line. The speaker relives the experience. Both
the language ("her kids loved it," "we grinned
inside," "We were tickled") and symbolism (the
comparison of suits to carcasses and shoe tips to
noses) used here suggest that this is a child's
perspective on the situation. This portion is
also spoken in the past tense. In the second
portion we hear a more reflective and
contemplative adult. It is spoken in the present
tense ("Now I . . ." [line 17]), and combines
both the speaker's bitterness (which dominates
the first portion) as well as her pity and sense
of guilt towards her father.

The two portions are framed by similar phrases:
"She took it and took it, in silence . . ." (line
1), "She had taught us to take it, to hate you

and take it . . ." (line 15), "I wonder who took
it and took it from them in silence . . ." (lines
23–24). In the final lines of the poem these words
take on a deep meaning and enable the reader to
read the poem in a completely different manner.

When we first read the words "took it and took
it in silence" we assume the mother took some
sort of abuse in silence. She taught her children
to take the abuse in silence and to hate their
father. The final repetition of that phrase: "I
wonder who took it and took it from them in
silence until they had given it all away and had
nothing left but this" (lines 23–26), reminds us
of the meaning of the word "take." "Taking it"
can mean taking abuse, but it can also mean
taking in the ordinary sense as in taking money
or a gift or love. One is active and one is
passive. If we adopt the active form, the poem is
still meaningful, only this time it is the father
who is the victim. He is the one who gave all he
had. The mother took and took (money, love,
attention) and taught her children to take and to
hate. One hint to support this interpretation
might be the first line of the poem, which
suggests that the mother was something more
than a passive victim ("When mother divorced
you . . . ," ". . . kicked you out . . ."). Again
the ambiguity of the phrase strengthens the sense
of ambivalence which a child must feel when her
parents divorce. It is never clear who "the
Victims" are in the poem, perhaps all of them.

Silence is another strong theme in the poem. Note the following examples: "took it, in silence" (line 2), "we grinned inside . . ." (line 5), "I wonder . . ." (line 23), "took it from them in silence . . ." (line 24). The strongest example of the silence, the lack of communication, and the alienation comes in the last section and the metaphor of the bums in doorways. The speaker compares her father to the drunken bums she sees and describes them in such a way that the image of fish or sunken ships becomes vivid ("white slugs of their bodies," "slits in their suits of compressed silt," "stained flippers," "underwater fire of their eyes"). The father is in some other, "underwater" world where sounds from the outside are inaudible. The only sound we hear in this poem is the speaker's voice. Silence and alienation predominated in her childhood, and now as an adult she is still unable to reach her father.

While on the surface this poem seems to be one of anger and accusation, a closer reading indicates a deeper, more complex view of human experience. Things are seldom as clearly defined and one-sided as they appear to a child.

---

1. It is not apparent whether the speaker is male or female. I chose to refer to her as a female simply because the poet is a female. It seems that the experience and feelings related are not exclusive to one sex or the other.

7 EXTERNAL FORM

Most poems of more than a few lines are divided into **stanzas,** groups of lines divided from other groups by white space on the page. Putting some space between groupings of lines has the effect of sectioning the poem, giving its physical appearance a series of divisions that often mark breaks in thought, changes of scenery or imagery, or other shifts in structure or direction. In "The Flea" (p. 90), for example, the stanza divisions mark distinctive stages in the action; between the first and second stanzas, the speaker stops his companion from killing the flea, and between the second and third stanzas, the companion follows through on her intention and kills the flea. In "The Goose Fish" (p. 207), the stanzas mark stages in the self-perception of the lovers; each of the stanzas is a more or less distinct scene, and the scenes unfold almost like a series of slides. Not all stanzas are quite so neatly patterned as are the ones in these two poems, but any formal division of a poem into stanzas is important to consider—what appear to be gaps or silences may be structural indicators.

Historically, stanzas have most often been organized by patterns of rhyme, and thus stanza divisions have been a visual indicator of patterns in sound. In most traditional stanza forms, the pattern of rhyme is repeated in stanza after stanza throughout the poem, until voice and ear become familiar with the pattern and come to expect it and, in a sense, to depend on it. The accumulation of pattern allows us to "hear" variations as well, just as we do in music. The rhyme thus becomes an organizational device in the poem—a formal, external determiner of organization, as distinguished from the internal, structural determiners we considered in Chapter 6—and ordinarily the metrical patterns stay constant from stanza to stanza. In Shelley's "Ode to the West Wind," for example, the first and third lines in each stanza rhyme, and the middle line then rhymes with the first and third lines of the next stanza. (In indicating rhyme, a different letter of the alphabet is conventionally used to represent each sound; in the following example, if we begin with "being" as *a* and "dead" as *b*, then "fleeing" is also *a*, and "red" and "bed" are *b*.)

O wild West Wind, thou breath of Autumn's being,	*a*
Thou, from whose unseen presence the leaves dead	*b*
Are driven, like ghosts from an enchanter fleeing,	*a*
Yellow, and black, and pale, and hectic red,	*b*
Pestilence-stricken multitudes: O thou,	*c*

Who chariotest to their dark wintry bed	*b*
The wingéd seeds, where they lie cold and low,	*c*
Each like a corpse within its grave, until	*d*
Thine azure sister of the Spring shall blow	*c*

In this stanza form, known as **terza rima,** the stanzas are linked to each other by a common sound: one rhyme sound from each stanza is picked up in the next stanza, and so on to the end of the poem or one section of the poem. This stanza form was used by the great Italian poet Dante in *The Divine Comedy,* written in the early 1300s. Terza rima is not all that common in English because it is a rhyme-rich stanza form—that is, it requires many rhymes—and English is, relatively speaking, a rhyme-poor language (not as rich in rhyme possibilities as such languages as Italian or French). One reason for this is that English derives from so many different language families that it has fewer similar word endings than languages that have remained more "pure," i.e., more dependent for vocabulary on the roots and patterns found in a single language family.

Contemporary poets seldom use rhyme, finding it neither necessary nor appealing, but until the twentieth century the music of rhyme was central to both the sound and the formal conception of most poems. Because poetry was originally an oral art (and its texts not always written down) various kinds of **memory devices** (sometimes called **mnemonic devices**) were built into poems to help reciters remember them. Rhyme was one such device, and most people still find it easier to memorize poetry that rhymes. The simple pleasure of hearing familiar sounds repeated may also help to account for the traditional popularity of rhyme, and perhaps plain habit (for both poets and hearers) had a lot to do with why rhyme flourished for so many centuries as a standard expectation. No doubt, too, rhyme helped to give poetry a special quality that distinguished it from prose, a significant advantage in ages that worried about decorum and propriety and were anxious to preserve a strong sense of poetic tradition. Some ages have been very concerned that poetry should not in any way be mistaken for prose or made to serve prosaic functions, and the literary critics and theorists in those ages made extraordinary efforts to emphasize the distinctions between poetry, which was thought to be artistically superior, and prose, which was thought to be primarily utilitarian. A pride in elitism and a fear that an expanded reading public could ultimately dilute the possibilities of traditional art forms have been powerful cultural forces in Western civilization, and if such forces were not themselves responsible for creating rhyme in poetry, they at least helped to preserve a sense of its necessity.

But there are at least two other reasons for rhyme. One is complex and hard to state justly without long explanations. It involves traditional ideas about the symmetrical relationship of different aspects of the world and the function of poetry to reflect the universe as human learning understood it. Most poets in earlier centuries assumed that rhyme was proper to verse, perhaps even essential. They would have felt themselves eccentric to compose poems any other way. Some poets did experiment—very successfully—with **blank verse** (that is, verse that did not rhyme but that nevertheless had strict metrical requirements), but the cultural pressure for rhyme was almost constant. Why? As noted above, custom or habit may account for part of the assumption that rhyme was necessary, but probably not all of it. Rather, the poets' sense that poetry was an imitation of larger relationships in the universe made it seem natural to use rhyme to represent or re-create a sense of harmony, correspondence, symmetry, and order. The sounds of poetry were thus reminders of the harmonious cosmos, of the music of the spheres that animated the planets, the processes of nature, the interrelationship of all created things and beings. Probably poets never said to themselves, "I shall now tunefully emulate the harmony of God's carefully ordered universe," but the tendency to use rhyme and other repetitions or re-echoings of sound (such as **alliteration** or **assonance**) nevertheless stemmed ultimately from basic assumptions about how the universe worked. In a modern world increasingly perceived as fragmented, rambling, and unrelated, there is of course less of a tendency to testify to a sense of harmony and symmetry. It would be too easy and too mechanical to think that rhyme in a poem specifically means that the poet has a firm sense of cosmic order, and that an unrhymed poem testifies to chaos, but cultural assumptions do affect the expectations of both poets and readers, and cultural tendencies create a kind of pressure upon the individual creator. If you take a survey course (or a series of related "period" courses in English or American literature), you will readily notice the diminishing sense of the need for—or relevance of—rhyme.

One other reason for using rhyme is that it provides a kind of discipline for the poet, a way of harnessing poetic talents and keeping a rein on the imagination, so that the results are ordered, controlled, put into some kind of meaningful and recognizable form. Robert Frost used to be fond of saying that writing poems without rhyme was like playing tennis without a net. Writing good poetry does require a lot of discipline, and Frost speaks for many (perhaps most) traditional poets in suggesting that rhyme can be a major source of that discipline. But it is not the only possible source, and more recent poets have usually felt they would rather play by new rules or invent their own as they go along; they have therefore sought their sources of discipline elsewhere, preferring the more spare tones that unrhymed poetry provides. It is not that contemporary poets cannot think of rhyme words or that they do not care about the sounds of their poetry; rather, recent poets have consciously decided not to work with rhyme and to use instead other aural devices and other strategies for organizing stanzas, just as they have chosen to work with experimental and variable rhythms instead of writing primarily in the traditional English meters. Some few modern poets, though, have protested the abandonment of rhyme and have continued to write rhymed verse successfully in a more or less traditional way.

The amount and density of rhyme vary widely in stanza and verse forms, from elaborate and intricate patterns of rhyme to more casual or spare sound repetitions. The **Spenserian stanza,** for example, is even more rhyme rich than terza rima, using only three rhyme sounds in nine rhymed lines, as in Keats's *The Eve of St. Agnes:*

Her falt'ring hand upon the balustrade,	*a*
Old Angela was feeling for the stair,	*b*
When Madeline, St. Agnes' charméd maid,	*a*
Rose, like a missioned spirit, unaware:	*b*
With silver taper's light, and pious care,	*b*
She turned, and down the agéd gossip led	*c*
To a safe level matting. Now prepare,	*b*
Young Porphyro, for gazing on that bed;	*c*
She comes, she comes again, like ring dove frayed and fled	*c*

On the other hand, the **ballad stanza** has only one set of rhymes in four lines; lines 1 and 3 in each stanza do not rhyme at all (from "Sir Patrick Spens"):

The king sits in Dumferling toune,	*a*
Drinking the blude-reid wine:	*b*
"O whar will I get guid sailor,	*c*
To sail this ship of mine?"	*b*

Most stanzas have a metrical pattern as well as a rhyme scheme. Terza rima, for example, involves iambic meter (unstressed and stressed syllables alternating regularly) and each line has five beats (pentameter). Most of the Spenserian stanza (the first eight lines) is also in iambic pentameter, but the ninth line in each stanza has one extra foot (it is iambic hexameter). The ballad stanza, also iambic, as are most English stanza and verse forms, alternates three-beat and four-beat lines; lines 1 and 3 are unrhymed iambic tetrameter, and lines 2 and 4 are rhymed iambic trimeter.

Stanza Forms

Many stanza forms are represented in this book. Some have names because they have been used over and over by different poets. Others were invented for a particular use in a particular poem and may never be repeated again. Most traditional stanzas are based on rhyme schemes, but some use other kinds of predictable sound patterns; early English poetry, for example, used alliteration to construct a balance between the first and second half of each line (see Earle Birney's "Anglosaxon Street" [p. 262] for a modern imitation of this principle). Sometimes, especially when a strong community of poets interacts with each other, highly elaborate *verse forms* have been developed that set up stanzas as part of a scheme for the whole poem. The poets of medieval Provence were especially inventive, subtle, and elaborate in their construction of complex verse forms, some of which have been copied by poets ever since. The **sestina,** for example, depends on the measured repetition of words in particular places; see, for example, "Sestina" (p. 252), and try to decipher the pattern. (There are also double and even triple sestinas, tough tests of a poet's ingenuity.) And the **villanelle,** another Provençal form, depends on the patterned repetition of whole lines (see Dylan Thomas's "Do Not Go Gentle into That Good Night" [p. 250]). Different cultures and different languages develop their own patterns and measures—not all poetries are parallel to English poetry—and they vary from age to age as well as nation to nation.

You can probably deduce the principles involved in each of the following stanza or verse forms by looking carefully at a poem that uses it; if you have trouble, look at the definitions in the glossary on p. 263.

heroic couplet	"Sound and Sense"	p. 179
tetrameter couplet	"To His Coy Mistress"	p. 355
limerick	["A staid schizophrenic named Struther"]	p. 183
free verse	"Dirge"	p. 177
blank verse	from *Paradise Lost*	p. 137

What are stanza forms good for? What use is it to recognize them? Why do poets bother? Matters discussed in this chapter so far have suggested two reasons: 1. Breaks between stanzas provide convenient pauses for reader and writer, something roughly equivalent to paragraphs in prose. The eye thus picks up the places where some kind of pause or break occurs. 2. Poets sometimes use stanza forms, as they do rhyme itself, as a discipline: writing in a certain kind of stanza form imposes a shape on their act of imagination. But visual spaces and unexpected print divisions also mean that poems sometimes *look* unusual and require special visual attention, attention that does not always follow the logic of sound patterns or syntax. At the end of this chapter (just after a detailed consideration of one kind of verse form—the sonnet—you will find poems that employ special configurations and shapes to establish their meanings and effects.

The Sonnet

The **sonnet** is one of the most persistent verse forms. From its origins in the Middle Ages as a prominent form in Italian and French poetry, it dominated English poetry in the late sixteenth and early seventeenth centuries and then was revived several times from the early nineteenth century onward. A sonnet, except for some early experiments with length, is always fourteen lines long and is usually written in iambic pentameter. It is usually printed as if it were a *single* stanza, although in reality it has several formal divisions that represent its rhyme schemes and formal breaks. As a popular and traditional verse form in English for more than four centuries, the sonnet has been surprisingly resilient even in ages that largely reject rhyme. It continues to attract a variety of poets, including (curiously) radical and even revolutionary poets who find its firm structure very useful. Its uses, although quite varied, can be illustrated fairly precisely. As a verse form, the sonnet is contained, compact, demanding; whatever it does, it must do concisely and quickly. To be effective, it must take advantage of the possibilities inherent in its shortness and its relative rigidity. It is best suited to intensity of feeling and concentration of expression. Not too surprisingly, one subject it frequently discusses is confinement itself.

WILLIAM WORDSWORTH

Nuns Fret Not

Nuns fret not at their convent's narrow room;
And hermits are contented with their cells;
And students with their pensive citadels;
Maids at the wheel, the weaver at his loom,
Sit blithe and happy; bees that soar for bloom,
High as the highest Peak of Furness-fells,[1]
Will murmur by the hour in foxglove bells:[2]

5

1. Mountains in England's Lake District, where Wordsworth lived.   2. Flowers from which digitalis (a heart medicine) began to be made in 1799.

In truth the prison, unto which we doom
Ourselves, no prison is: and hence for me,
In sundry moods, 'twas pastime to be bound   10
Within the sonnet's scanty plot of ground;
Pleased if some souls (for such there needs must be)
Who have felt the weight of too much liberty,
Should find brief solace there, as I have found.   1807

Most sonnets are structured according to one of two principles of division. On one principle, the sonnet divides into three units of four lines each and a final unit of two lines, and sometimes the line spacing reflects this division. On the other, the fundamental break is between the first eight lines (called an octave) and the last six (called a sestet). The 4-4-4-2 sonnet is usually called the **English** or **Shakespearean sonnet,** and ordinarily its rhyme scheme reflects the structure: the scheme of *abab cdcd efef gg* is the classic one, but many variations from that pattern still reflect the basic 4-4-4-2 division. The 8-6 sonnet is usually called the **Italian** or **Petrarchan sonnet** (the Italian poet Petrarch was an early master of this structure), and its "typical" rhyme scheme is *abbaabba cdecde*, although it too produces many variations that still reflect the basic division into two parts.

The two kinds of sonnet structures are useful for two different sorts of argument. The 4-4-4-2 structure works very well for constructing a poem that wants to make a three-step argument (with a quick summary at the end), or for setting up brief, cumulative images. "That time of year thou mayst in me behold" (p. 141), for example, uses the 4-4-4-2 structure to mark the progressive steps toward death and the parting of friends by using three distinct images, then summarizing. "Let me not to the marriage of true minds" (p. 19) works very similarly, following the kind of organization that in Chapter 6 was referred to as the 1-2-3 structure—and doing it compactly and economically.

Here, on the other hand, is a poem that uses the 8-6 pattern:

HENRY CONSTABLE

[My lady's presence makes the roses red]

My lady's presence makes the roses red,
Because to see her lips they blush for shame.
The lily's leaves, for envy, pale became,
And her white hands in them this envy bred.

5
        The marigold the leaves abroad doth spread,
        Because the sun's and her power is the same.
        The violet of purple colour came,
        Dyed in the blood she made my heart to shed.
        In brief: all flowers from her their virtue take;
10
        From her sweet breath their sweet smells do proceed;
        The living heat which her eyebeams doth make
        Warmeth the ground and quickeneth the seed.
        The rain, wherewith she watereth the flowers,
        Falls from mine eyes, which she dissolves in showers.   1594

The first eight lines argue that the lady's presence is responsible for the color of all of nature's flowers, and the final six lines summarize and extend that argument to smells and heat—and finally to the rain that the lady draws from the speaker's eyes. That kind of two-part structure, in which the octave states a proposition or generalization and the sestet provides a particularization or application of it, has a variety of uses. The final lines may, for example, reverse the first eight and achieve a paradox or irony in the poem, or the poem may nearly balance two comparable arguments. Basically, the 8-6 structure lends itself to poems with two points to make, or to those that wish to make one point and then illustrate it.

Sometimes the neat and precise structure I have described is altered—either slightly, as in "Nuns Fret Not" above (where the 8-6 structure is more of an 8½-5½ structure), or more radically as particular needs or effects may demand. And the two basic structures certainly do not define all the structural possibilities within a fourteen-line poem, even if they do suggest the most traditional ways of taking advantage of the sonnet's compact and well-kept container.

The sonnets in this chapter by Sidney, Shakespeare, and Constable survive from a golden age of English sonnet writing in the late sixteenth century, an age that set the pattern for expectations in the English tradition of form, subject matter, and tone. The sonnet came to England from Italy via France, and imitations of Petrarch's famous sonnet sequence to Laura became the rage. Thousands upon thousands of sonnets were written in those years, often in sequences of a hundred or more sonnets each; the sequences explored the many moods of love and usually had a light thread of narrative that purported to recount a love affair between the male poet and a female lover who was almost always golden-haired, beautiful, disdainful, and inaccessible. Her beauty was described in a series of exaggerated comparisons: her eyes were like the sun ("When Nature made her chief work, Stella's eyes"), her teeth like pearls, her cheeks like roses, her skin like ivory, and so on, but the adherence to these conventions was always playful, and it became a game of wit to play variations upon expectations ("My lady's presence makes the roses red" and "My mistress' eyes are nothing like the sun"). Sometimes the female lover was disdainful, unavailable, or rejecting, and sometimes male friendship or homosexual love rivaled the usual male / female relationship. Almost always teasing and witty, these poems were not necessarily as true to life as they pretended, but they provided historically an expectation of what sonnets were to be.

Many modern sonnets continue to be about love or private life, and many continue to use a personal, apparently open and sincere tone. But poets often find the sonnet's compact form and rigid demands equally useful for many varieties of subject, theme, and tone. Besides love, sonnets often treat other subjects: politics, philosophy, discovery of a new world. And tones vary widely too, from the anger and remorse of "Th' expense of spirit in a waste of shame" (p. 461) and righteous outrage of "On the Late Massacre in Piedmont" (p. 94) to the tender awe of "How Do I Love Thee?" (p. 2). Many poets seem to take the kind of comfort Wordsworth describes in the careful limits of the form, finding in its two basic variations (the English sonnet such as "My mistress' eyes" [p. 249] and the Italian sonnet such as "On First Looking into Chapman's Homer" [p. 293]) a sufficiency of convenient ways to organize their materials into coherent structures.

▼   ▼   ▼

JOHN KEATS

On the Sonnet

If by dull rhymes our English must be chained,
And like Andromeda,[3] the sonnet sweet
Fettered, in spite of painéd loveliness,
Let us find, if we must be constrained,
Sandals more interwoven and complete   5
To fit the naked foot of Poesy:[4]
Let us inspect the lyre, and weigh the stress
Of every chord,[5] and see what may be gained

3. Who, according to Greek myth, was chained to a rock so that she would be devoured by a sea monster. She was rescued by Perseus, who married her. When she died she was placed among the stars.   4. In a letter that contained this sonnet, Keats expressed impatience with the traditional Petrarchan and Shakespearean sonnet forms: "I have been endeavoring to discover a better sonnet stanza than we have."   5. Lyre-string.

By ear industrious, and attention meet;
Misers of sound and syllable, no less
Than Midas[6] of his coinage, let us be
Jealous of dead leaves in the bay-wreath crown;[7]
So, if we may not let the Muse be free,
She will be bound with garlands of her own.

1819

LOUISE BOGAN

Single Sonnet

Now, you great stanza, you heroic mould,
Bend to my will, for I must give you love:
The weight in the heart that breathes, but cannot move,
Which to endure flesh only makes so bold.

Take up, take up, as it were lead or gold
The burden; test the dreadful mass thereof.
No stone, slate, metal under or above
Earth, is so ponderous, so dull, so cold.

Too long as ocean bed bears up the ocean,
As earth's core bears the earth, have I borne this;
Too long have lovers, bending for their kiss,
Felt bitter force cohering without motion.

Staunch meter, great song, it is yours, at length,
To prove how stronger you are than my strength.

1937

WILLIAM WORDSWORTH

The World Is Too Much with Us

The world is too much with us; late and soon,
Getting and spending, we lay waste our powers:
Little we see in Nature that is ours;
We have given our hearts away, a sordid boon![8]
This Sea that bares her bosom to the moon;
The winds that will be howling at all hours,
And are up-gathered now like sleeping flowers;
For this, for every thing, we are out of tune;

---

6. The legendary king of Phrygia who asked, and got, the power to turn all he touched to gold.
7. The bay tree was sacred to Apollo, god of poetry, and bay wreaths came to symbolize true poetic achievement. The withering of the bay tree is sometimes considered an omen of death. *Jealous:* suspiciously watchful.   8. Gift.

It moves us not.—Great God! I'd rather be
A Pagan suckled in a creed outworn;
So might I, standing on this pleasant lea,
Have glimpses that would make me less forlorn;
Have sight of Proteus rising from the sea;
Or hear old Triton[9] blow his wreathed horn.

1802–04   1807

HELEN CHASIN

Joy Sonnet in a Random Universe

Sometimes I'm happy: la la la la la la la
la la la la la la la la la la la la la la la la la la
la la la la. Tum tum ti tum. La la la la la la
la la la la la la la la la la la la la la la la la la.
Hey nonny nonny. La la la la la la la la la
la la la la la la la la la la la. Vo do di o do.
Poo poo pi doo. La la la la la la la la la la
la la la la la la la la la la la la la la la la la la
la la. Whack a doo. La la la la la la la. Sh-
boom, sh-boom. La la la la la la la la la la   10
la la la la la la la la la la la la la la la la la la
la la. Dum di dum. La la la la la la la la la
la la la la la la la la la. Tra la la. Tra la la
la la la la la la la la la. Yeah yeah yeah.   1968

PERCY BYSSHE SHELLEY

Ozymandias[1]

I met a traveler from an antique land
Who said: Two vast and trunkless legs of stone
Stand in the desert. . . . Near them, on the sand,
Half sunk, a shattered visage lies, whose frown,
And wrinkled lip, and sneer of cold command,   5
Tell that its sculptor well those passions read
Which yet survive, stamped on these lifeless things,
The hand that mocked them, and the heart that fed:
And on the pedestal these words appear:

9. A sea deity, usually represented as blowing on a conch shell. *Proteus*: an old man of the sea who (in *The Odyssey*) could assume a variety of shapes.   1. The Greek name for Rameses II, 13th-century B.C. pharaoh of Egypt. According to a first-century B.C. Greek historian, Diodorus Siculus, the largest statue in Egypt was inscribed: "I am Ozymandias, king of kings; if anyone wishes to know what I am and where I lie, let him surpass me in some of my exploits."

10   "My name is Ozymandias, King of Kings:
     Look on my works, ye Mighty, and despair!"
     Nothing beside remains. Round the decay
     Of that colossal wreck, boundless and bare
     The lone and level sands stretch far away.   1818

WILLIAM WORDSWORTH

London, 1802

     Milton! thou should'st be living at this hour:
     England hath need of thee: she is a fen
     Of stagnant waters: altar, sword, and pen,
     Fireside, the heroic wealth of hall and bower,
5   Have forfeited their ancient English dower
     Of inward happiness. We are selfish men;
     Oh! raise us up, return to us again;
     And give us manners, virtue, freedom, power.
     Thy soul was like a star, and dwelt apart:
10   Thou hadst a voice whose sound was like the sea:
     Pure as the naked heavens, majestic, free,
     So didst thou travel on life's common way,
     In cheerful godliness; and yet thy heart
1802 The lowliest duties on herself did lay.

HELENE JOHNSON

Sonnet to a Negro in Harlem

     You are disdainful and magnificent—
     Your perfect body and your pompous gait,
     Your dark eyes flashing solemnly with hate,
     Small wonder that you are incompetent
5   To imitate those whom you so despise—
     Your shoulders towering high above the throng,
     Your head thrown back in rich, barbaric song,
     Palm trees and mangoes stretched before your eyes.
     Let others toil and sweat for labor's sake
10   And wring from grasping hands their meed of gold.
     Why urge ahead your supercilious feet?
     Scorn will efface each footprint that you make.
     I love your laughter arrogant and bold.
     You are too splendid for this city street.   p. 1927

CLAUDE McKAY

The Harlem Dancer

Applauding youths laughed with young prostitutes
And watched her perfect, half-clothed body sway;
Her voice was like the sound of blended flutes
Blown by black players upon a picnic day.
She sang and danced on gracefully and calm,   5
The light gauze hanging loose about her form;
To me she seemed a proudly-swaying palm
Grown lovelier for passing through a storm.
Upon her swarthy neck black shiny curls
Luxuriant fell; and tossing coins in praise,   10
The wine-flushed, bold-eyed boys, and even the girls,
Devoured her shape with eager, passionate gaze;
But looking at her falsely-smiling face,
I knew her self was not in that strange place.   1922

JOHN MILTON

[When I consider how my light is spent]

When I consider how my light is spent,
    Ere half my days, in this dark world and wide,
    And that one talent which is death to hide[2]
    Lodged with me useless, though my soul more bent
To serve therewith my Maker, and present   5
    My true account, lest he returning chide;
    "Doth God exact day-labor, light denied?"
    I fondly ask; but Patience to prevent[3]
That murmur, soon replies, "God doth not need
    Either man's work or his own gifts; who best   10
    Bear his mild yoke, they serve him best. His state
Is kingly. Thousands at his bidding speed
    And post o'er land and ocean without rest:
1652?   They also serve who only stand and wait."   1673

2. In the parable of the talents (Matthew 25), the servants who earned interest on their master's money (his talents) while he was away were called "good and faithful"; the one who hid the money and simply returned it was condemned and sent away. Usury, a deadly sin under Catholicism, was regarded by Puritans as a metaphor for attaining salvation.   3. Forestall. *Fondly:* foolishly.

ARCHIBALD LAMPMAN

Winter Evening

To-night the very horses springing by
Toss gold from whitened nostrils. In a dream
The streets that narrow to the westward gleam
Like rows of golden palaces; and high
From all the crowded chimneys tower and die
A thousand aureoles. Down in the west
The brimming plains beneath the sunset rest,
One burning sea of gold. Soon, soon shall fly
The glorious vision, and the hours shall feel
A mightier master; soon from height to height,
With silence and the sharp unpitying stars,
Stern creeping frosts, and winds that touch like steel,
Out of the depth beyond the eastern bars,
Glittering and still shall come the awful night.   1899

SIR CHARLES G. D. ROBERTS

The Potato Harvest

A high bare field, brown from the plough, and borne
    Aslant from sunset; amber wastes of sky
    Washing the ridge; a clamor of crows that fly
In from the wide flats where the spent tides mourn
To yon their rocking roosts in pines wind-torn;
    A line of grey snake-fence that zigzags by
    A pond and cattle; from the homestead nigh
The long deep summonings of the supper horn.
Black on the ridge, against that lonely flush,
    A cart, and stoop-necked oxen; ranged beside
        Some barrels; and the day-worn harvest-folk,
Here emptying their baskets, jar the hush
    With hollow thunders. Down the dusk hillside
        Lumbers the wain; and day fades out like smoke.   1886

ROBERT FROST

Once by the Pacific

The shattered water made a misty din.
Great waves looked over others coming in,

And thought of doing something to the shore
That water never did to land before.
The clouds were low and hairy in the skies,   5
Like locks blown forward in the gleam of eyes.
You could not tell, and yet it looked as if
The shore was lucky in being backed by cliff,
The cliff in being backed by continent;
It looked as if a night of dark intent   10
Was coming, and not only a night, an age.
Someone had better be prepared for rage.
There would be more than ocean-water broken
Before God's last *Put out the Light* was spoken.   1926

GWENDOLYN BROOKS

First Fight. Then Fiddle.

First fight. Then fiddle. Ply the slipping string
With feathery sorcery; muzzle the note
With hurting love; the music that they wrote
Bewitch, bewilder. Qualify to sing
Threadwise. Devise no salt, no hempen thing   5
For the dear instrument to bear. Devote
The bow to silks and honey. Be remote
A while from malice and from murdering.
But first to arms, to armor. Carry hate
In front of you and harmony behind.   10
Be deaf to music and to beauty blind.
Win war. Rise bloody, maybe not too late
For having first to civilize a space
Wherein to play your violin with grace.   1949

LOUIS MacNEICE

Sunday Morning

Down the road someone is practicing scales,
The notes like little fishes vanish with a wink of tails,
Man's heart expands to tinker with his car
For this is Sunday morning, Fate's great bazaar;
Regard these means as ends, concentrate on this Now,   5
And you may grow to music or drive beyond Hindhead⁴ anyhow,
Take corners on two wheels until you go so fast

4. In Surrey; the direction of a typical Sunday outing from London.

That you can clutch a fringe or two of the windy past,
That you can abstract this day and make it to the week of time
A small eternity, a sonnet self-contained in rhyme.
But listen, up the road, something gulps, the church spire
Opens its eight bells out, skulls' mouths which will not tire
To tell how there is no music or movement which secures
Escape from the weekday time. Which deadens and endures.   1935

10 (left margin, aligned to line 3)

CLAUDE McKAY

The White House

Your door is shut against my tightened face,
And I am sharp as steel with discontent;
But I possess the courage and the grace
To bear my anger proudly and unbent.
The pavement slabs burn loose beneath my feet,
And passion rends my vitals as I pass,
A chafing savage, down the decent street,
Where boldly shines your shuttered door of glass.
Oh, I must search for wisdom every hour,
Deep in my wrathful bosom sore and raw,
And find in it the superhuman power
To hold me to the letter of your law!
Oh, I must keep my heart inviolate
Against the poison of your deadly hate.   1937

SIR PHILIP SIDNEY

[When Nature made her chief work, Stella's eyes][5]

When Nature made her chief work, Stella's eyes,
In color black[6] why wrapped she beams so bright?
Would she in beamy black, like painter wise,
Frame daintiest luster mixed of shades and light?
Or did she else that sober hue devise,
In object best to knit and strength our sight,
Lest if no veil those brave gleams did disguise,
They sunlike should more dazzle than delight?
Or would she her miraculous power show,

5. From Sidney's sonnet sequence *Astrophel and Stella*, usually credited with having started the vogue of sonnet sequences in Elizabethan England.   6. Black was frequently used in the Renaissance to mean absence of light, and ugly or foul (see line 10).

That, whereas black seems Beauty's contrary,   10
She even in black doth make all beauties flow?
Both so and thus: she, minding[7] Love should be
Placed ever there, gave him this mourning weed
1582   To honor all their deaths who for her bleed.

WILLIAM SHAKESPEARE

[My mistress' eyes are nothing like the sun]

My mistress' eyes are nothing like the sun;
Coral is far more red than her lips' red;
If snow be white, why then her breasts are dun;[8]
If hairs be wires, black wires grow on her head.
I have seen roses damasked[9] red and white,   5
But no such roses see I in her cheeks;
And in some perfumes is there more delight
Than in the breath that from my mistress reeks.
I love to hear her speak, yet well I know
That music hath a far more pleasing sound;   10
I grant I never saw a goddess go;[1]
My mistress, when she walks, treads on the ground.
And yet, by heaven, I think my love as rare
As any she belied with false compare.   1609

DIANE ACKERMAN

Sweep Me Through Your Many-Chambered Heart

Sweep me through your many-chambered heart
if you like, or leave me here, flushed
amid the sap-ooze and blossom: one more dish
in the banquet called April, or think me hard-
won all your days full of women. Weeks   5
later, till I felt your arms around
me like a shackle, heard all the sundown
wizardries the fired body speaks.
Tell me why, if it was no more than this,
the unmuddled tumble, the renegade kiss,   10

---

7. Remembering that.   8. Mouse-colored.   9. Variegated.   1. Walk.

today, rapt in a still life and unaware,
my paintbrush dropped like an amber hawk;
thinking I'd heard your footfall on the stair,
I listened, heartwise, for the knock.   1978

EDNA ST. VINCENT MILLAY

[What lips my lips have kissed, and where, and why]

What lips my lips have kissed, and where, and why,
I have forgotten, and what arms have lain
Under my head till morning; but the rain
Is full of ghosts tonight, that tap and sigh
5 Upon the glass and listen for reply,
And in my heart there stirs a quiet pain
For unremembered lads that not again
Will turn to me at midnight with a cry.
Thus in the winter stands the lonely tree,
10 Nor knows what birds have vanished one by one,
Yet knows its boughs more silent than before:
I cannot say what loves have come and gone;
I only know that summer sang in me
A little while, that in me sings no more.   1923

Examples of Stanza Forms

DYLAN THOMAS

Do Not Go Gentle into That Good Night[2]

Do not go gentle into that good night,
Old age should burn and rave at close of day;
Rage, rage against the dying of the light.

Though wise men at their end know dark is right,
Because their words had forked no lightning they
5 Do not go gentle into that good night.

Good men, the last wave by, crying how bright
Their frail deeds might have danced in a green bay,
Rage, rage against the dying of the light.

2. Written during the final illness of the poet's father.

Wild men who caught and sang the sun in flight,   10
And learn, too late, they grieved it on its way,
Do not go gentle into that good night.

Grave men, near death, who see with blinding sight
Blind eyes could blaze like meteors and be gay,
Rage, rage against the dying of the light.   15

And you, my father, there on the sad height,
Curse, bless, me now with your fierce tears, I pray.
Do not go gentle into that good night.
Rage, rage against the dying of the light.   1952

MARIANNE MOORE

Poetry

I, too, dislike it: there are things that are important beyond all this fiddle.
     Reading it, however, with a perfect contempt for it, one discovers in
     it after all, a place for the genuine.
          Hands that can grasp, eyes
          that can dilate, hair that can rise   5
               if it must, these things are important not because a

high-sounding interpretation can be put upon them but because they are
     useful. When they become so derivative as to become unintelligible,
     the same thing may be said for all of us, that we
          do not admire what   10
          we cannot understand: the bat
               holding on upside down or in quest of something to

eat, elephants pushing, a wild horse taking a roll, a tireless wolf under
     a tree, the immovable critic twitching his skin like a horse that feels a flea, the base-
     ball fan, the statistician—   15
          nor is it valid
               to discriminate against "business documents and

school-books"[3]; all these phenomena are important. One must make a distinction
     however: when dragged into prominence by half poets, the result is not poetry,
     nor till the poets among us can be   20
          "literalists of
          the imagination"[4]—above
               insolence and triviality and can present

3. "*Diary of Tolstoy*, p. 84: 'Where the boundary between prose and poetry lies, I shall never be able to understand. The question is raised in manuals of style, yet the answer to it lies beyond me. Poetry is verse: prose is not verse. Or else poetry is everything with the exception of business documents and school books.' " (Moore's note)   4. " 'Literalists of the imagination.' Yeats, *Ideas of Good and Evil* (A. H. Bullen, 1903), p. 182. 'The limitation of his view was from the very intensity of his vision; he was a too literal realist of imagination, as others are of nature; and because he believed that the figures seen by the mind's eye, when exalted by inspiration, were 'eternal existences," symbols of divine essences, he hated every grace of style that might obscure their lineaments.' " (Moore's note)

for inspection, "imaginary gardens with real toads in them," shall we have
it. In the meantime, if you demand on the one hand,
the raw material of poetry in
all its rawness and
that which is on the other hand
genuine, you are interested in poetry.   1921

ELIZABETH BISHOP

Sestina

September rain falls on the house.
In the failing light, the old grandmother
sits in the kitchen with the child
beside the Little Marvel Stove,
reading the jokes from the almanac,
laughing and talking to hide her tears.

She thinks that her equinoctial tears
and the rain that beats on the roof of the house
were both foretold by the almanac,
but only known to a grandmother.
The iron kettle sings on the stove.
She cuts some bread and says to the child,

It's time for tea now; but the child
is watching the teakettle's small hard tears
dance like mad on the hot black stove,
the way the rain must dance on the house.
Tidying up, the old grandmother
hangs up the clever almanac

on its string. Birdlike, the almanac
hovers half open above the child,
hovers above the old grandmother
and her teacup full of dark brown tears.
She shivers and says she thinks the house
feels chilly, and puts more wood in the stove.

It was to be, says the Marvel Stove.
I know what I know, says the almanac.
With crayons the child draws a rigid house
and a winding pathway. Then the child
puts in a man with buttons like tears
and shows it proudly to the grandmother.

But secretly, while the grandmother
busies herself about the stove,
the little moons fall down like tears

from between the pages of the almanac
into the flower bed the child
has carefully placed in the front of the house.   35

Time to plant tears, says the almanac.
The grandmother sings to the marvellous stove
and the child draws another inscrutable house.   1965

ISHMAEL REED

beware : do not read this poem

tonite   ,   thriller was
abt an ol woman   , so vain she
surrounded herself w /
   many mirrors

it got so bad that finally she   5
locked herself indoors & her
whole life became the
   mirrors

one day the villagers broke
into her house   ,   but she was too   10
swift for them   .   she disappeared
   into a mirror

each tenant who bought the house
after that   ,   lost a loved one to
   the ol woman in the mirror :   15
   first a little girl
   then a young woman
   then the young woman / s husband

the hunger of this poem is legendary
it has taken in many victims   20
back off from this poem
it has drawn in yr feet
back off from this poem
it has drawn in yr legs

back off from this poem   25
it is a greedy mirror
you are into this poem   .   from
   the waist down
nobody can hear you can they   ?
this poem has had you up to here   30
   belch
this poem aint got no manners

you cant call out frm this poem
relax now & go w / this poem
35 move & roll on to this poem
do not resist this poem
this poem has yr eyes
this poem has his head
this poem has his arms
40 this poem has his fingers
this poem has his fingertips
this poem is the reader & the
reader this poem

statistic   :   the us bureau of missing persons reports
45 that in 1968 over 100,000 people disappeared
leaving no solid clues
nor trace   only
a space   in the lives of their friends   1970

ARCHIBALD MacLEISH

Ars Poetica[5]

A poem should be palpable and mute
As a globed fruit,

Dumb
As old medallions to the thumb,

5 Silent as the sleeve-worn stone
Of casement ledges where the moss has grown—

A poem should be wordless
As the flight of birds.

A poem should be motionless in time
10 As the moon climbs.

Leaving, as the moon releases
Twig by twig the night-entangled trees,

Leaving, as the moon behind the winter leaves,
Memory by memory the mind—

15 A poem should be motionless in time
As the moon climbs.

A poem should be equal to:
Not true.

---

5. "The Art of Poetry," title of a poetical treatise by the Roman poet Horace (65–8 B.C.).

For all the history of grief
An empty doorway and a maple leaf.   20

For love
The leaning grasses and two lights above the sea—

A poem should not mean
But be.   1926

The Way a Poem Looks

Stanza breaks and other kinds of print spaces are important, primarily to
guide the voice and mind to a clearer sense of sound and meaning. But there
are exceptions. A few poems are written to be seen rather than heard, and their
appearance on the page is crucial to their effect. The poem "l(a," for example,
tries to visualize typographically what the poet asks you to see in your mind's
eye. Occasionally, too, poems are composed in a specific shape so that the
poem looks like a physical object. The poems that follow in this chapter—
some old, some new—illustrate ways in which visual effects may be created.
Even though poetry has traditionally been thought of as oral—words to be said,
sung, or performed rather than looked at—the idea that poems can also be
related to painting and the visual arts is an old one. Theodoric in ancient
Greece is credited with inventing **technopaegnia**—that is, the construction of
poems with visual appeal. Once, the shaping of words to resemble an object
was thought to have mystical power, but more recent attempts at **concrete
poetry** or **shaped verse** are usually playful exercises (such as Robert Holland-
er's "You Too? Me Too—Why Not? Soda Pop" [p. 361], which is shaped like a
Coke bottle) that attempt to supplement (or replace) verbal meanings with
devices from painting and sculpture.

Reading a poem like "Easter Wings" aloud wouldn't make much sense.
Our eyes are everything for a poem like that. A more frequent poetic device
involves asking the eyes to become a guide for the voice. The following poem
depends upon recognition of some standard typographical symbols and knowl-
edge of their names. We have to say those names to read the poem.

FRANKLIN P. ADAMS

Composed in the Composing Room

At stated .ic times
I love to sit and—off rhymes
Till ,tose at last I fall
Exclaiming "I don't ∧ all."

Though I'm an * objection
By running this in this here §
This ☞ of the Fleeting Hour,
This lofty -ician Tower—

A ¶er's hope dispels
All fear of deadly ‖.
You think these [ ] are a pipe?
Well, not on your †eotype.   1914

We create the right term here when we verbalize, putting the visual signs together with the words or letters printed in the poem, for example making the word "periodic" out of ".ic" or "high Phoenician" out of "-ician." Like "Easter Wings," "Composed in the Composing Room" uses typography in an extreme way; here the eyes (and mind) are drawn into a punlike game that offers more puzzle-solving pleasure than emotional effect. More often poets give us—by the visual placement of sounds—a guide to reading, inviting us to regulate the pace of our reading, notice pauses or silences, pay attention both to the syntax of the poem and to the rhetoric of the voice, thus providing us a kind of musical score for reading.

E. E. CUMMINGS

[Buffalo Bill 's][1]

Buffalo Bill 's
defunct
            who used to
            ride a watersmooth-silver
                                    stallion
and break onetwothreefourfive pigeonsjustlikethat
                                                    Jesus

---

1. Portraits XXI.

he was a handsome man
                and what i want to know is
how do you like your blueeyed boy   10
Mister Death   1923

The unusual spacing of words here, with some run together and others widely separated, provides a guide to reading, regulating both speed and sense, so that the poem can capture aloud some of the excitement and wonder of a boy's enthusiasm for a theatrical act as spectacular as that of Buffalo Bill. A good reader-aloud, with only this typographical guidance, can capture some of the wide-eyed boy's responses, remembered now in retrospect long after Buffalo Bill himself is dead.

In prose, syntax and punctuation are the main guides to the voice of a reader, providing indicators of emphasis, pace, and speed; in poetry as well they are more conventional and more common guides than extreme forms of typography, such as in "Buffalo Bill 's." Reading a poem sensitively is in some ways a lot like reading a piece of prose sensitively: one has to pay close attention to the way the sentences are put together and how they are punctuated. A good reader makes use of appropriate pauses as well as thundering emphasis; silence as well as sound is part of any poem, and reading punctuation is as important as knowing how to say the words.

Beyond punctuation, the placement and spacing of lines on the page may be helpful to a reader even when that placement is not as radical as it is in "Buffalo Bill 's." The fact that poetry looks different from prose is not an accident; decisions to make lines one length instead of another have as much to do with vocal breaks and phrasing as with functions of syntax or meaning. In a good poem, there are few accidents, not even in the way the poem meets the eye, for as readers our eyes are the most direct route to our voices; they are our scanner and director, our prompter and guide.

The eye also may help the ear in poetry in another way—guiding us to notice repeated sounds by repeated visual patterns in letters. The most common rhymes in poems occur at the ends of lines, and the arrangement of lines (the typography of the poem) often calls attention to the pattern of sounds because of the similar appearance of line-ending words, as in sonnets and other traditional verse forms and sometimes in radically unconventional patterns. Not all words that rhyme have similar spellings, of course, but similarities of word appearance seem to imply a relationship of sound too, and many poems hint at their stanza patterns and verse forms by their spatial arrangement and repeated patterns at ends of lines. The following poem takes advantage of such expectations and plays with them by forcing a letter into arbitrary line relationships, forcing words ("stew," line 2) in order to create rhymes, setting up rhyme patterns and then breaking them (lines 9–11), using false or near rhymes (lines 10–11), and creating long lines with multisyllabic rhymes that seem silly (the final two lines).

STEVIE SMITH

The Jungle Husband

Dearest Evelyn, I often think of you
Out with the guns in the jungle stew
Yesterday I hittapotamus
I put the measurements down for you but they got lost in the fuss
It's not a good thing to drink out here
You know, I've practically given it up dear.
Tomorrow I am going alone a long way
Into the jungle. It is all grey
But green on top
Only sometimes when a tree has fallen
The sun comes down plop, it is quite appalling.
You never want to go in a jungle pool
In the hot sun, it would be the act of a fool
Because it's always full of anacondas, Evelyn, not looking ill-fed
I'll say. So no more now, from your loving husband, Wilfred.   1957

Visual devices are often entertainments to amuse, puzzle, or tease readers of poetry whose chief expectations are about sound, but sometimes poets achieve surprising (and lasting) original effects by manipulations of print space. Stanzas—visual breaks in poems that indicate some kind of unit of meaning or measurement—ultimately are more than visual devices, for they point to structural questions and ultimately frame and formalize the content of poems. But they involve—as do the similar visual patterns of words that rhyme—part of the "score" of poems, and suggest one more way that sight becomes a guide to sound in many poems.

▼   ▼   ▼

GEORGE HERBERT

Easter Wings

Lord, who createdst man in wealth and store,[2]
Though foolishly he lost the same,
Decaying more and more,
Till he became
Most poor:
With thee
O let me rise
As larks,[3] harmoniously,
And sing this day thy victories:
Then shall the fall further the flight in me.

My tender age in sorrow did begin;
And still with sicknesses and shame
Thou didst so punish sin,
That I became
Most thin.
With thee
Let me combine,
And feel this day thy victory;
For, if I imp[4] my wing on thine,
Affliction shall advance the flight in me.

1633

ROBERT HERRICK

The Pillar of Fame

Fame's pillar here, at last, we set,
Out-during *Marble, Brass,* or *Jet*,[5]
   Charmed and enchanted so,
    As to withstand the blow
      Of   overthrow: 5
     Nor shall the seas,
     Or   OUTRAGES
    Of storms o'erbear
    What we up-rear;
    Tho Kingdoms fall,
  This   pillar   never   shall   10
  Decline or waste at all;
But stand for ever by his own
Firm and well fixed foundation.

1648

2. In plenty.   **3.** Which herald the morning.   **4.** Engraft. In falconry, to engraft feathers in a damaged wing, so as to restore the powers of flight (OED).   **5.** Black lignite or black marble. *Out-during:* outlasting.

BARBARA HOWES

Mirror Image: Port-au-Prince

Au petit
Salon de Coiffeur,
Monique's / hands fork
like lightning, like a baton
rise / to lead her client's hair
in *repassage:* she irons out the kinks.
Madame's brown cheek / is dusted over with a
paler shade / of costly powder. Nails and lips are red.

Her matching lips and nails incarnadined, / in the
next booth Madam consults her face / imprisoned
in the glass. Her lovely tan / is almost
gone. Oh, watch Yvonne's astute /
conductor fingers set the
permanent, / *In little*
Drawing-room of
        Hairdresser!   1954

E. E. CUMMINGS

[l(a]

l(a

le
af
fa

ll

s)
one
l

iness   1958

NORA DAUENHAUER

Tlingit Concrete Poem

```
                           t ' a   n
                      a                i
                  a    k
        x ' a a x ' x ' a a x ' x ' a a x ' x ' a a x ' x ' a a x
         a a x ' x ' a a x ' x ' a a x ' x ' a a x ' x ' a a x ' x ' a a x ' x
        ' x ' a a x ' x ' a a x ' x ' a a x ' x ' a a x ' x ' a a x ' x ' a
       x ' x ' a a x ' x ' a a x ' x ' a a x ' x ' a a x ' x ' a a x ' x ' a a x
      a a x ' x ' a a x ' x ' a a x ' x ' a a x ' x ' a a x ' x ' a a x ' x ' a a x '
     ' a a x ' x ' a a x ' x ' a a x ' x ' a a x ' x ' a a x ' x ' a a x ' x ' a a x ' x
    x ' a a x ' x ' a a x ' x ' a a x ' x ' a a x ' x ' a a x ' x ' a a x ' x ' a a x ' x '
   ' x ' a a x ' x ' a a x ' x ' a a x ' x ' a a x ' x ' a a x ' x ' a a x ' x ' a a x ' x '
   ' x ' a a x ' x ' a a x ' x ' a a x ' x ' a a x ' x ' a a x ' x ' a a x ' x ' a a x ' x ' a
   ' x ' a a x ' x ' a a x ' x ' a a x ' x ' a a x ' x ' a a x ' x ' a a x ' x ' a a x ' x ' a
  x ' x ' a a x ' x ' a a x ' x ' a a x ' x ' a a x ' x ' a a x ' x ' a a x ' x ' a a x ' x ' a
  x ' x ' a a x ' x ' a a x ' x ' a a x ' x ' a a x ' x ' a a x ' x ' a a x ' x ' a a x ' x ' a
  x ' x ' a a x ' x ' a a x ' x ' a a x ' x ' a a x ' x ' a a x ' x ' a a x ' x ' a a x ' x ' a
  x ' x ' a a x ' x ' a a x ' x ' a a x ' x ' a a x ' x ' a a x ' x ' a a x ' x ' a a x ' x ' a
   ' x ' a a x ' x ' a a x ' x ' a a x ' x ' a a x ' x ' a a x ' x ' a a x ' x ' a a x ' x ' a
   ' x ' a a x ' x ' a a x ' x ' a a x ' x ' a a x ' x ' a a x ' x ' a a x ' x ' a a x ' x '
   ' x ' a a x ' x ' a a x ' x ' a a x ' x ' a a x ' x ' a a x ' x ' a a x ' x ' a a x ' x '
    x ' a a x ' x ' a a x ' x ' a a x ' x ' a a x ' x ' a a x ' x ' a a x ' x ' a a x ' x '
     ' a a x ' x ' a a x ' x ' a a x ' x ' a a x ' x ' a a x ' x ' a a x ' x ' a a x ' x
      ' a a x ' x ' a a x ' x ' a a x ' x ' a a x ' x ' a a x ' x ' a a x ' x ' a a x '
       a a x ' x ' a a x ' x ' a a x ' x ' a a x ' x ' a a x ' tɬ ' u k w x ' a a x ' x ' a a x '
        a x ' x ' a a x ' x ' a a x ' x ' a a x ' x ' a a x ' x ' a a x ' x ' a a x
         x ' x ' a a x ' x ' a a x ' x ' a a x ' x ' a a x ' x ' a a x ' x ' a a
          ' x ' a a x ' x ' a a x ' x ' a a x ' x ' a a x ' x ' a a x ' x ' a
           ' a a x ' x ' a a x ' x ' a a x ' x ' a a x ' x ' a a x ' x
            a x ' x ' a a x ' x ' a a x ' x ' a a x ' x ' a a x ' x ' a a x
             ' x ' a a x ' x ' a a x ' x ' a a x ' x ' a a x ' x ' a
              ' a a x ' x ' a a x ' x ' a a x ' x ' a a x ' x '
               ' x ' a a x ' x ' a a x ' x ' a a
                ' x ' a a
```

akat'ani = stem
x'aax' = apple
tl'ukwx = worm

1984

JOHN HOLLANDER

A State of Nature

Some broken
Iroquois adze
prounded southward
and resembled this
outlined once But now
boundaries foul-lines
and even sea-coasts are
naturally involved with
mappers and followers of
borders So that we who grew
up here might think That steak is
shaped too much like New York to be real And like
the shattered flinty implement whose ghost lives
inside our sense of what this rough chunk should
by right of history recall the language spoken by
its shapers now inhabits only streams and lakes and
hills The natural names are only a chattering and mean
only the land they label How shall we live in a forest of
such murmurs with
no ideas but in
forms a state
whose name
passes
for
a city

1969

EARLE BIRNEY

Anglosaxon Street

Dawn drizzle ended dampness steams from
blotching brick and blank plasterwaste
Faded housepatterns hoary and finicky
unfold stuttering stick like a phonograph

Here is a ghetto gotten for goyim
O with care denuded of nigger and kike
No coonsmell rankles reeks only cellarrot
Ottar[6] of carexhaust catcorpse and cookinggrease
Imperial hearts heave in this haven
Cracks across windows are welded with slogans
There'll Always Be An England enhances geraniums
and V's for Victory vanquish the housefly

6. Roselike fragrance.

Ho! with climbing sun march the bleached beldames
festooned with shopping bags farded[7] flatarched
bigthewed Saxonwives stepping over buttrivers   15
waddling back wienerladen to suckle smallfry

Hoy! with sunslope shrieking over hydrants
flood from learninghall the lean fingerlings
Nordic nobblecheeked[8] not all clean of nose
leaping Commandowise into leprous lanes   20

What! after whistleblow! spewed from wheelboat
after daylight doughtiness dire handplay
in sewertrench or sandpit come Saxonthegns
Junebrown Jutekings[9] jawslack for meat

Sit after supper on smeared doorsteps   25
not humbly swearing hatedeeds on Huns
profiteers politicians pacifists Jews

Then by twobit magic to muse in movie
unlock picturehoard or lope to alehall
soaking bleakly in beer skittleless   30

Home again to hotbox and humid husbandhood
in slumbertrough adding sleepily to Anglekin
Alongside in lanenooks carling and leman[1]
caterwaul and clip[2] careless of Saxonry
with moonglow and haste and a higher heartbeat   35

Slumbers now slumtrack unstinks cooling
waiting brief for milkmaid mornstar and worldrise

Toronto 1942, revised 1966

▼ ▼ ▼

EXTERNAL FORM A Glossary

alliteration: the repetition of sounds in nearby words; alliteration usually involves the initial consonant sounds of words (and sometimes internal consonants in stressed syllables)

assonance: the repetition of vowel sounds in a line or series of lines; assonance often affects pace (by unbalancing short and long vowel patterns) and the way words included in the pattern tend to seem underscored

---

7. Rouged. 8. Pimpled. 9. Refers to the Jutes, the German tribe that invaded England in the fifth century and spearheaded the Anglo-Saxon conquest. *Saxonthegns:* Freemen who provided military services for the Saxon lords. 1. Lover. *Carling:* old woman. 2. Embrace.

ballad stanza: a four-line stanza, the second and fourth lines of which are iambic trimeter and rhyme with each other; the first and third lines, in iambic tetrameter, do not rhyme

blank verse: unrhymed iambic pentameter

concrete poetry/shaped verse: an attempt to supplement (or replace) verbal meaning with visual devices from painting and sculpture

English or **Shakespearian sonnet:** three four-line stanzas and a couplet (two lines), rhymed *abab cdcd efef gg*

free verse: poetry that avoids regularized meter and has no significant recurrent stress rhythms, although it may use other repetitive patterns— of words, phrases, or structures

heroic couplet: a pair of rhymed lines of iambic pentameter

Italian or **Petrarchan sonnet:** an octave (eight lines) and a sestet (six lines); typically rhymed *abbaabba cdecde*, although it has many variations that still reflect the basic division into two parts

limerick: two lines of rhymed trimeter, two lines of rhymed dimeter, and an additional line of trimeter, the last word of which is the same as, or rhymes with, the last word of the first line

memory devices / mnemonic devices: forms, such as rhyme, built into poems to help reciters remember them

sestina: six six-line stanzas and a final three-line stanza, all unrhymed; but the final word in each line of the first stanza then becomes the final word in other stanzas (though in a different specific pattern); the final stanza uses these words again in a specified way, one in each half line

sonnet: a form, usually only a single stanza, that offers several related possibilities for its rhyme scheme, but is always fourteen lines long and usually written in iambic pentameter

Spenserian stanza: eight lines of iambic pentameter and a ninth line of iambic hexameter, called an alexandrine, rhymed *ababbcbcc*

stanzas: groups of lines with a specific cogency of their own and usually set off from one another by a space

syllabic verse: a form in which the poet establishes a precise number of syllables to a line and repeats them in subsequent stanzas

technopaegnia: the construction of poems with visual appeal

terza rima: the three-line stanza in which Dante wrote *The Divine Comedy*; each iambic pentameter stanza *(aba)* interlocks with the next through rhyme *(bcb, cdc, ded,* etc.)

tetrameter couplet: a pair of rhymed, four-beat lines

villanelle: contains five three-line stanzas and a final four-line stanza; only two rhyme sounds are permitted in the entire poem, and the first and third lines of the first stanza are repeated, alternately, as the third line of subsequent stanzas until the last

QUESTIONS

1. Chart the rhyme scheme of Keats's "On the Sonnet," and then, after a careful reading of the poem aloud, mark the major structural breaks in the poem. At what points do the structural breaks and the breaks in rhyme pattern coincide? At what points do they conflict? Can you account for the variations in terms of the poem's meaning?

2. Describe the structure of "Ozymandias." In what sense is it an Italian sonnet? Why do some of the rhythm sounds in the first eight lines contrast with rhymes in the last six?

3. What justification is there for calling "Joy Sonnet in a Random Universe" a sonnet?

4. What conventions of description is "My mistress' eyes are nothing like the sun" working against? How can you tell? Describe the tone of the poem. What strategies, beyond the basic one of inverting conventions, help to create the poem's special tone?

5. Characterize the "you" in "Sonnet to a Negro in Harlem." Describe the speaker's tone toward him. Describe the function of setting in the poem.

6. What principles seem to determine the form of "Anglosaxon Street"? How do sound patterns in the poem relate to its form?

WRITING SUGGESTIONS

1. Consider the structure of "The White House" and the poem's themes of confinement and exclusion. In what specific ways does the poem use the tight restrictions of the sonnet form? Write an essay of about two pages on the way content and form interact in the poem.

2. Compare "The Harlem Dancer" (also by Claude McKay) with "The White House," considering the very different uses the sonnet form accommodates. Write a parallel essay to that above in which you show how "The Harlem Dancer" uses the sonnet form to further its themes and tones.

3. Consider carefully the structure and sequencing in "First Fight. Then Fiddle." Notice how various uses of sound in the poem (rhyme, onomatapoeia, and alliteration, for example) help to enforce its themes and tones. In an essay of about 600 words, show the relationship between "sound and sense" in the poem.

8 THE WHOLE TEXT

I n the previous seven chapters, we have been thinking about one thing at a time—symbolism, meter, stanza form, and so on—and each poem has been read and discussed primarily in terms of a single problem. Learning to deal with one problem at a time is good educational practice and in the long run will make you a more careful and more effective reader of poems. Still, the elements of poems do not work individually but in combination, and in considering even the simplest elements (speaker, for example, or setting) we have noticed how categories overlap—how, for example, the question of setting in "Cherrylog Road" quickly merges into questions about the speaker, his state of mind, his personality, his distance from the central events in the poem. Thinking about a single issue never fully does justice to an individual poem; no poem depends for all its effects on just one device or one element of craft. Poems are complex wholes that demand varieties of attention, and ultimately *all* the questions you have been learning to ask need to be applied to any poem you read. Reading any poem fully and well involves all the questions about craft, form, and tradition that you can think to ask. Not all questions are equally relevant to all poems, of course, but moving systematically through your whole list of questions will ultimately enable you to get beyond the fragmentation of particular issues and approach the whole poem. It is now time to think about how the various elements of poems work together to create the effects of the whole poem.

Here is a short poem in which several of the issues we have considered come up almost simultaneously:

ELIZABETH JENNINGS

Delay

The radiance of that star that leans on me
Was shining years ago. The light that now
Glitters up there my eye may never see
And so the time lag teases me with how

Love that loves now may not reach me until
Its first desire is spent. The star's impulse

Must wait for eyes to claim it beautiful
And love arrived may find us somewhere else.   1953

In most poems, several issues come up more or less at once, and the ana-
lytic practice of separating issues is a convenience rather than an assertion of
priority or order. In "Delay," a lot of the basic questions (about speaker, situa-
tion, and setting, for example) seem to be put on hold in the beginning, but if
we proceed systematically the poem begins to open itself to us. The first line
identifies the "I" (or rather, in this case, "me") of the poem as an observer of
the bright star that is the main object in the poem and the principal source of
its imagery, its "plot," and its analogical argument. But we learn little detail
about the speaker. She surfaces again in lines 4 and 5 and with someone else
("us") in line 8, but she is always in the objective case—acted on rather than
acting. All that is certain about her is that she has some knowledge of the time
it takes light from the stars to reach her and that she contemplates deeply and
at length about the meaning and effect of such time lags. We are given even
less detail about setting and situation; somewhere the speaker is watching a
bright star and meditating on the fact that she is seeing it long, long after its
actual light was sent forth. Her location is not specified, and the time, though
probably night, could be any night (we do know that the speaker lives in the
age of modern astronomy, i.e., that the speed of light and the distance of the
stars from Earth are understood); the only other explicit clues we have about
situation involves the "us" of the final line and the fact that the speaker's con-
cern with time seems oddly personal, something that matters to her emotional
life—not merely a matter of stellar knowledge.

The poem's language helps us understand much more about the speaker
and her situation, as does the poem's structure and stanza form. The most cru-
cial word in the first stanza is probably the verb "leans" (line 1); certainly it is
the most unusual and surprising word. Because a star cannot literally *lean* on
its observer, the word seems to suggest the speaker's perception of her relation-
ship to the star. Perhaps she feels that the star impinges on her, that she is
somehow *subject* to its influence, though not in the popular, astrological sense.
Here the star influences the speaker because she understands something about
the way the universe works and can apply her knowledge of light and light
years in an analogical way to her own life: it "leans" because it tells her some-
thing about how observers are affected by their relationships to what they
observe. And it is worth noticing how fully the speaker thinks of herself as
object rather than actor. Here, as throughout the poem, she is acted upon;
things happen *to* her—the star leans on her, the time lag teases her (line 4),

love may not reach her (line 5), and she (along with someone else) is the object sought in the final line.

Other crucial words also help clarify the speaker and her situation. The words "radiance" (line 1) and "[g]litters" (line 3) are fairly standard ones to describe stars, but here their standard meanings are carefully qualified by their position in time. The radiance is from years ago and seems to be unavailable to the speaker, who now sees only glitter, something far less warm and resonant. And the word "impulse" in line 6 invokes technical knowledge about light. Here a star is not impulsive or quickly spent but must "wait" for its reception in the eye of the beholder where it becomes "beautiful"; in physics, an impulse combines force and duration. Hence, the receiver of light—the beholder, the acted upon—becomes important, and we begin to see why the speaker always appears as object: she is the receiver and interpreter, and the light is not complete—its duration not established—until she receives and interprets it. The star does, after all, *lean* on (depend on) her in some objective sense as well as the subjective one in which she first seems to report it.

The stanza form suggests that the poem may have stages and that its meaning may emerge in two parts, a suggestion that is in fact confirmed by the poem's form and structure. The first stanza is entirely about stars and stargazing, but the second stanza establishes the analogy with love that becomes the poem's central metaphor. Now, too, more becomes clear about the speaker and her situation. Her concern is about delay, "time lag" (line 4), and the fact that "Love that loves now may not reach me until / Its first desire is spent" (lines 5–6), a strong indication that her initial observation of the star is driven by feeling and her emotional context. Her attempt to put the remoteness of feeling into a perspective that will enable understanding and patience becomes the "plot" of the poem, and her final calm recognition about "us"—that "love arrived may find us somewhere else"—is, if not comforting, nevertheless a recognition that patience is important and that some things do last. Even the sounds of the poem—in this case the way rhyme is used—help support the meaning of the poem and the tone it achieves. The rhymes in the first part of the poem reflect perfectly the stable sense of ancient stars, while in the second stanza the sounds involve near-rhyme: there is harmony here, but in human life and emotion nothing is quite perfect.

Here is another short poem that deserves similar detailed attention to its several elements:

ANONYMOUS

Western Wind

Western wind, when wilt thou blow,
    The small rain down can rain?
Christ, if my love were in my arms
    And I in my bed again!   15th century

Perhaps the most obvious thing here is the poem's structure: its first two
lines seem to have little to do with the last two. How are we to account for
these two distinct and apparently unrelated directions, the calm concern with
natural processes in the first part and the emotional outburst about loneliness
and lovelessness in the second? The best route to the whole poem is still to
begin with the most simple of questions—who? when? where? what is happen-
ing?—and proceed to more difficult and complex ones.

As in "Delay," the speaker here offers little explicit autobiography. In the
first two lines, there is no personal information. The question these lines ask
could be delivered quite impersonally; they could be part of a philosophical
meditation. The abbreviated syntax at the end of line 1 (the question of causal-
ity is not fully stated, and we have to supply the "so that" implied at the end of
the line) may suggest strong feeling and emotional upset, but it tells us nothing
intimate and offers little information except that the time is spring (that's when
the western wind blows). No place is indicated, no year, no particulars of situa-
tion. But the next two lines, while remaining inexplicit about exact details,
make the speaker's situation clear enough: his love is no longer in his arms,
and he wishes she were. (We don't really know genders here, and my guess is
based on typical practice in the fifteenth century.)

The poem's language is a study in contrast, and it guides us to see the two-
part structure clearly. The question asked of the wind in the first two lines
involves straightforward, steady language, but the third line bursts with agony
and personal despair. The power of the first word of the third line—especially
in an age of belief—suggests a speaker ready to state his loss in the strongest
possible terms, and the parallel statements of loss in lines 3 and 4 suggest not
only the speaker's physical relationship to his love but also his displacement
from home: he is deprived of both place and love, human contact and contact
with his past. His longing for a world ordered according to his past experience
is structured to parallel his longing for the spring wind that brings the world
back to life. The two parts of the poem both express a desire for return—to life,

to order, to causal relationships within the world. Setting has in fact become a central theme in the poem, and what the poem expresses tonally involves a powerful desire for stability and belonging—an effect that grows out of our sense of the speaker's situation and character. Speaker, setting, language, and structure here intertwine to create the intense focus of the poem.

Here is another short poem in which the several elements noticeably interrelate:

ROBERT HERRICK

Upon Julia's Clothes

Whenas in silks my Julia goes
Then, then, methinks, how sweetly flows
That liquefaction of her clothes.

Next, when I cast mine eyes, and see
That brave[1] vibration, each way free,
O, how that glittering taketh me!

5

1648

The poem is unabashed in its admiration of the way Julia looks, and nearly everything in its six short lines contributes to its celebratory tone. Perhaps the most striking thing about the poem involves its unusual, highly suggestive use of words. "[G]oes" at the end of line 1 may be the first word to call special attention to itself, though we will return in a minute to the very first word of the poem. "Walks" or "moves" would seem to be more obvious choices; "goes" is more neutral and less specific and in most circumstances would seem an inferior choice, but here the point seems to be to describe Julia in a kind of seamless and unspecified motion and from a specific angle, because the poem is anxious to record the effect of Julia's movement on the speaker (already a second element becomes crucial) rather than the specifics of Julia herself. Another word that seems especially important is "liquefaction" (line 3), also an unusual and suggestive word about motion. Again it implies no specific kind of motion, just smoothness and seamlessness, and it is applied not to Julia but to her clothes—the kind of indirection that doesn't really fool anybody. Other words that might repay a close look include "vibration" in line 5 (the speaker is finally willing to be a little more direct), "brave" and "free" (also in line 5), and "glittering" and "taketh" in line 6.

Had we begun conventionally by thinking about speaker, situation, and set-

1. Handsome, showy.

ting, we would have quickly noticed the precise way that the speaker chose to clothe Julia: "in silks," which move almost as one with her body. And we would have noticed that the speaker positions himself almost as voyeur (standing for us as observers, of course, but also for himself as the central figure in the poem). Not much detail about situation or setting is given (and the speaker is characterized only as a viewer and appreciator), but one thing about the scene is crucial. It takes us back to the first word of the poem, "whenas." The slightly quaint quality of the word may at first obscure, to a modern reader, just what it tells us about the situation, that it is a *kind* of scene rather than a single event. "Whenas" is very close to "whenever"; the speaker's claim seems to be that he responds this way *whenever* Julia dons her silks—apparently fairly often, at least in his memory or imagination.

Most of the speaker's language is sensual and rather provocative (he is anxious to share his responses with others so that *everyone* will know just how "taking" Julia is), but there is one rather elaborate (though somewhat disguised) metaphor that suggests his awareness of his own calculation and its consequences. In the beginning of the second stanza he describes how he "cast" his eyes: it is a metaphor from fishing, a frequent one in love poetry about luring, chasing, and catching. Julia is the object. The metaphor continues two lines later, but the angler is himself caught: he is taken by the "glittering" lure. This turning of the tables, drawing as it does on a traditional, common image that is then modified to help characterize the speaker, gives a little depth to the show: whatever the slither and glitter, there is not just showing off and sensuality but a catch in this angling.

Many other elements in the poem are worth comment, especially because they quickly relate to each other. Consider the way the poet uses sounds, first of all in picking words like "liquefaction" that are themselves virtually onomatopoeic, but then also using rhyme very cleverly. There are only two rhyme sounds in the poem, one in the first stanza, the other in the second. The long *ee* of the second becomes almost exclamatory, and the three words of the first seem to become linked in a kind of separate grammar of their own, as if "goes," "flows," and "clothes" were all part of a single action—pretty much what the poem claims on a thematic level. A lot is going on in this short and simple poem, and although a reader can get at it step by step by thinking about element after element, the interlocking of the elements is finally what is most impressive. It's easy to see that the plot here reenacts the familiar stances of woman as object and man as gazer, but we need to be flexible enough in our analysis and reading to consider not only all the analytical categories, but also the ways in which they work together.

Going back to poems read earlier in the course—with the methods and approaches you have learned since then—can be a useful exercise in seeing how different elements of poems interrelate. Look, for example, at the stanza divisions in "Cherrylog Road" and consider how the neatly spaced, apparently discrete units work against the sometimes frantic pacing of the poem. Or consider the character of the speaker, or the fundamental metaphor of "wreckage" that sponsors the poem, relative to the idea of speaker. Go back and read "Woodchucks" while thinking about structural questions, or consider how the effaced speaker works in "Aunt Jennifer's Tigers"; or think about metaphor in "The Vacuum."

Here are seven new poems to analyze. As you read them, think about the elements discussed in the first seven chapters—but rather than thinking about a single element at a time, try to consider relationships, how the different elements combine to make you respond not to a single device but to a complex set of strategies and effects.

▼ ▼ ▼

W. H. AUDEN

Musée des Beaux Arts[2]

About suffering they were never wrong,
The Old Masters: how well they understood
Its human position; how it takes place
While someone else is eating or opening a window or just walking dully along;
5 How, when the aged are reverently, passionately waiting
For the miraculous birth, there always must be
Children who did not specially want it to happen, skating
On a pond at the edge of the wood:
They never forgot
10 That even the dreadful martyrdom must run its course
Anyhow in a corner, some untidy spot
Where the dogs go on with their doggy life and the torturer's horse
Scratches its innocent behind on a tree.

In Brueghel's *Icarus*,[3] for instance: how everything turns away
15 Quite leisurely from the disaster; the plowman may

2. The Museum of the Fine Arts, in Brussels.   3. *Landscape with the Fall of Icarus*, by Pieter Brueghel the elder (1525?–1569), located in the Brussels Museum. According to Greek myth, Daedalus and his son Icarus escaped from imprisonment by using homemade wings of wax; but Icarus flew too near the sun, the wax melted, and he fell into the sea and drowned. In the Brueghel painting the central figure is a peasant plowing, and several other figures are more immediately

Have heard the splash, the forsaken cry,
But for him it was not an important failure; the sun shone
As it had to on the white legs disappearing into the green
Water; and the expensive delicate ship that must have seen
Something amazing, a boy falling out of the sky,   20
Had somewhere to get to and sailed calmly on.

1938

GEORGE HERBERT

The Collar

I struck the board[4] and cried, "No more;
        I will abroad!
What? shall I ever sigh and pine?
My lines[5] and life are free, free as the road,
    Loose as the wind, as large as store.[6]   5
        Shall I be still in suit?[7]
Have I no harvest but a thorn
To let me blood, and not restore
What I have lost with cordial[8] fruit?
        Sure there was wine   10
Before my sighs did dry it; there was corn
    Before my tears did drown it.
Is the year only lost to me?
    Have I no bays[9] to crown it,
No flowers, no garlands gay? All blasted?   15
        All wasted?
Not so, my heart; but there is fruit,
        And thou hast hands.
Recover all thy sigh-blown age
On double pleasures: leave thy cold dispute   20
Of what is fit, and not. Forsake thy cage,
        Thy rope of sands,[1]
Which petty thoughts have made, and made to thee
    Good cable, to enforce and draw,
        And be thy law,   25
While thou didst wink[2] and wouldst not see.
        Away! take heed;
        I will abroad.
Call in thy death's-head[3] there; tie up thy fears.

noticeable than Icarus who, disappearing into the sea, is easy to miss in the lower right-hand corner. Equally ignored by the figures is a dead body in the woods.   **4.** Table.   **5.** Lot.   **6.** A storehouse; i.e., in abundance.   **7.** In service to another.   **8.** Reviving, restorative.   **9.** Wreaths of triumph.   **1.** Moral restrictions.   **2.** I.e., close your eyes to the weaknesses of such restrictions.   **3.** *Memento mori*, a skull intended to remind people of their mortality.

He that forbears
To suit and serve his need,
Deserves his load."
But as I raved and grew more fierce and wild
At every word,
Methought I heard one calling, *Child!*
And I replied, *My Lord.*

1633

ANNE SEXTON

With Mercy for the Greedy

for my friend, Ruth, who urges me to make an appointment
for The Sacrament of Confession

Concerning your letter in which you ask
me to call a priest and in which you ask
me to wear The Cross that you enclose;
your own cross,
your dog bitten cross,
no larger than a thumb,
small and wooden, no thorns, this rose.

I pray to its shadow,
that gray place
where it lies on your letter . . . deep, deep.
I detest my sins and I try to believe
in The Cross. I touch its tender hips, its dark jawed face,
its solid neck, its brown sleep.

True. There is
a beautiful Jesus.
He is frozen to his bones like a chunk of beef.
How desperately he wanted to pull his arms in!
How desperately I touch his vertical and horizontal axes!
But I can't. Need is not quite belief.

All morning long
I have worn
your cross, hung with package string around my throat.
It tapped me lightly as a child's heart might,
tapping second hand, softly waiting to be born.
Ruth, I cherish the letter you wrote.

My friend, my friend, I was born
doing reference work in sin, and born
confessing it. This is what poems are:
with mercy

for the greedy; 30
they are the tongue's wrangle,
the world's pottage, the rat's star. p. 1961

EMILY DICKINSON

[My Life had stood—a Loaded Gun—]

My Life had stood—a Loaded Gun—
In Corners—till a Day
The Owner passed—identified—
And carried Me away—

And now We roam in Sovereign Woods— 5
And now We hunt the Doe—
And every time I speak for Him—
The Mountains straight reply—

And do I smile, such cordial light
Upon the Valley glow— 10
It is as a Vesuvian face
Had let its pleasure through—

And when at Night—Our good Day done—
I guard My Master's Head—
'Tis better than the Eider-Duck's 15
Deep Pillow—to have shared—

To foe of His—I'm deadly foe—
None stir the second time—
On whom I lay a Yellow Eye—
Or an emphatic Thumb— 20

Though I than He—may longer live
He longer must—than I—
For I have but the power to kill,
ca. 1863 Without—the power to die—

ROBERT FROST

Design

I found a dimpled spider, fat and white,
On a white heal-all,[4] holding up a moth

4. A plant, also called the "all-heal" and "self-heal," with tightly clustered violet-blue flowers.

Like a white piece of rigid satin cloth—
Assorted characters of death and blight
5 Mixed ready to begin the morning right,
Like the ingredients of a witches' broth—
A snow-drop spider, a flower like a froth,
And dead wings carried like a paper kite.

What had that flower to do with being white,
10 The wayside blue and innocent heal-all?
What brought the kindred spider to that height,
Then steered the white moth thither in the night?
What but design of darkness to appall?—
If design govern in a thing so small.   1936

ROBERT HASS

The Feast

The lovers loitered on the deck talking,
the men who were with men and the men who were with new women,
a little shrill and electric, and the wifely women
who had repose and beautifully lined faces
5 and coppery skin. She had taken the turkey from the oven
and her friends were talking on the deck
in the steady sunshine. She imagined them
drifting toward the food, in small groups, finishing
sentences, lifting a pickle or a sliver of turkey,
10 nibbling a little with unconscious pleasure. And
she imagined setting it out artfully, the white meat,
the breads, antipasto, the mushrooms and salad
arranged down the oak counter cleanly, and how they all came
as in a dance when she called them. She carved meat
15 and then she was crying. Then she was in darkness
crying. She didn't know what she wanted.   1974

ADRIENNE RICH

Living in Sin

She had thought the studio would keep itself;
no dust upon the furniture of love.
Half heresy, to wish the taps less vocal,
the panes relieved of grime. A plate of pears,
5 a piano with a Persian shawl, a cat
stalking the picturesque amusing mouse

had risen at his urging.
Not that at five each separate stair would writhe
under the milkman's tramp; that morning light
so coldly would delineate the scraps   10
of last night's cheese and three sepulchral bottles;
that on the kitchen shelf among the saucers
a pair of beetle-eyes would fix her own—
envoy from some village in the moldings . . .
Meanwhile, he, with a yawn,   15
sounded a dozen notes upon the keyboard,
declared it out of tune, shrugged at the mirror,
rubbed at his beard, went out for cigarettes;
while she, jeered by the minor demons,
pulled back the sheets and made the bed and found   20
a towel to dust the table-top,
and let the coffee-pot boil over on the stove.
By evening she was back in love again,
though not so wholly but throughout the night
she woke sometimes to feel the daylight coming   25
like a relentless milkman up the stairs.   1955

ANONYMOUS

[My love in her attire doth show her wit]

My love in her attire doth show her wit,
    It doth so well become her;
For every season she hath dressings fit,
    For winter, spring, and summer.
    No beauty she doth miss   5
    When all her robes are on;
    But beauty's self she is
    When all her robes are gone.   1602

▼ ▼ ▼

QUESTIONS

1. Consider the setting of "Musée des Beaux Arts" both in the sense of the painting and of its location in the museum. In what different ways do the two settings become important? How does the use of setting relate to the way the speaker is conceived? Define the role played by all of the other characters in

the poem, including the people on the ship. Whose attitudes (or perhaps words) are being echoed or parodied in line 20? Describe the poem's structure.

2. Consider the elements of speaker and situation simultaneously when you analyze "The Collar."

3. Consider the interrelation of the elements of speaker, words and word order, and stanza form in "My Life had stood—a Loaded Gun—."

4. Consider the interrelationships among speaker, structure, stanza form, and tone in "Design."

5. Compare Herrick's "Upon Julia's Clothes" with the anonymous "My love in her attire." In what ways does sound affect feeling in each? In what way does sound affect meaning? tone?

WRITING SUGGESTIONS

1. Find a reproduction of the Brueghel painting on which Auden's poem is based. "Read" the painting carefully, and notice which details Auden mentions and which he does not. What aspect(s) of the painting does he choose to emphasize? What does he ignore? Write a three-page essay in which you show exactly how Auden *uses* the Brueghel painting in his poem.

2. Consider "Design" as a sonnet. What features of the sonnet seem especially important to the effects Frost achieves here? Consider the structure, rhyme scheme, and imagery of the poem. Now look at another Frost poem, "Range-Finding" (p. 494), and ask the same questions about this poem. Which poem seems to you to use the sonnet form more effectively? why?

Write a four- to five-page essay, comparing the two poems and evaluating their use of the sonnet form.

STUDENT WRITING

Below is a whole-text analysis of Maxine Kumin's "Woodchucks" (p. 36). In it, the student addresses the setting, language, tone, structure, rhythm, and, finally, the meaning of the poem.

Tragedy in Five Stanzas: "Woodchucks"

Meaghan E. Parker

Maxine Kumin's poem, "Woodchucks," is not, as the title might suggest, about cute, furry woodchucks, but instead describes how the speaker changes as she tries to kill them, revealing aspects of human attitudes towards killing. The speaker undergoes an internal conflict as she realizes her capacity for murder during her battle with the woodchucks. She is caught up in the age-old struggle of humans against nature, except that this time, it takes place in the modern, technological world. This battle is presented in five dramatic scenes, marked by six-line stanzas; the poem's structure echoes the format of a classical tragedy in five acts. The poem is subtly organized, each stanza rhyming *abcacb,* and more or less employing a pentameter line, mixing iambs with anapests. Although the rhyme and meter remain mostly constant over the course of this highly structured poem, the tone and pacing change with each stanza, as the speaker's attitudes transform during the struggle with the woodchucks. The poet indicates the development of the speaker's internal conflict by employing word choice to change the tone from slightly humorous and relaxed to indignant martial righteousness and finally to a harsh and primitive hunter's voice, and utilizing pacing and meter to build the action to its climax.

The poem is set in small-town North America, where the speaker grows marigolds, broccoli, carrots, roses and chard in her garden. Although the speaker buys the gas bomb from the "Feed and Grain Exchange," she is not a farmer, since she has only a "vegetable patch" (lines 2 and 11). Therefore, her killing of the woodchucks is not an occupational or economic necessity; the woodchucks were merely a nuisance, and the speaker is sort of dabbling in killing. The first line states that the "gassing . . . didn't turn out right," not that it didn't work, emphasizing with this understatement the dilettantish air of the speaker's activities (line 1). The first stanza employs a playful humor: the gas is called a "knockout bomb," like some comic-book weapon, and the speaker makes a pun on the word "airtight" (lines 2–4). The store "featured" the bomb, as if it were displayed and advertised as a consumer desirable, not as a agent of death (line 3). Line 3 utilizes anapestic feet to add to the humorous tone, and most of the lines of stanza 1 are composed of long clauses, creating an even, calm pacing. The speaker and her compatriots ("we") had a made a "case against them," suggesting that the decision to kill the woodchucks was a calm, rational, legal event, yet the woodchucks evade the law by escaping "out of range" underground (lines 4–6). The escalation of the battle is indicated by the military term "range" and the woodchucks' refusal to play by the rules (line 6).

The second stanza is less light-hearted; even though the irrepressible woodchucks "turned up again" "up to scratch," they are now unmistakably opponents to the "we," who attacked them with "cyanide" (lines 7–9). The weapon seems more sinister now; not just gas from a "merciful" "knockout bomb," but murderous cyanide. The last three lines are a litany of the woodchuck's crimes against nature, each one described as increasing in savagery and wanton destruction. First, they merely "brought down the marigolds," but in a "matter of course," thoughtless way, then they "took over" the vegetables, as if they were marauding bandits conquering the speaker's territory (lines 10–11). The speaker is horrified at the "nipping" and "beheading" of the vegetables; the use of the execution-style word "beheading" to create indignation at the death of a plant is ironic, probably consciously on the part of the speaker, since she had tried to execute the woodchuck (line 12). The litany of crimes is reeled off in quick anapestic feet, subtly hinting at the irony of the speaker's anger at the woodchucks and the ridiculousness of the escalating battle.

The action picks up pace in stanza 3, the center of the poem and the point at which the speaker makes her transformation from silent killer to murderous hunter. She indignantly implies that the woodchucks would steal "the food from our mouths": a cliché that is supposed to indicate what heartless criminals the woodchucks are, even though the poem does not indicate that the speaker is a subsistence farmer who would starve without the vegetables (line 13). Even so, she enjoys the feel of the gun, "righteously thrilling" to have the weapon of her justified revenge in her hands (line 13). The ".22" and the "bullets' neat noses" feel right and good, and while the woodchucks are depersonalized into the enemy, the bullets gain "noses" (line 14). The killer is "righteous," "fallen from grace" and "puffed with Darwinian pieties"; these heavy-handed, Bible-thumping words echo religious and political leaders' sermons against evil enemies. The pace of the first four lines of this stanza is heavy and martial, booming with polysyllabic words and stirring phrases. The meter is the most irregular in this stanza, with the two stressed syllables and similar sounds of "*lapsed*" and "*pacifist*" pounding the contrast home between the speaker's current manifestation as righteous killer and her former beliefs (line 15). Lines 15 and 16 begin with a stress, on "I" and "puffed"; the majority of the other lines in the poem begin with an unstressed syllable, so this pair of exceptions stands out, at the exact center of the poem, and present the turning point of her attitudes towards killing. Now "fallen from grace," she is "puffed" like a self-righteous windbag, and exchanges her pacifism for the maxim of survival of the fittest (lines 15–16). Line 17 begins the switch in tone from martial sloganeering to impersonal, hunting slang, as the speaker "drew a bead" on a woodchuck and kills him. His death is contrasted with the perennialness of the "everbearing roses," for whose sake he dies; this phrase indicates an undercurrent of regret at the killing of the woodchuck (line 18).

The fourth stanza speeds up, using short, harsh clashing words in short simple clauses, instead of the sermonizing phrases of the last stanza. The speaker says she "dropped the mother": "drop" is a crude, impersonal, and unfeeling word for "shot dead," and indicates the speaker's new callous attitude towards the killing of the woodchucks (line 19). Similarly, the description of the woodchuck "flipflopp[ing] in the air" is gratuitous and violent, and the stress on "flip," since the first syllable of the line should be unstressed, emphasizes the visual image of the helpless, blown-away woodchuck (line 20). The speaker immediately moves on: "another baby next" is killed without comment (line 22). In the same line, she counts down "O one-two-three" for the three woodchucks she's killed, and the three strong stresses lead into the climax of the poem, where she announces what she's become: "murderer" and "hawkeye killer" (lines 23–24). The killer comes "on stage forthwith," as the speaker appears fully transformed by her killing, her capability for murderous action arising from her nature to triumph over her professed pacifism. The stage metaphor reinforces the five-act tragic structure that the poem mirrors and line 24 brings the poem to its climax in the fourth stanza.

Throughout the poem, the poet uses the directions down and up to contrast life and death. The woodchucks "turn up" alive (line 7), "up to scratch" (line 9) from their "sub-sub-basement," but then they "brought down the marigolds" (line 10), so they "died down in the . . . roses" (line 18), "flipflopped and fell" after being "dropped" (lines 19–20). The speaker, on the other hand, was "up to scratch" (line 9) but "[fell] from grace" (line 15), so the "murderer inside [her] rose up hard," as her former pacifist self died down and was reborn as a killer (line 23). In the final stanza, the speaker, now living as this new self, describes her continuing struggle with the woodchuck and the tolls this battle is taking on her, as she remains "cocked and ready day after day after day" and her obsession with hunting this elusive prey keeps her awake at night, dreaming of shooting (lines 26-28). The pacing slows, as the action falls from the climax, and an unenumerated amount of time elapses, but still there is not resolution and thus no victory; the speaker realizes she has lost already to the woodchucks; the tragedy is that they have already stolen her former innocence of murder and killing and now she will never have peace. The final two lines echo the beginning of the poem: "gassing" from line 1 and "gassed" from line 30 are each stressed syllables beginning a line, thus neatly bookending the poem. The speaker suggests that if the woodchucks had died from the gas, she would not have directly confronted the woodchucks and their deaths and thus undergone this tragic change into an obsessive hunter. However, this statement contains a telling historical allusion which suggests that the gassing wouldn't have been an easy moral way out either: the speaker wishes they had died "gassed underground the quiet Nazi way" (line 30). The speaker wished the deaths had been quiet, efficient, clean, non-confrontational and unwitnessed by her, so she could deny any complicity to her conscience. However, this indicates an important contradiction: gassing is still murder, as the Nazis made abundantly clear, no matter how "merciful." The poet draws a parallel between what we consider the "mercy killing" of animals and the "murder" of human beings, and thus the

poem describes how delusions of righteousness
cause people to wield unnecessary power over
others, and how this damages and changes their
sense of self as they realize and accept the
human capability for acts of murder.

Exploring Contexts

9 THE AUTHOR'S WORK AS CONTEXT: JOHN KEATS

Poems are not all written in the same style, as if they were produced by a corporation or put together in a committee. Even though all poets share the same medium (language) and usually have some common notions of their craft, they put the unique resources of their individual minds and consciousnesses into what they create. A poet may rely on tradition extensively and use devices that others have developed without surrendering his or her own individuality, just as the integrity and uniqueness of an individual are not compromised by characteristics the individual may share with others—political affiliations, religious beliefs, tastes in clothes and music. Sometimes this uniqueness is hard to define—what exactly is it that defines the singular personality of an individual?—but it is always there, and we recognize and depend upon it in our relationships with other people. And so with poets: most don't make a conscious effort to put an individual stamp on their work; they don't have to. The stamp is there, just in the way they choose subjects, words, configurations. Every individual's consciousness uniquely marks what it records, imagines, and decides to print. The poems of John Keats, for example, are among the most distinctive in the English language. In this chapter, we will (after considering what makes the poems of any poet distinctive) look at the features of his poems that stamp them specifically as his own, and in the next chapter (on the poems of Adrienne Rich), we will look at how development and change occur *within* the continuity of a poet's consciousness.

Experienced readers can often identify a poem as the distinctive work of an individual poet even though they may never have seen the poem before, much as experienced listeners can identify a particular composer, singer, or group after hearing only a few phrases of a piece of new music. Such an ability depends upon a lot of reading of that author, or a lot of listening to music, but any reasonably sensitive reader can learn to do it with great accuracy. Developing this ability, however, is not really an end in itself; rather, it is a by-product of learning to notice the particular, distinctive qualities in the workmanship of any poet. Once you've read several poems by the same poet, you will usually begin to notice some features that the poems all have in common, and gradually you may come to think of those features as characteristic. The poem that follows was written by Howard Nemerov, whose work you have read in some earlier chapters. Before you read it, you may want to look back at his poems printed earlier in this book and remind yourself of what those poems were like, or to compare other of his poems later in the book. (The index will help you find them all.)

HOWARD NEMEROV

A Way of Life

It's been going on a long time.
For instance, these two guys, not saying much, who slog
Through sun and sand, fleeing the scene of their crime,
Till one turns, without a word, and smacks
His buddy flat with the flat of an axe,   5
Which cuts down on the dialogue
Some, but is viewed rather as normal than sad
By me, as I wait for the next ad.

It seems to me it's been quite a while
Since the last vision of blonde loveliness   10
Vanished, her shampoo and shower and general style
Replaced by this lean young lunk-
head parading along with a gun in his back to confess
How yestereve, being drunk
And in a state of existential despair,   15
He beat up his grandma and pawned her invalid chair.

But here at last is a pale beauty
Smoking a filter beside a mountain stream,

Brief interlude, before the conflict of love and duty
Gets moving again, as sheriff and posse expound,   20
Between jail and saloon, the American Dream
Where Justice, after considerable horsing around,
Turns out to be Mercy; when the villain is knocked off,
A kindly uncle offers syrup for my cough.

And now these clean-cut athletic types   25
In global hats are having a nervous debate
As they stand between their individual rocket ships
Which have landed, appropriately, on some rocks
Somewhere in Space, in an atmosphere of hate
Where one tells the other to pull up his socks   30
And get going, he doesn't say where; they fade,
And an angel food cake flutters in the void.

I used to leave now and again;
No more. A lot of violence in American life
These days, mobsters and cops all over the scene.   35
But there's a lot of love, too, mixed with the strife,
And kitchen-kindness, like a bedtime story
With rich food and a more kissable depilatory.
Still, I keep my weapons handy, sitting here
Smoking and shaving and drinking the dry beer.   1967   40

What does this poem have in common with Nemerov's other poems? The
concern with contemporary life, the tendency to concentrate on modern conve-
niences and luxuries, and the interest in isolating and defining aspects of the
distinctively modern sensibility are all characteristic of Nemerov, as is the ten-
dency to create a short drama, with a speaker who is not altogether admirable.
Several of Nemerov's other poems also share an attitude that seems deeply
imbedded in this poem, a kind of antiromanticism that emerges when some-
one tries to sound or feel *too* proud or cheerful and is shown, by events in the
poem, to be part of a grimmer reality instead. The concentration upon one or
more physical objects is also characteristic, and often (as in "The Vacuum")
the main object is a mechanical one that symbolizes modernity and our mod-
ern dependency on things rather than our concern with human relationships.
Americanness is emphasized here too, as if the poem were concerned to help
us define our culture and its habits and values. The mood of loneliness is also
typical of Nemerov, and so is the poem's witty conversational style. The verbal
wit here—although not as prominent as the puns and double-entendres of
"Boom!" (p. 358)—is characteristically informal. Often it seems to derive
from the language of commercials and street speech, and the undercutting of

this language by the poet—having a paranoid and simple-minded speaker talk about a gangster in "a state of existential despair"—is similar to the strategy of "Boom!" or "The Vacuum." The regular stanzas, rhymed but not in a traditional or regular way and with a number of near-rhymes, are also typical (look, for example, at "The Goose Fish," p. 207). Nemerov's thematic interests and ideas, his verbal style, and his cast of mind are all plainly visible in "A Way of Life."

Noticing common features does not mean that every poem by a particular author will be predictable and contain all these features. Most poets like to experiment with new subjects, tones, forms, and various kinds of poetic strategies and devices. But a characteristic way of thinking—the distinct stamp imposed by a unique consciousness—is likely to be visible anyway. The work of any writer will have certain *tendencies* that are identifiable, although not all of them will show up in any one poem.

Of what practical use is it to notice the distinctive voice and mind of a particular poet? One use (not the most important one for the casual reader, but one that nonetheless gives pleasure) is the pleasant surprise that occurs when you recognize something familiar. Reading a new poem by a familiar poet is a bit like meeting an old friend whose face or conversation reminds you of experiences you have had together. Poetic friendships can be treasures just as personal friendships are, even though they are necessarily more distant and somewhat more abstract. Just as novelty—meeting something or someone altogether new to you—is one kind of pleasure, so revisiting or recalling the familiar is another, its equal and opposite. Just *knowing* and *recognizing* often feel good—in and of themselves.

There are other reasons as well to look at the various works of a single writer. Just as you learn from watching other people—seeing how they react and respond to people and events, observing how they cope with various situations—you also learn from watching poets at work, seeing how they learn and develop, how they change their minds, how they discover the reach and limits of their imaginations and talents, how they find their distinctive voices and come to terms with their own identities. Watching someone at work over a period of years (as you can Adrienne Rich in the next chapter) is a little like watching an autobiography unfold, except that the individual poems continue to exist separately and for themselves at the same time they provide a record of a distinctive but gradually changing and evolving consciousness.

A third reason to study in some detail the work of an individual is a very practical one: the more you know about the poet, the better a reader you are likely to be of any individual poem by that poet. It is not so much that the external facts of a writer's life find their way into whatever he or she writes—be it poem, essay, letter, or autobiography—but that a reader gets used to habits and manners, and learns what to expect. Coming to a new poem by a poet you already know is not completely a new experience. You adjust faster, know what to look for, have some specific expectations (although they may be unconscious and unarticulated) of what the poem will be like. The more poems you read by any author, the better a reader you are likely to be of any one poem.

Before you read the following poem by John Donne, look at the poems by him that appear elsewhere in this book (check the index of authors). What features in these poems seem most striking and distinctive to you as you review them as a group?

JOHN DONNE

The Sun Rising

Busy old fool, unruly sun,
Why dost thou thus,
Through windows, and through curtains, call on us?
Must to thy motions lovers' seasons run?
    Saucy pedantic wretch, go chide   5
    Late schoolboys, and sour prentices,[1]
Go tell court-huntsmen that the king will ride,
Call country ants[2] to harvest offices;
Love, all alike, no season knows, nor clime,
Nor hours, days, months, which are the rags of time.   10

    Thy beams, so reverend and strong
    Why shouldst thou think?
I could eclipse and cloud them with a wink,
But that I would not lose her sight so long:
    If her eyes have not blinded thine,   15
    Look, and tomorrow late, tell me
Whether both the Indias[3] of spice and mine
Be where thou left'st them, or lie here with me.
Ask for those kings whom thou saw'st yesterday,
And thou shalt hear, all here in one bed lay.   20

    She is all states, and all princes I,
    Nothing else is.

1. Apprentices.   2. Farmworkers.   3. The East and West Indies, commercial sources of spices and gold.

Princes do but play us; compared to this,
All honor's mimic, all wealth alchemy.[4]
      Thou, sun, art half as happy as we,
        In that the world's contracted thus;
   Thine age asks[5] ease, and since thy duties be
     To warm the world, that's done in warming us.
Shine here to us, and thou art every where;
This bed thy center[6] is, these walls thy sphere.   1633

25

30

Is "The Sun Rising" somewhat easier to read than the first Donne poem you read this term? What kind of expectations did you have of the poem, knowing it was by the same author as other poems you had read? How conscious were you of those expectations? Did they enable you to ask more intelligent questions of the poem as you read it? How conscious were you, as you read, of the subject matter of other Donne poems? of their themes? tone? style? form? sound effects? of other poetic devices? Did you consciously expect a speaker and a dramatic situation? How quickly did you decide what the situation was? How quickly did you identify the setting? Did you find that you had certain expectations of the speaker once you had sensed the poem's subject and situation? In retrospect, how similar to other Donne poems does this one seem? In what specific ways? In what ways were your responses to this poem conditioned by what you already knew from other Donne poems?

The skills involved here are progressive: they don't come all at once like a flash of lightning. Rather, they develop over time, as do most of the more sophisticated contextual reading skills we will be considering in the later chapters of this book, and they develop in conjunction with skills you have already worked on in earlier chapters. Don't worry if you still have difficulty with a new Donne poem. You are in good company: Donne isn't easy. But the more you read, the better you will get. Reading ten or a dozen poems by a single author is better than reading three or four, not only because your generalizations and the expectations they create will be more reliable but also because you will feel increasingly comfortable. Spending some hours in the library reading several new poems by a poet you like and admire can be a very satisfying experience; work with any author long enough, and you will begin to feel positively at home. But even then, a good poet will still surprise you in every new poem, at least to some extent. Being reliable and distinctive is not the same as being predictable.

The poems that follow—all written by John Keats—vary quite a bit in sub-

---

4. Imposture, like the "scientific" procedures for turning base metals into gold. *Mimic:* hypocritical.
5. Requires.   6. Of orbit.

ject matter, tone, choice of verse form, and length. But they also have a coherence that derives from their having been conceived by the same imagination—the experiences of one young man in the early nineteenth century inform them all. As you read them over, you will note what they have in common, how they repeatedly suggest the pervasive sensuous and sensual quality of his work, his fascination with medieval times and gothic states of mind, his attraction both to nature and to highly ornate artifices, his distinctive patterns of phrasing and use of poetic devices, and the recurrent contrasts in his work between an external world of "objective" reality and internal states of "subjective" consciousness. Prose selections from a preface and from several of Keats's personal letters underscore some of his most persistent poetic and personal concerns. The poems are arranged chronologically, and a chronology of his life suggests the potential relevance of biographical information.

▼   ▼   ▼

JOHN KEATS

On First Looking into Chapman's Homer[7]

Much have I traveled in the realms of gold,
And many goodly states and kingdoms seen;
Round many western islands have I been
Which bards in fealty[8] to Apollo hold.
Oft of one wide expanse had I been told   5
That deep-browed Homer ruled as his demesne;
Yet did I never breathe its pure serene[9]
Till I heard Chapman speak out loud and bold:
Then felt I like some watcher of the skies
When a new planet swims into his ken;[1]   10
Or like stout Cortez[2] when with eagle eyes
He stared at the Pacific—and all his men
Looked at each other with a wild surmise—
Silent, upon a peak in Darien.   1816

7. George Chapman's were among the most famous Renaissance translations; his *Iliad* was completed in 1611, *The Odyssey* in 1616. Keats wrote the sonnet after being led to Chapman by his former teacher and reading *The Iliad* all night long.   8. Literally, the loyalty owed by a vassal to his feudal lord. Apollo was the Greek god of poetry and music.   9. Atmosphere.   1. Range of vision.   2. Actually, Balboa; he first viewed the Pacific from Darien, in Panama.

On the Grasshopper and the Cricket

The poetry of earth is never dead:
When all the birds are faint with the hot sun,
And hide in cooling trees, a voice will run
From hedge to hedge about the new-mown mead;
5   That is the grasshopper's—he takes the lead
In summer luxury—he has never done
With his delights; for when tired out with fun
He rests at ease beneath some pleasant weed.
The poetry of earth is ceasing never:
10   On a lone winter evening, when the frost
Has wrought a silence, from the stove there shrills
The cricket's song, in warmth increasing ever,
And seems to one in drowsiness half lost,
The grasshopper's among some grassy hills.

December 30, 1816

On Seeing the Elgin Marbles[3]

My spirit is too weak—mortality
Weighs heavily on me like unwilling sleep,
And each imagined pinnacle and steep
Of godlike hardship tells me I must die
5   Like a sick eagle looking at the sky.
Yet 'tis a gentle luxury to weep
That I have not the cloudy winds to keep
Fresh for the opening of the morning's eye.
Such dim-conceived glories of the brain
10   Bring round the heart an indescribable feud;
So do these wonders a most dizzy pain,
That mingles Grecian grandeur with the rude
Wasting of old Time—with a billowy main—
1817   A sun—a shadow of a magnitude.

---

3. Figures and friezes from the Athenian Parthenon. They were purchased from the Turks (who controlled Athens) by Lord Elgin, brought to England in 1806, and then sold to the British Museum, where Keats saw them.

from Endymion (Book I)[4]

A thing of beauty is a joy for ever:
Its loveliness increases; it will never
Pass into nothingness; but still will keep
A bower quiet for us, and a sleep
Full of sweet dreams, and health, and quiet breathing.   5
Therefore, on every morrow, are we wreathing
A flowery band to bind us to the earth,
Spite of despondence, of the inhuman dearth
Of noble natures, of the gloomy days,
Of all the unhealthy and o'er-darkened ways   10
Made for our searching: yes, in spite of all,
Some shape of beauty moves away the pall
From our dark spirits. Such the sun, the moon,
Trees old, and young sprouting a shady boon
For simple sheep; and such are daffodils   15
With the green world they live in; and clear rills
That for themselves a cooling covert make
'Gainst the hot season; the mid forest brake,[5]
Rich with a sprinkling of fair musk-rose blooms:
And such too is the grandeur of the dooms[6]   20
We have imagined for the mighty dead;
All lovely tales that we have heard or read:
An endless fountain of immortal drink,
Pouring unto us from the heaven's brink.
    Nor do we merely feel these essences   25
For one short hour; no, even as the trees
That whisper round a temple become soon
Dear as the temple's self, so does the moon,
The passion poesy, glories infinite,
Haunt us till they become a cheering light   30
Unto our souls, and bound to us so fast,
That, whether there be shine, or gloom o'ercast,
They always must be with us, or we die.

1817

When I Have Fears

When I have fears that I may cease to be
Before my pen has gleaned my teeming brain,
Before high-piléd books, in charact'ry,
Hold like rich garners the full-ripened grain;

4. Keats's long poem about the myth of a mortal (Endymion) loved by the goddess of the moon.
5. Thicket. 6. Judgments.

5   When I behold, upon the night's starred face,
Huge cloudy symbols of a high romance,
And think that I may never live to trace
Their shadows, with the magic hand of chance;
And when I feel, fair creature of an hour!
10   That I shall never look upon thee more,
Never have relish in the faery power
Of unreflecting love!—then on the shore
Of the wide world I stand alone, and think
1818   Till Love and Fame to nothingness do sink.

To Sleep

O soft embalmer of the still midnight,
Shutting, with careful fingers and benign,
Our gloom-pleased eyes, embowered from the light,
Enshaded in forgetfulness divine;
5   O soothest[7] Sleep! if so it please thee, close,
In midst of this thine hymn, my willing eyes,
Or wait the amen, ere thy poppy[8] throws
Around my bed its lulling charities;
Then save me, or the passéd day will shine
10   Upon my pillow, breeding many woes;
Save me from curious conscience, that still lords[9]
Its strength for darkness, burrowing like a mole;
Turn the key deftly in the oiléd wards,[1]
And seal the hushéd casket of my soul.

April 1819

Ode to a Nightingale

I

My heart aches, and a drowsy numbness pains
    My sense, as though of hemlock I had drunk,
Or emptied some dull opiate to the drains
    One minute past, and Lethe-wards[2] had sunk:
5 'Tis not through envy of thy happy lot,
    But being too happy in thine happiness,

---

7. Softest.   8. Because opium derives from it, the poppy was associated with sleep.   9. Marshals. *Curious:* scrupulous.   1. Ridges in a lock that distinguish proper from improper keys.
2. Toward the river of forgetfulness (Lethe) in Hades.

That thou, light-wingéd Dryad[3] of the trees,
   In some melodious plot
Of beechen green, and shadows numberless,
   Singest of summer in full-throated ease.   10

II

O, for a draught of vintage! that hath been
   Cooled a long age in the deep-delvéd earth,
Tasting of Flora[4] and the country green,
   Dance, and Provençal song,[5] and sunburnt mirth!
O for a beaker full of the warm South,   15
   Full of the true, the blushful Hippocrene,[6]
      With beaded bubbles winking at the brim,
         And purple-stainéd mouth;
That I might drink, and leave the world unseen,
   And with thee fade away into the forest dim: 20

III

Fade far away, dissolve, and quite forget
   What thou among the leaves hast never known,
The weariness, the fever, and the fret
   Here, where men sit and hear each other groan;
Where palsy shakes a few, sad, last gray hairs,   25
   Where youth grows pale, and specter-thin, and dies;
      Where but to think is to be full of sorrow
         And leaden-eyed despairs,
Where Beauty cannot keep her lustrous eyes,
   Or new Love pine at them beyond tomorrow.   30

IV

Away! away! for I will fly to thee,
   Not charioted by Bacchus and his pards,[7]
But on the viewless[8] wings of Poesy,
   Though the dull brain perplexes and retards:
Already with thee! tender is the night,   35
   And haply the Queen-Moon is on her throne,
      Clustered around by all her starry Fays;[9]
         But here there is no light,
Save what from heaven is with the breezes blown
   Through verdurous glooms and winding mossy ways.   40

---

3. Wood nymph.   4. Roman goddess of flowers.   5. The medieval troubadors of Provence were famous for their love songs.   6. The fountain of the Muses on Mt. Helicon, whose waters bring poetic inspiration.   7. The Roman god of wine was sometimes portrayed in a chariot drawn by leopards.   8. Invisible.   9. Fairies.

V

I cannot see what flowers are at my feet,
   Nor what soft incense hangs upon the boughs,
But, in embalméd[1] darkness, guess each sweet
   Wherewith the seasonable month endows
45   The grass, the thicket, and the fruit-tree wild;
      White hawthorn, and the pastoral eglantine;[2]
         Fast fading violets covered up in leaves;
           And mid-May's eldest child,
   The coming musk-rose, full of dewy wine,
50   The murmurous haunt of flies on summer eves.

VI

Darkling[3] I listen; and, for many a time
   I have been half in love with easeful Death,
Called him soft names in many a muséd rhyme,
   To take into the air my quiet breath;
55   Now more than ever seems it rich to die,
     To cease upon the midnight with no pain,
       While thou art pouring forth thy soul abroad
         In such an ecstasy!
   Still wouldst thou sing, and I have ears in vain—
60   To thy high requiem become a sod.

VII

Thou wast not born for death, immortal Bird!
   No hungry generations tread thee down;
The voice I hear this passing night was heard
   In ancient days by emperor and clown:
65   Perhaps the selfsame song that found a path
     Through the sad heart of Ruth,[4] when, sick for home,
       She stood in tears amid the alien corn;
         The same that ofttimes hath
   Charmed magic casements, opening on the foam
70   Of perilous seas, in faery lands forlorn.

VIII

Forlorn! the very word is like a bell
   To toll me back from thee to my sole self!

---

1. Fragrant, aromatic.   2. Sweetbriar or honeysuckle.   3. In the dark.   4. A virtuous Moabite widow who, according to the Old Testament Book of Ruth, left her own country to accompany her mother-in-law Naomi back to Naomi's native land. She supported herself as a gleaner.

Adieu! the fancy cannot cheat so well
 As she is famed to do, deceiving elf.
Adieu! adieu! thy plaintive anthem fades   75
 Past the near meadows, over the still stream,
  Up the hillside; and now 'tis buried deep
   In the next valley-glades:
 Was it a vision, or a waking dream?
  Fled is that music:—Do I wake or sleep?   80

May 1819

Ode on a Grecian Urn

I

Thou still unravished bride of quietness,
 Thou foster-child of silence and slow time,
Sylvan[5] historian, who canst thus express
 A flowery tale more sweetly than our rhyme:
What leaf-fringed legend haunts about thy shape   5
 Of deities or mortals, or of both,
  In Tempe or the dales of Arcady?[6]
What men or gods are these? What maidens loath?
 What mad pursuit? What struggle to escape?
  What pipes and timbrels? What wild ecstasy?   10

II

Heard melodies are sweet, but those unheard
 Are sweeter; therefore, ye soft pipes, play on;
Not to the sensual[7] ear, but, more endeared,
 Pipe to the spirit ditties of no tone:
Fair youth, beneath the trees, thou canst not leave   15
 Thy song, nor ever can those trees be bare;
  Bold Lover, never, never canst thou kiss,
Though winning near the goal—yet, do not grieve
 She cannot fade, though thou hast not thy bliss,
  For ever wilt thou love, and she be fair!   20

5. Rustic. The urn depicts a woodland scene.   6. Arcadia. Tempe is a beautiful valley near Mt. Olympus in Greece, and the valley ("dales") of Arcadia a picturesque section of the Peloponnesus; both came to be associated with the pastoral ideal.   7. Of the senses, as distinguished from the "ear" of the spirit or imagination.

III

Ah, happy, happy boughs! that cannot shed
    Your leaves, nor ever bid the Spring adieu;
And, happy melodist, unweariéd,
    For ever piping songs for ever new;
25 More happy love! more happy, happy love!
    For ever warm and still to be enjoyed,
      For ever panting, and for ever young;
All breathing human passion far above,
    That leaves a heart high-sorrowful and cloyed,
30   A burning forehead, and a parching tongue.

IV

Who are these coming to the sacrifice?
    To what green altar, O mysterious priest,
Lead'st thou that heifer lowing at the skies,
    And all her silken flanks with garlands dressed?
35 What little town by river or sea shore,
    Or mountain-built with peaceful citadel,
      Is emptied of this folk, this pious morn?
And, little town, thy streets for evermore
    Will silent be; and not a soul to tell
40   Why thou art desolate, can e'er return.

V

O Attic shape! Fair attitude! with brede[8]
    Of marble men and maidens overwrought,[9]
With forest branches and the trodden weed;
    Thou, silent form, dost tease us out of thought
45 As doth eternity: Cold Pastoral!
    When old age shall this generation waste,
      Thou shalt remain, in midst of other woe
Than ours, a friend to man, to whom thou say'st,
    Beauty is truth, truth beauty[1] —that is all
50   Ye know on earth, and all ye need to know.

May 1819

---

8. Woven pattern. *Attic:* Attica was the district of ancient Greece surrounding Athens.   9. Ornamented all over.   1. In some texts of the poem "Beauty is truth, truth beauty" is in quotation marks and in some texts it is not, leading to critical disagreements about whether the last line and a half are also inscribed on the urn or spoken by the poet.

Ode on Melancholy

I

No, no, go not to Lethe,[2] neither twist
   Wolfsbane, tight-rooted, for its poisonous wine;[3]
Nor suffer thy pale forehead to be kissed
   By nightshade, ruby grape of Proserpine;
Make not your rosary of yew-berries,[4]   5
     Nor let the beetle, nor the death-moth be
        Your mournful Psyche,[5] nor the downy owl
A partner in your sorrow's mysteries;
     For shade to shade will come too drowsily,
        And drown the wakeful anguish of the soul.   10

II

But when the melancholy fit shall fall
   Sudden from heaven like a weeping cloud,
That fosters the droop-headed flowers all,
   And hides the green hill in an April shroud;
Then glut thy sorrow on a morning rose,   15
     Or on the rainbow of the salt sand-wave,
        Or on the wealth of globéd peonies;
Or if thy mistress some rich anger shows,
     Emprison her soft hand, and let her rave,
        And feed deep, deep upon her peerless eyes.   20

III

She[6] dwells with Beauty—Beauty that must die;
   And Joy, whose hand is ever at his lips
Bidding adieu; and aching Pleasure nigh,
   Turning to poison while the bee-mouth sips:
Ay, in the very temple of Delight   25
     Veiled Melancholy has her sov'reign shrine,
        Though seen of none save him whose strenuous tongue
Can burst Joy's grape against his palate fine;[7]
     His soul shall taste the sadness of her might,
        And be among her cloudy trophies hung.[8]   30

May 1819

2. The river of forgetfulness in Hades.   3. Like nightshade (line 4), wolfsbane is a poisonous plant. *Proserpine*: queen of Hades.   4. Which often grow in cemeteries and which are traditionally associated with death.   5. *Psyche* means both "soul" and "breath," and sometimes it was anciently represented by a moth leaving the mouth at death. Owls and beetles were also traditionally associated with darkness and death.   6. The goddess Melancholy, whose chief place of worship ("shrine") is described in lines 25–26.   7. Sensitive, discriminating.   8. The ancient Greeks and Romans hung trophies in their gods' temples.

To Autumn

I

Season of mists and mellow fruitfulness,
    Close bosom-friend of the maturing sun;
Conspiring with him how to load and bless
    With fruit the vines that round the thatch-eves run;
To bend with apples the mossed cottage-trees,
    And fill all fruit with ripeness to the core;
        To swell the gourd, and plump the hazel shells
With a sweet kernel; to set budding more,
    And still more, later flowers for the bees,
    Until they think warm days will never cease,
        For Summer has o'er-brimmed their clammy cells.

II

Who hath not seen thee oft amid thy store?
    Sometimes whoever seeks abroad may find
Thee sitting careless on a granary floor,
    Thy hair soft-lifted by the winnowing wind;[9]
Or on a half-reaped furrow sound asleep,
    Drowsed with the fume of poppies, while thy hook[1]
        Spares the next swath and all its twinéd flowers:
And sometimes like a gleaner thou dost keep
    Steady thy laden head across a brook;
    Or by a cider-press, with patient look,
        Thou watchest the last oozings hours by hours.

III

Where are the songs of Spring? Ay, where are they?
    Think not of them, thou hast thy music too—
While barréd clouds bloom the soft-dying day,
    And touch the stubble-plains with rosy hue;
Then in a wailful choir the small gnats mourn
    Among the river sallows,[2] borne aloft
        Or sinking as the light wind lives or dies;
And full-grown lambs loud bleat from hilly bourn;[3]
    Hedge-crickets sing; and now with treble soft
    The red-breast whistles from a garden-croft;[4]
        And gathering swallows twitter in the skies.

September 19, 1819

9. Which sifts the grain from the chaff.   1. Scythe or sickle.   2. Willows.   3. Domain.
4. An enclosed garden near a house.

The Eve of St. Agnes[5]

1

St. Agnes' Eve—Ah, bitter chill it was!
The owl, for all his feathers, was a-cold;
The hare limp'd trembling through the frozen grass,
And silent was the flock in woolly fold:
Numb were the Beadsman's[6] fingers, while he told   5
His rosary, and while his frosted breath,
Like pious incense from a censer old,
Seem'd taking flight for heaven, without a death,
Past the sweet Virgin's picture, while his prayer he saith.

2

His prayer he saith, this patient, holy man;   10
Then takes his lamp, and riseth from his knees,
And back returneth, meagre, barefoot, wan,
Along the chapel aisle by slow degrees:
The sculptur'd dead, on each side, seem to freeze,
Emprison'd in black, purgatorial rails: 15
Knights, ladies, praying in dumb orat'ries,[7]
He passeth by; and his weak spirit fails
To think[8] how they may ache in icy hoods and mails.

3

Northward he turneth through a little door,
And scarce three steps, ere Music's golden tongue   20
Flatter'd[9] to tears this aged man and poor;
But no—already had his deathbell rung;
The joys of all his life were said and sung:
His was harsh penance on St. Agnes' Eve:
Another way he went, and soon among   25
Rough ashes sat he for his soul's reprieve,
And all night kept awake, for sinners' sake to grieve.

4

That ancient Beadsman heard the prelude soft;
And so it chanc'd, for many a door was wide,

5. Martyred early in the fourth century at the age of 13, St. Agnes became the patron saint of virgins. According to popular belief, if a virgin performed the proper ritual on St. Agnes' Eve (January 20), she would dream of her future husband.   6. Someone paid to pray for the soul of another. "told": counted his beads.   7. Silent chapels inside the larger chapel.   8. When he thinks. "mails": suits of armor.   9. Coaxed, beguiled.

30 From hurry to and fro. Soon, up aloft,
The silver, snarling trumpets 'gan to chide:
The level chambers, ready with their pride,[1]
Were glowing to receive a thousand guests:
The carved angels, ever eager-eyed,
35 Star'd, where upon their heads the cornice rests,
With hair blown back, and wings put cross-wise on their breasts.

5

At length burst in the argent revelry,[2]
With plume, tiara, and all rich array,
Numerous as shadows haunting fairily
40 The brain, new stuff'd, in youth, with triumphs gay
Of old romance. These let us wish away,
And turn, sole-thoughted, to one Lady there,
Whose heart had brooded, all that wintry day,
On love, and wing'd St. Agnes' saintly care,
45 As she had heard old dames full many times declare.

6

They told her how, upon St. Agnes' Eve,
Young virgins might have visions of delight,
And soft adorings from their loves receive
Upon the honey'd middle of the night,
50 If ceremonies due they did aright;
As, supperless to bed they must retire,
And couch supine their beauties, lily white;
Nor look behind, nor sideways, but require
Of heaven with upward eyes for all that they desire.

7

55 Full of this whim was thoughtful Madeline:
The music, yearning like a god in pain,
She scarcely heard: her maiden eyes divine,
Fix'd on the floor, saw many a sweeping train
Pass by—she heeded not at all: in vain
60 Came many a tiptoe, amorous cavalier,
And back retir'd, not cool'd by high disdain;
But she saw not: her heart was otherwhere:
She sigh'd for Agnes' dreams, the sweetest of the year.

1. Splendor.   2. Silver-clad revelers.

8

She danc'd along with vague, regardless eyes,
Anxious her lips, her breathing quick and short: 65
The hallow'd hour was near at hand: she sighs
Amid the timbrels,[3] and the throng'd resort
Of whisperers in anger, or in sport;
'Mid looks of love, defiance, hate, and scorn,
Hoodwink'd with faery fancy; all amort,[4]
Save to St. Agnes and her lambs unshorn,[5]
And all the bliss to be before to-morrow morn.

9

So, purposing each moment to retire,
She linger'd still. Meantime, across the moors,
Had come young Porphyro, with heart on fire   75
For Madeline. Beside the portal doors,
Buttress'd from moonlight,[6] stands he, and implores
All saints to give him sight of Madeline,
But for one moment in the tedious hours,
That he might gaze and worship all unseen;   80
Perchance speak, kneel, touch, kiss—in sooth such things have been.

10

He ventures in: let no buzz'd whisper tell:
All eyes be muffled, or a hundred swords
Will storm his heart, Love's fev'rous citadel:
For him, those chambers held barbarian hordes,   85
Hyena foemen, and hot-blooded lords,
Whose very dogs would execrations howl
Against his lineage:[7] not one breast affords
Him any mercy, in that mansion foul,
Save one old beldame,[8] weak in body and in soul.   90

11

Ah, happy chance! the aged creature came,
Shuffling along with ivory-headed wand,[9]
To where he stood, hid from the torch's flame,
Behind a broad hall-pillar, far beyond

---

3. Small hand drums or tambourines.   4. Deadened: oblivious.   5. At the feast of St. Agnes
the next day, lamb's wool was traditionally offered; later, nuns wove it into cloth (lines 115–
17).   6. Shaded by the wall supports.   7. Because of the feud between his family and Made-
line's.   8. Old, usually ugly, woman.   9. Walking stick, cane.

95   The sound of merriment and chorus bland:[1]
He startled her; but soon she knew his face,
And grasp'd his fingers in her palsied hand,
Saying, "Mercy, Porphyro! hie thee from this place;
They are all here to-night, the whole blood-thirsty race!

12

100   "Get hence! get hence! there's dwarfish Hildebrand;
He had a fever late, and in the fit
He cursed thee and thine, both house and land:
Then there's that old Lord Maurice, not a whit
More tame for his gray hairs—Alas me! flit!
105   Flit like a ghost away."—"Ah, Gossip[2] dear,
We're safe enough; here in this arm-chair sit,
And tell me how"—"Good Saints! not here, not here;
Follow me, child, or else these stones will be thy bier."

13

He follow'd through a lowly arched way,
110   Brushing the cobwebs with his lofty plume,
And as she mutter'd "Well-a—well-a-day!"
He found him in a little moonlight room,
Pale, lattic'd, chill, and silent as a tomb.
"Now tell me where is Madeline," said he,
115   "O tell me, Angela, by the holy loom
Which none but secret sisterhood may see,
When they St. Agnes' wool are weaving piously."

14

"St. Agnes! Ah! it is St. Agnes' Eve—
Yet men will murder upon holy days:
120   Thou must hold water in a witch's sieve,
And be liege-lord of all the Elves and Fays,
To venture so:[3] it fills me with amaze
To see thee, Porphyro!—St. Agnes' Eve!
God's help! my lady fair the conjuror plays[4]
125   This very night: good angels her deceive!
But let me laugh awhile, I've mickle[5] time to grieve."

15

Feebly she laugheth in the languid moon,
While Porphyro upon her face doth look,

1. Soothing.   2. Old friend.   3. I.e., Porphyro would need to be a magician to take such chances.   4. In trying to evoke the image of her lover.   5. Plenty of.

Like puzzled urchin on an aged crone
Who keepeth clos'd a wond'rous riddle-book,
As spectacled she sits in chimney nook.   130
But soon his eyes grew brilliant, when she told
His lady's purpose; and he scarce could brook[6]
Tears, at the thought of those enchantments cold,
And Madeline asleep in lap of legends old.   135

16

Sudden a thought came like a full-blown rose,
Flushing his brow, and in his pained heart
Made purple riot: then doth he propose
A stratagem, that makes the beldame start:
"A cruel man and impious thou art: 140
Sweet lady, let her pray, and sleep, and dream
Alone with her good angels, far apart
From wicked men like thee. Go, go!—I deem
Thou canst not surely be the same that thou didst seem."

17

"I will not harm her, by all saints I swear,"   145
Quoth Porphyro: "O may I ne'er find grace
When my weak voice shall whisper its last prayer,
If one of her soft ringlets I displace,
Or look with ruffian passion in her face:
Good Angela, believe me by these tears;   150
Or I will, even in a moment's space,
Awake, with horrid shout, my foemen's ears,
And beard[7] them, though they be more fang'd than wolves and bears."

18

"Ah! why wilt thou affright a feeble soul?
A poor, weak, palsy-stricken, churchyard thing,   155
Whose passing-bell[8] may ere the midnight toll;
Whose prayers for thee, each morn and evening,
Were never miss'd."—Thus plaining,[9] doth she bring
A gentler speech from burning Porphyro;
So woful, and of such deep sorrowing,   160
That Angela gives promise she will do
Whatever he shall wish, betide her weal or woe.[1]

---

6. Hold back.   7. Defy, affront.   8. Bell that rings for death.   9. Complaining.
1. Whatever happens to her, good or bad.

19

Which was, to lead him, in close secrecy,
Even to Madeline's chamber, and there hide
165　Him in a closet, of such privacy
That he might see her beauty unespied,
And win perhaps that night a peerless bride,
While legion'd fairies pac'd the coverlet,
And pale enchantment held her sleepy-eyed.
170　Never on such a night have lovers met,
Since Merlin paid his Demon all the monstrous debt.[2]

20

"It shall be as thou wishest," said the Dame:
"All cates[3] and dainties shall be stored there
Quickly on this feast-night: by the tambour frame[4]
175　Her own lute thou wilt see: no time to spare,
For I am slow and feeble, and scarce dare
On such a catering trust my dizzy head.
Wait here, my child, with patience; kneel in prayer
The while: Ah! thou must needs the lady wed,
180　Or may I never leave my grave among the dead."

21

So saying, she hobbled off with busy fear.
The lover's endless minutes slowly pass'd;
The dame return'd, and whisper'd in his ear
To follow her; with aged eyes aghast
185　From fright of dim espial. Safe at last,
Through many a dusky gallery, they gain
The maiden's chamber, silken, hush'd, and chaste;
Where Porphyro took covert, pleas'd amain.[5]
His poor guide hurried back with agues in her brain.

22

190　Her falt'ring hand upon the balustrade,
Old Angela was feeling for the stair,
When Madeline, St. Agnes' charmed maid,
Rose, like a mission'd spirit,[6] unaware:
With silver taper's light, and pious care,
195　She turn'd, and down the aged gossip led
To a safe level matting. Now prepare,

2. Merlin was a powerful magician in the Arthurian legends; the incident referred to here has not been identified.　3. Delicacies.　4. Embroidery frame.　5. Greatly.　6. Angel on a mission.

Young Porphyro, for gazing on that bed;
She comes, she comes again, like ring-dove fray'd[7] and fled.

23

Out went the taper as she hurried in;
Its little smoke, in pallid moonshine, died: 200
She clos'd the door, she panted, all akin
To spirits of the air, and visions wide:
No uttered syllable, or, woe betide!
But to her heart, her heart was voluble,
Paining with eloquence her balmy side;   205
As though a tongueless nightingale should swell
Her throat in vain, and die, heart-stifled, in her dell.

24

A casement[8] high and triple-arch'd there was,
All garlanded with carven imag'ries
Of fruits, and flowers, and bunches of knot-grass,   210
And diamonded with panes of quaint device,
Innumerable of stains and splendid dyes,
As are the tiger-moth's deep-damask'd wings;
And in the midst, 'mong thousand heraldries,
And twilight saints, and dim emblazonings,   215
A shielded scutcheon blush'd with blood of queens and kings.

25

Full on this casement shone the wintry moon,
And threw warm gules[9] on Madeline's fair breast,
As down she knelt for heaven's grace and boon;[1]
Rose-bloom fell on her hands, together prest,   220
And on her silver cross soft amethyst,
And on her hair a glory,[2] like a saint:
She seem'd a splendid angel, newly drest,
Save wings, for heaven: — Porphyro grew faint:
She knelt, so pure a thing, so free from mortal taint.   225

26

Anon his heart revives: her vespers done,
Of all its wreathed pearls her hair she frees;
Unclasps her warmed jewels one by one;
Loosens her fragrant boddice; by degrees

7. Frightened.   8. Window, in which are stained-glass representations of many kinds, including a royal coat of arms (line 216).   9. Heraldic red.   1. Gift, blessing.   2. Halo.

230   Her rich attire creeps rustling to her knees:
         Half-hidden, like a mermaid in sea-weed,
         Pensive awhile she dreams awake, and sees,
         In fancy, fair St. Agnes in her bed,
     But dares not look behind, or all the charm is fled.

27

235   Soon, trembling in her soft and chilly nest,
         In sort of wakeful swoon, perplex'd she lay,
         Until the poppied warmth of sleep oppress'd
         Her soothed limbs, and soul fatigued away;
         Flown, like a thought, until the morrow-day;
240   Blissfully haven'd both from joy and pain;
         Clasp'd like a missal where swart Paynims[3] pray;
     As though a rose should shut, and be a bud again.

28

         Stol'n to this paradise, and so entranced,
245   Porphyro gazed upon her empty dress,
         And listen'd to her breathing, if it chanced
         To wake into a slumberous tenderness;
         Which when he heard, that minute did he bless,
         And breath'd himself: then from the closet crept,
250   Noiseless as fear in a wide wilderness,
         And over the hush'd carpet, silent, stept,
     And 'tween the curtains peep'd, where, lo!—how fast she slept.

29

         Then by the bed-side, where the faded moon
         Made a dim, silver twilight, soft he set
255   A table, and, half anguish'd, threw thereon
         A cloth of woven crimson, gold, and jet:—
         O for some drowsy Morphean amulet![4]
         The boisterous, midnight, festive clarion,[5]
         The kettle-drum, and far-heard clarionet,
260   Affray his ears, though but in dying tone:—
     The hall door shuts again, and all the noise is gone.

30

         And still she slept an azure-lidded sleep,
         In blanched linen, smooth, and lavender'd,
         While he from forth the closet brought a heap
265   Of candied apple, quince, and plum, and gourd;

---

3. Pagans.   4. A charm of Morpheus, god of sleep.   5. Trumpet.

With jellies soother than the creamy curd,
And lucent syrops, tinct with cinnamon;
Manna[6] and dates, in argosy[7] transferr'd
From Fez, and spiced dainties, every one,
From silken Samarcand to cedar'd Lebanon.   270

31

These delicates he heap'd with glowing hand
On golden dishes and in baskets bright
Of wreathed silver: sumptuous they stand
In the retired quiet of the night,
Filling the chilly room with perfume light. —   275
"And now, my love, my seraph[8] fair, awake!
Thou art my heaven, and I thine eremite:
Open thine eyes, for meek St. Agnes' sake,
Or I shall drowse beside thee, so my soul doth ache."

32

Thus whispering, his warm, unnerved arm   280
Sank in her pillow. Shaded was her dream
By the dusk curtains: — 'twas a midnight charm
Impossible to melt as iced stream:
The lustrous salvers in the moonlight gleam;
Broad golden fringe upon the carpet lies: 285
It seem'd he never, never could redeem
From such a stedfast spell his lady's eyes;
So mus'd awhile, entoil'd[9] in woofed phantasies.

33

Awakening up, he took her hollow lute, —
Tumultuous, — and, in chords that tenderest be,   290
He play'd an ancient ditty, long since mute,
In Provence call'd, "La belle dame sans mercy":[1]
Close to her ear touching the melody; —
Wherewith disturb'd, she utter'd a soft moan:
He ceased — she panted quick — and suddenly   295
Her blue affrayed eyes wide open shone:
Upon his knees he sank, pale as smooth-sculptured stone.

---

6. Sweet gum.   7. Merchant ships. Fez, Samarcand, and Lebanon are in Morocco, central Asia,
and the Levant, respectively.   8. The highest order of angel. "eremite": devotee.   9. Entan-
gled. "woofèd": woven.   1. "The beautiful lady without pity," the kind of love song played or
sung in medieval Provence.

34

Her eyes were open, but she still beheld,
Now wide awake, the vision of her sleep:
There was a painful change, that nigh expell'd
The blisses of her dream so pure and deep:
At which fair Madeline began to weep,
And moan forth witless words with many a sigh;
While still her gaze on Porphyro would keep;
Who knelt, with joined hands and piteous eye,
Fearing to move or speak, she look'd so dreamingly.

35

"Ah, Porphyro!" said she, "but even now
Thy voice was at sweet tremble in mine ear,
Made tuneable with every sweetest vow;
And those sad eyes were spiritual and clear:
How chang'd thou art! how pallid, chill, and drear!
Give me that voice again, my Porphyro,
Those looks immortal, those complainings dear!
Oh leave me not in this eternal woe,
For if thou diest, my love, I know not where to go."

36

Beyond a mortal man impassion'd far
At these voluptuous accents, he arose,
Ethereal, flush'd, and like a throbbing star
Seen mid the sapphire heaven's deep repose;
Into her dream he melted, as the rose
Blendeth its odor with the violet,—
Solution sweet: meantime the frost-wind blows
Like Love's alarum pattering the sharp sleet
Against the window-panes; St. Agnes' moon hath set.

37

'Tis dark: quick pattereth the flaw-blown[2] sleet:
"This is no dream, my bride, my Madeline!"
'Tis dark: the iced gusts still rave and beat:
"No dream, alas! alas! and woe is mine!
Porphyro will leave me here to fade and pine.—
Cruel! what traitor could thee hither bring?
I curse not, for my heart is lost in thine,

300

305

310

315

320

325

330

2. Gust-blown.

Though thou forsakest a deceived thing;—
A dove forlorn and lost with sick unpruned wing."

38

"My Madeline! sweet dreamer! lovely bride!
Say may I be for aye[3] thy vassal blest?   335
Thy beauty's shield, heart-shap'd and vermeil[4] dyed?
Ah, silver shrine, here will I take my rest
After so many hours of toil and quest,
A famish'd pilgrim,—saved by miracle.
Though I have found, I will not rob thy nest   340
Saving of thy sweet self; if thou think'st well
To trust, fair Madeline, to no rude infidel.

39

"Hark! 'tis an elfin-storm from faery land,
Of haggard[5] seeming, but a boon indeed:
Arise—arise! the morning is at hand;—   345
The bloated wassaillers[6] will never heed:—
Let us away, my love, with happy speed;
There are no ears to hear, or eyes to see,—
Drown'd all in Rhenish and the sleepy mead:[7]
Awake! arise! my love, and fearless be,   350
For o'er the southern moors I have a home for thee."

40

She hurried at his words, beset with fears,
For there were sleeping dragons all around,
At glaring watch, perhaps, with ready spears—
Down the wide stairs a darkling way they found.—   355
In all the house was heard no human sound.
A chain-droop'd lamp was flickering by each door;
The arras,[8] rich with horseman, hawk, and hound,
Flutter'd in the besieging wind's uproar;
And the long carpets rose along the gusty floor.   360

41

They glide, like phantoms, into the wide hall;
Like phantoms, to the iron porch, they glide;
Where lay the Porter, in uneasy sprawl,
With a huge empty flaggon by his side:
The wakeful bloodhound rose, and shook his hide,   365

3. Forever.   4. Vermilion: bright red.   5. Wild.   6. Drunken revelers.   7. Liquor
made from honey. "Rhenish": rhine wine.   8. Tapestry.

But his sagacious eye an inmate[9] owns:
By one, and one, the bolts full easy slide:—
The chains lie silent on the footworn stones;—
The key turns, and the door upon its hinges groans.

42

370 And they are gone: ay, ages long ago
These lovers fled away into the storm.
That night the Baron dreamt of many a woe,
And all his warrior-guests, with shade and form
Of witch, and demon, and large coffin-worm,
375 Were long be-nightmar'd. Angela the old
Died palsy-twitch'd, with meagre face deform;
The Beadsman, after thousand aves[1] told,
For aye unsought for slept among his ashes cold.

Jan.–Feb. 1819   1820

from Letter to Benjamin Bailey, November 22, 1817[2]

* * * I am certain of nothing but of the holiness of the Heart's affections and the truth of Imagination—What the imagination seizes as Beauty must be truth—whether it existed before or not—for I have the same Idea of all our Passions as of Love they are all in their sublime, creative of essential Beauty * * The Imagination may be compared to Adam's dream[3]—he awoke and found it truth. I am the more zealous in this affair, because I have never yet been able to perceive how any thing can be known for truth by consequitive reasoning—and yet it must be—Can it be that even the greatest Philosopher ever ~~when~~ arrived at his goal without putting aside numerous objections—However it may be, O for a Life of Sensations rather than of Thoughts! It is "a Vision in the form of Youth" a Shadow of reality to come—and this consideration has further conv[i]nced me for it has come as auxiliary to another favorite Speculation of mine, that we shall enjoy ourselves here after by having what we called happiness on Earth repeated in a finer tone and so repeated—And yet such a fate can only befall those who delight in sensation rather than hunger as you do after Truth—Adam's dream will do here and seems to be a conviction that Imagination and its empyreal reflection is the same as human Life and its spiritual repetition. But as I was saying—the simple imaginative Mind may have its rewards in the repeti[ti]on of its own silent Working coming continually on the spirit with a fine suddenness—to compare great things with small—have you

---

9. Member of the household. "owns": recognizes.   1. Ave Maria's: Hail Mary's.   2. Keats's private letters, often carelessly written, are reprinted uncorrected.   3. In *Paradise Lost*, VIII, 460–90.

never by being surprised with an old Melody—in a delicious place—by a delicious voice, fe[l]t over again your very speculations and surmises at the time it first operated on your soul—do you not remember forming to yourself the singer's face more beautiful that [*for* than] it was possible and yet with the elevation of the Moment you did not think so—even then you were mounted on the Wings of Imagination so high—that the Prototype must be here after—that delicious face you will see—What a time! I am continually running away from the subject—sure this cannot be exactly the case with a complex Mind—one that is imaginative and at the same time careful of its fruits—who would exist partly on sensation partly on thought—to whom it is necessary that years should bring the philosophic Mind—such an one I consider your's and therefore it is necessary to your eternal Happiness that you not only ~~have~~ drink this old Wine of Heaven which I shall call the redigestion of our most ethereal Musings on Earth; but also increase in knowledge and know all things. * * *

from Letter to George and Thomas Keats, December 21, 1817

* * * I spent Friday evening with Wells[4] & went the next morning to see *Death on the Pale horse.*[5] It is a wonderful picture, when West's age is considered; But there is nothing to be intense upon; no women one feels mad to kiss, no face swelling into reality. the excellence of every Art is its intensity, capable of making all disagreeables evaporate, from their being in close relationship with Beauty & Truth—Examine King Lear & you will find this examplified throughout; but in this picture we have unpleasantness without any momentous depth of speculation excited, in which to bury its repulsiveness—The picture is larger than Christ rejected—I dined with Haydon the sunday after you left, & had a very pleasant day, I dined too (for I have been out too much lately) with Horace Smith & met his two Brothers with Hill & Kingston & one Du Bois,[6] they only served to convince me, how superior humour is to wit in respect to enjoyment—These men say things which make one start, without making one feel, they are all alike; their manners are alike; they all know fashionables; they have a mannerism in their very eating & drinking, in their mere handling a Decanter—They talked of Kean[7] & his low company—Would I were with that company instead of yours said I to myself! I know such like acquaintance will never do for me & yet I am going to Reynolds, on wednesday—Brown & Dilke walked with me & back from the Christmas pantomime. I had not a dispute but a disquisition with Dilke, on various subjects; several things dovetailed in my mind, & at once it struck me, what quality went to form a Man of Achievement

---

4. Charles Wells (1800–1879), an author.   5. By Benjamin West (1738–1820), American painter and president of the Royal Academy; *Christ Rejected* (mentioned below) is also by West.
6. Thomas Hill (1760–1840), a book collector, and Edward duBois (1774–1850), a journalist.
7. Edmund Kean (1789–1833), a famous Shakespearean actor.

especially in Literature & which Shakespeare possessed so enormously—I mean *Negative Capability*, that is when man is capable of being in uncertainties, Mysteries, doubts, without any irritable reaching after fact & reason—Coleridge, for instance, would let go by a fine isolated verisimilitude caught from the Penetralium of mystery, from being incapable of remaining content with half knowledge. This pursued through Volumes would perhaps take us no further than this, that with a great poet the sense of Beauty overcomes every other consideration, or rather obliterates all consideration.

Letter to John Hamilton Reynolds, February 19, 1818

I have an idea that a Man might pass a very pleasant life in this manner—let him on any certain day read a certain Page of full Poesy or distilled Prose and let him wander with it, and muse upon it, and reflect from it, and bring home to it, and prophesy upon it, and dream upon it—untill it becomes stale—but when will it do so? Never—When Man has arrived at a certain ripeness in intellect any one grand and spiritual passage serves him as a starting post towards all "the two-and-thirty Pallaces"[8] How happy is such a "voyage of conception," what delicious diligent Indolence! A doze upon a Sofa does not hinder it, and a nap upon Clover engenders ethereal finger-pointings—the prattle of a child gives it wings, and the converse of middle age a strength to beat them—a strain of musick conducts to "an odd angle of the Isle",[9] and when the leaves whisper it puts a girdle round the earth",[1] Nor will this sparing touch of noble Books be any irreverence to their Writers—for perhaps the honors paid by Man to Man are trifles in comparison to the Benefit done by great Works to the "Spirit and pulse of good" by their mere passive existence. Memory should not be called knowledge—Many have original minds who do not think it—they are led away by Custom—Now it appears to me that almost any Man may like the Spider spin from his own inwards his own airy Citadel—the points of leaves and twigs on which the Spider begins her work are few and she fills the Air with a beautiful circuiting: man should be content with as few points to tip with the fine Webb of his Soul and weave a tapestry empyrean—full of Symbols for his spiritual eye, of softness for his spiritual touch, of space for his wandering of distinctness for his Luxury—But the Minds of Mortals are so different and bent on such diverse Journeys that it may at first appear impossible for any common taste and fellowship to exist ~~bettween~~ between two or three under these suppositions—It is however quite the contrary—Minds would leave each other in contrary directions, traverse each other in Numberless points, and all [*for* at] last greet each other at the Journeys end—An old Man and a child would talk together and the old

8. "Places of delight" in Buddhism.   9. *The Tempest*, Act I, scene 2, 223.   1. The phrase is from *A Midsummer Night's Dream*, Act II, scene 1, 175.

Man be led on his Path, and the child left thinking—Man should not dispute or assert but whisper results to his neighbor, and thus by every germ of Spirit sucking the Sap from mould ethereal every human might become great, and Humanity instead of being a wide heath of Furse[2] and Briars with here and there a remote Oak or Pine, would become a grand democracy of Forest Trees. It has been an old Comparison for our urging on—the Bee hive—however it seems to me that we should rather be the flower than the Bee—for it is a false notion that more is gained by receiving than giving—no, the receiver and the giver are equal in their benefits—The f[l]ower I doubt not receives a fair guerdon from the Bee—its leaves blush deeper in the next spring—and who shall say between Man and Woman which is the most delighted? Now it is more noble to sit like Jove that [*for* than] to fly like Mercury—let us not therefore go hurrying about and collecting honey bee like, buzzing here and there impatiently from a knowledge of what is to be arrived at; but let us open our leaves like a flower and be passive and receptive—budding patiently under the eye of Apollo and taking hints from every noble insect that favors us with a visit—sap will be given us for Meat and dew for drink—I was led into these thoughts, my dear Reynolds, by the beauty of the morning operating on a sense of Idleness—I have not read any Books—the Morning said I was right—I had no Idea but of the Morning, and the Thrush said I was right—seeming to say—

> O thou whose face hath felt the Winter's wind,
> Whose eye has seen the snow-clouds hung in mist,
> And the black elm tops 'mong the freezing stars,
> To thee the spring will be a harvest-time.
> O thou, whose only book has been the light
> Of supreme darkness which thou feddest on
> Night after night when Phœbus was away,
> To thee the spring shall be a triple morn.
> O fret not after knowledge—I have none,
> And yet my song comes native with the warmth.
> O fret not after knowledge—I have none,
> And yet the Evening listens. He who saddens
> At thought of idleness cannot be idle,
> And he's awake who thinks himself asleep.

Now I am sensible all this is a mere sophistication, however it may neighbor to any truths, to excuse my own indolence—so I will not deceive myself that Man should be equal with jove—but think himself very well off as a sort of scullion-Mercury, or even a humble Bee—It is not [*for* no] matter whether I am right or wrong either one way or another, if there is sufficient to lift a little time from your Shoulders.

---

2. *The Tempest*, Act II, scene 1, 68–69.

from Letter to John Taylor, February 27, 1818

* * * It is a sorry thing for me that any one should have to overcome Prejudices in reading my Verses—that affects me more than any hyper-criticism on any particular Passage. In *Endymion* I have most likely but moved into the Go-cart from the leading strings. In Poetry I have a few Axioms, and you will see how far I am from their Centre. 1st I think Poetry should surprise by a fine excess and not by Singularity—it should strike the Reader as a wording of his own highest thoughts, and appear almost a Remembrance—2nd Its touches of Beauty should never be half way therby making the reader breathless instead of content: the rise, the progress, the setting of imagery should like the Sun come natural natural too him—shine over him and set soberly although in magnificence leaving him in the Luxury of twilight—but it is easier to think what Poetry should be than to write it—and this leads me on to another axiom. That if Poetry comes not as naturally as the Leaves to a tree it had better not come at all. However it may be with me I cannot help looking into new countries with "O for a Muse of fire to ascend!"[3]—If Endymion serves me as a Pioneer perhaps I ought to be content. I have great reason to be content, for thank God I can read and perhaps understand Shakspeare to his depths, and I have I am sure many friends, who, if I fail, will attribute any change in my Life and Temper to Humbleness rather than to Pride—to a cowering under the Wings of great Poets rather than to a Bitterness that I am not appreciated. I am anxious to get Endymion printed that I may forget it and proceed. * * *

from the Preface to *Endymion*, dated April 10, 1818

The imagination of a boy is healthy, and the mature imagination of a man is healthy; but there is a space of life between, in which the soul is in a ferment, the character undecided, the way of life uncertain, the ambition thick-sighted: thence proceeds mawkishness, and all the thousand bitters which those men I speak of must necessarily taste in going over the following pages.

I hope I have not in too late a day touched the beautiful mythology of Greece, and dulled its brightness: for I wish to try once more, before I bid it farewell.

3. *Henry V*, Prologue, 1.

CHRONOLOGY

1795   John Keats born October 31 at Finsbury, just north of London, the eldest child of Thomas and Frances Jennings Keats. Thomas Keats was head ostler at a livery stable.

1797–1803   Birth of three younger brothers and sisters: George in 1797, Thomas in 1799, Frances Mary (Fanny) in 1803.

1803   With George, begins school in Enfield.

1804   Father killed by a fall from his horse, April 15. On June 27 his mother remarries, and the children go to live with their maternal grandparents at Enfield. The grandfather dies a year later, and the children move with their grandmother to Lower Edmonton.

1809   Begins a literary friendship with Charles Cowden Clarke, the son of the headmaster at the Enfield school, and develops a strong interest in reading.

1810   Mother dies of tuberculosis, after a long illness.

1811   Leaves school to become apprenticed to an apothecary-surgeon in Edmonton; completes a prose translation of the *Aeneid*, begun at school.

1814   Earliest known attempts at writing verse. In December his grandmother dies, and the family home is broken up.

1815   In October moves to next stage of his medical training at Guy's Hospital, south of the Thames in London.

1816   On May 5 his first published poem, "O Solitude," appears in Leigh Hunt's *Examiner*. In October writes "On First Looking into Chapman's Homer," published in December. Meets Hunt, Benjamin Haydon, John Hamilton Reynolds, and Shelley. By the spring of 1817, gives up the idea of medical practice.

1817   In March, moves with brothers to Hampstead, sees the Elgin Marbles with Haydon, and publishes his first collection of *Poems*. Composes *Endymion* between April and November. Reads Milton, Shakespeare, and Coleridge and rereads Wordsworth during the year.

1818   *Endymion* published in April, unfavorably reviewed in September, defended by Reynolds in October. During the summer goes on walking tour of the lake country and Scotland, but returns to London in mid-August with a sore throat and severe chills. His brother Tom also seriously ill by late summer, dying on December 1. In September, Keats first meets Fanny Brawne (eighteen years old), with whom he arrives at an "understanding" by Christmas.

1819   Writes *The Eve of St. Agnes* in January, revises it in September. Fanny Brawne and her mother move into the other half of the double house in which Keats lives in April. During April and May writes "La Belle Dame sans Merci" and all the major odes except "To Autumn," written in September. Rental arrangements force separation from Fanny Brawne during the summer (Keats on Isle of Wight from June to August), and in the fall he tries to break his dependence on her, but they become engaged by Christmas. Earlier in December suffers a recurrence of his sore throat.

1820   In February has a severe hemorrhage and in June an attack of blood-spitting. In July his doctor orders him to Italy for the winter; he sails in September and finally arrives in Rome on November 15. In July a volume of

poems published, *Lamia, Isabella, The Eve of St. Agnes and Other Poems.*
Fanny Brawne nurses him through the late summer.

1821   Dies at 11 P.M., February 23. Buried in the English Cemetery at Rome.

▾   ▾   ▾

QUESTIONS

1. Once you have read at least half a dozen poems by Keats, make a list of
the ideas that you have found in more than one poem. Make a list as well of
any distinctive stylistic features you have noticed. What kinds of experiences or
events does he tend to write about? Do you notice any pattern in his use of
speaker? Does he have favorite words that he uses in a particular way? What
about metaphors? What are his habits in putting poems together? (You might
want to look ahead to some examples of his revisions in Chapter 13.) In which
poems do you feel as if you want to know more about the author and his experi-
ences before you can interpret them confidently?

2. What stanza forms does Keats seem especially fond of? How do you
explain his fondness for repeated rhymes? What kinds of tonal effects are pro-
duced by the rhyme-rich sound patterns of the poem? What effect on meaning
does the emphasis on rhyme have?

3. What kinds of images dominate Keats's poems? What kinds of settings?
Do Keats's poems tend to have a distinctive, describable speaker? What tones
are characteristic of Keats?

WRITING SUGGESTION

Pick out *one* poem that seems to you "typical" in that it uses many of the
strategies found in other poems by Keats and displays themes that seem central
to his work. Write a detailed paper (of eight to ten pages) in which you analyze
the poem you have chosen, showing how it is typical of Keats's work.

10 THE AUTHOR'S WORK IN CONTEXT: ADRIENNE RICH

The poet featured in this chapter, Adrienne Rich, has had a long and very distinguished career. By many readers and critics, she is regarded as the best poet writing today. And a careful reader of her work will find similarities of interest, strategy, and taste from her earliest poems—published shortly after World War II, in 1951—to her newest ones. There is a distinctive mind and orientation at work in all her poems; one can speak about character-istic features in Rich's poetry just as surely as one does about characteristic fea-tures in the work of Donne, Keats, or Nemerov. Throughout her career of more than forty years so far, Rich has, for example, steadfastly remained inter-ested in social and political issues and has often concentrated on themes relat-ing to women's consciousness and the societal roles of women. Furthermore, her poems have always been conceived with a powerful sense of functional structure and cast into lyric modes that reflect sensitively their respective moods and tones. And the voice has always been firm and clear, setting out images vividly and taking a stand in matters of conscience. But over the years the voice has changed quite a lot too, and Rich's views on a number of issues have modified and developed. Many of the changes in Rich's ideas and atti-tudes reflect changing concerns among American (and especially women) intellectuals in the second half of the twentieth century, and her poems repre-sent both changed social conditions and sharply altered social, political, and philosophical attitudes. But they also reflect altered personal circumstances and changes in lifestyle and expressions of sexual preference. Rich married in her early twenties and had three children by the time she was thirty; many of her early poems are about heterosexual love, and some of them are quite explicitly about sex (see, for example, "Two Songs," p. 148). More recently she has been involved in a long-term lesbian relationship and has written, again quite explicitly, about sex between women (see, for example, "My mouth hovers," p. 77). In her poems one can trace not only the contours of her changing personal and political life and commitments, but (even more important for the study of poetry generally) one can see as well how changes *within* the poet and *in her social and cultural context* alter the themes and

directions of her work and even change the formal nature of what she tries
to do.

In addition to the poems gathered in this chapter, there are seven other
poems by Adrienne Rich printed elsewhere in the book. If you have been pro-
ceeding linearly through the book, you have already read most of these poems
and may have noticed both the cogency of mind they show and the variations
in theme and attitude as Rich has developed and changed during her life and
career. One way to study Rich as an "author in context" is to read carefully
what she has to say about herself and her poems: she is unusually straightfor-
ward, explicit, and articulate, and to read her describing her own development
is to be guided carefully through her changing ideas about what is important
both to the individual subjective consciousness and to societal attitudes and
changing roles. Gathered at the end of this chapter are a series of excerpts
from Rich's writing about herself and about poetry more generally, and you
can use these self-conscious reflections as a kind of commentary on the poems
included here and elsewhere in the book.

Here is a chronological list of all the poems and prose commentary
included elsewhere in this book; you can deal with the issues of an author in
context in one of three ways: 1) read the commentary, then the poems; 2) read
the poems, then the commentary; or 3) read the poems and commentary inter-
mixed, in chronological order. Each selection is dated, usually (as throughout
this volume) by publication date below the poem on the right, but sometimes
(when Rich herself has been insistent about it) by the date of composition
listed below the poem on the left.

Aunt Jennifer's Tigers	(1951)	p. 37
Living in Sin	(1955)	p. 276
Two Songs	(1964)	p. 148
[My mouth hovers across your breasts]	(1986)	p. 77
Letters in the Family	(1989)	p. 59
Walking down the Road	(1989)	p. 100
Delta	(1989)	p. 436

An even better way to study Adrienne Rich (or any poet) is to go to the
library and read all (or as much as you can find) of her writing, and consider
in detail how the various texts interact. Most poets, even John Keats, who lived
only to age twenty-five, change a lot during their careers, and many of the
changes correspond to larger social and cultural changes in their own time and
nation. The best way to think about the contexts of a poet's life and career is to
read as much as possible of their own work along with that of relevant contem-
poraries. Watching a poet develop within various traditions and contexts can

lead to a far more balanced assessment of a particular career and also to a more exact assessment of what poetry is about in a particular time, era, or culture.

Studying Rich's career in context suggests a number of larger literary, cultural, and historical issues— the kinds of issues that will be explored more fully in the next two chapters. You may well want to think about Adrienne Rich again after you have read the poems in the other chapters—especially the poems in the *Ideas and Consciousness* section of Chapter 12.

▼ ▼ ▼

ADRIENNE RICH

At a Bach Concert

Coming by evening through the wintry city
We said that art is out of love with life.
Here we approach a love that is not pity.

This antique discipline, tenderly severe,
Renews belief in love yet masters feeling,   5
Asking of us a grace in what we bear.

Form is the ultimate gift that love can offer—
The vital union of necessity
With all that we desire, all that we suffer.

A too-compassionate art is half an art.   10
Only such proud restraining purity
Restores the else-betrayed, too-human heart.   1951

Storm Warnings

The glass has been falling all the afternoon,
And knowing better than the instrument
What winds are walking overhead, what zone
Of gray unrest is moving across the land,
I leave the book upon a pillowed chair   5
And walk from window to closed window, watching
Boughs strain against the sky

And think again, as often when the air
Moves inward toward a silent core of waiting,
How with a single purpose time has traveled   10

By secret currents of the undiscerned
Into this polar realm. Weather abroad
And weather in the heart alike come on
Regardless of prediction.

15   Between foreseeing and averting change
Lies all the mastery of elements
Which clocks and weatherglasses cannot alter.
Time in the hand is not control of time,
Nor shattered fragments of an instrument
20   A proof against the wind; the wind will rise,
We can only close the shutters.

I draw the curtains as the sky goes black
And set a match to candles sheathed in glass
Against the keyhole draught, the insistent whine
25   Of weather through the unsealed aperture.
This is our sole defense against the season;
These are the things that we have learned to do
Who live in troubled regions.   1951

Snapshots of a Daughter-in-Law

1

You, once a belle in Shreveport,
with henna-colored hair, skin like a peachbud,
still have your dresses copied from that time,
and play a Chopin prelude
5   called by Cortot: *"Delicious recollections*
float like perfume through the memory."

Your mind now, mouldering like wedding-cake,
heavy with useless experience, rich
with suspicion, rumor, fantasy,
10   crumbling to pieces under the knife-edge
of mere fact. In the prime of your life.

Nervy, glowering, your daughter
wipes the teaspoons, grows another way.

2

Banging the coffee-pot into the sink
15   she hears the angels chiding, and looks out
past the raked gardens to the sloppy sky.
Only a week since They said: *Have no patience.*

The next time it was: *Be insatiable.*
Then: *Save yourself; others you cannot save.*[1]
Sometimes she's let the tapstream scald her arm,   20
a match burn to her thumbnail,

or held her hand above the kettle's snout
right in the woolly steam. They are probably angels,
since nothing hurts her any more, except
each morning's grit blowing into her eyes.   25

3

A thinking woman sleeps with monsters.
The beak that grips her, she becomes. And Nature,
that sprung-lidded, still commodious
steamer-trunk of *tempora* and *mores*[2]
gets stuffed with it all: the mildewed orange-flowers,   30
the female pills, the terrible breasts
of Boadicea[3] beneath flat foxes' heads and orchids.

Two handsome women, gripped in argument,
each proud, acute, subtle, I hear scream
across the cut glass and majolica   35
like Furies[4] cornered from their prey:
The argument *ad feminam*,[5] all the old knives
that have rusted in my back, I drive in yours,
ma semblable, ma soeur![6]

4

Knowing themselves too well in one another: 40
their gifts no pure fruition, but a thorn,
the prick filed sharp against a hint of scorn . . .
Reading while waiting
for the iron to heat,
writing, *My Life had stood—a Loaded Gun—*[7]   45
in that Amherst pantry while the jellies boil and scum,

1. According to Matthew 27:42, the chief priests, scribes, and elders mocked the crucified Jesus by saying, "He saved others; himself he cannot save."   2. Times and customs.   3. Queen of the ancient Britons. When her husband died, the Romans seized the territory he ruled and scourged Boadicea; she then led a heroic but ultimately unsuccessful revolt.   4. In Roman mythology, the three sisters were the avenging spirits of retributive justice.   5. "To the woman" (Latin). The *argumentum ad hominem* (literally, argument to the man) is (in logic) an argument aimed at a person's individual prejudices or special interests.   6. "My mirror-image [or "double"], my sister." Baudelaire, in the prefatory poem to *Les Fleurs du Mal*, addresses (and attacks) his "hypocrite reader" as "mon semblable, mon frère" ("my double, my brother").   7. " 'My Life had stood—a Loaded Gun—' [Poem No. 754], Emily Dickinson, *Complete Poems*, ed. T. H. Johnson, 1960, p. 369." (Rich's note)

or, more often,
iron-eyed and beaked and purposed as a bird,
dusting everything on the whatnot every day of life.

5

50   *Dulce ridens, dulce loquens,*[8]
she shaves her legs until they gleam
like petrified mammoth-tusk.

6

When to her lute Corinna sings[9]
neither words nor music are her own;
55   only the long hair dipping
over her cheek, only the song
of silk against her knees
and these
adjusted in reflections of an eye.

60   Poised, trembling and unsatisfied, before
an unlocked door, that cage of cages,
tell us, you bird, you tragical machine—
is this *fertilisante douleur?*[1] Pinned down
by love, for you the only natural action,
65   are you edged more keen
to prise the secrets of the vault? has Nature shown
her household books to you, daughter-in-law,
that her sons never saw?

7

"To have in this uncertain world some stay
70   *which cannot be undermined, is*
of the utmost consequence."[2]
              Thus wrote
a woman, partly brave and partly good,
who fought with what she partly understood.
Few men about her would or could do more,
75   hence she was labeled harpy, shrew and whore.

---

8. "Sweet [or "winsome"] laughter, sweet chatter." The phrase (slightly modified here) concludes Horace's Ode, 1, 22, describing the appeal of a mistress.   9. The opening line of a famous Elizabethan lyric (by Thomas Campion) in which Corinna's music is said to control totally the poet's happiness or despair.   1. "Enriching pain" (French).   2. " '. . . is of the utmost consequence,' from Mary Wollstonecraft, *Thoughts on the Education of Daughters*, London, 1787." (Rich's note)

8

"You all die at fifteen," said Diderot,[3]
and turn part legend, part convention.
Still, eyes inaccurately dream
behind closed windows blankening with steam.
Deliciously, all that we might have been,   80
all that we were—fire, tears,
wit, taste, martyred ambition—
stirs like the memory of refused adultery
the drained and flagging bosom of our middle years.

9

Not that it is done well, but   85
that it is done at all?[4] Yes, think
of the odds! or shrug them off forever.
This luxury of the precocious child,
Time's precious chronic invalid,—
would we, darlings, resign it if we could?   90
Our blight has been our sinecure:
mere talent was enough for us—
glitter in fragments and rough drafts.

Sigh no more, ladies.
                    Time is male
and in his cups drinks to the fair.   95
Bemused by gallantry, we hear
our mediocrities over-praised,
indolence read as abnegation,
slattern thought styled intuition,
every lapse forgiven, our crime   100
only to cast too bold a shadow
or smash the mould straight off.

For that, solitary confinement,
tear gas, attrition shelling.
Few applicants for that honor.

3. " 'Vous mourez toutes a quinze ans,' from the *Lettres à Sophie Volland,* quoted by Simone de Beauvoir in *Le Deuxième Sexe,* vol. II, pp. 123–4." (Rich's note) Editor of the *Encyclopédie* (the central document of the French Enlightenment), Diderot became disillusioned with the traditional education of women and undertook an experimental education for his own daughter.   4. Samuel Johnson's comment on women preachers: "Sir, a woman's preaching is like a dog's walking on his hinder legs. It is not done well, but you are surprised to find it done at all." (Boswell's *Life of Johnson,* ed. L. F. Powell and G. B. Hill, Oxford: Clarendon, 1934–64, I, 463) (Rich's note)

10

105   Well,
she's long about her coming, who must be
more merciless to herself than history.[5]
Her mind full to the wind, I see her plunge
breasted and glancing through the currents,
110   taking the light upon her
at least as beautiful as any boy
or helicopter,
             poised, still coming,
her fine blades making the air wince

but her cargo
115   no promise then:
delivered
palpable
ours.

1958–60

In *When We Dead Awaken*, Rich describes her consciousness during the time she was writing this poem:

> Over two years I wrote a 10-part poem called "Snapshots of a Daughter-in-Law," in a longer, looser mode than I've ever trusted myself with before. It was an extraordinary relief to write that poem. It strikes me now as too literary, too dependent on allusion; I hadn't found the courage yet to do without authorities, or even to use the pronoun "I"—the woman in the poem is always "she." One section of it, #2, concerns a woman who thinks she is going mad; she is haunted by voices telling her to resist and rebel, voices which she can hear but not obey.

Orion

Far back when I went zig-zagging
through tamarack pastures
you were my genius, you
my cast-iron Viking, my helmed
5   lion-heart king in prison.
Years later now you're young

---

5. "Cf. *Le Deuxième Sexe*, vol. II, p. 574: '. . . elle arrive du fond des ages, de Thèbes, de Minos, de Chichen Itza; et elle est aussi le totem planté au coeur de la brousse africaine; c'est un helicoptère et c'est un oiseau; et voilà la plus grande merveille: sous ses cheveux peints le bruissement des feuillages devient une pensée et des paroles s'échappent de ses seins.' " (Rich's note)

my fierce half-brother, staring
down from that simplified west
your breast open, your belt dragged down
by an oldfashioned thing, a sword   10
the last bravado you won't give over
though it weighs you down as you stride

and the stars in it are dim
and maybe have stopped burning.
But you burn, and I know it;   15
as I throw back my head to take you in
an old transfusion happens again:
divine astronomy is nothing to it.

Indoors I bruise and blunder,
break faith, leave ill enough   20
alone, a dead child born in the dark.
Night cracks up over the chimney,
pieces of time, frozen geodes
come showering down in the grate.

A man reaches behind my eyes   25
and finds them empty
a woman's head turns away
from my head in the mirror
children are dying my death
and eating crumbs of my life.   30

Pity is not your forte.
Calmly you ache up there
pinned aloft in your crow's nest,
my speechless pirate!
You take it all for granted   35
and when I look you back

it's with a starlike eye
shooting its cold and egotistical spear
where it can do least damage.
Breathe deep! No hurt, no pardon   40
out here in the cold with you
you with your back to the wall.   1965

In *When We Dead Awaken*, Rich describes "Orion" as

a poem of reconstruction with a part of myself I had felt I was losing—the active
principle, the energetic imagination, the "half-brother" whom I projected, as I had
for many years, into the constellation Orion. It's no accident that the words "cold
and egotistical" appear in this poem, and are applied to myself. The choice still
seemed to be between "love"—womanly, maternal love, altruistic love—a love

defined and ruled by the weight of an entire culture—and egotism—a force directed by men into creation, achievement, ambition, often at the expense of others, but justifiably so. For weren't they men, and wasn't that their destiny as womanly love was ours? I know now that the alternatives are false ones—that the word "love" is itself in need of re-vision.

Leaflets

1

The big star, and that other
lonely on black glass
overgrown with frozen
lesions, endless night
the Coal Sack gaping
black veins of ice on the pane
spelling a word:
                    Insomnia
not manic but ordinary
to start out of sleep
turning off and on
this seasick neon
vision, this
division

the head clears of sweet smoke
and poison gas

life without caution
the only worth living
love for a man
love for a woman
love for the facts
protectless

that self-defense be not
the arm's first motion

memory not only
cards of identity

that I can live half a year
as I have never lived up to this time—[6]

6. Quoted from a letter by Anton Chekhov to I. L. Scheglov, March 22, 1890, explaining his forthcoming visit to Saghalien, an island penal colony. Chekhov (1860–1904), the Russian playwright and short story writer, had contracted tuberculosis at age 23 (see line 28).

Chekhov coughing up blood almost daily
the steamer edging in toward the penal colony
chained men dozing on deck   30
five forest fires lighting the island

lifelong that glare, waiting.

                                    2

Your face
            stretched like a mask
                        begins to tear
as you speak of Che Guevara[7]
Bolivia, Nanterre   35
I'm too young to be your mother
you're too young to be my brother

your tears are not political
they are real water, burning
as the tears of Telemachus   40
burned

Over Spanish Harlem the moon
swells up, a fire balloon
fire gnawing the edge
of this crushed-up newspaper   45

                        now
the bodies come whirling
coal-black, ash-white
out of torn windows
and the death columns blacken
                        whispering   50
Who'd choose this life?

We're fighting for a slash of recognition,
a piercing to the pierced heart.
Tell me what you are going through —[8]

but the attention flickers   55
                        and will flicker
a matchflame in poison air
a thread, a hair of light
                        sum of all answer
to the *Know that I exist!* of all existing things.   60

---

7. Latin American revolutionary theorist and an early leader in the Castro regime in Cuba. Guevara was killed in the abortive Bolivian revolution in 1967. *Nanterre*: one site of the 1968 French student uprising.   8. "Simone Weil: 'The love of a fellow-creature in all its fullness consists simply in the ability to say to him: "What are you going through" ' — *Waiting For God.*" (Rich's note)

3

If, says the Dahomeyan devil,[9]
someone has courage to enter the fire
the young man will be restored to life.

If, the girl whispers,
65 I do not go into the fire
I will not be able to live with my soul.

(Her face calm and dark as amber
under the dyed butterfly turban
her back scarified in ostrich-skin patterns.)

4

70 Crusaders' wind glinting
off linked scales of sea
ripping the ghostflags
galloping at the fortress
Acre, bloodcaked, lionhearted
75 raw vomit curdling in the sun
gray walkers walking
straying with a curbed intentness
in and out the inclosures
the gallows, the photographs
80 of dead Jewish terrorists, aged 15
their fading faces wide-eyed
and out in the crusading sunlight
gray strayers still straying
dusty paths
85 the mad who live in the dried-up moat
of the War Museum

what are we coming to
what wants these things of us
who wants them

5

90 The strain of being born
        over and over has torn your smile into pieces
Often I have seen it broken
        and then re-membered
and wondered how a beauty
95   so anarch, so ungelded
will be cared for in this world.

9. Legba the trickster.

I want to hand you this
leaflet streaming with rain or tears
    but the words coming clear
something you might find crushed into your hand   100
    after passing a barricade
and stuff in your raincoat pocket.
    I want this to reach you
who told me once that poetry is nothing sacred
    —no more sacred that is   105
than other things in your life—
    to answer yes, if life is uncorrupted
no better poetry is wanted.

    I want this to be yours
in the sense that if you find and read it   110
    it will be there in you already
and the leaflet then merely something
   to leave behind, a little leaf
in the drawer of a sublet room.
    What else does it come down to   115
but handing on scraps of paper
    little figurines or phials
no stronger than the dry clay they are baked in
    yet more than dry clay or paper
because the imagination crouches in them.   120
    If we needed fire to remind us
that all true images
    were scooped out of the mud
where our bodies curse and flounder
    then perhaps that fire is coming   125
to sponge away the scribes and time-servers
    and much that you would have loved will be lost as well
before you could handle it and know it
    just as we almost miss each other
in the ill cloud of mistrust, who might have touched   130
    hands quickly, shared food or given blood
for each other. I am thinking how we can use what we have
    to invent what we need.

Winter–Spring 1968

Planetarium

(Thinking of Caroline Herschel, 1750–1848,
astronomer, sister of William; and others)

A woman in the shape of a monster
a monster in the shape of a woman
the skies are full of them

a woman   "in the snow
among the Clocks and instruments
or measuring the ground with poles"

in her 98 years to discover
8 comets

she whom the moon ruled
like us
levitating into the night sky
riding the polished lenses

Galaxies of women, there
doing penance for impetuousness
ribs chilled
in those spaces   of the mind

An eye,
          "virile, precise and absolutely certain"
          from the mad webs of Uranisborg
                              encountering the NOVA

every impulse of light exploding
from the core
as life flies out of us

          Tycho[1] whispering at last
          "Let me not seem to have lived in vain"

What we see, we see
and seeing is changing

the light that shrivels a mountain
and leaves a man alive

Heartbeat of the pulsar
heart sweating through my body

---

1. Tycho Brahe (1546–1601), Danish astronomer whose cosmology tried to fuse the Ptolemaic and Copernican systems. He discovered and described (*De Nova Stella*, 1573) a new star in what had previously been considered a fixed star-system. Uranisborg (line 19) was Tycho's famous and elaborate palace-laboratory-observatory.

The radio impulse
pouring in from Taurus
      I am bombarded yet   I stand

I have been standing all my life in the   35
direct path of a battery of signals
the most accurately transmitted most
untranslatable language in the universe
I am a galactic cloud so deep   so invo-
luted that a light wave could take 15   40
years to travel through me   And has
taken   I am an instrument in the shape
of a woman trying to translate pulsations
into images   for the relief of the body
and the reconstruction of the mind.   45

1968

Rich describes this poem, in *When We Dead Awaken*, as a "companion poem to 'Orion,' " above:

at last the woman in the poem and the woman writing the poem become the same person. . . . It was written after a visit to a real planetarium, where I read an account of the work of Caroline Herschel, the astronomer, who worked with her brother William, but whose name remained obscure, as his did not.

Dialogue

She sits with one hand poised against her head, the
other turning an old ring to the light
for hours our talk has beaten
like rain against the screens
a sense of August and heat-lightning   5
I get up, go to make tea, come back
we look at each other
then she says (and this is what I live through
over and over)—she says: *I do not know*
if sex is an illusion   10

I do not know
who I was when I did those things
or who I said I was
or whether I willed to feel
what I had read about   15
or who in fact was there with me

> *or whether I knew, even then*
> *that there was doubt about these things*

1972

Diving into the Wreck

First having read the book of myths,
and loaded the camera,
and checked the edge of the knife-blade,
I put on
5 the body-armor of black rubber
the absurd flippers
the grave and awkward mask.
I am having to do this
not like Cousteau with his
10 assiduous team
aboard the sun-flooded schooner
but here alone.

There is a ladder.
The ladder is always there
15 hanging innocently
close to the side of the schooner.
We know what it is for,
we who have used it.
Otherwise
20 it's a piece of maritime floss
some sundry equipment.

I go down.
Rung after rung and still
the oxygen immerses me
25 the blue light
the clear atoms
of our human air.
I go down.
My flippers cripple me,
30 I crawl like an insect down the ladder
and there is no one
to tell me when the ocean
will begin.

First the air is blue and then
35 it is bluer and then green and then
black I am blacking out and yet
my mask is powerful
it pumps my blood with power
the sea is another story

the sea is not a question of power   40
I have to learn alone
to turn my body without force
in the deep element.

And now: it is easy to forget
what I came for   45
among so many who have always
lived here
swaying their crenellated fans
between the reefs
and besides   50
you breathe differently down here.

I came to explore the wreck.
The words are purposes.
The words are maps.
I came to see the damage that was done   55
and the treasures that prevail.
I stroke the beam of my lamp
slowly along the flank
of something more permanent
than fish or weed   60

the thing I came for:
the wreck and not the story of the wreck
the thing itself and not the myth
the drowned face always staring
toward the sun   65
the evidence of damage
worn by salt and sway into this threadbare beauty
the ribs of the disaster
curving their assertion
among the tentative haunters.   70

This is the place.
And I am here, the mermaid whose dark hair
streams black, the merman in his armored body
We circle silently
about the wreck   75
we dive into the hold.
I am she: I am he
whose drowned face sleeps with open eyes
whose breasts still bear the stress
whose silver, copper, vermeil cargo lies   80
obscurely inside barrels
half-wedged and left to rot
we are the half-destroyed instruments
that once held to a course

85
        the water-eaten log
        the fouled compass

        We are, I am, you are
        by cowardice or courage
        the one who find our way
90
        back to this scene
        carrying a knife, a camera
        a book of myths
        in which
        our names do not appear.

1972

Power

Living   in the earth-deposits   of our history

Today a backhoe divulged   out of a crumbling flank of earth
one bottle   amber   perfect   a hundred-year-old
cure for fever   or melancholy   a tonic
5
for living on this earth   in the winters of this climate

Today I was reading about Marie Curie:
she must have known she suffered   from radiation sickness
her body bombarded for years   by the element
she had purified
10
It seems she denied to the end
the source of the cataracts on her eyes
the cracked and suppurating skin   of her finger-ends
till she could no longer hold   a test-tube or a pencil

She died   a famous woman   denying
15
her wounds
denying
her wounds   came   from the same source as her power

1974   1978

Origins and History of Consciousness

I

Night-life. Letters, journals, bourbon
sloshed in the glass. Poems crucified on the wall,
dissected, their bird-wings severed

like trophies. No one lives in this room
without living through some kind of crisis. 5

No one lives in this room
without confronting the whiteness of the wall
behind the poems, planks of books,
photographs of dead heroines.
Without contemplating last and late 10
the true nature of poetry. The drive
to connect. The dream of a common language.

Thinking of lovers, their blind faith, their
experienced crucifixions,
my envy is not simple. I have dreamed of going to bed 15
as walking into clear water ringed by a snowy wood
white as cold sheets, thinking, *I'll freeze in there.*
My bare feet are numbed already by the snow
but the water
is mild, I sink and float 20
like a warm amphibious animal
that has broken the net, has run
through fields of snow leaving no print;
this water washes off the scent—
You are clear now 25
of the hunter, the trapper
the wardens of the mind—

yet the warm animal dreams on
of another animal
swimming under the snow-flecked surface of the pool, 30
and wakes, and sleeps again.

No one sleeps in this room without
the dream of a common language.

II

It was simple to meet you, simple to take your eyes
into mine, saying: these are eyes I have known 35
from the first. . . . It was simple to touch you
against the hacked background, the grain of what we
had been, the choices, years. . . . It was even simple
to take each other's lives in our hands, as bodies.

What is not simple: to wake from drowning 40
from where the ocean beat inside us like an afterbirth
into this common, acute particularity
these two selves who walked half a lifetime untouching—
to wake to something deceptively simple: a glass
sweated with dew, a ring of the telephone, a scream 45

of someone beaten up far down in the street
causing each of us to listen to her own inward scream

knowing the mind of the mugger and the mugged
as any woman must who stands to survive this city,
50 this century, this life . . .

each of us having loved the flesh in its clenched or loosened beauty
better than trees or music (yet loving those too
as if they were flesh—and they are—but the flesh
of beings unfathomed as yet in our roughly literal life).

III

55 It's simple to wake from sleep with a stranger,
dress, go out, drink coffee,
enter a life again. It isn't simple
to wake from sleep into the neighborhood
of one neither strange nor familiar
60 whom we have chosen to trust. Trusting, untrusting,
we lowered ourselves into this, let ourselves
downward hand over hand as on a rope that quivered
over the unsearched. . . . We did this. Conceived
of each other, conceived each other in a darkness
65 which I remember as drenched in light.
                                I want to call this, life.

But I can't call it life until we start to move
beyond this secret circle of fire
where our bodies are giant shadows flung on a wall
70 where the night becomes our inner darkness, and sleeps
like a dumb beast, head on her paws, in the corner.

1972–74   1978

For the Record

The clouds and the stars didn't wage this war
the brooks gave no information
if the mountain spewed stones of fire into the river
it was not taking sides
5   the raindrop faintly swaying under the leaf
had no political opinions

and if here or there a house
filled with backed-up raw sewage
or poisoned those who lived there
10 with slow fumes, over years

the houses were not at war
nor did the tinned-up buildings

intend to refuse shelter
to homeless old women and roaming children
they had no policy to keep them roaming   15
or dying, no, the cities were not the problem
the bridges were non-partisan
the freeways burned, but not with hatred

Even the miles of barbed-wire
stretched around crouching temporary huts   20
designed to keep the unwanted
at a safe distance, out of sight
even the boards that had to absorb
year upon year, so many human sounds

so many depths of vomit, tears   25
slow-soaking blood
had not offered themselves for this
The trees didn't volunteer to be cut into boards
nor the thorns for tearing flesh
Look around at all of it   30

and ask whose signature
is stamped on the orders, traced
in the corner of the building plans
Ask where the illiterate, big-bellied
women were, the drunks and crazies,   35
the ones you fear most of all: ask where you were.   1983

from Talking with Adrienne Rich[2]

* * * I think of myself as using poetry as a chief means of self-exploration—one of several means, of which maybe another would be dreams, really thinking about, paying attention to dreams, but the poem, like the dream, does this through images and it is in the images of my poems that I feel I am finding out more about my own experience, my sense of things. But I don't think of myself as having a position or a self-description which I'm then going to present in the poem.

When I started writing poetry I was tremendously conscious of, and very much in need of, a formal structure that could be obtained from outside, into which I could pour whatever I had, whatever I thought I had to express. But I think that was a part of a whole thing that I see, now as a teacher, very much

2. A transcript of a conversation recorded March 9, 1971, and printed in the *Ohio Review*, Fall 1971.

with young writers, of using language more as a kind of façade than as either self-revelation or as a probe into one's own consciousness. I think I would attribute a lot of the change in my poetry simply to the fact of growing older, undergoing certain kinds of experiences, realizing that formal metrics were not going to suffice me in dealing with those experiences, realizing that experience itself is much more fragmentary, much more sort of battering, much ruder than these structures would allow, and it had to find its own form.

I have a very strong sense about the existence of poetry in daily life and poetry being part of the world as it is, and that the attempt to reduce poetry to what is indited on a page just limits you terribly. . . . The poem is the poetry of things lodged in the innate shape of the experience. My saying "The moment of change is the only poem" is the kind of extreme statement you feel the need to make at certain times if only to force someone to say, "But I always thought a poem is something written on a piece of paper," you know, and to say: "But look, how did those words get on that piece of paper." There had to be a mind; there had to be an experience; the mind had to go through certain shocks, certain stresses, certain strains, and if you're going to carry the poem back to its real beginnings it's that moment of change. I feel that we are always writing.

When I was in my twenties * * * I was going through a very sort of female thing—of trying to distinguish between the ego that is capable of writing poems, and then this other kind of being that you're asked to be if you're a woman, who is, in a sense, denying that ego. I had great feelings of split about that for many years actually, and there are a lot of poems I couldn't write even, because I didn't want to confess to having that much aggression, that much ego, that much sense of myself. I had always thought of my first book as being a book of very well-tooled poems of a sort of very bright student, which I was at that time, but poems in which the unconscious things never got to the surface. But there's a poem in that book about a woman who sews a tapestry and the tapestry has figures of tigers on it. But the woman is represented as being completely—her hand is burdened by the weight of the wedding band, and she's meek, and she's fearful, and the only way in which she can express any other side of her nature is in embroidering these tigers. Well, I thought of that as almost a formal exercise, but when I go back and look at that poem I really think it's saying something about what I was going through. And now that's lessened a great deal for all sorts of reasons—that split.

from An Interview with Adrienne Rich[3]

I would have said ten or fifteen years ago that I would not even want to identify myself as a woman poet. That term *has* been used pejoratively; I just don't think

3. By David Kalstone, in the *Saturday Review*, April 22, 1972.

it can be at this point. You know, for a woman the act of creation is prototypically to produce children, while the act of creating with language—I'm not saying that women writers haven't been accepted; certainly, more have been accepted than women lawyers or doctors. Still, a woman writer feels, she is going against the grain—or there has been this sense until very recently (if there isn't still). Okay, it's all right to be a young thing and write verse. But a friend of mine was telling me about meeting a noted poet at a cocktail party. She'd sent him a manuscript for a contest he was judging. She went up to him and asked him about it, and he looked at her and said, "Young girls *are* poems; they shouldn't write them." This attitude toward women poets manifests itself so strongly that you are made to feel you are becoming the thing you are not.

If a man is writing, he's gone through all the nonsense and said "Okay, I am a poet and I'm still a man. They don't cancel each other out or, if they do, then I'll opt to be a poet." He's not writing for a hostile sex, a breed of critics who by virtue of their sex are going to look at his language and pass judgment on it. That does happen to a woman. I don't know why the woman poet has been slower than the woman novelist in taking risks though I'm very grateful that this is no longer so. I feel that I dare to think further than I would have dared to think ten years ago—and *that* certainly is going to affect my writing. And I now dare to entertain thoughts and speculations that then would have seemed unthinkable.

Many of the male writers whom I very much admire—Galway Kinnell, James Wright, W. S. Merwin—are writing poetry of such great desolation. They come from different backgrounds, write in different ways, and yet all seem to write out of a sense of doom, as if we were fated to carry on these terribly flawed relationships. I think it's expressive of a feeling that "we, the masters, have created a world that's impossible to live in and that probably may not be livable in, in a very literal sense. What we thought, what we'd been given to think is our privilege, our right, and our sexual prerogative has led to this, to our doom." I guess a lot of women—if not a lot of women poets—are feeling that there has to be some other way, that human life is messed-up but that it doesn't have to be *this* desolate.

Today, much poetry by women is charged with anger and uses voices of rage and anger that I don't think were ever used in poetry before. In poets like Sylvia Plath and Diane Wakoski, say, those voices are so convincing that it is impossible to describe them by using those favorite adjectives of phallic criticism—shrill and hysterical. Well, Sylvia Plath is dead. I always maintained from the first time I read her last poems that her suicide was not necessary, that she could have gone on and written poems that would have given us even more insight into the states of anger and willfulness, even of self-destructiveness, that women experience. She didn't need literally to destroy herself in order to reflect and express those things. Diane Wakoski is a young woman. She's changing a lot and will continue to change. What I admire in her, besides her energy and dynamism and quite a beautiful gift for snatching the image that she wants out of the air, is her honesty. No woman has written before about her face and said she hated it, that it had served her ill, that she wished she could throw acid in it. That's very shocking. But I think all women, even the most beautiful women, at times have felt that in a kind of self-hatred. Because the *face* is supposed to be the *woman*.

A lot of poetry is becoming more oral. Certainly, it's true of women and black poets. Reading black poetry on the printed page gives no sense of the poem, if you're going to look at that poetry the way you look at poems by Richard Wilbur. Yet you can hear these poets read and realize it's the oldest kind of poetry.

I think the energy of language comes somewhat from the pressure and need and unbearableness of what's being done to you. It's not the same energy you find in the blues. The blues are a grief language, a lost language, and a cry of pain, usually in a woman's voice, which is interesting. For a long time you sing the blues, and then you begin to say, "I'm tired of singing the blues. I want something else." And that's what you're hearing now. There seems to be a connection between an oppressed condition and having access to certain kinds of energy, vitality, and subjectivity. For women as well as blacks. Though I don't feel there is a necessary cause-and-effect relationship; what seems to happen is that being on top, being in a powerful position leads to a divorce between one's unruly, chaotic, revolutionary sensitivity and one's reason, sense of order and of maintaining a hold. And, therefore, you have at the bottom of the pile, so to speak, a kind of churning energy that gets lost up there among the administrators.

I don't know how or whether poetry changes anything. But neither do I know how or whether bombing or even community organizing changes anything when we are pitted against a massive patriarchal system armed with supertechnology. I believe in subjectivity—that a lot of male Left leaders have turned into Omnipotent Administrators, because their "masculinity" forced them to deny their subjectivity. I believe in dreams and visions and "the madness of art." And at moments I can conceive of a women's movement that will show the way to humanizing technology and fusing dreams and skills and visions and reason to begin the healing of the human race. But I don't want women to take over the world and run it the way men have, or to take on—yet again!—the burden of carrying the subjectivity of the race. Women are a vanguard now, and I believe will increasingly become so, because we have—Western women, Third World women, all women—known and felt the pain of the human condition most consistently. But in the end it can't be women alone.

from When We Dead Awaken: Writing as Re-Vision[4]

Most, if not all, human lives are full of fantasy—passive daydreaming which need not be acted on. But to write poetry or fiction, or even to think well, is not to fantasize, or to put fantasies on paper. For a poem to coalesce, for a character or an action to take shape, there has to be an imaginative transformation of reality which is in no way passive. And a certain freedom of the mind is needed—freedom to press on, to enter the currents of your thought like a glider pilot, knowing that your motion can be sustained, that the buoyancy of your attention will not be suddenly snatched away. Moreover, if the imagination is to transcend and transform experience it has to question, to challenge, to conceive of alternatives, perhaps to the very life you are living at that moment. You have to be free to play around with the notion that day might be night, love might be hate, nothing can be too sacred for the imagination to turn into its opposite or to call experimentally by another name. For writing is re-naming. Now, to be maternally with small children all day in the old way, to be with a man in the old way of marriage, requires a holding-back, a putting-aside of that imaginative activity, and demands instead a kind of conservatism. I want to make it clear that I am *not* saying that in order to write well, or think well, it is necessary to become unavailable to others, or to become a devouring ego. This has been the myth of the masculine artist and thinker; and I do not accept it. But to be a female human being trying to fulfill traditional female functions in a traditional way *is* in direct conflict with the subversive function of the imagination. The word traditional is important here. There must be ways, and we will be finding out more and more about them, in which the energy of creation and the energy of relation can be united. But in those earlier years I always felt the conflict as a failure of love in myself. I had thought I was choosing a full life: the life available to most men, in which sexuality, work, and parenthood could coexist. But I felt, at twenty-nine, guilt toward the people closest to me, and guilty toward my own being.

I wanted, then, more than anything, the one thing of which there was never enough: time to think, time to write. The fifties and early sixties were years of rapid revelations: the sit-ins and marches in the South, the Bay of Pigs, the early antiwar movement, raised large questions—questions for which the masculine world of the academy around me seemed to have expert and fluent answers. But I needed to think for myself—about pacifism and dissent and violence, about poetry and society, and about my own relationship to all these things. For about ten years I was reading in fierce snatches, scribbling in notebooks, writing poetry in fragments; I was looking desperately for clues, because if there were no clues then I thought I might be insane. I wrote in a notebook about this time:

---

4. First published in *College English* in 1972; this version slightly revised, is included in *On Lies, Secrets, and Silence: Selected Prose: 1966–1978* (1979).

> Paralyzed by the sense that there exists a mesh of relationships—e.g., between my
> anger at the children, my sensual life, pacifism, sex (I mean sex in its broadest sig-
> nificance, not merely sexual desire)—an interconnectedness which, if I could see it,
> make it valid, would give me back myself, make it possible to function lucidly and
> passionately. Yet I grope in and out among these dark webs.

I think I began at this point to feel that politics was not something "out there"
but something "in here" and of the essence of my condition.

In the late fifties I was able to write, for the first time, directly about experi-
encing myself as a woman. The poem was jotted in fragments during children's
naps, brief hours in a library, or at 3 A.M. after rising with a wakeful child. I
despaired of doing any continuous work at this time. Yet I began to feel that my
fragments and scraps had a common consciousness and a common theme, one
which I would have been very unwilling to put on paper at an earlier time
because I had been taught that poetry should be "universal," which meant, of
course, nonfemale. Until then I had tried very much *not* to identify myself as a
female poet.

How Does a Poet Put Bread on the Table?[5]

But how does a poet put bread on the table? Rarely, if ever, by poetry alone. Of
the four lesbian poets at the Nuyorican Poets Café about whose lives I know
something, one directs an underfunded community arts project, two are unten-
ured college teachers, one an assistant dean of students at a state university. Of
other poets I know, most teach, often part time, without security but year round;
two are on disability; one does clerical work; one cleans houses; one is a paid
organizer; one has a paid editing job. Whatever odd money comes in erratically
from readings and workshops, grants, permissions fees, royalties, prizes can be
very odd money indeed, never to be counted on and almost always small: checks
have to be chased down, grants become fewer and more competitive in a wors-
ening political and economic climate. Most poets who teach at universities are
untenured, without pension plans or group health insurance, or are employed
at public and community colleges with heavy teaching loads and low salaries.
Many give unpaid readings and workshops as part of their political "tithe."

Inherited wealth accounts for the careers of some poets: to inherit wealth is
to inherit time. Most of the poets I know, hearing of a sum of money, translate
it not into possessions, but into time—that precious immaterial necessity of our
lives. It's true that a poem can be attempted in brief interstitial moments, pulled
out of the pocket and worked on while waiting for a bus or riding a train or
while children nap or while waiting for a new batch of clerical work or blood
samples to come in. But only certain kinds of poems are amenable to these

5. From *What Is Found There: Notebooks on Poetry and Politics* (1993).

conditions. Sometimes the very knowledge of coming interruption dampens the flicker. And there is a difference between the ordinary "free" moments stolen from exhausting family strains, from alienating labor, from thought chained by material anxiety, and those other moments that sometimes arrive in a life being lived at its height though under extreme tension; perhaps we are waiting to initiate some act we believe will catalyze change but whose outcome is uncertain; perhaps we are facing personal or communal crisis in which everything unimportant seems to fall away and we are left with our naked lives, the brevity of life itself, and words. At such times we may experience a speeding-up of our imaginative powers, images and voices rush together in a kind of inevitability, what was externally fragmented is internally recognized, and the hand can barely keep pace.

But such moments presuppose other times: when we could simply stare into the wood grain of a door, or the trace of bubbles in a glass of water as long as we wanted to, *almost* secure in the knowledge that there would be no interruption—times of slowness, or purposelessness.

Often such time feels like a luxury, guiltily seized when it can be had, fearfully taken because it does not seem like work, this abeyance, but like "wasting time" in a society where personal importance—even job security—can hinge on acting busy, where the phrase "keeping busy" is a common idiom, where there is, for activists, so much to be done.

Most, if not all, of the names we know in North American poetry are the names of people who have had some access to freedom in time—that privilege of some which is actually a necessity for all. The struggle to limit the working day is a sacred struggle for the worker's freedom in time. To feel herself or himself, for a few hours or a weekend, as a free being with choices—to plant vegetables and later sit on the porch with a cold beer, to write poetry or build a fence or fish or play cards, to walk without a purpose, to make love in the daytime. To sleep late. Ordinary human pleasures, the self's re-creation. Yet every working generation has to reclaim that freedom in time, and many are brutally thwarted in the effort. Capitalism is based on the abridgment of that freedom.

Poets in the United States have either had some kind of private means, or help from people with private means, have held full-time, consuming jobs, or have chosen to work in low-paying, part-time sectors of the economy, saving their creative energies for poetry, keeping their material wants simple. Interstitial living, where the art itself is not expected to bring in much money, where the artist may move from a clerical job to part-time, temporary teaching to subsistence living on the land to waitressing or doing construction or translating, typesetting, or ghostwriting. In the 1990s this kind of interstitial living is more difficult, risky, and wearing than it has ever been, and this is a loss to all the arts—as much as the shrinkage of arts funding, the censorship-by-clique, the censorship by the Right, the censorship by distribution.

A Communal Poetry[6]

One day in New York in the late 1980s, I had lunch with a poet I'd known for more than twenty years. Many of his poems were—are—embedded in my life. We had read together at the antiwar events of the Vietnam years. Then, for a long time, we hardly met. As a friend, he had seemed to me withheld, defended in a certain way I defined as masculine and with which I was becoming in general impatient; yet often, in their painful beauty, his poems told another story. On this day, he was as I had remembered him: distant, stiff, shy perhaps. The conversation stumbled along as we talked about our experiences with teaching poetry, which seemed a safe ground. I made some remark about how long it was since last we'd talked. Suddenly, his whole manner changed: *You disappeared! You simply disappeared.* I realized he meant not so much from his life as from a landscape of poetry to which he though we both belonged and were in some sense loyal.

If anything, those intervening years had made me feel more apparent, more visible—to myself and to others—as a poet. The powerful magnet of the women's liberation movement—and the women's poetry movement it released—had drawn me to coffeehouses where women were reading new kinds of poems; to emerging "journals of liberation" that published women's poems, often in a context of political articles and the beginnings of feminist criticism; to bookstores selling chapbooks and pamphlets from the new women's presses; to a woman poet's workshops with women in prison; to meetings with other women poets in Chinese restaurants, coffee shops, apartments, where we talked not only of poetry, but of the conditions that make it possible or impossible. It had never occurred to me that I was disappearing—rather, that I was, along with other women poets, beginning to appear. In fact, we were taking part in an immense shift in human consciousness.

My old friend had, I believe, not much awareness of any of this. It was, for him, so off-to-the-edge, so out-of-the-way; perhaps so dangerous, it seemed I had sunk, or dived, into a black hole. Only later, in a less constrained and happier meeting, were we able to speak of the different ways we had perceived that time.

He thought there had been a known, defined poetic landscape and that as poetic contemporaries we simply shared it. But whatever poetic "generation" I belonged to, in the 1950s I was a mother, under thirty, raising three small children. Notwithstanding the prize and the fellowship to Europe that my first book of poems had won me, there was little or no "appearance" I then felt able to claim as a poet, against that other profound and as yet unworded reality.

---

6. From *What Is Found There: Notebooks on Poetry and Politics* (1993).

CHRONOLOGY

1929   Born in Baltimore, Maryland, May 16. Began writing poetry as a child under the encouragement and supervision of her father, Dr. Arnold Rich, from whose "very Victorian, pre-Raphaelite" library, Rich later recalled, she read Tennyson, Keats, Arnold, Blake, Rossetti, Swinburne, Carlyle, and Pater.

1951   A.B., Radcliffe College. Phi Beta Kappa. *A Change of World* chosen by W. H. Auden for the Young Poets Award and published.

1952–53   Guggenheim Fellowship; travel in Europe and England. Marriage to Alfred H. Conrad, an economist who taught at Harvard. Residence in Cambridge, Massachusetts, 1953–66.

1955   Birth of David Conrad. Publication of *The Diamond Cutters and Other Poems*, which won the Ridgely Torrence Memorial Award of the Poetry Society of America.

1957   Birth of Paul Conrad.

1959   Birth of Jacob Conrad.

1960   National Institute of Arts and Letters Award for poetry. Phi Beta Kappa poet at William and Mary College.

1961–62   Guggenheim Fellowship; residence with family in the Netherlands.

1962   Bollingen Foundation grant for translation of Dutch poetry.

1962–63   Amy Lowell Travelling Fellowship.

1963   *Snapshots of a Daughter-in-Law* published. Bess Hokin Prize of *Poetry* magazine.

1965   Phi Beta Kappa poet at Swarthmore College.

1966   *Necessities of Life* published, nominated for the National Book Award. Phi Beta Kappa poet at Harvard College. Move to New York City, where Alfred Conrad taught at City College of New York. Residence there from 1966 on. Increasingly active politically in protests against the Indochina war.

1966–68   Lecturer at Swarthmore College.

1967–69   Adjunct Professor of Writing in the Graduate School of the Arts, Columbia University.

1967   *Selected Poems* published in Britain. Litt.D., Wheaton College.

1968   Eunice Tietjens Memorial Prize of *Poetry* magazine. Began teaching in the SEEK and Open Admissions Programs at City College of New York.

1969   *Leaflets* published.

1970   Death of Alfred Conrad.

1971   *The Will to Change* published. Shelley Memorial Award of the Poetry Society of America. Increasingly identifies with the women's movement as a radical feminist.

1972–73   Fanny Hurst Visiting Professor of Creative Literature at Brandeis University.

1973   *Diving into the Wreck* published.

1973–74   Ingram Merrill Foundation research grant; began work on a book on the history and myths of motherhood.

1974   National Book Award for *Diving into the Wreck*. Rich rejected the award as an individual, but accepted it, in a statement written with Audre Lorde and Alice Walker, two other nominees, in the name of all women:

> We . . . together accept this award in the name of all the women whose voices have gone and still go unheard in a patriarchal world, and in the name of those who, like us, have been tolerated as token women in this

culture, often at great cost and in great pain. . . . We symbolically join here in refusing the terms of patriarchal competition and declaring that we will share this prize among us, to be used as best we can for women. . . . We dedicate this occasion to the struggle for self-determination of all women, of every color, identification or derived class . . . the women who will not understand yet; the silent women whose voices have been denied us, the articulate women who have given us strength to do our work.

Professor of English, City College of New York.

1975 *Poems: Selected and New* published.

1976 Professor of English at Douglass College. *Of Woman Born: Motherhood as Experience and Institution* published. *Twenty-one Love Poems* published.

1978 *The Dream of a Common Language: Poems 1974–1977* published.

1979 *On Lies, Secrets, and Silence: Selected Prose 1966–1978* published. Leaves Douglass College and New York City; moves to Montague, Massachusetts; edits, with Michelle Cliff, the lesbian-feminist journal, *Sinister Wisdom*.

1981 *A Wild Patience Has Taken Me This Far: Poems 1978–1981* published.

1984 *The Fact of a Doorframe: Poems Selected and New 1950–1984* published. Moves to Santa Cruz, California.

1986 *Blood, Bread, and Poetry: Selected Prose 1979–1985* published. Professor of English at Stanford University.

1989 *Time's Power: Poems 1985–1988* published.

1990 Member of the Department of Literature of the American Academy and Institute of Arts and Letters.

1991 *An Atlas of the Difficult World* published.

1992 Wins *Los Angeles Times* Book Prize for *An Atlas of the Difficult World*, the Lenore Marshall/*Nation* Prize for Poetry, and Nicholas Roerich Museum Poet's Prize; is co-winner of the Frost Silver Medal for distinguished lifetime achievement.

1993 *What Is Found There: Notebooks on Poetry and Politics* published.

1994 Awarded MacArthur fellowship.

▼   ▼   ▼

QUESTION

What significant differences do you notice among the poems by Adrienne Rich that appear throughout this volume? Can you tell quickly an early Rich poem from a later one? What are the differences in subject matter? in style? in situation? in strategies of argument? Try to read all the Rich poems in the book at one sitting, working in poems to be found elsewhere in the text in their appropriate chronological place. Characterize, as fully as you can, the voice of the poems written in the 1950s; in the '60s; '70s; '80s. In what ways does the voice seem to change? What similarities do you see in her work from beginning to end?

WRITING SUGGESTIONS

1. In what sense is "At a Bach Concert" typical of Rich's early poetry? Compare "Storm Warnings" and "Aunt Jennifer's Tigers" in terms of the comments Rich makes about her early work in the passage quoted from *When We Dead Awaken: Writing as Re-Vision* (p. 345). What "typical" features do the poems share? Write a detailed analysis (about 1,500 words) of "At a Bach Concert" showing how it is (or is not) typical of Rich's early work.

2. Carefully considering plot, characterization, and structure, write an essay in which you detail the ways "Diving into the Wreck" is and is not typical of Rich's recent work. (Alternate version: Are there other poems that strike you as more typical of later Rich? If so, choose one and show how it is characteristic of Rich's later ideas and strategies.)

11 LITERARY TRADITION AS CONTEXT

T he more poetry you read, the better a reader of poetry you are likely to be. This is not just because your skills will improve and develop, but also because you will come to know more about the poetic tradition and can thus understand more fully how poets draw upon each other. Poets are conscious of other poets, and often they refer to each other's work or use it as a starting point for their own, in ways that may not be immediately obvious to an outsider. Poetry can be treated as a form of argument: poets agree or disagree over basic matters. Sometimes a quiet (or even noisy) competitiveness is at the bottom of their concern with what other poems have done or can do; at other times, playfulness and a sense of humor about poetic possibilities take over, and the competitiveness dwindles to fun and poetic games. And often poets want to tap the rich mine of artistic expression in order to share in the bounty of our heritage. In any case, a poet's consciousness of what others have done leads to a sense of tradition that is often hard to articulate but nevertheless is very important to the effects of poetry—and this sense of tradition is something of a problem for a relatively new reader of poetry. How can I possibly read this poem intelligently, we are likely to ask sometimes in exasperation, until I've read all the other poems ever written? It's a real problem. Poets don't actually expect that all of their readers have Ph.D.'s in literature, but sometimes it *seems* as if they do. For some poets—Milton, T. S. Eliot, and Richard Wilbur are examples—it does help if one has read practically everything imaginable.

Why are poets so dependent on each other? What is the point of their relentless consciousness of what has already been done by others? Why do they repeatedly answer, allude to, and echo other poems? Why is a sense of tradition so important to them?

A sense of common task, a kind of communality of purpose, accounts for some traditional poetic practice, and the competitive desire of individual poets to achieve a place in the English and American poetic tradition accounts for more. Many poets are anxious to be counted among those who achieve, through their writing, a place in history; and a way of establishing that place is to define for oneself the relationship between one's own work and that of others whose place is already secure. There is, for many poets, a sense of a serious and abiding cultural tradition that they wish to share and pass on; but also important is a shared sense of playfulness, a kind of poetic gamesmanship. Making words dance on the page or in our heads provides in itself a satisfaction and delight for many writers—pride in craft that is like the pride of a painter or potter or tennis player. Often poets set themselves a particular task to see what they can do. One way of doing that is to introduce a standard traditional **motif** (a recurrent device, formula, or situation that deliberately connects a poem with common patterns of existing thought), and then to play variations on it much as a musician might do. Another way is to provide an alternative answer to a question that has repeatedly been asked and answered in a traditional way. Poetic playfulness by no means excludes serious intention—the poems in this chapter often make important statements about their subject, however humorous they may be in their method. Some teasing of the tradition and of other poets is pure fun, a kind of kidding among good friends; some is rather more harsh and represents an attempt to see the world very differently—to define and articulate a very different set of attitudes and values.

The English poetic tradition is a rich and varied heritage, and individual poets draw upon it in countless ways. You have probably noticed, in the poems you have read so far, a number of allusions, glances at the tradition or at individual expressions of it. The more poems you read, the more you will notice and the more you will yourself become a comfortable member of the audience poets write for. Poets do expect a lot from readers—not always but often enough to make a new reader feel nervous and sometimes inadequate. The other side of that discomfort comes when you begin to notice things that other readers don't. The groups of poems in this chapter illustrate some of the ways that the tradition energizes individual poets and suggest some of the things poets like to do with their heritage.

Echo and Allusion

The poems in this group illustrate the familiar poetic strategy of echoing or alluding to other texts as a way of importing meaning into a particular poem, similar to the strategy of "sampling" words in rap music. An **echo** may simply recall a word, phrase, or sound in another text as a way of associating what is going on in *this* poem with something in another, familiar text. The familiarity itself may sometimes be the point: writers often like to associate what they do with what has already been thought or expressed, especially if they can sound like a text that is already much admired. Echoes of Shakespeare (or other much admired writers) often have the function of implying that this new text shares concerns (and therefore insight or quality?) with something that has gone before. An **allusion** more insistently connects a particular word, phrase, or section of a poem with some similar formulation in a previous text; it *invokes* a previous text as a kind of gloss on this one; that is, it asks the reader to interpret this text in the light of some previous one, depending explicitly on the reader's recognition of the previous text and asking for interpretation based on the implied similarity.

Strategies of echo and allusion can be very complicated, for the question of just how much of one text can carry over—or be forcibly brought over—into another one cannot be answered categorically.

Often poets quote—or echo with variations—a passage from another text in order to suggest some thematic, ideological, tonal, or other link. Sometimes the purpose is simply to invoke an idea or attitude from another text, another place, or another culture. Thus, in Adrienne Rich's "Two Songs" (p. 148) Chaucer's familiar formulation of the rites of spring (with its description of all things coming to life, their vital juices flowing, as they follow the natural progress of the seasons) is introduced into the text to suggest the way the sap rises and bodies merge in ordinary lusty human beings. The speaker's attraction to a lover is thus put into a larger human perspective, and her sense of herself as a subject and object of lust comes to seem ordinary, part of the natural course of events.

The second poem in *Echo and Allusion* belongs, uncomfortably, in the *carpe diem* ("seize the day") tradition; but unlike ordinary *carpe diem* poems it is moralistic. It undercuts the speaker by having him allude to familiar biblical passages that imply a condemnation of live-for-today attitudes and ideas. By echoing Satan's tempting addresses to Eve in Genesis, the speaker in "Come, My Celia" condemns himself in the eyes of readers and becomes a seducer-tempter instead of a libertine-hero. The other poems here variously recall individual lines, passages, poems, ideas, or traditions in order to establish a particular stance or develop a position or attitude. The meaning of each poem derives primarily from a sorting through of the allusion.

Poems do not necessarily need earlier texts to exist or have meaning, but prior texts may set up what happens in a particular poem or govern how it is to be construed. Allusion is the strategy of using one text to comment on—and influence the interpretation of—another. It is one of the most popular, familiar, and frequent strategies that poets use.

ANDREW MARVELL

To His Coy Mistress

Had we but world enough, and time,
This coyness,[1] lady, were no crime.
We would sit down, and think which way
To walk, and pass our long love's day.
Thou by the Indian Ganges' side   5
Shouldst rubies[2] find: I by the tide
Of Humber[3] would complain. I would
Love you ten years before the Flood,
And you should if you please refuse
Till the conversion of the Jews.[4]   10
My vegetable love[5] should grow
Vaster than empires, and more slow;
An hundred years should go to praise
Thine eyes, and on thy forehead gaze;
Two hundred to adore each breast,   15
But thirty thousand to the rest.
An age at least to every part,
And the last age should show your heart.
For, lady, you deserve this state;[6]
Nor would I love at lower rate.   20
    But at my back I always hear
Time's wingéd chariot hurrying near;
And yonder all before us lie
Deserts of vast eternity.
Thy beauty shall no more be found,   25
Nor, in thy marble vault, shall sound
My echoing song; then worms shall try
That long preserved virginity,
And your quaint honor turn to dust,
And into ashes all my lust: 30
The grave's a fine and private place,
But none, I think, do there embrace.
    Now therefore, while the youthful hue
Sits on thy skin like morning dew,[7]
And while thy willing soul transpires[8]   35
At every pore with instant fires,

1. Hesitancy, modesty (not necessarily suggesting calculation).   2. Talismans that are supposed to preserve virginity.   3. A small river that flows through Marvell's home town of Hull. *Complain:* write love complaints, conventional songs lamenting the cruelty of love.   4. Which, according to popular Christian belief, will occur just before the end of the world.   5. Which is capable only of passive growth, not of consciousness. The "vegetable soul" is lower than the other two divisions of the soul, "animal" and "rational."   6. Dignity.   7. The text reads "glew." "Lew" (warmth) has also been suggested as an emendation.   8. Breathes forth.

Now let us sport us while we may,
And now, like am'rous birds of prey,
Rather at once our time devour
40 Than languish in his slow-chapped[9] pow'r.
Let us roll all our strength and all
Our sweetness up into one ball,
And tear our pleasures with rough strife
Thorough[1] the iron gates of life.
45 Thus, though we cannot make our sun
Stand still,[2] yet we will make him run.[3]   1681

BEN JONSON

Come, My Celia[4]

Come, my Celia, let us prove,[5]
While we can, the sports of love;
Time will not be ours forever:
He at length our good will sever.
5 Spend not, then, his gifts in vain;
Suns that set may rise again,
But if once we lose this light,
'Tis with us perpetual night.
Why should we defer our joys?
10 Fame and rumor are but toys.
Cannot we delude the eyes
Of a few poor household spies?
Or his easier ears beguile,
Thus removéd by our wile?
15 'Tis no sin love's fruits to steal,
But the sweet thefts to reveal;
To be taken, to be seen,
These have crimes accounted been.   1606

9. Slow-jawed. Chronos (Time), ruler of the world in early Greek myth, devoured all of his children except Zeus, who was hidden. Later, Zeus seized power (see line 46 and note).   1. Through.
2. To lengthen his night of love with Alcmene, Zeus made the sun stand still.   3. Each sex act was believed to shorten life by one day.   4. A song from *Volpone*, sung by the play's villain and would-be seducer. Part of the poem paraphrases *Catullus*, V.   5. Try.

DANNIE ABSE

Brueghel in Naples

> About suffering they were never wrong,
> The Old Masters . . .
>   —W. H. AUDEN

Ovid would never have guessed how far
and father's notion about wax melting, bah!
It's ice up there. Freezing.
Soaring and swooping over solitary altitudes
I was breezing along (a record I should think)   5
when my wings began to moult not melt.
These days, workmanship, I ask you.
Appalling.

There's a mountain down there on fire
and I'm falling, falling away from it.   10
Phew, the sun's on the horizon
or am I upside down?

Great Bacchus, the sea is rearing
up. Will I drown? My white legs
the last to disappear? (I have no trousers on)   15
A little to the left the ploughman,
a little to the right a galleon,
a sailor climbing the rigging,
a fisherman casting his line,
and now I hear a shepherd's dog barking.   20
I'm that near.

Lest I have no trace
but a few scattered feathers on the water
show me your face, sailor,
look up, fisherman,   25
look this way, shepherd,
turn around, ploughman.
Raise the alarm! Launch a boat!

My luck. I'm seen
only by a jackass of an artist   30
interested in composition, in the green
tinge of the sea, in the aesthetics
of disaster—not in me.

I drown, bubble by bubble,
(Help, Save me!)   35
while he stands ruthlessly

before the canvas, busy busy,
intent on becoming an Old Master.   1991

MARIANNE MOORE

Love in America?

Whatever it is, it's a passion—
a benign dementia that should be
engulfing America, fed in a way
   the opposite of the way
5   in which the Minotaur[6] was fed.
It's a Midas[7] of tenderness;
   from the heart;
nothing else. From one with ability
to bear being misunderstood—
10   take the blame, with "nobility
   that is action,"[8] identifying itself with
pioneer unperfunctoriness

without brazenness[9] or
bigness of overgrown
15   undergrown shallowness.

Whatever it is, let it be without
affectation.

Yés, yes, yes, *yes*.   1967

HOWARD NEMEROV

Boom!

SEES BOOM IN RELIGION, TOO

Atlantic City, June 23, 1957 (AP).—President Eisenhower's pastor
said tonight that Americans are living in a period of "unprece-
dented religious activity" caused partially by paid vacations, the
eight-hour day and modern conveniences.
    "These fruits of material progress," said the Rev. Edward L. R.

---

6. "The Minotaur demanded a virgin to devour once a year." (Moore's note)   7. "Midas, who
had the golden touch, was inconvenienced when eating or picking things up." (Moore's no-
te)   8. "Unamuno said that what we need as a cure for unruly youth is 'nobility that is action.' "
(Moore's note)   9. "*without brazenness or bigness* . . . Winston Churchill: 'Modesty becomes a
man.' " (Moore's note)

Elson of the National Presbyterian Church, Washington, "have
provided the leisure, the energy, and the means for a level of
human and spiritual values never before reached."

Here at the Vespasian-Carlton,[1] it's just one
religious activity after another; the sky
is constantly being crossed by cruciform
airplanes, in which nobody disbelieves
for a second and the tide, the tide   5
of spiritual progress and prosperity
miraculously keeps rising, to a level
never before attained. The churches are full,
the beaches are full, and the filling-stations
are full, God's great ocean is full   10
of paid vacationers praying an eight-hour day
to the human and spiritual values, the fruits,
the leisure, the energy, and the means, Lord,
the means for the level, the unprecedented level,
and the modern conveniences, which also are full.   15
Never before, O Lord, have the prayers and praises
from belfry and phonebooth, from ballpark and barbecue
the sacrifices, so endlessly ascended.

It was not thus when Job in Palestine
sat in the dust and cried, cried bitterly;[2]   20
when Damien kissed the lepers on their wounds
it was not thus;[3] it was not thus
when Francis worked a fourteen-hour day
strictly for the birds;[4] when Dante took
a week's vacation without pay and it rained   25
part of the time,[5] O Lord, it was not thus.

But now the gears mesh and the tires burn
and the ice chatters in the shaker and the priest
in the pulpit and Thy Name, O Lord,
is kept before the public, while the fruits   30
ripen and religion booms and the level rises
and every modern convenience runneth over,
that it may never be with us as it hath been

---

1. Vespasian was emperor of Rome 70–79, shortly after the reign of Nero. In French, *vespasienne*
means public toilet.   2. According to the Book of Job, he was afflicted with the loss of prosperity,
children, and health as a test of his faith. His name means, in Hebrew, "he cries"; see especially
Job 2:7–13.   3. "Father Damien" (Joseph Damien de Veuster, 1840–1889), a Roman Catholic
missionary from Belgium, was known for his work among lepers in Hawaii; he ultimately contracted
leprosy himself and died there.   4. St. Francis of Assisi, 13th-century founder of the Franciscan
order, was noted for his love of all living things, and one of the most famous stories about him tells
of his preaching to the birds. *Strictly for the birds*: a mid-20th-century expression for worthless or
unfashionable activity.   5. Dante's journey through Hell, Purgatory, and Paradise (in *The Divine
Comedy*) takes a week, beginning on Good Friday, 1300. It rains in the third chasm of Hell.

with Athens and Karnak and Nagasaki,[6]
35 nor Thy sun for one instant refrain from shining
on the rainbow Buick by the breezeway
or the Chris Craft with the uplift life raft;
that we may continue to be the just folks we are,
plain people with ordinary superliners and
40 disposable diaperliners, people of the stop'n'shop
'n'pray as you go, of hotel, motel, boatel,
the humble pilgrims of no deposit no return
and please adjust thy clothing, who will give to Thee,
if Thee will keep us going, our annual
45 Miss Universe, for Thy Name's Sake, Amen.   1960

6. Athens, the cultural center of ancient Greek civilization; Karnak, a village on the Nile, built on
the site of ancient Thebes; Nagasaki, a large Japanese port city, virtually destroyed by a U.S. atomic
bomb in 1945.

ROBERT HOLLANDER

You Too? Me Too—Why Not?
Soda Pop

I am
look
ing at
the Co
caCola
bottle
which is
green wi
th ridges
just–like

c   c   c
o   o   o
l   l   l
u   u   u
m   m   m
n   n   n
s   s   s

and on itself it says

COCA-COLA
reg.u.s.pat.off.

exactly like an art pop
statue of that kind of
bottle but not so green
that the juice inside
gives other than the co-
lor it has when I pour
it out in a clear glass
glass on this table top
(It's making me thirsty
all this winking and
beading of Hippocrene
please let me pause
drinking the fluid in)
ah! it is enticing how each
color is the same
brown in green bottle
brown in uplifted glass
making each utensil on
the table laid a brown
fork in a brown shade
making me long to watch
them harvesting the crop
which makes the deep-aged
rich brown wine of America
that is to say which makes
soda   pop

p. 1968

WILLIAM BLAKE

The Lamb

Little Lamb, who made thee?
Dost thou know who made thee?
Gave thee life, and bid thee feed
By the stream and o'er the mead;
Gave thee clothing of delight,
Softest clothing woolly bright;
Gave thee such a tender voice,
Making all the vales rejoice?
Little Lamb, who made thee?
Dost thou know who made thee?

Little Lamb, I'll tell thee!
Little Lamb, I'll tell thee:
He is callèd by thy name,
For he calls himself a Lamb,
He is meek and he is mild;
He became a little child.
I a child and thou a lamb,
We are callèd by his name.
Little Lamb, God bless thee!
Little Lamb, God bless thee!   1789

WILLIAM SHAKESPEARE

[Not marble, nor the gilded monuments]

Not marble, nor the gilded monuments
Of princes, shall outlive this powerful rhyme;
But you shall shine more bright in these conténts
Than unswept stone, besmeared with sluttish time.
When wasteful war shall statues overturn,
And broils root out the work of masonry,
Nor Mars his sword nor war's quick fire shall burn
The living record of your memory.
'Gainst death and all-oblivious enmity
Shall you pace forth; your praise shall still find room
Even in the eyes of all posterity
That wear this world out to the ending doom.[7]
So, till the judgment that yourself arise,
You live in this, and dwell in lovers' eyes.   1609

7. Judgment Day.

Poetic "Kinds"

There are all sorts of poems. By now you have experienced poems on a variety of subjects and with all kinds of tones—short poems, long poems, poems that rhyme and poems that don't. And there are, of course, many other sorts of poems that we haven't looked at. Some poems, for example, are thousands of lines long and differ rather substantially from the poems that can be included in a book like this.

Poems may be classified in a variety of ways, by subject, topic, or theme; by their length, appearance, and formal features; by the way they are organized; by the level of language they use; by the poet's intention and what kinds of effects the poem tries to generate.

Classification may be, of course, simply an intellectual exercise. Recognizing a poem that is, for example, an elegy (like *Lycidas* [p. 510]), a parody, or a satire, may be very much like the satisfaction involved in recognizing a scarlet tanager, a weeping willow, a French phrase, or a 1967 Ford Thunderbird. Just *knowing* what others don't know gives us a sense of importance, accomplishment, and power. But there are also *uses* for classification: we can experience a poem more fully if we understand early on exactly what kind of poem we are dealing with. A fuller response is possible because the poet has consciously chosen to play by certain defined rules, and the **conventions** he or she employs indicate certain standard ways of saying things to achieve certain expected effects. The **tradition** that is involved in a particular poetic kind is thus employed by the poet in order to produce predictable standard responses.

A poem that calls itself an "elegy," for example, gives us fair warning of what to expect: its label tells that it will be a serious poem memorializing the death of someone, and we may reasonably expect that its tone will be sad or angry about the death, reflective about the meaning and direction of the dead person's life, and perhaps ruminative about the implications of the death itself. For example, much of the humor and fun in the following poem is premised on the assumption that readers will recognize the kind of poem they are reading.

CHRISTOPHER MARLOWE

The Passionate Shepherd to His Love

Come live with me and be my love,
And we will all the pleasures prove[1]
That valleys, groves, hills, and fields,
Woods, or steepy mountain yields.

5   And we will sit upon the rocks,
Seeing the shepherds feed their flocks,
By shallow rivers to whose falls
Melodious birds sing madrigals.

And I will make thee beds of roses
10 And a thousand fragrant posies,
A cap of flowers, and a kirtle[2]
Embroidered all with leaves of myrtle;

A gown made of the finest wool
Which from our pretty lambs we pull;
15 Fair lined slippers for the cold,
With buckles of the purest gold;

A belt of straw and ivy buds,
With coral clasps and amber studs:
And if these pleasures may thee move,
20 Come live with me, and be my love.

The shepherd swains[3] shall dance and sing
For thy delight each May morning:
If these delights thy mind may move,
Then live with me and be my love.   1600

A beginning reader of poetry might easily protest that a plea such as this one is unrealistic and fanciful and thus feel unsure of the poem's tone. What could such a reader think of a speaker who constructs his argument in such a dreamlike way? But the traditions behind the poem and the conventions of the poetic kind make its intention and effects quite clear. "The Passionate Shepherd" is a pastoral poem, a poetic kind that concerns itself with the simple life of country folk and describes that life in stylized, idealized terms. The people in a pastoral poem are usually (as here) shepherds, although they may be fishermen or other rustics who lead an outdoor life and are involved in tending to basic human needs in a simplified society; the world of the poem is one of sim-

1. Try.   2. Gown.   3. Youths.

plicity, beauty, music, and love. The world always seems timeless in pastoral; people are eternally young, and the season is always spring, usually May. Nature seems endlessly green and the future entirely golden. Difficulty, frustration, disappointment, and obligation do not belong in this world at all; it is blissfully free of problems. Shepherds sing instead of tending sheep, and they make love and play music instead of having to watch out for wolves in the night. If only the shepherd boy and shepherd girl can agree with each other to make love joyously and passionately, they will live happily ever after. The language of pastoral is informal and fairly simple, although always a bit more sophisticated than that of real shepherds with real problems and real sheep.

Unrealistic? Of course. No real shepherd gets to spend even a single whole day like that, and certainly the world of simple country folk includes ferocities of nature, human falsehood and knavery, disease, bad weather, old age, moments that are not all green and gold. And probably no poet ever thought that shepherds really live that way, but it is an attractive fantasy, and poets who write pastoral simply choose one formulaic way to isolate a series of idealized moments. Fantasies can be personal and private, of course, but there is also a certain pleasure in shared public fantasies, and one central moment is that moment in a love relationship when two people are contemplating the joys of ecstatic love. The vision here is self-consciously constructed by poets in order to present a certain tone, attitude, and wholeness; it is a world that is self-existent, self-contained, and self-referential.

Pastoral poems are not written by shepherds. No doubt shepherds have fantasies too, but theirs probably involve ways of life far removed from sheepfolds and nights outdoors. Pastoral poems are usually written, as here, by city poets who are consciously indulging their "isn't it pretty to think so" thoughts. Pastoral poems involve an urban fantasy of rural bliss. It can be lovely to contemplate a world in which the birds sing only for our delight and other shepherds take care of the sheep, a world in which there is no work that does not turn into magic and in which the lambs bring themselves to us so that we can transform their wool instantly into a beautiful gown. It is also fun to "answer" such a vision. The next subsection of this chapter contains three poems that directly "answer" Marlowe's poem and thus offer a kind of critique of the pastoral vision. But in a sense none is necessary; the pastoral poet builds an awareness of artificiality into the whole idea of the poem. It is conceived in full consciousness that its fantasy avoids implication, and in filtering that implication carefully out of the poem, poets implicitly provide their own criticism of the fantasy world. Satire is, in a sense, the other side of the pastoral world—a city poet who fantasizes about being a shepherd usually knows all about dirt and grime and human failure and urban corruption—and satire and pastoral are often seen as complementary poetic kinds.

Several other poetic kinds are exemplified in this book; and each has its own characteristics and conventions that have become established by tradition, repetition, and habit.

epic	from *Paradise Lost*	p. 137
pastoral	"The Passionate Shepherd to His Love"	p. 364
elegy	*Lycidas*	p. 510
lyric	"The Lamb"	p. 362
ballad	"Sir Patrick Spens"	p. 218
protest poem	"Hard Rock Returns . . ."	p. 331
aubade	"The Sun Rising"	p. 291
confessional poem	"Skunk Hour"	p. 504
meditation	"Love Calls Us . . ."	p. 444
dramatic monologue	"My Last Duchess"	p. 101
soliloquy	"Soliloquy of the Spanish Cloister"	p. 61

You will find definitions and brief descriptions of these poetic kinds in the glossary. Each of these established kinds is worthy of detailed discussion and study, and your teacher may want to examine in depth how the conventions of several different kinds work. Here, we have chosen to examine in depth one particular poetic kind, the **epigram,** by including quite a few poems that typify it.

The poems that follow are all epigrams, and together they add up almost to a definition of that poetic kind. Like most poetic kinds, the epigram has a history that shaped its form and content. Originally, an epigram was an inscription upon some object such as a monument, triumphal arch, tombstone, or gate; hence brevity and conciseness were absolutely necessary. But over a period of time, the term "epigram" came to mean a short poem that tried to attract concentrated attention in the same way that an inscription attracts the eyes of passersby.

As the poems here suggest, epigrams have been popular over a long period of time. The modern tradition of epigrams has two more or less separate ancient sources, one in Greece, one in Rome. In classical Greece, epigrams were composed over a period of two thousand years; the earliest surviving ones date from the eighth century B.C. Apparently there were several anthologies of epigrams in early times, and fragments of these anthologies were later preserved, especially in large collections like the so-called *Greek Anthology,* which dates from the tenth century A.D. Largely short inscriptions, these epigrams also included some love poems (including many on homosexual love), comments on life and morality, riddles, etc. The father of the Roman tradition is generally agreed to be Martial (Marcus Valerius Martialis, A.D. 40?–104?), whose epigrams are witty and satirical. Modern epigrams have more frequently followed Martial's lead, but occasionally the distinctive influence of the older Greek tradition can be seen in the sadder poignancy of such poems as "Parting in Wartime."

Knowing what to do with a poem often is aided by knowing what it is, or what it means to be. Many modern poems are not consciously conceived in terms of a traditional kind, and not all older poems are either, but a knowledge of kind can often provide one more way of deciding what to look for in a poem, helping one to find the right questions to ask.

▼ ▼ ▼

SAMUEL TAYLOR COLERIDGE

What Is an Epigram?

What is an epigram? a dwarfish whole,
Its body brevity, and wit its soul.   p. 1802

BEN JONSON

Epitaph on Elizabeth, L. H.

Wouldst thou hear what man can say
In a little? Reader, stay.
Underneath this stone doth lie
As much beauty as could die;
Which in life did harbor give   5
To more virtue than doth live.
If at all she had a fault,
Leave it buried in this vault.
One name was Elizabeth;
Th' other, let it sleep with death: 10
Fitter, where it died, to tell,
Than that it lived at all. Farewell.   1616

MARTIAL

[You've told me, Maro, whilst you live][4]

You've told me, Maro, whilst you live
You'd not a single penny give,
But that whene'er you chanced to die,
You'd leave a handsome legacy;
You must be mad beyond redress,
If my next wish you cannot guess.

5

ca. 100

MARTIAL

[Fair, rich, and young? How rare is her perfection][5]

Fair, rich, and young? How rare is her perfection,
Were it not mingled with one foul infection?
I mean, so proud a heart, so cursed a tongue,
As makes her seem, nor fair, nor rich, nor young.

ca. 80–85

JOHN GAY

My Own Epitaph

Life is a jest; and all things show it.
I thought so once; but now I know it.

1720

RICHARD CRASHAW

An Epitaph upon a Young Married Couple, Dead and Buried Together

To these, whom death again did wed,
This grave's their second marriage-bed.
For though the hand of fate could force
'Twixt soul and body a divorce,
It could not sunder man and wife
'Cause they both livéd but one life.

5

---

4. Translated from the Latin by F. Lewis.   5. Translated from the Latin by Sir John Harington.

Peace, good reader. Do not weep.
Peace, the lovers are asleep.
They, sweet turtles,[6] folded lie
In the last knot love could tie.   10
And though they lie as they were dead,
Their pillow stone, their sheets of lead,
(Pillow hard, and sheets not warm)
Love made the bed; they'll take no harm;
Let them sleep, let them sleep on.   15
Till this stormy night be gone,
Till th' eternal morrow dawn;
Then the curtains will be drawn
And they wake into a light,
Whose day shall never die in night.   1646   20

X. J. KENNEDY

Epitaph for a Postal Clerk

Here lies wrapped up tight in sod
Henry Harkins c/o God.
On the day of Resurrection
May be opened for inspection.   1961

COUNTEE CULLEN

For a Lady I Know

She even thinks that up in heaven
Her class lies late and snores,
While poor black cherubs rise at seven
To do celestial chores.   1925

J. V. CUNNINGHAM

History of Ideas

God is love. Then by inversion
Love is God, and sex conversion.   1947

6. Turtledoves.

WENDY COPE

Another Christmas Poem

Bloody Christmas, here again.
Let us raise a loving cup:
Peace on earth, goodwill to men,
And make them do the washing-up.   1986

WALTER SAVAGE LANDOR

The Georges[7]

George the First was always reckoned
Vile, but viler George the Second;
And what mortal ever heard
Any good of George the Third?
5   When from earth the Fourth descended
(God be praised!) the Georges ended.   p. 1855

PETER PINDAR

Epigram

Midas, they say, possessed the art of old
Of turning whatsoe'er he touched to gold;
This modern statesmen can reverse with ease—
ca. 1780   Touch *them* with gold, *they'll turn to what you please.*

HOWARD NEMEROV

Epigram: Political Reflexion

loquitur the sparrow in the zoo[8]

No bars are set too close, no mesh too fine
To keep me from the eagle and the lion,
Whom keepers feed that I may freely dine.
This goes to show that if you have the wit
5   To be small, common, cute, and live on shit,
Though the cage fret kings, you may make free with it.   1958

7. British kings who ruled successively from 1714 to 1830.   8. I.e., the sparrow is the speaker.

EDNA ST. VINCENT MILLAY

First Fig

My candle burns at both ends;
   It will not last the night;
But ah, my foes, and oh, my friends —
   It gives a lovely light!   1920

Second Fig

Safe upon the solid rock the ugly houses stand:
Come and see my shining palace built upon the sand!   1920

FRANCES CORNFORD

Parting in Wartime

How long ago Hector[9] took off his plume,
Not wanting that his little son should cry,
Then kissed his sad Andromache good-bye —
And now we three in Euston[1] waiting-room.   1948

Imitating and Answering

Poems often respond directly — sometimes point by point or even line by line or word by word — to another poem. Often the point is teasing or comic, but often too there is a real issue behind the idea of such a facetious answer, a serious criticism perhaps of the poem's point or the tradition it represents, or sometimes an attempt to provide a different way of looking at the issue. Sometimes poems follow their models rather slavishly in order to emphasize their likeness; sometimes key words or details are substituted so that readers will easily notice the differences in tone or attitude.

Often these poems seem rather self-conscious — as if the poets who write

9. The noblest chieftain in ancient Troy and husband to Andromache.   1. A London railway station.

them are aware of the tradition they share and are each trying to do something a little bit different. However "sincere" these poems may be, their sense of play is equally important. The first three poems playfully pick on Christopher Marlowe's "The Passionate Shepherd to His Love" (p. 364). In effect, all of them provide "answers" to that poem. It is as if "his love" were telling the shepherd what is the matter with his argument, and the poets are answering Marlowe, too. These poets know full well what Marlowe was doing in the fantasy of his original poem, and they clearly have a lot of fun telling him how people in various circumstances might feel about his fantasy. There is in the end a lot of joy in their "realistic" deflation of his magic, and not much hostility. The poems by Koch, Skirrow, Hecht, and Cope poke gentle fun at other famous works, offering a summary or another version of what might have happened in each (see, respectively, "This Is Just to Say" [p. 546], "Ode on a Grecian Urn" [p. 299], "Dover Beach" [p. 99], and "Not marble, nor the gilded monuments" [p. 362]).

A **parody** is a poem that imitates another poem closely but changes details for a comic or critical effect. Strictly speaking, only two of the poems that follow (those by Koch and Cope) are parodies—that is, they pretend to write in the style of the original poem but comically exaggerate that style and change the content. The others make fun of an original in less direct phraseological ways, but they share a similar objective of answering an original, even though they use very different styles to alter, totally, the poetic intention of that original. "Ode on a Grecian Urn Summarized" teases Keats as well as the whole notion of poetic summaries; the effects of the summary are not very much like those of the Keats poem. "The Dover Bitch," on the other hand, is as its subtitle suggests much more than just a different perspective on the situation presented in "Dover Beach"; it uses the tradition to criticize art and life.

All these poems offer a revised version of what reality may be like (as does one of the poems in the next subsection, "Penelope," by telling a familiar literary story from a different—in this case the woman's—point of view). Poems like these may have a serious purpose, but their method is comic and usually light. And fun is not always easy to explain intellectually or to demonstrate.

SIR WALTER RALEGH

The Nymph's Reply to the Shepherd

If all the world and love were young,
And truth in every shepherd's tongue,

These pretty pleasures might me move
To live with thee and be thy love.

Time drives the flocks from field to fold,   5
When rivers rage, and rocks grow cold,
And Philomel[1] becometh dumb;
The rest complain of cares to come.

The flowers do fade, and wanton fields
To wayward winter reckoning yields: 10
A honey tongue, a heart of gall,
Is fancy's spring, but sorrow's fall.

Thy gowns, thy shoes, thy beds of roses,
Thy cap, thy kirtle, and thy posies
Soon break, soon wither, soon forgotten;   15
In folly ripe, in reason rotten.

Thy belt of straw and ivy buds,
Thy coral clasps and amber studs,
All these in me no means can move
To come to thee and be thy love.   20

But could youth last, and love still breed,
Had joys no date,[2] nor age no need,
Then these delights my mind might move
To live with thee and be thy love.   1600

WILLIAM CARLOS WILLIAMS

Raleigh Was Right

We cannot go to the country
for the country will bring us no peace
What can the small violets tell us
that grow on furry stems in
the long grass among lance shaped leaves?   5

Though you praise us
and call to mind the poets
who sung of our loveliness
it was long ago!
long ago! when country people   10
would plow and sow with
flowering minds and pockets at ease—
if ever this were true.

1. The nightingale.   2. End.

Not now. Love itself a flower
15   with roots in a parched ground.
Empty pockets make empty heads.
Cure it if you can but
do not believe that we can live
today in the country
20   for the country will bring us no peace.   1941

E. E. CUMMINGS

[(ponder,darling,these busted statues]

(ponder,darling,these busted statues
of yon motheaten forum be aware
notice what hath remained
—the stone cringes
5   clinging to the stone,how obsolete

lips utter their extant smile. . . .
remark .

a few deleted of texture
or meaning monuments and dolls

10   resist Them Greediest Paws of careful
time all of which is extremely
unimportant)whereas Life

matters if or

when the your- and my-
15   idle vertical worthless
self unite in a peculiarly
momentary

partnership(to instigate
constructive
20   Horizontal
business. . . . even so,let us make
haste
—consider well this ruined aqueduct

lady,
which used to lead something into somewhere)   1926

PETER DE VRIES

To His Importunate Mistress

ANDREW MARVELL UPDATED

Had we but world enough, and time,
My coyness, lady, were a crime,
But at my back I always hear
Time's wingèd chariot, striking fear
The hour is nigh when creditors   5
Will prove to be my predators.
As wages of our picaresque,
Bag lunches bolted at my desk
Must stand as fealty to you
For each expensive rendezvous.   10
Obeisance at your marble feet
Deserves the best-appointed suite,
And would have, lacked I not the pelf
To pleasure also thus myself;
But aptly sumptuous amorous scenes   15
Rule out the rake of modest means.

Since mistress presupposes wife,
It means a doubly costly life;
For fools by second passion fired
A second income is required,   20
The earning which consumes the hours
They'd hoped to spend in rented bowers.
To hostelries the worst of fates
That weekly raise their daily rates!
I gather, lady, from your scoffing   25
A bloke more solvent in the offing.
So revels thus to rivals go
For want of monetary flow.
How vexing that inconstant cash
The constant suitor must abash,   30
Who with excuses vainly pled
Must rue the undishevelled bed,
And that for paltry reasons given
His conscience may remain unriven.   p. 1986

C. DAY LEWIS

Song

Come, live with me and be my love,
And we will all the pleasures prove
Of peace and plenty, bed and board,
That chance employment may afford.

I'll handle dainties on the docks
And thou shalt read of summer frocks:
At evening by the sour canals
We'll hope to hear some madrigals.

Care on thy maiden brow shall put
A wreath of wrinkles, and thy foot
Be shod with pain: not silken dress
But toil shall tire thy loveliness.

Hunger shall make thy modest zone
And cheat fond death of all but bone—
If these delights thy mind may move,
Then live with me and be my love.

1935

KENNETH KOCH

Variations on a Theme by William Carlos Williams

1

I chopped down the house that you had been saving to live in next
   summer.
I am sorry, but it was morning, and I had nothing to do
and its wooden beams were so inviting.

2

We laughed at the hollyhocks together
and then I sprayed them with lye.
Forgive me. I simply do not know what I am doing.

3

I gave away the money that you had been saving to live on for the
   next ten years.
The man who asked for it was shabby
and the firm March wind on the porch was so juicy and cold.

4

Last evening we went dancing and I broke your leg.   10
Forgive me. I was clumsy, and
I wanted you here in the wards, where I am the doctor!   1962

DESMOND SKIRROW

Ode on a Grecian Urn Summarized

Gods chase
Round vase.
What say?
What play?
Don't know.   5
Nice, though.   p. 1960

ANTHONY HECHT

The Dover Bitch

A CRITICISM OF LIFE

for Andrews Wanning

So there stood Matthew Arnold and this girl
With the cliffs of England crumbling away behind them,
And he said to her, "Try to be true to me,
And I'll do the same for you, for things are bad
All over, etc., etc."   5
Well now, I knew this girl. It's true she had read
Sophocles in a fairly good translation
And caught that bitter allusion to the sea,[3]
But all the time he was talking she had in mind
The notion of what his whiskers would feel like   10
On the back of her neck. She told me later on
That after a while she got to looking out
At the lights across the channel, and really felt sad,
Thinking of all the wine and enormous beds
And blandishments in French and the perfumes.   15
And then she got really angry. To have been brought
All the way down from London, and then be addressed
As a sort of mournful cosmic last resort

---

3. In Sophocles' *Antigone*, lines 583–91. See "Dover Beach," lines 9–18.

Is really tough on a girl, and she was pretty.
20   Anyway, she watched him pace the room
And finger his watch-chain and seem to sweat a bit,
And then she said one or two unprintable things.
But you mustn't judge her by that. What I mean to say is,
She's really all right. I still see her once in a while
25   And she always treats me right. We have a drink
And I give her a good time, and perhaps it's a year
Before I see her again, but there she is,
Running to fat, but dependable as they come.
And sometimes I bring her a bottle of *Nuit d'Amour.*   1968

WENDY COPE

[Not only marble, but the plastic toys]

Not only marble, but the plastic toys
From cornflake packets will outlive this rhyme:
I can't immortalize you, love—our joys
Will lie unnoticed in the vault of time.
5   When Mrs Thatcher has been cast in bronze
And her administration is a page
In some O-level text-book,[4] when the dons
Have analysed the story of our age,
When travel firms sell tours of outer space
10   And aeroplanes take off without a sound
And Tulse Hill has become a trendy place
And Upper Norwood's on the underground[5]
Your beauty and my name will be forgotten—
My love is true, but all my verse is rotten.   1986

Mythology and Myth

The poems in this group draw on a tradition that is larger than just
"literary." Mythologies involve whole systems of belief, usually cultural in
scope, and the familiar literary formulations of these mythologies are just the
surface articulations of a larger view of why the world works the way it does.

Every culture develops stories to explain itself. These stories, about who we
are and why we are the way we are, constitute what are often called **myths.**

4. A text designed to prepare secondary school students for the first hurdle in entrance exams for
British universities. *Dons:* academics.   5. London subway.

Calling something a myth does not mean that it is false. In fact, it means nearly the opposite, for cultures that subscribe to various myths, or that have ever subscribed to particular myths about culture or history, become infused with and defined by those views. Myth, in the sense in which it is used here, involves explanations of life that are more or less universally shared within a particular culture; it is a frame of reference that people within the culture understand and share. A sharing of this frame of reference does not mean that all people within a culture are carbon copies of each other or that popular stereotypes represent reality accurately, nor does it mean that every individual in the culture *knows* the perceived history and can articulate its events, ideas, and values. But it does mean that a shared history and a shared set of symbols lie behind any particular culture and that the culture is to some extent aware of its distinctiveness from other cultures.

A **culture** may be of many sizes and shapes. Often we think of a nation as a culture (and so speak of American culture, American history, the myth of America, the American dream, the American frame of reference), and it is equally useful to make smaller and larger divisions—as long as there is some commonality of history and some cohesiveness of purpose within the group. One can speak of southern culture, for example, or of urban culture, or of the drug culture, or of the various popular music cultures, or of a culture associated with a particular political belief, economic class, or social group. Most of us belong, willingly or not, to a number of such cultures at one time, and to some extent our identity and destiny are linked with the distinctive features of those cultures and with the ways each culture perceives its identity, values, and history. Some of these cultures we choose to join; some are thrust upon us by birth and circumstances. It is these larger and more persistent forms of culture—not those chosen by an individual—that are illustrated in this chapter.

Poets, aware of their heritage, often like to probe its history and beliefs and plumb its depths, just as they like to articulate and play variations on the poetic tradition they feel a part of. For poetry written in the English language over the last four hundred years or so, both the Judeo-Christian frame of reference and the classical frame of reference (drawing on the civilizations of ancient Greece and Rome) have been quite important. Western culture, a broad culture that includes many nations and many religious and social groups, is largely defined within these two frames of reference—or it has been until quite recently. As religious belief in the west has eroded over the past two or three centuries, and as classical civilization has been less emphasized and less studied, poets have felt increasingly less comfortable in assuming that their audiences share a knowledge of their systems, but they have often continued to use them to isolate and articulate human traits that have cultural continuity and importance. More recently, poets have drawn on other cultural myths—Native American, African, and Asian, for example—to expand our sense of common heritage and give new meaning to the "American" and "Western" experience. The poems that follow draw on details from different myths and do so in a variety of different ways and tones.

JOHN HOLLANDER

Adam's Task

And Adam gave names to all cattle, and to the fowl of the air, and to every beast of the field . . .

—Gen. 2:20

Thou, paw-paw-paw; thou, glurd; thou, spotted
   Glurd; thou, whitestap, lurching through
The high-grown brush; thou, pliant-footed,
   Implex; thou, awagabu.

5   Every burrower, each flier
   Came for the name he had to give:
Gay, first work, ever to be prior,
   Not yet sunk to primitive.

Thou, verdle; thou, McFleery's pomma;
10   Thou; thou; thou—three types of grawl;
Thou, flisket; thou, kabasch; thou, comma-
   Eared mashawk; thou, all; thou, all.

Were, in a fire of becoming,
   Laboring to be burned away,
15   Then work, half-measuring, half-humming,
   Would be as serious as play.

Thou, pambler; thou, rivarn; thou, greater
   Wherret, and thou, lesser one;
Thou, sproal; thou, zant; thou, lily-eater.
20   Naming's over. Day is done.   1971

SUSAN DONNELLY

Eve Names the Animals

To me, *lion* was sun on a wing
over the garden. *Dove,*

a burrowing, blind creature.

I swear that man
never knew animals. Words   5
he lined up according to size,

while elephants slipped flat-eyed
through water

and trout
hurtled from the underbrush, tusked   10
and ready for battle.

The name he gave me stuck
me to him. He did it to comfort me,
for not being first.

Mornings, while he slept,   15
I got away. Pickerel
hopped on the branches above me.
Only spider accompanied me,

nosing everywhere,
running up to lick my hand.   20

Poor finch. I suppose I was
woe to him—
the way he'd come looking for me,
not wanting either of us
to be ever alone   25

But to myself I was
palomino
        raven
            fox . . .

I strung words   30
by their stems and wore them
as garlands on my long walks.

The next day
I'd find them withered.

I liked change.   1985   35

CHRISTINA ROSSETTI

Eve

"While I sit at the door,
Sick to gaze within,

Mine eye weepeth sore
For sorrow and sin:
As a tree my sin stands
To darken all lands;
Death is the fruit it bore.

"How have Eden bowers grown
Without Adam to bend them!
How have Eden flowers blown,
Squandering their sweet breath,
Without me to tend them!
The Tree of Life was ours,
Tree twelvefold-fruited,[1]
Most lofty tree that flowers,
Most deeply rooted:
I chose the Tree of Death.[2]

"Hadst thou but said me nay,
    Adam, my brother,
I might have pined away—
    I, but none other:
God might have let thee stay
Safe in our garden,
By putting me away
Beyond all pardon.

"I, Eve, sad mother
Of all who must live,
I, not another,
Plucked bitterest fruit to give
My friend, husband, lover.
O wanton eyes run over!
Who but I should grieve?—
Cain hath slain his brother:[3]
Of all who must die mother,
Miserable Eve!"

Thus she sat weeping,
Thus Eve our mother,
Where one lay sleeping
Slain by his brother.
Greatest and least
Each piteous beast
To hear her voice
Forgot his joys
And set aside his feast.

1. The tree of life is so described in Revelation 22:2, 14, but the account there is of the New Jerusalem, not of Eden.   2. The Genesis account distinguishes between the tree of life and the tree of the knowledge of good and evil; the latter is forbidden, and eating of it brings labor, sickness, and death into the world. See Genesis 2:9, 3:1–24.   3. Abel (see Genesis 4:1–15).

The mouse paused in his walk   45
And dropped his wheaten stalk:
Grave cattle wagged their heads
In rumination;
The eagle gave a cry
From his cloud station: 50
Larks on thyme beds
Forbore to mount or sing;
Bees dropped upon the wing;
The raven perched on high
Forgot his ration;   55
The conies[4] in their rock,
A feeble nation,
Quaked sympathetical;
The mocking-bird left off to mock;
Huge camels knelt as if   60
In deprecation;
The kind hart's tears were falling;
Chattered the wistful stork;
Dove-voices with a dying fall
Cooed desolation   65
Answering grief by grief.

Only the serpent in the dust,
Wriggling and crawling,
Grinned an evil grin, and thrust
His tongue out with its fork.   70

1865

ROBERT FROST

Never Again Would Birds' Song
Be the Same

He would declare and could himself believe
That the birds there in all the garden round
From having heard the daylong voice of Eve
Had added to their own an oversound,
Her tone of meaning but without the words.   5
Admittedly an eloquence so soft
Could only have had an influence on birds
When call or laughter carried it aloft.
Be that as may be, she was in their song.
Moreover her voice upon their voices crossed   10
Had now persisted in the woods so long

---

4. A common term for rabbits, but here probably the small pachyderms mentioned in Proverbs
30:26.

That probably it never would be lost.
Never again would birds' song be the same.
And to do that to birds was why she came.   1942

ALFRED, LORD TENNYSON

Ulysses[5]

It little profits that an idle king,
By this still hearth, among these barren crags,
Matched with an agéd wife,[6] I mete and dole
Unequal laws unto a savage race,
5   That hoard, and sleep, and feed, and know not me.

I cannot rest from travel; I will drink
Life to the lees.[7] All times I have enjoyed
Greatly, have suffered greatly, both with those
That loved me, and alone; on shore, and when
10   Through scudding drifts the rainy Hyades[8]
Vexed the dim sea. I am become a name;
For always roaming with a hungry heart
Much have I seen and known—cities of men
And manners, climates, councils, governments,
15   Myself not least, but honored of them all—
And drunk delight of battle with my peers,
Far on the ringing plains of windy Troy.
I am a part of all that I have met;
Yet all experience is an arch wherethrough
20   Gleams that untraveled world, whose margin fades
For ever and for ever when I move.
How dull it is to pause, to make an end,
To rust unburnished, not to shine in use!
As though to breathe were life. Life piled on life
25   Were all too little, and of one to me
Little remains; but every hour is saved
From that eternal silence, something more,
A bringer of new things; and vile it were
For some three suns to store and hoard myself,
30   And this gray spirit yearning in desire
To follow knowledge like a sinking star,
Beyond the utmost bound of human thought.

5. After the end of the Trojan War, Ulysses (or Odysseus), king of Ithaca and one of the Greek heroes of the war, returned to his island home (line 34). Homer's account of the situation is in *The Odyssey*, Book XI, but Dante's account of Ulysses in *The Inferno*, XXVI, is the more immediate background of the poem.   6. Penelope.   7. All the way down to the bottom of the cup. 8. A group of stars that were supposed to predict rain when they rose at the same time as the sun.

This is my son, mine own Telemachus,
To whom I leave the scepter and the isle—
Well-loved of me, discerning to fulfill 35
This labor by slow prudence to make mild
A rugged people, and through soft degrees
Subdue them to the useful and the good.
Most blameless is he, centered in the sphere
Of common duties, decent not to fail 40
In offices of tenderness, and pay
Meet adoration to my household gods,
When I am gone. He works his work, I mine.

    There lies the port; the vessel puffs her sail:
There gloom the dark, broad seas. My mariners, 45
Souls that have toiled, and wrought, and thought with me—
That ever with a frolic welcome took
The thunder and the sunshine, and opposed
Free hearts, free foreheads—you and I are old;
Old age hath yet his honor and his toil. 50
Death closes all; but something ere the end,
Some work of noble note, may yet be done,
Not unbecoming men that strove with Gods.
The lights begin to twinkle from the rocks;
The long day wanes; the slow moon climbs; the deep 55
Moans round with many voices. Come, my friends.
'Tis not too late to seek a newer world.
Push off, and sitting well in order smite
The sounding furrows; for my purpose holds
To sail beyond the sunset, and the baths 60
Of all the western stars, until I die.
It may be that the gulfs will wash us down;[9]
It may be we shall touch the Happy Isles,[1]
And see the great Achilles, whom we knew.
Though much is taken, much abides; and though 65
We are not now that strength which in old days
Moved earth and heaven, that which we are, we are:
One equal temper of heroic hearts,
Made weak by time and fate, but strong in will
To strive, to seek, to find, and not to yield. 70

1833

---

9. Beyond the Gulf of Gibraltar was supposed to be a chasm that led to Hades.   1. Elysium, the
Islands of the Blessed, where heroes like Achilles (line 64) abide after death.

JAMES HARRISON

Penelope[2]

for Ken

Oh, I have no illusions as to what
he's been up to all these years—a sea
nymph here, a minor goddess there, and a free
for all with the odd monster to give the plot
5   the necessary epic tone. Not
that I'm saying he goes out of his way to be
led astray. It happens quite naturally,
I'm sure. But it happens.
                  So, since suitors squat
on my doorstep, why so squeamish? In the first
10   place because it's the property they're out
to get, with me as an afterthought perhaps.
Then they're so callow. But mostly, having nursed
forebearance for twenty years, I'm not about
to have him forgiving me my only lapse.   1983

MIRIAM WADDINGTON

Ulysses Embroidered

You've come
at last from
all your journeying
to the old blind woman
5   in the tower,
Ulysses.

After all adventurings
through seas and
mountains through
10   giant battles,
storms and death,
from pinnacles
to valleys;

Past sirens
15   naked on rocks

---

2. "*Penelope*—wife of Ulysses, stuck at home the ten years he spent fighting Troy, and the further ten it took him to find his way back to Ithaca." (Harrison's note)

between Charybdis
and Scylla, from
dragons' teeth,
from sleep in
stables choking 20
on red flowers
walking through weeds
and through shipwreck.

And now you are
climbing the stairs, 25
taking shape,
a figure in shining
thread rising from
a golden shield:
a medallion 30
emblazoned in
tapestry you grew
from the blind hands
of Penelope.

Her tapestry 35
saw everything,
her stitches
embroidered the
painful colors
of her breath the 40
long sighing touch
of her hands.

She made many
journeys. 1992

EDNA ST. VINCENT MILLAY

An Ancient Gesture

I thought, as I wiped my eyes on the corner of my apron:
Penelope did this too.
And more than once: you can't keep weaving all day
And undoing it all through the night;
Your arms get tired, and the back of your neck gets tight 5
And along towards morning, when you think it will never be light,
And your husband has been gone, and you don't know where, for years,
Suddenly you burst into tears;
There is simply nothing else to do.
And I thought, as I wiped my eyes on the corner of my apron: 10

This is an ancient gesture, authentic, antique,
In the very best tradition, classic, Greek;
Ulysses did this too.
But only as a gesture,—a gesture which implied
To the assembled throng that he was much too moved to speak.
He learned it from Penelope . . .
Penelope, who really cried.

1954

LANGSTON HUGHES

The Negro Speaks of Rivers

I've known rivers:
I've known rivers ancient as the world and older than the flow of human blood
  in human veins.

My soul has grown deep like the rivers.

I bathed in the Euphrates when dawns were young.
I built my hut near the Congo and it lulled me to sleep.
I looked upon the Nile and raised the pyramids above it.
I heard the singing of the Mississippi when Abe Lincoln went down to New
  Orleans, and I've seen its muddy bosom turn all golden in the sunset.

I've known rivers:
Ancient, dusky rivers.

My soul has grown deep like the rivers.

1926

JUNE JORDAN

Something Like a Sonnet for Phillis Miracle Wheatley

Girl from the realm of birds florid and fleet
flying full feather in far or near weather
Who fell to a dollar lust coffled like meat
Captured by avarice and hate spit together
Trembling asthmatic alone on the slave block
built by a savagery travelling by carriage
viewed like a species of flaw in the livestock
A child without safety of mother or marriage

Chosen by whimsy but born to surprise
They taught you to read but you learned how to write
Begging the universe into your eyes:

They dressed you in light but you dreamed with the night.
From Africa singing of justice and grace,
Your early verse sweetens the fame of our Race.   1989

MAYA ANGELOU

Africa

Thus she had lain
sugar cane sweet
deserts her hair
golden her feet
mountains her breasts   5
two Niles her tears
Thus she has lain
Black through the years.

Over the white seas
rime white and cold   10
brigands ungentled
icicle bold
took her young daughters
sold her strong sons
churched her with Jesus   15
bled her with guns.
Thus she has lain.

Now she is rising
remember her pain
remember the losses   20
her screams loud and vain
remember her riches
her history slain
now she is striding
although she had lain.   1975   25

DEREK WALCOTT

A Far Cry from Africa

A wind is ruffling the tawny pelt
Of Africa. Kikuyu,[3] quick as flies,

---

3. An East African tribe whose members, as Mau Mau fighters, conducted an eight-year terrorist campaign against British colonial settlers in Kenya.

Batten upon the bloodstreams of the veldt.[4]
Corpses are scattered through a paradise.
5   Only the worm, colonel of carrion, cries:
"Waste no compassion on these separate dead!"
Statistics justify and scholars seize
The salients of colonial policy.
What is that to the white child hacked in bed?
10   To savages, expendable as Jews?

Threshed out by beaters,[5] the long rushes break
In a white dust of ibises whose cries
Have wheeled since civilization's dawn
From the parched river or beast-teeming plain.
15   The violence of beast on beast is read
As natural law, but upright man
Seeks his divinity by inflicting pain.
Delirious as these worried beasts, his wars
Dance to the tightened carcass of a drum,
20   While he calls courage still that native dread
Of the white peace contracted by the dead.

Again brutish necessity wipes its hands
Upon the napkin of a dirty cause, again
A waste of our compassion, as with Spain,[6]
25   The gorilla wrestles with the superman.
I who am poisoned with the blood of both,
Where shall I turn, divided to the vein?
I who have cursed
The drunken officer of British rule, how choose
30   Between this Africa and the English tongue I love?
Betray them both, or give back what they give?
How can I face such slaughter and be cool?
How can I turn from Africa and live?   1962

ISHMAEL REED

I Am a Cowboy in the Boat of Ra

The devil must be forced to reveal any such physical evil (potions,
charms, fetishes, etc.) still outside the body and these must be
burned.
    —*Rituale Romanum*, published 1947, endorsed by the coat of
    arms and introduction letter from Francis Cardinal Spellman

---

4. Open country, neither cultivated nor forest (Afrikaans).   5. In big-game hunting, natives are
hired to beat the brush, driving birds—such as ibises—and animals into the open.   6. The Span-
ish Civil War (1936–39), in which the Loyalists were supported by liberals in the West and militarily
by Soviet Communists, and the rebels by Nazi Germany and Fascist Italy.

I am a cowboy in the boat of Ra,[7]
sidewinders in the saloons of fools
bit my forehead   like   O
the untrustworthiness of Egyptologists
Who do not know their trips. Who was that   5
dog-faced man?[8] they asked, the day I rode
from town.

School marms with halitosis cannot see
the Nefertiti[9] fake chipped on the run by slick
germans, the hawk behind Sonny Rollins' head or   10
the ritual beard of his axe,[1] a longhorn winding
its bells thru the Field of Reeds.

I am a cowboy in the boat of Ra. I bedded
down with Isis,[2] Lady of the Boogaloo, dove
down deep in her horny, stuck up her Wells-Far-ago   15
in daring midday get away. "Start grabbing the
blue," i said from top of my double crown.

I am a cowboy in the boat of Ra. Ezzard Charles[3]
of the Chisholm Trail. Took up the bass but they
blew off my thumb. Alchemist in ringmanship but a   20
sucker for the right cross.

I am a cowboy in the boat of Ra. Vamoosed from
the temple i bide my time. The price on the wanted
poster was a-going down, outlaw alias copped my stance
and moody greenhorns were making me dance; while my mouth's   25
shooting iron got its chambers jammed.

I am a cowboy in the boat of Ra. Boning-up in
the ol West i bide my time. You should see
me pick off these tin cans whippersnappers. I
write the motown long plays for the comeback of   30
Osiris.[4] Make them up when stars stare at sleeping
steer out here near the campfire. Women arrive
on the backs of goats and throw themselves on
my Bowie.[5]

I am a cowboy in the boat of Ra. Lord of the lash,   35
the Loup Garou[6] Kid. Half breed son of Pisces and

---

7. Chief of the ancient Egyptian gods, creator and protector of humans and vanquisher of Evil.
8. The Egyptian god of the dead, Anubis was usually depicted as a man with the head of a dog or
jackal.   9. Fourteenth-century B.C. Egyptian queen; elsewhere Reed says that German scholars
are responsible for the notion that her dynasty was white.   1. Saxophone. *Sonny Rollins*: jazz
great of the late 1950s and early 1960s.   2. Principal goddess of ancient Egypt.   3. World
heavyweight boxing champion, 1949–51.   4. Husband of Isis and constant foe of his brother Set
(line 48). Tricked by Set, he died violently but later rose from the dead.   5. Large hunting knife.
6. French for werewolf; in voodoo, a priest who has run amok or gone mad.

Aquarius. I hold the souls of men in my pot. I do
the dirty boogie with scorpions. I make the bulls
keep still and was the first swinger to grape the taste.

40 I am a cowboy in his boat. Pope Joan[7] of the
Ptah Ra. C / mere a minute willya doll?
Be a good girl and
Bring me my Buffalo horn of black powder
Bring me my headdress of black feathers
45 Bring me my bones of Ju-Ju snake
Go get my eyelids of red paint.
Hand me my shadow
I'm going into town after Set

I am a cowboy in the boat of Ra
50 look out Set   here i come Set
to get Set   to sunset Set
to unseat Set   to Set down Set
usurper of the Royal couch
imposter RAdio of Moses' bush[8]
55 party pooper O hater of dance
vampire outlaw of the milky way   1969

JUDITH ORTIZ COFER

How to Get a Baby

To receive the *waiwaia* (spirit children) in the water seems to be
the most usual way of becoming pregnant. . . . They come along
on large tree trunks, and they may be attached to seascum and
dead leaves floating on the surface.
—BRONISLAW MALINOWSKI,
Baloma: The Spirits of the Dead in the Trobriand Islands

Go to the sea
the morning after a rainstorm,
preferably
fresh from your man's arms—
5 the *waiwaia* are drawn
to love smell.
They are tiny luminous fish

7. Mythical female pope, supposed to have succeeded to the papacy in 855. *Ptah Ra*: chief god of
Memphis, capital of ancient Egypt.   8. Which, according to Exodus 3:2, burned but was not
consumed and from which Moses heard the voice of God telling him to lead the Israelites out of
Egypt.

and blind. You must call
the soul of your child
in the name of your ancestors: 10
Come to me, little fish, come
to Tamala, Tudava, come to me.
Sit in shallow water
up to your waist until the tide
pulls away from you   15
like an exhausted lover.
You will by then
be carrying new life.
Make love that night,
and every night,   20
to let the little one
who chooses you know
she is one with your joy.   1993

ALBERTO ALVARO RÍOS

Advice to a First Cousin

The way the world works is like this:
for the bite of scorpions, she says,
my grandmother to my first cousin,
because I might die and someone must know,
go to the animal jar   5
the one with the soup of green herbs
mixed with the scorpions I have been putting in
still alive. Take one out
put it on the bite. It has had time to think
there with the others—put the lid back tight—   10
and knows that a biting is not the way to win
a finger or a young girl's foot.
It will take back into itself the hurting
the redness and the itching and its marks.

But the world works like this, too: 15
look out for the next scorpion you see,
she says, and makes a big face to scare me
thereby instructing my cousin, look out!
for one of the scorpion's many
illegitimate and unhappy sons.   20
It will be smarter, more of the devil.
It will have lived longer than these dead ones.
It will know from them something more
about the world, in the way mothers know
when something happens to a child, or how   25
I knew from your sadness you had been bitten.

It will learn something stronger than biting.
Look out most for that scorpion, she says,
making a big face to scare me again and it works
30   I go—crying—she lets me go—they laugh,
the way you must look out for men
who have not yet bruised you.   1985

DUNCAN CAMPBELL SCOTT

The Onondaga⁹ Madonna

She stands full-throated and with careless pose,
This woman of a weird and waning race,
The tragic savage lurking in her face,
Where all her pagan passion burns and glows;
5   Her blood is mingled with her ancient foes,
And thrills with war and wildness in her veins;
Her rebel lips are dabbled with the stains
Of feuds and forays and her father's woes.
And closer in the shawl about her breast,
10   The latest promise of her nation's doom,
Paler than she her baby clings and lies,
The primal warrior gleaming from his eyes;
He sulks, and burdened with his infant gloom,
He draws his heavy brows and will not rest.   1898

CATHY SONG

A Mehinaku Girl in Seclusion

When the pequi fruit blossomed,
I went into seclusion.
A red flower
dropped out of my body
5   and stained the red dirt of the earth
one color. With one color
I became married to the earth.
I went to live by myself
in the hut at the end of the village.

10   There no one must see me.
For three years,
no one must touch me.

9. One of the five groups of Native Americans forming what became known as the League of Five Nations, or the Iroquois Confederacy, the Onondaga originated in upper New York State; many moved to Canada after the American Revolution and now form part of the Six Nations Reserve near Brantford, Ontario.

The men carve the spirit birds
and dream of me
becoming beautiful in the dark. 15
They say my skin
will be as delicate as the light
that touches the spider's web.
The women walk to the river
and bathe and time passes. 20

One woman, the old one,
brings me news of the harvest,
the names of the children who are born.
The children are taught
to make babies out of mud, 25
babies in the shape of gourds.
The children cry when the rains come.

When the rain comes I slip out
and circle the dirt plaza.
I pause as if to drink at each door. 30
At each door,
the sound of the sleeping.
I return before the first
hint of light,
return to hear 35
the click of my spinning.

I will learn to become
mistress of the hammocks.
The man who will be my husband
shall be proud. 40
When I walk beside him
to bathe in the river,
I will say with my body,
He is mine.
The manioc bread he eats 45
becomes the children I will bear.
His hammocks are not tattered.
Ask him. Yes, ask him.
I am learning to say this
with my body.   1988   50

LOUISE ERDRICH

Jacklight

The same Chippewa word is used both for flirting and hunting
game, while another Chippewa word connotes both using force
in intercourse and also killing a bear with one's bare hands.

—DUNNING 1959

We have come to the edge of the woods,
out of brown grass where we slept, unseen,
out of knotted twigs, out of leaves creaked shut,
out of hiding.

At first the light wavered, glancing over us.
Then it clenched to a fist of light that pointed,
searched out, divided us.
Each took the beams like direct blows the heart answers.
Each of us moved forward alone.

We have come to the edge of the woods,
drawn out of ourselves by this night sun,
this battery of polarized acids,
that outshines the moon.

We smell them behind it
but they are faceless, invisible,
We smell the raw steel of their gun barrels,
mink oil on leather, their tongues of sour barley.
We smell their mother buried chin-deep in wet dirt.

We smell their fathers with scoured knuckles,
teeth cracked from hot marrow.
We smell their sisters of crushed dogwood, bruised apples,
of fractured cups and concussions of burnt hooks.

We smell their breath steaming lightly behind the jacklight.
We smell the itch underneath the caked guts on their clothes.
We smell their minds like silver hammers
cocked back, held in readiness
for the first of us to step into the open.

We have come to the edge of the woods,
out of brown grass where we slept, unseen,
out of leaves creaked shut, out of our hiding.
We have come here too long.

It is their turn now,
their turn to follow us. Listen,
they put down their equipment.
It is useless in the tall brush.
And now they take the first steps, not knowing
how deep the woods are and lightless.
How deep the woods are.

1984

LESLIE MARMON SILKO

[Long time ago]

Long time ago
in the beginning
there were no white people in this world
there was nothing European.
And this world might have gone on like that   5
except for one thing:
witchery.
This world was already complete
even without white people.
There was everything   10
including witchery.

Then it happened.
These witch people got together.
Some came from far far away
across oceans   15
across mountains.
Some had slanty eyes
others had black skin.
They all got together for a contest
the way people have baseball tournaments nowadays   20
except this was a contest
in dark things.

So anyway
they all got together
witch people from all directions   25
witches from all the Pueblos
and all the tribes.
They had Navajo witches there,
some from Hopi, and a few from Zuni.
They were having a witches' conference,   30
that's what it was
Way up in the lava rock hills
north of Cañoncito
they got together
to fool around in caves   35
with their animal skins.
Fox, badger, bobcat, and wolf
they circled the fire
and on the fourth time
they jumped into that animal's skin.   40

But this time it wasn't enough
and one of them

maybe a Sioux or some Eskimos
started showing off.
45   "That wasn't anything,
watch this."

The contest started like that.
Then some of them lifted the lids
on their big cooking pots,
50   calling the rest of them over
to take a look:
dead babies simmering in blood
circles of skull cut away
all the brains sucked out.
55   Witch medicine
to dry and grind into powder
for new victims.
Others untied skin bundles of disgusting objects:
dark flints, cinders from burned hogans where the
60   dead lay
Whorls of skin
cut from fingertips
sliced from the penis end and clitoris tip.

Finally there was only one
65   who hadn't shown off charms or powers.
The witch stood in the shadows beyond the fire
and no one ever knew where this witch came from
which tribe
or if it was a woman or a man.
70   But the important thing was
this witch didn't show off any dark thunder charcoals
or red ant-hill beads.
This one just told them to listen:
"What I have is a story."

75   At first they all laughed
but this witch said
Okay
go ahead
laugh if you want to
80   *but as I tell the story*
it will begin to happen.

Set in motion now
set in motion by our witchery
to work for us.

85   *Caves across the ocean*
in caves of dark hills
white skin people

*like the belly of a fish
covered with hair.*

Then they grow away from the earth   90
*then they grow away from the sun
then they grow away from the plants and animals.
They see no life
When they look
they see only objects.*   95
*The world is a dead thing for them
the trees and rivers are not alive
the mountains and stones are not alive.
The deer and bear are objects
They see no life.*   100
*They fear
They fear the world.
They destroy what they fear.
They fear themselves.*

The wind will blow them across the ocean   105
*thousands of them in giant boats
swarming like larva
out of a crushed ant hill.*

*They will carry objects
which can shoot death*   110
faster than the eye can see.

*They will kill the things they fear
all the animals
the people will starve.*

They will poison the water   115
*they will spin the water away
and there will be drought
the people will starve.*

*They will fear what they find
They will fear the people*   120
They kill what they fear.

*Entire villages will be wiped out
They will slaughter whole tribes.
Corpses for us
Blood for us*   125
Killing killing killing killing.

*And those they do not kill
will die anyway
at the destruction they see
at the loss*   130

at the loss of the children
the loss will destroy the rest.

Stolen rivers and mountains
the stolen land will eat their hearts
135   *and jerk their mouths from the Mother.*
The people will starve.

They will bring terrible diseases
the people have never known.
Entire tribes will die out
140   *covered with festered sores*
shitting blood
vomiting blood.
Corpses for our work

Set in motion now
145   *set in motion by our witchery*
set in motion
to work for us.

They will take this world from ocean to ocean
they will turn on each other
150   *they will destroy each other*
Up here
in these hills
they will find the rocks,
rocks with veins of green and yellow and black.
155   *They will lay the final pattern with these rocks*
they will lay it across the world
and explode everything.

Set in motion now
set in motion
160   *To destroy*
To kill
Objects to work for us
objects to act for us
Performing the witchery
165   *for suffering*
for torment
for the stillborn
the deformed
the sterile
170   *the dead.*

Whirling
Whirling
Whirling
Whirling

set into motion now   175
set into motion.

So the other witches said
"Okay you win; you take the prize,
but what you said just now—
it isn't so funny   180
It doesn't sound so good.
We are doing okay without it
we can get along without that kind of thing.
Take it back.
Call that story back."   185

But the witch just shook its head
at the others in their stinking animal skins, fur
and feathers.
It's already turned loose.
It's already coming.   190
It can't be called back.   1981

GREGORY ORFALEA

Arab and Jew in Alaska

For Gordon Massman

. . . on the surface of the desert were fine
flakes like hoarfrost. The Israelites asked
one another, "What is this?" Moses told them,
"This is the bread which the Lord has given you to eat."
                                              Exodus 16:14–15

God's light is an olive
that is neither of the East nor of the West
whose oil wellnigh would shine, even if no fire touched it.
                                              Koran, Sura XXIV

1

Two sons of Sem,[1] called by an unknown
we drove separate over gravel—North.
Leaves shuddered down. Gold
radiated up to our faces and went cold.

1. Shem, one of Noah's sons, from whom Semites, Arabs and Jews, are said to have descended.

5   In no-man's land we met. You pulled
out sheaves of poems, and your voice quavered.
My feet pawed on the other side
of the table as you read
from the Book of Lamentations,[2]
10   twentieth century-style: aborted
life, walled death—Rothschild's screeching
fiddle,[3] I thought. And when you threatened
to kill off the reader, I bristled.
Did you have the whole corner
15   on suffering? I wondered,
wondered, and watched the snow
drop into blistering
cold dunes . . .

2

Winter fell hard on the harder earth,
20   aged it quiet
and did its work on the warm-blooded.

Hoarfrost did not discriminate
between our moustaches. White
ice clung to our eyebrows, lashes
25   and dripped from our noses, so that our mouths
shut. We joined in Fairbanks
from opposite directions, shivering
breath-clouds
indoors, gasping
30   with poems.

3

Warm and lone as wolves, barking
our art, we withdrew
each boiling his own despair
on the crossed logs.
35   Waiting . . .
At night in the woods
Moses and Joshua trailed past my cabin,
pointing—and Ishmael,
father of Bedouins.
40   The desert does things to people
like latitude. But the heart
beats in longitude.

---

2. Book of the Bible that mourns the destruction of Jerusalem.   3. The name of a great European Jewish banking family whose empire was plundered in World War II; "Rothschild's Fiddle," a short story by Anton Chekhov.

A Bedouin is born on a dune—
if it doesn't crest and crash
to shore, he will burn   45
his soles to get to another dune.
He will tell his feet: *Water*
even if they rupture. Like Aaron's rod:[4]
Water is my flower that splits the rocks!

4

Cold tar poured over the North   50
and I begged God spare the last
quivering light . . .
                    outside, huge in parka,
inflated shoes, I banged the empty
oil drums—darkness
hit my face   55
like sand. Darkness felt: *khamsin*,[5]
the Pharoah's Ninth Plague,[6]
a dark to be rubbed by the hands.

5

And how does one row   60
in a black vortex?
—Straight back into the soul,
flaring the wick of rare life
where others, too, are raw.

From separate vigils, we brought each other   65
what glowed in the dark:
the blue of snow that pulls
the soul out of the lung,
a woman's sequins on the moonlit branches.
I walked a long way from the lost   70
gold mines at Ester,[7] legs block-ice,
to tell you there was no gold
but the Aurora, our new Ark of the Covenant.

For here—in the tremor of discovering
the other—Arab and Jew   75
disappear.

---

4. From the Book of Exodus, the rod cast by Aaron before Pharoah, which became a serpent, and was later used by Moses to split the rock that brought forth water.   5. A hot south wind from the Sahara that blows in the Near East from late March to early May.   6. Of the ten plagues brought down against the Pharoah and his people in the Book of Exodus, the ninth was a thick darkness lasting three days.   7. Small village west of Fairbanks, Alaska.

6

The next year we camped near
an ice-filled port. Anchorage
mornings you'd trudge in the dark
80   grasping poems, gray sparrows, breathing
on the wings and calling, "Here! Quickly!"

Goliath gloves held the poem like a membrane:
This is the best one yet, hot off the griddle.
The mercury held forty-below zero.

85   That year a dagger rose from the snow
you recognized, helped pull it out
of me, scarred birch, brother.
Frozen sparrows of your life you held as evidence
and began laughing so strangely
90   I understood. We kicked up snow
with our *dabkah*,[8] our *hora*,[9]

a laughing dance to fill the abyss!

7

If I could sculpt the world
the path we wore back and forth in the snow
95   under the dark, over the skeptic ice,
poems on their toes
with our breath—
If I could hold that feet-on-feet way
in the white that sees a light
100   that vaults the past—

I would take the sculpture,
call it Minimal Art—
and place it in Sinai, the Golan Heights,[1]
Jerusalem, leading from temple to church to mosque—
105   A wave sculpture like a ray
that would freeze the hearts of men
such they would want melting
over anything
without country, religion, any claim but:

110   "Heat us—light."

8

It is raining today on the Pacific
and you are on the gulf, rain-years away.

---

8. Arab folk dance.   9. Israeli folk dance.   1. A territory in southwest Syria captured in the
1967 June War and annexed by Israel in 1981.

I hold over the cloud of tea and marvel
at such a cold California day.

Friend, where is our homeland? 115
We were born in America, set adrift
on what it started.
Our veins often wander
at the smell of mint,
the sound of a goat . . . but 120
where, dear friend, where?

I know, at times, even in the hottest
blood, I hear an echo,
a thin icy rasping, the sash
of the sky undoing— 125

the sound of color, all together,
and alone. Someday, again,

home. 1988

▼ ▼ ▼

LITERARY TRADITION AS CONTEXT A Glossary

aubade: a morning song in which the coming of dawn is either celebrated or denounced as a nuisance

ballad: a narrative poem that is, or originally was, meant to be sung; characterized by repetition and often by a repeated refrain (recurrent phrase or series of phrases), ballads were originally a folk creation, transmitted orally from person to person and age to age

confessional poem: a relatively new (or recently defined) kind in which the speaker describes a confused, chaotic state of mind, which becomes a metaphor for the larger world

conventions: standard ways of saying things in verse, employed to achieve certain expected effects

dramatic monologue: a monologue set in a specific situation and spoken to someone

echo: a reference that recalls a word, phrase, or sound in another text

elegy: in classical times, any poem on any subject written in "elegiac" meter, but since the Renaissance usually a formal lament for the death of a particular person

epic: a poem that celebrates, in a continuous narrative, the achievements of mighty heroes and heroines, usually in founding a nation or developing a culture, and uses elevated language and a grand, high style

epigram: originally any poem carved in stone (on tombstones, buildings, gates, etc.), but in modern usage a very short, usually witty verse with a quick turn at the end

lyric: originally designated poems meant to be sung to the accompaniment of a lyre; now a short poem in which the speaker expresses intense personal emotion rather than describing a narrative or dramatic situation

meditation: a contemplation of some physical object as a way of reflecting upon some larger truth, often (but not necessarily) a spiritual one

motif: a recurrent device, formula, or situation that deliberately connects a poem with common patterns of existing thought

myth: stories that are more or less universally shared within a culture to explain its history, traditions

pastoral: a poem (also called an eclogue, a bucolic, or an idyll) that describes the simple life of country folk, usually shepherds who live a timeless, painless (and sheepless) life in a world that is full of beauty, music, and love, and that remains forever green

protest poem: an attack, sometimes indirect, on institutions or social injustices

soliloquy: a monologue in which the character is alone and speaking only to him- or herself

tradition: an inherited, established, or customary practice

QUESTIONS

1. How, specifically, is the speaker undercut in Jonson's "Come, My Celia"? Explain how the strategy of allusion works in this poem.

2. Are Moore's notes to "Love in America" adequate to explain the allusions in her poem? What other information do you wish to have? After you have unearthed that information in your college library, show in detail how each separate allusion in the poem works. How would you paraphrase the poem? Why is there a question mark in the poem's title?

3. List all the metaphors you can find in "An Epitaph upon a Young Married Couple, Dead and Buried Together." How closely are the metaphors related to each other? Which metaphors seem especially appropriate to an epitaph? to the epigram as a poetic kind?

4. Which epitaph in the chapter seems to you the most likely actually to end up on a tombstone? Why? What features would prevent most of the "epitaphs" here from actually being used? Which epitaph here seems to you the wittiest? In what, exactly, does the wit consist? Do you like the epigrams better or worse that have a "sting" at the end? Why?

5. Read through a number of the very short poems in this book and pick out one of no more than eight lines that does not seem to you to qualify as an

epigram. What features of the poem make that label inappropriate? On the basis of what you know about poetic kinds, can you assign a label to it?

6. Read the Cummings poem "(ponder,darling,these busted statues" closely in relation to "To His Coy Mistress." In what specific ways does it echo Marvell's poem? Which images are specifically derived from Marvell? In what specific ways does the Cummings poem undercut the argument of the Marvell poem? In what ways does it undercut its own argument? to what purpose?

7. Indicate the specific ways in which Ralegh's poem "replies" to Marlowe's. In what points does Williams agree with Ralegh? What, exactly, is "unfair" about Skirrow's summary of Keats? How do you think Keats would justify himself against Skirrow's summary?

8. What attitudes toward Adam and Eve are displayed in the Donnelly, Hollander, and Rossetti poems? Which poems develop the strongest negative attitudes toward their "heroes" or "heroines"? How does Harrison's version of the Ulysses story differ from Tennyson's? How do Waddington's and Millay's versions differ? What values are associated with Africa in the Hughes, Angelou, and Reed poems? What is the "cowboy" doing in Reed's poem?

WRITING SUGGESTIONS

1. In what specific ways is "To His Coy Mistress" anchored to its historical or cultural context? Can you tell that it is written by a 17th-century poet? How? What historical or cultural "allusions" anchor the poem to its specific moment in time? to its philosophical or thematic contexts? In what specific ways does the de Vries poem establish itself as contemporary? Write a short (500–700 word) essay in which you show how de Vries undercuts the assumptions of Marvell. (Alternative: write a short essay in which you show how Cummings undercuts the assumptions of Marvell.)

2. Choose randomly any six of the epigrams in this chapter, and try to decide on the basis of them what a good definition of the epigram might be. Write down your definition, mentioning any features of epigram that seem to you crucial to the kind. Then choose a seventh poem from the chapter, one that seems to you entirely typical of the epigram kind, and write a brief, three-paragraph analysis of it, showing exactly how it uses features mentioned in your definition.

3. Using one of the poems in this chapter as your model, try your hand at writing an epigram (of no more than four lines) of your own. When you have completed your poem, write a brief paragraph about it, describing how you have used features characteristic of the poetic kind.

4. Using a poetry index (available in the reference section of your college library), find half a dozen poems that use the term "elegy" in their titles, and compare their tones and strategies. Try to decide what features and expectations seem to be central to the poetic kind. Then look back at "On My First Son" (p. 9), often said to be a typical elegy, and write a brief (two-page) analysis of the poem in which you show how it uses and transforms the expectations associated with the elegy as a poetic kind.

5. In an essay of about three pages, show how the primary effects of "I Am a Cowboy in the Boat of Ra" relate to its use of cultural myths. (Alternative: apply this same question to Rossetti's "Eve," Tennyson's "Ulysses," or Song's "A Mehinaku Girl in Seclusion.")

12 HISTORY AND CULTURE AS CONTEXT

The more you know, the better a reader of poetry you are likely to be. And that goes for general knowledge as well as knowledge of other poetry and literary traditions. Poems often draw upon a larger fund of human knowledge about all sorts of things, asking us to bring to bear on a poem facts and values we have taken on from earlier reading or from our experiences in the world more generally. The first section of this book—the introductory chapter on *Reading, Responding, and Writing* and the first eight chapters—suggests how practice makes interpretation easier and better: the more you read and the more close analysis you do, the better interpreter you are likely to become. But in this "contextual" section we are concerned with information you need to read richly and fully—information about authors, about events that influenced them or became the inspiration or basis for their writing, and about literary traditions that provide a context for their work. Poets always write in a specific time, under particular circumstances, and with some awareness of the world around them, whether or not they specifically refer to it in a particular poem. In this chapter, our concern is with the specifically historical and cultural—events, movements, ideas that directly influence poets or that poets in some way represent in the poems they write.

Very little that you know will ultimately go to waste in your reading of poetry. The best potential reader of poetry is someone who has already developed reading skills to perfection, read everything, thought deeply about all kinds of things, and who is wise beyond belief—wise enough to know exactly how to apply what she or he knows accurately to a given text. But that is the ideal reader we all strive to be, not the one any of us actually is. Although no poet really expects any reader to be all those things, good readers try. And sometimes poets seem to write as if they expect such skills and knowledge. Poems can be just as demanding—or at least requestful—of readers about historical information as about the intricacies of language and form. Poems not only *refer to* people, places, and events—things that exist in time—but they also *are* themselves products of given moments, participating in both the potentialities and the limitations of the times in which they were created.

Things that happen every day frequently find their way into poetry in an easy and yet often forceful manner. Making love in a junkyard, as in "Cherrylog Road," is one kind of example; a reader doesn't need to know what particular junkyard was involved—or imaginatively involved—in order to understand the poem, but a reader does need to know what an auto junkyard was like in the mid-twentieth century, with more or less whole car bodies being scattered in various states of disarray over a large plot of ground. But what if, over the next generation or two, junkyards completely disappear as other ways are found to dispose of old cars? Already a lot of old cars are crushed into small metal blocks, especially in large cities. But what if the metal is all melted down, or the junk is orbited into space? If that should happen, readers then will have never seen a junkyard, and they will need a footnote to explain what such junkyards were like. The history of junkyards will not be lost—there will be pictures, films, records, and someone will write definitive books about the forms and functions of junkyards, probably even including the fact that lovers occasionally visited them—but the public memory of junkyards will soon disappear. No social customs, nothing that is made, no institutions or sites last forever.

Readers may still be able to experience "Cherrylog Road" when junkyards disappear, but they will need some help, and they may think its particulars a little quaint, much as we regard literature that involves horses and buggies—or even making love in the back seat of a parked car—as quaint now. Institutions change, habits change, times change, places and settings change—all kinds of particulars change, even when people's wants, needs, and foibles pretty much go on in the same way. Footnotes never provide a precise or adequate substitute for the ease and pleasure that come from already knowing, but they can help us understand and pave the way for feeling and experience. A kind of imaginative historical sympathy can be simulated and in fact created, for poems from earlier times that refer to specific contemporary details (and that have now become to us, in our own time, *historical* details) often describe human nature and human experiences very much as we still know and experience them. Today's poem may need tomorrow's footnote, but the poem need not be tomorrow's puzzle or only a curiosity or fossil.

The following poem, not many years old, already requires some explanation, not only because the factual details of its occasion may not be known to every reader, but also because the whole spirit of the poem may be difficult to appreciate unless one knows its circumstances.

RAYMOND R. PATTERSON

You Are the Brave

You are the brave who do not break
In the grip of the mob when the blow comes straight
To the shattered bone; when the sockets shriek;
When your arms lie twisted under your back.

Good men holding their courage slack   5
In their frightened pockets see how weak
The work that is done; and feel the weight
Of your blood on the ground for their spirits' sake;

And build their anger, stone on stone;
1962   Each silently, but not alone.   10

I can remember teaching this poem in class during the Vietnam War and
finding that a lot of students were hostile to it because they assumed it to be a
poem in praise of patriotism and war. More recently it has seemed to some
readers to be about Lebanon, or Bosnia, or a variety of other sites of painful vio-
lence. Sometimes the difficulty about factual information is that one doesn't
know that one *needs* specific information. In a poem like "You Are the Brave,"
it is fairly easy to assume (incorrectly, but understandably) that the conflict
involved is a war and that the speaker addresses, and honors, a group of sol-
diers. Actually, there are clues in the poem that this conflict is, if as bitter as
war, one in which mob violence (line 2) and enforced restraint (line 4) are
involved. The date of the poem is a clue too—1962, when the American civil
rights struggle was at its height. Once that "fact" is noticed, the whole histori-
cal context of the poem, if not its *immediate* occasion in terms of one specific
civil rights march in one place on one day, becomes clear. In fact, since the
poem doesn't mention a particular time and place, we may assume that it is
not about the particulars of one specific incident, but instead gathers the kind
of details that characterized many moments of the early 1960s. The poem's
details (generalized details about mob resentments and brutalities in a situation
of passive resistance), its metaphors in the second and third stanzas, and its dig-
nified tone of praise for "the brave" all make sense readily when the right infor-
mation is available. The poem does not mention specific time and place
because its concern is not confined to one event, but its location in time is
important to finding what it refers to. Poems may be referential to one single
event or moment, or to some larger situation that may span weeks, months, or
even years. The amount of particularity in the poem will tell you.

How do you know what you need to know? The easiest clue is your own puzzlement. When it seems that something is happening in a poem that you don't recognize—and yet the poem makes no apparent effort to clarify it—you have a clue that readers at the time the poem was written must have recognized something that is not now such common knowledge. Once you know you don't know, it only takes a little work to find out: most college libraries contain far more information than you will ever need, and the trick is to search efficiently. Your ability to find the information will depend upon how well you know the written reference materials and computer searches available to you. Practice helps. Knowledge accumulates. Most poems printed in textbooks like this one will be annotated for you with basic facts, but often you may need additional information to interpret the poem's full meaning and resonance. An editor, trying to satisfy the needs of a variety of readers, may not always decide to write the footnote you in particular may need, so there could be digging to do in the library for any poem you read, certainly for those you come upon in magazines and books of poetry without footnotes. Few poets like to footnote their own work (they'd rather let you struggle a little to appreciate them), and besides, many things that now need footnotes didn't when they were written, as in "You Are the Brave."

The two poems that follow both require from the reader some specific "referential" information, but they differ considerably in their emphasis on the particularities of time and place. The first poem, "Channel Firing," reflects and refers to a moment just before the outbreak of World War I when British naval forces were preparing for combat by taking gunnery practice in the English Channel. The second, "Sonnet: The Ladies' Home Journal," reflects a longer cultural moment in which attitudes and assumptions, rather than some specific event, are crucial to understanding the poem.

THOMAS HARDY

Channel Firing

That night your great guns, unawares,
Shook all our coffins as we lay,
And broke the chancel window squares,[1]
We thought it was the Judgment-day

5   And sat upright. While drearisome
Arose the howl of wakened hounds:

---

1. The windows near the altar in a church.

The mouse let fall the altar-crumb,[2]
The worms drew back into the mounds,

The glebe cow[3] drooled. Till God called, "No;
It's gunnery practice out at sea   10
Just as before you went below;
The world is as it used to be:

"All nations striving strong to make
Red war yet redder. Mad as hatters
They do no more for Christés sake   15
Than you who are helpless in such matters.

"That this is not the judgment-hour
For some of them's a blessed thing,
For if it were they'd have to scour
Hell's floor for so much threatening . . .   20

"Ha, ha. It will be warmer when
I blow the trumpet (if indeed
I ever do; for you are men,
And rest eternal sorely need)."

So down we lay again. "I wonder,   25
Will the world ever saner be,"
Said one, "than when He sent us under
In our indifferent century!"

And many a skeleton shook his head.
"Instead of preaching forty year,"   30
My neighbor Parson Thirdly said,
"I wish I had stuck to pipes and beer."

Again the guns disturbed the hour,
Roaring their readiness to avenge.
As far inland as Stourton Tower,   35
April 1914   And Camelot, and starlit Stonehenge.[4]

2. Breadcrumbs from the Blessed Sacrament.   3. Parish cow pastured on the meadow next to the churchyard.   4. Stourton Tower, built in the 18th century to commemorate King Alfred's ninth-century victory over the Danes, in Stourhead Park, Wiltshire. Camelot is the legendary site of King Arthur's court, said to have been in Cornwall or Somerset. Stonehenge, a circular formation of upright stones dating from about 1800 B.C., is on Salisbury Plain, Wiltshire; it is thought to have been a ceremonial site for political and religious occasions or an early scientific experiment in astronomy.

SANDRA GILBERT

Sonnet: The Ladies' Home Journal

The brilliant stills of food, the cozy
glossy, bygone life—mashed potatoes
posing as whipped cream, a neat mom
conjuring shapes from chaos, trimming the flame—
how we ached for all that,
that dance of love in the living room,
those paneled walls, that kitchen golden
as the inside of a seed: how we leaned
on those shiny columns of advice,
stroking the *thank yous*, the firm thighs, the wise
closets full of soap.

        But even then
we knew it was the lies we loved, the lies
we wore like Dior coats,[5] the clean-cut airtight
lies that laid out our lives in black and white.   1984

"Channel Firing" is not ultimately *about* World War I, for its emphasis is
finally on how human behavior stays the same from age to age, but it begins
from a particular historical vantage point. It would be difficult to make much
sense of the poem if the reader were not to recognize the importance of that
specific reference, and the poem's situation (with a waking corpse as the main
speaker) is difficult enough to sort out even with the clue of the careful dating
at the end (the date here is actually a part of the poem, recorded on the manu-
script by the author and always printed as part of the text). The firing of the
guns has awakened the dead who are buried near the channel, and in their
puzzlement they assume it is Judgment Day, time for them to arise, until God
enters and tells them what is happening. Much of the poem's effect depends
on character portrayal—a God who laughs and sounds cynical, a parson who
regrets his selfless life and wishes he had indulged himself more—as well as
the sense that nothing ever changes. But particularity of time and place are cru-
cial to this sense of changelessness; even so important a contemporary moment
as the beginning of a world war—a moment viewed by most people at the time
as unique and world-changing—fades into a timeless parade of moments that
stretches over centuries of history. The geographical particulars cited at the
end—as the sound of the guns moves inland to be heard in place after place—

5. Designer coats by Christian Dior.

make the same point. Great moments in history are all encompassed in the sound of the guns and its message about human behavior. Times, places, and events, however important they seem, all become part of some larger pattern that denies individuality or uniqueness.

The particulars in "Sonnet: The Ladies' Home Journal" work rather differently—to remind us not of a specific time that readers need to identify but to characterize a way of seeing and thinking. The referentiality here is more cultural than historical; it is based more on ideas and attitudes characteristic of a particular period than on a specific moment or location. The pictures in the magazine stand for a whole way of thinking about women that was characteristic of the time when the *Ladies' Home Journal* flourished as a popular magazine. The poem implicitly contrasts the "lies" (line 12) of the magazine with the truth of the present—that women's lives and values are not to be seen as some fantasized sense of beautiful food, motherhood, social rituals, and commercial products. Two vastly different cultural attitudes—that of the poem's present, with its skeptical view of traditional women's roles, and that of a past that equated the superficiality of glossy photographs with gender identity—are at the heart of the poem. It is about cultural attitudes and their effects on actual human beings. Readers need to know what the *Ladies' Home Journal* was like in order to understand the poem; we do not need to know the date or contents of a specific issue, only that this popular magazine reflected the attitudes and values of a whole age and culture. The referentiality of this poem involves information about ideas and consciousness more than time and event.

To get at appropriate factual, cultural, and historical information, it is important to learn to ask three kinds of questions. One kind is obvious: it is the "Do I understand the reference to . . . ?" kind. When events, places, or people unfamiliar to you come up, you will need to find out what or who they are. The second kind of question is more difficult: How do you know, in a poem like "You Are the Brave," that you need to know more? When there are no specific references to look up, no people or events to identify, how do you know that there is a specific context? To get at this sort of question, you have to trust two people: the poet, and yourself. Learning to trust yourself, your own responses, is the more difficult—you can just decide to trust the poet. Usually, good poets know what they are doing. If they do, they will not want to puzzle you more than necessary, so that you can safely assume that something that is not self-explanatory will merit close attention and possibly some digging in the library. (Poets do make mistakes and miscalculations about their readers, but in an introductory way it is usually safe to assume they know what they are doing and why they are doing it.) References that are not in themselves clear (such as "the grip of the mob" or the "arms . . . twisted under your back" in "You Are the Brave") provide a strong clue that you need more information. And that is why you need to trust yourself: when something doesn't click, when the information given you does not seem enough, you need to trust your puzzlement and try to find the missing facts that will allow the poem to make sense. But how? Often the date of the poem is a help, as in "You Are the Brave." Sometimes the title gives a clue or a point of departure. Sometimes you can discover, by reading about the author, some of the things he or she was interested in or concerned about. There is no single all-purpose way to discover what to look for, but that kind of research—looking for clues, adding up the evidence—can be interesting in itself and very rewarding when it is successful.

The third question is why? For every factual reference, one needs to ask why. Why does the poem refer to this particular person instead of some other? What function does the reference serve?

Beyond the level of simply understanding that a particular poem is about an event or place or movement is the matter of developing a full sense of historical context, a sense of the larger significance and resonance of the historical occurrence or attitude referred to. Often a poem expects you to bring with you some sense of that significance; just as often it works to continue your education, telling you more, wanting you to understand and appreciate on the level of feeling some further things about this occurrence.

What we need to bring to our reading varies from poem to poem. For example, "Dulce et Decorum Est" (below), needs our knowledge that poison gas was used in World War I; the green tint through which the speaker sees the world in lines 13–14 comes from green glass in the goggles of the gas mask he has just put on. But some broader matters are important as well. Harder to specify but probably even more important is the climate of opinion that surrounded the war. To idealists, it was "the war to end all wars," and many participants—as well as politicians and propagandists—considered it a sacred mission, regarding the threat of Germany's expansionist policy as dangerous to Western civilization. No doubt you will read the poem more intelligently—and with more feeling—the more you know about World War I, and the same is true of poems about any historical occurrence or that refer to things that happen or situations that exist in a temporal or spatial context. But it is also true that your sense of these events will grow as a result of reading sensitively and thoughtfully the poems themselves. Facts are no substitute for skills. Once you have read individually the poems in this section, try taking a breather; and then at one sitting read them all again. Reading poetry can be a form of gaining knowledge as well as an aesthetic experience. One doesn't go to poetry to seek information as such, but poems often give us more than we came for. The ways to wisdom are paved with facts, and although poetry is not primarily a data-conscious art, it often requires us to be aware, sometimes in detail, of its referents in the real world.

Times, Places, and Events

IRVING LAYTON

From Colony to Nation

A dull people,
but the rivers of this country
are wide and beautiful

A dull people
enamoured of childish games,   5
but food is easily come by
and plentiful

Some with a priest's voice
in their cage of ribs: but
on high mountain-tops and in thunderstorms   10
the chirping is not heard

Deferring to beadle and censor;
not ashamed for this,
but given over to horseplay,
the making of money   15

A dull people, without charm or
ideas,
settling into the clean empty look
of a Mountie or dairy farmer
as into a legacy   20

One can ignore them
(the silences, the vast distances help)
and suppose them at the bottom
of one of the meaner lakes,
their bones not even picked for souvenirs.   1956   25

HENRY WADSWORTH LONGFELLOW

The Jewish Cemetery at Newport

How strange it seems! These Hebrews in their graves,
    Close by the street of this fair seaport town,
Silent beside the never-silent waves,
    At rest in all this moving up and down!

The trees are white with dust, that o'er their sleep
    Wave their broad curtains in the southwind's breath,
While underneath these leafy tents they keep
    The long, mysterious Exodus of Death.

And these sepulchral stones, so old and brown,
    That pave with level flags their burial-place,
Seem like the tablets of the Law, thrown down
    And broken by Moses at the mountain's base.

The very names recorded here are strange,
    Of foreign accent, and of different climes;
Alvares and Rivera interchange
    With Abraham and Jacob of old times.

"Blessed be God! for he created Death!"
    The mourners said, "and Death is rest and peace";
Then added, in the certainty of faith,
    "And giveth Life that nevermore shall cease."

Closed are the portals of their Synagogue,
    No Psalms of David now the silence break,
No Rabbi reads the ancient Decalogue
    In the grand dialect the Prophets spake.

Gone are the living, but the dead remain,
    And not neglected; for a hand unseen,
Scattering its bounty, like a summer rain,
    Still keeps their graves and their remembrance green.

How came they here? What burst of Christian hate,
    What persecution, merciless and blind,
Drove o'er the sea—the desert desolate—
    These Ishmaels and Hagars of mankind?

They lived in narrow streets and lanes obscure,
    Ghetto and Judenstrass,[1] in mirk and mire;
Taught in the school of patience to endure
    The life of anguish and the death of fire.

5

10

15

20

25

30

35

---

1. German for "Street of Jews."

All their lives long, with the unleavened bread
    And bitter herbs of exile and its fears,
The wasting famine of the heart they fed,
    And slaked its thirst with marah[2] of their tears.   40

Anathema maranatha![3] was the cry
    That rang from town to town, from street to street;
At every gate the accursed Mordecai[4]
    Was mocked and jeered, and spurned by Christian feet.

Pride and humiliation hand in hand   45
    Walked with them through the world wher'er they went;
Trampled and beaten were they as the sand,
    And yet unshaken as the continent.

For in the background figures vague and vast
    Of patriarchs and of prophets rose sublime,   50
And all the great traditions of the Past
    They saw reflected in the coming time.

And thus forever with reverted look
    The mystic volume of the world they read,
Spelling it backward, like a Hebrew book,   55
    Till life became a Legend of the Dead.

But ah! what once has been shall be no more!
    The growing earth in travail and in pain
Brings forth its races, but does not restore,
    And the dead nations never rise again.   1852   60

DONALD JUSTICE

Children Walking Home from School Through Good Neighborhood

They are like figures held in some glass ball,
One of those in which, when shaken, snowstorms occur;
But this one is not yet shaken.
    And they go unaccompanied still,
Out along this walkway between two worlds,   5
This almost swaying bridge.
    October sunlight checkers their path;

2. The Hebrew word for "bitter" or "bitterness"; salt water (symbolizing tears), unleavened bread, and bitter herbs are all part of the Passover meal.   3. A Greek-Aramaic phrase signifying a terrible curse, applied specifically to the Jews.   4. A Jew whose foster daughter, Esther, became the queen of Ahasuerus (Xerxes), king of Persia. When Haman, Ahasuerus' favored advisor, sought to destroy Mordecai and the Jews, Mordecai stood at the king's gate crying out against the persecution.

It frets their cheeks and bare arms now with shadow
Almost too pure to signify itself.
And they progress slowly, somewhat lingeringly,   10
Independent, yet moving all together,
Like polyphonic voices that crisscross
In short-lived harmonies.

    Today, a few stragglers.
One, a girl, stands there with hands spaced out, so—   15
A gesture in a story. Someone's school notebook spills,
And they bend down to gather up the loose pages.
(Bright sweaters knotted at the waist; solemn expressions.)
Not that they would shrink or hold back from what may come,
For now they all at once run to meet it, a little swirl of colors,   20
Like the leaves already blazing and falling farther north.   1987

CLAUDE McKAY

America

Although she feeds me bread of bitterness,
And sinks into my throat her tiger's tooth,
Stealing my breath of life, I will confess
I love this cultured hell that tests my youth!
Her vigor flows like tides into my blood,   5
Giving me strength erect against her hate.
Her bigness sweeps my being like a flood.
Yet as a rebel fronts a king in state,
I stand within her walls with not a shred
Of terror, malice, not a word of jeer.   10
Darkly I gaze into the days ahead,
And see her might and granite wonders there,
Beneath the touch of Time's unerring hand,
Like priceless treasures sinking in the sand.   1922

LANGSTON HUGHES

Harlem (A Dream Deferred)

What happens to a dream deferred?

    Does it dry up
    like a raisin in the sun?
    Or fester like a sore—
    And then run?   5

Does it stink like rotten meat?
Or crust and sugar over—
like a syrupy sweet?

Maybe it just sags
like a heavy load. 10

Or does it explode? 1951

JAMES A. EMANUEL

Emmett Till[5]

I hear a whistling
Through the water.
Little Emmett
Won't be still.
He keeps floating 5
Round the darkness,
Edging through
The silent chill.
Tell me, please,
That bedtime story 10
Of the fairy
River Boy
Who swims forever,
Deep in treasures,
Necklaced in 15
A coral toy. 1968

ROBERT HAYDEN

Frederick Douglass[6]

When it is finally ours, this freedom, this liberty, this beautiful
and terrible thing, needful to man as air,
usable as earth; when it belongs at last to all,
when it is truly instinct, brain matter, diastole, systole,
reflex action; when it is finally won; when it is more 5
than the gaudy mumbo jumbo of politicians:
this man, this Douglass, this former slave, this Negro

5. In 1955, Till, a fourteen-year-old from Chicago, was lynched in Mississippi for allegedly making sexual advances toward a white woman.   6. Frederick Douglass (1817–1895), escaped slave. Douglass was involved in the Underground Railroad, and became the publisher of the famous abolitionist newspaper the *North Star*, in Rochester, N.Y.

beaten to his knees, exiled, visioning a world
where none is lonely, none hunted, alien,
this man, superb in love and logic, this man
shall be remembered. Oh, not with statues' rhetoric,
not with legends and poems and wreaths of bronze alone,
but with the lives grown out of his life, the lives
fleshing his dream of the beautiful, needful thing.

10

1966

THOMAS HARDY

The Convergence of the Twain

LINES ON THE LOSS OF THE "TITANIC"[7]

I

In a solitude of the sea
Deep from human vanity,
And the Pride of Life that planned her, stilly couches she.

II

Steel chambers, late the pyres
Of her salamandrine[8] fires,
Cold currents thrid,[9] and turn to rhythmic tidal lyres.

5

III

Over the mirrors meant
To glass the opulent
The sea-worm crawls—grotesque, slimed, dumb, indifferent.

IV

Jewels in joy designed
To ravish the sensuous mind
Lie lightless, all their sparkles bleared and black and blind.

10

V

Dim moon-eyed fishes near
Gaze at the gilded gear
And query: "What does this vaingloriousness down here?" . . .

15

7. On the night of April 14, 1912, the *Titanic*, the largest ship afloat and on her maiden voyage to New York from Southampton, collided with an iceberg in the North Atlantic and sank in less than three hours; 1,500 of 2,206 passengers were lost.   8. Bright red; the salamander was supposed to be able to live in fire.   9. Thread.

VI

Well: while was fashioning
This creature of cleaving wing,
The Immanent Will that stirs and urges everything

VII

Prepared a sinister mate
For her—so gaily great—   20
A Shape of Ice, for the time far and dissociate.

VIII

And as the smart ship grew
In stature, grace, and hue,
In shadowy silent distance grew the Iceberg too.

IX

Alien they seemed to be: 25
No mortal eye could see
The intimate welding of their later history,

X

Or sign that they were bent
By paths coincident
On being anon twin halves of one august event,   30

XI

Till the Spinner of the Years
Said "Now!" And each one hears,
And consummation comes, and jars two hemispheres.   1914

WILFRED OWEN

Dulce et Decorum Est[1]

Bent double, like old beggars under sacks,
Knock-kneed, coughing like hags, we cursed through sludge,
Till on the haunting flares we turned our backs
And towards our distant rest began to trudge.
Men marched asleep. Many had lost their boots   5

1. Part of a phrase from Horace, quoted in full in the last lines: "It is sweet and proper to die for one's country."

But limped on, blood-shod. All went lame; all blind;
Drunk with fatigue; deaf even to the hoots
Of disappointed shells that dropped behind.

Gas! Gas! Quick, boys!—An ecstasy of fumbling,
Fitting the clumsy helmets just in time;
But someone still was yelling out and stumbling
And floundering like a man in fire or lime.—
Dim, through the misty panes and thick green light
As under a green sea, I saw him drowning.

In all my dreams, before my helpless sight,
He plunges at me, guttering, choking, drowning.

If in some smothering dreams you too could pace
Behind the wagon that we flung him in,
And watch the white eyes writhing in his face,
His hanging face, like a devil's sick of sin;
If you could hear, at every jolt, the blood
Come gargling from the froth-corrupted lungs,
Obscene as cancer, bitter as the cud
Of vile, incurable sores on innocent tongues,—
My friend, you would not tell with such high zest
To children ardent for some desperate glory,
The old Lie: Dulce et decorum est
Pro patria mori.

1917

RICHARD EBERHART

The Fury of Aerial Bombardment

You would think the fury of aerial bombardment
Would rouse God to relent; the infinite spaces
Are still silent. He looks on shock-pried faces.
History, even, does not know what is meant.

You would feel that after so many centuries
God would give man to repent; yet he can kill
As Cain could, but with multitudinous will,
No farther advanced than in his ancient furies.

Was man made stupid to see his own stupidity?
Is God by definition indifferent, beyond us all?
Is the eternal truth man's fighting soul
Wherein the Beast ravens in its own avidity?

Of Van Wettering I speak, and Averill,
Names on a list, whose faces I do not recall

But they are gone to early death, who late in school   15
Distinguished the belt feed lever from the belt holding pawl.[2]   1947

ROBERT BRINGHURST

For the Bones of Josef Mengele, Disinterred June 1985

Master of Auschwitz, angel of death,
murderer, deep in Brazil they are breaking
your bones—or somebody's bones: my
bones, your bones, his bones, whose
bones does not matter. Deep in Brazil they are breaking   5
bones like loaves of old bread. The angel
of death is not drowning but eating.

Speak! they are saying. *Speak! speak!*
If you don't speak we will open and read you!
Something you too might have said in your time.   10
Are these bones guilty? they say. And the bones
are already talking. The bones, with guns
to their heads, are already saying, *Yes!*
Yes! It is true, we are guilty!

Butcher, baker, lampshade and candlestick   15
maker: yes, it is true. But the bones? The bones,
earth, metals, teeth, the body?
These are not guilty. The minds of the dead
are not to be found in the bones of the dead.
The minds of the dead are not anywhere to be found,   20
outside the minds of the living.   1986

MARY JO SALTER

Welcome to Hiroshima

is what you first see, stepping off the train:
a billboard brought to you in living English
by Toshiba Electric. While a channel
silent in the TV of the brain

projects those flickering re-runs of a cloud   5
that brims its risen columnful like beer

2. Machine-gun parts.

and, spilling over, hangs its foamy head,
you feel a thirst for history: what year

it started to be safe to breathe the air,
10   and when to drink the blood and scum afloat
on the Ohta River. But no, the water's clear,
they pour it for your morning cup of tea

in one of the countless sunny coffee shops
whose plastic dioramas advertise
15   mutations of cuisine behind the glass:
a pancake sandwich; a pizza someone tops

with a maraschino cherry. Passing by
the Peace Park's floral hypocenter (where
how bravely, or with what mistaken cheer,
20   humanity erased its own erasure),

you enter the memorial museum
and through more glass are served, as on a dish
of blistered grass, three mannequins. Like gloves
a mother clips to coatsleeves, strings of flesh

25   hang from their fingertips; or as if tied
to recall a duty for us, *Reverence*
the dead whose mourners too shall soon be dead,
but all commemoration's swallowed up

in questions of bad taste, how re-created
30   horror mocks the grim original,
and thinking at last *They should have left it all*
you stop. This is the wristwatch of a child.

Jammed on the moment's impact, resolute
to communicate some message, although mute,
35   it gestures with its hands at eight-fifteen
and eight-fifteen and eight-fifteen again

while tables of statistics on the wall
update the news by calling on a roll
of tape, death gummed on death, and in the case
40   adjacent, an exhibit under glass

is glass itself: a shard the bomb slammed in
a woman's arm at eight-fifteen, but some
three decades on—as if to make it plain
hope's only as renewable as pain,

45   and as if all the unsung
debasements of the past may one day come
rising to the surface once again—
worked its filthy way out like a tongue.

1984

WILLIAM STAFFORD

At the Bomb Testing Site

At noon in the desert a panting lizard
waited for history, its elbows tense,
watching the curve of a particular road
as if something might happen.

It was looking at something farther off   5
than people could see, an important scene
acted in stone for little selves
at the flute end of consequences.

There was just a continent without much on it
under a sky that never cared less.   10
Ready for a change, the elbows waited.
The hands gripped hard on the desert.   1966

DUDLEY RANDALL

Ballad of Birmingham

*(On the bombing of a church in
Birmingham, Alabama, 1963)*

"Mother dear, may I go downtown
Instead of out to play,
And march the streets of Birmingham
In a Freedom March today?"

"No, baby, no, you may not go,   5
For the dogs are fierce and wild,
And clubs and hoses, guns and jails
Aren't good for a little child."

"But, mother, I won't be alone.
Other children will go with me,   10
And march the streets of Birmingham
To make our country free."

"No, baby, no, you may not go,
For I fear those guns will fire.
But you may go to church instead   15
And sing in the children's choir."

She has combed and brushed her night-dark hair,
And bathed rose petal sweet,

And drawn white gloves on her small brown hands,
And white shoes on her feet.

20 The mother smiled to know her child
Was in the sacred place,
But that smile was the last smile
To come upon her face.

25 For when she heard the explosion,
Her eyes grew wet and wild.
She raced through the streets of Birmingham
Calling for her child.

She clawed through bits of glass and brick,
30 Then lifted out a shoe.
"Oh, here's the shoe my baby wore,
But, baby, where are you?"   1969

AI

Riot Act, April 29, 1992

I'm going out and get something.
I don't know what.
I don't care.
Whatever's out there, I'm going to get it.
5 Look in those shop windows at boxes
and boxes of Reeboks and Nikes
to make me fly through the air
like Michael Jordan
like Magic.
10 While I'm up there, I see Spike Lee.
Looks like he's flying too
straight through the glass
that separates me
from the virtual reality
15 I watch everyday on TV.
I know the difference between
what it is and what it isn't.
Just because I can't touch it
doesn't mean it isn't real.
20 All I have to do is smash the screen,
reach in and take what I want.
Break out of prison.
South Central homey's newly risen
from the night of living dead,
25 but this time he lives,
he gets to give the zombies

a taste of their own medicine.
Open wide and let me in,
or else I'll set your world on fire,
but you pretend that you don't hear.   30
You haven't heard the word is coming down
like the hammer of the gun
of this black son, locked out of the big house,
while massa looks out the window and sees only smoke.
Massa doesn't see anything else,   35
not because he can't,
but because he won't.
He'd rather hear me talking about mo' money,
mo' honeys and gold chains
and see me carrying my favorite things   40
from looted stores
than admit that underneath my Raiders' cap,
the aftermath is staring back
unblinking through the camera's lens,
courtesy of CNN,   45
my arms loaded with boxes of shoes
that I will sell at the swap meet
to make a few cents on the declining dollar.
And if I destroy myself
and my neighborhood   50
"ain't nobody's business, if I do,"
but the police are knocking hard
at my door
and before I can open it,
they break it down   55
and drag me in the yard.
They take me in to be processed and charged,
to await trial,
while Americans forget
the day the wealth finally trickled down   60
to the rest of us.   1993

Ideas and Consciousness

ANNA LAETITIA BARBAULD

Washing-Day

The Muses are turned gossips; they have lost
The buskined step, and clear high-sounding phrase,

Language of gods. Come then, domestic Muse,
In slipshod measure loosely prattling on
Of farm or orchard, pleasant curds and cream,
Or drowning flies, or shoe lost in the mire
By little whimpering boy, with rueful face;
Come, Muse, and sing the dreaded Washing-Day.
Ye who beneath the yoke of wedlock bend,
With bowèd soul, full well ye ken the day
Which week, smooth sliding after week, brings on
Too soon;—for to that day nor peace belongs
Nor comfort;—ere the first grey streak of dawn,
The red-armed washers come and chase respose.
Nor pleasant smile, nor quaint device of mirth,
E'er visited that day: the very cat,
From the wet kitchen scared, and reeking hearth,
Visits the parlor,—an unwonted guest.
The silent breakfast-meal is soon dispatched;
Uninterrupted, save by anxious looks
Cast at the lowering sky, if sky should lower.
From that last evil, O preserve us, heavens!
For should the skies pour down, adieu to all
Remains of quiet: then expect to hear
Of sad disasters—dirt and gravel stains
Hard to efface, and loaded lines at once
Snapped short—and linen-horse by dog thrown down,
And all the petty miseries of life.
Saints have been calm while stretched upon the rack,
And Guatimozin smiled on burning coals;
But never yet did housewife notable
Greet with a smile a rainy washing-day.
—But grant the welkin fair, require not thou
Who call'st thyself perchance the master there,
Or study swept, or nicely dusted coat,
Or usual 'tendance;—ask not, indiscreet,
Thy stockings mended, though the yawning rents
Gape wide as Erebus; nor hope to find
Some snug recess impervious: shouldst thou try
The 'customed garden walks, thine eye shall rue
The budding fragrance of thy tender shrubs,
Myrtle or rose, all crushed beneath the weight
Of coarse-checked apron—with impatient hand
Twitched off when showers impend: or crossing lines
Shall mar thy musings, as the wet cold sheet
Flaps in thy face abrupt. Woe to the friend
Whose evil stars have urged him forth to claim
On such a day the hospitable rites!
Looks, blank at best, and stinted courtesy,
Shall he receive. Vainly he feeds his hopes

With dinner of roast chicken, savoury pie,
Or tart or pudding: — pudding he nor tart
That day shall eat; nor, though the husband try,
Mending what can't be helped, to kindle mirth
From cheer deficient, shall his consort's brow   55
Clear up propitious: — the unlucky guest
In silence dines, and early slinks away.
I well remember, when a child, the awe
This day struck into me; for then the maids,
I scarce knew why, looked cross, and drove me from them: 60
Nor soft caress could I obtain, nor hope
Usual indulgencies; jelly or creams,
Relic of costly suppers, and set by
For me their petted one; or buttered toast,
When butter was forbid; or thrilling tale   65
Of ghost, or witch, or murder — so I went
And sheltered me beside the parlour fire:
There my dear grandmother, eldest of forms,
Tended the little ones, and watched from harm,
Anxiously fond, though oft her spectacles   70
With elfin cunning hid, and oft the pins
Drawn from her ravelled stocking, might have soured
One less indulgent. —
At intervals my mother's voice was heard,
Urging dispatch: briskly the work went on,   75
All hands employed to wash, to rinse, to wring,
To fold, and starch, and clap, and iron, and plait.
Then would I sit down, and ponder much
Why washings were. Sometimes through hollow bowl
Of pipe amused we blew, and sent aloft   80
The floating bubbles; little dreaming then
To see, Montgolfier, thy silken ball
Ride buoyant through the clouds — so near approach
The sports of children and the toils of men.
Earth, air, and sky, and ocean, hath its bubbles,   85
And verse is one of them — this most of all.   1797

DORIANNE LAUX

The Laundromat

My clothes somersault in the dryer. At thirty
I float in and out of a new kind of horniness,
the kind where you get off on words and gestures;
long talks about art are foreplay, the climax
is watching a man eat a Napoleon while he drives.   5

Across from me a fifty year old matron folds clothes,
her eyes focused on the nipples of a young man in
silk jogging shorts. He looks up, catching her.
She giggles and blurts out, "Hot, isn't it?"
A man on my right eyes the line of my shorts, waiting
for me to bend over. I do. An act of animal kindness.
A long black jogger swings in off the street to
splash his face in the sink and I watch the room
become a sweet humid jungle. We crowd around
the Amazon at the watering hole, twitching our noses
like wildebeests or buffalo, snorting, rooting out
mates in the heat. I want to hump every moving thing
in this place. I want to lie down in the dry dung
and dust and twist to scratch my back. I want to
stretch and prowl and grow lazy in the shade. I want
to have a slew of cubs. "Do you have change for
a quarter?" he asks, scratching the inside of his thigh.
Back in the laundromat my socks are sticking to my
sheets. Caught in the crackle of static electricity,
I fold my underwear. I notice the honey-colored
stains in each silk crotch. Odd-shaped, like dreams,
I make my panties into neat squares and drop them,
smiling, into the wicker basket.

10

15

20

25

1990

MARGE PIERCY

What's That Smell in the Kitchen?

All over America women are burning dinners.
It's lambchops in Peoria; it's haddock
in Providence; it's steak in Chicago;
tofu delight in Big Sur; red
rice and beans in Dallas.
All over America women are burning
food they're supposed to bring with calico
smile on platters glittering like wax.
Anger sputters in her brainpan, confined
but spewing out missiles of hot fat.
Carbonized despair presses like a clinker
from a barbecue against the back of her eyes.
If she wants to grill anything, it's
her husband spitted over a slow fire.
If she wants to serve him anything
it's a dead rat with a bomb in its belly
ticking like the heart of an insomniac.
Her life is cooked and digested,

5

10

15

nothing but leftovers in Tupperware.
Look, she says, once I was roast duck   20
on your platter with parsley but now I am Spam.
Burning dinner is not incompetence but war.   1983

ELIZABETH[1]

When I Was Fair and Young

When I was fair and young, and favor graced me,
    Of many was I sought, their mistress for to be;
But I did scorn them all, and answered them therefore,
    "Go, go, go, seek some otherwhere,
        Importune me no more!"   5

How many weeping eyes I made to pine with woe,
    How many sighing hearts, I have no skill to show;
Yet I the prouder grew, and answered them therefore,
    "Go, go, go, seek some otherwhere,
        Importune me no more!"   10

Then spake fair Venus' son, that proud victorious boy,[2]
    And said: "Fine dame, since that you be so coy,
I will so pluck your plumes that you shall say no more,
    'Go, go, go, seek some otherwhere,
        Importune me no more!' "   15

When he had spake these words, such change grew in my breast
    That neither night nor day since that, I could take any rest.
Then lo! I did repent that I had said before,
    "Go, go, go, seek some otherwhere,
ca. 1585?   Importune me no more!"   20

KATHERINE PHILIPS

L'amitié: To Mrs. M. Awbrey

Soul of my soul, my Joy, my crown, my friend!
A name which all the rest doth comprehend;
How happy are we now, whose souls are grown,
By an incomparable mixture, One:
Whose well acquainted minds are now as near   5
As Love, or vows, or secrets can endear.

---

1. The attribution of this poem to Queen Elizabeth I of England (1533–1603) is likely but not certain.
2. Cupid.

I have no thought but what's to thee reveal'd,
Nor thou desire that is from me conceal'd.
Thy heart locks up my secrets richly set,
10   And my breast is thy private cabinet.
Thou shedst no tear but what my moisture lent,
And if I sigh, it is thy breath is spent.
United thus, what horror can appear
Worthy our sorrow, anger, or our fear?
15   Let the dull world alone to talk and fight,
And with their vast ambitions nature fright;
Let them despise so innocent a flame,
While Envy, Pride, and Faction play their game:
But we by Love sublim'd so high shall rise,
20   To pity Kings, and Conquerors despise,
Since we that sacred union have engrossed,
Which they and all the sullen world have lost.   1667

EDNA ST. VINCENT MILLAY

[Women have loved before as I love now]

Women have loved before as I love now;
At least, in lively chronicles of the past—
Of Irish waters by a Cornish prow
Or Trojan waters by a Spartan mast
5   Much to their cost invaded—here and there,
Hunting the amorous line, skimming the rest,
I find some woman bearing as I bear
Love like a burning city in the breast.
I think however that of all alive
10   I only in such utter, ancient way
Do suffer love; in me alone survive
The unregenerate passions of a day
When treacherous queens, with death upon the tread,
Heedless and wilful, took their knights to bed.   1931

ANNE SEXTON

The Farmer's Wife

From the hodge porridge
of their country lust,
their local life in Illinois,
where all their acres look

like a sprouting broom factory,   5
they name just ten years now
that she has been his habit;
as again tonight he'll say
honey bunch let's go
and she will not say how there   10
must be more to living
than this brief bright bridge
of the raucous bed or even
the slow braille touch of him
like a heavy god grown light,   15
that old pantomime of love
that she wants although
it leaves her still alone,
built back again at last,
mind's apart from him, living   20
her own self in her own words
and hating the sweat of the house
they keep when they finally lie
each in separate dreams
and then how she watches him,   25
still strong in the blowzy bag
of his usual sleep while
her young years bungle past
their same marriage bed
and she wishes him cripple, or poet,   30
or even lonely, or sometimes,
better, my lover, dead.   1960

LIZ ROSENBERG

Married Love

The trees are uncurling their first
green messages: Spring, and some man
lets his arm brush my arm in a darkened
theatre. Faint-headed, I fight the throb.
Later I dream   5
the gas attendant puts a cool hand
on my breast, asking a question.
Slowly I rise through the surface of the dream,
brushing his hand and my own heat away.

Young, I burned to marry. Married,   10
the smolder goes on underground,
clutching at weeds, writhing everywhere.
I'm trying to talk to a friend on burning

issues, flaming from the feet up,
drinking in his breath, touching his wrist.
I want to grab the pretty woman
on the street, seize the falcon
by its neck, beat my way into whistling steam.

I turn to you in the dark, oh husband,
watching your lit breath circle the pillow.
Then you turn to me, throwing first one limb
and then another over me, in the easy brotherly
lust of marriage. I cling to you
as if I were a burning ship and you
could save me, as if I won't go sliding down
beneath you soon; as if our lives are made of rise
and fall, and we could ride this out forever,
with longing's thunder rolling heavy in our arms.

1986

ADRIENNE RICH

Delta

If you have taken this rubble for my past
raking through it for fragments you could sell
know that I long ago moved on
deeper into the heart of the matter

If you think you can grasp me, think again:
my story flows in more than one direction
a delta springing from the riverbed
with its five fingers spread

1989

JUDITH ORTIZ COFER

Unspoken

When I hug you tight at bedtime
you wince in pain for the tender
swelling of new breasts.
Nothing is said, both of us aware
of the covenant of silence
we must maintain through the rending
apart that is adolescence.
            But it won't always
be confusion and hurting, the body
will find itself through this pain;

remember Michelangelo, who believed
that in marble, form already exists,
the artist's hands simply pulling it out
into the world.
          I want to tell you about men: 15
the pleasure of a lover's hands on skin
you think may rip at elbows and knees
stretching over a frame like clothes
you've almost outgrown; of the moment
when a woman first feels   20
a baby's mouth at her breast, opening her
like the hand of God in Genesis, the moment
when all that led to this seems right.
          Instead I say, *sweet dreams,*
for the secrets hidden under the blanket   25
like a forbidden book

I'm not supposed to know you've read.   1993

SHARON OLDS

The Elder Sister

When I look at my elder sister now
I think how she had to go first, down through the
birth canal, to force her way
head-first through the tiny channel,
the pressure of Mother's muscles on her brain,   5
the tight walls scraping her skin.
Her face is still narrow from it, the long
hollow cheeks of a Crusader on a tomb,
and her inky eyes have the look of someone who has
been in prison a long time and   10
knows they can send her back. I look at her
body and think how her breasts were the first to
rise, slowly, like swans on a pond.
By the time mine came along, they were just
two more birds in the flock, and when the hair   15
rose on the white mound of her flesh, like
threads of water out of the ground, it was the
first time, but when mine came
they knew about it. I used to think
only in terms of her harshness, sitting and   20
pissing on me in bed, but now I
see I had her before me always
like a shield. I look at her wrinkles, her clenched
jaws, her frown-lines—I see they are

25 the dents on my shield, the blows that did not reach me.
She protected me, not as a mother
protects a child, with love, but as a
hostage protects the one who makes her
escape as I made my escape, with my sister's
30 body held in front of me.   1984

ERICA JONG

Penis Envy

I envy men who can yearn
with infinite emptiness
toward the body of a woman,

hoping that the yearning
5 will make a child,
that the emptiness itself
will fertilize the darkness.

Women have no illusions about this,
being at once
10 houses, tunnels,
cups & cupbearers,
knowing emptiness as a temporary state
between two fullnesses,
& seeing no romance in it.

15 If I were a man
doomed to that infinite emptiness,
& having no choice in the matter,
I would, like the rest, no doubt,
find a woman
20 & christen her moonbelly,
madonna, gold-haired goddess
& make her the tent of my longing,
the silk parachute of my lust,
the blue-eyed icon of my sacred sexual itch,
25 the mother of my hunger.

But since I am a woman,
I must not only inspire the poem
but also type it,
not only conceive the child
30 but also bear it,
not only bear the child
but also bathe it,

not only bathe the child
but also feed it,
not only feed the child
but also carry it   35
everywhere, everywhere . . .

while men write poems
on the mysteries of motherhood.

I envy men who can yearn   40
with infinite emptiness.   1975

DOROTHY PARKER

Indian Summer

In youth, it was a way I had
    To do my best to please,
And change, with every passing lad,
    To suit his theories.

But now I know the things I know,   5
    And do the things I do;
And if you do not like me so,
    To hell, my love, with you!   1937

RUTH STONE

Second-Hand Coat

I feel
in her pockets; she wore nice cotton gloves,
kept a handkerchief box, washed her undies,
ate at the Holiday Inn, had a basement freezer,
belonged to a bridge club.   5
I think when I wake in the morning
that I have turned into her.
She hangs in the hall downstairs,
a shadow with pulled threads.
I slip her over my arms, skin of a matron.   10
Where are you? I say to myself, to the orphaned body,
and her coat says,
Get your purse, have you got your keys?   1987

KAY SMITH

Annunciation

for Kathy

In all the old paintings
The Virgin is reading—
No one knows what,
When she is disturbed
By an angel with a higher mission,
Beyond books.

She looks up reluctantly,
Still marking the place with her finger.
The angel is impressive,
With red shoes and just
A hint of wing and shine everywhere.
Listening to the measured message
The Virgin bows her head,
Her eyes aslant
Between the angel and the book.

At the Uffizi[3]
We stood
Before a particularly beautiful angel
And a hesitant Sienese Virgin,
We two sometimes women.
Believing we could ignore
All messages,
Unobliged to wings or words,
We laughed in the vibrant space
Between the two,
Somewhere in the angled focus
Of the Virgin's eye.

Now, in the harder times,
I do not laugh so often;
Still the cheap postcard in my room
Glints with the angel's robe.
I look with envy
At the angel and the book,
Wishing I had chosen
One or the other,
Anything but the space between.

1986

---

3. The richest art gallery in Italy, located in Florence. Its collection includes a painting of the Annunciation by the 14th-century Sienese painter Simone Martini.

PAULETTE JILES

Paper Matches

My aunts washed dishes while the uncles
squirted each other on the lawn with
   garden hoses. Why are we in here,
I said, and they are out there.
   That's the way it is,
   said Aunt Hetty, the shrivelled-up one.   5
   I have the rages that small animals have,
being small, being animal.
   Written on me was a message,
"At Your Service" like a book of   10
paper matches. One by one we were
taken out and struck.
   We come bearing supper.
our heads on fire.   1973

▼ ▼ ▼

QUESTIONS

1. What additional information would you like to have about the events referred to in "Frederick Douglass" and "Ballad of Birmingham"? What details in these poems seem to require additional information about the events on which each is based? What details about the life and writings of Frederick Douglass, and about his character, would help your reading of "Frederick Douglass"? What do you make of the mention of "dogs," "clubs," and "hoses" in "Ballad of Birmingham"? What did "Freedom March" mean in 1969? Given the poem's structure and its portrayal of children's voices and attitudes, what difference might it make to your reading of the poem if you had factual information about the actual casualties of the bombing? If you were editing this poem, what other footnotes would you provide? Reread "Sir Patrick Spens" (p. 218). In what ways does Randall's poem allude to it? why?

2. What details about the physical suffering from poison gas are specifically suggested in "Dulce et Decorum Est"? what details about the physical effects of atomic explosions in "Welcome to Hiroshima"? How accurate are these representations? Using the reference resources in your college library, look up news accounts of gassings in World War I and the atomic bombing of Hiroshima, and compare the journalistic details with those given in the poems.

How careful does each poet seem to have been in representing historical events? What evidence do you find of distortion or "poetic license"? Which details are specifically chosen for powerful rhetorical effects in each poem?

3. Compare the images of fire and burning in "What's That Smell in the Kitchen?," "Married Love," and "Paper Matches." How are the images used differently in each poem? What common thread of meaning informs the images in these poems? On what kind of cultural assumptions about women and their roles do these images seem to be based? In what ways are these images like other images of passion in other poems you have read? In what ways are the images like other images of destruction?

4. What is the relationship between burning "to marry" (line 10), "burning issues" (lines 13–14), and the "burning ship" (line 24) in "Married Love"? What, exactly, is the dramatic situation in the poem? In what specific ways does the speaker's attitude change in the course of the poem? How do you interpret the poem's "as ifs" in final stanza? What is the poem's ultimate attitude toward "married love"?

5. Which poems in the *Ideas and Consciousness* group are especially concerned to suggest the importance of physical space? In what ways do they portray its absence? In what ways do they represent the male sense of a woman's "place"? How does the image of "rubble" in "Delta" (line 1) relate to the images of place, material evidence, and destruction in other poems? Why does the speaker of "Delta" describe herself and her past as ungraspable (line 5)? In what sense has she "moved on" (line 3) beyond the "rubble"? Explain the ironies in the phrase "the heart of the matter" (line 4). Explain the poem's title.

6. What images of passivity, deferentiality, and compliance can you find about women in the poems in this group? How is each image treated in the individual poem? In what ways do images of assertion and resistance compete with these images?

WRITING SUGGESTIONS

1. Using reference materials available in your college's library, construct a short but detailed narrative (of about 500–700 words) of the Birmingham bombing. Then "read" the poem in the context of the full story, showing how the poem uses specific details of the incident to create its effects.

2. Compare the speaker of Millay's "Women have loved before as I love now" with Jong's "Penis Envy." In an essay of about 800 words, show how each speaker characterizes herself through attitudes toward other people.

13 THE PROCESS OF CREATION

Poems do not write themselves. Even if the idea for a poem comes in a flash (as it sometimes does), poets often struggle to get the final effect just right. For some poems that means draft after draft, and sometimes poets write more than one version of a poem and allow them to compete as rival authorized texts, or later revise the poem and alter it in some crucial way. Often a study of the manuscript or of the several drafts suggests the various kinds of decisions a poet may make as a poem moves toward its final form. In this chapter you will find examples of several poems as they take shape—or take different forms—in the poet's mind.

The first example involves early drafts of the first stanza of Richard Wilbur's "Love Calls Us to the Things of This World," which in its finished form is printed right after the drafts. Wilbur is one of the most careful craftsmen writing today, and in the early drafts of the first stanza we can see him moving toward the brilliant and surprising effects he achieves in the "final" version, that is, the version the poet decided to publish. Someone is just awaking, and through a window sees laundry on a clothesline blowing in the breeze. But he is not quite awake and not quite sure what he sees: his body and soul, the poet says playfully in lines 26 and 27, are not yet quite reunited, and he seems for a moment still suspended in a world of spirit and dream; the blowing clothes look like disembodied angels. Ultimately, the poem captures that sense of suspension between worlds, the uncertainty of where one is and what is happening in that first half-conscious moment when normal physical laws don't seem to apply. It is a delicate moment to catch, and in the six successive drafts printed below we can see the poet moving toward the more precise effect of the completed poem.

In the first three drafts the speaker seems to speak about himself—not quite right because that device makes him too conscious, and part of the basic effect of the poem involves a lack of consciousness and control. By the fourth draft "My eyes came open" has become "The eyes open," and the effect of being a little lost and unsure of identity is becoming clearer. Another major change in the early drafts is that the sound of the laundry pulley changes from "squeak" to "shriek" to "cry": the first two words capture the shrill sound of a moving pulley faithfully, but "cry" makes it seem personal and human, and now it is as if the pulleys were in fact calling the speaker from sleep. The image changes too: in the first draft the world of sleep is a brothel, but those connotations are eliminated in later drafts, and instead by the sixth draft the "spirit" has become "soul" and is bodiless. Every new draft changes the conception just a little, and in the drafts printed here we can see effects gradually getting clearer in the poet's mind and falling into place. Notice how rhyme appears in draft and then disappears again, notice how the poet tries out and rejects words that don't have quite the right connotation: "wallow" (draft c), "frothing" (draft d), "rout" (draft f). In a detailed set of drafts like this one, we can see the poet weighing different visual and verbal possibilities, choosing every single word with care.

The other poems and passages similarly give us a chance to compare the effects of more than one version of a poem or passage. In several cases, a poem is "finished" in more than one version, and the poets invite us to choose among the competing versions instead of choosing one themselves. In each selection a few crucial words create significant differences in the text.

▼ ▼ ▼

1. Early drafts of the first stanza of "Love Calls Us to the Things of This World," reprinted by permission of the author:

(a) My eyes came open to the squeak of pulleys
My spirit, shocked from the brothel of itself

(b) My eyes came open to the shriek of pulleys,
And the soul, spirited from its proper wallow,
Hung in the air as bodiless and hollow

(c) My eyes came open to the pulleys' cry.
The soul, spirited from its proper wallow,
Hung in the air as bodiless and hollow
As light that frothed upon the wall opposing;
But what most caught my eyes at their unclosing
Was two gray ropes that yanked across the sky.
One after one into the window frame
. . . the hosts of laundry came

(d)   The eyes open to a cry of pulleys,
And the soul, so suddenly spirited from sleep,
As morning sunlight frothing on the floor,
While just outside the window
The air is solid with a dance of angels.

(e)   The eyes open to a cry of pulleys,
And spirited from sleep, the astounded soul
Hangs for a moment bodiless and simple
As dawn light in the moment of its breaking:
    Outside the open window
The air is crowded with a

(f)   The eyes open to a cry of pulleys,
And spirited from sleep, the astounded soul
Hangs for a moment bodiless and simple
As false dawn
    Outside the open window,
Their air is leaping with a rout of angels.
    Some are in bedsheets, some are in dresses,
    it does not seem to matter

Final Version, 1956

The eyes open to a cry of pulleys,
And spirited from sleep, the astounded soul
Hangs for a moment bodiless and simple
As false dawn.
        Outside the open window   5
The morning air is all awash with angels.

Some are in bed-sheets, some are in blouses,
Some are in smocks: but truly there they are.
Now they are rising together in calm swells
Of halcyon[1] feeling, filling whatever they wear   10
With the deep joy of their impersonal breathing;
    Now they are flying in place,[2] conveying
The terrible speed of their omnipresence, moving
And staying like white water; and now of a sudden
They swoon down into so rapt a quiet   15
That nobody seems to be there.
        The soul shrinks

From all that it is about to remember,
From the punctual rape of every blessèd day,
And cries,   20
    "Oh, let there be nothing on earth but laundry,
Nothing but rosy hands in the rising steam
And clear dances done in the sight of heaven."

Yet, as the sun acknowledges
With a warm look the world's hunks and colors,

---

1. Serene.   2. Like planes in a formation.

The soul descends once more in bitter love
To accept the waking body, saying now
In a changed voice as the man yawns and rises,

    "Bring them down from their ruddy gallows;
Let there be clean linen for the backs of thieves;
Let lovers go fresh and sweet to be undone,
And the heaviest nuns walk in a pure floating
Of dark habits,
          keeping their difficult balance."

30

2. Two versions of Keats's "Bright star! would I were stedfast as thou art!"

Original Version, 1819

Bright star! would I were stedfast as thou art!
Not in lone splendor hung amid the night;
Not watching, with eternal lids apart,
Like Nature's devout sleepless Eremite,
The morning waters at their priestlike task
Of pure ablution round earth's human shores;
Or, gazing on the new soft fallen mask
Of snow upon the mountains and moors:—
No;—yet still stedfast, still unchangeable.
Cheek-pillow'd on my Love's white ripening breast,
To touch, for ever, its warm sink and swell,
Awake, for ever, in a sweet unrest;
To hear, to feel her tender taken breath,
Half-passionless, and so swoon on to death.

5

10

Revised Version, 1820

Bright star! would I were steadfast as thou art—
   Not in lone splendor hung aloft the night
And watching, with eternal lids apart,
   Like nature's patient, sleepless Eremite,
The moving waters at their priestlike task
   Of pure ablution round earth's human shores,
Or gazing on the new soft fallen mask
   Of snow upon the mountains and the moors—
No—yet still steadfast, still unchangeable,
   Pillowed upon my fair love's ripening breast,
To feel for ever its soft fall and swell,
   Awake for ever in a sweet unrest,
Still, still to hear her tender-taken breath,
And so live ever—or else swoon to death.

5

10

3. Two published versions of Keats's "La Belle Dame sans Merci: A Ballad."

Original Version, 1819

I

O what can ail thee, knight-at-arms,
 Alone and palely loitering?
The sedge has withered from the lake,
 And no birds sing.

II

O what can ail thee, knight-at-arms,   5
 So haggard and so woe-begone?
The squirrel's granary is full,
 And the harvest's done.

III

I see a lily on thy brow,
 With anguish moist and fever dew,   10
And on thy cheeks a fading rose
 Fast withereth too.

IV

I met a lady in the meads[3]
 Full beautiful—a faery's child,
Her hair was long her foot was light,   15
 And her eyes were wild.

V

I made a garland for her head,
 And bracelets too, and fragrant zone,[4]
She looked at me as she did love,
 And made sweet moan.   20

VI

I set her on my pacing steed,
 And nothing else saw all day long,
For sidelong would she bend, and sing
 A faery's song.

VII

She found me roots of relish sweet   25
 And honey wild, and manna dew,
And sure in language strange she said,
 "I love thee true."

3. Meadows. 4. Girdle.

VIII

She took me to her elfin grot,
    And there she wept, and sighed full sore,
And there I shut her wild wild eyes
    With kisses four.

IX

And there she lullèd me asleep,
    And there I dreamed—Ah! woe betide!
The latest[5] dream I ever dreamed
    On the cold hill side.

Revised Version, 1820

I

Ah, what can ail thee, wretched wight,
    Alone and palely loitering;
The sedge is withered from the lake,
    And no birds sing.

II

Ah, what can ail thee, wretched wight,
    So haggard and so woe-begone?
The squirrel's granary is full,
    And the harvest's done.

III

I see a lily on thy brow,
    With anguish moist and fever dew;
And on thy cheek a fading rose
    Fast withereth too.

IV

I met a lady in the meads
    Full beautiful, a fairy's child;
Her hair was long, her foot was light,
    And her eyes were wild.

V

I set her on my pacing steed,
    And nothing else saw all day long;
For sideways would she lean, and sing
    A fairy's song.

5. Last.

VI

I made a garland for her head,
  And bracelets too, and fragrant zone:
She looked at me as she did love,
  And made sweet moan.

VII

She found me roots of relish sweet,   25
  And honey wild, and manna dew;
And sure in language strange she said,
  "I love thee true."

VIII

She took me to her elfin grot,
  And there she gazéd and sighéd deep,   30
And there I shut her wild sad eyes—
  So kissed to sleep.

IX

And there we slumbered on the moss,
  And there I dreamed, ah woe betide,
The latest dream I ever dreamed   35
  On the cold hill side.

X

I saw pale kings and princes too,
  Pale warriors, death-pale were they all;
They cried—"La Belle Dame sans Merci
  Hath thee in thrall!"   40

XI

I saw their starved lips in the gloam,
  With horrid warning gapéd wide,
And I awoke and found me here,
  On the cold hill's side.

XII

And this is why I sojourn here,   45
  Alone and palely loitering,
Though the sedge has withered from the lake,
  And no birds sing.

4. Three versions of Alexander Pope's "Ode on Solitude."

1709 Manuscript Version

Happy the man, who free from care,
The business and the noise of towns,
Contented breathes his native air,
  In his own grounds.

5   Whose herds with milk, whose fields with bread,
    Whose flocks supply him with attire,
    Whose trees in summer yield him shade,
              In winter fire.

    Blest! who can unconcern'dly find
10 His years slide silently away,
    In health of body, peace of mind,
              Quiet by day,

    Repose at night; study and ease
    Together mix'd; sweet recreation,
15 And innocence, which most does please,
              With meditation.

    Thus let me live, unseen, unknown;
    Thus unlamented let me die;
    Steal from the world, and not a stone
20   Tell where I lie.

First Printed Version, 1717

    How happy he, who free from care,
    The rage of courts, and noise of towns;
    Contented breathes his native air,
              In his own grounds.
5   Whose herds with milk, whose fields with bread,
    Whose flocks supply him with attire.
    Whose trees in summer yield him shade,
              In winter fire.
    Blest! who can unconcern'dly find
10 Hours, days, and years slide swift away,
    In health of body, peace of mind,
              Quiet by day,
    Sound sleep by night; study and ease
    Together mix'd; sweet recreation,
15 And innocence, which most does please,
              With meditation.
    Thus let me live, unheard, unknown;
    Thus unlamented let me die;
    Steal from the world, and not a stone
20   Tell where I lie.

Final Version, 1736

    Happy the man, whose wish and care
    A few paternal acres bound,
    Content to breathe his native air,
              In his own ground.

Whose herds with milk, whose fields with bread,   5
Whose flocks supply him with attire,
Whose trees in summer yield him shade,
    In winter fire.
Blest! who can unconcern'dly find
Hours, days, and years slide soft away,   10
In health of body, peace of mind,
    Quiet by day,
Sound sleep by night; study and ease
Together mix'd; sweet recreation,
And innocence, which most does please,   15
    With meditation.
Thus let me live, unseen, unknown;
Thus unlamented let me die;
Steal from the world, and not a stone
    Tell where I lie.   20

5. This famous folk ballad was sung and recited in many variations; here
are two written versions. Neither version can be dated precisely.

"O where ha' you been, Lord Randal, my son?
And where ha' you been, my handsome young man?"
"I ha' been at the greenwood; mother, mak my bed soon,
For I'm wearied wi' huntin', and fain wad[6] lie down."

"And wha met ye there, Lord Randal, my son?   5
And wha met you there, my handsome young man?"
"O I met wi' my true-love; mother, mak my bed soon,
For I'm wearied wi' huntin', and fain wad lie down."

"And what did she give you, Lord Randal, my son?
And what did she give you, my handsome young man?"   10
"Eels fried in a pan; mother, mak my bed soon,
For I'm wearied wi' huntin', and fain wad lie down."

"And wha gat your leavin's, Lord Randal, my son?
And wha gat your leavin's, my handsome young man?"
"My hawks and my hounds; mother, mak my bed soon,   15
For I'm wearied wi' huntin', and fain wad lie down."

"And what becam of them, Lord Randal, my son?
And what becam of them, my handsome young man?"
"They stretched their legs out and died; mother, mak my bed soon,
For I'm wearied wi' huntin', and fain wad lie down."   20

"O I fear you are poisoned, Lord Randal, my son!
I fear you are poisoned, my handsome young man!"

6. Would like to.

"O yes, I am poisoned; mother, mak my bed soon,
For I'm sick at the heart, and I fain wad lie down."

25 "What d'ye leave to your mother, Lord Randal, my son?
What d'ye leave to your mother, my handsome young man?"
"Four and twenty milk kye;[7] mother, mak my bed soon,
For I'm sick at the heart, and I fain wad lie down."

"What d'ye leave to your sister, Lord Randal, my son?
30 What d'ye leave to your sister, my handsome young man?"
"My gold and my silver; mother, mak my bed soon,
For I'm sick at the heart, and I fain wad lie down."

"What d'ye leave to your brother, Lord Randal, my son?
What d'ye leave to your brother, my handsome young man?"
35 "My houses and my lands; mother, mak my bed soon,
For I'm sick at the heart, and I fain wad lie down."

"What d'ye leave to your true-love, Lord Randal, my son?
What d'ye leave to your true-love, my handsome young man?"
"I leave her hell and fire; mother, mak my bed soon,
40 For I'm sick at the heart, and I fain wad lie down."

Shorter Version

"O where hae ye been, Lord Randal, my son?
O where hae ye been, my handsome young man?"
"I hae been to the wild wood; mother, make my bed soon,
For I'm weary wi' hunting, and fain wald lie down."

5 "Where gat ye your dinner, Lord Randal, my son?
Where gat ye your dinner, my handsome young man?"
"I dined wi' my true-love; mother, make my bed soon,
For I'm weary wi' hunting, and fain wald lie down."

"What gat ye to your dinner, Lord Randal, my son?
10 What gat ye to your dinner, my handsome young man?"
"I gat eels boiled in broo; mother, make my bed soon,
For I'm weary wi' hunting, and fain wald lie down."

"What became of your bloodhounds, Lord Randal, my son?
What became of your bloodhounds, my handsome young man?"
15 "O they swelled and they died; mother, make my bed soon,
For I'm weary wi' hunting, and fain wald lie down."

"O I fear ye are poisoned, Lord Randal, my son!
O I fear ye are poisoned, my handsome young man!"
"O yes! I am poisoned; mother, make my bed soon,
20 For I'm sick at the heart, and I fain wald lie down."

7. Cows.

6. "Poetry," by Marianne Moore, appears on page 251 in a version that was originally published in 1921. Here are two later versions.

The 1925 Version

I too, dislike it:
there are things that are important beyond all this fiddle.
The bat, upside down; the elephant pushing,
the tireless wolf under a tree,
the base-ball fan, the statistician—   5
"business documents and schoolbooks"—
these phenomena are pleasing,
but when they have been fashioned
into that which is unknowable,   10
we are not entertained.
It may be said of all of us
that we do not admire what we cannot understand;
enigmas are not poetry.

The version Moore chose to print in her *Complete Poems* in 1967:

I, too, dislike it.
    Reading it, however, with a perfect contempt for it, one discovers in
it after all, a place for the genuine.

7. Two versions of Emily Dickinson's "Safe in their Alabaster Chambers–":

1859 Version

Safe in their Alabaster Chambers—
Untouched by Morning
And untouched by Noon—
Sleep the meek members of the Resurrection—
Rafter of satin,   5
And Roof of stone.

Light laughs the breeze
In her Castle above them—
Babbles the Bee in a stolid Ear,
Pipe the Sweet Birds in ignorant cadence—   10
Ah, what sagacity perished here!

1861 Version

Safe in their Alabaster Chambers—
Untouched by Morning—
And untouched by Noon—
Lie the meek members of the Resurrection—
Rafter of Satin—and Roof of Stone!   5

> Grand go the Years—in the Crescent—above them—
> Worlds scoop their Arcs—
> And Firmaments—row—
> Diadems—drop—and Doges—surrender—
> Soundless as dots—on a Disc of Snow—

10

8. Two versions of Wordsworth's "The Reverie of Poor Susan," the first titled, simply, "Poor Susan":

Original Version, 1800

> At the corner of Wood-Street, when day-light appears,
> There's a Thrush that sings loud, it has sung for three years:
> Poor Susan has pass'd by the spot and has heard
> In the silence of morning the song of the bird.
>
> 'Tis a note of enchantment; what ails her? She sees
> A mountain ascending, a vision of trees;
> Bright volumes of vapour through Lothbury glide,
> And a river flows on through the vale of Cheapside.
>
> Green pastures she views in the midst of the dale,
> Down which she so often has tripp'd with her pail,
> And a single small cottage, a nest like a dove's,
> The only one dwelling on earth that she loves.
>
> She looks, and her heart is in Heaven, but they fade,
> The mist and the river, the hill and the shade;
> The stream will not flow, and the hill will not rise,
> And the colours have all pass'd away from her eyes.
>
> Poor Outcast! return—to receive thee once more
> The house of thy Father will open its door,
> And thou once again, in thy plain russet gown,
> May'st hear the thrush sing from a tree of its own.

5

10

15

20

Final Version, 1802

> At the corner of Wood-Street, when day-light appears,
> There's a Thrush that sings loud, it has sung for three years:
> Poor Susan has pass'd by the spot and has heard
> In the silence of morning the song of the bird.
>
> 'Tis a note of enchantment; what ails her? She sees
> A mountain ascending, a vision of trees;
> Bright volumes of vapour through Lothbury glide,
> And a river flows on through the vale of Cheapside.
>
> Green pastures she views in the midst of the dale,
> Down which she so often has tripp'd with her pail,

5

10

And a single small cottage, a nest like a dove's,
The one only dwelling on earth that she loves.

She looks, and her heart is in Heaven, but they fade,
The mist and the river, the hill and the shade;
The stream will not flow, and the hill will not rise,   15
And the colours have all pass'd away from her eyes.

9. Drafts of "The Tyger" by William Blake. The final version, published in 1790, can be found on page 52.

First Draft[8]
     The Tyger

1   Tyger Tyger burning bright
        In the forests of the night
        What immortal hand or eye
     ~~Dare~~ Could frame thy fearful symmetry

          Burnt in
2   ~~In what~~ distant deeps or skies
  ~~The cruel~~ ~~Burnt the~~ fire of thine eyes
        On what wings dare he aspire
        What the hand dare sieze the fire

3   And what shoulder & what art
        Could twist the sinews of thy heart
        And when thy heart began to beat
        What dread hand & what dread feet

        ~~Could fetch it from the furnace deep~~
        ~~And in thy horrid ribs dare steep~~
        ~~In the well of sanguine woe~~
        ~~In what clay & what mould~~
        ~~Were thy eyes of fury rolld~~

        Where   where
4   ~~What~~ the hammer ~~what~~ the chain
        In what furnace was thy brain
                   dread grasp
        What the anvil what ~~the arm~~ arm grasp ~~clasp~~
  Dare ~~Could~~ its deadly terrors ~~clasp~~ ~~grasp~~ clasp

6   Tyger Tyger burning bright
        In the forests of the night

8. These drafts have been taken from a notebook used by William Blake, called the Rossetti MS because it was once owned by Dante Gabriel Rossetti, the Victorian poet and painter; David V. Erdman's edition of *The Notebook of William Blake* (1973) contains a photographic facsimile. The stanza numbers were written by Blake in the manuscript.

What immortal hand & eye
       frame
Dare ~~form~~ thy fearful symmetry

Trial Stanzas

Burnt in distant deeps or skies
The cruel fire of thine eye,
Could heart descend or wings aspire
What the hand dare sieze the fire

          dare he ~~smile laugh~~
5 ~~3~~   And ~~did he laugh~~ his work to see
          ankle
    ~~What the shoulder what the knee~~
    Dare
4   ~~Did~~ he who made the lamb make thee
1   When the stars threw down their spears
2   And waterd heaven with their tears

Second Full Draft

Tyger Tyger burning bright
In the forests of the night
What Immortal hand & eye
Dare frame thy fearful symmetry

And what shoulder & what art
Could twist the sinews of thy heart
And when thy heart began to beat
What dread hand & what dread feet

When the stars threw down their spears
And waterd heaven with their tears
Did he smile his work to see
Did he who made the lamb make thee

Tyger Tyger burning bright
In the forests of the night
What immortal hand & eye
Dare frame thy fearful symmetry

▽ ▽ ▽

Evaluating Poetry

How do you know a good poem when you see one? This is not an easy question to answer—partly because deciding about the *value* of poems is a complex, difficult, and often lengthy process, and partly because there is no single and absolute criterion that will measure texts and neatly divide the good from the not so good. People who long for a nice, infallible sorter—some test that will automatically pick out the best poems and distinguish variations of quality much as a litmus test separates acids from bases—often are frustrated at what they perceive to be the "relativity" of judgment in evaluating poems. But because an issue is complex does not mean it is impossible, and even if there is no easy and absolute standard to be discovered, there are nevertheless distinctions to be made. Some poems are better—that is, more consistently effective with talented and experienced readers—than others. Even if we cannot sensibly rate poems on a 1 to 10 scale or agree on the excellence of a single poem, it is possible to set out some criteria that are helpful to readers who may not yet have developed confidence in their own judgments. It isn't necessary, of course, to spend all of our time asking about quality and being judgmental about poetry. But because life isn't long enough to read everything, it is often useful to separate those poems that are likely to be worth your time from those that aren't. Besides, the process of sorting—in which you begin to articulate your own judgments and poetic values—can be a very useful strategy in making yourself a better reader and a more informed, better-educated, and wiser person. Evaluating poems can be, among other things, a way to learn more about yourself, for what you like in poetry has a lot to say about where your own values really lie.

"I like it." That simple, unreflective statement about a poem is often a way to begin the articulation of standards—as long as your next move is to ask yourself why. Answers to *why* questions are often, at first, quite simple, even for experienced and sophisticated readers. "I like the way it sounds" or "I like its rhythm and pace" might be good, if partial, reasons for liking a poem. The popularity of nursery rhymes and simple childish ditties, or even the haunting, predictable, and repeated sounds and phrases of a poem like "The Raven" owe a lot (if not necessarily everything) to the use of sound. Another frequent answer might be: "because it is TRUE" or "because I agree with what it says." All of us are apt to like sentiments or ideas that resemble our own more than those that challenge or disturb us, though bad formulations of some idea we treasure, like bad behavior in someone we love, can sometimes be more embarrassing than comforting. But the longer we struggle with our reasons for liking a poem, the more complex and revealing our answers are likely to be: "I like the *way* it expresses something I had thought but had never quite been able to articulate." "I like the way its sounds and rhythms imitate the sounds of what is being described." "I like the way it presents conflicting emotions, balancing negative and positive feelings that seem to exist at the same time in about equal intensity." "I like its precision in describing just how something like that affects a person." Such statements as "I like . . ." begin to quietly cross the border into the area of "I admire," and to include a second clause, beginning with "because," that offers complex reasons for that admiration.

What kinds of reasons might we expect different readers to agree on? *Groups* of readers might well agree on certain ideas—questions of politics or economics or religion, for example—but not readers across the board. More likely to generate consensus are technical criteria, questions of craft. How precise are the word choices at crucial moments in the poem? How rich, suggestive, and resonant are the words that open up the poem to larger statements and claims? How appropriate are the metaphors and other figures of speech? How original and imaginative? How carefully is the poem's situation set up? How clearly? How full and appropriate is the characterization of the speaker? How well-matched are the speaker, situation, and setting with the poem's sentiments and ideas? How consistent is the poem's tone? How appropriate to its themes? How carefully worked out is the poem's structure? How appropriate to the desired effects are the line breaks, the stanza breaks, and the pattern of rhythms and sounds?

One way of seeing how good a poem is in its various aspects is to look at what it is not—to consider the choices *not* made by the poet. Often it is possible to consider what a poem would be like if a different artistic choice had been made, as a way of seeing the importance of the choice actually made. What if, for example, Sylvia Plath had described a black *crow* in rainy weather instead of a rook? What if William Carlos Williams had described a *white* wheelbarrow? Sometimes we have the benefit, if we have a working manuscript or an autobiographical account of composition, of actually watching the process of selection. Look again, for example, at the several drafts of the first stanza of "Love Calls Us to the Things of This World":

> (a) My eyes came open to the squeak of pulleys
>   My spirit, shocked from the brothel of itself

> (b) My eyes came open to the shriek of pulleys,
>   And the soul, spirited from its proper wallow,
>   Hung in the air as bodiless and hollow

> (c) My eyes came open to the pulleys' cry.
>   The soul, spirited from its proper wallow,
>   Hung, in the air as bodiless and hollow
>   As light that frothed upon the wall opposing;
>   But what most caught my eyes at their unclosing
>   Was two gray ropes that yanked across the sky.
>   One after one into the window frame
>   . . . the hosts of laundry came

> (d)   The eyes open to a cry of pulleys,
>   And the soul, so suddenly spirited from sleep,
>   As morning sunlight frothing on the floor,
>   While just outside the window
>   The air is solid with a dance of angels.

> (e)   The eyes open to a cry of pulleys,
>   And spirited from sleep, the astounded soul
>   Hangs for a moment bodiless and simple
>   As dawn light in the moment of its breaking:
>   Outside the open window
>   The air is crowded with a

> (f)   The eyes open to a cry of pulleys,
>   And spirited from sleep, the astounded soul
>   Hangs for a moment bodiless and simple
>   As false dawn
>   Outside the open window,
>   Their air is leaping with a rout of angels.
>   Some are in bedsheets, some are in dresses,
>   it does not seem to matter.

Notice how much more appropriate to the total poem is the choice of "cry" over "shriek" or "squeak" to describe the sound of pulleys or how much more effective than the metaphor of a spirit's "brothel" is the image of the soul hanging "bodiless." Notice the things Wilbur excised from the early drafts as well as the things he added when the poem became more clear and more of a piece in his mind. Read some of the other revised versions of poems or passages printed in Chapter 13. Do you think all the revisions improve on the originals? in what specific way? What are your criteria for deciding? Do any of the revisions seem pointless to you—or (worse) make the poem less than it was?

Let's look again at one of the first poems we discussed, Adrienne Rich's "Aunt Jennifer's Tigers" (p. 37). Some of the power of this poem comes from the poet's clear and sympathetic engagement with Aunt Jennifer's situation, but the effects are carefully generated through a series of specific technical choices. Rich herself may or may not have made all these choices consciously; her later comments on the poem suggest that her creative instincts, as well as her then-repressed sense of gender, may have governed some decisions more fully than her own deliberate calculations. But however conscious, the choices of speaker, situation, metaphor, and connotative words work brilliantly together to create a strong feminist statement, almost a manifesto on the subject of mastery and compliance.

In a sense there is no speaker in this poem, no specified personality—only a faceless niece who observes the central character—but the effacing of this speaker in the light of the vivid Jennifer amounts to a brilliant artistic decision. Jennifer, powerless to articulate and possibly even to understand her own plight, nevertheless is allowed almost to speak for herself, primarily through her hands. The seeming refusal of the narrator to do more than simply describe Jennifer's hands and their product gives Jennifer the crucial central role; she is the center of attention throughout, and the poem emphasizes only what one sees, with little apparent "editorial" comment (though the speaker does make three evaluative statements, saying that Jennifer was "mastered" by her ordeals [line 10], and noting that her hands are "terrified" [line 9] and that the wedding band "sits heavily" [line 9] on one of them). The tigers are ultimately more eloquent than the speaker seems to be: they "prance" (lines 1 and 12) and "pace" (line 4), and they are "proud" (line 12) and unafraid of men (lines 3 and 12), embodying the guarded message Jennifer sends to the world even though she herself is "mastered" and "ringed" (line 10). The brightly conceived colors in the tapestry, the expressive description of Jennifer's fingers and hands (note especially the excitement implied in "fluttering" [line 5]), and the action of the panel itself combine with the characterization of Jennifer to present a strong statement of generational repression—and boldness. The image of knitting as art, suggestive of the way the classical Fates determine the future and the nature of things, also hints at what is involved in Rich's art. The quality of the poem lies in the care, precision, and imaginativeness of Rich's craftsmanship. In later years, Rich has become clearer and more vocal about her values, but the direction and intensity of her vision are already apparent in this excellent poem taken from her first book, published more then forty years ago.

Here is another celebrated poem that similarly accomplishes a great deal in a short space:

WILLIAM SHAKESPEARE

[Th' expense of spirit in a waste of shame]

Th' expense[1] of spirit in a waste[2] of shame
Is lust in action; and, till action, lust
Is perjured, murderous, bloody, full of blame,
Savage, extreme, rude, cruel, not to trust;
Enjoyed no sooner but despiséd straight: 5
Past reason hunted; and no sooner had,
Past reason hated, as a swallowed bait,
On purpose laid to make the taker mad:
Mad in pursuit, and in possession so;
Had, having, and in quest to have, extreme;   10
A bliss in proof;[3] and proved, a very woe;
Before, a joy proposed; behind, a dream.
All this the world well knows; yet none knows well
To shun the heaven that leads men to this hell.   1609

Here the speaker *is* fully characterized, and the economical skill with which the characterization is achieved is one of the most striking aspects of the poem. The poem sets up its situation carefully and, at first, not altogether clearly. But the delay in clarity is functional: we do not know for a while just what disturbs the speaker so much, except that it has to do with "lust in action" (line 2). What we do know quickly is how powerful his feeling is. The two explosive *p*'s in the first half of the first line get the poem off to a fast and powerful start, and by the fourth line the speaker has listed nine separate unpleasant human characteristics driven by lust. He virtually spits them out. Here is one angry speaker, and it swiftly becomes clear that he is speaking from (undescribed) personal experience.

But the poem is not only angry and negative about lust. It also admits that there are definite, and powerful, pleasures in lust: it is "enjoyed" (line 5) at the time ("a bliss in proof," line 11), and anticipated with pleasure ("a joy proposed," line 12). Such inconsistencies (or at least complexities) in the speaker's

1. Expending.   2. Using up; also, desert.   3. In the act.

opinion are characteristic of the poem. Everything about his views, and according to him about lust itself, is "extreme" (line 10). There are no easy conclusions about lust in the first twelve lines of the poem, just a confusing movement back and forth between positives and negatives. The powerful condemnation of lust in the beginning—detailed in terms of how it makes people feel about themselves and how it affects their actions—quickly shifts into admissions of pleasure and joy, but then shifts back again. No opinion sticks for long. The only consistent thing about the speaker's feelings is his certainty of lust's power—to drive individuals to behavior that they may love or hate. Only at the end is there any kind of reasoned conclusion, and the "moral" is hardly comforting: everybody knows what I've been saying, the speaker says, and yet nobody knows how to avoid lust and its consequences because its pleasures are so sensational, both in prospect and in actual experience ("the heaven that leads men to this hell").

The vacillation of the speaker's opinions and moods is not the only confusing thing about the poem's organization. His account of lust repeatedly skips around in time. Are we talking here about lust at the time it is being satisfied ("lust in action")? Or are we talking about desire and anticipation? Or are we talking about what happens afterward? The answer is all three, and the discussion is hardly systematic. The first line and a half describe the present, and the meter of the first line even imitates the rhythms and force of male ejaculation: note how the basic iambic pentameter strategy of the poem does not regularize until near the end of the second line. But soon we are talking about what happens before lust in action ("till action," line 2), and by line 5, after. Lines 6 and 7 contrast before and after, and line 9 compares before and during. Line 10 describes all three positions in time ("Had, having, and in quest to have"). Line 11 compares during and after, line 12 before and after. The poem, or rather the speaker, does not seem able to decide exactly what he wants to talk about and what he thinks of his subject.

All this shifting around in focus and in feelings could easily be regarded as a serious flaw. Don't we expect a short poem, and especially a sonnet, to be very carefully organized and carefully focused toward a single end? Shouldn't the poet make up his mind about what he thinks and what the poem is about? It would be easy to construct an argument, on the basis of consistency or clarity of purpose, that this is not a very good poem, that perhaps the greatest poet in the English language was not, here, at the top of his form. But doing so would ignore the power of the poem's effects and underrate another principle of consistency—that of character. If we regard the poem as representative of a mind wrestling with the complex feelings brought about by lust—someone out of control because of lust, conscious enough to see his plight but unable to do anything about it—we can see a higher consistency here that helps explain the poem's powerful effect on many readers. Here is an account of a human mind grappling with a universal human experience, the subject of many much longer works of literature. Lust is beautiful but terrifying, certainly to be avoided but impossible to avoid. Shakespeare has managed, in the unlikely space of fourteen lines and in a form in which we expect tight organization and intense focus, to portray succinctly the human recognition of confusion and powerlessness in the face of a passion larger than our ability to control it.

Here is a parody of Shakespeare's poem:

WENDY COPE

[The expense of spirits is a crying shame]

The expense of spirits is a crying shame,
So is the cost of wine. What bard[4] today
Can live like old Khayyám?[5] It's not the same—
A loaf and Thou and Tesco's Beaujolais.
I had this bird[6] called Sharon, fond of gin—   5
Could knock back six or seven. At the price
I paid a high wage for each hour of sin
And that was why I only had her twice.
Then there was Tracy, who drank rum and Coke,
So beautiful I didn't mind at first   10
But love grows colder. Now some other bloke
Is subsidizing Tracy and her thirst.
I need a woman, honest and sincere,
Who'll come across on half a pint of beer.   1986

Gone here are, among other things, the agony and the complexity. In one sense, this poem makes fun of both the emotion and the tortured uncertainty in the Shakespeare original: here the speaker is clear, and simple, in what he wants, and there is no negotiation or kidding oneself about the urgency and value of sex. Cope creates a very different kind of poem, one that stands on its own in depicting sexual and economic values, but that also retains a close

---

4. Poet.   **5.** In Edward Fitzgerald's poem *The Rubáiyat of Omar Khayyám* (more or less a translation of an Arab original), the poet longs for "a loaf of bread, a jug of wine, and Thou." *Tesco's:* a British supermarket that sells a cheap house-brand of Beaujolais.   **6.** British slang for female sex object.

dependence, quite beyond the verbal phrasing, on the Shakespeare original. Had there not been the anxiety, anger, desire, and hesitation in the original poem, this poem could not have existed: the original makes the parody possible in more than just the sense of being a point to take off from or a model to react against.

But just as Shakespeare's poem is a basis for Cope's, the Cope poem becomes a criticism and interpretation of Shakespeare's. Not only does Cope tease Shakespeare about excessive agonizing and debilitating uncertainty; she also, through her own simplifications of situation and theme, calls strong attention to the complexities in the psychology of Shakespeare's speaker and to the elaborate structure of Shakespeare's sonnet—grossly and comically simplified in the Cope speaker, who just wants to get somebody into bed no matter what. There are no afterthoughts in Cope, no hesitations; there is no self-consciousness or awareness of larger consequences or feelings. Cope's poem leads us, as sensitive parodies very often do, to notice details in the original—details that may actually help us with analysis.

Is the Cope poem in itself a good one? Certainly it's clever in its use of verbal patterns that exist in the original, in getting a lot of mileage out of the different meanings of "expense" and "spirit," and in turning the direction of the whole poem in a way that responds dramatically to (or answers) the original. But ultimately a full evaluation of Cope's parody would consider not just its witty changing of expectations, clever word play, and tonal manipulation, but also its commentary on the Shakespeare original—and the insights it offers about why poems are created and what they can do.

Here is another poem that is something of a challenge to evaluate:

JOHN DONNE

Song

Go, and catch a falling star,
    Get with child a mandrake root,[7]
Tell me, where all past years are,
    Or who cleft the devil's foot,
Teach me to hear mermaids singing
Or to keep off envy's stinging,
        And find
        What wind
Serves to advance an honest mind.

7. The forked mandrake root is said to look vaguely human.

If thou beest born to strange sights,[8]   10
  Things invisible to see,
Ride ten thousand days and nights,
  Till age snow white hairs on thee;
Thou, when thou return'st, wilt tell me
All strange wonders that befell thee,   15
    And swear
    No where
Lives a woman true, and fair.

If thou find'st one, let me know:
  Such a pilgrimage were sweet.   20
Yet do not, I would not go,
  Though at next door we might meet:
Though she were true when you met her,
And last till you write your letter,
    Yet she   25
    Will be
False, ere I come, to two, or three.   1633

One immediate problem to confront here is the irregular, jerky rhythm. In a poem called "Song," we are likely to expect music, harmony, something pleasant and (within limits) predictable in its rhythm and movement. But this "song" is nothing like that. At first its message sounds lyrical and romantic: to go and catch a falling star is, if impossible, a romantic thing to propose, a motif that often comes up (and has for centuries) in love poems and popular songs; and lines 3 and 5 propose similar traditional romantic activities that evoke wonder and pleasure in contemplation. But the activities suggested in the alternate lines (2, 4, and 6) contrast sharply; they are just as bold in their unromantic or antiromantic sentiments. Making a mandrake root pregnant does not sound like an especially pleasant male activity, however much such a root may look like a female body, and knowledge of the devil's cleft foot or envy's stinging are not usually the stuff of romantic poems or songs. Besides, the strange interruptions of easy rhythm (indicated by commas) in otherwise pleasant lines like 1 and 3 suggest that something less than lyrical is going on there too.

By the time we get to the last stanza, what is going on is a lot clearer. We have here a portrait of an angry and disillusioned man who is obsessed with the infidelity of women. He is talking to another man, apparently someone who has far more positive, perhaps even romantic, notions of women, and the poem is a kind of argument, except that the disillusioned speaker does all the talking. He pretends to take into account some traditional romantic rhetoric

8. I.e., if you have supernatural powers.

but turns it all on its head, intermixing the traditional impossible quests of lovers with a quest of his own—to find a "woman true, and fair" (line 18). But he knows cynically—he would probably say from experience, though he offers no evidence of his experience and no account of why he feels the way he does— that all these quests are impossible. This is one bitter man, and the song he sings has nothing to do with love or romance.

If we were to evaluate this "song" on the basis of harmonic and romantic expectations, looking for evenness of rhythms, pleasant sounds, and an attractive series of images consonant with romantic attitudes, we would certainly find it wanting. But again (as with the Shakespeare poem above) a larger question of appropriateness begs to be applied. Is the musical, imagistic, and organizational strategy consonant with the poem's total focus and force? Do the sounds and tone of the poem "work" in terms of the speaker portrayed here and the kind of artistic project this poem represents? The displeasure we feel in the speaker's words, images, feelings, and attitudes ultimately needs to be directed toward the speaker; the poet has done a good job of portraying a character whose bitterness, however generated, is unpleasant and off-putting. The poem "works" on its own terms. We may or may not like to hear attitudes like this expressed in a poem; we may or may not approve of using a pretended "song" to mouth such sentiments. But whether or not we "like" the poem in terms of what it says, we can evaluate, through close analysis of its several different elements (much as we have been doing analytically in earlier chapters), how *well* it does what it does. There are, of course, still larger questions of whether what it tries to do is worth doing, and readers of different philosophical or political persuasions may differ widely in their opinions and evaluations of that matter.

Different people do admire different things, and when we talk about criteria for evaluating poetry, we are talking about, at best, elements that a fairly large number of people have, over a long period of time, agreed on as important. There may be substantial agreement about political or social values in a particular group, and a consensus may exist among, say, misogynists or feminists about the value of such a poem as Donne's "Song." But more general agreements that bridge social and ideological divisions are more likely to involve the kinds of matters that have come up for analysis in earlier chapters, matters involving how well a poem *works*, how well it uses the resources it has within its conceptual limits. For some readers, ideology is everything, and there is no such thing as quality beyond political views or moral conclusions. But for others, different, more pluralistic evaluations can be made about accomplishment and quality.

Consistency. Appropriateness. Coherence. Effectiveness. Such terms are likely to be key ones for most readers in making their evaluations—as they have been in this discussion. But individual critics or readers will often have their own emphases, their own axes to grind. For some critics in past generations, "organic unity" was the key to all evaluation, whether a poem achieved, like something grown in nature, a wholeness of conception and effect. For others, the key term may be "tension" or "ambiguity" or "complexity" or "simplicity" or "authenticity" or "cultural truth" or "representation" or "psychological accuracy." With experience, you will develop your own set of criteria that may or may not involve a single ruling concept or term. But wherever (and whenever) you come out, you will learn something about yourself and your values in the process of articulating exactly what you like and admire—and why.

▼   ▼   ▼

IRVING LAYTON

Street Funeral

Tired of chewing
the flesh
of other animals;
Tired of subreption and conceit;
of the child's   5
bewildered conscience
fretting the sly man;
Tired of holding down
a job; of giving insults,
taking insults;   10
Of excited fornication,
failing heart valves,
septic kidneys . . .

This frosty morning,
the coffin wood bursting   15
into brilliant flowers,
Is he glad
that after all the lecheries,
betrayals, subserviency,
After all the lusts,   20
false starts, evasions
he can begin

the unobstructed change
into clean grass
25   Done forever
with the insult
of birth,
the long adultery
with illusion?   1956

REGINA BARRECA

Nighttime Fires

When I was five in Louisville
we drove to see nighttime fires. Piled seven of us,
all pajamas and running noses, into the Olds,
drove fast toward smoke. It was after my father
5   lost his job, so not getting up in the morning
gave him time: awake past midnight, he read old newspapers
with no news, tried crosswords until he split the pencil
between his teeth, mad. When he heard
the wolf whine of the siren, he woke my mother,
10   and she pushed and shoved
us all into waking. Once aroused we longed for burnt wood
and a smell of flames high into the pines. My old man liked
driving to rich neighborhoods best, swearing in a good mood
as he followed fire engines that snaked like dragons
15   and split the silent streets. It was festival, carnival.

If there were a Cadillac or any car
in a curved driveway, my father smiled a smile
from a secret, brittle heart.
His face lit up in the heat given off by destruction
20   like something was being made, or was being set right.
I bent my head back to see where sparks
ate up the sky. My father who never held us
would take my hand and point to falling cinders that
covered the ground like snow, or, excited, show us
25   the swollen collapse of a staircase. My mother
watched my father, not the house. She was happy
only when we were ready to go, when it was finally over
and nothing else could burn.
Driving home, she would sleep in the front seat
30   as we huddled behind. I could see his quiet face in the
rearview mirror, eyes like hallways filled with smoke.   1986

GEOFFREY HILL

In Memory of Jane Fraser

When snow like sheep lay in the fold
And winds went begging at each door
And the far hills were blue with cold
And a cold shroud lay on the moor

She kept the siege. And every day   5
We watched her brooding over death
Like a strong bird above its prey.
The room filled with the kettle's breath.

Damp curtains glued against the pane
Sealed time away. Her body froze   10
As if to freeze us all and chain
Creation to a stunned repose.

She died before the world could stir.
In March the ice unloosed the brook
And water ruffled the sun's hair.   15
Dead cones upon the altar shook.   1959

GALWAY KINNELL

Blackberry Eating

I love to go out in late September
among the fat, overripe, icy, black blackberries
to eat blackberries for breakfast,
the stalks very prickly, a penalty
they earn for knowing the black art   5
of blackberry-making; and as I stand among them
lifting the stalks to my mouth, the ripest berries
fall almost unbidden to my tongue,
as words sometimes do, certain peculiar words
like *strengths* or *squinched*,   10
many-lettered, one-syllabled lumps,
which I squeeze, squinch open, and splurge well
in the silent, startled, icy, black language
of blackberry-eating in late September.   1980

EMILY DICKINSON

[The Brain—is wider than the Sky—]

The Brain—is wider than the Sky—
For—put them side by side—
The one the other will contain
With ease—and You—beside—

The Brain is deeper than the sea—
For—hold them—Blue to Blue—
The one the other will absorb—
As Sponges—Buckets—do—

The Brain is just the weight of God—
For—Heft them—Pound for Pound—
And they will differ—if they do—
As Syllable from Sound—

5

10

ca. 1862

SARAH N. CLEGHORN

The Golf Links

The golf links lie so near the mill
That almost every day
The laboring children can look out
And see the men at play.

1917

▾   ▾   ▾

QUESTIONS

1. What seems to you the most important single factor in whether you like or dislike a poem? Read back over the poems in the course that you have liked most; what do they have in common?

2. How adaptable do you think you are in adjusting to a poem's emphases? Which poems have you liked though you didn't especially like the conclusions they came to?

3. How important to you is the *precision* of words in a poem? Do you tend to like poems better if they are definite and explicit in what they say? if they are ambiguous, uncertain, or complex?

4. Which chapters in the first section of this textbook (up through Chapter

8) have you found most useful? most surprising? Which did you enjoy most? From which did you learn the most about yourself and your tastes and values?

5. What do you value most in poetry generally? Do you read poems that are not assigned? Do you read poems outside this textbook or outside the course? If so, what kinds of poems do you tend to seek out?

6. How important to you is the *tone* of a poem? Do you tend to like funny poems more than serious ones? tragic situations more than comic ones? unusual treatments of standard or predictable subjects and themes?

7. Which poem in this chapter did you most enjoy reading? Which one did you like best after reading the commentary about it? Are there any poems you have read this term that you have violently disliked? What about them particularly irritated you?

8. Are certain subjects or themes always appealing to you? always unappealing? What variable seems to you most important in determining whether you will like or dislike a poem?

WRITING SUGGESTIONS

1. Choose one poem that you especially admire and one that you do not. Write a two- or three-page essay about each in which you try to show what specific accomplishments (or lack of them) lead you to your evaluative conclusions. Treat each poem in detail, and suggest fully not only how but *why* things "work" — or don't work. Try to construct your argument as "objectively" as possible, so that you are not simply pitting your personal judgment against someone else's. (Alternative: find two poems that are very much alike in subject matter, theme, or situation, but that seem to you to succeed to different degrees. Write one *comparative* essay in which you account for the difference in quality by showing in detail the difference between what works and what does not.)

2. Discuss with classmates a variety of poems you have read this term, and choose one poem about which a number of you disagree. Discuss among yourselves the different perspectives you have on the poem, and try to sort out in the discussion exactly what issues are at stake. Take notes on the discussion, trying to be clear about how your position differs from that of other students. Once you believe that you have the issues sorted out and can be clear about your own position, write a two- or three-page personal letter to your instructor in which you outline a position contrary to your own and then answer it point by point. Be sure to make clear in your letter the *grounds* for your evaluative

position, positive or negative—that is, the principles or values on which you base your evaluation. (Hint: in the conversation with classmates, try to steer the discussion to a clear disagreement on no more than two or three points, and in your letter focus carefully on these points. State the arguments of your classmates as effectively and forcefully as you can so that your own argument will be as probing and sophisticated as you can make it.)

3. Choose a poem you have read this term that you admire but really don't like very much. In thinking over the poem again, try to account for the conflict between your feelings and judgment: what questions of content or form, social or political assumption, personal style, or manner of argument in the poem seem to make it less attractive to you? In a personal letter to a friend who is not in the class and who thus has not heard the class discussions of the issues, describe your dilemma, being careful to first outline why you think the poem is admirable. Say frankly what your personal reservations about the poem are, and at the end use the discussion of the poem to talk about your own values, in poetry and in general.

Reading More Poetry

W. H. AUDEN

In Memory of W. B. Yeats

(d. January, 1939)

I

He disappeared in the dead of winter:
The brooks were frozen, the airports almost deserted,
And snow disfigured the public statues;
The mercury sank in the mouth of the dying day.
What instruments we have agree   5
The day of his death was a dark cold day.

Far from his illness
The wolves ran on through the evergreen forests,
The peasant river was untempted by the fashionable quays;
By mourning tongues   10
The death of the poet was kept from his poems.

But for him it was his last afternoon as himself,
An afternoon of nurses and rumors;
The provinces of his body revolted,
The squares of his mind were empty,   15
Silence invaded the suburbs,
The current of his feeling failed; he became his admirers.

Now he is scattered among a hundred cities
And wholly given over to unfamiliar affections,
To find his happiness in another kind of wood   20
And be punished under a foreign code of conscience.
The words of a dead man
Are modified in the guts of the living.

But in the importance and noise of tomorrow
When the brokers are roaring like beasts on the floor of the Bourse,[1]
And the poor have the sufferings to which they are fairly accustomed,
And each in the cell of himself is almost convinced of his freedom,
A few thousand will think of this day
As one thinks of a day when one did something slightly unusual.
What instruments we have agree
The day of his death was a dark cold day.

II

You were silly like us; your gift survived it all:
The parish of rich women, physical decay,
Yourself. Mad Ireland hurt you into poetry.
Now Ireland has her madness and her weather still,
For poetry makes nothing happen: it survives
In the valley of its making where executives
Would never want to tamper, flows on south
From ranches of isolation and the busy griefs,
Raw towns that we believe and die in; it survives,
A way of happening, a mouth.

III

Earth, receive an honored guest:
William Yeats is laid to rest.
Let the Irish vessel lie
Emptied of its poetry.

In the nightmare of the dark
All the dogs of Europe bark,
And the living nations wait,
Each sequestered in its hate;

Intellectual disgrace
Stares from every human face,
And the seas of pity lie
Locked and frozen in each eye.

Follow, poet, follow right
To the bottom of the night,
With your unconstraining voice
Still persuade us to rejoice;

With the farming of a verse
Make a vineyard of the curse,
Sing of human unsuccess
In a rapture of distress;

1. The Paris stock exchange.

In the deserts of the heart
Let the healing fountain start,
In the prison of his days
1939   Teach the free man how to praise.   65

ELIZABETH BISHOP

The Armadillo

for Robert Lowell

This is the time of year
when almost every night
the frail, illegal fire balloons appear.
Climbing the mountain height,

rising toward a saint   5
still honored in these parts,
the paper chambers flush and fill with light
that comes and goes, like hearts.

Once up against the sky it's hard
to tell them from the stars—   10
planets, that is—the tinted ones:
Venus going down, or Mars,

or the pale green one. With a wind,
they flare and falter, wobble and toss;
but if it's still they steer between   15
the kite sticks of the Southern Cross,

receding, dwindling, solemnly
and steadily forsaking us,
or, in the downdraft from a peak,
suddenly turning dangerous.   20

Last night another big one fell.
It splattered like an egg of fire
against the cliff behind the house.
The flame ran down. We saw the pair

of owls who nest there flying up   25
and up, their whirling black-and-white
stained bright pink underneath, until
they shrieked up out of sight.

The ancient owls' nest must have burned.
Hastily, all alone,   30

a glistening armadillo left the scene,
rose-flecked, head down, tail down,

and then a baby rabbit jumped out,
short-eared, to our surprise.
35   So soft!—a handful of intangible ash
with fixed, ignited eyes.

Too pretty, dreamlike mimicry!
O falling fire and piercing cry
and panic, and a weak mailed fist
40   *clenched ignorant against the sky!*   1965

SAMUEL TAYLOR COLERIDGE

Kubla Khan: or, a Vision in a Dream[2]

In Xanadu did Kubla Khan
   A stately pleasure-dome decree:
Where Alph, the sacred river, ran
Through caverns measureless to man
5   Down to a sunless sea.
So twice five miles of fertile ground
With walls and towers were girdled round:
And here were gardens bright with sinuous rills
Where blossomed many an incense-bearing tree;
10   And here were forests ancient as the hills,
Enfolding sunny spots of greenery.
But oh! that deep romantic chasm which slanted
Down the green hill athwart a cedarn cover![3]
A savage place! as holy and enchanted
15   As e'er beneath a waning moon was haunted
By woman wailing for her demon-lover![4]
And from this chasm, with ceaseless turmoil seething,
As if this earth in fast thick pants were breathing,
A mighty fountain momently was forced,
20   Amid whose swift half-intermitted burst
Huge fragments vaulted like rebounding hail,
Or chaffy grain beneath the thresher's flail:
And 'mid these dancing rocks at once and ever
It flung up momently the sacred river.
25   Five miles meandering with a mazy motion

---

2. Coleridge said he wrote this fragment immediately after waking from an opium dream and that after he was interrupted by a caller he was unable to finish the poem.   **3.** From side to side of a cover of cedar trees.   **4.** In a famous and often imitated German ballad, the lady Lenore is carried off on horseback by the specter of her lover and married to him at his grave.

Through wood and dale the sacred river ran,
Then reached the caverns measureless to man,
And sank in tumult to a lifeless ocean:
And 'mid this tumult Kubla heard from far
Ancestral voices prophesying war! 30

 The shadow of the dome of pleasure
 Floated midway on the waves;
 Where was heard the mingled measure
 From the fountain and the caves.
It was a miracle of rare device, 35
A sunny pleasure-dome with caves of ice!
 A damsel with a dulcimer
 In a vision once I saw:
 It was an Abyssinian maid,
 And on her dulcimer she played, 40
 Singing of Mount Abora.
 Could I revive within me
 Her symphony and song,
 To such a deep delight 'twould win me,
That with music loud and long, 45
I would build that dome in air,
That sunny dome! those caves of ice!
And all who heard should see them there,
And all should cry, Beware! Beware!
His flashing eyes, his floating hair! 50
Weave a circle round him thrice,
And close your eyes with holy dread,
For he on honey-dew hath fed,
And drunk the milk of Paradise. 1798

HART CRANE

To Emily Dickinson

 You who desired so much—in vain to ask—
 Yet fed your hunger like an endless task,
 Dared dignify the labor, bless the quest—
 Achieved that stillness ultimately best,

 Being, of all, least sought for: Emily, hear! 5
 O sweet, dead Silencer, most suddenly clear
 When singing that Eternity possessed
 And plundered momently in every breast;

 —Truly no flower yet withers in your hand.
 The harvest you descried and understand 10

Needs more than wit to gather, love to bind.
Some reconcilement of remotest mind—

Leaves Ormus rubyless, and Ophir⁵ chill.
Else tears heap all within one clay-cold hill.   1933

Exile

(after the Chinese)

My hands have not touched pleasure since your hands,—
No,—nor my lips freed laughter since 'farewell',
And with the day, distance again expands
Voiceless between us, as an uncoiled shell.

5 Yet love endures, though starving and alone.
A dove's wings cling about my heart each night
With surging gentleness, and the blue stone
Set in the tryst-ring has but worn more bright.   p. 1918

Episode of Hands

The unexpected interest made him flush.
Suddenly he seemed to forget the pain,—
Consented,—and held out
One finger from the others.

5 The gash was bleeding, and a shaft of sun
That glittered in and out among the wheels,
Fell lightly, warmly, down into the wound.

And as the fingers of the factory owner's son,
That knew a grip for books and tennis
10 As well as one for iron and leather,—
As his taut, spare fingers wound the gauze
Around the thick bed of the wound,
His own hands seemed to him
Like wings of butterflies
15 Flickering in sunlight over summer fields.

The knots and notches,—many in the wide
Deep hand that lay in his,—seemed beautiful.

---

5. An ancient country from which Solomon secured gold and precious stones. *Ormus:* Presumably Ormuz, an ancient city on the Persian Gulf.

They were like the marks of wild ponies' play,—
Bunches of new green breaking a hard turf.

And factory sounds and factory thoughts   20
Were banished from him by that larger, quieter hand
That lay in his with the sun upon it.
And as the bandage knot was tightened
1920   The two men smiled into each other's eyes.

E. E. CUMMINGS

[anyone lived in a pretty how town]

anyone lived in a pretty how town
(with up so floating many bells down)
spring summer autumn winter
he sang his didn't he danced his did.

Women and men(both little and small)   5
cared for anyone not at all
they sowed their isn't they reaped their same
sun moon stars rain

children guessed(but only a few
and down they forgot as up they grew   10
autumn winter spring summer)
that noone loved him more by more

when by now and tree by leaf
she laughed his joy she cried his grief
bird by snow and stir by still   15
anyone's any was all to her

someones married their everyones
laughed their cryings and did their dance
(sleep wake hope and then)they
said their nevers they slept their dream   20

stars rain sun moon
(and only the snow can begin to explain
how children are apt to forget to remember
with up so floating many bells down)

one day anyone died i guess   25
(and noone stooped to kiss his face)
busy folk buried them side by side
little by little and was by was

all by all and deep by deep
and more by more they dream their sleep   30

noone and anyone earth by april
wish by spirit and if by yes.

Women and men(both dong and ding)
summer autumn winter spring
35   reaped their sowing and went their came
sun moon stars rain   1940

WARING CUNEY

No Images

She does not know
Her beauty,
She thinks her brown body
Has no glory.

5   If she could dance
Naked,
Under palm trees
And see her image in the river
She would know.

10   But there are no palm trees
On the street,
And dish water gives back no images.   p. 1926

H. D. (HILDA DOOLITTLE)

Sea Rose

Rose, harsh rose,
marred and with stint of petals,
meagre flower, thin,
sparse of leaf,

5   more precious
than a wet rose
single on a stem—
you are caught in the drift.

Stunted, with small leaf,
10   you are flung on the sand,
you are lifted
in the crisp sand
that drives in the wind.

Can the spice-rose
drip such acrid fragrance   15
hardened in a leaf?   1916

Garden

I

You are clear
O rose, cut in rock,
hard as the descent of hail.

I could scrape the color
from the petals   5
like spilt dye from a rock.

If I could break you
I could break a tree.
If I could stir
I could break a tree—   10
I could break you.

II

O wind, rend open the heat,
cut apart the heat,
rend it to tatters.

Fruit cannot drop   15
through this thick air—
fruit cannot fall into heat
that presses up and blunts
the points of pears
and rounds the grapes.   20

Cut the heat—
plough through it,
turning it on either side
of your path.   1916

EMILY DICKINSON

[Because I could not stop for Death—]

Because I could not stop for Death—
He kindly stopped for me—
The Carriage held but just Ourselves—
And Immortality.

5   We slowly drove—He knew no haste
And I had put away
My labor and my leisure too,
For His Civility—

We passed the School, where Children strove
10   At Recess—in the Ring—
We passed the Fields of Gazing Grain—
We passed the Setting Sun—

Or rather—He passed Us—
The Dews drew quivering and chill—
15   For only Gossamer,⁶ my Gown—
My Tippet—only Tulle⁷—

We paused before a House that seemed
A Swelling of the Ground—
The Roof was scarcely visible—
20   The Cornice—in the Ground—

Since then—'tis Centuries—and yet
Feels shorter than the Day
I first surmised the Horses' Heads
ca. 1863   Were toward Eternity—

[I reckon—when I count at all—]

I reckon—when I count at all—
First—Poets—Then the Sun—
Then Summer—Then the Heaven of God—
And then—the List is done—

5   But, looking back—the First so seems
To Comprehend the Whole—
The Others look a needless Show—
So I write—Poets—All—

---

6. A soft sheer fabric.   7. A fine net fabric. *Tippet:* scarf.

Their Summer—lasts a Solid Year—
They can afford a Sun   10
The East—would deem extravagant—
And if the Further Heaven—

Be Beautiful as they prepare
For Those who worship Them—
It is too difficult a Grace—   15
ca. 1862   To justify the Dream—

[My life closed twice before its close—]

My life closed twice before its close—
It yet remains to see
If Immortality unveil
A third event to me

So huge, so hopeless to conceive   5
As these that twice befell.
Parting is all we know of heaven,
And all we need of hell.   1896

[We do not play on Graves—]

We do not play on Graves—
Because there isn't Room—
Besides—it isn't even—it slants
And People come—

And put a Flower on it—   5
And hang their faces so—
We're fearing that their Hearts will drop—
And crush our pretty play—

And so we move as far
As Enemies—away—
Just looking round to see how far   10
ca. 1862   It is—Occasionally—

[Wild Nights—Wild Nights!]

Wild Nights—Wild Nights!
Were I with thee

Wild Nights should be
Our luxury!

Futile—the Winds—
To a Heart in port—
Done with the Compass—
Done with the Chart!

Rowing in Eden—
Ah, the Sea!
Might I but moor—Tonight—
In Thee!

ca. 1861

[She dealt her pretty words like Blades—]

She dealt her pretty words like Blades—
How glittering they shone—
And every One unbared a Nerve
Or wantoned with a Bone—

She never deemed—she hurt—
That—is not Steel's Affair—
A vulgar grimace in the Flesh—
How ill the Creatures bear—

To Ache is human—not polite—
The Film upon the eye
Mortality's old Custom—
Just locking up—to Die.

1862

[The Wind begun to knead the Grass—]

The Wind begun to knead the Grass—
As Women do a Dough—
He flung a Hand full at the Plain—
A Hand full at the Sky—
The Leaves unhooked themselves from Trees—
And started all abroad—
The Dust did scoop itself like Hands—
And throw away the Road—
The Wagons quickened on the Street—
The Thunders gossiped low—

The Lightning showed a Yellow Head—
And then a livid Toe—
The Birds put up the Bars to Nests—
The Cattle flung to Barns—
Then came one drop of Giant Rain—   15
And then, as if the Hands
That held the Dams—had parted hold—
The Waters Wrecked the Sky—
But overlooked my Father's House—
1864   Just Quartering a Tree—   20

JOHN DONNE

The Canonization

For God's sake hold your tongue and let me love!
    Or chide my palsy or my gout,
My five gray hairs or ruined fortune flout;
With wealth your state, your mind with arts improve,
    Take you a course, get you a place,   5
    Observe his Honor or his Grace,
Or the king's real or his stampéd face[8]
    Contemplate; what you will, approve,
        So you will let me love.

Alas, alas, who's injured by my love?   10
    What merchant's ships have my sighs drowned?
Who says my tears have overflowed his ground?
When did my colds a forward spring remove?
    When did the heats which my veins fill
    Add one man to the plaguy bill?[9]   15
Soldiers find wars, and lawyers find out still
    Litigious men which quarrels move,
        Though she and I do love.

Call us what you will, we are made such by love.
    Call her one, me another fly,   20
We're tapers[1] too, and at our own cost die;
And we in us find th' eagle and the dove.[2]
    The phoenix riddle[3] hath more wit[4]

8. On coins.   9. List of plague victims.   1. Which consume themselves. To "die" is Renais-
sance slang for consummating the sexual act, which was popularly believed to shorten life by one
day. *Fly*: a traditional symbol of transitory life.   2. Traditional symbols of strength and purity.
3. According to tradition, only one phoenix existed at a time, dying in a funeral pyre of its own
making and being reborn from its own ashes. The bird's existence was thus a riddle akin to a
religious mystery (line 27), and a symbol sometimes fused with Christian representations of immor-
tality.   4. Meaning.

By us; we two, being one, are it.
25   So to one neutral thing both sexes fit,
        We die and rise the same, and prove
           Mysterious by this love.

We can die by it, if not live by love;
           And if unfit for tombs and hearse
30   Our legend be, it will be fit for verse;[5]
And if no piece of chronicle we prove,
           We'll build in sonnets[6] pretty rooms
           (As well a well-wrought urn becomes[7]
The greatest ashes, as half-acre tombs),
35   And by these hymns all shall approve
              Us canonized for love.

And thus invoke us: "You whom reverent love
           Made one another's hermitage,
You to whom love was peace, that now is rage,
40   Who did the whole world's soul extract, and drove[8]
           Into the glasses of your eyes
           (So made such mirrors and such spies
That they did all to you epitomize)
           Countries, towns, courts; beg from above
45   A pattern of your love!"   1633

[Death, be not proud, though some have calléd thee]

Death, be not proud, though some have calléd thee
Mighty and dreadful, for thou art not so;
For those whom thou think'st thou dost overthrow
Die not, poor Death, nor yet canst thou kill me.
From rest and sleep, which but thy pictures[9] be,
Much pleasure; then from thee much more must flow,
And soonest[1] our best men with thee do go,
Rest of their bones, and soul's delivery.[2]
Thou art slave to Fate, Chance, kings, and desperate men,
And dost with Poison, War, and Sickness dwell;
And poppy or charms can make us sleep as well,
And better than thy stroke; why swell'st[3] thou then?
One short sleep past, we wake eternally
And death shall be no more; Death, thou shalt die.   1633

---

5. I.e., if we don't turn out to be an authenticated piece of historical narrative.   6. Love poems.
In Italian, *stanza* means room.   7. Befits.   8. Compressed.   9. Likenesses.   1. Most
willingly.   2. Deliverance.   3. Puff with pride.

A Valediction: Forbidding Mourning

As virtuous men pass mildly away,
    And whisper to their souls to go,
Whilst some of their sad friends do say,
    "The breath goes now," and some say, "No,"

So let us melt, and make no noise,   5
    No tear-floods, nor sigh-tempests move;
'Twere profanation of our joys
    To tell the laity our love.

Moving of the earth[4] brings harms and fears,
    Men reckon what it did and meant;   10
But trepidation of the spheres,[5]
    Though greater far, is innocent.

Dull sublunary[6] lovers' love
    (Whose soul is sense) cannot admit
Absence, because it doth remove   15
    Those things which elemented[7] it.

But we, by a love so much refined
    That our selves know not what it is,
Inter-assured of the mind,
    Care less, eyes, lips, and hands to miss.   20

Our two souls therefore, which are one,
    Though I must go, endure not yet
A breach, but an expansion,
    Like gold to airy thinness beat.

If they be two, they are two so   25
    As stiff twin compasses are two:
Thy soul, the fixed foot, makes no show
    To move, but doth, if the other do;

And though it in the center sit,
    Yet when the other far doth roam,   30
It leans, and hearkens after it,
    And grows erect, as that comes home.

Such wilt thou be to me, who must,
    Like the other foot, obliquely run;
Thy firmness makes my circle[8] just,   35
    And makes me end where I begun.

1611?

4. Earthquakes.   5. The Renaissance hypothesis that the celestial spheres trembled and thus caused unexpected variations in their orbits. Such movements are "innocent" because earthlings do not observe or fret about them.   6. Below the moon: i.e., changeable. According to the traditional cosmology that Donne invokes here, the moon was considered the dividing line between the immutable celestial world and the earthly mortal one.   7. Comprised.   8. A traditional symbol of perfection.

RITA DOVE

Parsley[9]

1. THE CANE FIELDS

There is a parrot imitating spring
in the palace, its feathers parsley green.
Out of the swamp the cane appears

to haunt us, and we cut it down. El General
5   searches for a word; he is all the world
there is. Like a parrot imitating spring,

we lie down screaming as rain punches through
and we come up green. We cannot speak an R—
out of the swamp, the cane appears

10   and then the mountain we call in whispers *Katalina*.[1]
The children gnaw their teeth to arrowheads.
There is a parrot imitating spring.

El General has found his word: *perejil*.
Who says it, lives. He laughs, teeth shining
15   out of the swamp. The cane appears

in our dreams, lashed by wind and streaming.
And we lie down. For every drop of blood
there is a parrot imitating spring.
Out of the swamp the cane appears.

2. THE PALACE

20   The word the general's chosen is parsley.
It is fall, when thoughts turn
to love and death; the general thinks
of his mother, how she died in the fall
and he planted her walking cane at the grave
25   and it flowered, each spring stolidly forming
four-star blossoms. The general

pulls on his boots, he stomps to
her room in the palace, the one without
curtains, the one with a parrot
30   in a brass ring. As he paces he wonders
Who can I kill today. And for a moment

9. "On October 2, 1957, Rafael Trujillo (1891–1961), dictator of the Dominican Republic, ordered 20,000 blacks killed because they could not pronounce the letter 'r' in *perejil*, the Spanish word for parsley." (Dove's note)   1. I.e., "Katarina."

the little knot of screams
is still. The parrot, who has traveled

all the way from Australia in an ivory
cage, is, coy as a widow, practising   35
spring. Ever since the morning
his mother collapsed in the kitchen
while baking skull-shaped candies
for the Day of the Dead,[2] the general
has hated sweets. He orders pastries   40
brought up for the bird; they arrive

dusted with sugar on a bed of lace.
The knot in his throat starts to twitch;
he sees his boots the first day in battle
splashed with mud and urine   45
as a soldier falls at his feet amazed—
how stupid he looked—at the sound
of artillery. *I never thought it would sing*
the soldier said, and died. Now

the general sees the fields of sugar   50
cane, lashed by rain and streaming.
He sees his mother's smile, the teeth
gnawed to arrowheads. He hears
the Haitians sing without R's
as they swing the great machetes: 55
Katalina, they sing, *Katalina*,

mi madle, mi amol en muelte.[3] God knows
his mother was no stupid woman; she
could roll an R like a queen. Even
a parrot can roll an R! In the bare room   60
the bright feathers arch in a parody
of greenery, as the last pale crumbs
disappear under the blackened tongue. Someone

calls out his name in a voice
so like his mother's, a startled tear   65
splashes the tip of his right boot.
My mother, my love in death.
The general remembers the tiny green sprigs
men of his village wore in their capes
to honor the birth of a son. He will   70
order many, this time, to be killed

for a single, beautiful word.   1983

---

2. All Souls' Day, November 1.   3. Line 67 translates this phrase.

JOHN DRYDEN

[Why should a foolish marriage vow][4]

Why should a foolish marriage vow,
   Which long ago was made,
Oblige us to each other now
   When passion is decayed?
5 We loved, and we loved, as long as we could,
   Till our love was loved out in us both;
But our marriage is dead when the pleasure is fled:
   'Twas pleasure first made it an oath.

If I have pleasures for a friend,
10   And farther love in store,
What wrong has he whose joys did end,
   And who could give no more?
'Tis a madness that he should be jealous of me,
   Or that I should bar him of another:
15 For all we can gain is to give ourselves pain,
   When neither can hinder the other.

                                                     1671

PAUL LAWRENCE DUNBAR

We Wear the Mask

We wear the mask that grins and lies,
It hides our cheeks and shades our eyes, —
This debt we pay to human guile;
With torn and bleeding hearts we smile,
5 And mouth with myriad subtleties.

Why should the world be over-wise,
In counting all our tears and sighs?
Nay, let them only see us, while
   We wear the mask.

10 We smile, but, O great Christ, our cries
To thee from tortured souls arise.
We sing, but oh the clay is vile
Beneath our feet, and long the mile;
But let the world dream otherwise,
15   We wear the mask!

                                                     1896

---

4. A song from Dryden's play, *Marriage à la Mode.*

T. S. ELIOT

The Love Song of J. Alfred Prufrock

*S'io credesse che mia risposta fosse
A persona che mai tornasse al mondo,
Questa fiamma staria senza piu scosse.
Ma perciocche giammai di questo fondo
Non torno vivo alcun, s'i'odo il vero,
Senza tema d'infamia ti rispondo.*[5]

Let us go then, you and I,
When the evening is spread out against the sky
Like a patient etherized upon a table;
Let us go, through certain half-deserted streets,
The muttering retreats   5
Of restless nights in one-night cheap hotels
And sawdust restaurants with oyster-shells:
Streets that follow like a tedious argument
Of insidious intent
To lead you to an overwhelming question . . .   10
Oh, do not ask, "What is it?"
Let us go and make our visit.

　　In the room the women come and go
Talking of Michelangelo.

　　The yellow fog that rubs its back upon the window-panes,   15
The yellow smoke that rubs its muzzle on the window-panes
Licked its tongue into the corners of the evening,
Lingered upon the pools that stand in drains,
Let fall upon its back the soot that falls from chimneys,
Slipped by the terrace, made a sudden leap,   20
And seeing that it was a soft October night,
Curled once about the house, and fell asleep.

　　And indeed there will be time[6]
For the yellow smoke that slides along the street,

5. Dante's *Inferno*, XXVII, 61–66. In the Eighth Chasm, Dante and Vergil meet Count Guido de Montefeltrano, one of the False Counselors. The spirits there are in the form of flames, and Guido speaks from the trembling tip of the flame, responding to Dante's request that he tell his life story: "If I thought that my answer were to someone who would ever go back to Earth, this flame would be still, without any more movement. But because no one has ever gone back alive from this chasm (if what I hear is true) I answer you without fear of infamy."　6. See Ecclesiastes 3:1 ff.: "To everything there is a season, and a time to every purpose under the heaven: A time to be born, and a time to die; a time to plant, and a time to pluck up that which is planted; A time to kill, and a time to heal. . . ." Also see Marvell's "To His Coy Mistress": "Had we but world enough and time. . . ."

25 Rubbing its back upon the window-panes;
There will be time, there will be time
To prepare a face to meet the faces that you meet;
There will be time to murder and create,
And time for all the works and days[7] of hands
30 That lift and drop a question on your plate;
Time for you and time for me,
And time yet for a hundred indecisions,
And for a hundred visions and revisions,
Before the taking of a toast and tea.

35   In the room the women come and go
Talking of Michelangelo.

    And indeed there will be time
To wonder, "Do I dare?" and, "Do I dare?"
Time to turn back and descend the stair,
40 With a bald spot in the middle of my hair—
(They will say: "How his hair is growing thin!")
My morning coat, my collar mounting firmly to the chin,
My necktie rich and modest, but asserted by a simple pin—
(They will say: "But how his arms and legs are thin!")
45 Do I dare
Disturb the universe?

In a minute there is time
For decisions and revisions which a minute will reverse.

    For I have known them all already, known them all:—
50 Have known the evenings, mornings, afternoons,
I have measured out my life with coffee spoons;
I know the voices dying with a dying fall
Beneath the music from a farther room.
    So how should I presume?

55   And I have known the eyes already, known them all—
The eyes that fix you in a formulated phrase,
And when I am formulated, sprawling on a pin,
When I am pinned and wriggling on the wall,
Then how should I begin
50 To spit out all the butt-ends of my days and ways?
    And how should I presume?

    And I have known the arms already, known them all—
Arms that are braceleted and white and bare
(But in the lamplight, downed with light brown hair!)
65 Is it perfume from a dress
That makes me so digress?

7. Hesiod's ancient Greek didactic poem *Works and Days* prescribed in practical detail how to conduct one's life.

Arms that lie along a table, or wrap about a shawl.
   And should I then presume?
   And how should I begin?

. . . . .

Shall I say, I have gone at dusk through narrow streets   70
And watched the smoke that rises from the pipes
Of lonely men in shirt-sleeves, leaning out of windows? . . .

   I should have been a pair of ragged claws
Scuttling across the floors of silent seas

. . . . .

And the afternoon, the evening, sleeps so peacefully!   75
Smoothed by long fingers,
Asleep . . . tired . . . or it malingers,
Stretched on the floor, here beside you and me.
Should I, after tea and cakes and ices,
Have the strength to force the moment to its crisis?   80
But though I have wept and fasted, wept and prayed,
Though I have seen my head (grown slightly bald) brought in upon a platter,[8]
I am no prophet—and here's no great matter;
I have seen the moment of my greatness flicker,
And I have seen the eternal Footman hold my coat, and snicker,   85
And in short, I was afraid.

   And would it have been worth it, after all,
After the cups, the marmalade, the tea,
Among the porcelain, among some talk of you and me,
Would it have been worth while,   90
To have bitten off the matter with a smile,
To have squeezed the universe into a ball[9]
To roll it toward some overwhelming question,
To say: "I am Lazarus,[1] come from the dead,
Come back to tell you all, I shall tell you all"—   95
If one, settling a pillow by her head,
   Should say: "That is not what I meant at all.
   That is not it, at all."

   And would it have been worth it, after all,
Would it have been worth while,   100
After the sunsets and the dooryards and the sprinkled streets,
After the novels, after the teacups, after the skirts that trail along the floor—
And this, and so much more?—
It is impossible to say just what I mean!

8. See Matthew 14:1–12 and Mark 6:17–29: John the Baptist was decapitated, upon Salome's request and at Herod's command, and his head delivered on a platter.   9. See Marvell's "To His Coy Mistress," lines 41–42: "Let us roll all our strength and all / our sweetness up into one ball. . . .   1. One Lazarus was raised from the dead by Jesus (see John 1:1 to 2:2), and another (in the parable of the rich man Dives) is discussed in terms of returning from the dead to warn the living (Luke 16:19–31).

105 But as if a magic lantern[2] threw the nerves in patterns on a screen:
Would it have been worth while
If one, settling a pillow or throwing off a shawl,
And turning toward the window, should say:
     "That is not it at all,
110   That is not what I meant, at all."

                              . . . . .

No! I am not Prince Hamlet, nor was meant to be;
Am an attendant lord,[3] one that will do
To swell a progress,[4] start a scene or two,
Advise the prince; no doubt, an easy tool,
115 Deferential, glad to be of use,
Politic, cautious, and meticulous;
Full of high sentence, but a bit obtuse;
At times, indeed, almost ridiculous—
Almost, at times, the Fool.

120   I grow old . . . I grow old . . .
I shall wear the bottoms of my trousers rolled.

     Shall I part my hair behind? Do I dare to eat a peach?
I shall wear white flannel trousers, and walk upon the beach.
I have heard the mermaids singing, each to each.

125   I do not think that they will sing to me.

     I have seen them riding seaward on the waves
Combing the white hair of the waves blown back.
When the wind blows the water white and black.

     We have lingered in the chambers of the sea
130 By sea-girls wreathed with seaweed red and brown
Till human voices wake us, and we drown.   1917

ROBERT FROST

Range-Finding

          The battle rent a cobweb diamond-strung
          And cut a flower beside a groundbird's nest
          Before it stained a single human breast.
          The stricken flower bent double and so hung.
5   And still the bird revisited her young.
          A butterfly its fall had dispossessed,
          A moment sought in air his flower of rest,
          Then lightly stooped to it and fluttering clung.

2. A nonelectric projector used as early as the 17th century.   3. Like Polonius in *Hamlet*, who is full of maxims ("high sentence," line 117).   4. Procession of state.

On the bare upland pasture there had spread
O'ernight 'twixt mullein⁵ stalks a wheel of thread   10
And straining cables wet with silver dew.
A sudden passing bullet shook it dry.
The indwelling spider ran to greet the fly,
But finding nothing, sullenly withdrew.   1916

The Road Not Taken

Two roads diverged in a yellow wood,
And sorry I could not travel both
And be one traveler, long I stood
And looked down one as far as I could
To where it bent in the undergrowth;   5

Then took the other, as just as fair,
And having perhaps the better claim,
Because it was grassy and wanted wear;
Though as for that the passing there
Had worn them really about the same,   10

And both that morning equally lay
In leaves no step had trodden black.
Oh, I kept the first for another day!
Yet knowing how way leads on to way,
I doubted if I should ever come back.   15

I shall be telling this with a sigh
Somewhere ages and ages hence:
Two roads diverged in a wood, and I—
I took the one less traveled by,
And that has made all the difference.   1916   20

Stopping by Woods on a Snowy Evening

Whose woods these are I think I know.
His house is in the village, though;
He will not see me stopping here
To watch his woods fill up with snow.

My little horse must think it queer   5
To stop without a farmhouse near

5. Weed.

Between the woods and frozen lake
The darkest evening of the year.

He gives his harness bells a shake
10   To ask if there is some mistake.
The only other sound's the sweep
Of easy wind and downy flake.

The woods are lovely, dark, and deep,
But I have promises to keep,
15   And miles to go before I sleep,
And miles to go before I sleep.   1923

THOMAS HARDY

The Darkling Thrush

I leant upon a coppice gate
   When Frost was specter gray,
And Winter's dregs made desolate
   The weakening eye of day.
5   The tangled bine-stems scored the sky
   Like strings of broken lyres,
And all mankind that haunted nigh
   Had sought their household fires.

The land's sharp features seemed to be
10   The Century's corpse outleant,
His crypt the cloudy canopy,
   The wind his death-lament.
The ancient pulse of germ and birth
   Was shrunken hard and dry,
15   And every spirit upon earth
   Seemed fervorless as I.

At once a voice arose among
   The bleak twigs overhead
In a full-hearted evensong
20   Of joy illimited;
An aged thrush, frail, gaunt, and small,
   In blast-beruffled plume,
Had chosen thus to fling his soul
   Upon the growing gloom.

25   So little cause for carolings
   Of such ecstatic sound
Was written on terrestrial things

Afar or nigh around,
That I could think there trembled through
His happy good-night air   30
Some blessed Hope, whereof he knew
And I was unaware.

December 31, 1900

During Wind and Rain

They sing their dearest songs—
He, she, all of them—yea,
Treble and tenor and bass,
    And one to play;
With the candles mooning each face. . . .   5
    Ah, no; the years O!
How the sick leaves reel down in throngs!

They clear the creeping moss—
Elders and juniors—aye,
Making the pathway neat   10
    And the garden gay;
And they build a shady seat. . . .
    Ah, no; the years, the years;
See, the white stormbirds wing across!

They are blithely breakfasting all—   15
Men and maidens—yea,
Under the summer tree,
    With a glimpse of the bay,
While pet fowl come to the knee. . . .
    Ah, no; the years O!   20
And the rotten rose is ripped from the wall.

They change to a high new house,
He, she, all of them—aye,
Clocks and carpets, and chairs
    On the lawn all day,   25
And brightest things that are theirs. . . .
    Ah, no; the years, the years;
Down their carved names the rain drop ploughs.   1917

GERARD MANLEY HOPKINS

God's Grandeur

The world is charged with the grandeur of God.
　　It will flame out, like shining from shook foil;[6]
　　It gathers to a greatness, like the ooze of oil
Crushed. Why do men then now not reck his rod?[7]
Generations have trod, have trod, have trod;
　　And all is seared with trade; bleared, smeared with toil;
　　And wears man's smudge and shares man's smell: the soil
Is bare now, nor can foot feel, being shod.

And for all this, nature is never spent;
　　There lives the dearest freshness deep down things;
And though the last lights off the black West went
　　Oh, morning, at the brown brink eastward, springs—
Because the Holy Ghost over the bent
　　World broods with warm breast and with ah! bright wings.

1918

The Windhover[8]

to Christ our Lord

I caught this morning morning's minion,[9] king-
　　dom of daylight's dauphin,[1] dapple-dawn-drawn Falcon, in his riding
　　Of the rolling level underneath him steady air, and striding
High there, how he rung upon the rein of a wimpling[2] wing
In his ecstasy! then off, off forth on swing,
　　As a skate's heel sweeps smooth on a bow-bend: the hurl and gliding
　　Rebuffed the big wind. My heart in hiding
Stirred for a bird,—the achieve of, the mastery of the thing!

Brute beauty and valor and act, oh, air, pride, plume, here
　　Buckle![3] AND the fire that breaks from thee then, a billion
Times told lovelier, more dangerous, O my chevalier![4]

---

6. "I mean foil in its sense of leaf or tinsel. . . . Shaken goldfoil gives off broad glares like sheet lightning and also, and this is true of nothing else, owing to its zig-zag dints and creasings and network of small many cornered facets, a sort of fork lightning too." *Letters of Gerard Manley Hopkins to Robert Bridges,* ed. C. C. Abbott, 1955, p. 169.　　7. Heed his authority.　　8. A small hawk, the kestrel, which habitually hovers in the air, headed into the wind.　　9. Favorite, beloved.　　1. Heir to regal splendor.　　2. Rippling.　　3. Several meanings may apply: to join closely, to prepare for battle, to grapple with, to collapse.　　4. Horseman, knight.

No wonder of it: sheér plód makes plow down sillion[5]
Shine, and blue-bleak embers, ah my dear,
   Fall, gall themselves, and gash gold-vermilion.

1877

LANGSTON HUGHES

Theme for English B

The instructor said,

   Go home and write
   a page tonight.
   And let that page come out of you—
   Then, it will be true.   5

I wonder if it's that simple?
I am twenty-two, colored, born in Winston-Salem.
I went to school there, then Durham,[6] then here
to this college[7] on the hill above Harlem.
I am the only colored student in my class.   10
The steps from the hill lead down into Harlem,
through a park, then I cross St. Nicholas,[8]
Eighth Avenue, Seventh, and I come to the Y,
the Harlem Branch Y, where I take the elevator
up to my room, sit down, and write this page: 15

It's not easy to know what is true for you or me
at twenty-two, my age. But I guess I'm what
I feel and see and hear, Harlem, I hear you:
hear you, hear me—we two—you, me, talk on this page.
(I hear New York, too.) Me—who?   20

Well, I like to eat, sleep, drink, and be in love.
I like to work, read, learn, and understand life.
I like a pipe for a Christmas present,
or records—Bessie,[9] bop, or Bach.
I guess being colored doesn't make me *not* like   25
the same things other folks like who are other races.
So will my page be colored that I write?

Being me, it will not be white.
But it will be
a part of you, instructor.   30

5. The narrow strip of land between furrows in an open field divided for separate cultivation.
6. Winston-Salem and Durham are cities in North Carolina.   7. Columbia University.
8. An avenue east of Columbia University.   9. Bessie Smith (1898?–1937), famous blues singer.

You are white—
yet a part of me, as I am a part of you.
That's American.
Sometimes perhaps you don't want to be a part of me.
35   Nor do I often want to be a part of you.
But we are, that's true!
As I learn from you,
I guess you learn from me—
although you're older—and white—
40   and somewhat more free.

This is my page for English B.   1959

BEN JONSON

To Penshurst[1]

Thou art not, Penshurst, built to envious show,
Of touch[2] or marble; nor canst boast a row
Of polished pillars, or a roof of gold;
Thou hast no lantern[3] whereof tales are told,
5   Or stair, or courts; but stand'st an ancient pile,
And, these grudged at,[4] art reverenced the while.
Thou joy'st in better marks, of soil, of air,
Of wood, of water; therein thou art fair.
Thou hast thy walks for health, as well as sport;
10   Thy mount, to which the dryads do resort,
Where Pan and Bacchus[5] their high feasts have made
Beneath the broad beech and the chestnut shade,
That taller tree, which of a nut was set
At his great birth[6] where all the Muses met.
15   There in the writhéd bark are cut the names
Of many a sylvan, taken with his flames;[7]
And thence the ruddy satyrs oft provoke
The lighter fauns to reach thy Lady's Oak.[8]
Thy copse too, named of Gamage,[9] thou hast there,
20   That never fails to serve thee seasoned deer

1. The country seat (in Kent) of the Sidney family, owned by Sir Robert, brother of the poet, Sir Philip. Jonson's celebration of the estate is one of the earliest "house" poems and a prominent example of topographical or didactic-descriptive poetry.   2. Touchstone: basanite, a smooth dark stone similar to black marble.   3. A glassed or open tower or dome atop the roof.   4. I.e., although these (more pretentious structures) are envied. *The while*: anyway.   5. Ancient gods of nature and wine, both associated with spectacular feasting and celebration.   6. Sir Philip Sidney's, on November 30, 1554; the tree stood for nearly 150 years.   7. Inspired by Sidney's love poetry.   8. Where, according to legend, a former lady of the house (Lady Leicester) began labor pains. *Satyrs*: half-men, half-goats who participated in the rites of Bacchus.   9. The maiden name of the owner's wife. *Copse*: thicket.

When thou wouldst feast, or exercise, thy friends.
The lower land, that to the river bends,
Thy sheep, thy bullocks, kine, and calves do feed;
The middle grounds thy mares and horses breed.
Each bank doth yield thee conies;[1] and the tops,   25
Fertile of wood, Ashore and Sidney's copse,
To crown thy open table, doth provide
The purpled pheasant with the speckled side;
The painted partridge lies in every field,
And for thy mess is willing to be killed.   30
And if the high-swollen Medway[2] fail thy dish,
Thou hast thy ponds that pay thee tribute fish,
Fat agéd carps that run into thy net,
And pikes, now weary their own kind to eat,
As loath the second draught[3] or cast to stay,   35
Officiously[4] at first themselves betray;
Bright eels that emulate them, and leap on land
Before the fisher, or into his hand.
Then hath thy orchard fruit, thy garden flowers,
Fresh as the air, and new as are the hours.   40
The early cherry, with the later plum,
Fig, grape, and quince, each in his time doth come:
The blushing apricot and woolly peach
Hang on thy walls, that every child may reach.
And though thy walls be of the country stone,   45
They're reared with no man's ruin, no man's groan;
There's none that dwell about them wish them down,
But all come in, the farmer and the clown,[5]
And no one empty-handed, to salute
Thy lord and lady, though they have no suit.[6]   50
Some bring a capon, some a rural cake,
Some nuts, some apples; some that think they make
The better cheeses bring 'em, or else send
By their ripe daughters, whom they would commend
This way to husbands, and whose baskets bear   55
An emblem of themselves in plum or pear.
But what can this (more than express their love)
Add to thy free[7] provisions, far above
The need of such? whose liberal board doth flow
With all that hospitality doth know;   60
Where comes no guest but is allowed to eat,
Without his fear, and of thy lord's own meat;
Where the same beer and bread, and selfsame wine,
That is his lordship's shall be also mine.

---

1. Rabbits.   2. A river bordering the estate.   3. Of a net. *Stay:* await.   4. Oblig-
ingly.   5. Rustic, peasant.   6. Request for favors.   7. Generous.

65 　 And I not fain[8] to sit (as some this day
　　　 At great men's tables), and yet dine away.[9]
　　　 Here no man tells[1] my cups; nor, standing by,
　　　 A waiter doth my gluttony envý,
　　　 But gives me what I call, and lets me eat;
70 　 He knows below he shall find plenty of meat.
　　　 Thy tables hoard not up for the next day;
　　　 Nor, when I take my lodging, need I pray
　　　 For fire, or lights, or livery;[2] all is there,
　　　 As if thou then wert mine, or I reigned here:
75 　 There's nothing I can wish, for which I stay.
　　　 That found King James when hunting late this way
　　　 With his brave son, the prince,[3] they saw thy fires
　　　 Shine bright on every hearth, as the desires
　　　 Of thy Penates had been set on flame
80 　 To entertain them; or the country came
　　　 With all their zeal to warm their welcome here.
　　　 What (great I will not say, but) sudden cheer
　　　 Didst thou then make 'em! and what praise was heaped
　　　 On thy good lady then! who therein reaped
85 　 The just reward of her high housewifery;[4]
　　　 To have her linen, plate, and all things nigh,
　　　 When she was far; and not a room but dressed
　　　 As if it had expected such a guest!
　　　 These, Penshurst, are thy praise, and yet not all.
90 　 Thy lady's noble, fruitful, chaste withal.
　　　 His children thy great lord may call his own,
　　　 A fortune in this age but rarely known.
　　　 They are, and have been, taught religion; thence
　　　 Their gentler spirits have sucked innocence.
95 　 Each morn and even they are taught to pray,
　　　 With the whole household, and may, every day,
　　　 Read in their virtuous parents' noble parts
　　　 The mysteries of manners, arms, and arts.
　　　 Now, Penshurst, they that will proportion[5] thee
100 　 With other edifices, when they see
　　　 Those proud, ambitious heaps, and nothing else,
　　　 May say, their lords have built, but thy lord dwells.　　　　1616

8. Obliged.　　9. Possibly, "elsewhere," because they do not get enough to eat; or "away" in the sense of far from the party of honor.　　1. Counts.　　2. Provisions (or, possibly, servants). 3. Prince Henry, who died in 1612.　　4. Domestic economy.　　5. Compare.

A. M. KLEIN

Heirloom

My father bequeathed me no wide estates;
No keys and ledgers were my heritage;
Only some holy books with *yahrzeit*[6] dates
Writ mournfully upon a blank front page—

Books of the Baal Shem Tov,[7] and of his wonders;   5
Pamphlets upon the devil and his crew;
Prayers against road demons, witches, thunders;
And sundry other tomes for a good Jew.

Beautiful: though no pictures on them, save
The scorpion crawling on a printed track;   10
The Virgin floating on a scriptural wave,
Square letters twinkling in the Zodiac.

The snuff left on this page, now brown and old,
The tallow stains of midnight liturgy—
These are my coat of arms, and these unfold   15
My noble lineage, my proud ancestry!

And my tears, too, have stained this heirloomed ground,
When reading in these treatises some weird
Miracle, I turned a leaf and found
A white hair fallen from my father's beard.   1940   20

RICHARD LOVELACE

To Amarantha, that She Would Dishevel Her Hair

Amarantha sweet and fair,
Ah, braid no more that shining hair!
As my curious hand or eye
Hovering round thee, let it fly.

Let it fly as unconfined   5
As its calm ravisher, the wind,
Who hath left his darling, th' East,
To wanton o'er that spicy nest.

---

6. Anniversary of the death of a parent or near relative.   7. A title given to someone who possesses the secret knowledge of Jewish holy men and who therefore could work miracles.

Every tress must be confessed
But neatly tangled at the best,
   Like a clue[8] of golden thread,
Most excellently raveléd.

Do not then wind up that light
In ribands, and o'ercloud in night;
   Like the sun in's early ray,
But shake your head and scatter day.

See, 'tis broke! Within this grove,
The bower and the walks of love,
   Weary lie we down and rest
And fan each other's panting breast.

Here we'll strip and cool our fire
In cream below, in milk-baths higher;
   And when all wells are drawn dry,
I'll drink a tear out of thine eye.

Which our very joys shall leave,
That sorrows thus we can deceive;
   Or our very sorrows weep,
That joys so ripe so little keep.   1649

ROBERT LOWELL

Skunk Hour

for Elizabeth Bishop

Nautilus Island's hermit
heiress still lives through winter in her Spartan cottage;
her sheep still graze above the sea.
Her son's a bishop. Her farmer
is first selectman[9] in our village,
she's in her dotage.

Thirsting for
the hierarchic privacy
of Queen Victoria's century,
she buys up all
the eyesores facing her shore,
and lets them fall.

8. Ball.   9. An elected New England town official.

The season's ill—
we've lost our summer millionaire,
who seemed to leap from an L. L. Bean[1]   15
catalogue. His nine-knot yawl
was auctioned off to lobstermen.
A red fox stain covers Blue Hill.

And now our fairy
decorator brightens his shop for fall,   20
his fishnet's filled with orange cork,
orange, his cobbler's bench and awl,
there is no money in his work,
he'd rather marry.

One dark night,   25
my Tudor Ford climbed the hill's skull,
I watched for love-cars. Lights turned down,
they lay together, hull to hull,
where the graveyard shelves on the town. . . .
My mind's not right.   30

A car radio bleats,
"Love, O careless Love. . . ."[2] I hear
my ill-spirit sob in each blood cell,
as if my hand were at its throat. . . .
I myself am hell;   35
nobody's here—

only skunks, that search
in the moonlight for a bite to eat.
They march on their soles up Main Street:
white stripes, moonstruck eyes' red fire   40
under the chalk-dry and spar spire
of the Trinitarian Church.

I stand on top
of our back steps and breathe the rich air—
a mother skunk with her column of kittens swills the garbage pail.   45
She jabs her wedge head in a cup
of sour cream, drops her ostrich tail,
and will not scare.   1959

---

1. Famous old Maine sporting goods firm.   2. A popular song.

ANDREW MARVELL

The Garden

How vainly men themselves amaze[3]
To win the palm, the oak, or bays,[4]
And their incessant labors see
Crowned from some single herb, or tree,
Whose short and narrow-vergèd[5] shade   5
Does prudently their toils upbraid;
While all flowers and all trees do close[6]
To weave the garlands of repose!

Fair Quiet, have I found thee here,
And Innocence, thy sister dear?   10
Mistaken long, I sought you then
In busy companies of men.
Your sacred plants,[7] if here below,
Only among the plants will grow;
Society is all but rude[8]   15
To[9] this delicious solitude.

No white nor red was ever seen
So am'rous as this lovely green.
Fond lovers, cruel as their flame,
Cut in these trees their mistress' name: 20
Little, alas, they know, or heed
How far these beauties hers exceed!
Fair trees, wheresoe'er your barks I wound,
No name shall but your own be found.

When we have run our passion's heat,   25
Love hither makes his best retreat.
The gods, that mortal beauty chase,
Still in a tree did end their race:
Apollo hunted Daphne so,
Only that she might laurel grow;   30
And Pan did after Syrinx speed,
Not as a nymph, but for a reed.[1]

What wondrous life is this I lead!
Ripe apples drop about my head;
The luscious clusters of the vine   3
Upon my mouth do crush their wine;

3. Become frenzied.   4. Awards for athletic, civic, and literary achievements.   5. Narrowly
cropped.   6. Unite.   7. Cuttings.   8. Barbarous.   9. Compared to.   1. In Ovid's *Meta-
morphoses*, Daphne, pursued by Apollo, is turned into a laurel, and Syrinx, pursued by Pan, into a
reed that Pan makes into a flute.

The nectarine and curious[2] peach
Into my hands themselves do reach;
Stumbling on melons, as I pass,
Insnared with flowers, I fall on grass. 40

   Meanwhile the mind, from pleasure less,
Withdraws into its happiness;[3]
The mind, that ocean where each kind
Does straight its own resemblance find;[4]
Yet it creates, transcending these, 45
Far other worlds and other seas,
Annihilating[5] all that's made
To a green thought in a green shade.

   Here at the fountain's sliding foot,
Or at some fruit tree's mossy root, 50
Casting the body's vest[6] aside,
My soul into the boughs does glide:
There, like a bird, it sits and sings,
Then whets[7] and combs its silver wings,
And, till prepared for longer flight, 55
Waves in its plumes the various[8] light.

   Such was that happy garden-state,
While man there walked without a mate:
After a place so pure, and sweet,
What other help could yet be meet![9] 60
But 'twas beyond a mortal's share
To wander solitary there:
Two paradises 'twere in one
To live in paradise alone.

   How well the skillful gardener drew 65
Of flowers and herbs this dial[1] new,
Where, from above, the milder sun
Does through a fragrant zodiac run;
And as it works, th' industrious bee
Computes its time as well as we! 70
How could such sweet and wholesome hours
Be reckoned but with herbs and flowers? 1681

---

2. Exquisite.   3. I.e., the mind withdraws from lesser sense pleasure into contemplation.
4. All land creatures were supposed to have corresponding sea-creatures.   5. Reducing to noth-
ing by comparison.   6. Vestment, clothing; the flesh is being considered as simply clothing for
the soul.   7. Preens.   8. Many-colored.   9. Appropriate.   1. A garden planted in the
shape of a sundial, complete with zodiac.

The Mower, Against Gardens

Luxurious[2] man, to bring his vice in use,
    Did after him the world seduce,
And from the fields the flowers and plants allure,
    Where Nature was most plain and pure.
He first enclosed within the gardens square   5
    A dead and standing pool of air,
And a more luscious earth for them did knead,
    Which stupefied them while it fed.
The pink[3] grew then as double as his mind;
    The nutriment did change the kind.   10
With strange perfumes he did the roses taint;
    And flowers themselves were taught to paint.[4]
The tulip white did for complexion seek,
    And learned to interline its cheek;
Its onion root[5] they then so high did hold,   15
    That one was for a meadow sold:[6]
Another world was searched through oceans new,
    To find the Marvel of Peru;[7]
And yet these rarities might be allowed
    To man, that sov'reign thing and proud,   20
Had he not dealt[8] between the bark and tree,
    Forbidden mixtures there to see.
No plant now knew the stock from which it came;
    He grafts upon the wild the tame,
That the uncertain and adult'rate fruit   25
    Might put the palate in dispute.
His green seraglio has its eunuchs too,
    Lest any tyrant him outdo;
And in the cherry he does Nature vex,
    To procreate without a sex.   30
'Tis all enforced,[9] the fountain and the grot,
    While the sweet fields do lie forgot,
Where willing Nature does to all dispense
    A wild and fragrant innocence;
And fauns and fairies do the meadows till   35
    More by their presence than their skill.
Their statues polished by some ancient hand
    May to adorn the gardens stand;
But, howsoe'er the figures do excel,
    The gods themselves with us do dwell.   1681   40

---

2. Self-indulgent.   3. A *Dianthus* flower; figuratively, the embodiment of perfection.   4. Use artificial coloring.   5. Bulb.   6. In the 17th century tulips were held in extremely high regard, so much so that some countries were said to have tulip-omania.   7. The "four-o'clock" plant.   8. Artificially placed.   9. Imposed.

On a Drop of Dew

See how the orient[1] dew,
Shed from the bosom of the morn
   Into the blowing roses,
Yet careless of its mansion new
For[2] the clear region where 'twas born   5
   Round in itself incloses,
   And in its little globe's extent
Frames as it can its native element;
   How it the purple flow'r does slight,
   Scarce touching where it lies,   10
But gazing back upon the skies,
   Shines with a mournful light
      Like its own tear,
Because so long divided from the sphere.[3]
   Restless it rolls and unsecure,   15
     Trembling lest it grow impure,

   Till the warm sun pity its pain,
And to the skies exhale it back again.
     So the soul, that drop, that ray
Of the clear fountain of eternal day,   20
Could it within the human flower be seen,
   Rememb'ring still its former height,
   Shuns the sweet leaves and blossoms green;
   And, recollecting its own light,
Does, in its pure and circling thoughts, express   25
The greater Heaven in an Heaven less.
   In how coy[4] a figure wound,
   Every way it turns away;
   So the world excluding round,
   Yet receiving in the day: 30
   Dark beneath, but bright above,
   Here disdaining, there in love.

   How loose and easy hence to go,
   How girt and ready to ascend;
   Moving but on a point below,   35
   It all about does upwards bend.
Such did the manna's sacred dew distill,
White and entire, though congealed and chill;[5]
Congealed on earth, but does, dissolving, run
Into the glories of th' almighty sun.   1681   40

---

1. Shining.   2. By reason of.   3. Of heaven.   4. Reserved, withdrawn, modest.   5. In the wilderness, the Israelites fed upon manna from heaven (distilled from the dew; see Exodus 16:10–21); manna became a traditional symbol for divine grace.

JOHN MILTON

Lycidas[6]

In this monody the author bewails a learned friend, unfortunately
drowned in his passage from Chester on the Irish Seas, 1637.[7] And
by occasion foretells the ruin of our corrupted clergy then in their
height.

Yet once more, O ye laurels, and once more
Ye myrtles brown, with ivy never sere,[8]
I come to pluck your berries harsh and crude,[9]
And with forced fingers rude,
Shatter your leaves before the mellowing year.   5
Bitter constraint, and sad occasion dear,[1]
Compels me to disturb your season due:
For Lycidas is dead, dead ere his prime,
Young Lycidas, and hath not left his peer.
Who would not sing for Lycidas? He knew   10
Himself to sing, and build the lofty rhyme.
He must not float upon his wat'ry bier
Unwept, and welter[2] to the parching wind,
Without the meed[3] of some melodious tear.
   Begin then, sisters of the sacred well,[4]   15
That from beneath the seat of Jove doth spring,
Begin, and somewhat loudly sweep the string.
Hence with denial vain and coy excuse;
So may some gentle muse[5]
With lucky words favor my destined urn,   20
And as he passes turn,
And bid fair peace be to my sable shroud.
For we were nursed upon the self-same hill,
Fed the same flock, by fountain, shade, and rill.
   Together both, ere the high lawns[6] appeared   25
Under the opening eyelids of the morn,
We drove afield, and both together heard
What time the gray-fly winds[7] her sultry horn,
Batt'ning[8] our flocks with the fresh dews of night,
Oft till the star that rose, at ev'ning, bright,   30

6. The name of a shepherd in Vergil's *Eclogue*, III. Milton's elegy works from the convention of treating the dead man as if he were a shepherd and also transforms other details to a pastoral setting and situation.   7. Edward King, a student with Milton at Cambridge, and at the time of his death a young clergyman. *Monody:* a song sung by a single voice.   8. Withered. The laurel, myrtle, and ivy were all materials used to construct traditional evergreen garlands signifying poetic accomplishment. *Brown:* dusky, dark.   9. Unripe.   1. Dire.   2. Tumble about.   3. Tribute. 4. The muses, who lived on Mt. Helicon. At the foot of the mountain were two fountains, or wells, where the muses danced around Jove's altar.   5. Poet.   6. Grasslands: pastures.   7. Blows; i.e., the insect hum of midday.   8. Fattening.

Towards Heav'n's descent had sloped his westering wheel.
Meanwhile the rural ditties were not mute,
Tempered to the oaten flute;⁹
Rough satyrs danced, and fauns with clov'n heel,
From the glad sound would not be absent long,   35
And old Damaetas¹ loved to hear our song.
     But O the heavy change, now thou art gone,
Now thou art gone, and never must return!
Thee, shepherd, thee the woods and desert caves,
With wild thyme and the gadding² vine o'ergrown,   40
And all their echoes mourn.
The willows and the hazel copses³ green
Shall now no more be seen,
Fanning their joyous leaves to thy soft lays.
As killing as the canker⁴ to the rose,   45
Or taint-worm to the weanling herds that graze,
Or frost to flowers, that their gay wardrobe wear,
When first the white-thorn blows:⁵
Such, Lycidas, thy loss to shepherd's ear.
     Where were ye, nymphs,⁶ when the remorseless deep   50
Closed o'er the head of your loved Lycidas?
For neither were ye playing on the steep,
Where your old Bards, the famous Druids, lie,
Nor on the shaggy top of Mona high,
Nor yet where Deva spreads her wizard stream:⁷   55
Ay me, I fondly⁸ dream!
Had ye been there—for what could that have done?
What could the Muse⁹ herself that Orpheus bore,
The Muse herself, for her enchanting¹ son
Whom universal nature did lament,   60
When by the rout that made the hideous roar,
His gory visage down the stream was sent,
Down the swift Hebrus to the Lesbian shore?
     Alas! What boots² it with uncessant care
To tend the homely slighted shepherd's trade,   65
And strictly meditate the thankless Muse?
Were it not better done, as others use³
To sport with Amaryllis in the shade,

9. Shepherds' pipes.   1. A traditional pastoral name, possibly referring here to a Cambridge tutor.
2. Wandering.   3. Thickets.   4. Cankerworm.   5. Blossoms.   6. Nature deities.
7. The River Dee, reputed to have prophetic powers. *Mona:* the Isle of Anglesey. The steep (line
52) may be a burial ground, in northern Wales, for Druids, ancient priests and magicians; all three
locations are near the place where King drowned.   8. Foolishly.   9. Calliope, the muse of
epic poetry, whose son Orpheus was torn limb from limb by frenzied orgiasts. His head, thrown into
the Hebrus (lines 62–63), floated into the sea and finally to Lesbos, where it was buried.   1. Or-
pheus was reputed to be able to charm even inanimate things with his music; he once persuaded
Pluto to release his dead wife, Eurydice, from the infernal regions.   2. Profits.   3. Customar-
ily do. Amaryllis (line 68) and Neaera (line 69) are stock names of women celebrated in pastoral
love poetry.

Or with the tangles of Neaera's hair?
70 Fame is the spur that the clear spirit doth raise
(That last infirmity of noble mind)
To scorn delights, and live laborious days;
But the fair guerdon[4] when we hope to find,
And think to burst out into sudden blaze,
75 Comes the blind Fury[5] with th' abhorréd shears,
And slits the thin-spun life. "But not the praise,"
Phoebus[6] replied, and touched my trembling ears:
"Fame is no plant that grows on mortal soil,
Nor in the glistering foil[7]
80 Set off to th' world, nor in broad rumor lies,
But lives and spreads aloft by those pure eyes
And perfect witness of all-judging Jove;
As he pronounces lastly on each deed,
Of so much fame in Heav'n expect thy meed."
85   O fountain Arethuse,[8] and thou honored flood,
Smooth-sliding Mincius, crowned with vocal reeds,
That strain I heard was of a higher mood.
But now my oat[9] proceeds,
And listens to the herald of the sea,[1]
90 That came in Neptune's plea.
He asked the waves and asked the felon-winds,
What hard mishap hath doomed this gentle swain,[2]
And questioned every gust of rugged wings
That blows from off each beakéd promontory.
95 They knew not of his story,
And sage Hippotades[3] their answer brings:
That not a blast was from his dungeon strayed;
The air was calm, and on the level brine,
Sleek Panopë[4] with all her sisters played.
100 It was that fatal and perfidious bark
Built in th' eclipse, and rigged with curses dark,
That sunk so low that sacred head of thine,
        Next Camus,[5] reverend sire, went footing slow,
His mantle hairy, and his bonnet sedge,
105 Inwrought with figures dim, and on the edge

4. Reward.   5. Atropos, the Fate who cuts the threads of human life after they are spun and measured by her two sisters.   6. Apollo, god of poetic inspiration. In Roman tradition, touching the ears of one's hearers meant asking them to remember what they heard.   7. Flashy setting, used to make inferior gems glitter.   8. A Sicilian fountain, associated with the pastoral poetry of Theocritus. The River Mincius (line 86) is associated with Vergil's pastorals.   9. Oaten pipe: pastoral song.   1. Triton, who maintains the innocence of Neptune, the Roman god of the sea, in the death of Lycidas.   2. Youth, shepherd, poet.   3. Aeolus, god of the winds and son of Hippotas.   4. According to Vergil, the greatest of the Nereids (sea nymphs).   5. God of the River Cam, which flows through Cambridge.

Like to that sanguine flower inscribed with woe.[6]
"Ah! who hath reft," quoth he, "my dearest pledge?"
Last came, and last did go,
The pilot of the Galilean Lake;[7]
Two massy keys he bore of metals twain   110
(The golden opes, the iron shuts amain).
He shook his mitered locks, and stern bespake:
"How well could I have spared for thee, young swain,
Enow[8] of such as for their bellies' sake
Creep and intrude, and climb into the fold![9]   115
Of other care they little reck'ning make,
Than how to scramble at the shearers' feast,
And shove away the worthy bidden guest.
Blind mouths! that scarce themselves know how to hold
A sheep-hook,[1] or have learned aught else the least   120
That to the faithful herdman's art belongs!
What recks it[2] them? What need they? They are sped,[3]
And when they list,[4] their lean and flashy songs
Grate on their scrannel[5] pipes of wretched straw.
The hungry sheep look up and are not fed,   125
But swoln with wind, and the rank mist they draw,
Rot inwardly, and foul contagion spread,
Besides what the grim wolf with privy paw[6]
Daily devours apace, and nothing said;
But that two-handed engine[7] at the door   130
Stands ready to smite once, and smite no more."
   Return, Alpheus,[8] the dread voice is past,
That shrunk thy streams; return, Sicilian Muse,
And call the vales, and bid them hither cast
Their bells and flowrets of a thousand hues.   135
Ye valleys low, where the mild whispers use,[9]
Of shades and wanton winds and gushing brooks,
On whose fresh lap the swart star[1] sparely looks,

---

6. The hyacinth, which was supposed to bear marks that meant "alas" because the flower was created by Phoebus from the blood of a youth he had killed accidentally.   7. St. Peter, a fisherman before he became a disciple. According to Matthew 16:19, Christ promised him "the keys of the kingdom of heaven"; he was traditionally regarded as the first head of the Church, hence the bishop's miter in line 112.   8. The old plural of "enough."   9. According to John 10:1, "He that entereth not by the door into the sheepfold, but climbeth up some other way . . . is a thief and a robber."   1. A bishop's staff was shaped like a sheephook to suggest his role as "pastor" (shepherd) of the flock of saints.   2. Does it matter to.   3. Have attained their purpose—but also, destroyed.   4. Desire.   5. Feeble.   6. The Roman Catholic Church.   7. Not identified. Guesses include the two-handed sword of the archangel Michael, the two houses of Parliament, and St. Peter's keys.   8. A river god who, according to Ovid, fell in love with Arethusa. She fled in the form of an underground stream and became a fountain in Sicily, but Alpheus dived under the sea and at last his waters mingled with hers. See above, line 85. *Sicilian Muse*: the muse of Theocritus.   9. Frequent.   1. Sirius, the Dog Star, which supposedly withers plants in late summer.

Throw hither all your quaint enameled eyes,
140 That on the green turf suck the honeyed showers,
And purple all the ground with vernal flowers.
Bring the rathe[2] primrose that forsaken dies,
The tufted crow-toe, and pale jessamine,
The white pink, and the pansy freaked[3] with jet,
145 The glowing violet,
The musk-rose, and the well-attired woodbine,
With cowslips wan that hang the pensive head,
And every flower that sad embroidery wears.
Bid amaranthus[4] all his beauty shed,
150 And daffodillies fill their cups with tears,
To strew the laureate hearse[5] where Lycid lies.
For so to interpose a little ease,
Let our frail thoughts dally with false surmise.
Ay me! Whilst thee the shores and sounding seas
155 Wash far away, where'er thy bones are hurled,
Whether beyond the stormy Hebrides,[6]
Where thou perhaps under the whelming tide
Visit'st the bottom of the monstrous world;[7]
Or whether thou to our moist vows denied,
160 Sleep'st by the fable of Bellerus old,[8]
Where the great vision of the guarded mount
Look toward Namancos and Bayona's hold;
Look homeward, Angel, now, and melt with ruth.[9]
And, O ye dolphins,[1] waft the hapless youth.
165   Weep no more, woeful shepherds, weep no more,
For Lycidas your sorrow is not dead,
Sunk though he be beneath the wat'ry floor,
So sinks the day-star[2] in the ocean bed,
And yet anon repairs his drooping head,
170 And tricks[3] his beams, and with new-spangled ore
Flames in the forehead of the morning sky:
So Lycidas sunk low, but mounted high,
Through the dear might of him that walked the waves,[4]
Where, other groves and other streams along,
175 With nectar pure his oozy locks he laves,
And hears the unexpressive nuptial song,[5]
In the blest kingdoms meek of joy and love.

2. Early.   3. Flecked.   4. A legendary flower that cannot fade.   5. Bier.   6. Islands off
Scotland, the northern edge of the sea where King drowned.   7. World where monsters li-
ve.   8. A legendary giant, supposedly buried at Land's End in Cornwall. At the tip of Land's End
is St. Michael's Mount (line 161), from which the archangel is pictured looking south across the
Atlantic toward Spanish (Catholic) strongholds (Namancos and Bayona, line 162).   9. Pity.
1. According to Roman legend, dolphins brought the body of a drowned youth, Melicertes, to
land, where a temple was erected to him as the protector of sailors.   2. The sun.
3. Dresses.   4. Christ. See Matthew 14:25–26.   5. Sung at the "marriage of the Lamb," ac-
cording to Revelation 19, *unexpressive*: inexpressible.

There entertain him all the saints above,
In solemn troops and sweet societies
That sing, and singing in their glory move,   180
And wipe the tears forever from his eyes.
Now, Lycidas, the shepherds weep no more;
Henceforth thou art the genius[6] of the shore,
In thy large recompense, and shalt be good
To all that wander in that perilous flood.   185
    Thus sang the uncouth swain[7] to th' oaks and rills,
While the still morn went out with sandals gray;
He touched the tender stops of various quills,[8]
With eager thought warbling his Doric[9] lay.
And now the sun had stretched out all the hills,   190
And now was dropped into the western bay.
At last he rose, and twitched his mantle blue:
Tomorrow to fresh woods, and pastures new.   1637

MICHAEL ONDAATJE

King Kong Meets Wallace Stevens

Take two photographs—
Wallace Stevens and King Kong
(Is it significant that I eat bananas as I write this?)

Stevens is portly, benign, a white brush cut
striped tie. Businessman but   5
for the dark thick hands, the naked brain
the thought in him.

Kong is staggering
lost in New York streets again
a spawn of annoyed cars at his toes.   10
The mind is nowhere.
Fingers are plastic, electric under the skin.
He's at the call of Metro-Goldwyn-Mayer.

Meanwhile W. S. in his suit
is thinking chaos is thinking fences.
In his head—the seeds of fresh pain   15
his exorcising,
the bellow of locked blood.

The hands drain from his jacket,
pose in the murderer's shadow.   1979   20

---

6. Protecting deity.   7. Unlettered shepherd: i.e., Milton.   8. Reeds in the shepherd's pipes.
9. The Greek dialect of Theocritus, Bion, and Moschus, the first writers of pastoral.

SYLVIA PLATH

Black Rook in Rainy Weather

On the stiff twig up there
Hunches a wet black rook
Arranging and rearranging its feathers in the rain.
I do not expect a miracle
5   Or an accident

To set the sight on fire
In my eye, nor seek
Any more in the desultory weather some design,
But let spotted leaves fall as they fall,
10   Without ceremony, or portent

Although, I admit, I desire,
Occasionally, some backtalk
From the mute sky, I can't honestly complain:
A certain minor light may still
15   Leap incandescent

Out of kitchen table or chair
As if a celestial burning took
Possession of the most obtuse objects now and then—
Thus hallowing an interval
20   Otherwise inconsequent

By bestowing largesse, honor,
One might say love. At any rate, I now walk
Wary (for it could happen
Even in this dull, ruinous landscape); skeptical,
25   Yet politic; ignorant

Of whatever angel may choose to flare
Suddenly at my elbow. I only know that a rook
Ordering its black feathers can so shine
As to seize my senses, haul
30   My eyelids up, and grant

A brief respite from fear
Of total neutrality. With luck,
Trekking stubborn through this season
Of fatigue, I shall
35   Patch together a content

Of sorts. Miracles occur,
If you care to call those spasmodic
Tricks of radiance miracles. The wait's begun again,
The long wait for the angel,
40   For that rare, random descent.[1]   1960

---

1. According to Acts 2, the Holy Ghost at Pentecost descended like a dove upon Jesus' disciples.

Lady Lazarus

I have done it again.
One year in every ten
I manage it—

A sort of walking miracle, my skin
Bright as a Nazi lampshade,   5
My right foot

A paperweight,
My face a featureless, fine
Jew linen.

Peel off the napkin   10
O my enemy.
Do I terrify?—

The nose, the eye pits, the full set of teeth?
The sour breath
Will vanish in a day.   15

Soon, soon the flesh
The grave cave ate will be
At home on me

And I a smiling woman.
I am only thirty.   20
And like the cat I have nine times to die.

This is Number Three.
What a trash
To annihilate each decade.

What a million filaments.   25
The peanut-crunching crowd
Shoves in to see

Them unwrap me hand and foot—
The big strip tease.
Gentlemen, ladies   30

These are my hands
My knees.
I may be skin and bone,

Nevertheless, I am the same, identical woman.
The first time it happened I was ten.   35
It was an accident.

The second time I meant
To last it out and not come back at all.
I rocked shut

40 As a seashell.
They had to call and call
And pick the worms off me like sticky pearls.

Dying
Is an art, like everything else.
45 I do it exceptionally well.

I do it so it feels like hell.
I do it so it feels real.
I guess you could say I've a call.

It's easy enough to do it in a cell.
50 It's easy enough to do it and stay put.
It's the theatrical

Comeback in broad day
To the same place, the same face, the same brute
Amused shout:

55 "A miracle!"
That knocks me out.
There is a charge

For the eyeing of my scars, there is a charge
For the hearing of my heart—
60 It really goes.

And there is a charge, a very large charge
For a word or a touch
Or a bit of blood

Or a piece of my hair or my clothes.
65 So, so Herr Doktor.
So, Herr Enemy.

I am your opus,
I am your valuable,
The pure gold baby

70 That melts to a shriek.
I turn and burn.
Do not think I underestimate your great concern

Ash, ash—
You poke and stir.
75 Flesh, bone, there is nothing there—

A cake of soap,
A wedding ring,
A gold filling.

Herr God, Herr Lucifer
80 Beware
Beware.

Out of the ash
I rise with my red hair
And I eat men like air.

1965

EZRA POUND

The Garden

En robe de parade.
—SAMAIN[2]

Like a skein of loose silk blown against a wall
She walks by the railing of a path in Kensington Gardens,[3]
And she is dying piece-meal
     of a sort of emotional anæmia.

And round about there is a rabble   5
Of the filthy, sturdy, unkillable infants of the very poor.
They shall inherit the earth.

In her is the end of breeding.
Her boredom is exquisite and excessive.
She would like some one to speak to her,   10
And is almost afraid that I
     will commit that indiscretion.

1916

In a Station of the Metro[4]

The apparition of these faces in the crowd;
Petals on a wet, black bough.

p. 1913

A Virginal

No, no! Go from me. I have left her lately.
I will not spoil my sheath with lesser brightness,
For my surrounding air hath a new lightness;
Slight are her arms, yet they have bound me straitly
And left me cloaked as with a gauze of aether;   5
As with sweet leaves; as with a subtle clearness.

2. Albert Samain, late 19th-century French poet. The phrase is from the first line of the prefatory poem in his first book of poems, *Au Jardin de l'Infante:* "Mon âme est une infante en robe de parade" ("My soul is an Infanta in ceremonial dress"). An "Infanta" is a daughter of the Spanish royal family, which, long inbred, had for many years been afflicted with a rare blood disease, hemophilia.   **3.** A fashionable park near the center of London.   **4.** The Paris subway.

Oh, I have picked up magic in her nearness
To sheathe me half in half the things that sheathe her.
No, no! Go from me, I have still the flavor,
Soft as spring wind that's come from birchen bowers.
Green come the shoots, aye April in the branches,
As winter's wound with her sleight hand she staunches,
Hath of the trees a likeness of the savor:
As white their bark, so white this lady's hours.

1912

JOHN CROWE RANSOM

Bells for John Whiteside's Daughter

There was such speed in her little body,
And such lightness in her footfall,
It is no wonder her brown study[5]
Astonishes us all.

Her wars were bruited in our high window.
We looked among orchard trees and beyond
Where she took arms against her shadow,
Or harried unto the pond

The lazy geese, like a snow cloud
Dripping their snow on the green grass,
Tricking and stopping, sleepy and proud,
Who cried in goose, Alas,

For the tireless heart within the little
Lady with rod that made them rise
From their noon apple-dreams and scuttle
Goose-fashion under the skies!

But now go the bells, and we are ready,
In one house we are sternly stopped
To say we are vexed at her brown study,
Lying so primly propped.

1924

THEODORE ROETHKE

The Dream

1

I met her as a blossom on a stem
Before she ever breathed, and in that dream

5. Stillness, as if in meditation or deep thought.

The mind remembers from a deeper sleep:
Eye learned from eye, cold lip from sensual lip.
My dream divided on a point of fire;   5
Light hardened on the water where we were;
A bird sang low; the moonlight sifted in;
The water rippled, and she rippled on.

2

She came toward me in the flowing air,
A shape of change, encircled by its fire.   10
I watched her there, between me and the moon;
The bushes and the stones danced on and on;
I touched her shadow when the light delayed;
I turned my face away, and yet she stayed.
A bird sang from the center of a tree;   15
She loved the wind because the wind loved me.

3

Love is not love until love's vulnerable.
She slowed to sigh, in that long interval.
A small bird flew in circles where we stood;
The deer came down, out of the dappled wood.   20
All who remember, doubt. Who calls that strange?
I tossed a stone, and listened to its plunge.
She knew the grammar of least motion, she
Lent me one virtue, and I live thereby.

4

She held her body steady in the wind;   25
Our shadows met, and slowly swung around;
She turned the field into a glittering sea;
I played in flame and water like a boy
And I swayed out beyond the white seafoam;
Like a wet log, I sang within a flame.   30
In that last while, eternity's confine,
I came to love, I came into my own.   1958

I Knew a Woman

I knew a woman, lovely in her bones,
When small birds sighed, she would sigh back at them;
Ah, when she moved, she moved more ways than one:
The shapes a bright container can contain!
Of her choice virtues only gods should speak;   5

Or English poets who grew up on Greek
(I'd have them sing in chorus, cheek to cheek).

How well her wishes went! She stroked my chin,
She taught me Turn, and Counter-turn, and Stand;[6]
10   She taught me Touch, that undulant white skin;
I nibbled meekly from her proffered hand;
She was the sickle; I, poor I, the rake,
Coming behind her for her pretty sake
(But what prodigious mowing we did make).

15   Love likes a gander, and adores a goose:
Her full lips pursed, the errant note to seize;
She played it quick, she played it light and loose;
My eyes, they dazzled at her flowing knees;
Her several parts could keep a pure repose,
20   Or one hip quiver with a mobile nose
(She moved in circles, and those circles moved).

Let seed be grass, and grass turn into hay:
I'm martyr to a motion not my own;
What's freedom for? To know eternity.
25   I swear she cast a shadow white as stone.
But who would count eternity in days?
These old bones live to learn her wanton ways:
(I measure time by how a body sways).   1958

The Waking

I wake to sleep, and take my waking slow.
I feel my fate in what I cannot fear.
I learn by going where I have to go.

We think by feeling. What is there to know?
5   I hear my being dance from ear to ear.
I wake to sleep, and take my waking slow.

Of those so close beside me, which are you?
God bless the Ground! I shall walk softly there,
And learn by going where I have to go.

10   Light takes the Tree; but who can tell us how?
The lowly worm climbs up a winding stair;
I wake to sleep, and take my waking slow.

Great Nature has another thing to do
To you and me; so take the lively air,
15   And, lovely, learn by going where to go.

6. Literary terms for the parts of a Pindaric ode.

This shaking keeps me steady. I should know.
What falls away is always. And is near.
I wake to sleep, and take my waking slow.
I learn by going where I have to go.   1953

MURIEL RUKEYSER

Reading Time : 1 Minute 26 Seconds

The fear of poetry is the
fear : mystery and fury of a midnight street
of windows whose low voluptuous voice
issues, and after that there is no peace.

That round waiting moment in the   5
theatre : curtain rises, dies into the ceiling
and here is played the scene with the mother
bandaging a revealed son's head.   The bandage is torn off.
Curtain goes down.   And here is the moment of proof.

That climax when the brain acknowledges the world,   10
all values extended into the blood awake.
Moment of proof.   And as they say Brancusi did,
building his bird to extend through soaring air,
as Kafka planned stories that draw to eternity
through time extended.   And the climax strikes.   15

Love touches so, that months after the look of
blue stare of love, the footbeat on the heart
is translated into the pure cry of birds
following air-cries, or poems, the new scene.
Moment of proof.   That strikes long after act.   20

They fear it.   They turn away, hand up palm out
fending off moment of proof, the straight look, poem.
The prolonged wound-consciousness after the bullet's shot.
The prolonged love after the look is dead,
the yellow joy after the song of the sun.   1939   25

Myth

Long afterward, Oedipus, old and blinded, walked the
roads.   He smelled a familiar smell.   It was
the Sphinx.   Oedipus said, "I want to ask one question.
Why didn't I recognize my mother?"   "You gave the
wrong answer," said the Sphinx.   "But that was what   5

made everything possible," said Oedipus.   "No," she said.
"When I asked, What walks on four legs in the morning,
two at noon, and three in the evening, you answered,
Man.   You didn't say anything about woman."

10   "When you say Man," said Oedipus, "you include women
too. Everyone knows that."   She said, "That's what
you think."

1973

WILLIAM SHAKESPEARE

[Hark, hark! the lark at heaven's gate sings][7]

Hark, hark! the lark at heaven's gate sings,
    And Phoebus'[8] gins arise,
His steeds to water at those springs
    On chaliced[9] flowers that lies;
5   And winking Mary-buds[1] begin
    To ope their golden eyes:
With every thing that pretty is,
    My lady sweet, arise!
ca. 1610   Arise, arise!

[Two loves I have of comfort and despair]

Two loves I have of comfort and despair,
Which like two spirits do suggest[2] me still:
The better angel is a man right fair,
The worser spirit a woman, color'd ill.[3]
5   To win me soon to hell, my female evil
Tempteth my better angel from my side,
And would corrupt my saint to be a devil,
Wooing his purity with her foul pride.
And whether that my angel be turn'd fiend
10   Suspect I may, but not directly tell
But being both from me,[4] both to each friend,
I guess one angel in another's hell:
    Yet this shall I ne'er know, but live in doubt,
    Till my bad angel fire[5] my good one out.

1609

---

7. From *Cymbeline*, Act II, scene 3.   8. Apollo, the sun god.   9. Cup-shaped.   1. Buds of
marigolds.   2. Tempt. *Still:* constantly.   3. Badly.   4. Away from me. *Both to each friend:*
friends to each other.   5. Drive out with fire ("fire" was Elizabethan slang for venereal disease).

Spring[6]

When daisies pied and violets blue
   And ladysmocks all silver-white
And cuckoobuds of yellow hue
   Do paint the meadows with delight,
The cuckoo then, on every tree,   5
Mocks married men;[7] for thus sings he,
            Cuckoo;
Cuckoo, cuckoo: Oh word of fear,
Unpleasing to a married ear!

When shepherds pipe on oaten straws,   10
   And merry larks are plowmen's clocks,
When turtles tread,[8] and rooks, and daws,
   And maidens bleach their summer smocks,
The cuckoo then, on every tree,
Mocks married men; for thus sings he,   15
            Cuckoo;
Cuckoo, cuckoo: Oh word of fear,
Unpleasing to a married ear!

ca. 1595

Winter

When icicles hang by the wall
   And Dick the shepherd blows[9] his nail,
And Tom bears logs into the hall,
   And milk comes frozen home in pail.
When blood is nipped and ways be foul,   5
Then nightly sings the staring owl,
            Tu-who;
Tu-whit, tu-who: a merry note,
While greasy Joan doth keel[1] the pot.

When all aloud the wind doth blow,   10
   And coughing drowns the parson's saw,[2]
And birds sit brooding in the snow,
   And Marian's nose looks red and raw,
When roasted crabs[3] hiss in the bowl,
Then nightly sings the staring owl,   15
            Tu-who;
Tu-whit, tu-who: a merry note
ca. 1595   While greasy Joan doth keel the pot.

---

6. Like "Winter" (below), a song from *Love's Labors Lost*, Act V, scene 2.
7. By the resemblance of its call to the word "cuckold."   8. Copulate. *Turtles:* turtle-doves.   9. Breathes on for warmth. *Nail:* fingernail; i.e., hands.   1. Cool: stir to keep it from boiling over.   2. Maxim, proverb.   3. Crabapples.

WALLACE STEVENS

Anecdote of the Jar

I placed a jar in Tennessee,
And round it was, upon a hill.
It made the slovenly wilderness
Surround that hill.

The wilderness rose up to it,
And sprawled around, no longer wild.
The jar was round upon the ground
And tall and of a port in air.

It took dominion everywhere.
The jar was gray and bare.
It did not give of bird or bush,
Like nothing else in Tennessee.   1923

The Emperor of Ice-Cream

Call the roller of big cigars,
The muscular one, and bid him whip
In kitchen cups concupiscent curds.[4]
Let the wenches dawdle in such dress
As they are used to wear, and let the boys
Bring flowers in last month's newspapers.
Let be be finale of seem.[5]
The only emperor is the emperor of ice-cream.

Take from the dresser of deal,
Lacking the three glass knobs, that sheet
On which she embroidered fantails[6] once
And spread it so as to cover her face.
If her horny feet protrude, they come
To show how cold she is, and dumb.
Let the lamp affix its beam.
The only emperor is the emperor of ice-cream.   1923

4. "The words 'concupiscent curds' have no genealogy; they are merely expressive: at least, I hope they are expressive. They express the concupiscence of life, but, by contrast with the things in relation in the poem, they express or accentuate life's destitution, and it is this that gives them something more than a cheap lustre." Wallace Stevens, *Letters* (New York: Knopf, 1966), p. 500.   5. ". . . the true sense of Let be be the finale of seem is let being become the conclusion of denouement of appearing to be: in short, ice cream is an absolute good. The poem is obviously not about ice cream, but about being as distinguished from seeming to be." Stevens, *Letters*, p. 341. 6. Fantail pigeons.

Sunday Morning

I

Complacencies of the peignoir, and late
Coffee and oranges in a sunny chair,
And the green freedom of a cockatoo
Upon a rug mingle to dissipate
The holy hush of ancient sacrifice.   5
She dreams a little, and she feels the dark
Encroachment of that old catastrophe,[7]
As a calm darkens among water-lights.
The pungent oranges and bright, green wings
Seem things in some procession of the dead,   10
Winding across wide water, without sound,
The day is like wide water, without sound,
Stilled for the passing of her dreaming feet
Over the seas, to silent Palestine,
Dominion of the blood and sepulchre.   15

II

Why should she give her bounty to the dead?
What is divinity if it can come
Only in silent shadows and in dreams?
Shall she not find in comforts of the sun,
In pungent fruit and bright, green wings, or else   20
In any balm or beauty of the earth,
Things to be cherished like the thought of heaven.
Divinity must live within herself:
Passions of rain, or moods in falling snow;
Grievings in loneliness, or unsubdued   25
Elations when the forest blooms; gusty
Emotions on wet roads on autumn nights;
All pleasures and all pains, remembering
The bough of summer and the winter branch.
These are the measures destined for her soul.   30

III

Jove in the clouds has his inhuman birth.
No mother suckled him, no sweet land gave
Large-mannered motions to his mythy mind
He moved among us, as a muttering king,
Magnificent, would move among his hinds,[8]   35
Until our blood, commingling, virginal,

7. The Crucifixion.   8. Lowliest rural subjects.

With heaven, brought such requital to desire
The very hinds discerned it, in a star.[9]
Shall our blood fail? Or shall it come to be
40   The blood of paradise? And shall the earth
Seem all of paradise that we shall know?
The sky will be much friendlier then than now,
A part of labor and a part of pain,
And next in glory to enduring love,
45   Not this dividing and indifferent blue.

IV

She says, "I am content when wakened birds,
Before they fly, test the reality
Of misty fields, by their sweet questionings;
But when the birds are gone, and their warm fields
50   Return no more, where, then, is paradise?"
There is not any haunt of prophecy,
Nor any old chimera of the grave,
Neither the golden underground, nor isle
Melodious, where spirits gat[1] them home,
55   Nor visionary south, nor cloudy palm
Remote on heaven's hill, that has endured
As April's green endures, or will endure
Like her remembrance of awakened birds,
Or her desire for June and evening, tipped
60   By the consummation of the swallow's wings.

V

She says, "But in contentment I still feel
The need of some imperishable bliss."
Death is the mother of beauty; hence from her,
Alone, shall come fulfillment to our dreams
65   And our desires. Although she strews the leaves
Of sure obliteration on our paths,
The path sick sorrow took, the many paths
Where triumph rang its brassy phrase, or love
Whispered a little out of tenderness,
70   She makes the willow shiver in the sun
For maidens who were wont to sit and gaze
Upon the grass, relinquished to their feet.
She causes boys to pile new plums and pears
On disregarded plate.[2] The maidens taste
75   And stray impassioned in the littering leaves.

---

9. The star of Bethlehem.   1. Got.   2. "Plate is used in the sense of so-called family plate. Disregarded refers to the disuse into which things fall that have been possessed for a long time. I mean, therefore, that death releases and renews. What the old have come to disregard, the young inherit and make use of." Stevens, *Letters*, pp. 183–84.

VI

Is there no change of death in paradise?
Does ripe fruit never fall? Or do the boughs
Hang always heavy in that perfect sky,
Unchanging, yet so like our perishing earth,
With rivers like our own that seek for seas   80
They never find, the same receding shores
That never touch with inarticulate pang?
Why set the pear upon those river-banks
Or spice the shores with odors of the plum?
Alas, that they should wear our colors there,   85
The silken weavings of our afternoons,
And pick the strings of our insipid lutes!
Death is the mother of beauty, mystical,
Within whose burning bosom we devise
Our earthly mothers awaiting, sleeplessly.   90

VII

Supple and turbulent, a ring of men
Shall chant in orgy[3] on a summer morn
Their boisterous devotion to the sun,
Not as a god, but as a god might be,
Naked among them, like a savage source.   95
Their chant shall be a chant of paradise,
Out of their blood, returning to the sky;
And in their chant shall enter, voice by voice,
The windy lake wherein their lord delights,
The trees, like serafin,[4] and echoing hills,   100
That choir among themselves long afterward.
They shall know well the heavenly fellowship
Of men that perish and of summer morn.
And whence they came and whither they shall go
The dew upon their feet shall manifest.   105

VIII

She hears, upon that water without sound,
A voice that cries, "The tomb in Palestine
Is not the porch of spirits lingering.
It is the grave of Jesus, where he lay."
We live in an old chaos of the sun,   110
Or old dependency of day and night,
Or island solitude, unsponsored, free,
Of that wide water, inescapable.
Deer walk upon our mountains, and the quail

---

3. Ceremonial revelry.   4. Seraphim, the highest of the nine orders of angels.

115 Whistle about us their spontaneous cries;
Sweet berries ripen in the wilderness;
And, in the isolation of the sky,
At evening, casual flocks of pigeons make
Ambiguous undulations as they sink,
120 Downward to darkness, on extended wings.

1915

ALFRED, LORD TENNYSON

Tears, Idle Tears[5]

Tears, idle tears, I know not what they mean,
Tears from the depth of some divine despair
Rise in the heart, and gather to the eyes,
In looking on the happy autumn-fields,
5 And thinking of the days that are no more.

Fresh as the first beam glittering on a sail,
That brings our friends up from the underworld,
Sad as the last which reddens over one
That sinks with all we love below the verge;
10 So sad, so fresh, the days that are no more.

Ah, sad and strange as in dark summer dawns
The earliest pipe of half-awakened birds
To dying ears, when unto dying eyes
The casement slowly grows a glimmering square;
15 So sad, so strange, the days that are no more.

Dear as remembered kisses after death,
And sweet as those by hopeless fancy feigned
On lips that are for others; deep as love,
Deep as first love, and wild with all regret;
20 O Death in Life, the days that are no more!

1847

Tithonus[6]

The woods decay, the woods decay and fall,
The vapors weep their burthen to the ground,
Man comes and tills the field and lies beneath,

5. A song from *The Princess*, a long narrative poem about what the mid-19th century called the "new woman."   6. Prince of Troy. He is loved by Aurora, goddess of the dawn, to whom he speaks the poem. Aurora obtained for him the gift of eternal life but forgot to ask for eternal youth.

And after many a summer dies the swan.
Me only cruel immortality 5
Consumes; I wither slowly in thine arms,
Here at the quiet limit of the world,
A white-haired shadow roaming like a dream
The ever-silent spaces of the East,
Far-folded mists, and gleaming halls of morn. 10
   Alas! for this gray shadow, once a man—
So glorious in his beauty and thy choice,
Who madest him thy chosen, that he seemed
To his great heart none other than a God!
I asked thee, "Give me immortality." 15
Then didst thou grant mine asking with a smile,
Like wealthy men who care not how they give.
But thy strong Hours indignant worked their wills,
And beat me down and marred and wasted me,
And though they could not end me, left me maimed 20
To dwell in presence of immortal youth,
Immortal age beside immortal youth,
And all I was in ashes. Can thy love,
Thy beauty, make amends, though even now,
Close over us, the silver star, thy guide, 25
Shines in those tremulous eyes that fill with tears
To hear me? Let me go; take back thy gift.
Why should a man desire in any way
To vary from the kindly race of men,
Or pass beyond the goal of ordinance 30
Where all should pause, as is most meet for all?
   A soft air fans the cloud apart; there comes
A glimpse of that dark world where I was born.
Once more the old mysterious glimmer steals
From thy pure brows, and from thy shoulders pure, 35
And bosom beating with a heart renewed.
Thy cheek begins to redden through the gloom,
Thy sweet eyes brighten slowly close to mine,
Ere yet they blind the stars, and the wild team
Which love thee, yearning for thy yoke, arise, 40
And shake the darkness from their loosened manes,
And beat the twilight into flakes of fire.
   Lo! ever thus thou growest beautiful
In silence, then before thine answer given
Departest, and thy tears are on my cheek. 45
   Why wilt thou ever scare me with thy tears,
And make me tremble lest a saying learnt,
In days far-off, on that dark earth, be true?
"The Gods themselves cannot recall their gifts."
   Ay me! ay me! with what another heart 50
In days far-off, and with what other eyes

I used to watch—if I be he that watched—
The lucid outline forming round thee; saw
The dim curls kindle into sunny rings;
55 Changed with thy mystic change, and felt my blood
Glow with the glow that slowly crimsoned all
Thy presence and thy portals, while I lay,
Mouth, forehead, eyelids, growing dewy-warm
With kisses balmier than half-opening buds
60 Of April, and could hear the lips that kissed
Whispering I knew not what of wild and sweet,
Like that strange song I heard Apollo sing,
While Ilion like a mist rose into towers.
      Yet hold me not forever in thine East;
65 How can my nature longer mix with thine?
Coldly thy rosy shadows bathe me, cold
Are all thy lights, and cold my wrinkled feet
Upon thy glimmering thresholds, when the steam
Floats up from those dim fields about the homes
70 Of happy men that have the power to die,
And grassy barrows of the happier dead.
Release me, and restore me to the ground.
Thou seest all things, thou wilt see my grave;
Thou wilt renew thy beauty morn by morn,
75 I earth in earth forget these empty courts,
And thee returning on thy silver wheels.   1860

DYLAN THOMAS

Fern Hill

Now as I was young and easy under the apple boughs
About the lilting house and happy as the grass was green,
      The night above the dingle starry,
            Time let me hail and climb
5   Golden in the heydays of his eyes,
And honored among wagons I was prince of the apple towns
And once below a time I lordly had the trees and leaves
            Trail with daisies and barley
      Down the rivers of the windfall light.

10 And as I was green and carefree, famous among the barns
About the happy yard and singing as the farm was home,
      In the sun that is young once only,
            Time let me play and be
      Golden in the mercy of his means,
15 And green and golden I was huntsman and herdsman, the calves
Sang to my horn, the foxes on the hills barked clear and cold,

And the sabbath rang slowly
In the pebbles of the holy streams.

All the sun long it was running, it was lovely, the hay
Fields high as the house, the tunes from the chimneys, it was air   20
    And playing, lovely and watery
        And fire green as grass.
    And nightly under the simple stars
As I rode to sleep the owls were bearing the farm away,
All the moon long I heard, blessed among stables, the nightjars[7]   25
    Flying with the ricks,[8] and the horses
        Flashing into the dark.

And then to awake, and the farm, like a wanderer white
With the dew, come back, the cock on his shoulder: it was all
    Shining, it was Adam and maiden,
        The sky gathered again   30
    And the sun grew round that very day.
So it must have been after the birth of the simple light
In the first, spinning place, the spellbound horses walking warm
    Out of the whinnying green stable   35
        On to the fields of praise.

And honored among foxes and pheasants by the gay house
Under the new made clouds and happy as the heart was long,
    In the sun born over and over,
        I ran my heedless ways,   40
    My wishes raced through the house-high hay
And nothing I cared, at my sky-blue trades, that time allows
In all his tuneful turning so few and such morning songs
    Before the children green and golden
    Follow him out of grace,   45

Nothing I cared, in the lamb white days, that time would take me
Up to the swallow-thronged loft by the shadow of my hand,
    In the moon that is always rising,
        Nor that riding to sleep
    I should hear him fly with the high fields   50
And wake to the farm forever fled from the childless land.
Oh as I was young and easy in the mercy of his means,
    Time held me green and dying
    Though I sang in my chains like the sea.   1946

In My Craft or Sullen Art

In my craft or sullen art
Exercised in the still night

---

7. Birds.   8. Haystacks.

When only the moon rages
And the lovers lie abed
5 With all their griefs in their arms,
I labor by singing light
Not for ambition or bread
Or the strut and trade of charms
On the ivory stages
10 But for the common wages
Of their most secret heart.

Not for the proud man apart
From the raging moon I write
On these spindrift⁹ pages
15 Nor for the towering dead
With their nightingales and psalms
But for the lovers, their arms
Round the griefs of the ages,
Who pay no praise or wages
20 Nor heed my craft or art.   1946

JEAN TOOMER

Song of the Son¹

Pour O pour that parting soul in song,
O pour it in the sawdust glow of night,
Into the velvet pine-smoke air tonight,
And let the valley carry it along.
5 And let the valley carry it along.

O land and soil, red soil and sweet-gum tree,
So scant of grass, so profligate of pines,
Now just before an epoch's sun declines
Thy son, in time, I have returned to thee,
10 Thy son, I have in time returned to thee.

In time, for though the sun is setting on
A song-lit race of slaves, it has not set;
Though late, O soil, it is not too late yet
To catch thy plaintive soul, leaving, soon gone,
15 Leaving, to catch thy plaintive soul soon gone.

O Negro slaves, dark purple ripened plums,
Squeezed, and bursting in the pine-wood air,
Passing, before they strip the old tree bare
One plum was saved for me, one seed becomes

---

9. Literally, wind-driven sea spray.   1. From the novel *Cane*.

An everlasting song, a singing tree,   20
Caroling softly souls of slavery,
What they were, and what they are to me,
Caroling softly souls of slavery.   1923

DIANE WAKOSKI

A Poet Recognizing the Echo
of the Voice

I. ISOLATION OF BEAUTIFUL WOMEN

"How were you able to get ten of the world's
most beautiful women to marry you?"
"I just asked them. You know, men all over
the world dream about Lana Turner, desire
her, want to be with her. But very very
few ever ask her to marry them."
                    —paraphrase of an interview with
                    ARTIE SHAW

We are burning
in our heads
at night,
bonfires of our own bodies.
Persia reduces our heads   5
to star sapphires and lapis lazuli.[2]
Silver threads itself
into the lines of our throats
and glitters every time we speak.

Old alchemical riddles[3]   10
are solved in the dreams of men
who marry other women and think of us.
Anyone who sees us
will hold our small hands,
like mirrors in which they see themselves,   15
and try to initial our arms
with desperation.
Everyone wants to come close to
the cinnamon of our ears.
Every man wants to explore our bodies   20
and fill up our minds.
Riding their motorcycles along collapsing grey highways,

---

2. Blue gems.   3. Problems. Alchemy was devoted to finding an elixir that would turn baser
metals to gold (line 31).

they sequester their ambivalent hunting clothes
between our legs,
25 reminding themselves of their value
by quoting mining stock prices, and ours.
But men do not marry us,
do not ask us to share their lives,
do not survive the bonfires
30 hot enough to melt steel.
To alchemize rubies.

We live the loneliness
that men run after,
and we,
35 the precious rocks of the earth
are made harder,
more fiery
more beautiful,
more complex,
40 by all the pressing,
the burying,
the plundering;

even your desertions,
your betrayals,
45 your failure to understand and love us,
your unwillingness to face the world
as staunchly as we do;
these things
which ravage us,
50 cannot destroy our lives,
though they often take our bodies.
We are the earth.
We wake up
finding ourselves
55 glinting in the dark
after thousands of years
of pressing.

II. MOVEMENT TO ESTABLISH MY IDENTITY

> I know what wages beauty gives,
> How hard a life her servant lives . . .
> —"To A Young Beauty," W. B. YEATS

A woman wakes up
finds herself
glinting in the dark;
60 the earth holds her

as a precious rock
in a mine

her breath is a jumble
of sediments,   65
of mixed strata,
of the valuable,
beautiful,
of bulk.

All men are miners;   70
willing to work hard
and cover themselves with pit dirt;
to dig out;
to weigh;
to possess.   75

Mine is a place.
Mine is a designation.
A man says, "it is mine,"
but he hacks,
chops apart the mine   80
to discover,
to plunder,
what's in it / Plunder,
that is the word.
Plunder.   85

A woman wakes up
finds herself
scarred
but still glinting
in the dark.   90

III. Beauty

> only God, my dear,
> Could love you for yourself alone
> And not your yellow hair.
> —"For Anne Gregory," w. b. yeats

and if I cut off my long hair,
if I stopped speaking,
if I stopped dreaming for other people about parts of the car,
stopped handing them tall creamy flowered silks
and loosing the magnificent hawks to fly in their direction,   95
stopped exciting them with the possibilities
of a thousand crystals under the fingernail
to look at while writing a letter,
if I stopped crying for the salvation of the tea ceremony,

100 stopped rushing in excitedly with a spikey bird-of-paradise,[4]
and never let them see how accurate my pistol shooting is,
who would I be?

Where is the real me
I want them all to love?

105 We are all the textures we wear.

We frighten men with our steel;
we fascinate them with our silk;
we seduce them with our cinnamon;
we rule them with our sensuous voices;
110 we confuse them with our submissions.
Is there anywhere
a man
who
will not punish us
115 for our beauty?

He is the one
we all search for,
chanting names for exotic oceans of the moon.

He is the one
120 we all anticipate,
pretending these small pedestrians
jaywalking into our lives
are he.
He is the one
125 we all anticipate;
beauty looks for its match,
confuses the issue
with a mystery that does not exist:
the rock
130 that cannot burn.

We are burning
in our heads at night
the incense of our histories, finding
you have used our skulls
135 for ashtrays.   1970

---

4. A bright, spectacular plant.

WALT WHITMAN

Facing West from California's Shores

Facing west, from California's shores,
Inquiring, tireless, seeking what is yet unfound,
I, a child, very old, over waves, towards the house of maternity,[5] the land of
    migrations, look afar,
Look off the shores of my Western sea, the circle almost circled:
For starting westward from Hindustan, from the vales of Kashmere,   5
    From Asia, from the north, from the God, the sage, and the hero,
From the south, from the flowery peninsulas and the spice islands,
Long having wandered since, round the earth having wandered,
Now I face home again, very pleased and joyous;
(But where is what I started for, so long ago?   10
    And why is it yet unfound?)   1860

I Hear America Singing

I hear America singing, the varied carols I hear,
Those of mechanics, each one singing his as it should be blithe and strong,
The carpenter singing his as he measures his plank or beam,
The mason singing his as he makes ready for work, or leaves off work,
The boatman singing what belongs to him in his boat, the deckhand singing on
    the steamboat deck,   5
    The shoemaker singing as he sits on his bench, the hatter singing as he
    stands,
The wood-cutter's song, the ploughboy's on his way in the morning, or at noon
    intermission or at sundown,
The delicious singing of the mother, or of the young wife at work, or of the girl
    sewing or washing,
Each singing what belongs to him or her and to none else,
The day what belongs to the day—at night the party of young fellows, robust,
    friendly,   10
Singing with open mouths their strong melodious songs.   1860

A Noiseless Patient Spider

A noiseless patient spider,
I marked where on a little promontory it stood isolated,

5. Asia, as the supposed birthplace of the human race.

Marked how to explore the vacant vast surrounding,
It launched forth filament, filament, filament, out of itself,
5   Ever unreeling them, ever tirelessly speeding them.

      And you O my soul where you stand,
Surrounded, detached, in measureless oceans of space,
Ceaselessly musing, venturing, throwing, seeking the spheres to connect them,
Till the bridge you will need be formed, till the ductile anchor hold,
10 Till the gossamer thread you fling catch somewhere, O my soul.   1881

When Lilacs Last in the Dooryard Bloomed⁶

1

When lilacs last in the dooryard bloomed,
And the great star early drooped in the western sky in the night,
I mourned, and yet shall mourn with ever-returning spring.

Ever-returning spring, trinity sure to me you bring,
5   Lilac blooming perennial and drooping star in the west,
And thought of him I love.

2

O powerful western fallen star!
O shades of night—O moody, tearful night!
O great star disappeared—O the black murk that hides the star!
10 O cruel hands that hold me powerless—O helpless soul of me!
O harsh surrounding cloud that will not free my soul.

3

In the dooryard fronting an old farm-house near the white-washed palings,
Stands the lilac-bush tall-growing with heart-shaped leaves of rich green,
With many a pointed blossom rising delicate, with the perfume strong I love,
15 With every leaf a miracle—and from this bush in the dooryard,
With delicate-colored blossoms and heart-shaped leaves of rich green,
A sprig with its flower I break.

4

In the swamp in secluded recesses,
A shy and hidden bird is warbling a song.

6. The "occasion" of the poem is the assassination of Abraham Lincoln.

Solitary the thrush,   20
The hermit withdrawn to himself, avoiding the settlements,
Sings by himself a song.

Song of the bleeding throat,
Death's outlet song of life (for well dear brother I know,
If thou wast not granted to sing thou would'st surely die).   25

                                    5

Over the breast of the spring, the land, amid cities,
Amid lanes and through old woods, where lately the violets peeped from the
    ground, spotting the gray debris,
Amid the grass in the fields each side of the lanes, passing the endless grass,
Passing the yellow-speared wheat, every grain from its shroud in the dark-
    brown fields uprisen,
Passing the apple-tree blows of white and pink in the orchards,   30
Carrying a corpse to where it shall rest in the grave,
Night and day journeys a coffin.

                                    6

Coffin that passes through lanes and streets,[7]
Through day and night with the great cloud darkening the land,
With the pomp of the inlooped flags with the cities draped in black,   35
    With the show of the States themselves as of crepe-veiled women standing,
With processions long and winding and the flambeaus of the night,
With the countless torches lit, with the silent sea of faces and the unbared
    heads,
With the waiting depot, the arriving coffin, and the somber faces,
With dirges through the night, with the thousand voices rising strong and
    solemn,
    With all the mournful voices of the dirges poured around the coffin,   40
The dim-lit churches and the shuddering organs—where amid these you
    journey,
With the tolling tolling bells' perpetual clang,
Here, coffin that slowly passes,
I give you my sprig of lilac.   45

                                    7

(Nor for you, for one alone,
Blossoms and branches green to coffins all I bring,
For fresh as the morning, thus would I chant a song for you O sane and
    sacred death.

---

7. The funeral cortege stopped at many towns between Washington and Springfield, Illinois, where
Lincoln was buried.

All over bouquets of roses,
50 O death, I cover you over with roses and early lilies,
But mostly and now the lilac that blooms the first,
Copious I break, I break the sprigs from the bushes,
With loaded arms I come, pouring for you,
For you and the coffins all of you O death.)

8

55 O western orb sailing the heaven,
Now I know what you must have meant as a month since I walked,
As I walked in silence the transparent shadowy night,
As I saw you had something to tell as you bent to me night after night,
As you drooped from the sky low down as if to my side (while the other stars
all looked on),
As we wandered together the solemn night (for something I know not what
60 kept me from sleep),
As the night advanced, and I saw on the rim of the west how full you were
of woe,
As I stood on the rising ground in the breeze in the cool transparent night,
As I watched where you passed and was lost in the netherward black of the
night,
65 As my soul in its trouble dissatisfied sank, as where you sad orb,
Concluded, dropped in the night, and was gone.

9

Sing on there in the swamp,
O singer bashful and tender, I hear your notes, I hear your call,
I hear, I come presently, I understand you,
But a moment I linger, for the lustrous star has detained me,
70 The star my departing comrade holds and detains me.

10

O how shall I warble myself for the dead one there I loved?
And how shall I deck my song for the large sweet soul that has gone?
And what shall my perfume be for the grave of him I love?
Sea-winds blown from east and west,
Blown from the Eastern sea and blown from the Western sea, till there on
75 the prairies meeting,
These and with these and the breath of my chant,
I'll perfume the grave of him I love.

11

O what shall I hang on the chamber walls?
And what shall the pictures be that I hang on the walls,
To adorn the burial-house of him I love?

80

Pictures of growing spring and farms and homes,
With the Fourth-month eve at sundown, and the gray smoke lucid and
    bright,
With floods of the yellow gold of the gorgeous, indolent, sinking sun, burn-
    ing, expanding the air,
With the fresh sweet herbage under foot, and the pale green leaves of the
    trees prolific,
In the distance the flowing glaze, the breast of the river, with a wind-dapple
    here and there,   85
    With ranging hills on the banks, with many a line against the sky, and
    shadows,
And the city at hand with dwellings so dense, and stacks of chimneys,
And all the scenes of life and the workshops, and the workmen homeward
    returning.

                                    12

Lo, body and soul—this land,
My own Manhattan with spires, and the sparkling and hurrying tides, and
    the ships,   90
    The varied and ample land, the South and the North in the light, Ohio's
    shores and flashing Missouri,
And ever the far-spreading prairies covered with grass and corn.

Lo, the most excellent sun so calm and haughty,
The violet and purple morn with just-felt breezes,
The gentle soft-born measureless light,   95
    The miracle spreading bathing all, the fulfilled noon,
The coming eve delicious, the welcome night and the stars,
Over my cities shining all, enveloping man and land.

                                    13

Sing on, sing on you gray-brown bird,
Sing from the swamps, the recesses, pour your chant from the bushes,   100
Limitless out of the dusk, out of the cedars and pines.

Sing on dearest brother, warble your reedy song,
Loud human song, with voice of uttermost woe.

O liquid and free and tender!
O wild and loose to my soul—O wondrous singer!   105
You only I hear—yet the star holds me (but will soon depart),
Yet the lilac with mastering odor holds me.

                                    14

Now while I sat in the day and looked forth,
In the close of the day with its light and the fields of spring, and the farmers
    preparing their crops,
In the large unconscious scenery of my land with its lakes and forests,   110

In the heavenly aerial beauty (after the perturbed winds and the storms),
Under the arching heavens of the afternoon swift passing, and the voices of
    children and women.
The many-moving sea-tides, and I saw the ships how they sailed,
And the summer approaching with richness, and the fields all busy with
    labor,
And the infinite separate houses, how they all went on, each with its meals
115   and minutia of daily usages,
And the streets how their throbbings throbbed, and the cities pent—lo, then
    and there,
Falling upon them all and among them all, enveloping me with the rest,
Appeared the cloud, appeared the long black trail,
And I knew death, its thought, and the sacred knowledge of death.

120 Then with the knowledge of death as walking one side of me,
And the thought of death close-walking the other side of me,
And I in the middle as with companions, and as holding the hands of com-
    panions,
I fled forth to the hiding receiving night that talks not,
Down to the shores of the water, the path by the swamp in the dimness,
125 To the solemn shadowy cedars and ghostly pines so still.

And the singer so shy to the rest received me,
The gray-brown bird I know received us comrades three,
And he sang the carol of death, and a verse for him I love.

From deep secluded recesses,
130 From the fragrant cedars and the ghostly pines so still,
Came the carol of the bird.

And the charm of the carol rapt me,
As I held as if by their hands my comrades in the night,
And the voice of my spirit tallied the song of the bird.

135 *Come lovely and soothing death,*
Undulate round the world, serenely arriving, arriving,
In the day, in the night, to all, to each,
Sooner or later delicate death.

Praised be the fathomless universe,
140 *For life and joy, and for objects and knowledge curious,*
And for love, sweet love—but praise! praise! praise!
For the sure-enwinding arms of cool-enfolding death.

Dark mother always gliding near with soft feet,
Have none chanted for thee a chant of fullest welcome?
145 *Then I chant it for thee, I glorify thee above all,*
I bring thee a song that when thou must indeed come, come unfalteringly.

Approach strong deliveress,
When it is so, when thou hast taken them I joyously sing the dead,
Lost in the loving floating ocean of thee,
150 *Laved in the flood of thy bliss O death.*

From me to thee glad serenades,
Dances for thee I propose saluting thee, adornments and feastings for thee,
And the sights of the open landscape and the high-spread sky are fitting,
And life and the fields, and the huge and thoughtful night.

The night in silence under many a star,   155
The ocean shore and the husky whispering wave whose voice I know,
And the soul turning to thee O vast and well-veiled death,
And the body gratefully nestling close to thee.

Over the tree-tops I float thee a song,
Over the rising and sinking waves, over the myriad fields and the prairies wide,   160
Over the dense-packed cities all and the teeming wharves and ways,
I float this carol with joy, with joy to thee O death.

15

To the tally of my soul,
Loud and strong kept up the gray-brown bird,
With pure deliberate notes spreading filling the night.   165

Loud in the pines and cedars dim,
Clear in the freshness moist and the swamp-perfume,
And I with my comrades there in the night.

While my sight that was bound in my eyes unclosed,
As to long panoramas of visions.   170

And I saw askant[8] the armies,
I saw as in noiseless dreams hundreds of battle-flags,
Borne through the smoke of the battles and pierced with missiles I saw them,
And carried hither and yon through the smoke, and torn and bloody,
And at last but a few shreds left on the staffs (and all in silence),   175
And the staffs all splintered and broken.

I saw battle-corpses, myriads of them,
And the white skeletons of young men, I saw them,
I saw the debris and debris of all the slain soldiers of the war,
But I saw they were not as was thought,   180
They themselves were fully at rest, they suffered not,
The living remained and suffered, the mother suffered,
And the wife and the child and the musing comrade suffered,
And the armies that remained suffered.

16

Passing the visions, passing the night,   185
Passing, unloosing the hold of my comrades' hands,
Passing the song of the hermit bird and the tallying song of my soul,
Victorious song, death's outlet song, yet varying ever-altering song,

8. Askance: sideways.

As low and wailing, yet clear the notes, rising and falling, flooding the night,
Sadly sinking and fainting, as warning and warning, and yet again bursting
190   with joy,
Covering the earth and filling the spread of the heaven,
As that powerful psalm in the night I heard from recesses,
Passing, I leave thee lilac with heart-shaped leaves,
I leave thee there in the door-yard, blooming, returning with spring.

195 I cease from my song for thee,
From my gaze on thee in the west, fronting the west, communing with thee,
O comrade lustrous with silver face in the night.

Yet each to keep and all, retrievements out of the night,
The song, the wondrous chant of the gray-brown bird,
200 And the tallying chant, the echo aroused in my soul,
With the lustrous and drooping star with the countenance full of woe,
With the holders holding my hand nearing the call of the bird,
Comrades mine and I in the midst, and their memory ever to keep, for the
    dead I loved so well,
For the sweetest, wisest soul of all my days and lands—and this for his dear
    sake,
205 Lilac and star and bird twined with the chant of my soul,
There in the fragrant pines and the cedars dusk and dim.   1865–66

WILLIAM CARLOS WILLIAMS

This Is Just to Say

I have eaten
the plums
that were in
the icebox

5 and which
you were probably
saving
for breakfast

Forgive me
10 they were delicious
so sweet
and so cold   1934

WILLIAM WORDSWORTH

Lines Composed a Few Miles above Tintern Abbey on Revisiting the Banks of the Wye During a Tour, July 13, 1798[9]

Five years have passed; five summers, with the length
Of five long winters! and again I hear
These waters, rolling from their mountain-springs
With a soft inland murmur. Once again
Do I behold these steep and lofty cliffs,   5
That on a wild secluded scene impress
Thoughts of more deep seclusion; and connect
The landscape with the quiet of the sky.
The day is come when I again repose
Here, under this dark sycamore, and view   10
These plots of cottage-ground, these orchard tufts,
Which at this season, with their unripe fruits,
Are clad in one green hue, and lose themselves
'Mid groves and copses.[1] Once again I see
These hedge-rows, hardly hedge-rows, little lines   15
Of sportive wood run wild: these pastoral farms,
Green to the very door; and wreaths of smoke
Sent up, in silence, from among the trees!
With some uncertain notice, as might seem
Of vagrant dwellers in the houseless woods,   20
Or of some hermit's cave, where by his fire
The hermit sits alone.
                                   These beauteous forms,
Through a long absence, have not been to me
As is a landscape to a blind man's eye;
But oft, in lonely rooms, and 'mid the din   25
Of towns and cities, I have owed to them,
In hours of weariness, sensations sweet,
Felt in the blood, and felt along the heart;
And passing even into my purer mind,
With tranquil restoration—feelings too   30
Of unremembered pleasure: such, perhaps,
As have no slight or trivial influence
On that best portion of a good man's life,
His little, nameless, unremembered acts
Of kindness and of love. Nor less, I trust,   35

9. Wordsworth had first visited the Wye valley and the ruins of the medieval abbey there in 1793, while on a solitary walking tour. He was 23 then, 28 when he wrote this poem.   1. Thickets.

To them I may have owed another gift,
Of aspect more sublime; that blessèd mood,
In which the burthen[2] of the mystery,
In which the heavy and the weary weight
40 Of all this unintelligible world,
Is lightened—that serene and blessèd mood,
In which the affections gently lead us on—
Until, the breath of this corporeal frame
And even the motion of our human blood
45 Almost suspended, we are laid asleep
In body, and become a living soul;
While with an eye made quiet by the power
Of harmony, and the deep power of joy,
We see into the life of things.
                                    If this
50 Be but a vain belief, yet, oh! how oft—
In darkness and amid the many shapes
Of joyless daylight; when the fretful stir
Unprofitable, and the fever of the world,
Have hung upon the beatings of my heart—
55 How oft, in spirit, have I turned to thee,
O sylvan Wye! thou wanderer through the woods,
How often has my spirit turned to thee!

    And now, with gleams of half-extinguished thought,
With many recognitions dim and faint,
60 And somewhat of a sad perplexity,
The picture of the mind revives again;
While here I stand, not only with the sense
Of present pleasure, but with pleasing thoughts
That in this moment there is life and food
65 For future years. And so I dare to hope,
Though changed, no doubt, from what I was when first
I came among these hills; when like a roe
I bounded o'er the mountains, by the sides
Of the deep rivers, and the lonely streams,
70 Wherever nature led: more like a man
Flying from something that he dreads than one
Who sought the thing he loved. For nature then
(The coarser[3] pleasures of my boyish days,
And their glad animal movements all gone by)
75 To me was all in all—I cannot paint
What then I was. The sounding cataract
Haunted me like a passion; the tall rock,
The mountain, and the deep and gloomy wood,
Their colors and their forms, were then to me
80 An appetite; a feeling and a love,

2. Burden.   3. Physical.

That had no need of a remoter charm.
By thought supplied, nor any interest
Unborrowed from the eye. That time is past,
And all its aching joys are now no more,
And all its dizzy raptures. Not for this   85
Faint I,[4] nor mourn nor murmur; other gifts
Have followed; for such loss, I would believe,
Abundant recompense. For I have learned
To look on nature, not as in the hour
Of thoughtless youth; but hearing oftentimes   90
The still, sad music of humanity,
Nor harsh nor grating, though of ample power
To chasten and subdue. And I have felt
A presence that disturbs me with the joy
Of elevated thoughts, a sense sublime   95
Of something far more deeply interfused,
Whose dwelling is the light of setting suns,
And the round ocean and the living air,
And the blue sky, and in the mind of man:
A motion and a spirit, that impels   100
All thinking things, all objects of all thought,
And rolls through all things. Therefore am I still
A lover of the meadows and the woods
And mountains; and of all that we behold
From this green earth; of all the mighty world   105
Of eye, and ear—both what they half create,
And what perceive; well pleased to recognize
In nature and the language of the sense
The anchor of my purest thoughts, the nurse,
The guide, the guardian of my heart, and soul   110
Of all my moral being.
                            Nor perchance,
If I were not thus taught, should I the more
Suffer my genial spirits[5] to decay:
For thou art with me here upon the banks
Of this fair river; thou my dearest Friend,[6]   115
My dear, dear Friend; and in thy voice I catch
The language of my former heart, and read
My former pleasures in the shooting lights
Of thy wild eyes. Oh! yet a little while
May I behold in thee what I was once,   120
My dear, dear Sister! and this prayer I make,
Knowing that Nature never did betray
The heart that loved her; 'tis her privilege,
Through all the years of this our life, to lead
From joy to joy: for she can so inform   125

---

4. Am I discouraged.   **5.** Natural disposition; i.e., the spirits that are part of his individual genius.   **6.** His sister Dorothy.

The mind that is within us, so impress
With quietness and beauty, and so feed
With lofty thoughts, that neither evil tongues,
Rash judgments, nor the sneers of selfish men,
130   Nor greetings where no kindness is, nor all
The dreary intercourse of daily life,
Shall e'er prevail against us, or disturb
Our cheerful faith that all which we behold
Is full of blessings. Therefore let the moon
135   Shine on thee in thy solitary walk;
And let the misty mountain-winds be free
To blow against thee: and, in after years,
When these wild ecstasies shall be matured
Into a sober pleasure; when thy mind
140   Shall be a mansion for all lovely forms,
Thy memory be as a dwelling-place
For all sweet sounds and harmonies; oh! then,
If solitude, or fear, or pain, or grief,
Should be thy portion, with what healing thoughts
145   Of tender joy wilt thou remember me,
And these my exhortations! No, perchance—
If I should be where I no more can hear
Thy voice, nor catch from thy wild eyes these gleams
Of past existence—wilt thou then forget
150   That on the banks of this delightful stream
We stood together; and that I, so long
A worshiper of Nature, hither came
Unwearied in that service; rather say
With warmer love—oh! with far deeper zeal
155   Of holier love. Nor wilt thou then forget,
That after many wanderings, many years
Of absence, these steep woods and lofty cliffs,
And this green pastoral landscape, were to me
More dear, both for themselves and for thy sake!   1798

W. B. YEATS

Easter 1916[7]

I have met them at close of day
Coming with vivid faces
From counter or desk among gray

7. On Easter Monday 1916, an Irish Republic was proclaimed by nationalist leaders, who launched an unsuccessful revolt against the British government. After a week of street fighting, the Easter Rebellion was put down. A number of prominent nationalists were executed, including the four leaders mentioned in lines 75–76, all of whom Yeats knew personally.

Eighteenth-century houses.
I have passed with a nod of the head   5
Or polite meaningless words,
Or have lingered awhile and said
Polite meaningless words,
And thought before I had done
Of a mocking tale or a gibe   10
To please a companion
Around the fire at the club,
Being certain that they and I
But lived where motley is worn:
All changed, changed utterly: 15
A terrible beauty is born.

That woman's[8] days were spent
In ignorant good-will,
Her nights in argument
Until her voice grew shrill.   20
What voice more sweet than hers
When, young and beautiful,
She rode to harriers?
This man[9] had kept a school
And rode our wingéd horse;[1]   25
This other[2] his helper and friend
Was coming into his force;
He might have won fame in the end,
So sensitive his nature seemed,
So daring and sweet his thought.   30
This other man[3] I had dreamed
A drunken, vainglorious lout.
He had done most bitter wrong
To some who are near my heart,
Yet I number him in the song;   35
He, too, has resigned his part
In the casual comedy;
He, too, has been changed in his turn,
Transformed utterly:
A terrible beauty is born.   40

8. Countess Constance Georgina Markiewicz, a beautiful and well-born young woman from County Sligo who became a vigorous and bitter nationalist. At first condemned to death, she later had her sentence commuted to life imprisonment, and she gained amnesty in 1917. 9. Patrick Pearse, who led the assault on the Dublin Post Office, from which the proclamation of a republic was issued. A schoolmaster by profession, he had vigorously supported the restoration of the Gaelic language in Ireland and was an active political writer and poet. 1. Pegasus, a traditional symbol of poetic inspiration. 2. Thomas MacDonagh, also a writer and teacher. 3. Major John MacBride, who had married Yeats's beloved Maud Gonne in 1903 but separated from her two years later.

Hearts with one purpose alone
Through summer and winter seem
Enchanted to a stone
To trouble the living stream.
45 The horse that comes from the road,
The rider, the birds that range
From cloud to tumbling cloud,
Minute by minute they change;
A shadow of cloud on the stream
50 Changes minute by minute;
A horse-hoof slides on the brim,
And a horse plashes within it;
The long-legged moor-hens dive,
And hens to moor-cocks call;
55 Minute by minute they live:
The stone's in the midst of all.

Too long a sacrifice
Can make a stone of the heart.
O when may it suffice?
60 That is Heaven's part, our part
To murmur name upon name,
As a mother names her child
When sleep at last has come
On limbs that had run wild.
65 What is it but nightfall?
No, no, not night but death;
Was it needless death after all?
For England may keep faith[4]
For all that is done and said.
70 We know their dream; enough
To know they dreamed and are dead;
And what if excess of love
Bewildered them till they died?
I write it out in a verse—
75 MacDonagh and MacBride
And Connolly[5] and Pearse
Now and in time to be,
Wherever green is worn,
Are changed, changed utterly;
80   1916 A terrible beauty is born.

4. Before the uprising the English had promised eventual home rule to Ireland.   5. James Connolly, the leader of the Easter uprising.

The Second Coming[6]

Turning and turning in the widening gyre[7]
The falcon cannot hear the falconer;
Things fall apart; the center cannot hold;
Mere anarchy is loosed upon the world,
The blood-dimmed tide is loosed, and everywhere   5
The ceremony of innocence is drowned;
The best lack all conviction, while the worst
Are full of passionate intensity.
Surely some revelation is at hand;
Surely the Second Coming is at hand.   10
The Second Coming! Hardly are those words out
When a vast image out of *Spiritus Mundi*[8]
Troubles my sight: somewhere in sands of the desert
A shape with lion body and the head of a man,
A gaze blank and pitiless as the sun,   15
Is moving its slow thighs, while all about it
Reel shadows of the indignant desert birds.[9]
The darkness drops again; but now I know
That twenty centuries of stony sleep
Were vexed to nightmare by a rocking cradle,   20
And what rough beast, its hour come round at last,
Slouches towards Bethlehem to be born?   p. 1920

Leda and the Swan[1]

A sudden blow: the great wings beating still
Above the staggering girl, her thighs caressed

6. The Second Coming of Christ, according to Matthew 24:29–44, will come after a time of "tribulation." Disillusioned by Ireland's continued civil strife, Yeats saw his time as the end of another historical cycle. In A *Vision* (1937) Yeats describes his view of history as dependent on cycles of about 2,000 years: the birth of Christ had ended the cycle of Greco-Roman civilization, and now the Christian cycle seemed near an end, to be followed by an antithetical cycle, ominous in its portents.   7. Literally, the widening spiral of a falcon's flight. "Gyre" is Yeats's term for a cycle of history, which he diagramed in terms of a series of interpenetrating cones.   8. Or *Anima Mundi*, the spirit or soul of the world. Yeats considered this universal consciousness or memory a fund from which poets drew their images and symbols.   9. Yeats later wrote of the "brazen winged beast . . . described in my poem *The Second Coming*" as "associated with laughing, ecstatic destruction." "Our civilization was about to reverse itself, or some new civilization about to be born from all that our age had rejected . . . ; because we had worshiped a single god it would worship many."
1. According to Greek myth, Zeus took the form of a swan to seduce Leda, who became the mother of Helen of Troy and also of Clytemnestra, Agamemnon's wife and murderer. Helen's abduction from her husband. Menelaus, brother of Agamemnon, began the Trojan War (line 10). Yeats described the visit of Zeus to Leda as an annunciation like that to Mary (see Luke 1:26–38): "I imagine the annunciation that founded Greece as made to Leda. . . ." (A *Vision*).

By the dark webs, her nape caught in his bill,
He holds her helpless breast upon his breast.

5 How can those terrified vague fingers push
The feathered glory from her loosening thighs?
And how can body, laid in that white rush,
But feel the strange heart beating where it lies?

A shudder in the loins engenders there
10 The broken wall, the burning roof and tower
And Agamemnon dead.
                              Being so caught up,
So mastered by the brute blood of the air,
Did she put on his knowledge with his power
1923 Before the indifferent beak could let her drop?

Sailing to Byzantium[2]

I

That[3] is no country for old men. The young
In one another's arms, birds in the trees
—Those dying generations—at their song,
The salmon-falls, the mackerel-crowded seas
5 Fish, flesh, or fowl, commend all summer long
Whatever is begotten, born, and dies.
Caught in that sensual music all neglect
Monuments of unaging intellect.

II

An aged man is but a paltry thing,
10 A tattered coat upon a stick, unless
Soul clap its hands and sing, and louder sing
For every tatter in its mortal dress,
Nor is there singing school but studying
Monuments of its own magnificence;
15 And therefore I have sailed the seas and come
To the holy city of Byzantium.

2. The ancient name of Istanbul, the capital and holy city of Eastern Christendom from the late fourth century until 1453. It was famous for its stylized and formal mosaics, its symbolic, nonnaturalistic art, and its highly developed intellectual life. Yeats repeatedly uses it to symbolize a world of artifice and timelessness, free from the decay and death of the natural and sensual world. 3. Ireland, as an instance of the natural, temporal world.

III

O sages standing in God's holy fire
As in the gold mosaic of a wall,
Come from the holy fire, perne in a gyre,[4]
And be the singing-masters of my soul.   20
Consume my heart away; sick with desire
And fastened to a dying animal
It knows not what it is; and gather me
Into the artifice of eternity.

IV

Once out of nature I shall never take   25
My bodily form from any natural thing,
But such a form as Grecian goldsmiths make
Of hammered gold and gold enameling
To keep a drowsy Emperor awake;[5]
Or set upon a golden bough[6] to sing   30
To lords and ladies of Byzantium
Of what is past, or passing, or to come.   1927

Among School Children

I

I walk through the long schoolroom questioning;
A kind old nun in a white hood replies;
The children learn to cipher and to sing,
To study reading-books and history,
To cut and sew, be neat in everything   5
In the best modern way—the children's eyes
In momentary wonder stare upon
A sixty-year-old smiling public man.[7]

---

4. I.e., whirl in a coiling motion, so that his soul may merge with its motion as the timeless world invades the cycles of history and nature. "Perne" is Yeats's coinage (from the noun "pirn"): to spin around in the kind of spiral pattern that thread makes as it comes off a bobbin or spool.   **5.** "I have read somewhere that in the Emperor's palace at Byzantium was a tree made of gold and silver, and artificial birds that sang." (Yeats's note)   **6.** In Book VI of *The Aeneid*, the sybil tells Aeneas that he must pluck a golden bough from a nearby tree in order to descend to Hades. There is only one such branch there, and when it is plucked an identical one takes its place.   **7.** At 60 (in 1925) Yeats had been a senator of the Irish Free State.

II

I dream of a Ledaean body,[8] bent
Above a sinking fire, a tale that she
Told of a harsh reproof, or trivial event
That changed some childish day to tragedy—
Told, and it seemed that our two natures blent
Into a sphere from youthful sympathy,
Or else, to alter Plato's parable,
Into the yolk and white of the one shell.[9]

III

And thinking of that fit of grief or rage
I look upon one child or t'other there
And wonder if she stood so at that age—
For even daughters of the swan can share
Something of every paddler's heritage—
And had that color upon cheek or hair,
And thereupon my heart is driven wild:
She stands before me as a living child.

IV

Her present image floats into the mind—
Did Quattrocento finger[1] fashion it
Hollow of cheek as though it drank the wind
And took a mess of shadows for its meat?
And I though never of Ledaean kind
Had pretty plumage once—enough of that,
Better to smile on all that smile, and show
There is a comfortable kind of old scarecrow.

V

What youthful mother, a shape upon her lap
Honey of generation[2] had betrayed,

8. Like that of Helen of Troy, daughter of Leda. The memory dream is of Maud Gonne (see also lines 29–30), with whom Yeats had long been hopelessly in love.   9. In Plato's *Symposium*, the origin of human love is explained by parable: Human beings were once spheres, but Zeus was fearful of their power and cut them in half; now each half longs to be reunited with its missing half. Helen and Pollux were hatched from one of two eggs born to Leda after her union with Zeus in the form of a swan; the other contained Castor and Clytemnestra. According to Yeats in *A Vision*, "from one of [Leda's] eggs came Love and from the other War."   1. The hand of a 15th-century artist. Yeats especially admired Botticelli, and in *A Vision* praises his "deliberate strangeness everywhere [that] gives one an emotion of mystery which is new to painting."   2. Porphyry, a third-century Greek scholar and neoplatonic philosopher, says "honey of generation" means the "pleasure arising from copulation" that draws souls "downward" to generation.

And that must sleep, shriek, struggle to escape   35
As recollection or the drug decide,
Would think her son, did she but see that shape
With sixty or more winters on its head,
A compensation for the pang of his birth,
Or the uncertainty of his setting forth?   40

VI

Plato thought nature but a spume that plays
Upon a ghostly paradigm of things;[3]
Solider Aristotle played the taws
Upon the bottom of a king of kings;[4]
World-famous golden-thighed Pythagoras[5]   45
Fingered upon a fiddle-stick or strings
What a star sang and careless Muses heard:
Old clothes upon old sticks to scare a bird.

VII

Both nuns and mothers worship images,
But those the candles light are not as those   50
That animate a mother's reveries
But keep a marble or a bronze repose.
And yet they too break hearts—O Presences
That passion, piety or affection knows,
And that all heavenly glory symbolize—   55
O self-born mockers of man's enterprise;

VIII

Labor is blossoming or dancing where
The body is not bruised to pleasure soul,
Nor beauty born out of its own despair,
Nor blear-eyed wisdom out of midnight oil.   60
O chestnut-tree, great-rooted blossomer,
Are you the leaf, the blossom or the bole?
O body swayed to music, O brightening glance,
How can we know the dancer from the dance?   1927

---

3. Plato considered the world of nature an imperfect and illusory copy of the ideal world.   4. Aristotle, the teacher of Alexander the Great, disciplined him with a strap ("taw," line 43). His philosophy, insisting on the interdependence of form and matter, took the world of nature far more seriously than did Plato's.   5. Pythagoras (580?–500? B.C.), the Greek mathematician and philosopher, was highly revered, and one legend describes his godlike golden thighs.

Byzantium

The unpurged images of day recede;
The Emperor's drunken soldiery are abed;
Night resonance recedes, night-walkers' song
After great cathedral gong;
5   A starlit or a moonlit dome[6] disdains
All that man is,
All mere complexities,
The fury and the mire of human veins.

Before me floats an image, man or shade,
10   Shade more than man, more image than a shade;
For Hades' bobbin bound in mummy-cloth
May unwind the winding path;
A mouth that has no moisture and no breath
Breathless mouths may summon;
15   I hail the superhuman;
I call it death-in-life and life-in-death.

Miracle, bird or golden handiwork,
More miracle than bird or handiwork,
Planted on the star-lit golden bough
20   Can like the cocks of Hades crow,[7]
Or, by the moon embittered, scorn aloud
In glory of changeless metal
Common bird or petal
And all complexities of mire or blood.

25   At midnight on the Emperor's pavement flit
Flames that no faggot feeds, nor steel has lit,
Nor storm disturbs, flames begotten of flame,
Where blood-begotten spirits come
And all complexities of fury leave,
30   Dying into a dance,
An agony of trance,
An agony of flame that cannot singe a sleeve.

Astraddle on the dolphin's mire and blood,[8]
Spirit after spirit! The smithies break the flood,
35   The golden smithies of the Emperor!
Marbles of the dancing floor

---

6. According to Yeats's philosophy, the full moon ("moonlit") represents the mind "completely absorbed in being."   7. As the bird of dawn, the cock has from antiquity been a symbol of rebirth and resurrection.   8. In ancient art, dolphins symbolize the soul moving from one state to another, and sometimes they provide a vehicle for the dead. Palaemon, for example, in Greek tradition is often mounted on a dolphin.

Break bitter furies of complexity,
Those images that yet
Fresh images beget,
That dolphin-torn, that gong-tormented sea.   1932   40

WRITING ABOUT POETRY

INTRODUCTION

Writing about literature ought to be easier than writing about anything else. When you write about painting, for example, you have to translate shapes and colors and textures into words. When you write about music, you have to translate various aspects and combinations of sounds into words. When you write about that complex, mysterious, fleeting thing called "reality" or "life," you have an even more difficult task. Worst of all, perhaps, is trying to put into words all that is going on at any given moment inside your particular and unique self. So you ought to be relieved to know that you are going to write about literature—that is, use words to write about words.

But writing about poetry will not be easy if you haven't learned to *read* poetry, for in order to write about anything you have to know that something rather well. Helping you to learn to read poetry is what the earlier chapters of this book is about; this chapter is about the writing. (But, as you will see, you cannot fully separate the writing from the reading.)

Another thing keeps writing about poetry from being easy: writing itself is not easy. Writing well requires a variety of language skills—a good working vocabulary, for example—and a sense of how to order your ideas, of how to link one idea or statement to another, of what to put in and what to leave out. Worse, writing is not a finite or definite skill or art; you never really "know how to write," you just learn how to write a little better about a little more. These very words you are reading have been written and revised several times, even though your editors have had a good many years of practice.

REPRESENTING THE LITERARY TEXT

Copying

I f writing about poetry is using words about words, what words should you use? Since most writers work very hard to get each word exactly right and in exactly the right order, there are no better words to use in discussing what the literature is about than those of the literary work itself. Faced with writing about a poem, then, you could just write the poem over again, word for word:

> Once upon a midnight dreary, while I pondered weak and weary,
> Over many a quaint and curious volume of forgotten lore. . . .

and so on until the end. **Copying** texts was useful in medieval monasteries, but in our electronic age, with printing, word processors, and Fax machines available to us, it would not seem to be very useful. Besides, if you try to copy a text, you will probably find that spelling or punctuation errors, reversed word order, and missing or added or just different words seem mysteriously to appear. Still, it's a good exercise for teaching yourself accuracy and attention to detail, and you will probably discover things about the text you are copying that you would be unlikely to notice otherwise. Early in a poetry course, particularly, copying can be a useful step in learning how to read and write about poetry; later, being able to copy a passage accurately will help when you want to quote a passage to illustrate or prove a point you are making. But copying is not, in itself, writing *about* poetry.

Reading aloud, a variation of copying, may be a more original and interpretive exercise than copying itself, since by tone, emphasis, and pace you are clarifying the text or indicating the way you understand the text. But it, too, is not *writing* about poetry, and you will not long be satisfied with merely repeating someone else's words. You will have perceptions, responses, and ideas that you will want to express for yourself about what you are reading. And having something to say and wanting to say or write it is the first and most significant step in learning to write about poetry.

Paraphrase

If you look away from the text for a while and then write the same material but in your own words, you are writing a **paraphrase.**

For example, let's try to paraphrase the first sentence of Jane Austen's *Pride and Prejudice*: "It is a truth universally acknowledged that a single man in possession of a good fortune, must be in want of a wife." We can start by making "It is a truth" a little less formal: *It's true that,* perhaps. Now "universally acknowledged": *everybody acknowledges,* or, a little more loosely, *everybody agrees.* Now we may choose to drop the whole first clause and begin, *Everybody agrees that* "a single man"—*a bachelor*—"in possession of a good fortune"—*rich*—"must be in want of a wife"—*wants a wife.* Or is it *needs a wife?* Okay, *Everybody agrees that a rich bachelor needs* (or *wants*) *a wife.* You can see that the process of paraphrase is something like that of translation. We are translating Austen's nineteenth-century formal English prose into twentieth-century informal American prose.

But what good is that? First of all, it enables us to test whether we really understand what we are reading. Second, certain elements of the text become clearer: we may see now that Austen's sentence is meant to be ironic or humorous, and we now understand the two possible meanings of "in want of." Third, we can check our paraphrase with those of others, our classmates' versions, for example, to compare our understanding of the passage with theirs. Finally, we have learned how dependent literature is upon words. A paraphrase, no matter how precise, can render only an approximate equivalent of the meaning of a text—how *good* Austen's sentence is, how *flat* our paraphrase.

Paraphrasing, like copying, is not in itself an entirely satisfactory way of writing about poetry, but, like copying, it can be a useful tool when you write about poetry in other ways. In trying to explain or clarify a literary text for someone, to illustrate a point you are making about that text, or to remind your readers of or to acquaint them with a text or passage, you will at times want to paraphrase. Unlike an exact copy, a paraphrase, being in your own words, adds something of yours to the text or passage—your emphasis, your perspective, your understanding.

Summary

Paraphrase follows faithfully the outlines of the text. But if you stand back far enough from the text so as not to see its specific words or smaller details and put down briefly in your own words what you believe the work is about, you will have a **summary**. How briefly? Well, you could summarize the one hundred eight lines of Poe's "The Raven" in about one hundred eighty words or so, like this, for example:

> The speaker of Poe's "The Raven" is sitting in his room late at night reading in order to forget the death of his beloved Lenore. There's a tap at the door; after some hesitation he opens it and calls Lenore's name, but there is only an echo. When he goes back into his room he hears the rapping again, this time at his window, and when he opens it a raven enters. He asks the raven its name, and it answers very clearly, "Nevermore." When the speaker says that the bird, like his friends, will leave, the raven again says, "Nevermore." As the speaker's thoughts run back to Lenore, he realizes the aptness of the raven's word: she shall sit there nevermore. But, he says, sooner or later he will forget her and the grief will lessen. "Nevermore," the raven says again, too aptly. Now the speaker wants the bird to leave, but "Nevermore," the raven says once again. At the end, the speaker knows he'll never escape the raven or its dark message.

Or you could summarize the story of *Hamlet* in a single sentence: "A young man, seeking to avenge the murder of his father by his uncle, kills his uncle, but he himself and others die in the process." Has *too* much been left out? What do you feel it essential to add? Let's try again: "In Denmark, many centuries ago, a young prince avenged the murder of his father, the king, by his uncle, who had usurped the throne, but the prince himself was killed as were others, and a well-led foreign army had no trouble successfully invading the decayed and troubled state." A classmate may have written this summary: "From the ghost of his murdered father a young prince learns that his uncle, who has married the prince's mother, much to the young man's shame and disgust, is the father's murderer, and he plots revenge, feigning madness, acting erratically—even to insulting the woman he loves—and, though gaining his revenge, causes the suicide of his beloved and the deaths of others and, finally, of himself."

The last two, though accurate enough, sound like two different plays, don't they? To summarize means to select and emphasize and so to interpret: that is, not to replicate the text in miniature, as a reduced photograph might replicate the original, but while reducing it to change the angle of vision and even the filter, to represent the essentials as the reader or summarizer sees them. When you write a summary you should try to be as objective as possible; nevertheless, your summary will reflect not only the literary text but also your own understanding and attitudes. There's nothing wrong with your fingerprints or "mindprints" appearing on the summary, so long as you recognize that in summarizing you are doing more than copying, paraphrasing, or merely reflecting the literary text. You might learn something about both literature and yourself by comparing your summaries of, say, three or four short poems with summaries of the same works by several of your classmates. As you read their summaries, try to understand how each viewed the text differently from you. You might then write a composite summary that would include all that any one reader felt important. You might try the same exercise again on different texts. Has the practice made you more careful? More inclusive? Is there a greater degree of uniformity or inclusiveness in your summaries?

A good summary can be a form of literary criticism. Though you will seldom be called upon merely to summarize a work, a good deal of writing about poetry requires that at some point or other you do summarize—a whole work, a particular incident or aspect, a stanza, chapter, or scene. But beware: a mere summary, no matter how accurate, will seldom fulfill an assignment for a critical essay.

REPLYING TO THE TEXT

Imitation and Parody

While paraphrase is something like translation—a faithful following of the original text but in different words—and summary is the faithful, but inevitably interpretive, reduction of the text, there is another kind of writing about poetry that faithfully follows the manner or matter or both of a literary text, but that does so for different ends. It's called **imitation.**

For many generations, students were taught to write by "writing from models"—imitating good writing. Many serious works are, in one way or another, imitations: *The Aeneid*, for example, may be said to be an imitation of *The Odyssey*, and, in a very different way, so might James Joyce's *Ulysses*. You too may be able to learn a good deal about writing—and reading—by trying your hand at an imitation.

To write an imitation, first analyze the original—that is, break it down into its characteristics or qualities—and decide just what you want to preserve in your version. Sometimes you can poke fun at a work by imitating it but at the same time exaggerating its style or prominent characteristics, or placing it in an inappropriate context; that kind of imitation, a kind that is still popular, is called a **parody.** The list of qualities and the model might be much the same for a serious imitation and for a parody, only in a parody you can exaggerate a little—or a lot.

To parody Poe's "The Raven," we may decide to stick closely to Poe's rhythms, his use of repetitive mood words or of several words that mean almost the same thing, and his frequent use of alliteration (words that begin with the same sound). We might want to exaggerate the characteristic stylistic devices as C. L. Edson does in his parody; it begins,

> Once upon a midnight dreary, eerie, scary,
> I was wary, I was weary, full of worry, thinking of my lost Lenore,
> Of my cheery, airy, faerie, fierie Dearie—(Nothing more).

We may choose another kind of parody, keeping the form as close as possible to the original but applying it to a ludicrously unsuitable subject, as Pope does in his mock epic "The Rape of the Lock," where he uses pretentious epic machinery in a poem about cutting off a lock of a woman's hair. In writing such a parody of "The Raven," we will keep the rhythm closer to Poe's and the subject matter less close. How about this?

> Once upon a midday murky, crunching on a Christmas turkey,
> And guzzling giant Jereboams of gin . . .

And maybe we could use the "Nevermore" refrain as if it were an antacid commercial.

You will have noticed that in order to write a good imitation or parody you must read and reread the original very carefully, examine it, and identify just those elements and qualities that make it a unique and recognizable text. Since you admire works you wish to imitate, such close study should be a pleasure. You may or may not greatly admire a work you wish to parody, but parody itself is fun to do and fun to read. In either case, you are having fun while gaining a deeper, more intimate knowledge of the nature and details of a work of literature. Moreover, such close attention to how a professional piece of writing is put together and how its parts function together along with your effort to reproduce the effects in your own imitation or parody are sure to help you understand the process of writing and so help you improve your own ability to write about literature knowledgeably.

Re-creation and Reply

Sometimes a poem will seem so partial, biased, or unrealistic that it will stimulate a response that is neither an imitation or a parody but a retort. While Christopher Marlowe's "shepherd" in "The Passionate Shepherd to His Love" paints an idyllic scene of love in the country for his beloved and pleads, "Come live with me and be my love," Sir Walter Ralegh apparently feels obliged to reply in the name of the beloved "nymph": it won't always be spring, she says in "The Nymph's Reply to the Shepherd"; we won't always be young, and, besides, I can scarcely trust myself to someone who offers me such a phony view of reality.

Ralegh's nymph confronts the invitation and the words of Marlowe's shepherd directly and almost detail for detail. You may have noticed that while retorts can often be witty, they are also serious. Usually they say not merely, "That's not how the story went," but "That's not what life is really like." Try to read literature initially with the aim of understanding it and taking it at its high-

est value (rather than reducing it and quibbling). Try to "hear" what it is say-
ing; avoid imposing your own notions of reality prematurely upon a work.
Open your mind to learning from the work and let it broaden your views.
Finally, read it critically as well, asking, "Is this the way things *really* are?" or,
more generously, "If I were standing over there, where the poet is, would
things really look that way?"

EXPLAINING THE TEXT

Description

To give an account of the form of a work or passage rather than merely a brief version of its content or plot (and a plot summary, even of a poem, is usually what we mean by "summary") you may wish to write a **description.** We have given a summary of Poe's "The Raven" earlier, concentrating there, as summaries tend to do, on subject and plot. A description, on the other hand, may concentrate on the form of the stanzas, the lines, the rhyme scheme, perhaps like this:

> Poe's "The Raven" is a poem of one hundred eight lines divided into eighteen six-line stanzas. If in describing the rhyme scheme you were to look just at the ends of the lines, you would notice only one or two unusual features: not only is there only one rhyme sound per stanza, lines 2, 4, 5, and 6 rhyming, but one rhyme sound is the same in all eighteen stanzas, so that there are seventy-two lines ending with the sound "ore"; in addition, the fourth and fifth lines of each stanza end with the identical word, and in six of the stanzas that word is "door" and in four others "Lenore." There is even more repetition: the last line of six of the first seven stanzas ends with the words "nothing more," and the last eleven stanzas end with the word "Nevermore." The rhyming lines—other than the last, which is very short—in each stanza are fifteen syllables long, the unrhymed lines sixteen. The longer lines give the effect of shorter ones, however, and add still further to the frequency of repeated sounds, for the first half of each opening line rhymes with the second half of the line, and so do the halves of line 3. There is still more: the first half of line 4 rhymes with the halves of line 3 (in the first stanza the rhymes are "dreary" /"weary" and "napping" / "tapping" /"rapping"). So at least nine words in each eight-line stanza are involved in the regular rhyme scheme, and in many stanzas there are added instances of rhyme or repetition. As if this were not enough, all the half-line rhymes are rich feminine rhymes, where both the accented and the following unaccented syllables rhyme—"drēarў" /"wēarў."

This is a detailed and complicated description of a complex and unusual pattern of rhymes. Though there are many other elements of the poem we could describe—images and symbols, for example—the unusual and dominant element in this poem is clearly the intricate and insistent pattern of rhyme and repetition. Moreover, this paragraph shows how you can describe at length, in depth, and with considerable complexity certain aspects of a work without mentioning the content at all.

Analysis

Like copying, paraphrase, and summary, a description of a work or passage rarely stands alone as a piece of writing about poetry. It is, instead, a tool, a means of supporting a point or opinion. Even the description we have given above borders on **analysis.** To analyze is to break something down into its parts to discover what they are, and, usually, how they function in and relate to the whole. The description of the rhyme scheme of "The Raven" tells you what that scheme or pattern is but says nothing about how it functions in the poem. If you were to add such an account to the description, then, you would have analyzed one aspect of the poem. In order to do so, however, you would first have to decide what, in a general way, the poem is about: what its *theme* is. If you defined the theme of "The Raven" as "inconsolable grief," you could then write an analytical paper suggesting how the rhyme scheme reinforces that theme. You might begin something like this:

Obsessive Rhyme in "The Raven"

We all know that gloomy poem with that gloomy bird, Edgar Allan Poe's "The Raven." The time is midnight, the room is dark, the bird is black, and the poem is full of words like "dreary," "sad," "mystery," and "ghastly." We all know too it has a rather sing-song rhythm and repeated rhymes, but we do not often stop to think how the rhymes contribute to the mood or meaning. Before we do so here, perhaps it would be a good idea to describe in detail just what that rhyme scheme is.

Then follow with the description of the rhyme scheme, and go on like this:

Of course the most obvious way in which the rhyme scheme reinforces the theme of inconsolable loss is through the emphatic repetition of "Nevermore." Since this refrain comes at the very end of each of the last stanzas it is even more powerful in its effect.

What is not so obvious as the effect of repeating "Nevermore" is the purpose of the over-all abundance and richness of rhyme. Some might say it is not abundant and rich but excessive and cloying. These harsh critics cynically add that in a way the rhymes and repetitions are appropriate to this poem because the whole poem is excessive and cloying: grief over loss, even intense grief, does, human experience tells us, pass away. This criticism is just, however, only if we have accurately defined the theme of the poem as "inconsolable sorrow." The very insistence of the rhyme and repetition, however, suggests we may need to adjust slightly our definition of that theme. Perhaps the poem is not about "inconsolable sorrow" in so neutral a way; maybe it would be better to say it is about obsessive grief. Then the insistent, pounding rhyme and repetition make sense (just as the closed-in dark chamber does). Obsessive repetition of words and sounds thus helps to create the meaning of the poem almost as much as the words themselves do.

Interpretation

Principles and Procedures

If you have been reading carefully, you may have noticed what looks like a catch: to turn description into analysis, you must relate what you are describing to the theme, the overall effect, and meaning of the poem. But how do you know what the theme is? If analysis relates the part to the whole, how can you know the "whole" before you have analyzed each part? But then, how can you analyze each part—relating it to the whole—if you don't know what that whole is?

Interpretation, or the expression of your understanding of a literary work and its meaning, involves an initial general impression that is then supported and, often, modified by analysis of the particulars. It involves looking at the whole, the part, the whole, the part, the whole, the part, in a series of approximations and adjustments. (Note, in particular, the need to keep your mind open for modifications or changes rather than forcing your analysis to confirm your first impressions.)

This procedure should in turn suggest something of the nature and even the form of the critical essay, or essay of interpretation. The essay should present the overall theme and support that generalization with close analyses of the major elements of the text (or, in some essays, an analysis of one significant element)—showing how one or more of such elements as rhyme or speaker, plot or setting reinforce, define, or modify the theme of the poem. Often the conclusion of such an essay will be a fuller, more refined statement of the theme.

Both the definition of and the procedures for interpreting a work suggest that a literary text is unified, probably around a theme, a meaning, and an effect. In interpreting, you therefore keep asking of each element or detail, "How does it fit? How does it contribute to *the* theme or whole?" In most instances, especially when you are writing on shorter works, if you dig hard and deep enough, you will find a satisfactory interpretation or central theme. Even after you have done your best, however, you must hold your "reading" or interpretation as a hypothesis rather than a final truth. Your experience of reading criticism has probably already shown you that more than one reading of a literary work is possible and that no reading exhausts the meaning and totality of a work. Nonetheless, you will want to begin reading a literary text as if it were going to make a central statement and create a single effect, no matter how complex. Try as conscientiously as you can to make sense of the work, to analyze it, show how its elements work together. In analyzing elements, you kept your initial sense of the whole as hypothesis and did not try to force evidence to fit your first impression. Here, too, you will want to hold your interpretation as a hypothesis even in its final stages, even at the end. It is, you must be sure, the fullest and best "reading" of the text you are capable of at this time, with the evidence and knowledge you have at this moment; but only that. In other words, an interpretation is "only an opinion." But just as your political and other opinions are not lightly held but are what you really feel and believe based on all you know and have experienced and all you have thought and felt, so your opinion or interpretation of a literary work should be as responsible as you can make it. Your opinions are a measure of your knowledge, intelligence, and sensibility. They should not be lightly changed but neither should they be obstinately and inflexibly held.

Reading and Theme Making

Because you need a sense of the whole text before you can analyze it, analysis and interpretation would seem to be possible only after repeated readings. Though obvious, logical, and partially true, this may not be *entirely* true. In reading, we actually anticipate theme or meaning much as we anticipate what will happen next. Often this anticipation or expectation of theme or effect begins with our first opening a book—or even before, in reading the title. Titles usually provide clues to give you some idea of what a poem is about. "The Raven" does not immediately imply a poem about inconsolable loss, but it introduces the main vehicle for the poem's statement, and titles such as "To His Coy Mistress," "The Passionate Shepherd to His Love," or "My Papa's Waltz" suggest situation, plot, and something of tone. Titles may of course be ironic—or misleading—and thus set the reader up for a surprise, but they almost always set our expectations in motion, providing at least some hint of the contours of possibility.

Just as we have more than one expectation of what may happen next as we read a poem, so we may have more than one expectation of what a poem is going to be "about" in the more general sense: as we read along we have expectations or hypotheses of meaning, and so we consciously or unconsciously try to fit together the pieces of elements of what we are reading into a pattern of significance. By the end of our first reading we should have a fairly well-defined sense of what a poem is "about," what it means, even how some of the elements have worked together to produce that meaning and effect. Indeed, isn't this the way we read when we are not reading for a class or performance? Don't most people read most works of literature only once? And don't we usually think we have understood what we have read? Shouldn't we be able to read a sonnet or a very short poem in class just once and immediately write an interpretive paper based on that first reading?

This is not to say that we cannot understand more about a work by repeated readings, or that there is some virtue or purity of response in the naive first reading that is lost in closer study. Our first "reading"—"reading" in the sense of both "casting our eye over" and "interpretation"—is almost certain to be modified or refined by rereading: if nothing else, we know from the beginning of our second reading what the speaker's situation is and why he is so prone to interpret a raven's song as significant, or what kind of coyness in his mistress the speaker is trying to overcome. The next time, then, we can concentrate on the speaker's state of mind, or the "logic" of the seduction argument, or how the language of the poem relates to the situation and theme. The theme or meaning is likely to be modulated by later readings, the way the elements function in defining or embodying meaning is likely to be clearer; the effect of the second reading is certain to be different from that of the first. It may be instructive to reread several times the short work we interpreted in class after a single reading, write a new interpretive essay, and see how our understanding has been changed and enriched by subsequent readings.

Opinions, Right and Wrong

Just as each of our separate readings is different, so naturally one reader's fullest and "final" reading, interpretation, or opinion will differ somewhat from another's. Seldom will readers agree entirely with any full statement of the theme of a literary text. Nor is one of these interpretations entirely "right" and all the others necessarily "wrong." For no thematic summary, no analysis or interpretation, no matter how full, can exhaust the affective or intellectual significance of a major literary text. There are various approximate readings of varying degrees of acceptability, various competent or "good" readings, not just one single "right" reading.

Anyone who has heard two accomplished musicians faithfully perform the same work, playing all the "same" notes; or anyone who has seen two performances of *Hamlet,* will recognize how "interpretations" can be both correct and different. You might try to get hold of several recordings of one or more of Hamlet's soliloquies—by John Barrymore, Sir John Gielgud, Richard Burton, Sir Laurence Olivier, or Mel Gibson, for example—and notice how each of these actors lends to identical passages his own emphasis, pacing, tone, color, his own effect, and so, ultimately, his own meaning. These actors reading the identical words are, in effect, "copying." They are not paraphrasing or putting Shakespeare's Elizabethan poetry into modern American prose, not "interpreting" as we have defined it, or putting his play into their own words. If merely performing or reading the words aloud generates significant differences in interpretation, it is no wonder that when you write an interpretive essay about literature, when you give your conception of the meaning and effect of the literary text in your own words, your interpretation will differ from other interpretations, even when each of the different interpretations is competent and "correct."

Any communication, even a work of literature, is refracted—that is, interpreted and modified—by the recipient. In one sense, it is not complete until it is received, just as, in a sense, a musical score is not "music" until it is played. Philip Roth reported, not too long ago, how perturbed he was by what the critics and other readers said of his first novel—that was not at all what he intended, what the novel really was, he thought at first. But then he realized that once he had had his say in the novel, it was "out there," and each reader had to understand it within the limits and range of his or her own perspectives and literary and life experiences. His novel, once in print, was no longer merely "his," and rightly so.

That quite different interpretations may be "correct" is not to say, with Alice's Humpty-Dumpty, that a word or a work "means just what I choose it to mean." Though there may not be one "right" reading, some readings are more appropriate and convincing than others and some readings are demonstrably wrong.

What would you say about this reading of *Hamlet?*

> The play is about the hero's sexual love for his mother. He sees his father's "ghost" because he feels guilty, somehow responsible for his father's death, more than likely because he had often wished his father dead. To free himself from this feeling of

guilt, he imagines that he sees his father's ghost and that the ghost tells him that his uncle murdered his father. He focuses upon his uncle because he is fiercely jealous that it is his uncle, not himself, who has replaced his father in his mother's bed. He so resents his mother's choice of so unworthy a mate, he attributes it not to love but to mere lust, clearly a projection of his own lust for his mother, which he calls love. His mother's lust so disgusts him that he hates all women now, even Ophelia. When his father was alive he could be fond of Ophelia, for his sexual feeling for his mother was deflected by his father-the-king's powerful presence. Now, however, he must alienate Ophelia not only because of his new hatred of women but because he has a chance of winning his mother, especially if he can get rid of Claudius, his uncle.

Such a reading explains more or less convincingly certain details in the play, but it wrenches some out of context and it leaves a good deal out and a good deal unexplained: why, for example, do others see the ghost of Hamlet's father if it is just a figment of his imagination? What are Horatio and Fortinbras and the political elements doing in the play? If you accept certain Freudian premises about human psychology and see life in Freudian terms; if you see literary texts as the *author's* psychic fantasy stimulating your own psychic fantasies and believe that interpretation of *Hamlet* is not merely a reading of the play itself but an analysis of Shakespeare's psyche, you may find this reading somewhat convincing. You will perhaps explain away some of the details of the play that do not seem to fit your Freudian reading as a cover-up, an attempt by Shakespeare to disguise the true but hidden meaning of his dramatic fantasy from others—and from himself. Such a reading is probably neither right nor wrong but only a way of interpreting *Hamlet* based on certain assumptions about psychology and about the way literature *means* and so it could seem "right" or acceptable to those who share those assumptions.

Suppose one of your ingenious classmates were to argue that the real subject of *Hamlet* is that the hero has tuberculosis. This would explain, your classmate would say, the hero's moodiness, his pretended madness that sometimes seems real, his rejection of Ophelia (he wouldn't want their children to suffer from the disease), his father's ghost (he, too, died of consumption), his anger at his uncle (who carries the disease, of course) for marrying Hamlet's mother, and so on. Your classmate might even argue that the text of the play is flawed, that it was just copied down during a performance by someone in the audience or was printed from an actor's imperfect copy. Therefore, "O that this too too *solid flesh*" should read "*sullied flesh*," as many scholars have argued (and might not "sullied flesh" suggest tuberculosis?). And, therefore, isn't it quite possible that the most famous soliloquy in the play really began or was meant to begin, "TB or not TB"? "No way!" we'd say. We would be reasonably sure that this is not just "not proved" but just plain *wrong*. It might be interesting and illuminating to rebut that reading in a paper of your own and to notice what kinds of evidence you bring to bear on an interpretive argument.

Reader and Text

If it is difficult to say exactly what a piece of literature *says*, it is usually not because it is vague or meaning*less* but because it is too specific and meaning*ful* to paraphrase satisfactorily in any language other than its own. Since no two human beings are identical and no two people can inhabit the same space at the same time, no two people can see exactly the same reality from the same angle and vantage point. Most of us get around this awkward truth by saying that we see what we are "supposed" to see, a generalized, common-sense approximation of reality. We are all, in effect, like Polonius in the third act of *Hamlet*, who sees in a cloud, a camel, a weasel, a whale—whatever Hamlet tells him he sees.

Some individuals struggle to see things as fully and clearly as possible from their own unique vantage point and to communicate to others their particular—even peculiar—vision. But here too we are individuated, for though we speak of our "common language," we each speak a unique language, made up of "dialects" that are not only regional and ethnic but also conditioned by our age group, our profession, our education, travel, reading—all our experiences. Yet if we want to express our unique vision to others who have different visions and different "languages," we have to find some medium that is both true to ourselves and understandable to others.

There is for these individuals—these writers of literature—a constant tug-of-war between the uniqueness of their individual visions and the generalizing nature of language. The battle does not always result in sheer loss, however. Often, in the very struggle to get their own perceptions into language, writers sharpen those perceptions or discover what they themselves did not know when they began to write. You have probably made similar discoveries in the process of writing a letter or an assigned paper. But writers also find that what they have written does not perfectly embody what they meant it to, just as you perhaps have found that your finished papers have been not quite so brilliant as your original idea.

"Understanding" is not a passive reception of a text but an active reaching out from our own experiences toward the text. At least at first we need to do so by meeting the author on the ground of a common or general language and set of conventions—things that everybody "knows." The first task of the reader, therefore, is to get not to the author's intention, but to the general statement that the work itself makes—that is, its theme or thesis. After a few readings we can usually make a stab at articulating the theme of a text. What a work says in the way of a general theme, however, is not necessarily its full or ultimate meaning; otherwise we would read theme summaries and not poems. The theme is the meaning accessible to all through close reading of the text and common to all, but a literary text is not all statement. There are often cloudy areas in the text where we cannot be sure what is **implication,** the suggestion of the text, and what is our **inference,** or interpretation, of the text. What is the speaker of "The Raven" doing, for example, in the opening lines of that poem? He is reading, or, rather, pondering over "many a quaint and curious volume of forgotten lore." Now why should a man so stricken by the death of a loved one be reading? The poem does not say, but we might infer from our own experience that he is trying to forget, to distract his attention from his loss, and indeed the final "message" of the raven is that he shall nevermore be able to escape his grief. But why is he reading quaint old educational or instuctional books instead of entertaining ones, if he is merely seeking to distract himself? No wonder he's weary. Words like "quaint," "curious," "forgotten," and "lore" in the context of his obsessive grief may suggest to you, especially if other maca-bre works of Poe's are part of your past reading experience, that he has been studying black magic, some way of raising or communicating with the dead Lenore. The black carrion-eating bird enters then to tell him there is no way, not even by magic; he will see Lenore nevermore. Poe's poem does not *say* what the volumes are about. Many readers, however, will find this inference convincing. If accepted, this changes the theme of the poem to some degree. Still, it need not be accepted; the poem does not, will never, say what those vol-umes contain. The meaning of the poem for the reader who is convinced will differ from the meaning for the reader who is not convinced.

The full meaning of a work for you is not only in its stated theme, one that everyone can agree on, but in the meaning you derive by bringing together that generalized theme, the precise language of the text, and your own response and experiences—including reading experience—and imagination. That "meaning" is not the total meaning of the work, not what the author origi-nally perceived and "meant to say"; it is the vision of the author as embodied in the work *and re-viewed from your own angle of vision.*

Your role in producing a meaning from the text does not free you from pay-ing very close attention to the precise language of the text, the words and their meanings, their order, the syntax of the sentences, and even such mundane details as punctuation. You cannot impose a meaning on the text, no matter how sincerely and intensely you feel it, in defiance of the rules of grammar and the nature of the language.

Still, the reader has to be an artist too, trying to experience the reality of the work as the author experienced reality, and with the same reverence and sense of responsibility for the original. To write about poetry you need to embody your reading experience—or interpretation—of the work in language. Alas, writing about poetry, using words about words, is not as easy as it sounds at first. But it is more exciting, giving you a chance to see with another's eyes, to explore another's perceptions or experiences, and to explore and more fully understand your own in the process, thus expanding the horizon of your experience, perception, consciousness.

When some rich works of literature, like *Hamlet*, seem to have more than one meaning or no entirely satisfactory meaning or universally agreed upon single theme, it is not that they are not saying something, and saying something very specific, but that what they are saying is too specific, and complex, and profound (and true, perhaps) to be generalized or paraphrased in a few dozen words. The literary work is meaning*ful*—that is, full of meaning or meanings; but it is the reader who produces each particular meaning from the work, using the work itself, the language of the community and of the work, and his or her own language, experience, and imagination.

As a reader trying to understand the unique perception and language of the author, you should try to translate the text as best you can into terms you can understand. Do your best to approach the text with an open, receptive mind.

An interpretation, then, is not a clarification of what the writer "was trying to say"; it is a process that itself says, in effect, "The way I am trying to understand this poem is . . . ."

CRITICAL APPROACHES

The way you read and talk about a literary text depends on your assumptions, usually unconscious or unarticulated, about what a work of literature is, what is it supposed to do, and what makes it good. Literary critics, however, often define their assumptions about literature and the proper way to go about reading it and writing about it. The results are critical theories or critical approaches. Looking at a few of these, you may recognize some of your own assumptions, see new and exciting ways of looking at literature, or, at the very least, become aware of your own critical premises and prejudices.

Objectivism

We might begin by asking just what, quite literally, a work of literature *is*. There are critics who think of it as a fixed and freestanding object made up of words on a page. It is "freestanding" in that it has no connection on the one hand with the author or his or her intention or life, or, on the other hand, with the historical or cultural context of the author or the reader. These we might call **objectivist** critics; they believe that a text is an independent object, free from the subjectivity of author and reader.

Formalism

Among the objectivist critics are the **formalists.** One common formalist conception is that a work is **autotelic,** that is, complete in itself, written for its own sake, and unified by its form—that which makes it a work of art. Content is less important than form. Literature involves a special kind of language that sets it apart from merely utilitarian writing; the formal strategies that organize and animate that language elevate literature and give it a special, almost religious character.

NEW CRITICISM   One group of formalists, the **New Critics,** dominated literary criticism in the middle of the twentieth century, and New Criticism remains an important influence today. Their critical practice is to demonstrate formal unity by showing how every part of a work—every word, every image, every element—contributes to a central unifying theme. Because the details of the work relate to a theme or idea, they are generally treated as *symbolic*, as figurative or allegorical, representations of that central, unifying idea. The kind of unity thus demonstrated, in which every part is related to the whole and the whole is reflected in each part, is called **organic unity.** The New Critics differentiate organic unity from (and much prefer it to) **mechanical unity,** the external, pre-conceived structure or rules that do not arise from the individuality of the work but from the type or genre. New Critical analysis, or **explication of the text,** is especially effective in the critical reading of lyric poetry. It has become so uni-versally accepted as *at least the first step* in the understanding of literature that it is almost everywhere the critical approach taught in introductory literature courses, even in those that do not share its fundamental autotelic assumption. It is, indeed, the basic approach of the "Understanding the Text" sections in *The Norton Introduction to Poetry.*

The New Critics' focus on theme or meaning as well as form signifies that for them literature is **referential:** it points to something outside itself, things in the real, external world or in human experience—a tree, a sound wave, love. The New Critics, in general, do not question the reality of the phenomenal world or the ability of language to represent it.

Structuralism

For many formalists, however, literature is not referential. The words in a story, poem, or play no longer point outward to the things, people, or world they are supposed to denote, as they might do in ordinary, "nonliterary" discourse, but point inward to each other and to the formal system they create. The critic still focuses on interrelatedness but is less concerned with "meaning"; words are treated not as referential symbols but as natural numbers; poetry is likened to mathematics or music.

Structuralism focuses on the text as an independent aesthetic object and also tends to detach literature from history and social and political implica-tions, but (much more than New Criticism) structuralism emphasizes system-atic analysis, aspiring to make literary criticism a branch of scientific inquiry. It sees every literary work as a separate "system" and seeks to discover the princi-ples or general laws that govern the interaction of parts within the system. Structuralism has its roots in modern linguistic theory; it looks especially to the work of Ferdinand de Saussure (1857–1913), who founded structural linguistics early in the twentieth century. Structuralism in criticism did not, however, flourish internationally until the early 1960s, when a combination of space-age preoccupation with science and cold-war fear of implication led to a view of literature as intellectually challenging yet socially and politically noncontroversial.

Although based on linguistic theory, structuralism tries to extend newly discovered principles about language to other aspects of literature. Drawing on the **semiotic** principle that a vast and intricate system of signs enables human beings to communicate through language, structuralism asks readers to consider the way that other kinds of sign systems within a work—structures all—combine to produce meaning. Language and its characteristic habits are important to structuralists, but it is not enough to consider any single part of a work or any single kind of sign—linguistic or otherwise—within it. Structuralism aspires to elucidate the meaning of a work of literature by seeing the way all of its parts work relationally toward some wholeness of structure and meaning. Like formalism, it shows little interest in the creative process as such and has virtually no interest in authors, their intentions, or the circumstances or contexts of creation. It takes texts to represent interactions of words and ideas apart from individual human identities or sociopolitical commitments, and concentrates its analytical attention on what can be said about how different elements or processes in a text operate in relation to one another. Structuralists are less likely than formalists to concentrate their attention on some single all-explaining characteristic of literature (such as Cleanth Brooks's "tension" or William Empson's "ambiguity") and its practitioners are less likely to privilege a particular text for its revelation or authority. Structuralism may be seen as a sort of secular equivalent of formalism; it is less mysterious and authoritarian, and it has both the advantage and disadvantage of seeming to be less arbitrary and more "objectively" reliable. But in some ways it seems to promise too much for method and "objectivity," and by the 1970s its insights into the ways of language were already beginning to be used against it to attack the certitudes it appeared to promise and to emphasize instead the uncertainties and indeterminateness of texts.

Post-Structuralism

Post-Structuralism is the broad term used to designate the several directions of literary criticism that, while depending crucially on the insights of science-based theory, attack the very idea that any kind of certitude can exist about the meaning, understandability, or sharability of texts. Post-structuralists, disturbed at the optimism of positivist philosophy in suggesting that the world is knowable and explainable, ultimately doubt the possibility of certainties of any kind, and they see language as especially elusive and unfaithful. Much of post-structuralism involves undoing; the best-known variety of post-structuralism, **deconstruction**, suggests as much in its very name.

DECONSTRUCTION   Deconstruction takes the observations of structuralism to their logical conclusion, arguing that the elaborate web of semiotic differentiations created by the principle of difference in language means that no text can ultimately have any stable, definite, or discoverable meaning.

For the deconstructionist, language consists just in black marks on a page that repeat or differ from each other and the reader is the only author, one who can find whatever can be found in, or be made to appear in, those detached, isolated marks. The deconstructionist conception of literature is thus very broad—almost any writing will do. While this may seem "subjective," in that the critical reader has great freedom, it is the object—the black marks on the blank page—that is the sole subject/object of intention/attention.

As practiced by its most famous proponent, the French philosopher Jacques Derrida (b. 1930), deconstruction endeavors to trace the way texts challenge or cancel their explicit meanings and wrestle themselves into stasis or neutrality. Many deconstructionists have strong radical political commitments (it is possible to argue that the radical counterculture of the 1960s and especially the political events in Paris of 1968 are the crucial context for understanding the origins of deconstructionism), but the retreat from meaning and denial of clear signification that characterizes deconstruction also has affinities with formalism and structuralism, particularly as deconstruction is practiced by American critics. Rather than emphasizing form over content, however, deconstruction tries to deny the possibility of content and places value instead on verbal play as a characteristic outlet of a fertile, adroit, and supple human mind. Like structuralism, it lives almost completely in a self-referential verbal world rather than a world in which texts represent some larger or other reality, but unlike structuralism it denies that the verbal world adds up to anything coherent, consistent, or meaningful in itself. Deconstruction also influences other varieties of post-structuralism with different kinds of interests in history and ideology. Michel Foucault (1926–1984), Julia Kristeva (b. 1941), and Jacques Lacan (1901–1981), though their disciplinary interests are in social history, feminist philosophy, and psychoanalysis, respectively, all come out of deconstructionist assumptions and carry the indeterminacies of post-structuralism (and of post-modernism more generally) into kinds of literary criticism with interests fundamentally different from those of structuralism.

Subjectivism

Opposed to objectivism is what might be called **subjectivism.** This loose term can be used to embrace many forms of psychological and self-, subject-, or reader-centered criticism.

Psychological Criticism

The assumption is that literature is the expression of the author's psyche, often his or her unconscious, and, like dreams, needs to be interpreted.

FREUDIAN CRITICISM   The dominant school is the **Freudian,** based on the work of Sigmund Freud (1856–1939). Many of its practitioners assert that the meaning of a literary work does not lie on its surface but in the psyche (some would even claim, in the neuroses) of the author. The value of the work, then, lies in how powerfully and convincingly it expresses the author's unconscious and how universal the psychological elements are. A well-known Freudian reading of *Hamlet,* for example, insists that Hamlet is upset because he is jealous of his uncle, for he, *like all male children,* unconsciously wants to go to bed with his mother. The ghost may then be a manifestation of Hamlet's unconscious desire; his madness is not just acting but is the result of this frustrated desire; his cruelly gross mistreatment of Ophelia is a deflection of his disgust at his mother's being "lecherous," "unfaithful" in her love for him. A Freudian critic may assume then that Hamlet is suffering from an Oedipus complex, a Freudian term for the desire of the son for his mother, its name derived from the Greek myth that is the basis of Sophocles' play *Oedipus the King.*

  Some Freudian critics stress the author's psyche and find *Hamlet* the expression of Shakespeare's own Oedipus complex. Others stress the effect on the reader, the work having a purgative or cleansing effect by expressing in socially and morally acceptable ways unconscious desires that would be unacceptable if expressed directly.

LACANIAN CRITICISM   As it absorbs the indeterminacies of post-structuralism under the influence of thinkers such as Jacques Lacan, psychological criticism has become increasingly complex. Accepting the Oedipal paradigm and the unconscious as the realm of repressed desire, Lacanian psychology (and the critical theory that comes from that psychology) conflates these concepts with the deconstructionist emphasis on language as expressing absence—you use a word to represent an absent object but you cannot make it present. The word, then, like the unconscious desire, is something that cannot be fulfilled. Language, reaching out with one word after the other, striving for but never reaching its object, is the arena of desire.

JUNGIAN CRITICISM Just as a Freudian assumes that human psyches have similar histories and structures, the **Jungian** critic assumes that we all share a universal or **collective unconscious** (as well as having a racial and individual unconscious). According to Carl Gustav Jung (1875–1961) and his followers, in the collective and in our individual unconscious are universal images, patterns, and forms of human experiences or **archetypes.** These archetypes can never be known directly, but they surface in art in an imperfect, shadowy way, taking the form of **archetypal images**—the snake with its tail in its mouth, rebirth, mother, the double, the descent into Hell. To get a sense of the archetype beneath the archetypal images or shadows in the characters, plot, language, and images of a work, to bring these together in an archetypal interpretation, is the function of the Jungian critic. He is guided by his belief that there is a central myth common to all literature. Just as, for the Freudian literary critic, the "family romance," out of which the Oedipus story comes, is central, so the Jungian assumes there is a **monomyth** that underlies the archetypal images and gives a clue as to how they can be related to suggest the archetypes themselves. The myth is that of the quest. In that all-encompassing myth the hero struggles to free himself (the gender of the pronoun is specific and significant) from the Great Mother, to become a separate, self-sufficient being who is then rewarded by union with his ideal other, the feminine *anima*.

Phenomenological Criticism

Another kind of subjectivist criticism is **phenomenology,** especially as it is practiced by **critics of consciousness.** They consider all the writings of an author—shopping lists and letters as well as lyrics—as the expression of his or her mindset or way of looking at reality. Such a critic looks for repeated or obsessive use of certain key words, incidents, patterns, and angles of vision, and, using these, maps out thereby the inner world of the writer.

Reader-Response Criticism

The formalists focus on the text. Though the psychological critics focus most frequently on the author, their assumptions about the similarity or universality of the human mind make them consider as well the role of the reader. There is another approach that, though not psychological in the usual sense of the word, also focuses on the reception of the text, on **reader response.** The conventional notion of reading is that a writer or speaker has an "idea," **encodes** it—that is, turns it into words—and the reader or listener **decodes** it, deriving, when successful, the writer/speaker's "idea." What the reader-response critic assumes, however, is that such equivalency between sender and receiver is impossible. The literary **work** therefore does *not* exist on the page; that is only the **text.** The text becomes a work only when it is read, just as a score becomes music only when it is played. And just as every musical performance, even of exactly the same notes, is somewhat different, a different "interpretation," so no two readers read or perform exactly the same work from identical texts. Besides the individual differences of readers, space is made for different readings or interpretations by **gaps** in a text itself. Some of these are temporary—such as the withholding of the name of the murderer until the end—and are closed by the text sooner or later, though each reader will in the meantime fill them differently. But others are permanent, and can never be filled with certainty; the result is a degree of uncertainty or **indeterminacy** in the text.

The reader-response critic's focus on the reading process is especially useful in the study of long works such as novels. The critic follows the text sequentially, observing what **expectations** are being aroused, how they are being satisfied or modified, how the reader recapitulates "evidence" from the portion of the text he has read to project forward a **configuration,** a tentative assumption of what the work as a whole will be and mean once it is done. The expectations are in part built by the text and in part by the repertoire of the reader, i.e., the reader's reading experience plus his or her social and cultural knowledge.

Historical Criticism

Dialogism

Another critical approach that gives a significant role to the reader and is particularly useful for long fiction is **dialogism,** largely identified with the work of Mikhail Bakhtin (1895–1975). The dialogic critic bases the study of language and literature on the individual utterance, taking into account the specific time, the place, the speaker, and the listener or reader. Such critics thus see language as a continuous dialogue, each utterance being a reply to what has gone before. Even thought, which they define as inner speech, is a dialogue between utterances that you have taken in. Even your own language (and thus thought) is itself dialogic, for it is made up of the dialogue in which you are engaged, that which you have heard from parents and peers, teachers and television, all kinds of social and professional discourse and reading. Indeed, you speak many "languages"—those of your ethnic, social, economic, national, professional, gender, and other identities. Your individual language consists in the combination of those languages. The literary form in which the dialogic is most interesting, complex, and significant is the novel, for there you have the languages not only of the characters (as you do in drama), but also that of a mediator or narrator and passages of description or analysis or information that seem to come from other voices—newspapers, whaling manuals, legal cases, and so on. Because the world is growing more interrelated and we have multiple voices rather than one dominant voice or language, the novel has become the most appropriate form for the representation of that world.

Because the dialogic sees utterances, including literary utterances or works, as specific to a time and place, one of its dimensions, unlike formalist, structuralist, or psychological criticism, is *historical*. Nineteenth-century **historical criticism** took the obvious fact that a work is created in a specific historical and cultural context and that the author is a part of that context in order to treat literature as a product of the culture. Formalists and others emphasizing the **aesthetic** value of literature saw this as reducing the literary work to the status of a mere historical document and the abandonment of literary study to history. The dialogic critic sees the work in relation to its host context, a part of the dialogue of the culture. The work in turn helps to create the context for other utterances, literary and otherwise. Some consider dialogic criticism a form of sociological criticism.

SOCIOLOGICAL CRITICISM   More recently, as scientists from psychology to physics recognized the role of the perceiver in perception, historians realized that they were not only discovering and looking at facts but were finding what they were looking for, selecting facts to fit preconceived views or interpretations. Literary historians or historical critics began to see literature not as a mere passive product of "history" but a contributor and even creator of history. An early form of this kind of historicism was **sociological criticism,** in which literature is seen as one aspect of the larger processes of history, especially those processes involving people acting in social groups or as members of social institutions or movements. Much sociological criticism uses literary texts to illustrate social attitudes and tendencies—and therefore has been strongly resisted by formalists, structuralists, and other "objectivist" critics as not being properly literary—but sociological criticism also attempts to relate what happens in texts to social events and patterns and is as concerned about the effects of texts on human events as about the effects of historical events on texts. Sociological criticism assumes that the most significant aspects of human beings are social and that the most important functions of literature thus involve the way that literature both portrays and influences human interactions. Much sociological criticism centers its attention on contemporary life and texts, seeking to affect both societal directions and literary ones in the present, but some sociological criticism is historical, concerned with differences in different times and places and anxious to interpret directions of literature in terms of historical emphases and patterns.

MARXIST CRITICISM The most insistent and vigorous historicism through most of the twentieth century has been **Marxism,** based on the work of Karl Marx (1818–1883). Marxist criticism, like other historical critical methods in the nineteenth century, treated literature as a passive product of the culture, specifically of the economic aspect, and therefore of class warfare. Economics, the underlying cause of history, was thus the *base,* and culture, including literature and the other arts, the *superstructure.* Viewed from the Marxist perspective, the literary works of a period would, then, reveal the state of the struggle between classes in the historical place and moment.

Marxist critics, however, early on recognized the role of perception. They insisted that all use of language, including literary and critical language, is **ideological,** that is, that it derives from and expresses preconceived ideas, particularly economic or class values. Criticism is thus not just the product of the culture but part of the discourse or "conversation" that we call history. Formalism and even the extreme apolitical position of **aestheticism,** "art for art's sake," by placing art in a realm above the grubbiness of everyday life—above such mundane things as politics and money—removes art from having any importance in that life. According to Marxists, this "bourgeois mystification of art" tends to support the class in power. Marxism has traditionally been sensitive to and articulate about power politics in both life and literature, and both its social and literary analyses have often been based on an explicit or implicit political agenda, though many Marxist critics are motivated more by theoretical than practical aims. In recent years, especially in the wake of post-structuralism and the psychoanalytical criticism of the 1970s and 1980s, Marxist criticism has become increasingly theoretical and less doctrinaire politically. Critics such as Raymond Williams, Fredric Jameson, Terry Eagleton, Pierre Macherey, Walter Benjamin, and Louis Althusser have gained wide audiences among readers with a variety of political and literary commitments. Over the course of the century, it has been Marxism that has most often and most consistently raised referential and historical issues about literature, and those readers who have been interested in the interactive relationship between literature and life have most often turned for their guidance on such issues to Marxist analysts, whether or not they share their philosophical or political assumptions. In the past decade, however, two other critical schools with strong commitments to historical and cultural issues have become very powerful intellectually and have attracted many practitioners and adherents. These two, feminism and new historicism, have (along with Marxism and, in its way, dialogism) turned critical attention powerfully toward historical and representational issues, and since the mid-1980s they have set the dominant directions in literary criticism.

FEMINIST CRITICISM   Like Marxist criticism, feminist criticism derives from firm political and ideological commitments and insists that literature both reflects and influences human behavior in the larger world. Feminist criticism often, too, has practical and political aims. Strongly conscious that most of recorded history has given grossly disproportionate attention to the interests, thoughts, and actions of men, feminist thought endeavors both to extend contemporary attention to distinctively female concerns, ideas, and accomplishments and to recover the largely unrecorded and unknown history of women in earlier times. Not all directions of feminist criticism are historical; feminism has, in fact, taken many different directions and forms in recent years, and it has many different concerns. French feminist criticism, for example, has been deeply influenced by psychoanalysis, especially Lacanian psychoanalysis, and by French post-structuralist emphasis on language. Beyond their common aim of explicating and furthering specifically female interests, feminist critics may differ substantially in their assumptions and emphases. Like Marxism, feminism draws creatively on various other approaches and theories for its several methodologies. The most common historical directions of American feminism in particular involve the recovery of neglected or forgotten texts written by women in earlier times, the redrawing of literary values to include forms of writing (letters and autobiography, for example) that women were able to create when more public and accepted forms were denied to them, the discovery of the roles (positive and negative) that reading played in the lives and consciousnesses of women when they were unable to pursue more "active" and "public" courses, and the sorting out of cultural values implicit in the way women are represented in the texts of particular times and places.

New Historicism

New historicism has less obvious ideological commitments than Marxism or feminism, but it shares their interest in the investigation of how power is distributed and used in different cultures. Drawing on the insights of modern anthropology (and especially on the work of Clifford Geertz), new historicism wishes to isolate the fundamental values in texts and cultures, and it regards texts both as evidence of basic cultural patterns and as forces in cultural and social change. Many of the most influential practitioners of the new historicism come out of the ranks of Marxism and feminism, and new historicists are usually knowledgeable about most varieties of literary theory. Like Marxists and feminists, they are anxious to uncover the ideological commitments in texts, and they care deeply about historical and cultural difference and the way texts represent it. But personal commitments and specific political agendas usually are less important—at least explicitly—to new historicists, and one of the main contentions between feminists and new historicists—or between Marxists and new historicists—involves disagreement about the role that one's own politics should play in the practice of criticism. Many observers regard new historicism as politically to the left in its analysis of traditional cultural values, but critics on the left are suspicious of new historicism, especially of its reluctance to state its premises openly, and they generally regard its assumptions as conservative. Whatever its fundamental political commitments, however (or whether its commitments can be fairly described as having a consistent and specifiable bias), new historicism is far more interested than any other literary approach in social groups generally ignored by literary historians, and it refuses to privilege "literature" over other printed, oral, or material texts. "Popular literature" often gets major attention in the work of new historicists, who see all texts in a culture as somehow expressive of its values and directions and thus as equally useful in determining the larger intellectual, epistemological, and ethical system of which any text is a part. Texts here are thus seen as less specifically individual and distinctive than in most objectivist criticisms, and although new historicists are sometimes interested in the psychology of authors or readers their main concern is with the prevailing tendencies shared across a culture and thus shared across all kinds of texts, whatever their class status, literary value, or political aim.

Pluralism

These classifications are not pigeonholes, and you will notice that many of the approaches overlap: many feminists, especially French feminist critics, are Lacanian or post-structuralist as well, while British feminists often lean toward sociological, especially Marxist, criticism; dialogic critics accept many of the starting points and methods of reader-response and sociological critics, and so on. These crossovers or combinations are generally enriching; they cause problems only when the critic seems to be operating out of contradictory assumptions.

There is a lively debate among critics and theorists at present involving the question of whether readers should bring together the insights and methods of different schools (practitioners of the mixing of methods are usually called **pluralists**) or whether they should commit themselves wholeheartedly to a single system. Pluralists contend that they make use of promising insights or methods wherever they find them and argue that putting together the values of different approaches leads to a more fair and balanced view of texts and their uses. Opponents—those who insist on a consistency of ideological commitment— argue that pluralists are simply unwilling to state or admit their real commitments, and that any mixing of methods leads to confusion, uncertainty, and inconsistency rather than fairness. Readers, conscious or not of their assumptions and their methods, make this basic choice—to follow one lead or many—and the kind of reading they do and the conclusions they come to depend not only on this basic choice but many others suggested by the dominant strands of recent criticism that have been described here. Not all critics are aware of their assumptions, methodologies, or values, and some would even deny that they begin with any particular assumptions or biases, but is is often useful, especially to readers newly learning to practice literary criticism, to sort out their own beliefs carefully and see exactly what kind of difference it makes in the way they read literature and ask questions of it.

Further Reading on Critical Approaches

For good introductions to the issues discussed here, see the following books from which we have drawn in our discussion and definitions:

Robert Alter, *The Pleasures of Reading in an Ideological Age*, New York, 1989

Jonathan Culler, *The Pursuit of Signs*, London, 1981

Jonathan Culler, *On Deconstruction*, London, 1983

Robert Con Davis and Ronald Schleifer, *Contemporary Literary Criticism*, 2d ed., New York, 1989

Mary Eagleton (ed.), *Feminist Literary Theory: A Reader*, Oxford, 1986

Terry Eagleton, *Literary Theory: An Introduction*, Minneapolis, 1983

Nannerl Keohane, Michelle Z. Rosaldo, and Barbara C. Gelpi (eds.), *Feminist Theory: A Critique of Ideology*, Chicago, 1982

Dominick LaCapra, *History and Criticism*, Ithaca, N.Y., 1985

Frank Lentricchia, *After the New Criticism*, Chicago, 1980

Frank Lentricchia and Thomas McLaughlin (eds.), *Critical Terms for Literary Study*, Chicago, 1990

Richard Macksey and Eugenio Donato (eds.), *The Structuralist Controversy: The Languages of Criticism and the Sciences of Man*, Baltimore, 1972

Toril Moi, *Sexual-Textual Politics*, New York, 1985

Jean Piaget (translated by Chanihan Maschler), *Structuralism*, New York, 1970

Tzvetan Todorov, *Mikhail Bakhtin: The Dialogic Principle*, Minneapolis, 1984

DECIDING WHAT TO
WRITE ABOUT

Having Something to Say

D eciding what to write about—what approach to use, which questions
to ask—seems like the first step in the process of writing a paper
about a work of poetry. It isn't. Before that, you have to have confi-
dence that you have something to say. If you are a beginner at this kind of writ-
ing, you are likely to have deep doubts about that. Developing confidence is
not, at first, easy. You may feel as if you can *never* begin and want to put off
the paper forever, or you may want to plunge in fast and get it over with.
Either of these approaches, though common and tempting, is a mistake: the
best way is to begin preparing for the paper as soon as possible—the moment
you know you have one to write—but not to hurry into the writing itself.

The first step is to get close enough to the work to feel comfortable with it.
Before you can tell anyone else about what you have read—and writing about
poetry is just another form of talking about poetry, although a more formal and
organized one—you need to "know" the work, to have a sure sense of what the
work itself is like, how its parts function, what ideas it expresses, how it creates
particular effects, and what your responses are. And the only way you will get
to know the work is to spend time with it, reading it carefully and thoughtfully
and turning it over in your mind. There is no substitute for reading, several
times and with care, the work you are going to write about *before* you pick up a
pen and prepare to write. And let your reading be of the *work itself*, not of
something *about* that work, at least at first; later, your instructor may steer you
to background materials or to critical readings about the work, but at first you
should encounter the work alone and become aware of your own private
responses to it.

Begin, then, by reading, several times, the work you are going to write
about. The first time, read it straight through at one sitting: read slowly, paus-
ing at its natural divisions—sections, stanzas, sentences, even at each line
break—to consider how you are responding to the work. Later, when your
knowledge of the work is more nearly complete and when you have the "feel"

of the whole, you can compare your early responses with your more considered thoughts, in effect "correcting" your first impressions in whatever way seems necessary on the basis of new and better knowledge. But if you are noncommittal at first, refusing to notice what you think and feel, you will have nothing to correct, and you may cut yourself off from the most direct routes of response. Feelings are not always reliable—about literature any more than about people—but they are always the first point of contact with a literary work: you feel before you think. Try to start with your mind open, as if it were a blank sheet of paper ready to receive an impression from what you read.

When you have finished a first reading, think about your first impressions. Think about how the work began, how it gained your interest, how it generated expectations, how its conflicts and issues were resolved, how it ended, how it made you feel from beginning to end. Write down any phrases or events that you remember especially vividly, anything you are afraid you might forget. Look back at any parts that puzzled you at first. Write down in one sentence what you think the story, poem, or play is about. Then read it again, this time much more slowly, making notes as you go on any passages that seem especially significant and pausing over any features or passages that puzzle you. Then write a longer statement—three or four sentences—summarizing the work and suggesting more fully what it seems to be about. Try to write the kind of summary described above on pages 563–65. If you get stuck, try brainstorming all of your ideas about the work for fifteen minutes, and then write the summary.

Stop. Do something else for a while, something as different as possible— see a movie, do math problems, ride a bicycle, listen to music, have a meal, take a nap, mow the lawn, build a loft. Do NOT do some other reading you have been meaning to do. When you go back to the work and finish reading it for the third time—rapidly and straight through—write down in a sentence the most important thing you would want to tell someone else who was about to read it for the first time: not just whether you liked it or not, but what exactly you liked, how the whole thing seems to have worked.

Now you are ready to choose a topic.

Choosing a Topic

Once you are ready to choose a topic, the chances are that you have already— quietly and unconsciously—chosen one. The clue is in the last statement you wrote. The desire to tell someone about a work of literature is a wonderful place to begin. Good papers almost always grow out of a desire to communicate. Desire is not enough, of course—the substance (and most of the work, sentence by sentence) is still ahead of you; but desire will get you started. Chances are that what you wrote down as the one thing you most wanted to say is close to the heart of the central issue in the work you are going to write about. Your statement will become, perhaps, in somewhat revised form, your thesis.

The next step is to convert your personal feelings and desire to communicate into a sentence or two that states your purpose—into an "objective" statement about the work, a statement that will mean something to someone else. This will be your thesis. Again, you may already be further along than you realize. Look at the "summary" you wrote after your second reading. The summary will probably sound factual, objective, and general about the work; the personal statement you wrote after the third reading will be more emotional, subjective, and particular about some aspect of the work. In combining the two successfully lies the key to a good paper: what you need to do is to write persuasively an elaboration and explanation of the last statement so that your reader comes to share the "objective" view of the whole work that your summary expresses. The summary you have written will, in short, be implicit in the whole essay; your total essay will suggest to your reader the wholeness of the work you are writing about, but it will do so by focusing its attention on some particular aspect of the work—on a part that leads to, or suggests, or represents the whole. What you want to do is build an essay on the basis of your first statement, taking a firm hold on the handle you have found. The summary is your limit and guide: it reminds you of where you will come out. Any good topic ultimately leads back to the crucial perceptions involved in a summary. Ultimately, any good writing about literature leads to a full and resonant sense of the central thrust of the work, but the most effective way to find that center is by discovering a pathway that particularly interests you. The best writing about poetry presents a clear—and well-argued—thesis about a work or works and presents it from the perspective of personal, individual perception. But the thesis should clarify the central thrust of the work, helping it to open itself up to readers more completely and more satisfyingly.

Topics often suggest themselves after a second or third reading, simply because one feature or problem stands out so prominently that it almost demands to be talked about. Sometimes you may be lucky: your instructor may *assign* a topic instead of asking you to choose your own. At first glance, that may not seem like a good break: it often feels confining to follow specific directions or to have to operate within limits and rules prescribed by someone else. The advantage is that it may save a lot of time and prevent floundering around. If your instructor assigns a topic, it is almost certain to be one that will work, one that has a payoff if you approach it creatively and without too much resentment at being directed so closely and precisely. It is time-consuming, even when you have tentatively picked a topic, to think through its implications and be sure it works. And an instructor's directions, especially if they are detailed and call attention to particular questions or passages, may aid greatly in helping you focus on particular issues or in leading you to evidence crucial to the topic.

If your instructor does *not* give you a topic and if no topic suggests itself to you after you have read a particular work three or four times, you may sometimes have to settle for the kind of topic that will—more or less—be safe for any literary work. Some topics are almost all-purpose. You can almost always write an adequate paper analyzing rhythm, or verse form, or imagery, or the connotations of key words. Such "fall-back" topics are, however, best used only as last resorts, when your instincts have failed you in a particular instance. When choice is free, a more lively and committed paper is likely to begin from a particular insight or question, something that grabs you and makes you want to say something, or solve a problem, or formulate a thesis. The best papers are usually very personal in origin; even when a topic is set by the assignment, the best papers come from a sense of having personally found an answer to a significant question. To turn a promising idea into a good paper, however, personal responses usually need to be supported by a considerable mass of evidence; the process often resembles the testing of "evidence" in a laboratory or the formulation of hypotheses and arguments in a law case. You may need to narrow your topic so that your thesis is focused and can be supported by examples from throughout the text. If your topic is too broad, your paper will likely become long, unwieldy, and overly general.

Here are some sample paper topics that have worked for other students. Most are particular to individual poems, suggesting features or strategies that are unique to a single work. But some are adaptable, or at least suggestive about how considering elements of a poem leads to a better appreciation of the whole.

1. Scene, Sequence, and Time in "Sir Patrick Spens"
2. Attitudes toward Authority in "Sir Patrick Spens"
3. Sir Partick Spens as a Tragic Hero
4. Birth and Death Imagery in "The Death of the Ball Turret Gunner"

5. Varieties of Violence in Frost's "Range-Finding"
6. The Characterization of God in "Channel Firing"
7. The Idea of Flight in "Ode to a Nightingale"
8. Attitudes toward the Past in "Mr. Flood's Party" and "They Flee from Me"
9. Satire of Distinctive American Traits in "Boom," "Dirge," and "What the Motorcycle Said"
10. Male and Female in "Diving into the Wreck"
11. Following the Argument in "The Canonization"
12. Bestial *versus* Human in "Burning the Cat"
13. Syntax as Strategy in "[anyone lived in a pretty how town]"
14. The Power of Complex Words in Blake's "London" (or Yeats's "Byzantium")

Most poems have key words and images. All poems contain attitudes, opinions, and stances. Many take surprising turns, leading readers where they did not necessarily mean to go. The starting question for most topics is "how," and the ultimate question is "why." If you can find a topic that addresses the basic things you find interesting in a particular poem—and that takes *your* reader to a central understanding of the poem itself—you are on your way to a successful paper.

Considering Your Audience

Thinking of your paper as an argument or an explanation will also help with one of the most sensitive issues in writing about literature. The issue: To whom are you writing? Who is your audience? The obvious answer is, your instructor, but in an important sense, that is the wrong answer. It is wrong because, although it could literally be true that your instructor will be the only person (besides you) who will ever read your paper, your object in writing about literature is to learn to write for an audience of peers, people a lot like yourself who are sensible, pretty well educated, and need to have something (in this case a literary work) explained to them so that they will be able to understand it more fully. Picture your ideal reader as someone about your own age and with about the same educational background. Assume that the person is intelligent and has some idea of what literature is like and how it works, but that he or she has just read this particular literary work for the first time and has not yet had a chance to think about it carefully. Don't be insulting and explain the obvious, but don't assume either that your reader has noticed and considered every detail. The object is to inform and convince your reader, not to try to impress.

Should you, then, altogether ignore the obvious fact that it is an instructor—probably with a master's degree or Ph.D. in literature—who is your actual reader? Not altogether: you don't want to get so carried away with speaking to people of your own age and interests that you slip into slang, or feel the need to explain what a stanza is, or leave an allusion to a rock star unexplained, and you do want to learn from the kind of advice your instructor has given in class or from comments he or she may have made on other papers you have written. But don't become preoccupied with the idea that you are writing for someone in "authority" or someone you need to please. Most of all, don't think of yourself as writing for a captive audience, for a reader who *has* to read what you write. It is not always easy to know exactly who your audience is or how interested your readers may be, so you have to make the most of every single word. It is your job to get the reader's attention. And you will have to do it subtly, making conscious assumptions about what your reader already knows and what he or she can readily understand. The tone of your paper should be serious and straightforward and its attitude respectful toward the reader, as well as toward the literary work. But its approach and vocabulary, while formal enough for academic writing, should be readily understandable by someone with your own background and reading experience. And it should be lively enough to interest someone like you. Try to imagine, as your ideal reader, the person in your class whom you most respect. Write to get, and hold, that person's serious attention. Try to communicate, try to teach.

FROM TOPIC TO ROUGH DRAFT

Writing about literature is very much like talking about literature. But there is one important difference. When we talk, we organize as we go—trying to get a handle, experimenting, working toward an understanding. And the early stages of preparing a paper—the notetaking, the outlining, the rough drafts—are much like that. A "finished" paper, however, has the uncertainties and tentativeness worked out and presents an argument that moves carefully and compellingly toward a conclusion. How does one get from here to there?

Once you have decided on a topic, the process of planning is fairly straightforward, but it can be time consuming and (often) frustrating. There are three basic steps in the planning process: first you gather the evidence, then you sort it into order, and (finally) you develop it into a convincing argument. The easiest way is to take these steps one by one.

Gathering Evidence

The first step involves accumulating evidence that supports the statement you have decided to make about your topic (that is, your thesis), and that takes you back to the text. But before you read the text again, look over the notes you have already made in the margin of that text or on separate pieces of paper. Which of them have something to do with the topic you have now defined? Which of them say something about your main point? Which ones can you now set aside as irrelevant to your topic?

Reading over the notes you have already made is a good preparation for re-reading the work again, for this time as you read it you will be looking at it in a new and quite specific way, looking for all the things in it that relate to the topic you have decided on. This time you will, in effect, be flagging everything—words, phrases, structural devices, changes of tone, anything—that bears upon your topic. As you read—very slowly and single-mindedly, with your topic always in mind—keep your pen constantly poised to mark useful points. Be ready to say something about the points as you come upon them; it's a good idea to write down, immediately, any sentences that occur to you as you reread this time. Some of these sentences will turn out to be useful when you actually begin to write your paper. Some will be incorporated in your paper; but some will not: you will find that a lot of the notes you take, like a lot of the footage shot in making a film, will end up on the cutting room floor.

No one can tell you exactly how to take notes but there are some general guidelines that may be useful. The notes you will need to take and how you take them will depend on the particulars of the paper you are about to write. Here are five hints toward successful notetaking.

1. Keep your topic and your thesis about your topic constantly in mind as you reread and take notes. Mark all passages in the text that bear on your topic, and for each one write on a note card a single sentence that describes how the passage relates to your topic and thesis. Add a "key" word that identifies the note at the top of the card to help you to organize the cards into clusters later in the process. Then indicate, for each passage, the specific location in the text—by line or stanza number. If you are taking notes on a computer, put page breaks between each one, so that when you print them out, there will be one note per page.

2. Keep rereading and taking notes until one of five things happens:
   a. You get too tired and lose your concentration. (If that happens, stop and then start again later, preferably the next day.)
   b. You stop finding relevant passages or perceive a noticeable drying up of your ideas. (Again, time to pause; give the work at least one more reading later when your mind is fresh and see whether the juices start anew. If they don't, you may be ready to outline and write.)
   c. You begin to find yourself annotating every single sentence or line, and the evidence all begins to run together into a single blob. (If this happens, your thesis is probably too broad. Try simplifying and narrowing it so that you don't try to include everything. Then go back to your notetaking and discriminate more carefully between what actually is important to your thesis and what only relates at some distance.)
   d. You become impatient with your notetaking and can't wait to get started writing. (Start writing. Use scrap paper, and be prepared to go back to systematic notetaking if your ideas or your energy fades. The chances are that the prose passages you write this way will find a place in your paper, but they may not belong exactly where you think they do when you first write them down.)
   e. You find that there is insufficient evidence for your thesis, that the evi-

dence points in another direction, or that the evidence contradicts your thesis. (Revise your topic to reflect the evidence, and begin re-reading once more.)

3. When you think you have finished your notetaking, read all your note cards over slowly, one by one, and jot down any further ideas as they occur to you, each one on a separate note card. Computer users can either read the file on screen and add notes as they wish, or print out all of the notes and read through them on paper. (Sometimes it will seem as if note cards beget note cards. Too much is better than too little at the notetaking stage: you can always discard them before the final draft. Don't worry if you seem to have too many notes and too much material. But later, when you boil down to essentials, you will have to be ruthless and omit some of your favorite ideas.)

4. Transfer all of your notes to pieces of paper—or note cards—that are all the same size, one note on each. It is easier to sort them this way when you get ready to organize and outline. If you like to write notes in the margin of your text (or on the backs of envelopes, or on dinner napkins, or shirtsleeves), systematically transfer every note to uniform sheets of paper or cards before you begin to outline. Having everything easily recorded on sortable cards that can be moved from one pile to another makes organizing easier later, especially when you change your mind (as you will) and decide to move a point from one part of your paper to another. Index cards—either 3 × 5, if you write small and make economical notes, or 4 × 6, if you need more space—are ideal for notetaking and sorting.

5. When you think you are done taking notes (because you are out of ideas, or out of time, or getting beyond a manageable number of pieces of evidence), read through the whole pile one more time, again letting any new ideas—or ideas that take on a fresh look because you combine them in a new way—spawn new sentences for new note cards.

How many times should you read a poem before you stop taking notes? There is no right answer. If you have read the work three times before settling on a topic, two more readings may do. But it could take several more. Common sense, endurance, and deadlines will all have an effect on how many rereadings you do. Let your conscience, your judgment, and your clock be your guides.

Organizing Your Notes

The notes you have taken will become, in the next few hours, almost the whole content of your paper. The task remaining is to give that content the form and shape that will make it appealing and persuasive. But it is not an easy task: the best content in the world isn't worth much if it isn't effectively presented. The key to the task is getting all your ideas into the right order, that is, into a sequence that will allow them to argue your thesis most persuasively.

In order to put your notes into a proper order, you will need (ironically) to get a little distance from your notes. (The key to good planning and writing—and to many other pursuits—is in knowing when to back away and get some perspective.) Set your notes aside, but not too far away. On a fresh sheet of paper, write down all the major points you want to be sure to make. Write them down randomly, as they occur to you. Now read quickly through your pack of note cards and add to your list any important points you have left out. Then decide which ideas should go first, which should go second, and so on.

Putting your points in order is something of a guess at this point. You may well want to reorder them before you begin to write—or later when you are writing a first (or even later) draft. But make your best guess. The easiest way to try out an order is to take your random list and put a 1 in front of the point you will probably begin with, a 2 before the probable second point, and so on. Then copy the list, in numerical order, onto a clean sheet of paper, revising (if you need to) as you go. Do not be surprised if later you have to revise your list further. Your next task is to match up your note cards (and the examples they contain) with the points on your outline. If you've added "key" words to the top of each card, you can make a "rough cut" according to these words.

Putting things in a particular order is a spatial problem, and by having your notes on cards or pieces of paper of a uniform size you can do much of your organizing physically. Do your sorting on a large table or sit in the middle of the floor. Prepare a title card for each point in your outline, writing on it the point and its probable place in your paper, then line them up on the table or floor in order before you begin writing. If you're using your computer, you can use the search function to find each instance of a key word, phrase, or name, and arrange your electronic "cards" under the headings on your list by blocking and moving your "cards" to new parts of the document.

Two-thirds of this exercise is quite easy: most examples and ideas you have written down will match quite easily with a particular point. But some cards will resist classification. Some cards will seem to belong in two or more places;

others will not seem to belong at all. If a card seems to belong to more than one point, put it in the pile with the lowest number (but write on it the number or numbers of other possible locations). If, for example, a card might belong in point 2 but could also belong in point 6 or 9, put it in the pile of 2's and write "maybe 6 or 9" on the card; if you don't use it in writing about point 2 move it to pile 6; if you don't use it in 6, move it to 9. Remember that you will work your way through the piles in numerical order, so that you have a safety system for notes that don't seem to belong where you first thought but that still belong somewhere in your paper. Move them to a possible later point, or put them in a special file (marked "?" or "use in revised draft") and, once you have completed a first draft on your paper, go through this file, carefully looking for places in your paper where these ideas may belong. Almost never will everything fit neatly into your first draft. If everything does seem to fit exactly as you had originally planned, you have either done an incredible job of planning and guessing about the organization of your paper, or you are forcing things into inappropriate places.

Don't be surprised if you have a large number of leftover note cards, that is, cards whose ideas you haven't yet used, after you have written your first draft. You will probably find places for many of these ideas later, but some just won't fit and won't be needed for the paper you ultimately write, no matter how good the ideas are. No paper will do everything it could do. Writing a paper is a *human* project; it has limits.

Before you actually start writing, you may want to develop a more elaborate outline, incorporating your examples and including topic sentences for each paragraph, or you may wish to work from your sketchy outline and the accompanying packs of cards. Do the more detailed outline if it seems right to you, but don't delay the writing too long. You are probably ready right now, and any exercises you invent to delay writing are probably just excuses.

Developing an Argument

Once you have decided on your major points and assembled your evidence, you have to decide how you are going to present your argument and how you are going to present *yourself*. What you say is, of course, more important than how you say it, but your manner of presentation can make a world of difference. Putting your evidence together effectively—in a coherent and logical order so that your readers' curiosities and questions are answered systematically and fully—is half the task in developing a persuasive argument. The other half involves your choice of a voice and tone that will make readers want to read on—and make them favorably disposed toward what you say.

The tone of your paper is the basis of your relationship with your reader. "I will be just *me*," you may say, "and write naturally." But writing is not a "natural" act, any more than swinging a tennis racket, carrying a football, or dancing a pirouette. The "me" you choose to present is only one of several possible me's; you will project a certain mood, a certain attitude toward your subject, a certain confidence. How do you want your readers to feel about you and your argument? Being too positive can make your readers fell stupid and inadequate and can turn them into defensive, resistant readers who will rebel at your every point. Friendship with your reader is better than an adversary relationship. Sounding like a nice person who is talking reasonably and sensibly is not enough if in fact you don't make sense or have nothing to say, but the purpose of the tone you choose is to make your reader receptive to your content, not hostile. The rest of the job depends on the argument itself.

It has been said that all good papers should be organized in the same way:

1. Tell 'em what you're going to tell 'em.
2. Tell 'em.
3. Tell 'em what you told 'em.

That description fits—in pretty general terms—the most common kind of organization, which includes an introduction, a body of argument, and a conclusion, but if it is followed too simplistically it can lead to a paper that sounds simple-minded. The beginning does need to introduce the subject, sort out the essential issues, and suggest what your perspective will be, and the conclusion does need to sum up what you have said in the main part of your paper, but the first paragraph shouldn't give *everything* away, nor should the final one simply repeat what is already clear. Lead into your subject clearly but with a little subtlety; arrange your main points in the most effective manner you can think of, building a logical argument and supporting your general points with clear textual evidence, concisely phrased and presented, and at the end *show how* your argument has added up—don't just *say* that it did.

There are, of course, other ways to organize than the basic Tell-3 method, but the imagination and originality that can be exercised in a straightforward Tell-3 paper are practically unlimited.

Writing the First Draft

It is now time to set pen to paper or fingers to keyboard. No one can help you much now for a while. The main thing is to get started right, with a clear first sentence that expresses your sense of direction and arrests the attention of your readers. (If you can't think of a good first sentence, don't pause over it too long. Write down a paraphrase of what you want it to say—something like the statement you wrote down after your third reading—and go on to start writing about your main points. Your "first" sentence may sometimes be the last one you will write.) And then you inch along, word by word and sentence by sentence, as you follow your outline from one paragraph to another. Keep at it. Struggle. Stare into space. Bite your pen when you feel like it. Get up and stride about the room. Scratch your head. Sharpen a pencil. Run your fingers through your hair. Groan. Snap your fingers. But keep writing.

It is often frustrating as you search for the right word or struggle to decide how the next sentence begins, but it is satisfying when you get it right. If you get stuck, try working out your ideas on a separate piece of paper or free writing for a while inside your computer document. Sometimes, working out an idea away from your draft can be helpful. Stay with your draft until you're reasonably satisfied with it. Write "The End" at the bottom and set it aside. Breathe a sigh of relief and put it away until tomorrow.

FROM ROUGH DRAFT TO
COMPLETED PAPER

Revising

This final stage of the process is the most important of all, and it is the easiest one to mismanage. There is a world of difference between a bunch of ideas that present a decent interpretation of a work of literature and a cogent, coherent, persuasive essay that will stir your readers to a nod of agreement and shared pleasure in a moment of insight. If you haven't done good literary analysis and sorted out your insights earlier, nothing you do at this stage will help much, but if what you have done so far is satisfactory, this is the stage that can turn your paper into something special.

The important thing is not to allow yourself to be too easily satisfied. If you have struggled with earlier stages, it may be tempting to think you are finished when you have put a period to the last sentence in your first draft. It will often feel as if you are done: you may feel drained, tired of the subject, anxious to get on to other things, such as sleep or food or friends or another project. And it *is* a good idea to take a break once you've finished a draft and let what you have done settle for a few hours, preferably overnight. (The Roman poet and critic Horace suggested putting a draft aside for nine years, but most instructors won't wait that long.) Rereading it "cold" may be discouraging, though: all those sentences that felt so good when you wrote them often seem flat and stale, or even worthless, when a little time has elapsed. The biggest struggle in moving from a first draft to a second one is to keep from throwing what you have written into a wastebasket. You've spent a lot of time on this already, and with some more work, you'll have a paper you can be proud of.

It may take *several* more drafts to produce your best work. Often it is tempting to cut corners—to smooth out a troublesome paragraph by obscuring the issue or by omitting the difficult point altogether instead of confronting it, or to ask a roommate or friend for help in figuring out what is wrong with a particular passage. But you will learn more in the long run—and probably do better in the short run as well—if you make yourself struggle a bit. When a particular word or phrase you have used turns out to be imprecise, or misleading, or ambiguous, search until you find the *right* word or phrase. (At the least put a big X in the margin so that you will come back and fix it later.) If a paragraph is incomplete or poorly organized, fill it out or reorganize it. If a transition from one point to another does not work, look again at your outline and see if another way of ordering your points would help. *Never* decide that the problem can best be solved by hoping that your reader will not notice. The satisfaction of finally solving the problem will build your confidence and sooner or later make your writing easier and better.

Reviewing Your Work and Revising Again

Precisely how you move from one draft to another is up to you and will depend on the ways you work best; the key is to find all the things that bother you (and that *should* bother you) and then gradually correct them, moving toward a better paper with each succeeding draft. Here are some things to watch for.

Thesis and central thrust: Is it clear what your main point is? Do you state it clearly, effectively, and early? Do you make clear what the work is about? Are you fair to the spirit and emphasis of the work? Do you make clear the relationship between your thesis and the central thrust of the work? Do you explain *how* the work creates its effect rather than just asserting it?

Organization: Does your paper move logically from beginning to end? Does your first paragraph set up the main issue you are going to discuss and suggest the direction of your discussion? Do your paragraphs follow each other in a coherent and logical order? Does the first sentence of each paragraph accurately suggest what that paragraph will contain? Does your final paragraph draw a conclusion that follows from the body of your paper? Do you resolve the issues you say you resolve?

Use of evidence: Do you use enough examples? Too many? Does each example prove what you say it does? Do you explain each example fully enough? Are the examples sufficiently varied? Are any of them labored, or over-explained, or made to bear more weight than they can stand? Have you left out any examples useful to your thesis? Do you include any gratuitous ones just because you like them? Have you achieved a good balance between examples and generalizations?

Tone: How does your voice sound in the paper? Confident? Does it show off too much? Is it too timid or self-effacing? Do you ever sound smug? Too tentative? Too dogmatic? Would a neutral reader be put off by any of your assertions? By your way of arguing? By your choice of examples? By the language you use?

Sentences: Does each sentence read clearly and crisply? Have you rethought and rewritten any sentences you can't explain? Is the first sentence of your paper a strong, clear one likely to gain the interest of a neutral reader? Is the first sentence of each paragraph an especially vigorous one? Are your sentences varied enough? Do you avoid the passive voice and "there is/there are" sentences?

Word Choice: Have you used any words whose meaning you are not sure of? In any cases in which you were not sure of what word to use, did you stay with the problem until you found the exact word? Do your metaphors and figures of speech make literal sense? Are all the idioms used correctly? Is your terminology correct? Are your key words always used to mean *exactly* the same thing? Have you avoided sounding repetitive by varying your sentences rather than using several different terms to mean precisely the same thing?

Conciseness: Have you eliminated all the padding you put in when you didn't think your paper would be long enough? Have you gone through your paper, sentence by sentence, to eliminate all the unnecessary words and phrases? Have you looked for sentences (or even paragraphs) that essentially repeat what you have already said—and eliminated all repetition? Have you checked for multiple examples and pared down to the best and most vivid ones? Have you got rid of all inflated phrasing calculated to impress readers? Have you eliminated all roundabout phrases and rewritten long, complicated, or confusing sentences into shorter, clearer ones? Are you convinced that you have trimmed every possible bit of excess and that you cannot say what you have to say any more economically?

Punctuation and mechanics: Have you checked the syntax in each *separate* sentence? Have you checked the spelling of any words that you are not sure of or that look funny? Have you examined each sentence separately for punctuation? Have you checked every quotation word by word against the original? Have you given proper credit for all material—written or oral—that you have borrowed from others? Have you followed the directions your instructor gave you for citations, footnotes, and form?

As you begin to revise it's a good idea to look first at the larger issues (your thesis, organization, and supporting evidence) to make sure you find and solve any major problems early on. Then, you're in a better position to work on your tone, sentences, choice of words, and punctuation and mechanics. In the final stages, the most effective way to revise is to read through your paper looking for one problem at a time, that is, to go through it once looking at paragraphing, another time looking at individual sentences, still another for word choice or problems of grammar. It is almost impossible to check too many things too often—although you can get so absorbed with little things that you overlook larger matters. With practice, you will learn to watch carefully for the kinds of mistakes you are most prone to. Everyone has individual weaknesses and flaws. Here are some of the most common stumbling blocks for beginning writers:

1. Haste. (Don't start too late, or finish too soon after you begin.)
2. Pretentiousness. (Don't use words you don't understand, tackle problems that are too big for you, or write sentences you can't explain; it is more important to make sense than to make a big, empty impression.)
3. Boredom. (The quickest way to bore others is to be bored yourself. If you think your paper will be a drag, you are probably right. It is hard to fake interest in something you can't get excited about; keep at it until you find a spark.)
4. Randomness. (Don't try to string together half a dozen unrelated ideas or insights and con yourself into thinking that you have written a paper.)
5. Imprecision. (Don't settle for approximation, either in words or ideas; something that is 50 percent right is also 50 percent wrong.)
6. Universalism. (Don't try to be a philosopher and make grand statements about life; stick to what is in the work you are writing about.)
7. Vagueness. (Don't settle for a general "sense" of the work you are talking about; get it detailed, get it right.)
8. Wandering. (Don't lose track of your subject or the work that you are talking about.)
9. Sloppiness. (Don't sabotage all your hard work on analysis and writing by failing to notice misspelled words, grammatical mistakes, misquotations, incorrect citations or references, or typographical errors. Little oversights make readers suspicious.)
10. Impatience. (Don't be too anxious to get done. Enjoy the experience; savor the process. Have fun watching yourself learn.)

Being flexible—being willing to rethink your ideas and reorder your argument as you go—is crucial to success in writing, especially in writing about poetry. You will find different (and better) ways to express your ideas and feelings as you struggle with revisions, and you will also find that—in the course of analyzing the work, preparing to write, writing, and rewriting—your response to the work itself will have grown and shifted somewhat. Part of the reason is that you will have become more knowledgeable as a result of the time and effort you have spent, and you will have a more subtle understanding of the work. But part of the reason will also be that the work itself will not be exactly the same. Just as a work is a little different for every reader, it is also a little different with every successive reading by the *same* reader, and what you will be capturing in your words is some of the subtlety of the work, its capacity to produce effects that are alive and that are therefore always changing just slightly. You need not, therefore, feel that you must say the final word about the work you are writing about—but you do want to say whatever word you have to say in the best possible way.

You can turn all this into a full-time job, of course, but you needn't. It is hard work, and at first the learning seems slow and the payoff questionable. A basketball novice watching the magic of Michael Jordan may find it hard to see the point of practicing lay-ups, but even creative geniuses have to go through those awful moments of sitting down and putting pen to paper (and then crossing out and rewriting again and again). But that's the way you learn to make it seem easy. Art is mostly craft, and craft means methodical work.

It *will* come more easily with practice. But you needn't aspire to professional writing to take pleasure in what you accomplish. Learning to write well about poetry will help you with all sorts of tasks, some of them having little to do with writing. Writing trains the mind, creates habits, teaches you procedures that will have all kinds of long-range effects that you may not immediately recognize or be able to predict. And ultimately it is very satisfying, even if it is not easy, to be able to stand back and say, "That is mine. Those are my words. I know what I'm talking about. I understand, and I can make someone else understand."

One final bit of advice: do not follow, too rigidly or too closely, anyone's advice, including ours. We have suggested some general strategies and listed some common pitfalls. But writing is a very personal experience, and you will have talents (and faults) that are a little different from anyone else's. Learn to play to your own strengths and avoid the weaknesses that you are especially prone to. Pay attention to your instructor's comments; learn from your own mistakes.

A SUMMARY OF THE PROCESS

Here, briefly, is a summary, step by step, of the stages we have suggested you move through in preparing a paper about poetry.

Stage One: Deciding what to write about

- Read the work straight through, thoughtfully. Make notes at the end on any points that caught your special attention.
- Read the work again more slowly, pausing to think through all the parts you don't understand. When you finish, write a three- or four-sentence summary.
- Read the work again, carefully but quite quickly. Decide what you feel most strongly about in the work, and write down the one thing you would most want to explain to a friend about how the poem works, or (if the work still puzzles you) the one question you would most like to be able to answer.
- Decide how the statement you made at the end of your third reading relates to the summary you wrote down after the second reading.
- Write a one-paragraph "promise" of what your paper is going to argue.

Stage Two: Planning and drafting your paper

- Read the work at least twice more and make notes on anything that relates to your thesis.
- Read through all your notes so far, and for each write a sentence articulating how it relates to your thesis.
- Transfer all your notes to note cards of uniform size.
- Read through all your notes again and record any new observations or ideas on additional note cards.
- Set aside your note cards for the moment, and make a brief outline of the major points you intend to make.
- Sort the note cards into piles corresponding to the major points in your outline. Sort the cards in each separate pile into the most likely order of their use in the paper.
- Make a more detailed outline (including the most significant examples) from your pile of note cards on each point.

- Reconsider your order of presentation and make any necessary adjustments.
- Write a first draft.

Stage Three: Rewriting

- Go over your writing, word by word, sentence by sentence, and paragraph by paragraph, in draft after draft until your paper expresses your ideas clearly and concisely.

Stage Four: Final preparation

- If you have not been working on a computer, type or word-process your paper.
- Proofread carefully for errors of all kinds—spelling, typing, etc.
- Proofread again. Find your mistakes before someone else does.
- Congratulate yourself on a job well done.

BIOGRAPHICAL SKETCHES[1]

AI (b. 1947)

Born to parents of Asian, African, and Native American heritage, Ai earned a B.A. in Oriental Studies from the University of Arizona and an M.F.A. from the University of California at Irvine. Her first collection of poetry, *Cruelty*, appeared in 1973. Notable for its dramatic monologues, Ai's subsequent collection, *Killing Floor* (1979), received the Lamont Poetry Prize. Her narrative poetry, most recently *Fate* (1991) and *Greed* (1993), invokes graphic images and defiant characters.

W. H. AUDEN (1907–1973)

A prolific writer of poems, plays, essays, and criticism, Wystan Hugh Auden was born in York, England, to a medical officer and a nurse. Auden studied at Oxford and taught at various universities in the United States, where he became a naturalized citizen in 1946. He won the Pulitzer Prize in 1948 for his collection of poems, *Age of Anxiety*, and is regarded as a poet of political and intellectual conscience. His long-term relationship with poet Chester Kallman has been the subject of several recent biographies.

ELIZABETH BISHOP (1911–1979)

Born in Worcester, Massachusetts, Bishop endured the death of her father before she was a year old and the institutionalization of her mother when she was five. Bishop was raised by her maternal grandmother in Nova Scotia, then by her paternal grandparents back in Worcester. Bishop attended Vassar College and met the poet Marianne Moore, who encouraged her to give up plans for medical school to pursue the life of a poet. Bishop traveled through Canada, Europe, and South America, finally settling in Rio de Janeiro, where she lived for nearly twenty years. Bishop produced only four volumes of poetry: *North and South* (1946); *A Cold Spring* (1955), which won the Pulitzer Prize; *Questions of Travel* (1965); and *Geography III* (1976), which won the National Book Critics' Circle Award.

WILLIAM BLAKE (1757–1828)

In defense of his unorthodox and original work, Blake once said: "That which can be made Explicit to the Idiot . . . is not worth my care." The son of a London haberdasher, he studied drawing at ten and at fourteen was apprenticed to an engraver for seven years. After a first book of poems, *Poetical Sketches* (1783), he began experimenting with what he called "illuminated printing"—the words and pictures of each page were engraved in relief on copper and the printed sheets partly colored by hand—a laborious and time-consuming process that resulted in books of singular beauty, no two of which were exactly alike. His great *Songs of Innocence* (1789) and *Songs of Experience* (1794) were printed in this manner, as were his increasingly mythic and prophetic books, which include *The Marriage of Heaven and Hell* (1793), *The Four Zoas* (1803), *Milton* (1804), and *Jerusalem* (1809). Blake devoted his later life to pictorial art, illustrating *The Canterbury Tales*, the Book of Job, and *The Divine Comedy*, on which he was hard at work when he died.

1. Biographical sketches are included for all poets represented by two or more poems.

LOUISE BOGAN (1897–1970)

Louise Bogan was born in Maine and attended Boston University. During her lifetime she was known chiefly as a critic; as poetry editor for *The New Yorker*, she wrote a biannual column called "The Season's Verse," which appeared from 1931 to 1969. She was elected to the National Institute of Arts and Letters and the American Academy of Arts and Letters. Her books include *Body of This Death* (1924), *Dark Summer* (1929), *The Blue Estuaries, Poems 1923–1968* (1968), and the prose work *Achievement in American Poetry, 1900–1950* (1951).

ROO BORSON (b. 1952)

While considered a Canadian poet, Ruth Elizabeth Borson was born in Berkeley, California. She later attended the University of California at Santa Barbara and earned her B.A. in 1973 from Gordon College. Four years later, she published her first collection of poetry, *Landfall*, in addition to receiving her M.F.A. from the University of British Columbia, where she was awarded the Macmillan Prize for Poetry. Borson's poetry suggests what she calls the "intricacy of the physical world" as it recognizes the powers of sensuality and memory. She has published a number of collections, including *The Whole Night Coming Home* (1984) and *Intent, or the Weight of the World* (1989).

GWENDOLYN BROOKS (b. 1917)

Brooks was born in Topeka, Kansas, and was raised in Chicago, where she began writing poetry at the age of seven. Her formal training began at the Southside Community Art Center, and she produced her first book of poems, *A Street in Bronzeville*, shortly after, in 1945. Her second book of poems, *Annie Allen* (1949), won Brooks the distinction of being the first African American to win the Pulitzer Prize for Poetry. Brooks's early poetry concentrated on what Langston Hughes called the "ordinary aspects of black life," but her work was transformed in the 1960s and Brooks became a passionate advocate for African American consciousness and activism.

ROBERT BROWNING (1812–1889)

Born in London, Browning was an aspiring but unknown poet and playwright when he met the already-famous poet, Elizabeth Barrett. After their elopement in 1846, the Brownings moved to Italy, where Elizabeth Barrett Browning authored the chronicle of their love, *Sonnets from the Portuguese* (1850). Browning wrote most of his great poems during this period, and after his wife's death in 1861, he returned to England and began to establish his own literary reputation for his fine dramatic monologues.

JUDITH ORTIZ COFER (b. 1952)

Born in 1952 in Hormigueros, Puerto Rico, Cofer spent her childhood between Puerto Rico and Patterson, New Jersey, where her father's family lived. This bicultural childhood is a common theme in both her poems and fiction. Cofer attended Augusta College in Georgia and received her M.A. in English from Florida Atlantic University. She received a fellowship to study at Oxford and subsequent scholarships to the Bread Loaf Writers' Conference, where she taught for a number of years. Her first collection of poetry, *Peregrina* (1985), won the Riverstone International Poetry Competition, and in 1989 Cofer was a National Endowment for the Arts Fellow in Poetry. Her novel, *The Line of the Sun* was published in 1989, and her most recent work, a collection of poetry and essays, is titled *The Latin Deli* (1993).

SAMUEL TAYLOR COLERIDGE (1772–1834)

Born in the small town of Ottery St. Mary, in rural Devonshire, England, Coleridge was one of the greatest and most original of the nineteenth-century Romantic poets. He wrote three of the most haunting poems in the English tradition—*The Rime of the Ancient Mariner* (1798), *Christabel* (1816), and *Kubla Khan* (1816)—as well as immensely influential literary criticism and a revolutionary treatise on biology, *Hints Towards the Formation of a More Comprehensive Theory of Life*. In 1795, in the midst of a failed experiment to establish a "Pantisocracy" (his form of ideal community), he met William Wordsworth, and in 1798 they published together their *Lyrical Ballads*, which was to influence the course of English Romanticism for decades to come. Coleridge's physical ailments, addiction to opium, and profound sense of despair have to this day shaped our sense of the poet suffering for the sake of art.

WENDY COPE (b. 1945)

Born in Kent, England, Cope studied history and learned to play the guitar at Oxford University. While working as a primary school teacher, she began writing poetry. Her first volume, *Making Cocoa for Kingsley Amis*, was published in 1986, and the following year, she received a Cholmondeley Award for Poetry. Her most recent collection, *Serious Concerns* (1992), includes her trademark optimistic and witty verses. Cope has also published a children's book and a narrative poem, *The River Girl* (1991), commissioned for performance.

HART CRANE (1899–1932)

Crane's vision of modernist poetry refused the popular pessimism of T. S. Eliot's *The Waste Land*, and called for "a more positive, or . . . ecstatic goal." Born in Garretsville, Ohio, Harold Hart Crane spent his childhood in Cleveland, and after adolescent visits to Cuba, Paris, and New York, he opted to leave high school and move to Greenwich Village. In spite of the artistic intensity of the Village, Crane was unable to support himself financially, and moved back to Cleveland to work for his father. While back in Ohio, Crane published a number of poems, and in 1923 he again moved to New York City, where he wrote extensively and published his first collection, *White Buildings*, in 1926. At the same time, he was working on his epic poem, *The Bridge*, which received *Poetry Magazine*'s annual award. Crane was awarded a Guggenheim Fellowship in 1931, but a year later he took his own life.

E. E. CUMMINGS (1894–1962)

Cummings's variety of modernism was distinguished by its playful sense of humor, its formal experimentation, its lyrical directness, and above all by its celebration of the individual against mass society. Born in Cambridge, Massachusetts, the son of a Congregationalist minister, Edward Estlin Cummings attended Harvard University, where he wrote poetry in the Pre-Raphaelite and Metaphysical traditions. He joined the ambulance corps in France the day after the United States entered World War I and was imprisoned by his own side for his outspoken letters and disdain for bureaucracy; he transmuted the experience into his first literary success, *The Enormous Room* (1922). After the war, Cummings established himself as a poet and artist in Greenwich Village, made frequent trips to France and New Hampshire, and showed little interest in wealth or his growing celebrity.

JAMES DICKEY (b. 1923)

Dickey did not become seriously interested in poetry until he joined the Air Force in 1942. When he returned from World War II, he earned a B.A. and an M.A. at Vanderbilt University, publishing his first poem in *Sewanee Review* his senior year. Since the publication of his first book of poems, *Into the Stone* (1960), Dickey, while primarily a poet, has engaged in diverse careers ranging from advertising writer and novelist to poetry teacher at various universities. His 1965 collection, *Buckdancer's Choice*, received the National Book Award, and from 1967 to 1969 Dickey was Consultant in Poetry to the Library of Congress. He is more popularly known for his best-selling novel, *Deliverance* (1970), which he later adapted for Hollywood. Most recently, he has published *The Whole Motion: Collected Poems 1949–1992* (1992) and a novel, *The White Sea* (1993).

EMILY DICKINSON (1830–1886)

From childhood on, Dickinson's life was sequestered and obscure. Yet her verse had a power and influence that has traveled far beyond the cultured yet relatively circumscribed environment in which she lived her life: her room, her father's house, her family, a few close friends, and the small town of Amherst, Massachusetts. Indeed, along with Walt Whitman, her far more public contemporary, she all but invented American poetry. Born in Amherst, the daughter of a respected lawyer and revered father ("His heart was pure and terrible," she once wrote), Dickinson studied for less than a year at the Mount Holyoke Female Seminary, returning permanently to Amherst. In later life she became more and more of a recluse, dressing in white, seeing no visitors, yet working without stint at her poems—nearly eighteen hundred in all, only a few of which were published during her lifetime.

JOHN DONNE (1572–1631)

The first and greatest of what came to be known as the "Metaphysical" school of poets, Donne wrote in a style, revolutionary at the time, that combined highly intellectual conceits with complex, compressed phrasing. Born into an old Roman Catholic family at a time when Catholics were subject to constant harassment, Donne quietly abandoned his religion and had a brilliant early career until a politically disastrous marriage ruined his worldly hopes and forced him to struggle for years to support a large and growing family; impoverished and despairing, he even wrote a treatise (*Biathanatos*) on the lawfulness of suicide. King James (who had ambitions for him as a preacher) eventually forced Donne to take Anglican orders in 1615, and indeed he became one of the great sermonizers of his day, rising to dean of St. Paul's Cathedral in 1621. Donne's private devotions were published in 1624, and he continued to write sacred poetry until a few years before his death.

RITA DOVE (b. 1952)

When Dove won the 1987 Pulitzer Prize for Poetry for *Thomas and Beulah* (1986), she became only the second African American poet (after Gwendolyn Brooks in 1950) to receive such high recognition. A native of Akron, Ohio, Dove attended Miami University in Ohio, studied for a year in West Germany as a Fulbright scholar, and received an M.F.A. in creative writing from the University of Iowa. She taught creative writing at Arizona State University and is now a professor of English at the University of Virginia as well as an associate editor of *Callaloo*, the journal of African-American and African arts and letters. Dove's books include *The Yellow House on the Corner* (1980), *Museum* (1983), *Grace Notes* (1989), *Selected Poems* (1993) and *Mother Love* (1995). From 1993–1995 she served as Poet Laureate of the United States.

JOHN DRYDEN (1631–1700)

Called "the father of English criticism" by Samuel Johnson, Dryden was a prolific poet and dramatist. He attended Trinity College, Cambridge, where he took his A.B. in 1654, and for most of his career, Dryden wrote nondramatic, occasional, and public poems, celebrating historical moments. In 1667 he wrote "Annus Mirabilis," which celebrated England's "year of wonders." During his middle years, Dryden focused mostly on creating popular drama and literary criticism. In 1677, he adapted Shakespeare's *Antony and Cleopatra* into a play called *All for Love*, and in "An Essay of Dramatic Poesy" (1668), he outlined new theoretical principles for drama. That same year he was named England's Poet Laureate. Later in his career, Dryden became known for his political satires, like the scathing mock-heroic, "MacFlecknoe" (1682) and "Absalom and Achitophel" (1681).

RICHARD EBERHART (b. 1904)

Richard Eberhart was born in Austin, Minnesota, the son of a wealthy businessman. He attended the University of Minnesota and received his B.A. from Dartmouth in 1926. After holding a variety of jobs he landed in England and took a second B.A. from St. John's College in Cambridge in 1929. He published his first book of poems the following year. During World War II he was an aerial gunner, and afterward he returned to Dartmouth as a teacher and poet-in-residence. Since 1970 he has held various visiting professorships, and he has received many prizes and honorary degrees. His recent books include *Maine Poems* (1988) and *Richard Eberhart, New and Selected Poems: 1930–1990* (1990).

T. S. ELIOT (1888–1965)

Thomas Stearns Eliot—from his formally experimental and oblique writings to his brilliant arguments in defense of "orthodoxy" and "tradition"—dominated the world of English poetry between the world wars. Born in St. Louis, Missouri, of New England stock, Eliot studied literature and philosophy at Harvard, and later in France and Germany. He came to England in 1914, read Greek philosophy at Oxford, and published his first major poem, "The Love Song of J. Alfred Prufrock," the next year. In 1922, with the help of his great supporter and adviser, Ezra Pound, Eliot published his long poem, *The Waste Land* (1922), which would profoundly influence a whole generation of poets. In his later work, particularly the *Four Quartets* (completed in 1945), Eliot explored religious questions in a quieter, more controlled idiom. He was awarded the Nobel Prize for Literature in 1948.

LOUISE ERDRICH (b. 1954)

Born in Little Falls, Minnesota, of German-American and Chippewa descent, Erdrich grew up in Wahpeton, North Dakota, as a member of the Turtle Mountain Band of Chippewa, and attended Dartmouth College. After graduation, she returned to teach in North Dakota's Poetry in the Schools Program. She received an M.A. in creative writing from Johns Hopkins University in 1979. In the same year, *Jacklight*, a collection of poetry, was published. Her first novel, *Love Medicine* (1984), has been praised as a landmark work in its depiction of the lives of contemporary Native Americans, and was the winner of the National Book Critics' Circle Award for Fiction. An expanded version was published in 1993. Erdrich has also published another collection of poetry, *Baptism of Desire* (1989), several novels in the North American series that includes *Love Medicine, The Beet Queen* (1986), *Tracks* (1988), and *The Bingo Palace* (1993), and jointly authored *The Crown of Columbus* (1991) with her husband Michael Dorris.

CAROLYN FORCHÉ (b. 1950)

Born in Detroit, Michigan, Forché studied creative writing and international relations at Michigan State University and did graduate study at Bowling Green State University. Her first book of poetry, *Gathering the Tribes* (1976), won the Yale Series of Younger Poets Award. Forché was a journalist for Amnesty International in El Salvador and Beirut correspondent for National Public Radio's "All Things Considered." She has taught at many universities and has published several volumes of poetry, including *The Country Between Us* (1981).

ROBERT FROST (1874–1963)

Though his poetry forever identified Frost with rural New England, he was born and lived to the age of eleven in San Francisco. Coming to New England after his father's death, Frost studied classics in high school, entered and dropped out of both Dartmouth and Harvard, and spent difficult years as an unrecognized poet before his first book, *A Boy's Will* (1913), was accepted and published in England. Frost's character was full of contradiction—he held "that we get forward as much by hating as by loving"—yet by the end of his long life he was one of the most honored poets of his time. In 1961, two years before his death, he was invited to read a poem at John F. Kennedy's presidential inauguration ceremony.

JOHN GAY (1685–1732)

After attending school in Devon, Gay moved to London to work as an apprentice; within five years he was involved in contemporary literary circles as well as the publishing world. Known for both his playfulness and his serious social commentary, Gay, with Pope, Swift, and Arbuthnot, founded the Scriblerus Club, which became famous for its literary satires and practical jokes. In addition to poems like "The Shepherd's Week" (1714) and "Trivia, or the Art of Walking the Streets of London" (1716), Gay wrote *The Beggar's Opera* (1728), a ballad-opera that satirized contemporary political corruption.

THOMAS HARDY (1840–1928)

In a preface dated 1901, Hardy called his poems "unadjusted impressions," which nevertheless might, by "humbly recording diverse readings of phenomena as they are forced upon us by chance and change," lead to a philosophy. Indeed, though he was essentially retrospective in his outlook, Hardy anticipated the concerns of modern poetry by treating the craft as an awkward, often skeptical means of penetrating the facade of language. Born at Upper Bockhampton in Dorset, England, the son of a master mason, Hardy began to write while in the midst of an architectural career. After a long and successful career as a novelist, he turned exclusively to poetry; he died in the midst of preparing his last book, *Winter Words* (1929), for publication.

ROBERT HAYDEN (1913–1980)

Hayden was born in Detroit, Michigan, and studied at Wayne State University and the University of Michigan. He taught at Fisk University for over twenty years and at the University of Michigan for more than ten. Although Hayden produced ten volumes of poetry he did not receive acclaim until late in life. In the 1960s, Hayden resisted pressure to express the militancy some African Americans wanted, and thus alienated himself from a growing body of African American literary tradition.

H.D. (HILDA DOOLITTLE) (1886–1961)

The only surviving daughter in a prominent family that included five sons, Hilda Doolittle grew up in Pennsylvania. She moved to London in 1911, in the footsteps of her friend and one-time fiancé Ezra Pound, who helped her begin her poetic career. Her first book of poems, *Sea Garden*, was published in 1916, followed by *Hymen* (1921), *Heliodora and Other Poems* (1924), *Collected Poems* (1925), and *Red Roses for Bronze* (1931), among others. After surviving the bombings of London in World War II, she wrote two major epics about war, *Trilogy* (1944–1946) and *Helen in Egypt* (1961). In 1960, she was given the Award of Merit Medal for Poetry from the American Academy of Arts and Letters.

GEORGE HERBERT (1593–1633)

After the early death of his Welsh father, Herbert was raised by his mother, a literary patron of John Donne. Herbert graduated with honors from Cambridge and was subsequently elected public orator at the University. He twice served as a member of Parliament in the 1620s, but his political career never flourished. Instead, he began to work for the church in 1626, married, and took holy orders in 1630. While living in Bemerton, he became known as "Holy Mr. Herbert" for his diligent care of the members of his ministry. He died of consumption in 1633, and his most famous poetry collection, *The Temple*, was published posthumously by a friend.

ROBERT HERRICK (1591–1674)

The son of a London goldsmith, Herrick would have liked nothing better than to live a life of leisured study, discussing literature and drinking sack with his hero, Ben Jonson. For a number of reasons, though, he decided to take religious orders and moved to a parish in Devonshire. Herrick eventually made himself at home there, inventing dozens of imaginary mistresses with exotic names (his housekeeper was prosaically named Prudence) and practicing, half-seriously, his own peculiar form of paganism. When the Puritans came to power, Herrick was driven from his post to London where, in 1648, he published a volume of over fourteen hundred poems with two titles, *Hesperides* for the secular poems and *Noble Numbers* for those with sacred subjects. Though they did not survive the harsh atmosphere of Puritanism and were virtually forgotten until the nineteenth century, Herrick was eventually restored to his post in Devonshire where he lived out his last years quietly.

JOHN HOLLANDER (b. 1929)

Known for his originality, wit, and keen perception of language, Hollander plays with words and shapes in his poetry. Hollander was born in New York City and later attended Columbia University, earning a B.A. in 1950 and an M.A. in 1952. He received his Ph.D. from Indiana University after serving as a Junior Fellow in the Society of Fellows at Harvard and teaching there. He now teaches at Yale. While he is most widely known as a poet, he has also written extensive criticism and created several children's books. His first book, *A Crackling of Thorns* (1958) was introduced by W. H. Auden as the 1958 volume in the Yale Series of Younger Poets. Hollander received the Bollingen Prize for Poetry in 1963, and his subsequent collections include *Types of Shape* (1969) and *Powers of Thirteen* (1983). In 1990, Hollander was made a Fellow of the MacArthur Foundation. He has two recent volumes, *Tessarae and Other Poems* and *Selected Poetry*; both were published in 1993.

GERARD MANLEY HOPKINS (1844–1889)

Hopkins's verse, in all its superbly controlled tension, strong rhythm, and sheer exuberance, has been championed by a number of modern poets—yet he made few attempts to publish what many of his contemporaries found nearly incomprehensible, and he was all but unknown until long after his death. Born the eldest of eight children of a marine-insurance adjuster (shipwrecks later figured in his poetry, particularly *The Wreck of the Deutschland*) Hopkins attended Oxford, where his ambition was to become a painter—until he was converted to Catholicism. He taught for a time, decided to become a Jesuit, burnt all his early poetry as too worldly, and was ordained in 1877. Near the end of his life Hopkins was appointed professor of Greek at University College, Dublin. Out of place and miserable, he died there of typhoid at the age of forty-four.

LANGSTON HUGHES (1902–1967)

Hughes, born in Joplin, Missouri, was a major figure of the intellectual and literary movement called the Harlem Renaissance. A graduate of Lincoln University in 1929, Hughes traveled through the world as a correspondent and columnist. He also founded theaters and produced plays, as well as authoring poems and novels. His works include *The Weary Blues* (1926), *Montage of a Dream Deferred* (1951), and *The Panther and the Lash: Poems of Our Time* (1961). Hughes has recently been incorporated into the gay

BEN JONSON (1572?–1637)

Poet, playwright, actor, scholar, critic, translator, and leader, for the first time in English, of a literary "school" (the "Cavalier" poets), Jonson was born the posthumous son of a clergyman and stepson to a master bricklayer of Westminster. He had an eventful early career, going to war against the Spanish, working as an actor and killing an associate in a duel, and converting to Catholicism (which made him an object of deep suspicion after the Gunpowder Plot of Guy Fawkes in 1605). Jonson wrote a number of plays in the midst of all this, including *Every Man in His Humor* (in which Shakespeare acted a leading role), *Volpone* (1606), and *The Alchemist* (1610). He spent the latter part of his life at the center of a vast literary circle. When in 1616 he published his collected works, *The Works of Benjamin Jonson*, it was the first time an English author had been so presumptuous as to consider writing a profession.

X. J. KENNEDY (b. 1929)

Kennedy's *Nude Descending a Staircase* (1961) is a *tour de force* performance, one of the most remarkable first volumes of poetry written in this century. Its range, from elegy to lyric to song to light verse, encompasses a great variety of tones and poetic kinds. Born Joseph Charles Kennedy in Dover, New Jersey, he was educated at Seton Hall College in New Jersey, Columbia University, and the Sorbonne in Paris. After serving in the U.S. Navy, he taught at several colleges and universities, was poetry editor of *Paris Review*, and edited anthologies of poetry, fiction, and essays. At present he works as a free-lance writer. His most recent volume, with Dorothy M. Kennedy, is *Talking Like the Rain: A First Book of Poems* (1992).

GALWAY KINNELL (b. 1927)

Born in Providence, Rhode Island, Kinnell writes poetry that calls attention to humanity's deep connection with nature. After earning a B.A. from Princeton in 1948 and an M.A. from the University of Rochester, he was a journalist, a civil rights field worker, and a teacher at numerous colleges and universities. With a keen sense of combining personal and national historical events, Kinnell's 1969 collection *Body Rags* calls upon the civil rights movement and, more recently, *The Past* (1985) speculates on the Hiroshima and Nagasaki bombings. His early poetry, collected in *What a Kingdom It Was* (1960) and *First Poems 1946–1954* (1970), is highly formal; his more recent work, however, invokes a more colloquial style. His *Selected Poems* (1982) received both a Pulitzer Prize and the American Book Award. Currently teaching creative writing at New York University, Kinnell has recently published a compilation of earlier work, *Three Books: Body Rags, Mortal Acts, Mortal Words, The Past* (1993).

ARCHIBALD LAMPMAN (1861–1899)

Born in Ontario to German parents, Lampman, as the son of a clergyman, was headed for the Anglican ministry. After graduating from the University of Toronto in 1882 with honors in languages, however, he went into the civil service where he worked as a clerk until the end of his life. Along with Duncan Campbell Scott and William Wilfred Campbell, Lampman was a member of the Confederation group, a number of Canadian nature poets who have been praised for their efforts to articulate a Canadian national literature. Inspired by music, Lampman wrote poetry as a peaceful mode of self-expression, and he published his first volume, *Among the Millet,* in 1888. Two subsequent collections appeared after his death, *Lyrics of Earth: Sonnets and Ballads* (1925) and *At the Long Sault and Other New Poems* (1943).

IRVING LAYTON (b. 1912)

Considered Canada's most prolific poet, Layton was born to Jewish parents in Romania in 1912. One year later, his family emigrated to Canada. After a series of unrelated jobs, Layton earned a degree in agriculture before embarking on a career writing poetry. He was critical of both literary tradition and the most representative modernist poetry like that of T. S. Eliot. Pivotal in rethinking the boundaries of poetic conventions, Layton has served on the editorial boards of a number of literary magazines, most prominently the *Black Mountain Review.* His irreverent career is collected in numerous volumes of poetry. Two recent works, *The Gucci Bag* (1983) and *A Spider Danced a Cozy Jig* (1984), highlight Layton's unique sense of humor.

AUDRE LORDE (1934–1992)

Born in New York City, Lorde grew up in Harlem and attended Hunter College and Columbia University. She later returned to Hunter College in 1980 as a professor of English. Lorde raised a son and a daughter in an interracial lesbian relationship and helped to start Kitchen Table: Women of Color Press. Her poetry publications include *The First Cities* (1968), *The Black Unicorn* (1987), and *Undersong: Chosen Poems Old and New* (1993). Lorde has also published two volumes of essays, *Sister Outsider* (1983) and *Burst of Light* (1988), as well as an autobiograhical novel, *Zami* (1980).

CLAUDE MCKAY (1890–1948)

Born in Sunny Ville, Jamaica, McKay became one of the most prominent figures of the Harlem Renaissance—the oldest as well as the first to publish. Always politically active, he was attracted to Communism and in 1922 met Lenin and Trotsky in Moscow, though he later repudiated this commitment with his 1942 conversion to Catholicism. "[To] have a religion," he wrote, "is very much like falling in love with a woman. You love her for her . . . beauty, which cannot be defined." McKay's conception of black experience, infused with social reform and a consciousness of ethnic vitality, made him a catalytic poet for his generation. His works include *If We Must Die* (1919), *Home to Harlem* (1928), and *A Long Way from Home* (1937).

MARTIAL (40?–104?)

Known for his witty epigrams, Marcus Valerius Martialis was born in Northeast Spain to Roman colonists in about 40 A.D. He received an excellent education and moved to Rome, discovering that he could find and keep patrons by writing compliments in verse. Early in his career, Martial performed his epigrams in private presentations, but after the spectacular inauguration at the Colosseum (80 A.D.), he published *Liber de Speactaculis (The Book of the Shows)*; he continued to write and publish until 96 A.D.

ANDREW MARVELL (1621–1678)

Marvell was born in Yorkshire, England and educated at Cambridge. He was a supporter of the Puritans and a member of the British Parliament. Marvell was known in his day for his satires in prose and verse, but today is better known for his less public poems.

EDNA ST. VINCENT MILLAY (1892–1950)

Winner of the 1923 Pulitzer Prize for Poetry, Millay was born in Maine and educated at Vassar. After college, with her reputation as a poet already established, Millay moved to Greenwich Village in New York and became notorious for her bohemian life and passionate love affairs.

JOHN MILTON (1608–1674)

Born in London, the elder son of a self-made businessman, Milton exhibited unusual literary and scholarly gifts at an early age; before entering Cambridge University, he was already adept at Latin and Greek and was well on his way to mastering Hebrew and most of the European languages. After graduation, he spent six more years reading, day and night, just about everything of importance written in English, Italian, Latin, and Greek— after which his father sent him abroad for another year of travel and study. Returning to England, Milton immediately embroiled himself in political controversy, writing pamphlets defending everything from free speech to the execution of Charles I by Cromwell and his followers. In the midst of this feverish activity, the monarchy was restored, and Milton was imprisoned and his property confiscated—but worst of all he lost his sight. Blind, impoverished, and isolated, he set about writing the great works of his later years: *Paradise Lost* (1667), *Paradise Regained* (1671), and *Samson Agonistes* (1671).

MARIANNE MOORE (1887–1972)

Of poetry, Moore self-consciously wrote, "I, too, dislike it"; the phrase captures her fascinating character. Born in Kirkwood, Missouri, near St. Louis, Moore's family moved to Pennsylvania, where she earned a degree from Bryn Mawr College in 1909. In 1918, she and her mother moved to Brooklyn, New York, where Moore became an avid Brooklyn Dodgers fan. While she began to write and publish poetry in college, she did not immediately devote herself to it full time. Instead, she studied business science, taught stenography, and eventually worked as branch librarian at the New York Public Library from 1921 to 1925. In addition to writing poetry, Moore was a prolific critic and served as the editor of the *Dial* from 1926 to 1929. Her *Collected Poems* (1951) were honored with the Bollingen, Pulitzer, and National Book awards. Her *Complete Poems* (1967), while hardly complete, reveal a poet whose constant revisions showed her changing relationship to both nature and language.

PAT MORA (b. 1942)

Born to Mexican-American parents in El Paso, Texas, Mora earned both her B.A. and M.A. from the University of Texas, El Paso. Her first two collections of poetry, *Chants* (1985) and *Borders* (1986), won Southwest Book Awards. Along with these books, her most recent volume of poetry, *Communion* (1991), reflects and addresses her Chicana and Southwestern background. She has recently compiled a collection of essays called *Nepantla: Essays from the Land in the Middle* (1993).

SUSAN MUSGRAVE (b. 1951)

Born in Santa Cruz, California in 1951, Musgrave now resides in Canada. *Songs of the Sea-Witch* (1970), her first collection, invokes nightmares and darkness where the speakers live on the border of madness. She was the writer-in-residence at the University of Waterloo in Ontario from 1983 until 1985, when she published *Cocktails at the Mausoleum*. Her work, most recently *The Embalmer's Art* (1991), includes many personal moments, and their explicitness invites confrontation. Musgrave has also written plays, novels, and poetry for children.

HOWARD NEMEROV (1920–1991)

Nemerov once called his poems "bad jokes, and even terrible jokes, emerging from the nature of things as well as from my propensity for coming at things a touch subversively, and from the blind side, or the dark side, the side everyone concerned with 'values' would just as soon forget." The resonance of his poetry may lie in his ability to balance this subversive, wayward imagination with lucid, precise language and traditional verse forms. Born in New York City, Nemerov graduated from Harvard University, served in the Air Force during World War II, and returned to New York to complete his first book, *The Image and the Law* (1948). He taught at a number of colleges and universities and published books of poetry, plays, short stories, novels, and essays. His *Collected Poems* won the Pulitzer Prize and the National Book Award in 1978. In addition, he served as Poet Laureate of the United States from 1988 to 1990. *Trying Conclusions: New and Selected Poems 1961–1991* was published in 1991.

SHARON OLDS (b. 1942)

Olds's poems might well be compared with those of the "confessional" poets (particularly Plath and Sexton) in their intense focus on and preoccupation with sexual and family relationships. Born in San Francisco, Olds studied at Stanford and Columbia universities, settling afterwards in New York City, where she teaches creative writing at New York University and the Goldwater Hospital (a public facility for the severely physically disabled). Olds's books include *Satan Says* (1980), *The Dead and the Living* (1983; National Book Critics Circle Award), and *The Gold Cell* (1987). She has received a National Endowment for the Arts Grant and a Guggenheim Fellowship. Her most recent volume, *The Father*, appeared in 1992.

DOROTHY PARKER (1893–1967)

Parker satirized the literary, social, and sexual pieties of her time with a sharp eye and sardonic exuberance. If "Brevity is the soul of Lingerie," as she announced in a *Vogue* advertisement, it is also the heart of her wit. There are a number of "Parkerisms"—brief, witty aphorisms—still in circulation. Parker was born in New York City and was friendly with several other prominent writers and humorists of the 1920s and 1930s, including Harold Ross, founder of the *New Yorker*. Author of poetry, criticism, screenplays, and short stories, she published a number of collections, including *Enough Rope* (1926), *Sunset Gun* (1928), *Death and Taxes* (1931), and *Not So Deep as a Well* (1936).

LINDA PASTAN (b. 1932)

Author of more than half a dozen volumes of poetry, Pastan was born in New York City and attended Radcliffe College and Brandeis University before settling in suburban Washington, D.C. Her books include *A Perfect Circle of Sun* (1971), *The Five Stages of Grief* (1978), *A Fraction of Darkness* (1985), and *The Imperfect Paradise* (1988). *PM / AM: New and Selected Poems* (1982) was nominated for the American Book Award. Her latest collection, *Heroes in Disguise*, was published in 1991.

MARGE PIERCY (b. 1936)

Piercy's earlier poetry examined the complex interplay between personal relationships and political forces, at the same time voicing the rage of women who have for so long been dominated and overwhelmed by men ("I imagine that I speak for a constituency, living and dead," she writes). Her later work, particularly the poems in *Stone, Paper, Knife* (1983), expresses also a sense of inclusiveness, of interconnection with all living things. Born in Detroit, Piercy studied at the University of Michigan and Northwestern University and taught for some time before the success of her novels allowed her to live a semirural life on Cape Cod. Her books of poetry include *Living in the Open* (1976), *The Moon Is Always Female* (1980), and *Available Light* (1988). In 1990 Piercy received the Golden Rose Award. Her most recent book of poetry, *Mars and Her Children*, was published in 1992.

SYLVIA PLATH (1932–1963)

Plath has attained the status of a cult figure as much for the splendid and beautiful agony of her poems as for her "martyrdom" to art. Her life, in all its outer banality and inner tragedy, might be seen as a confirmation that poetry is a dangerous vocation. Born the daughter of a Polish immigrant who died in 1940, Plath's early years were a vision of conventional success, including poetry prizes, scholarships at Smith College, and a *summa cum laude* graduation. She won a Fulbright Scholarship to Cambridge University, where she met and married the English poet, Ted Hughes, with whom she had two children. Yet beneath it all was a woman whose acute perceptions and intolerable pain led her to produce a novel, *The Bell Jar* (1963), and three volumes of poetry—and to commit suicide at the age of thirty.

EDGAR ALLAN POE (1809–1849)

Poe's actor father deserted his wife and son when Edgar was less than a year old. His mother died before he was three, and he and his younger sister were separated and taken into different families. The Allans (who gave Poe his middle name) moved, in 1815, to England, where Edgar had his early schooling. He studied briefly at the University of Virginia and in 1827 paid to have a volume of poems published in Boston (his birthplace); a second volume appeared in 1829 in Baltimore (where he was to die twenty years later). Having served for two years in the army, he was appointed to West Point in 1830 but apparently managed to have himself expelled within the year for cutting classes. Living in Baltimore with his grandmother, aunt, and cousin Virginia (whom he married in 1835 when she was thirteen), Poe began to attract critical attention but made very little money. For the twelve years of his bizarre marriage, he wrote, worked as journalist and editor, and drank. Not long after his wife died in 1847 he seemed to be straightening himself out when, on election day—October 3—he was found semiconscious near a polling place and died four days later without fully regaining consciousness. It is testimony to the continuing fame of his works that they need not be named here.

ALEXANDER POPE (1688–1744)

Born near London, Pope was delicate as a child and deformed early on by tuberculosis of the spine. He nevertheless was encouraged to read widely and exhibited a precocious talent for poetry; his first successes were the *Essay on Criticism* (1711) and *The Rape of the Lock* (1712 and 1714). Pope's Catholicism, which precluded him from attending a university, voting, holding public office, or receiving the sort of patronage commonly bestowed on writers of his generation, led him to embark on translations of Homer's *Iliad* and *Odyssey* in 1713, the success of which would eventually make him the only important writer of his generation to make his living solely by his craft. Pope's extraordinary career resulted in works as diverse as the *Dunciad* (1728 and 1743), his great verse satire, and the *Essay on Man* (1733–34), his exploration of ethics and philosophy.

EZRA POUND (1885–1972)

Pound's tremendous ambition—to succeed in his own work and to influence the development of poetry and Western culture in general—led him to found the Imagist school of poetry, to advise and assist a galaxy of great writers (Eliot, Joyce, Williams, Frost, and Hemingway, to name a few), and to write a number of highly influential critical works. It also led him to a charge of treason (Pound served as a propagandist for Mussolini during World War II), a diagnosis of insanity, and twelve years at St. Elizabeth's, an institution for the criminally insane. Born in Hailey, Idaho, Ezra Loomis Pound studied at the University of Pennsylvania and Hamilton College before traveling to Europe in 1908. He remained there, living in Ireland, England, France, and Italy, for much of his life. Pound's verse is collected in *Personae: The Collected Poems* (1949) and *The Cantos* (1976).

SIR WALTER RALEGH (1552–1618)

Clearly a man of immense versatility, Ralegh undertook a variety of adventures in his tumultuous life. Born in Devonshire, England, he briefly attended Oxford but withdrew to fight in the army. He is credited with bringing the potato to Ireland and tobacco to Europe, and through his many explorations, he became an investor in the North American colonies. He was knighted and named a member of Parliament, but after offending the Queen, Ralegh was imprisoned in the Tower of London. After his release in 1595, he charted a failed expedition to Guiana, and in 1603 he was again imprisoned on trumped-up treason charges. In prison, he began his unfinished *History of the World*. After another unsuccessful trip to Guiana, he was again imprisoned and executed on the orders of James I. His writings include the popular "The Nymph's Reply to the Shepherd," a response to Marlowe's "Passionate Shepherd," and some extensive writings on his findings in Guiana.

JAROLD RAMSEY (b. 1937)

Jarold Ramsey grew up on a ranch in central Oregon, and his work reflects his ongoing interest in the mythology and culture of Northwest Indians. He is currently a professor of english at the University of Rochester. His recent books include *Reading the Fire: Essays in the Traditional Indian Literatures of the Far West* (1983) and *Hand-Shadows* (1989).

ISHMAEL REED (b. 1938)

Born in Chattanooga, Tennessee, Reed attended the University of Buffalo. Considered a writer of the 1960s and 1970s counterculture, Reed, through his novels, essays, plays, songs, and poems, calls attention to the marginalization of nonwhite cultures and traditions in mainstream America. While he is probably best known for his satirical novel, *Mumbo Jumbo* (1972), Reed is a prolific poet. His first volume, *Catechism of D NeoAmerican Hoodoo Church*, was published in 1970. His most recent work is a novel, *Japanese by Spring* (1993). Reed has taught at a variety of colleges and universities; he currently teaches at the University of California, Berkeley.

ALBERTO ALVARO RÍOS (b. 1952)

Ríos was born in Nogales, Arizona, to a British mother and a Mexican father. He graduated from the University of Arizona and teaches at Arizona State University. He has recieved an NEA Fellowship and the 1981 Academy of American Poets Walt Whitman's Award for his collection of poems entitled *Whispering to Fool the Wind*. His other publications include three books of poetry, *Five Indiscretions* (1985), *The Lime Orchard Woman* (1988), and *Teodoro Luna's Two Kisses* (1990), as well as a collection of short stories, *The Iguana Killer: Twelve Stories of the Heart* (1984).

THEODORE ROETHKE (1908–1963)

Born in Saginaw, Michigan, Roethke grew up around his father's twenty-five-acre greenhouse complex—its associations with nurture and growth became an important subject in his later poetry. He worked for a time at Lafayette College, where he was professor of English and tennis coach, and later at the University of Washington, which appointed him poet-in-residence one year before he died. Roethke was an unhappy man, suffering from periodic mental breakdowns, yet the best of his poetry, with its reverence for and fear of the physical world, its quest for an ecstatic union with nature, seems destined to last. Roethke's books include *Open House* (1942), *Praise to the End!* (1951), and *The Far Field* (1964), which received a posthumous National Book Award.

MURIEL RUKEYSER (1913–1980)

Born in New York City, Rukeyser later attended Vassar College and Columbia University. Uncomfortable with her family's wealth, Rukeyser associated herself with more radical issues, namely the labor movement of the 1920s and 1930s. Her first collection of poetry, *Theory of Flight* (1935) was apparently inspired by her attendance at the Roosevelt Aviation School. In the 1940s Rukeyser wrote poetry highlighting the destruction of World War II. She later protested against U.S. involvement in Korea and Vietnam, and in the 1970s, she addressed feminist issues in her art. *The Collected Poems of Muriel Rukeyser* was published in 1978.

ANNE SEXTON (1928–1974)

Born in Newton, Massachusetts, Anne (Harvey) Sexton interrupted her attendance at Garland Junior College to marry. She wrote poetry as a child, abandoned it, and, on the advice of her doctors, began writing again after suffering a nervous breakdown. Sexton attended Boston University with fellow student Sylvia Plath, and she studied poetry with Robert Lowell. Published in 1960, her first book of poems, *To Bedlam and Part Way Back*, recounted her mental collapse and subsequent recovery period. A "confessional" poet, Sexton received many awards, most notably the Pulitzer Prize for *Live or Die* (1966). She committed suicide in 1974. That same year, she had published *Death Notebooks*; a posthumous volume, *The Awful Rowing toward God*, appeared in 1975.

WILLIAM SHAKESPEARE (1554–1616)

Considering the great and deserved fame of his work, surprisingly little is known of Shakespeare's life. We do know that between 1585 and 1592 he left his birthplace of Stratford for London to begin a career as playwright and actor. No dates of his professional career are recorded, however, nor can we be certain of the order in which he composed his plays and poetry. By 1594 he had established himself as a poet with two long works—*Venus and Adonis* and *The Rape of Lucrece*—but it was in the theater that he made his strongest reputation. Shakespeare produced perhaps thirty-five plays in twenty-five years, proving himself a master of many genres in works such as *Macbeth, King Lear, Othello,* and *Antony and Cleopatra* (tragedy); *Richard III* and *Henry IV* (historical drama); *Twelfth Night* and *As You Like It* (comedy); and *The Tempest* (romance). His more than one hundred fifty sonnets are supreme expressions of the form.

PERCY BYSSHE SHELLEY (1792–1822)

Born in Sussex to a wealthy member of Parliament, Shelley attended Eton and Oxford. An unconventional young man, Shelley was expelled from Oxford during his first year for collaborating with a friend, Thomas Jefferson Hogg, on a pamphlet entitled "The Necessity of Atheism" (1811). That same year, Shelley eloped with Harriet Westbrook, but within three years, he left her to be with Mary Wollstonecraft Godwin. After Harriet's suicide, Shelley married Mary and the couple and their children moved permanently to Italy. The death of their two children, coupled with financial difficulties, left Shelley in despair, and it was at this time (1819) that he wrote his most memorable poetry, namely "Prometheus Unbound" and "Ode to the West Wind." Shelley's important critical essay, "A Defence of Poetry," was published posthumously in 1840.

STEVIE SMITH (1902–1971)

Because of her small size, Florence Margaret Smith earned her nickname from a famous jockey, Steve Donoghue. At a young age, her family moved to a London suburb, and later Smith worked as a secretary at a publishing company and as a writer and broadcaster for the BBC. In the 1930s, she began publishing fiction and poetry, which she often illustrated. Her first novel, *Novel on Yellow Paper*, appeared in 1936, followed by her first collection of poetry, *A Good Time Was Had By All* (1937). Her fascination with death was collected in verse in a volume called *Not Waving But Drowning* (1957) in which she maintains her consistently witty voice. In 1966 she was given the Cholmondely Award, and in 1969, she received the Queen's Gold Medal for Poetry. Both her *Collected Poems* (1976) and *Me Again: The Uncollected Writings* (1981) were published after her death.

WALLACE STEVENS (1879–1955)

"I believe that with a bucket of sand and a wishing lamp I could create a world in half a second that would make this one look like a hunk of mud," Stevens once remarked to his wife. One of the great imaginative forces of this century, he was nevertheless an extraordinarily self-effacing public man, working for much of his adult life as an executive of the Hartford Accident and Indemnity Company while recreating the world at night in the "supreme fiction" of poetry. Born in Reading, Pennsylvania, Stevens attended Harvard University and New York Law School; his first book of poems, *Harmonium*, appeared in 1923. Stevens's poetry and prose can be found in *The Palm at the End of the Mind* (1971) and *The Necessary Angel: Essays on Reality and Imagination* (1951).

JONATHAN SWIFT (1667–1745)

Born to English parents in Dublin, Ireland, Swift later attended Trinity College. In 1689, he moved to England in the service of Sir William Temple. Swift later received an M.A. from Oxford, and in 1695 he took orders to become an Anglican clergyman. He became known for his scathing religious and political satires, and after writing "A Tale of a Tub" and "The Battle of the Books," he returned to Ireland and was named dean of Saint Patrick's Cathedral in Dublin. In his later years, Swift suffered from senility and was removed from his post. He is most popularly known for his 1726 book, *Gulliver's Travels*. His poetry, too, is masterfully satiric.

ALFRED, LORD TENNYSON (1809–1892)

Perhaps the most important and certainly the most popular of the Victorian poets, Tennyson demonstrated his talents at an early age; he published his first volume in 1827. Encouraged to devote his life to poetry by a group of undergraduates at Cambridge University known as the "Apostles," Tennyson was particularly close to Arthur Hallam, whose sudden death in 1833 inspired the long elegy, *In Memoriam* (1850). With that poem he achieved lasting fame and recognition; he was appointed Poet Laureate the year of its publication. Whatever the popularity of his "journalistic" poetry—"The Charge of the Light Brigade" (1854) is perhaps his best known—Tennyson's great theme was always the past, both personal (*In the Valley of Cauteretz*, 1864) and national (*Idylls of the King*, 1869).

DYLAN THOMAS (1914–1953)

In a note to his *Collected Poems* (1952), Thomas wrote: "These poems, with all their crudities, doubts, and confusions, are written for the love of Man and in praise of God, and I'd be a damn fool if they weren't." Given their somber undertones and often wrenching awareness of death, his poems are also rich verbal and visual celebrations of life and its sweetness. Born in Swansea, Wales, into what he called "the smug darkness of a provincial town," Thomas published his first book, *18 Poems* (1934), at the age of twenty. Thereafter he had a successful, though turbulent, career publishing poetry, short stories, and plays, including the highly successful *Under Milk Wood* (1954). In his last years he supported himself with lecture tours and poetry readings in the United States, but his extravagant drinking caught up with him and he died in New York City of chronic alcoholism.

JEAN TOOMER (1894–1967)

Born in Washington, D.C., Toomer later briefly attended a number of colleges and universities. He published poetry and fiction in a variety of small magazines, in addition to African American publications like *Crisis* and *Opportunity*. A crucial text of the Harlem Renaissance, Toomer's landmark, *Cane*, was published in 1923. *Cane* combines a variety of genres, and Toomer's juxtapositions of poetry, drama, and prose foreground his comparisons between rural and urban life for African Americans. After *Cane*, Toomer was unable to publish his work, and he primarily wrote for himself. In 1980, his previously unpublished works appeared in a volume called *The Wayward and the Seeking*.

WALT WHITMAN (1819–1892)

Born on a farm in West Hills, Long Island, to a British father and a Dutch mother, Whitman eventually worked as a journalist throughout New York for many years. After teaching for a while, he founded his own newspaper, *The Long Islander* in 1838, but he left journalism to work on *Leaves of Grass*, which was originally intended as a poetic treatise on American democratic idealism. Published privately in multiple editions from 1855 to 1874, the book originally failed to reach a mass audience. In 1881 Boston's Osgood and Company published another edition of *Leaves of Grass*, which sold well until the district attorney called it "obscene literature" and stipulated that Whitman remove certain poems and phrases. He refused, and many years later, his works were published in Philadelphia. Whitman's poetry creates tension between the self-conscious and political, the romantic and realistic, the mundane and mystical, and the collective and individual.

WILLIAM CARLOS WILLIAMS (1883–1963)

Williams influenced a generation of American poets—many of them still living—by bringing to poetry the sense that "life is above all things else at any moment subversive of life as it was the moment before—always new, irregular." Born in Rutherford, New Jersey, Williams attended school in Switzerland and New York, and studied medicine at the University of Pennsylvania, where he met Hilda Doolittle (H.D.) and Ezra Pound. Thereafter he spent most of his life in Rutherford, practicing medicine and crafting a poetry of palpable immediacy, written in vital, local language. His long poem, *Paterson* (completed in 1963), vividly expresses what lies at the heart of his work: "No ideas but in things."

WILLIAM WORDSWORTH (1770–1850)

Born in Cockermouth in the sparsely populated English Lake District (which Coleridge and he would immortalize), Wordsworth spent his early years "drinking in" (to use a favorite metaphor) a rural environment that would provide material for much of his later poetry. After study at Cambridge University, he spent a year in France, hoping to witness first-hand the French Revolution's "glorious renovation." Remarkably, he was able to establish "a saving intercourse with my true self"—and to write some of his finest poetry—after a love affair with a French woman whose sympathies were Royalist, his own disillusionment at the Revolution, a forced return to England, and near emotional collapse. Perhaps because he was, above all, a poet of remembrance (of "emotion recollected in tranquility"), and his own early experience was not an inexhaustible resource, Wordsworth had written most of his great work—including his masterpiece, *The Prelude*—by the time he was forty.

WILLIAM BUTLER YEATS (1865–1939)

Perhaps the greatest twentieth-century poet in English, Yeats was born in Dublin, attended art school for a time, and left to devote himself to poetry (at the start of his career, a self-consciously romantic poetry, dreamy and ethereal). Yeats's reading of

Nietzsche, his involvement with the Nationalist cause, and his desperate love for the actress (and Nationalist) Maud Gonne led to a tighter, more actively passionate verse and a number of innovative dramatic works. Bitter and disillusioned at the results of revolution and the rise of the Irish middle class, Yeats later withdrew from contemporary events to "Thoor Ballylee," his Norman Tower in the country, there to construct an elaborate mythology and to write poetry, at once realist, symbolist, and metaphysical, which explored what were, for Yeats, fundamental questions of history and identity. Of the progress of his life, Yeats once said: "Man can embody truth but cannot know it."

DANNIE ABSE: "Breughel in Naples." Reprinted by permission of Sheil Land Associates Ltd. for the author.

DIANE ACKERMAN: "Sweep Me Through Your Many-Chambered Heart" from *Jaguar of Sweet Laughter: New and Selected Poems* by Diane Ackerman. Copyright © 1991 by Diane Ackerman. Reprinted by permission of Random House, Inc.

FRANKLIN P. ADAMS: "Composed in the Composing Room" from *By and Large* by Franklin P. Adams. Copyright © 1914 by Franklin P. Adams. Reprinted by permission from Bantam Doubleday Dell.

AI: "Twenty-year Marriage" from *Cruelty* by Ai. Copyright © 1970, 1973 by Ai. Reprinted by permission from Houghton Mifflin Company. All rights reserved. "Riot Act, April 29, 1992" reprinted from *Greed* by Ai, by permission of W. W. Norton & Company, Inc. Copyright © 1993 by Ai. In *Greed*, the dramatic monologues are 100 percent fiction and are merely characters created by the poet. Some of them project the names of "real" public figures onto made-up characters in made-up circumstances. Where the names of corporate, media, or public or political figures are used in the monologues, those names are meant only to denote figures, images, the stuff of imagination; they do not denote or pretend to private information about actual persons, living, dead, or otherwise.

ELIZABETH ALEXANDER: "Boston Year" from *The Venus Hottentot*, edited by Charles Rowell. Copyright © 1990 by Elizabeth Alexander. Reprinted by permission of the University Press of Virginia.

AGHA SHAHID ALI: "The Dacca Gauzes" reprinted from *The Half-Inch Himalayas*, copyright © 1987 by Agha Shahid Ali, Wesleyan University Press. By permission of University Press of New England.

A. R. AMMONS: "Needs" reprinted from *Collected Poems, 1951–1971* by A. R. Ammons, by permission of W. W. Norton & Company, Inc. Copyright © 1972 by A. R. Ammons.

MAYA ANGELOU: "Africa" from *Oh Pray My Wings Are Gonna Fit Me Well* by Maya Angelou. Copyright © 1975 by Maya Angelou. Reprinted by permission of Random House, Inc.

RICHARD ARMOUR: "Hiding Place" from *Light Armour*. Copyright © 1954 by Richard Armour. Reprinted by permission of John Hawkins & Associates, Inc.

JOHN ASHBERY: "City Afternoon" from *Self-Portrait in a Convex Mirror* by John Ashbery. Copyright © 1974 by John Ashbery. Reprinted by permission of Viking Penguin, a division of Penguin Books USA Inc.

MARGARET ATWOOD: "Death of a Young Son by Drowning" from *The Journals of Susanna Moodie* by Margaret Atwood, © 1970 by Oxford University Press Canada. "Siren Song" from *You Are Happy*, © 1978 by Margaret Atwood. Reprinted by permission of Oxford University Press Canada and Houghton Mifflin Company.

W. H. AUDEN: "Musée des Beaux Arts" and "In Memory of W. B. Yeats" from *Collected Poems* by W. H. Auden, edited by Edward Mendelson. Copyright © 1940 W. H. Auden. Reprinted by permission of Faber & Faber Ltd. and Random House, Inc.

CAROL JANE BANGS: "Touching Each Other's Surfaces" from *The Bones of the Earth* by Carol Jane Bangs. Copyright © 1983 by Carol Jane Bangs. Reprinted by permission of New Directions Publishing Corporation.

REGINA BARRECA: "Nighttime Fires" by Regina Barreca, from *The Minnesota Review*, Fall 1986. Reprinted by permission of the author and The Minnesota Review.

APRIL BERNARD: "Praise Palm of the City-Dweller" from *Psalms* by April Bernard, by permission of W. W. Norton & Company, Inc. Copyright © 1993 by April Bernard.

JOHN BETJEMAN: "In Westminster Abbey" from *Collected Poems* by John Betjeman. Reprinted by permission of the author and John Murray (Publishers) Ltd.

EARLE BIRNEY: "Anglosaxon Street" from *The Collected Poems of Earle Birney*. Used by permission of the Canadian Publishers, McClelland & Stewart, Toronto.

ELIZABETH BISHOP: "Sestina" and "The Armadillo" from *The Complete Poems 1927–1979* by Elizabeth Bishop. Copyright © 1979, 1983 by Alice Helen Methfessel. Reprinted by permission of Farrar, Straus & Giroux, Inc.

LOUISE BOGAN: "Cartography" and "Single Sonnet" from *The Blue Estuaries* by Louise Bogan. Copyright © 1968 by Louise Bogan. Reprinted by permission of Farrar, Straus & Giroux, Inc.

ROO BORSON: "After a Death" and "Save Us From" from *Intent, or the Weight of the World* by Roo Borson. Used by permission of the Canadian Publishers, McClelland & Stewart, Toronto.

ROBERT BRINGHURST: "For the Bones of Joseph Mengele, Disinterred June 1985," copyright © 1986 by Robert Bringhurst, reprinted from *Pieces of Map, Pieces of Music*, by permission of McClelland & Stewart Ltd. and the author.

GWENDOLYN BROOKS: "We Real Cool," "Queen of the Blues," and "First Fight. Then Fiddle" from *Blacks*, by Gwendolyn Brooks. Copyright © 1991 by Third World Press, Chicago. Reprinted by permission from Gwendolyn Brooks.

HELEN CHASIN: "Joy Sonnet in a Random Verse" and "The Word *Plum*" from *Coming Close and Other Poems* by Helen Chasin. Copyright © 1968 by Helen Chasin. Reprinted by permission of Yale University Press.

MARILYN CHIN: "Aubade" from Dwarf Bamboo by Marilyn Chin. Reprinted by permission of Greenfield Review Press, Greenfield Review Literary Ctr.

JUDITH ORTIZ COFER: "How to Get a Baby" from *The Latin Deli* by Judith Ortiz Cofer. Reprinted by permission of the University of Georgia Press. "The Changling" and "Unspoken" from *Prairie Schooner*, Fall 1992, vol. 66, no. 3, pp. 28–29. Reprinted by permission of the University of Nebraska Press. Copyright © 1992 by the University of Nebraska Press.

WENDY COPE: "Emily Dickinson," "From Strugnell's Sonnets IV, 'Not only marble, but the plastic toys' " and "From Strugnell's Sonnets I, 'The expense of spirits is a crying shame' " from *Making Cocoa for Kingsley Amis* by Wendy Cope. "Another Christmas Poem" from *Serious Concerns* by Wendy Cope. Reprinted by permission of Faber & Faber, Ltd.

FRANCES CORNFORD: "Parting in Wartime" from *Collected Poems* by Frances Cornford. Reprinted by permission from Random House U.K. Limited.

HART CRANE: "Exile," "Forgetfulness," "Episode of Hands," "To Emily Dickinson" reprinted from *Complete Poems of Hart Crane*, edited by Marc Simon, by permission of Liveright Publishing Corporation. Copyright © 1933, 1958, 1966 by Liveright Publishing Corporation. Copyright © 1986 by Marc Simon.

COUNTEE CULLEN: "For a Lady I Know" from *Color* by Countee Cullen. Copyright © 1925 by Harper & Brothers; copyright renewed 1953 by Ida M. Cullen. Reprinted by permission of GRM Associates, Inc., Agents for the Estate of Ida M. Cullen.

E. E. CUMMINGS: "in Just-," "Buffalo Bill's," "l(a," "(ponder,darling,these busted statues," "anyone lived in a pretty how town" reprinted from *Complete Poems, 1904–1962* by E. E. Cummings, edited by George J. Firmage, by permission of Liveright Publishing Corporation. Copyright © 1923, 1926, 1940, 1951, 1954, 1958, 1968, 1986, 1991 by the Trustees for the E. E. Cummings Trust. Copyright © 1976, 1985 by George James Firmage.

WARING CUNEY: "No Images" by Waring Cuney. We have made diligent efforts to contact the copyright holder to obtain permission to reprint this selection. If you have information that would help us, please write W. W. Norton & Company, 500 Fifth Avenue, New York, NY 10110.

J. V. CUNNINGHAM: "History of Ideas" from *Collected Poems and Epigrams of J. V. Cunningham*. Reprinted by permission of Jessie C. Cunningham.

NORA DAUENHAUER: "Tlingit Concrete Poem" from *The Droning Shaman*. Copyright © 1988 by Nora Dauenhauer. Reprinted by permission of the author.

PETER DE VRIES: "To His Importunate Mistress" by Peter De Vries, originally published in *The New Yorker*. Reprinted by permission of the Watkins/Loomis Agency.

JAMES DICKEY: "Cherrylog Road" and "The Leap" reprinted from *Poems, 1957–1967*. Copyright © 1967 by James Dickey, Wesleyan University Press. Reprinted by permission of University Press of New England.

EMILY DICKINSON: "After great pain, a formal feeling comes—" "I dwell in Possibility—" "My Life had stood—a Loaded Gun—" "The Brain—is Wider than the Sky—" "I reckon—when I count it all—" "We do not play on Graves—" "She dealt her pretty words like blades—" "The Wind begun to knead the Grass" reprinted by permission of the publishers and the Trustees of Amherst College from *The Poems of Emily Dickinson*, Thomas H. Johnson, ed., Cambridge, Mass.: The Belknap Press of Harvard University Press. Copyright © 1951, 1955, 1983 by the President and Fellows of Harvard College. From *The Complete Works of Emily Dickinson*, edited by Thomas H. Johnson. Copyright © 1929, 1935 by Martha Dickinson Bianchi; copyright © renewed 1957, 1963 by Mary L. Hampson. By permission of Little, Brown and Company.

SUSAN DONNELLY: "Eve Names the Animals" from *Eve Names the Animals*. Copyright © 1985 by Susan Donnelly. Reprinted with permission of Northeastern University Press, Boston.

HILDA DOOLITTLE: "Sea Rose" and "Garden" from *Collected Poems 1912–1944* by Hilda Doolittle. Copyright © by the Estate of Hilda Doolittle. Reprinted by permission of New Directions Publishing Corporation.

RITA DOVE: "Daystar" from *Thomas and Beulah* by Rita Dove. Copyright © 1986 by Rita Dove. "Parsley" from *Museum, Poems* by Rita Dove. Copyright © 1983 by Rita Dove. Reprinted by permission of the author. "Fifth Grade Autobiography" reprinted from *Grace Notes, Poems* by Rita Dove, by permission of W. W. Norton & Company, Inc. Copyright © 1989 by Rita Dove.

ALAN DUGAN: "Elegy" from *New and Collected Poems 1961–1983*. Copyright © 1961, 1962, 1968, 1972, 1973, 1974, 1983 by Alan Dugan. First printed by The Ecco Press in 1983. Reprinted by permission.

STEPHEN DUNN: "Dancing with God" from *Between Angels* by Stephen Dunn. Copyright © 1989 by Stephen Dunn. Reprinted by permission of W.W. Norton & Company, Inc.

RICHARD EBERHARDT: "The Fury of Aerial Bombardment" and "The Groundhog" from *Collected Poems, 1930–1986* by Richard Eberhardt. Copyright © 1988 by Richard Eberhardt. Reprinted by permission of Oxford University Press, Inc.

T. S. ELIOT: "The Love Song of J. Alfred Prufrock" and "Journey of the Magi" from *Collected Poems 1909–1962* by T. S. Eliot. Copyright © 1936 by Harcourt Brace & Company, copyright © 1964, 1963 by T. S. Eliot, reprinted by permission of Harcourt Brace & Company, and Faber & Faber Ltd.

JAMES A. EMANUEL: "Emmett Till" from *Whole Grain: Collected Poems, 1958–1989*. Reprinted by permission of the author.

LOUISE ERDRICH: "Jacklight" from *Jacklight* by Louise Erdrich. Copyright © 1984 by Louise Erdrich. Reprinted by permission of Henry Holt and Company, Inc.

KENNETH FEARING: "Dirge" from *New and Selected Poems 1936–1976* by Kenneth Fearing. Copyright © 1976 by Kenneth Fearing. Reprinted with permission from Indiana University Press.

CAROLYN FORCHÉ: All lines from "Reunion" and "Taking Off My Clothes" from *The Country Between Us* by Carolyn Forché. Copyright © 1978, 1981 by Carolyn Forché. Reprinted by permission of HarperCollins Publishers, Inc.

ROBERT FRANCIS: "Hogwash" reprinted from *Robert Francis: Collected Poems, 1936–1976* (Amherst: University of Massachusetts Press, 1976), copyright © 1976 by Robert Francis.

ROBERT FROST: "Stopping by Woods on a Snowy Evening," "Design," "Once by the Pacific," "Never Again Would Birds' Song Be the Same," "Range-Finding," and "The Road Not Taken" from *The Poetry of Robert Frost*, edited by Edward Connery Lathem. Copyright © 1936, 1944, 1951 by Robert Frost. Copyright © 1964 by Lesley Frost Ballantine. Copyright © 1916, 1923, © 1969 by Henry Holt and Company, Inc. Reprinted by permission of Henry Holt and Company, Inc.

TESS GALLAGHER: "Sudden Journey," copyright © 1984 by Tess Gallagher. Reprinted from *Willingly* with the permission of Graywolf Press, Saint Paul, Minnesota.

SANDRA GILBERT: "Sonnet: The Ladies' Home Journal" reprinted from *Emily's Bread, Poems* by Sandra M. Gilbert, by permission of W. W. Norton & Company, Inc. Copyright © 1984 by Sandra M. Gilbert.

SUSAN GLICKMAN: "Beauty" from *Henry Moore's Sheep and Other Poems* by Susan Glickman. Reprinted by permission of Véhicule Press.

LOUISE GLÜCK: "Labor Day" from *Ararat* by Louise Gluck. Copyright © 1990 by Louise Gluck. Published by The Ecco Press. Reprinted by permission.

ROBERT GRAVES: "The Naked and the Nude" from *Collected Poems 1975* by Robert Graves. Copyright © 1975 by Robert Graves. Reprinted by permission of Oxford University Press, Inc.

JORIE GRAHAM: "The Geese" from *Hybrids of Plants and Ghosts* by Jorie Graham. Copyright © 1980 by Jorie Graham. Reprinted by permission of Princeton University Press.

MICHAEL HARPER: "Dear John, Dear Coltrane" from *Dear John, Dear Coltrane*. Reprinted by permission of the author.

JAMES HARRISON: "Penelope" from *The Flying Dutchman* by James Harrison. Reprinted by permission of Sono Nis press, Victoria, B.C. Canada.

ROBERT HASS: "The Feast" from *Praise*. Copyright © 1974, 1975, 1976, 1977, 1978, 1979 by Robert Hass. Reprinted by permission of the Ecco Press.

ROBERT HAYDEN: "Those Winter Sundays" and "Frederick Douglass" reprinted from *Angle of Ascent, New and Selected Poems*, by Robert Hayden, by permission of Liveright Publishing Corporation. Copyright © 1975, 1972, 1970, 1966 by Robert Hayden.

SEAMUS HEANEY: "The Outlaw" from *Poems, 1965–1975* by Seamus Heaney. Copyright © 1975, 1980 by Seamus Heaney. Reprinted by permission of Faber & Faber Ltd. and Farrar, Straus & Giroux, Inc.

ANTHONY HECHT: "The Dover Bitch" from *Collected Earlier Poems* by Anthony Hecht.

GEOFFREY HILL: "In Memory of Jane Fraser" from *Collected Poems* by Geoffrey Hill. Copyright © 1985 by Geoffrey Hill. Reprinted by permission of Oxford University Press, Inc.

JOHN HOLLANDER: "Adam's Task" from *Selected Poetry* by John Hollander. Copyright © 1993 by John Hollander. Reprinted by permission of Alfred A. Knopf, Inc. "A State of Nature" from *Types of Shape*. Copyright © 1967 by John Hollander. Reprinted by permission of Yale University Press.

ROBERT HOLLANDER: "You Too? Me Too—Why Not? Soda Pop" from *The Massachusetts Review*, vol. 9, no. 3. Copyright © 1968 by Robert Hollander. Reprinted with permission by The Massachusetts Review.

BARBARA HOWES: "Mirror Image: Port-au-Prince" reprinted from *Light and Dark*. Copyright © 1959 by Barbara Howes, Wesleyan University Press. By permission of University Press of New England.

LANGSTON HUGHES: "Theme for English B" from *Montage of a Dream Deferred*. Copyright © 1951 by Langston Hughes. Copyright renewed 1979 by George Houston Bass. Reprinted by permission from Harold Ober Associates, Inc. "The Negro Speaks of Rivers" from *Selected Poems of Langston Hughes* by Langston Hughes. Copyright © 1926 by Alfred A. Knopf, Inc. and renewed by Langston Hughes. "Harlem (A Dream Deferred)" from *The Panther and the Lash* by Langston Hughes. Copyright © 1951 by Langston Hughes. Reprinted by permission of Alfred A. Knopf, Inc.

RANDALL JARRELL: "The Death of the Ball Turret Gunner" from *The Complete Poems* by Randall Jarrell. Copyright © 1945, 1969 by Mrs. Randall Jarrell. Reprinted by permission from Farrar, Straus & Giroux, Inc.

ELIZABETH JENNINGS: "Delay" from *Collected Poems* by Elizabeth Jennings. Reprinted with permission from David Higham Associates, Inc.

PAULETTE JILES: "Paper Matches" from *Cousins* by Paulette Jiles. Copyright © 1992 by Paulette Jiles. Reprinted by permission of Alfred A. Knopf, Inc.

HELENE JOHNSON: "Sonnet to a Negro in Harlem" by Helene Johnson. We have made diligent efforts to contact the copyright holder to obtain permission to reprint this selection. If you have information that could help us, please write to W. W. Norton & Company, 500 Fifth Avenue, New York, NY 10110.

ERICA JONG: "Penis Envy" from *Loveroot* by Erica Jong. Copyright © 1968, 1969, 1973, 1974, 1975 by Erica Mann Jong. Reprinted by permission of Henry Holt and Company, Inc.

JUNE JORDAN: "Something Like a Sonnet for Phillis Miracle Wheatley" from *Naming Our Destiny* by June Jordan. Copyright © 1989 by June Jordan. Used by permission of the publisher, Thunder's Mouth Press.

DONALD JUSTICE: "Counting the Mad" from *Summer Anniversaries* by Donald Justice. Copyright © 1981 by Donald Justice, Wesleyan University Press. Reprinted by permission of University Press of New England. "Children Walking Home Through Good Neighborhood" from *The Sunset Maker*. Copyright © 1987 by Donald Justice. Reprinted by permission of the author.

X. J. KENNEDY: "Epitaph for a Postal Clerk" and "In a Prominent Bar in Secaucus One Day" from *Nude Descending a Staircase*. Copyright © 1961 by X. J. Kennedy. Reprinted by permission of Curtis Brown, Ltd.

GALWAY KINNELL: "Blackberry Eating," and "After Making Love We Hear Footsteps" from *Mortal Acts, Mortal Wounds* by Galway Kinnell. Copyright © 1980 by Galway Kinnell. Reprinted by permission of Houghton Mifflin Company. All rights reserved.

CAROLYN KIZER: "Bitch" from *Mermaids in the Basement* by Carolyn Kizer. Copyright © 1984 by Carolyn Kizer. Reprinted by permission of Copper Canyon Press.

A. M. KLEIN: "Heirloom," from *Complete Poems* by A. M. Klein, edited by Zailig Pollock. Copyright © 1990. Reprinted by permission of University of Toronto Press Incorporated.

ETHERIDGE KNIGHT: "Hard Rock Returns to Prison from the Hospital from the Criminal Insane" from *Poems From Prison*. Copyright © 1968 by Etheridge Knight. Reprinted by permission of Broadside Press.

KENNETH KOCH: "Variations on a Theme by William Carlos Williams" from *Thank You and Other Poems*. Copyright © 1962 by Kenneth Koch. Reprinted by permission of the author.

MAXINE KUMIN: "Woodchucks," copyright © 1971 by Maxine Kumin, from *Our Ground Time Here Will Be Brief* by Maxine Kumin. Used by permission of Viking Penguin, a division of Penguin Books USA Inc.

PHILIP LARKIN: "Church Going" by Philip Larkin, reprinted from *The Less Deceived* by permission of The Marvell Press, England and Australia.

DORIANNE LAUX: "The Laundromat" from *Awake*. Copyright © 1990 by Dorianne Laux. Reprinted by permission of BOA Editions, Ltd.

IRVING LAYTON: "The Way the World Ends," "From Colony to Nation," "Street Funeral" from *Collected Poems* by Irving Layton. Used by permission of the Canadian Publishers, McClelland & Stewart, Toronto.

LI-YOUNG LEE: "Persimmons" from *Rose* by Li-Young Lee. Copyright © 1986 by Li-Young Lee. Reprinted by permission of BOA Editions, Ltd., 92 Park Avenue, Brockport, NY 14420.

DENISE LEVERTOV: "What Were They Like?" from *Poems 1960–1967*. Copyright © 1964 by Denise Levertov Goodman. Reprinted by permission of New Directions Publishing Corporation.

C. DAY LEWS: "Song" from *Collected Poems*. Reprinted by permission.

DOROTHY LIVESAY: "Green Rain" by Dorothy Livesay. We have made diligent efforts to contact the copyright holder to obtain permission to reprint this selection. If you have information that would help us, please write W. W. Norton & Company, 500 Fifth Avenue, New York, NY 10110.

AUDRE LORDE: "Hanging Fire" and "Recreation" reprinted from *The Black Unicorn, Poems* by Audre Lorde, by permission of W. W. Norton & Company, Inc. Copyright © 1978 by Audre Lorde.

ROBERT LOWELL: "Skunk Hour" from *Life Studies* by Robert Lowell. Copyright © 1956, 1959 by Robert Lowell. Copyright renewed © 1987 by Harriet Lowell. Reprinted by permission of Farrar, Straus & Giroux, Inc.

ARCHIBALD MACLEISH: "Ars Poetica" from *Collected Poems 1917–1982* by Archibald MacLeish. Copyright © 1985 by the Estate of Archibald MacLeish. Reprinted by permission of Houghton Mifflin Company. All rights reserved.

WALTER DE LA MARE: "Slim Cunning Hands" from *Walter de la Mare: Slim Cunning Hands* by Walter de la Mare. Reprinted by permission of The Literary Trustees of Walter de la Mare, and The Society of Authors as their representative.

HEATHER MCHUGH: "Two St. Petersburgs" from *Hinge & Sign* by Heather McHugh. Copyright © 1994 Heather McHugh. Reprinted by permission of the author and University Press of New England.

CLAUDE MCKAY: "The Harlem Dancer," "The White House," and "America" from *Selected Poems of Claude McKay*. Copyright © 1981 by Harcourt Brace. Reprinted by permission of the Archives of Claude McKay, Carl Cowl Administrator.

LOUISE MACNEICE: "Sunday Morning" from *The Collected Poems of Louis MacNeice*. Reprinted by permission of Faber and Faber Ltd.

JAMES MERRILL: "Watching the Dance" from *Nights and Days* by James Merrill. Copyright © 1966, 1992 by James Merrill. Reprinted by permission of Alfred A. Knopf.

W. S. MERWIN: "Burning the Cat" from *Green with Beasts* by W. S. Merwin. Copyright © 1955, 1956 by W. S. Merwin. Reprinted by permission of Georges Borchardt, Inc. for the author.

EDNA ST. VINCENT MILLAY: "I, being born a woman and distressed," "What lips my lips have kissed, and where, and why," "Women have loved before as I love now," "An Ancient Gesture," "First Fig," and "Second Fig" by Edna St. Vincent Millay. From *Collected Poems*, HarperCollins. Copyright © 1923, 1931, 1951, 1954, 1958, 1982 by Edna St. Vincent Millay and Norma Millay Ellis. Reprinted by permission of Elizabeth Barnett, literary executor.

MARIANNE MOORE: "Poetry" from *Collected Poems of Marianne Moore*. Copyright 1935 by Marianne Moore, renewed 1963 by Marianne Moore and T. S. Eliot. Reprinted with permission of Simon &

Schuster. "Love in America," from *The Complete Poems of Marianne Moore* by Marianne Moore. Copyright © 1981 by Clive E. Driver, Literary Executor of the Estate of Marianne C. Moore. Used by permission of Viking Penguin, a division of Penguin Books USA Inc.

PAT MORA: "Gentle Communion," and "Sonrisas" by Pat Mora are printed with permission from the publishers of *Borders* (Houston: Arte Publico Press—University of Houston, 1986).

ERIN MOURÉ: "Thirteen Years" from *Furious* by Erin Mouré. Reprinted by permission of the author and Stoddart Publishing Co. Limited, Don Mills, Ontario.

SUSAN MUSGRAVE: "I Am Not a Conspiracy" from *Cocktails at the Mausoleum*, "Hidden Meaning" and "You Didn't Fit" from *Embalmer's Art*, both by Susan Musgrave. Reprinted by permission of the author.

HOWARD NEMEROV: "A Way of Life," "Epigram: Political Reflexion," "Boom!" "The Vacuum," "The Goose Fish," and "The Town Dump" from *The Collected Poems of Howard Nemerov*. Copyright © 1977 by Howard Nemerov. Reprinted with permission of the Howard Nemerov Trust and Margaret Nemerov.

SHARON OLDS: "Leningrad Cemetery, Winter of 1941" by Sharon Olds from *The New Yorker*, December 31, 1979. Reprinted by permission © 1979 of The New Yorker Magazine, Inc. "The Glass" and "The Lifting" from *The Father* by Sharon Olds. Copyright © 1992 by Sharon Olds. "Sex Without Love," "The Victims," and "The Elder Sister" from *The Dead and the Living* by Sharon Olds. Copyright © 1975, 1978, 1979, 1980, 1981, 1982, 1983 by Sharon Olds. Reprinted by permission of Alfred A. Knopf, Inc.

MICHAEL ONDAATJE: "King Kong Meets Wallace Stevens" from *The Cinnamon Peeler* by Michael Ondaatje. Copyright © 1989 by Michael Ondaatje. Reprinted by permission of the Canadian Publishers, McClelland & Stewart, Toronto and Alfred A. Knopf, Inc.

GREGORY ORFALEA: "Arab and Jew in Alaska" from *The Capital of Solitude* (Greenfield Center, NY: Ithaca House/Greenfield Review Press, 1988). Copyright © 1988 by Gregory Orfalea. Reprinted by permission of the author.

WILFRED OWEN: "Dulce et Decorum Est" from *Collected Poems of Wildred Owen*. Copyright © 1963 by Chatto & Windus, Ltd. Reprinted by permission of New Directions Publishing Corporation.

DOROTHY PARKER: "Comment," copyright 1926, renewed © 1954 by Dorothy Parker; "Indian Summer," copyright 1926, renewed © 1954 by Dorothy Parker; "One Perfect Rose," copyright 1929, renewed © 1957 by Dorothy Parker; "A Certain Lady," copyright 1928, renewed © 1956 by Dorothy Parker, from *The Portable Dorothy Parker* by Dorothy Parker, Introduction by Brendan Gill. Used by permission of Viking Penguin, a division of Penguin Books USA Inc.

LINDA PASTAN: "Marks" reprinted from *PM/AM, New and Selected Poems*, by Linda Pastan, by permission of W. W. Norton & Company, Inc. Copyright © 1982 by Linda Pastan. "To a Daughter Leaving Home," "Erosion," and "love poem" from *The Imperfect Paradise, Poems* by Linda Pastan, by permission of W. W. Norton & Company, Inc. Copyright © 1988 by Linda Pastan.

RAYMOND R. PATTERSON: "You Are the Brave" from *26 Ways of Looking at a Black Man* by Raymond R. Patterson. Copyright by Raymond Patterson. Reprinted with permission from Ayer Company Publishers, Inc.

RICARDO PAU-LLOSA: "Foreign Language" from *Bread of the Imagined* by Ricardo Pau-Llosa (Tempe: Bilingual Press, Arizona State University, 1992), originally appeared in *Kayak*, no. 64, May 1984. Reprinted with permission from the author.

MARGE PIERCY: "Barbie Doll" from *Circles on the Water* by Marge Piercy. Copyright © 1982 by Marge Piercy. "To Have Without Holding" from *The Moon Is Always Female* by Marge Piercy. Copyright © 1979 by Marge Piercy. "What's That Smell in the Kitchen?" from *Stone, Paper, Knife* by Marge Piercy. Copyright © 1980 by Marge Piercy. Reprinted by permission of Alfred A. Knopf, Inc.

SYLVIA PLATH: "Point Shirley" from *The Collossus and Other Poems*. Copyright © 1959 by Sylvia Plath. Reprinted by permission of Alfred A. Knopf, Inc. and Faber & Faber Ltd. "Daddy," "Black Rook in Rainy Weather," "Lady Lazarus," "Morning Song," and "Mirror," (originally appeared in *The New Yorker*) from *Collected Poems* by Sylvia Plath, edited by Ted Hughes. Reprinted with permission of Faber & Faber Ltd. and HarperCollins Publishers, Inc.

KATHA POLLITT: "Two Fish" from *Antarctic Traveller* by Katha Pollitt. Copyright © 1972 by Katha Pollitt. Reprinted by permission of Alfred A. Knopf, Inc.

EZRA POUND: "The River-Merchant's Wife: A Letter," "The Garden," "In a Station of the Metro," and "A Virginal" from *Personae* by Ezra Pound. Copyright © 1926 by Ezra Pound. Reprinted by permission of New Directions Publishing Corporation.

JAROLD RAMSEY: "The Tally Stick" and "Hunting Arrowheads" by Jarold Ramsey. Reprinted by permission of the author.

DUDLEY RANDALL: "Ballad of Birmingham" from *Poem Counter Poem* by Dudley Randall. Reprinted by permission of the Broadside Press.

JOHN CROWE RANSOM: "Bells for John Whiteside's Daughter" from *Selected Poems* by John Crowe Ransom. Copyright © 1924 by John Crowe Ransom. Reprinted by permission of Alfred A. Knopf, Inc.

HENRY REED: "Lessons of the War: Judging Distances," from *Henry Reed: Collected Poems*, edited by Jon Stallworthy (1991). Copyright © The Executor of Henry Reed's Estate. Reprinted by permission of Oxford University Press.

ISHMAEL REED: "beware: do not read this poem" and "I Am a Cowboy in the Boat of Ra" by Ishmael Reed. Copyright © 1972 by Ishmael Reed. Reprinted by permission of author and Whitman Breed Abbott & Morgan.

ADRIENNE RICH: "Origins and History of Consciousness" reprinted from *The Dream of a Common Language, Poems 1974–1977* by Adrienne Rich. "Walking Down the Road" and "Letters in the Family" reprinted from *Time's Power, Poems 1985–1988* by Adrienne Rich. Part 3, "My mouth hovers across your breasts," from *Contradictions: Tracking Poems*, reprinted from *Your Native Land, Your Life, Poems* by Adrienne Rich. "Dialogue," Delta," "Power," "Living in Sin," "Leaflets," "Planetarium," "Aunt Jennifer's Tigers," "At a Bach Concert," "Storm Warnings," and "Snapshots of a Daughter-in-Law," "Orion," "Diving into the Wreck," "Two Songs," and "For the Record" all reprinted from *The Fact of a Doorframe, Poems Selected and New, 1950–1984*, by Adrienne Rich. "How does a poet put bread on the table?" and an excerpt from "A communal poetry" reprinted from *What Is Found There, Notebooks on Poetry and Politics*, by Adrienne Rich. Excerpt from "When We Dead Awaken: Writing as Re-Vision" reprinted from *On Lies, Secrets, and Silence, Selected Prose 1966–1978* by Adrienne Rich, by permission of W. W. Norton & Company, Inc. Copyright © 1978 by W. W. Norton & Company, Inc. "Talking with Adrienne Rich," an interview with Wayne Dodd and Stanley Plumly, from *The Ohio Review*, no. 1. Used by permission of The Ohio Review.

ALBERTO RÍOS: "Advice to a First Cousin" from *Five Indiscretions* by Alberto Ríos. Copyright © 1985 The Sheep Meadow Press. Reprinted by permission. Riverdale-on-Hudson, New York.

EDWIN ARLINGTON ROBINSON: "Mr. Flood's Party" from *Collected Poems of Edwin Arlington Robinson*. Copyright © 1921 by Edwin Arlington Robinson, renewed 1949 by Ruth Nivision. Reprinted with permission of Simon & Schuster, Inc.

THEODORE ROETHKE: "Elegy for Jane," copyright 1950 by Theodore Roethke. "My Papa's Waltz," copyright 1942 by Hearst Magazines, Inc. "The Dream," copyright © 1955 by Theodore Roethke. "The Waking," copyright 1948 by Theodore Roethke. "I Knew a Woman," copyright 1954 by Theodore Roethke. Used by permission of Doubleday, a division of Bantam Doubleday Dell Publishing Group, Inc.

LIZ ROSENBERG: "Married Love" reprinted from *The Fire Music* by Liz Rosenberg, by permission of the University of Pittsburgh Press. Copyright © 1986 by Liz Rosenberg.

MURIEL RUKEYSER: "Reading Time : 1 Minute 26 Seconds" and "Myth" by Muriel Rukeyser. Reprinted by permission of William L. Rukeyser.

MARY JO SALTER: "Welcome to Hiroshima" from *Henry Purcell in Japan*, by Mary Jo Salter. Copyright © 1984 by Mary Jo Salter. Reprinted by permission of Alfred A. Knopf, Inc.

DUNCAN CAMPBELL SCOTT: "The Onondaga Madonna" from *Selected Poems of Duncan Campbell Scott* by Duncan Campbell Scott. Reprinted by permission of John G. Aylen.

ANNE SEXTON: "The Fury of Overshoes" from *The Death Notebooks* by Anne Sexton. Copyright © 1974 by Anne Sexton. "The Farmer's Wife" from *To Bedlam and Part Way Back* by Anne Sexton. Copyright © 1960 by Anne Sexton, renewed © 1988 by Linda G. Sexton. "With Mercy for the Greedy" from *All My Pretty Ones* by Anne Sexton. Copyright © 1962 by Anne Sexton, renewed © 1990 by Linda G. Sexton. Reprinted by permission from Houghton Mifflin Company. All rights reserved.

KARL SHAPIRO: "Auto Wreck," copyright © 1941, 1987 Karl Shapiro by arrangement with Wieser & Weiser, Inc. New York. Reprinted by permission of Weiser & Weiser, Inc.

LESLIE MARMON SILKO: "Long Time Ago." Copyright © 1981 by Leslie Marmon Silko. Reprinted by permission of Wylie, Aitken & Stone, Inc.

DESMOND SKIRROW: "Ode on a Grecian Urn Summarized" by Desmond Skirrow. Reprinted by permission of The New Statesman, Foundation House, Perserverance Works, London, England.

KAY SMITH: "Annunciations" by Kay Smith. Reprinted by permission of the author.

STEVIE SMITH: "Our Bog is Dood," "The Jungle Husband," and 'I Remember" from *Collected Poems of Stevie Smith*. Copyright © 1972 by Stevie Smith. Reprinted with permission of New Directions Publishing Corporation.

W. D. SNODGRASS: "Leaving the Motel" by W. D. Snodgrass. Reprinted by permission of the author.

RICHARD SNYDER: "A Mongoloid Child Handling Shells on the Beach" from *Practicing Our Sighs: The Collected Poems of Richard Snyder*, edited by Mary Snyder and Robert McGovern. Copyright © 1989 by Richard Snyder. Reprinted with permission of The Ashland Poetry Press, Ashland University.

CATHY SONG: "A Mehinaku Girl in Seclusion" reprinted from *Frameless Windows, Squares of Light, Poems* by Cathy Song, by permission of W. W. Norton & Company, Inc. Copyright © 1988 by Cathy Song.

WILLIAM STAFFORD: "At the Bomb Testing Site" from *The Rescued Year* by William Stafford. Copyright © 1960. Reprinted by permission of the estate of William Stafford.

WALLACE STEVENS: "Anecdote of the Jar," "The Emperor of Ice-Cream," and "Sunday Morning" from *The Collected Poems of Wallace Stevens* by Wallace Stevens. Copyright © 1923 and renewed 1951 by Wallace Stevens. Reprinted by permission of Alfred A. Knopf, Inc.

RUTH STONE: "Second-Hand Coat" from *Second-Hand Coat*. Reprinted by permission of the author.

DYLAN THOMAS: "Fern Hill," "In My Craft or Sullen Art," and "Do Not Go Gentle into That Good Night" from *The Poems* by Dylan Thomas. Copyright © 1939 by Dylan Thomas. Reprinted with permission of David Higham Associates, Ltd., and New Directions Publishing Corporation.

JEAN TOOMER: "Reapers" and "Song of the Son" reprinted from *Cane* by Jean Toomer, by permission of Liveright Publishing Corporation. Copyright © 1923 by Boni & Liveright. Copyright renewed 1951 by Jean Toomer.

MONA VAN DUYN: "What the Motorcycle Said" from *If It Be Not I* by Mona Van Duyn. Copyright © 1993 by Mona Van Duyn. Reprinted by permission of Alfred A. Knopf, Inc.

MIRIAM WADDINGTON: "Ulysses Embroidered" from *The Last Landscape* by Miriam Waddington. Copyright © 1992 by Miriam Waddington. Reprinted by permission of Oxford University Press Canada.

DAVID WAGONER: "My Father's Garden" from *Through the Forest*. Copyright © 1987 by David Wagoner. Used by permission of Grove/Atlantic, Inc.

DIANE WAKOSKI: "A Poet Recognizing the Echo of the Voice" by Diane Wakoski. Copyright © 1970 by Diane Wakoski. Reprinted by permission of the author.

DEREK WALCOTT: "A Far Cry from Africa" from *Collected Poems 1948–1984* by Derek Walcott. Copyright © 1986 by Derek Walcott. Reprinted by permission of Farrar, Straus & Giroux, Inc.

TOM WAYMAN: "Wayman in Love" by Tom Wayman. Reprinted by permission of Harbour Publishing Company, Limited.

RICHARD WILBUR: "Love Calls Us to the Things of This World" from *Things of This World*, copyright © 1956 and renewed by Richard Wilbur, reprinted by permission of Harcourt Brace & Company.

WILLIAM CARLOS WILLIAMS: "The Red Wheelbarrow" and "This Is Just to Say" from *Collected Poems 1909–1939, Vol. I*. Copyright © 1938 by New Directions Corporation. "Raleigh Was Right," "The Dance," and "Poem" from *Collected Poems 1939–1962, Vol. II*. Copyright © 1944, 1948, 1962 by William Carlos Williams. Reprinted by permission of New Directions Publishing Corporation.

YVOR WINTERS: "At the San Francisco Airport" from *The Collected Poems of Yvor Winters* (Ohio University Press/Swallow Press, 1980).

JAMES WRIGHT: "Arrangements with Earth for Three Dead Friends" reprinted from *Collected Poems* by James Wright. Copyright © 1971 by James Wright, Wesleyan University Press. By permission of University Press of New England.

JUDITH WRIGHT: " 'Dove-Love' " from *Collected Poems 1942–1970* by Judith Wright. Reprinted by kind permission of Angus & Robertson Publishers.

W. B. YEATS: "Byzantium" and "A Last Confession," copyright 1933 by Macmillan Publishing Company, renewed 1961 by Bertha Georgie Yeats. "Leda and the Swan," "Sailing to Byzantium," and "Among School Children," copyright 1928 by Macmillan Publishing Company, renewed 1956 by Georgie Yeats. "Easter 1916," "The Second Coming," copyright 1924 by Macmillan Publishing Company, renewed 1952 by Bertha Georgie Yeats. From *The Poems of W. B. Yeats: A New Edition*.

INDEX OF AUTHORS

INDEX OF TITLES AND FIRST LINES

INDEX OF LITERARY TERMS